UKCH Religious Trends No. 4 2003/2004

Edited by Dr Peter Brierley

Assistant Editor: Kim Miles

Vision Building, 4 Footscray Road, London SE9 2TZ

Tel: 020 8294 1989 Fax: 020 8294 0014
Email: admin@christian-research.org.uk

Websites: www.christian-research.org.uk www.ukchristianhandbook.org.uk

British Library Cataloguing in Publication Data

UK Christian Handbook Religious Trends No. 4 – 2003/2004
1. Great Britain Christian Church
I. Brierley, Peter, 1938
ISBN 1 85321 149 4

Christian Research aims to provide Christian leaders with factual information, surveys, and other resource material to help them in their strategic planning for evangelism and growth in the long-term, and with leadership training for greater efficiency, effectiveness and cost-effectiveness in the short-term. Christian Research also publishes and distributes related books and papers. The Christian Research Association is a registered charity, number 1017701.

Material similar to that in *Religious Trends* is published every other month in the Christian Research Association's bulletin, *Quadrant*. This is available only to members. Details of membership may be obtained from Gwen Gowers, Christian Research, Vision Building, 4 Footscray Road, Eltham, London SE9 2TZ. Email: admin@christian-research.org.uk.

Typeset by Paul Jones Associates, 98 Eden Way, Beckenham, Kent BR3 3DH.
Printed for Christian Research at the above address by Ebenezer Baylis.

Rt Rev Nigel McCulloch
Bishop of Manchester

It is said that Queen Elizabeth the First died "mildly like a lambe, easily like a ripe apple from the tree". Four hundred years later there are those who see the Christian Church in this country undergoing a similarly gentle demise and quiet death.

Such a departure of the Church from our national culture has been long predicted. However, in each generation, Christianity has shown a capacity for survival that has surprised many a harbinger of doom. Of that, the recent UK Government Census, showing nearly 72% of the population describing themselves as Christians, is the latest example.

It would be unwise to read too much into that statistic; and sensible to remember the dismissive comment of St Bernard about the twelfth century Irish who were, he averred, "Christian in name but pagan in fact". As this latest edition of *Religious Trends* demonstrates, there is a great numerical disparity between those who, in their census return, professed an allegiance to Christianity and those who translate that allegiance into regular commitment through worship.

Nevertheless, following the publication of the Census, the *Guardian* newspaper's leader column observed: "this is a Christian country simply in the unanswerable sense that most of its citizens think of themselves as Christians." It went on to say that the figures showed, at the very least, that the church provides an extensive institutional and collective bond for many more people than we might otherwise imagine – in what is often seen as an atomised and secular society.

The *Guardian* editorial also noted that the census figures are reminders that religion in general, and the Church in particular, are not marginal anachronisms doomed to terminal decline in our modern society. On the contrary, they seem to be remarkably resilient and enduring parts of the social order. The column concluded: "the Church has a more vital role to play in the search for community and personal peace than has sometimes been allowed for recently."

It is against this background that the up-to-date information provided in this new edition of *Religious Trends* is so helpful – not least in the special features that have been included for the first time. The major focus in this has been the obtaining of the latest available membership figures for each denomination (broken down by England, Wales, Scotland and Northern Ireland) so that the membership – and thus the percentage of the population who are church members – relate directly to each of these geographical areas. For example, detailed analysis is provided for church attendance in Scotland. This has been broken down for twenty-six of the thirty-two Council areas in that country, together with information for each major denominational group, as well as other analyses.

Extracts from the religion section of the 2001 Census are readily available from these pages too, with reference to the four countries and also the various Local Authority Districts. Included here as well are revised estimates of the number of people who are baptised into the Church of England. Furthermore, there is a new page of coloured maps of its dioceses showing some of their differing features.

There are also new references to the European dimension. Christian churches in the United Kingdom are beginning to realise there are significant religious implications in the gradual moves towards further political and economic integration within Europe and, in particular, the enlargement of the European Union. This edition of *Religious Trends* therefore includes several pages analysing the candidate countries and the Christian composition of each.

But the overall picture presented by this book serves to highlight the dilemma which Christian churches in the United Kingdom currently face. It has long been said that there is a yearning for spirituality across our countries, but until now the evidence has been largely anecdotal. What the Census has shown is that a huge majority of our population, in the privacy of their own homes and without any external pressure, have expressed a personal allegiance of some kind to the Christian faith. Unfortunately, as the trends noted in this book ably demonstrate, there is a seeming inability on the part of most Christian churches to understand and engage with that opportunity.

It is not the author's purpose to offer facile solutions or trite techniques. Rather, by providing the facts, *Religious Trends* invites us to pray and ponder in an informed manner – so that, under God, we may begin to engage intelligently in a style of evangelism that connects the Christian Church and the population of the United Kingdom in a manner that is not happening now.

There is, of course, an important caveat to all this – and one that must not be forgotten. How far can we equate attendance at religious services with the level of religious conviction? It is surely unwise to confuse quantity and quality. The Church as it really is must be defined not by the numbers attending its official worship, but by the nature of people's relationship with God, with themselves and with each other.

Nevertheless the Church, since New Testament times, has been charged with providing the prime witness to Jesus Christ; and at its earthly heart are the faithful few who gather for worship and scatter for service. The fact that, in so many places, they are becoming even fewer is a matter of the deepest concern. These pages provide evidence that underlines the urgency of the situation and the need for this generation, by God's grace, to build up the Church and extend the Kingdom.

We spend much thought and energy wondering how to build bridges into what we have perceived to be an almost wholly secular society; but we have often failed to recognise the bridges which others, from within society, have built towards us. Peter Brierley is to be congratulated on providing a resource that, wisely used, could help to close that gap between institutionalised religion and society's spiritual needs – and make sure that, under God, the UK Christian Church in this second Elizabethan age does not die.

+ Nigel McCulloch
Bishopscourt, Manchester

Contents

How to use *Religious Trends*

Religious Trends is primarily a reference book for those wanting information about church life in the UK or wider afield. It is not a book to read straight through! Like any resource book, the Index (Section 13) is a good place to start, especially as this gives cumulative references to the previous three volumes.

All the sections listed on the Contents Page 0.5 are flagged by bleeds at the edge of each page. Hold the book closed, and you will see them on the edge. The book operates around these sections (plus a fourteenth, numbered zero, which comprises the necessary introductory pages). Page numbers are given in terms of these sections, and are continuous within each section but not beyond it, since each new section begins with its own page 1.

This edition has a number of special features:

- Section 1 looks at European Christianity, especially because the European Union is about to be enlarged, and the Candidate Countries are separately identified and totalled.
- Section 4 displaces the usual demographic data by focusing specifically on the results of the 2001 Population Census with regard to Religion, as a means of helping the research and academic community have easy access to the data by local geographical entity. These are summarised on Pages 2.2 and 2.3.
- Section 12 focuses specifically on the results of the Scottish Church Census, whose general results are in the book *Turning the Tide*. This Section details the results by Council, and gives supplementary denominational analyses.
- This information provides the data for the maps in the coloured part of Section 2, although the final page displays Church of England data.
- Section 3 utilises a completely new method of collecting mission statistics, and much of this data has not appeared before.
- Sections 8 to 10 break down a vast amount of individual denominational statistics (Sections 8 and 9) and Other Religions statistics (Section 10) by the four constituent countries of the UK (updating the data in *Religious Trends* No 1 which included information for 1980 and 1985). This is all summarised on Pages 2.21 especially and Pages 2.22 and 2.23.
- As a consequence there has been no space for Sections 6 and 11! But Section 7 continues to list other religious research published in the past 2 years of which we are aware, and has its own subject index at the end of that section.

Each edition of *Religious Trends* is at least 90% different from the previous one. Numbers 1 and 3 are still in print should any reader wish to purchase back copies. Unlike previous editions, however, this is published separately from the *UK Christian Handbook,* although it is still linked to that volume by its title.

Peter Brierley
April 2003

Notes and definitions for statistics in sections 2, 8, 9 and 10

Page 2.21 is a **total summary** of all the data given in Sections 8 and 9. A repeat of the denominational totals are given on Pages 2.22 and 23 for ease of reference.

Membership figures were given in answer to the following request: "Total number of adult (aged 15 and over) members/adherents in the UK." Definitions of membership vary according to the church denomination or religious group in question. Adult church membership is defined as appropriate to each particular group, so that for example the Electoral Roll (not to be confused with the Local Authority Roll) has been used for the Church of England, whilst because there is no comparable equivalent to the Protestant definitions of membership, Roman Catholic adult mass attendance figures have mostly been used. Where adherents are defined as non-communicant members, as with some Scottish denominations, these have been added to the true members.

Active membership is normally taken as half the community where actual membership is unknown. For religions other than Christianity, the results of the 2001 Population Census have been used where necessary.

Ministers are full-time active clergy, ordained officials (including those in administration, chaplaincies, etc.) or other recognised leaders. Many of the Afro-Caribbean clergy are part-time.

Churches (or equivalent buildings for religions other than Christianity) are those religious buildings in regular use, normally wholly owned by the organisations. Numbers of buildings do not necessarily correspond to the number of congregations or groups within the particular denomination so the number of congregations has been used in some tables as indicated.

Estimates indicated by footnotes are always editorial estimates, rather than ones made by the individual denominations themselves, which are not identified in these tables.

Estimates **for the year 2005** are based on the data for the previous years shown in the text and on other information where available, generally using a dampened linear regression.

Revised figures refer to changes from the previous edition of *Religious Trends.*

Extensive **footnotes** are sometimes supplied to help those requiring more information.

1

European Christianity

Sources: Mainly the *Eurostat Yearbook,* 2002, and the *Statistical Yearbook on Candidate and south-east European countries* both Eurostat, European Commission, 2002 and *Population Trends,* Office for National Statistics, for UK data.

1.2 Population and Christianity of European Union countries

Table 1.2
Population and Christianity of European Union and other European countries

Country	Abb	Population (thousands) 2000	2001	2025	Annual percentage change 2000–2005 %	2000–2025 %	Total Christians (thousands) 2000	2025	Percentage of population 2000	2025	Number of churches 2000	2025
Austria	A	8,103	8,121	8,390	*+0.23*	*+0.14*	7,273	7,299	*89.8*	*87.0*	5,400	5,200
Belgium	B	10,239	10,262	10,343	*+0.23*	*+0.04*	9,038	8,843	*88.3*	*85.5*	5,500	5,000
Denmark	DK	5,330	5,349	5,604	*+0.36*	*+0.20*	4,847	4,674	*91.6*	*89.2*	3,010	2,900
Finland	FIN	5,171	5,181	5,217	*+0.19*	*+0.04*	4,804	4,747	*92.8*	*91.0*	1,740	1,900
France	F	59,226	59,521	64,337	*+0.50*	*+0.33*	41,889	43,620	*70.7*	*67.8*	43,000	42,000
Germany	D	82,164	82,193	77,181	*+0.04*	*–0.25*	62,368	56,882	*75.8*	*73.7*	47,500	45,000
Greece	EL	10,543	10,565	11,365	*+0.21*	*+0.30*	9,984	10,660	*94.7*	*93.8*	35,000	34,000
Ireland	IRL	3,777	3,820	4,006	*+1.14*	*+0.24*	3,671	3,846	*97.2*	*96.0*	2,850	3,200
Italy	I	57,680	57,844	55,177	*+0.28*	*–0.18*	47,355	44,086	*82.1*	*79.9*	38,000	21,000
Luxembourg	L	436	441	503	*+1.28*	*+0.57*	409	468	*93.9*	*93.0*	360	400
Netherlands	NL	15,864	15,983	17,116	*+0.75*	*+0.30*	12,755	13,231	*80.4*	*77.3*	10,000	12,000
Portugal	P	9,998	10,023	10,625	*+0.25*	*+0.24*	9,238	9,616	*92.4*	*90.5*	9,200	10,000
Spain	E	39,442	39,490	39,099	*+0.12*	*–0.03*	36,918	35,971	*93.6*	*92.0*	30,000	32,000
Sweden	S	8,861	8,883	9,313	*+0.24*	*+0.20*	6,017	6,175	*67.9*	*66.3*	9,500	10,000
United Kingdom	UK	58,602	58,789	60,388	*+0.35*	*+0.12*	42,079	41,789	*71.6*	*69.2*	48,820	46,170
Total	**EU-15**	**375,432**	**376,465**	**378,664**	***+0.28***	***+0.03***	**298,645**	**291,907**	***79.5***	***77.1***	**289,880**	**270,770**
Cyprus	CY	755	759	864	*+0.53*	*+0.54*	710	798	*94.1*	*92.4*	750	800
Czech Republic	CZ	10,278	10,267	9,512	*–0.11*	*–0.31*	6,457	7,102	*63.0*	*74.7*	6,100	6,200
Estonia	EE	1,372	1,367	1,131	*–0.37*	*–0.77*	887	800	*63.5*	*70.8*	580	600
Hungary	HU	10,043	10,005	8,900	*–0.38*	*–0.48*	8,764	8,078	*87.3*	*90.8*	6,800	7,100
Latvia	LV	2,380	2,366	1,936	*–0.58*	*–0.82*	1,578	1,509	*66.9*	*77.9*	1,000	900
Lithuania	LT	3,699	3,693	3,399	*–0.16*	*–0.34*	3,214	3,158	*87.6*	*92.9*	910	900
Malta	MT	389	391	430	*+0.67*	*+0.40*	382	420	*98.3*	*97.6*	160	190
Poland	PL	38,654	38,644	39,069	*–0.02*	*+0.04*	37,758	38,264	*97.4*	*97.9*	17,000	19,000
Slovakia	SK	5,399	5,403	5,409	*+0.06*	*+0.01*	4,624	4,784	*85.6*	*88.5*	3,100	3,300
Slovenia	SI	1,988	1,990	1,818	*+0.12*	*–0.36*	1,829	1,706	*92.1*	*93.8*	2,500	4,100
Total	**CN-10**	**74,957**	**74,885**	**72,468**	***–0.10***	***–0.13***	**66,203**	**66,619**	***88.3***	***91.9***	**38,900**	**43,090**
Grand total	**EU-25**	**450,391**	**451,350**	**451,132**	***+0.22***	***+0.01***	**364,848**	**357,992**	***81.0***	***79.4***	**328,780**	**313,860**
Bulgaria	BG	8,191	8,150	6,959	*–0.50*	*–0.65*	6,635	5,831	*81.0*	*83.8*	5,600	5,400
Romania	RO	22,456	22,430	20,060	*–0.11*	*–0.45*	19,753	18,235	*88.0*	*90.9*	38,000	43,000
Turkey	TR	64,815	65,784	85,526	*+1.50*	*+1.12*	378	428	*0.6*	*0.5*	1,370	1,800
Grand total	**EU-28**	**545,853**	**547,714**	**563,677**	***+0.34***	***+0.13***	**391,614**	**382,486**	***71.7***	***67.9***	**373,750**	**364,060**
Iceland	IS	279	283	319	*+1.43*	*+0.54*	271	306	*97.2*	*96.0*	410	600
Norway	NO	4,479	4,503	4,921	*+0.54*	*+0.38*	4,224	4,542	*94.3*	*92.3*	3,000	3,900
Switzerland	CH	7,164	7,206	7,609	*+0.59*	*+0.24*	6,333	6,612	*88.4*	*86.9*	6,900	7,300
Albania	AL	3,401	3,426[1]	4,173	*+0.74*	*+0.82*	1,203	1,835	*35.4*	*44.0*	1,010	2,000
Croatia	HR	4,568	4,548[1]	4,282	*–0.44*	*–0.26*	4,349	4,117	*95.2*	*96.1*	2,200	2,000
Macedonia	MK	2,022	2,031	2,256	*+0.45*	*+0.44*	1,287	1,399	*63.7*	*62.0*	1,000	1,100
Yugoslavia	YU	10,637	10,645	10,841	*+0.08*	*+0.08*	7,223	7,856	*67.9*	*72.5*	4,500	5,000
Grand total	**EU-35**	**578,403**	**580,356**	**598,078**	***+0.34***	***+0.13***	**416,504**	**409,153**	***71.9***	***68.4***	**392,770**	**385,960**

Abb = Official abbreviation   [1] Estimate

Sources: Population for 2000, 2001 and 2025 for EU-15 and for Iceland, Norway and Switzerland from *Eurostat Yearbook,* 2002, Eurostat, European Commission, 2002; Population for 2000 and 2001 for CN-10 and Bulgaria, Romania, Turkey, Albania, Croatia, Macedonia and Yugoslavia from the *Statistical Yearbook on Candidate and South-east European countries,* Eurostat, European Commission, 2002; Office for National Statistics and *Religious Trends* for UK statistics; Number of Christians, CN-10 and subsequent countries 2025 population and number of churches *World Christian Encyclopedia,* David Barrett, OUP, 2001, adjusted pro rata by actual 2000 population.

Figure 1.3.1
Percentage of population who are Christian, 2000

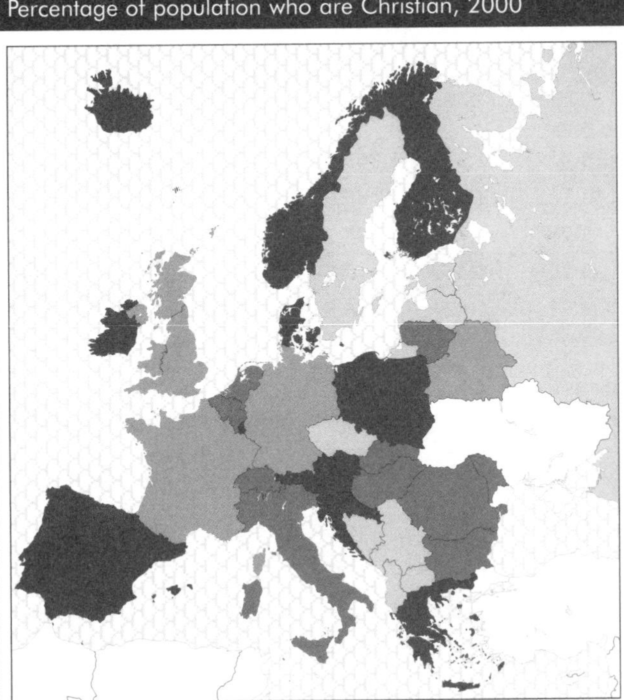

Figure 1.3.2 Percentage of Christians who are Evangelical, Pentecostal or Charismatic, 2000

The European Union (EU) currently involves just 15 countries (defined as EU-15), but a further 13 have applied to join in January 2004. However three of these (Bulgaria, Romania and Turkey) are not being allowed to proceed with membership immediately. When the other 10 join (defined as EU-25) then the combined population will move from 376 million in 2001 to 450 million, almost a fifth as big again. The EU is already the largest population block after China (1,273 million) and India (1,029 million) although a long way behind, and these new countries will simply reduce the difference.

Between 2000 and 2001 the EU-15 population grew by 1,049,000 people, comprised of a net natural increase (births over deaths) of 368,000 and a net migration increase of 681,000. However, the natural population is declining in 4 existing EU countries: Germany, Greece, Italy and Sweden, and in no less than 6 of the candidate countries: Czech Republic, Estonia, Hungary, Latvia, Lithuania, and Slovenia. Movements of migrant workers in **Table 1.2** may hide these changes. But the consequence of this decline is that the proportion the EU-25 is of the total world population will decrease over the next 50 years.

Table 1.2 gives the population of both the existing and candidate countries and the number of Christians in each, as given by David Barrett in his *World Christian Encyclopedia,* although using the latest UK figures. These figures are mapped in **Figure 1.3.1.**

Because of the dominance of Catholics in Poland, Europe becomes slightly more Christian when the 10 candidate countries join next year. If the other three eventually join, however, the Christian proportion decreases because so few of Turkey's population are Christian.

The Muslim proportion of the population in 2000 of the EU-15 countries is 3.3%, because of the high numbers in France and Germany especially, but also the United Kingdom. The number of Muslims in the 10 candidate countries is very small, so the Muslim percentage of the population in EU-25 drops to 2.8%. Were the other three to join this would become 14.1% due to the influence of Turkish Muslims.

Figure 1.3.2 shows the proportion of Evangelicals, Pentecostals and Charismatics (as defined by David Barrett) in the Christian community. The British Isles and Scandinavia have the highest percentages, with Belgium, Greece, Spain and some of the old East European countries the lowest.

1.4 Demographic and other data of European Union countries

Table 1.4
Demographic and other data of European Union and other European countries

Country	Abb	Percentage of population in 2000 who were: Under 15 %	15–24 %	25–64 %	65/65+ %	Percentage of population in 2000 who: Married %	Divorced %	No. of children per woman 1996	2000	Percentage of population in 1999 with a: Car %	Doctor %	GDP per person in 2000 in euros	Monthly wage of full-timers in 1999 in euros
Austria	A	17	12	55	16	0.48	0.24	1.42	1.32	49.4	0.37	24,570	1,905
Belgium	B	18	12	53	17	0.44	0.26	1.55	1.65	45.0	0.41	25,130	n/a
Denmark	DK	16	12	57	15	0.67[2]	0.25[2]	1.75	1.76	34.1	0.29[5]	27,140	3,281
Finland	FIN	18	13	54	15	0.51	0.27	1.76	1.73	40.7	0.31	23,200	2,109
France	F	19	13	52	16	0.52	0.20[2]	1.72	1.89	46.5	0.30	22,250	2,162
Germany	D	16	11	56	17	0.51	0.23[2]	1.32	1.34	51.5	0.36	23,540	2,688
Greece	EL	15	14	53	18	0.52[2]	0.09	1.30	1.30	27.5	0.43[4]	15,460	n/a
Ireland	IRL	22	17	49	12	0.50	n/a	1.89	1.89	34.6	0.23	26,800	n/a
Italy	I	14	12	56	18	0.48[2]	0.06	1.20	1.25	54.4	0.59	22,890	n/a
Luxembourg	L	19	11	56	14	0.49	0.23	1.76	1.78	61.0	0.26	43,750	3,213
Netherlands	NL	19	12	56	13	0.55	0.21	1.53	1.72	39.8	0.31	26,310	2,287
Portugal	P	17	15	52	16	0.64	0.19	1.43	1.54	33.0	0.32	16,770	645[4]
Spain	E	15	15	53	17	0.52[2]	0.09[2]	1.17	1.22	42.4	0.44	18,110	1,208
Sweden	S	19	12	52	17	0.45	0.24	1.60	1.54	44.0	0.28[4]	22,960	2,351
United Kingdom	UK	19	12	53	16	0.52	0.27	1.72	1.64	41.4	0.18[5]	23,560	2,707
Total	**EU-15**	**17**	**12**	**54**	**17**	**0.51**	**0.19**	**1.44**	**1.53**	**46.0**	**0.36**	**22,530**	**2,265**[4]
Cyprus	CY	23	15	48	14	1.23	0.17	2.08	1.83	34.0	0.28	14,200	1,342
Czech Republic	CZ	17	16	51	16	0.54	0.29	1.18	1.14	33.5	0.30	5,400	359
Estonia	EE	18	14	50	18	0.40	0.31	1.30	1.39	33.4	0.31	3,800	291
Hungary	HU	17	15	51	17	0.48	0.24	1.46	1.33	22.5	0.32	5,000	318
Latvia	LV	18	14	50	18	0.39	0.26	1.16	1.24	22.1	0.29	3,300	226
Lithuania	LT	20	14	50	16	0.46	0.29	1.42	1.33	29.4	0.39	3,300	251
Malta	MT	20	15	50	15	0.62	n/a	2.10	1.80	46.9	0.26	9,900	836
Poland	PL	19	17	50	14	0.55	0.11	1.58	1.34	24.0	0.23	4,400	442
Slovakia	SK	20	17	50	13	0.48	0.17	1.47	1.30	22.9	0.34	3,900	271
Slovenia	SI	16	15	53	16	0.37	0.11	1.28	1.25	42.7	0.22	9,800	809
Total	**CN-10**	**19**	**16**	**50**	**15**	**0.52**	**0.17**	**1.47**	**1.31**	**26.1**	**0.27**	**4,750**	**403**[4]
Total	**EU-25**	**17**	**13**	**53**	**17**	**0.51**	**0.19**	**1.44**	**1.49**	**42.7**	**0.35**	**18,790**	**1,955**[4]
Bulgaria	BG	16	15	51	18	0.42	0.13	1.24	1.25	23.3	0.35	1,600	110
Romania	RO	19	16	50	15	0.61	0.14	1.30	1.30	13.3	0.19	1,800	120
Turkey	TR	30	20	44	6	0.74[2]	0.05	2.59	2.50	6.3	0.12	3,200	407[4]
Total	**EU-28**	**18**	**14**	**52**	**16**	**0.54**	**0.17**	**1.57**	**1.60**	**36.9**	**0.32**	**15,980**	**1,668**[4]
Iceland	IS	23	15	50	12	0.63	0.19	2.12	2.08	54.2	0.33[3]	27,220	1,531
Norway	NO	20	12	53	15	0.53[2]	0.20[2]	1.89	1.85	40.8	0.31[3]	31,200	1,601
Switzerland	CH	17	12	56	15	0.55	0.15	1.50	1.50	46.2[5]	0.34	28,300	n/a
Albania	AL	32	17	44	7	0.76	0.05	2.70	2.10	27.1	0.13	1,210	87
Croatia	HR	20	14	51	15	0.50	0.10	1.70	1.40	23.3	0.24	4,150[2]	601
Macedonia	MK	23	16	50	11	0.70	0.07	1.90	1.90	14.3	0.22	1,910	279
Yugoslavia	YU	20	15	49	16	0.55	0.08	1.80	1.60	16.1	0.21	1,580[2]	n/a
Grand Total	**EU-35**	**18**	**14**	**52**	**16**	**0.54**	**0.17**	**1.58**	**1.60**	**36.4**	**0.32**	**15,760**	**1,644**[4]

Abb = Official abbreviation [1] Estimate [2] 1999 figure [3] 1997 figure [4] 1998 figure [5] 1996 figure

Sources: Population for 2000, 2001 and 2025 for EU-15 and for Iceland, orway and Switzerland *Eurostat Yearbook,* 2002, Eurostat, European Commission, 2002; Population for 2000 and 2001 for CN-10 and Bulgaria, Romania, Turkey from the *Statistical Yearbook on Candidate and South-east European countries,* Eurostat, European Commission, 2002; *Population Trends* Office for National Statistics.

Table 1.5
Strength of Christianity and other religions in the European Union and other European countries, 2000

Country	Abb	Area in sq. miles (thousands)	Percentage of Christians: 1 Anglican %	2 R Catholic %	3 Independent %	4 Orthodox %	5 Protestant %	6 Unaffiliated %	7 Marginal %	E/P/C %	Percentage of population: 8 Muslim %	9 Jew %	10 All others %	11 Non-R %
Austria	A	32.4	*0.0*	*84.1*	*1.0*	*2.1*	*5.6*	*6.3*	*0.9*	*4.7*	*2.2*	*0.1*	*0.2*	*7.7*
Belgium	B	12.0	*0.1*	*91.7*	*0.5*	*0.5*	*1.4*	*5.0*	*0.8*	*3.7*	*3.6*	*0.2*	*0.4*	*7.5*
Denmark	DK	16.6	*0.1*	*0.7*	*0.8*	*0.0*	*95.7*	*2.0*	*0.7*	*9.7*	*1.2*	*0.1*	*0.2*	*6.9*
Finland	FIN	117.8	*0.0*	*0.1*	*1.6*	*1.2*	*91.6*	*4.7*	*0.8*	*29.3*	*0.2*	*0.0*	*0.2*	*6.8*
France	F	210.0	*0.0*	*90.6*	*3.2*	*1.6*	*2.2*	*1.6*	*0.8*	*4.1*	*7.1*	*1.0*	*1.5*	*19.7*
Germany	D	137.8	*0.0*	*44.4*	*1.2*	*1.1*	*46.7*	*5.7*	*0.9*	*6.3*	*4.4*	*0.1*	*0.3*	*19.4*
Greece	EL	51.0	*0.0*	*0.6*	*2.3*	*96.3*	*0.2*	*0.2*	*0.4*	*1.3*	*3.3*	*0.1*	*0.0*	*1.9*
Ireland	IRL	27.0	*3.7*	*87.2*	*0.5*	*0.0*	*0.9*	*7.4*	*0.3*	*16.9*	*0.2*	*0.1*	*0.0*	*2.5*
Italy	I	116.2	*0.0*	*96.8*	*0.9*	*0.2*	*1.0*	*0.2*	*0.9*	*9.6*	*1.2*	*0.1*	*0.1*	*16.5*
Luxembourg	L	1.2	*0.1*	*96.1*	*0.5*	*0.3*	*1.9*	*0.4*	*0.7*	*5.2*	*1.0*	*0.2*	*0.3*	*4.6*
Netherlands	NL	13.1	*0.1*	*42.9*	*3.8*	*0.1*	*33.4*	*19.0*	*0.7*	*13.0*	*3.8*	*0.2*	*1.4*	*14.2*
Portugal	P	35.5	*0.0*	*94.0*	*3.0*	*0.0*	*1.5*	*0.4*	*1.1*	*8.2*	*0.2*	*0.0*	*0.9*	*6.5*
Spain	E	195.0	*0.0*	*98.2*	*0.9*	*0.0*	*0.3*	*0.1*	*0.5*	*3.2*	*0.5*	*0.0*	*0.2*	*5.7*
Sweden	S	158.7	*0.1*	*2.9*	*1.0*	*2.0*	*93.2*	*0.9*	*0.9*	*25.0*	*2.3*	*0.2*	*0.2*	*29.4*
United Kingdom	UK	94.2	*67.2*	*13.8*	*6.6*	*1.2*	*10.9*	*0.0*	*0.3*	*35.8*	*2.7*	*0.4*	*2.1*	*23.2*
Total	**EU-15**	**1,217.8**	***9.5***	***62.3***	***2.3***	***4.0***	***18.4***	***2.8***	***0.7***	***11.3***	***3.2***	***0.3***	***0.8***	***16.2***
Cyprus	CY	3.6	*0.6*	*1.7*	*0.1*	*92.9*	*0.8*	*2.5*	*1.4*	*1.1*	*1.0*	*0.0*	*0.2*	*4.7*
Czech Republic	CZ	30.5	*0.0*	*64.0*	*4.2*	*0.9*	*5.0*	*25.4*	*0.5*	*5.9*	*0.0*	*0.1*	*0.0*	*36.9*
Estonia	EE	17.5	*0.0*	*0.7*	*5.2*	*25.9*	*27.1*	*40.2*	*0.9*	*14.9*	*0.3*	*0.2*	*0.0*	*36.0*
Hungary	HU	35.9	*0.0*	*68.6*	*1.9*	*1.0*	*27.8*	*0.2*	*0.5*	*13.1*	*0.6*	*0.5*	*0.0*	*11.6*
Latvia	LV	24.9	*0.0*	*28.2*	*7.3*	*32.0*	*32.2*	*0.1*	*0.2*	*16.4*	*0.4*	*0.6*	*0.0*	*32.1*
Lithuania	LT	25.2	*0.0*	*94.0*	*1.0*	*3.5*	*1.4*	*0.0*	*0.1*	*1.9*	*0.2*	*0.2*	*0.0*	*12.0*
Malta	MT	0.1	*0.3*	*96.2*	*0.2*	*0.0*	*0.3*	*2.8*	*0.2*	*25.5*	*0.5*	*0.0*	*0.1*	*1.1*
Poland	PL	120.7	*0.0*	*94.7*	*0.9*	*2.7*	*0.5*	*0.7*	*0.5*	*5.7*	*0.0*	*0.0*	*0.1*	*2.5*
Slovakia	SK	18.9	*0.0*	*79.4*	*0.5*	*0.5*	*13.0*	*6.2*	*0.4*	*7.8*	*0.0*	*0.1*	*0.0*	*14.3*
Slovenia	SI	7.8	*0.0*	*90.7*	*1.7*	*0.7*	*1.7*	*5.1*	*0.1*	*4.6*	*0.1*	*0.0*	*0.0*	*7.8*
Total	**CN-10**	**285.1**	***0.0***	***83.2***	***1.5***	***4.1***	***6.6***	***4.1***	***0.5***	***7.1***	***0.1***	***0.1***	***0.1***	***11.4***
Total	**EU-25**	**1,502.9**	***7.8***	***66.1***	***2.1***	***4.0***	***16.3***	***3.0***	***0.7***	***10.5***	***2.7***	***0.3***	***0.7***	***15.4***
Bulgaria	BG	42.9	*0.0*	*1.4*	*8.7*	*88.3*	*1.4*	*0.1*	*0.1*	*3.9*	*11.9*	*0.1*	*0.0*	*7.0*
Romania	RO	92.0	*0.0*	*12.8*	*1.5*	*75.4*	*9.4*	*0.1*	*0.8*	*14.0*	*1.3*	*0.0*	*0.0*	*10.7*
Turkey	TR	297.1	*0.5*	*7.8*	*20.0*	*58.6*	*8.4*	*4.1*	*0.6*	*20.2*	*97.2*	*0.0*	*0.1*	*2.1*
Total	**EU-28**	**1,934.9**	***7.3***	***62.2***	***2.2***	***9.1***	***15.7***	***2.8***	***0.7***	***10.6***	***14.0***	***0.2***	***0.6***	***13.5***
Iceland	IS	38.6	*0.0*	*1.1*	*4.0*	*0.0*	*91.7*	*2.9*	*0.3*	*10.8*	*0.0*	*0.0*	*1.0*	*1.8*
Norway	NO	118.9	*0.1*	*1.1*	*3.2*	*0.0*	*94.8*	*0.2*	*0.6*	*41.2*	*1.0*	*0.0*	*2.2*	*2.5*
Switzerland	CH	15.4	*0.2*	*48.5*	*2.5*	*0.4*	*45.2*	*1.3*	*1.9*	*11.8*	*2.7*	*0.2*	*0.5*	*8.2*
Albania	AL	11.1	*0.0*	*47.3*	*1.6*	*45.4*	*1.8*	*2.8*	*1.1*	*9.6*	*38.8*	*0.0*	*0.2*	*25.6*
Croatia	HR	21.8	*0.0*	*93.0*	*0.2*	*5.9*	*0.6*	*0.1*	*0.2*	*3.2*	*2.3*	*0.1*	*0.0*	*2.4*
Macedonia	MK	9.9	*0.0*	*5.5*	*0.6*	*93.1*	*0.6*	*0.1*	*0.1*	*0.8*	*28.3*	*0.0*	*0.0*	*8.0*
Yugoslavia	YU	21.7	*0.0*	*7.6*	*2.5*	*83.7*	*1.4*	*4.7*	*0.1*	*4.0*	*16.2*	*0.0*	*0.0*	*15.9*
Grand Total	**EU-35**	**2,172.3**	***6.9***	***60.5***	***2.2***	***10.5***	***16.5***	***2.7***	***0.7***	***10.7***	***13.9***	***0.2***	***0.6***	***13.4***

Abb = Official abbreviation   Non-religious includes Atheists
1 square mile = 259 hectares or 2.59 km²
Independent = "Those rejecting control of churches by centralised denominational headquarters; separated from, uninterested in, and independent of historic denominationalist Christianity"
Unaffiliated = "Persons professing allegiance and commitment to Christ but who have no church affiliation"
Marginal = "Members affiliated to bodies holding mainstream Christian doctrines except on the nature of Christ, and existence of the Trinity; also professing a second source of revelation in addition to the Bible" (for example, Jehovah's Witnesses, Mormons)
E/P/C = Evangelical/Pentecostal/Charismatic; the percentage is the total of those in these persuasions across each of the previous 7 columns
Non R = Non-Religious

Columns (1) through (7) total 100% and relate to the Christian total in Table 1.2. Columns (8) through (11), with the Christian total, make up the entire population.

Sources: Area for EU-15 and Iceland, Norway and Switzerland from *Eurostat Yearbook, 2002,* Eurostat, European Commission, 2002; for CN-10 and Bulgaria, Romania, Turkey, Albania, Croatia, Macedonia and Yugoslavia from *Statistical Yearbook on Candidate and South-East European Countries,* Eurostat, European Commission, 2002; Office for National Statistics and *Religious Trends* for UK statistics; Data on Christians and other religions for all other countries from *World Christian Encyclopedia,* David Barrett, OUP, 2001.

1.6 European Christianity: Christianity in Malta

Malta, GC, has a special place in the history of the Second World War when on 15th April 1942 King George VI awarded the inhabitants a collective George Cross for being "bombed but not broken" (as their underground posters proclaimed) to encourage them in their strategic resistance.

Centuries earlier, St Paul was shipwrecked on the island. Catacombs today show where Paul might have lived the 3 months he was there, and on the outside wall of the church in St Paul's Bay is the inscription "I believe God that it will be just as it was told me" (Acts 27:25).

Malta is a small island of 246 sq km (95 square miles), twice the size of Jersey, or marginally bigger than the city of Peterborough. In 2000, 380,000 people lived there, 98% Maltese, growing at 1% per year. This represents an average population of 4,300 per church, 4 times as many in the UK! Gozo and Comino are smaller associated islands to the west, with a population of 30,000. 450,000 British tourists go each year for an average of 12 days, half the total.

Discern, the Institute for Research on the Signs of the Times in Malta has undertaken 3 church censuses of Catholic Mass attenders – in 1967, 1982 and 1995. The percentage has dropped as in the rest of Europe, from 82% to 73% to 62%, but even so is far higher than even in other Catholic countries. The figures exclude "twicers" (4% in 1995), and are therefore of attenders. Malta is 93% Catholic with 772 priests and 335 Catholic churches in 65 parishes.

Figure 1.6.1 Percentage attending Mass, by age-group

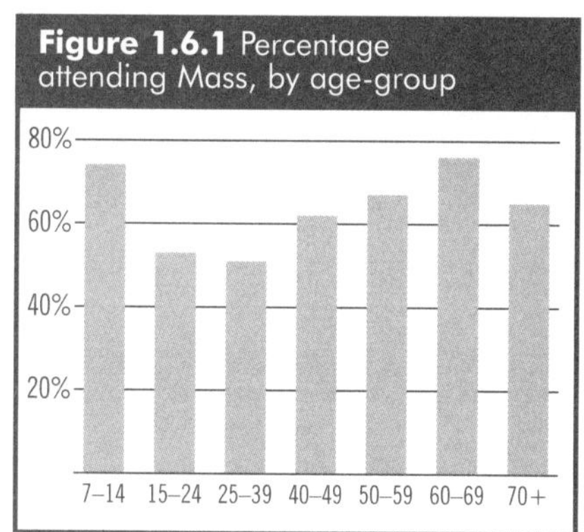

There are also 23 other churches: 2 Anglican, 2 Baptist churches (the Bible Baptist and the Evangelical Baptist), 8 Pentecostal (including two Full Gospel Praise Centres in Bugibba and Mosta), 3 Salvation Army, 1 Church of Scotland, 1 Greek Orthodox, 1 Methodist and 5 others. In 1995 there was a collective membership of these churches of 1,870, of which the Anglicans were half. If attendance is two-thirds of membership, this gives an average Sunday congregation of 30 for the non-Anglican churches (against an average of 175 per Mass, average 3 per Sunday, per Catholic church). There are also 5 Jehovah's Witness Kingdom Halls and small Jewish, Bahá'i, Buddhist and Muslim communities.

Streets are crowded in Malta, but that doesn't stop people going to the church they like rather than the one in whose parish they are situated. 27% of the Catholics went to Mass in another parish in 1995, twice the percentage in 1967. Such a high mobility points to people searching for ... what? Relevance?

Women go to Mass more than men, 56% to 44%, about the same as English Catholics. Rather more singles (+9%) and rather fewer married (–10%) are represented in church compared to the general population.

What percentage go to Mass in each age-group? **Table 1.6.1** indicates. The smallest percentage is amongst those aged 25 to 39, similar to churches in the UK (although with a far lower percentage!). Maltese churches still retain a high number of children, although drop considerably as they reach their later teens and early 20s. Older people are still the most faithful in attendance, only dropping off when old age prevents the going so often.

Figure 1.6.2
Sunday Mass and non-attending population, 1967–2010

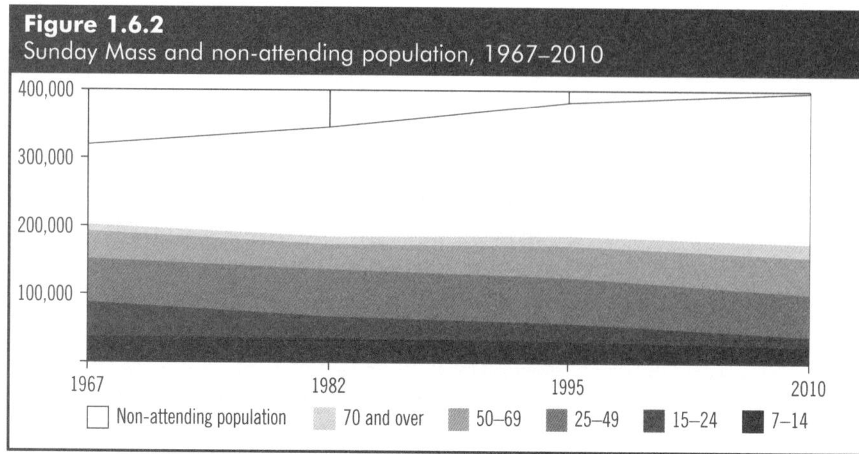

What of the future? What the trends suggest is reflected in **Figure 1.6.2,** which shows that the overall population of Malta is steadily increasing, and that the proportion attending Mass on a Sunday is declining, down to 44% on current trends by 2010, almost half the percentage of 1967. It also shows the age composition of those who are attending Mass, and show a clear decline in the numbers of children (aged 7 to 14), and young people aged 15 to 24. The number of Mass attenders aged 25 to 49 declines slightly, basically people whose parents were not regular Mass attenders, and who, when they became parents, would not send their children regularly to Mass. The numbers in their 50s and 60s increase slightly, as do those who are older still. The diagram shows there are clear challenges ahead for the leaders of the Catholic church in Malta.

Does the decline in Mass attendance mean a more open door for the Protestant churches, or are those not attending becoming in effect de-churched Catholics who are unlikely to try other churches? Will the increasing numbers of visitors and non-Maltese residents provide opportunities for the churches?

Focus Groups in 1995 explored what Sunday Mass meant to those who went. It was either a habit which "pulled people to church by some kind of cultural inertia", or "a social norm and tradition" (people would feel less acceptable to their families if they missed it), or "it was a social experience of belonging to the church community", or "it was a personal experience of contact... with God and His Christ."

These were not mutually exclusive, but the majority probably fell into the first two reasons – habit and norm. Those who went to Mass "were seeking quality" even if unconsciously (something reflected in research in UK churches). "Sunday Mass had to become more meaningful, in terms of education... homes and their jobs", concludes the Maltese report. The issue of relevance is central to UK church life also. "The level of belonging... has been falling."

The Focus Groups concluded that the quality of Sunday Mass had to change for the priests as well as the laity, and that the laity were looking primarily for relevant teaching, and a transcendent reality. They suggested that the test of a successful radical shift was when attenders enjoyed the Mass, because they celebrated it "in remembrance of ***Me.***"

Sources: Attendance at Sunday Mass, Report on the Third Census, Discern, Institute for Research on the Signs of the Times, Floriana, Malta, 1998; *Demographic Review 2000,* Official Statistics of Malta (OSM), National Statistics Office, Malta, 2001; personal observation; talk with OSM Librarian, June 2002; *Malta 2001/2 Highlights,* Thomson; *World Christian Encyclopedia,* 2nd edition, Dr David Barrett (editor), Oxford University Press, 2001; *The Malta Year Book,* 2001, Page 148; *Malta Trends,* 1993, Benjamin Tonna, Discern.

2

Churches in the UK

Sources: Individual denominations, Scottish Church Census 2002, Office for National Statistics, Research and Statistics Dept., Archbishops' Council and their publications.

2.2 Census: Questions on Religion

Table 2.2.1
UK Christian Community in millions, 1975–2005

Denominational Group	1975	1980	1985	1990	1995	2000	2005
Anglican	29.3[2]	29.0[2]	28.8[2]	28.6[2]	28.4[2]	28.3[2]	28.2[2]
Roman Catholic	5.6	5.7	5.7[2]	5.7[2]	5.9	5.8	5.8[2]
Orthodox	0.4	0.4	0.4	0.5	0.5	0.5	0.6
Presbyterian	3.4[2]	3.3[2]	3.2[2]	3.2[2]	3.1[2]	2.9[2]	2.9[2]
Baptist	0.5[2]	0.5[2]	0.5[2]	0.5[2]	0.5[2]	0.5[2]	0.5[2]
Methodist	1.7[2]	1.6[2]	1.5[2]	1.5[2]	1.4[2]	1.3[2]	1.2[2]
All other churches	1.0	1.2	1.3	1.2	1.3	1.4	1.3
TOTAL Trinitarian	**41.9**	**41.7**	**41.4**	**41.2**	**40.9**	**40.7**	**40.5**
Non-Trinitarian	0.7	0.8	1.0	1.1	1.3	1.4[2]	1.4
TOTAL Christian	**42.6**	**42.5**	**42.4**	**42.3**	**42.2**	**42.1**	**41.9**
Muslim	0.4	0.7[2]	1.0[2]	1.3[2]	1.4[2]	1.6[2]	1.7[2]
Hindu	0.4[2]	0.5[2]	0.5[2]	0.5[2]	0.5[2]	0.6[2]	0.6[2]
Sikh	0.1[2]	0.1[2]	0.2[2]	0.2[2]	0.3[2]	0.3[2]	0.4[2]
Jew	0.4	0.3	0.3	0.3	0.3	0.3	0.3
Buddhist[1]	0.0	0.1	0.1	0.1	0.1	0.2	0.2
Other religions[3]	0.1	0.1	0.1[2]	0.1[2]	0.2	0.2	0.2
TOTAL all religions	**44.0**	**44.3**	**44.6**	**44.8**	**45.0**	**45.2**	**45.3**
Percentage of population:							
Christian	*76%*	*76%*	*74%*	*74%*	*73%*	*72%*	*70%*
Muslim	*1%*	*1%*	*2%*	*2%*	*2%*	*3%*	*3%*
All other religions	*1%*	*2%*	*2%*	*2%*	*2%*	*2%*	*3%*
Total all religions	***78%***	***79%***	***78%***	***78%***	***77%***	***77%***	***76%***

[1] Estimate [2] Revised figure [3] Previously included Buddhists

Table 2.2.2
The Local Authority District where each religion was highest, 2001

Religion	District	County	% pop
Christianity	St Helens	Merseyside	*86.9*
Islam	Tower Hamlets	Greater London	*36.4*
Hindu	Harrow	Greater London	*19.6*
Sikh	Slough	Berkshire	*9.1*
Jew	Barnet	Greater London	*14.8*
Buddhist	Westminster	Greater London	*1.3*
Other religions	Harrow	Greater London	*2.0*
No Religion	Norwich	Norfolk	*27.8*
Did not answer	Haringey	Greater London	*12.1*

Table 2.2.3
Community by Christian Denomination, by country, millions, 2001

Denomination	England	Wales	Scotland	Ireland	UK	% of total
Anglican	27.2	0.9	0.0	0.2	**28.3**	*68*
Roman Catholic	4.1	0.2	0.8	0.7	**5.8**	*14*
Orthodox	0.5	0.0	0.0	0.0	**0.5**	*1*
Presbyterian	0.1	0.2	2.3	0.3	**2.9**	*7*
Baptist	0.3	0.1	0.1	0.0	**0.5**	*1*
Methodist	1.1	0.1	0.0	0.1	**1.3**	*3*
All other churches	0.8	0.4	0.1	0.1	**1.4**	*3*
Total Trinitarian	34.1	1.9	3.3	1.4	**40.7**	*97*
Non-Trinitarian	1.2	0.2	0.0	0.0	**1.4**	*3*
TOTAL Christian	**35.3**	**2.1**	**3.3**	**1.4**	**42.1**	***100***

Table 2.2.4
Scottish and Irish Denominations, 2001

Denomination	Scotland	N Ireland
Church of Scotland/ Ireland	2,146,251	257,788
Roman Catholic	803,732	678,462
Presbyterian Church in Ireland	n/a	348,742
Methodist Church in Ireland	n/a	59,173
Other Christian	344,562	102,221
Total Christian	**3,294,545**	**1,446,386**

Table 2.2.5
Number of baptised in Church of England in population in millions

1980	28.4	1995	27.9
1985	28.1	2000	27.8
1990	28.0	2005	27.8

Source: Estimated; Church House 1979 figure 27.0 million

The 2001 Census used different questions to ascertain a person's religion. In England and Wales the question was "What is your religion?" with 7 religious options (given in **Table 2.3.1**) and a no religion box. In Scotland it was "What religion, religious denomination or body do you belong to?" with the same options as in England and Wales but with Christian broken down into three components (given in **Table 2.2.4**). In Northern Ireland the question was "Do you regard yourself as belonging to any particular religion? If yes, ..." and then followed the Scottish question. Answers were as in Scotland except that "Christian" had five components. The breakdown of no religion/not stated given in **Table 2.3.1** is as given on the Office for National Statistics website.

The Local Authority District where each English answer was highest is shown in **Table 2.2.2.**

The number who ticked the Christian box was greater than many had expected. Earlier editions of *Religious Trends* had estimated the percentage as 63% in 2000, so revisions of previous figures are given in **Table 2.2.1**. The British Social Attitudes Report had put the figure at 53% in 1998 and European Values Study estimated it at 66% in 1999. Secular commentators were surprised that so many people had not reneged on their basic religious affiliation.

The large majority of the 37 million Christian people in England in 2001 are those who have been baptised in the Church of England. Estimates of the actual number baptised, based on numbers for 1962 and 1979 published by what is now the Research and Statistics Department in Church House were given in *Religious Trends* No 2, **Table 8.4.1.** That Table gave an estimate, known to be low, for the year 2000 of just under 26 million. **Table 2.2.1** has instead used the higher estimate of 28 million, and **Table 2.2.5** re-evaluates the Church of England component of these total UK Anglican estimates.

Source: April 2001 Census, Office for National Statistics, website www.statistics.gov.uk, accessed February 2003.

Table 2.3.1
Community numbers by Religion, by country, 2001

Religion	England	Wales	Scotland	N Ireland	TOTAL UK
Christianity	35,251,244	2,087,242	3,294,545	1,446,386	**42,079,417**
Islam	1,524,887	21,739	42,557	1,943	**1,591,126**
Hindu	546,982	5,439	5,564	825	**558,810**
Sikh	327,343	2,015	6,572	219	**336,149**
Jew	257,671	2,256	6,448	365	**266,740**
Buddhist	139,046	5,407	6,830	533	**151,816**
Other religions	143,811	6,909	26,974	1,143	**178,837**
No Religion	7,171,332	537,935	1,394,460	45,909	**9,149,636**
Not stated	3,776,515	234,143	278,061	187,944	**4,476,663**
TOTAL	49,138,831	2,903,085	5,062,011	1,685,267	**58,789,194**

Table 2.3.2
Community percentages by Religion, by country, 2001

Religion	England %	Wales %	Scotland %	N Ireland %	TOTAL UK %
Christianity	*71.74*	*71.90*	*65.08*	*85.83*	***71.58***
Islam	*3.10*	*0.75*	*0.84*	*0.12*	***2.71***
Hindu	*1.11*	*0.19*	*0.11*	*0.05*	***0.95***
Sikh	*0.67*	*0.07*	*0.13*	*0.01*	***0.57***
Jew	*0.52*	*0.08*	*0.13*	*0.02*	***0.45***
Buddhist	*0.28*	*0.18*	*0.14*	*0.03*	***0.26***
Other religions	*0.29*	*0.24*	*0.53*	*0.07*	***0.30***
No Religion	*14.60*	*18.53*	*27.55*	*2.72*	***15.56***
Not stated	*7.69*	*8.06*	*5.49*	*11.15*	***7.62***
Base	49,138,831	2,903,085	5,062,011	1,685,267	**58,789,194**

Christians

The 2001 Population Census included a voluntary question about religion for first time in 150 years. The basic finding was that nearly three-quarters, 72%, of the population in the UK said they were Christians, as may be seen in **Table 2.3.2**, the numbers behind which are given in **Table 2.3.1.** The overall proportions are depicted in **Figure 2.3.** A very solid Christian base is thus established.

The 37 million of these 42 million people who were in England and Wales is rather more than the 4 million who attend church every week, or the 6 million who come once a month, or even the 12 million who attend once a year, especially at Christmas. So there is an obvious yawning gap between profession and commitment in terms of church attendance.

Other Religions

Overall 5% of the UK population belong to other religions, of which half are Muslim. The large majority of these, 95%, live in England, where the percentage rises to 6.0%, against 1.8% of Scots, 1.5% of Welsh and 0.3% of the Irish. 96% of British Muslims live in England, as against 98% of Hindus and 97% of Sikhs and Jews, but only 92% of the country's Buddhists are in England and 80% of those belonging to other religions.

No religion

The 16% who said they had "no religion" contrasts with the 40% estimated in the 2002 British Social Attitudes Survey. Rather more in Scotland, 28%, said they had no religion than in other parts of the UK. Some 389,000 people ticked "Jedi", 0.7% (more than the number of Sikhs, Jews or Buddhists!), in the apparent belief that if 10,000 so ticked the form it would be counted as an official religion. Instead, the New Zealander National Statistician, Len Cook, treated them all as "no religion".

How far the 8% who did not answer this voluntary question (11% in Northern Ireland presumably because of security fears) should be treated as having the same proportions of religion or no religion as those who did tick the form is debatable. If they were, the Christian proportion would rise to 77%, and those of no religion to 17%. Those of other religions would then be 6%. Some Muslims and Jews have claimed many of those who did not answer were in fact Muslims or Jews, since their numbers seemed low by earlier estimates. However, it is probably safer, in the absence of any other knowledge, to treat those who did not reply as those of no religion.

Christian belief

The Census question gave no definition of Christian. So who are they? At best only a third are churchgoers, and half of these only come once a year. The majority of the remaining two-thirds of non-churchgoing Christians believe in Heaven, in God (and would call Him Father), and that Jesus Christ died for us and rose again from the dead. However, only a minority believe that the Holy Spirit can empower people today, and fewer still believe in the Trinity or in hell.

Can the church build on this rudimentary faith system in challenging people to go further in their faith? Yes, it can. Analysis of what makes churches grow would suggest growing deeper relationships between committed Christians and the non-committed. Ultimately people want friendship, and when churchgoers are involved in the community (as some 30% are) the opportunities for such friendships can flourish.

Christian values

The popularity of Church Schools stems not only from the fact that many are excellent academically, but also from the morals that are taught in them. Traditional morality is still regarded as hugely important at least for children, and while the Census showed a major dip in the proportion of married people (to only 50.7% of the population), that does not stop the desire for integrity, truth and honesty from being key values for the 21st century. The survey reported on **Page 5.9** among those aged 10 to 14 indicated that "tweenagers" also regard these as priority values.

The survey reported on **Page 5.8** (of the community in part of Manchester) showed that infidelity was regarded as a key sin. People yearn for commitment and sticking with it, and churchgoing Christians seem better able to do this, judging by the smaller percentage of divorces among them (as evidenced in Northern Ireland in 1991, the only statistics available). Some churches have found people are attracted to marriage seminars, parenting classes and the like.

Figure 2.3
Religions in the UK, 2001

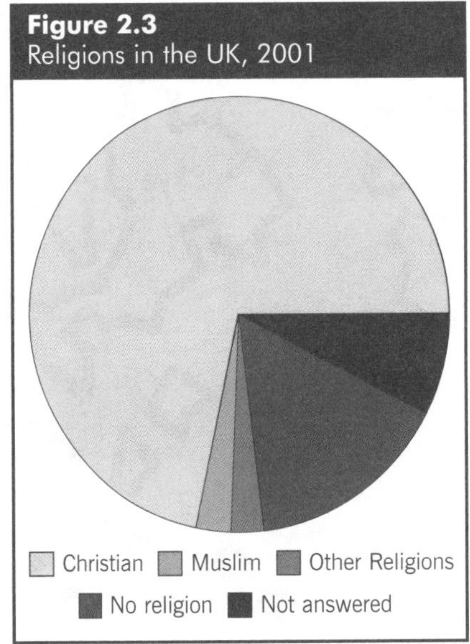

Source: April 2001 Census, Office for National Statistics, website www.statistics.gov.uk, accessed February 2003.

2.4 Scottish Church Census 2002: Councils of Scotland

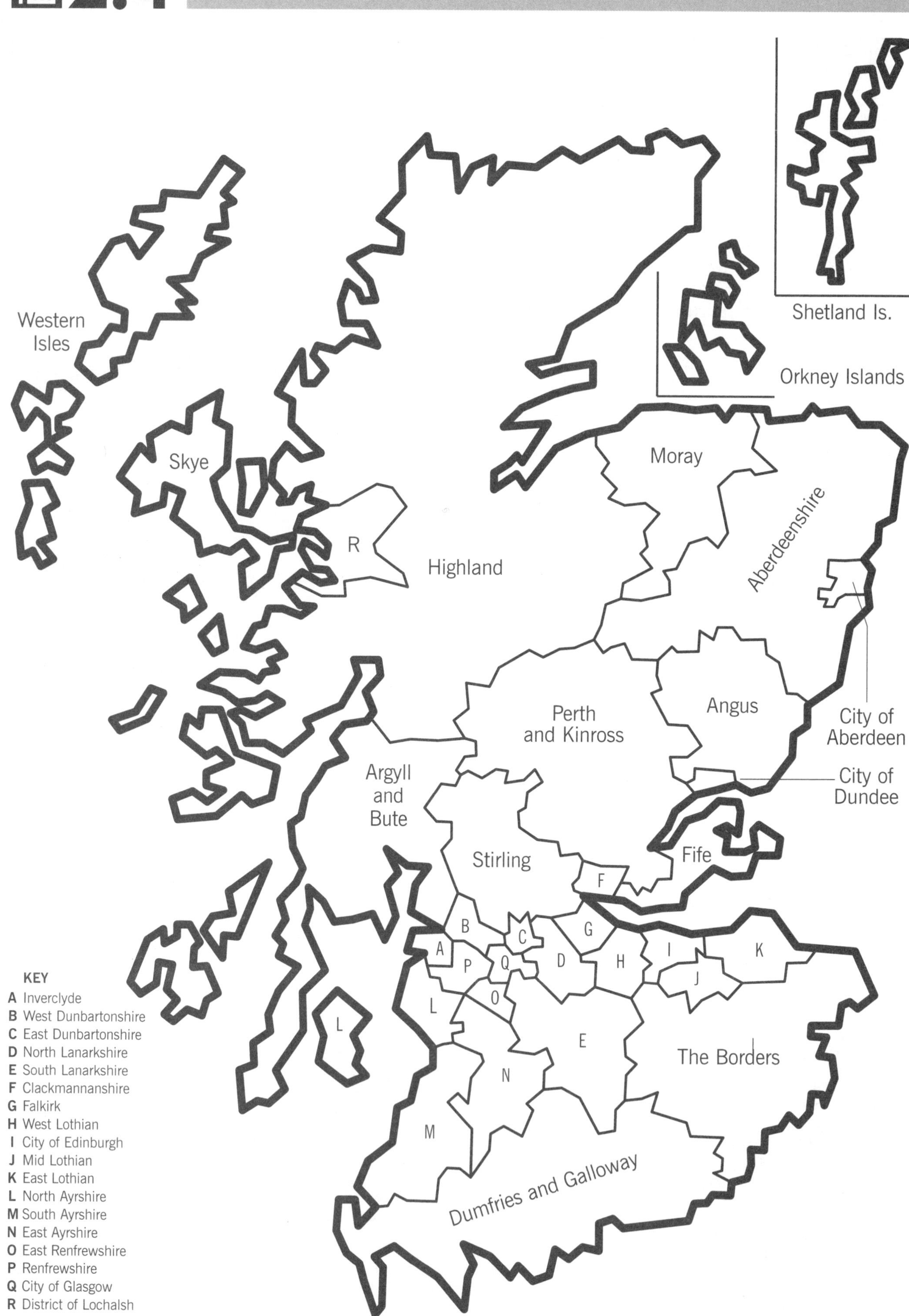

Figure 2.5.1 Sunday church attendance as % of population, 1984

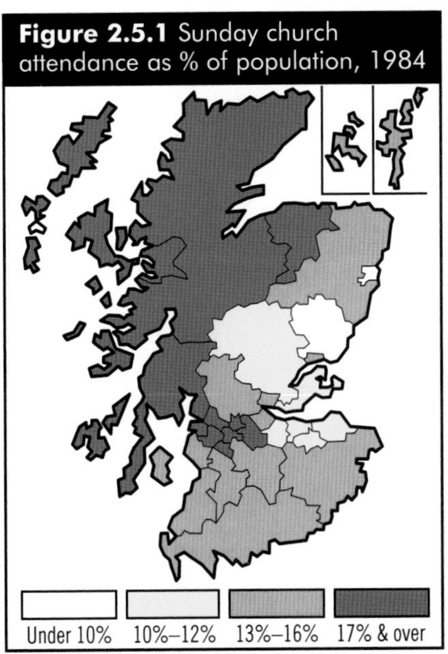

Figure 2.5.2 Sunday church attendance as % of population, 1994

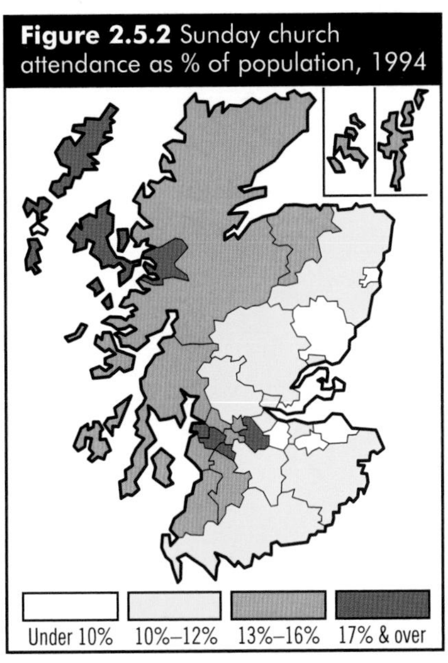

Figure 2.5.3 Sunday church attendance as % of population, 2002

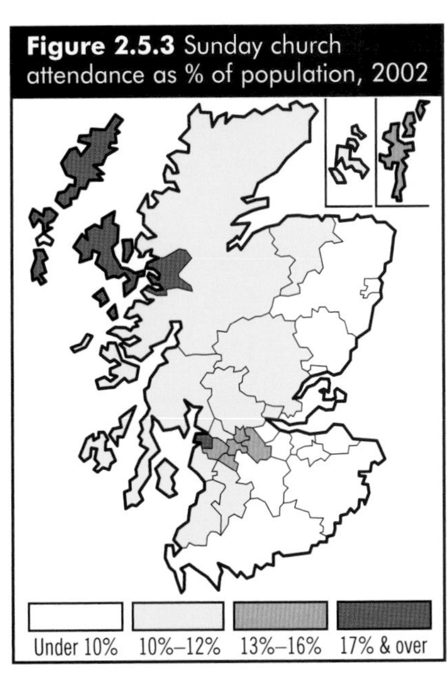

Figure 2.5.4 Changes in Sunday church attendance, 1984–1994

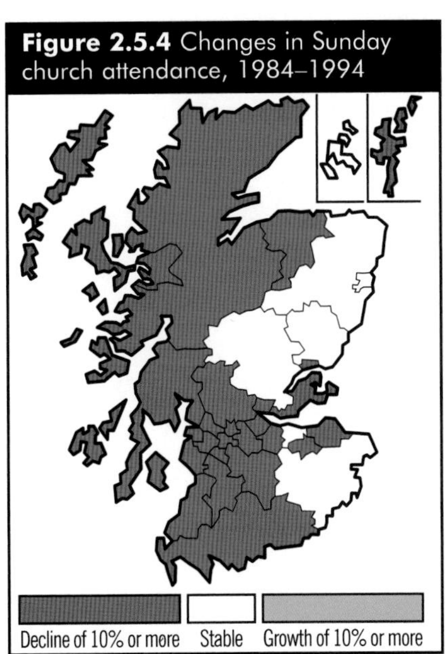

Figure 2.5.5 Sunday Church Attendance, by age, All Scotland, 1984, 1994 and 2002

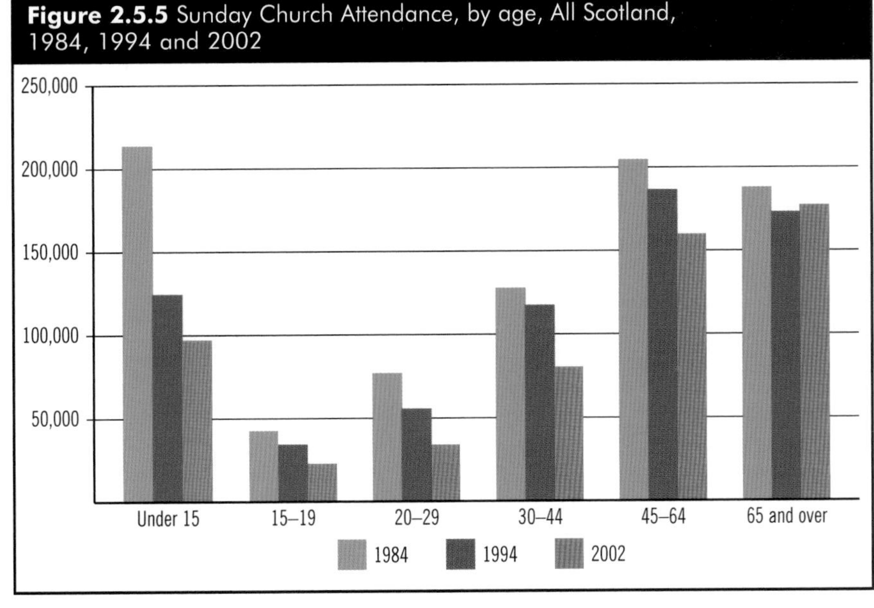

Figure 2.5.6 Changes in Sunday church attendance, 1994–2002

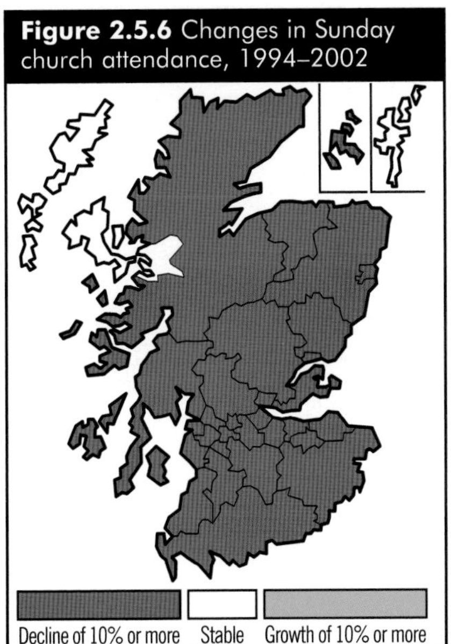

The strongest parts of Scottish Christianity (as measured by Sunday church attendance) is in the north and west of Scotland, the Highland and Argyll areas, together with Skye and the Western Isles. While this has diminished over the 18 years 1984 to 2002, it remains at a high level in Skye and Lochalsh (the district within the Highlands) and the Western Isles.

Conversely the weakest parts of Scottish church life, again as measured by Sunday church attendance, are in Aberdeen and Angus, something which has not changed in these 18 years, but which rather has spread across all the eastern and southern Councils. As **Figure 2.5.6** shows the decline has affected all parts of the country.

Figure 2.5.5 shows that the change was particularly in young people between 1984 and 1994, but in the 8 years 1994 to 2002 has been especially amongst those aged 30 to 44 and 45 to 64, age-groups often of parents of children who, it might be presumed, could drop out of church in the years ahead if they follow parental example.

Figure 2.5.7 indicates that there are many more church leaders aged 55 to 64 than there are pro rata adults attenders in their congregation, even if the average age for both is much the same (56 years). There are far fewer under 35.

Figure 2.5.7 Age of adult Sunday church attenders and leaders, 2002

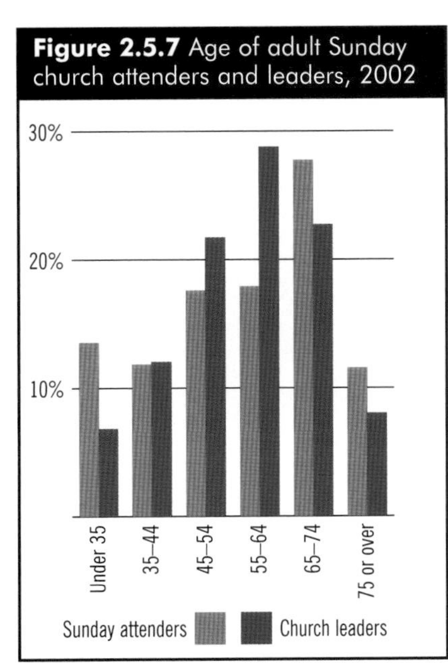

2.6 Scottish Church Census 2002: Church of Scotland

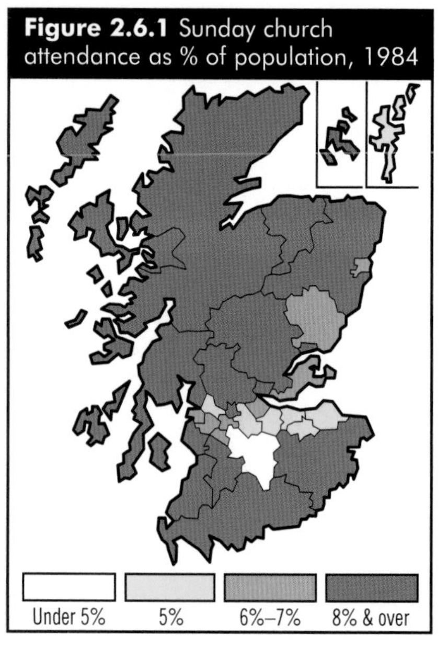

Figure 2.6.1 Sunday church attendance as % of population, 1984

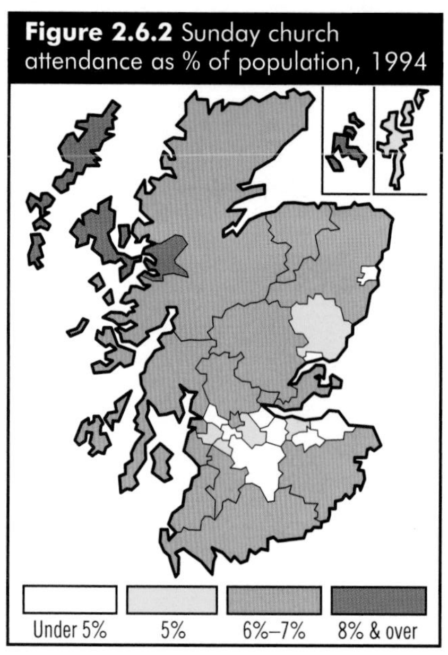

Figure 2.6.2 Sunday church attendance as % of population, 1994

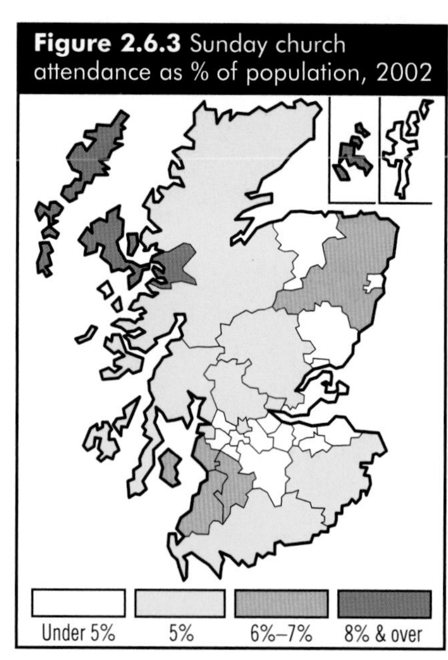

Figure 2.6.3 Sunday church attendance as % of population, 2002

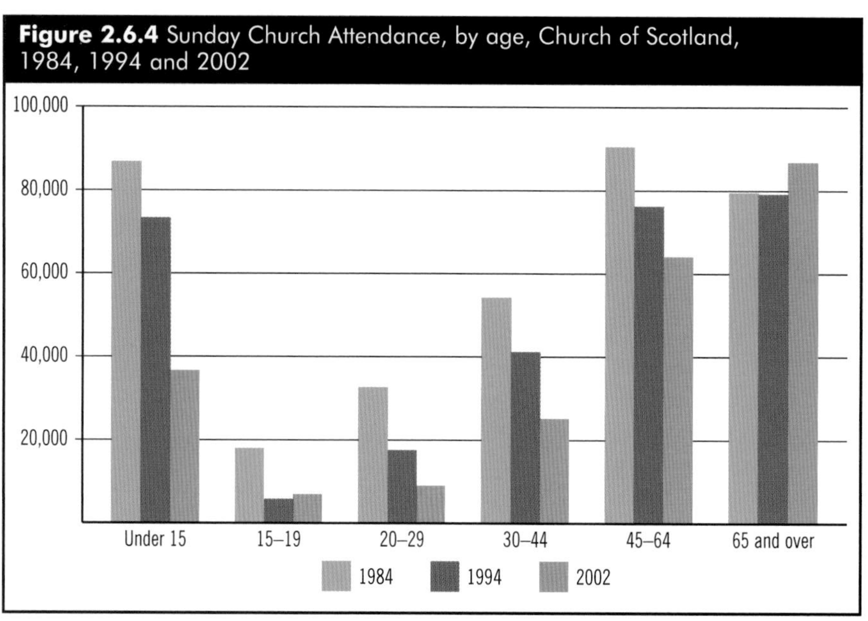

Figure 2.6.4 Sunday Church Attendance, by age, Church of Scotland, 1984, 1994 and 2002

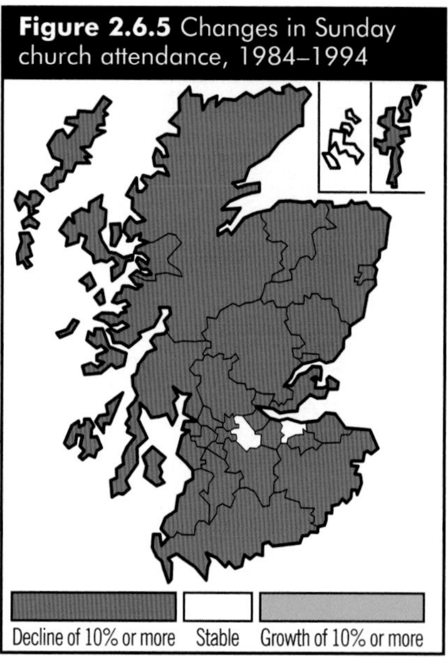

Figure 2.6.5 Changes in Sunday church attendance, 1984–1994

The Church of Scotland has seen Sunday church attendance declining between 1984 and 2002 in all areas except the Western Isles (with Skye and Lochalsh) and the Orkneys. The urban weakness apparent in 1994 in Aberdeen and Glasgow has continued by 2002 and extended to Dundee and Edinburgh also. The central band from Glasgow to Edinburgh has become progressively weaker in Church of Scotland church attendance over these 18 years.

However it has also weakened in the northern, central and southern more rural areas. **Figure 2.6.7** shows decline literally everywhere, with the steepest drops in East Dunbartonshire and Inverclyde (both 29% down in 2002 on 1994) and the least decline in the West Dunbartonshire and the Western Isles (both down 15%).

Figure 2.6.4 shows that the decline has partiucularly been seen amongst young people under 15, and more might have left had it not been for the mid-week youth clubs and the various Boys' Brigades that many churches have. It is interesting that there has been a marginal rise in the numbers of older teenagers attending.

Figure 2.6.6 reveals that there are almost twice as many Elders aged 55 to 64 pro rata than people in the congregation and far fewer aged under 35, but with an average age of 60 this but replicates the average of the adult congregation.

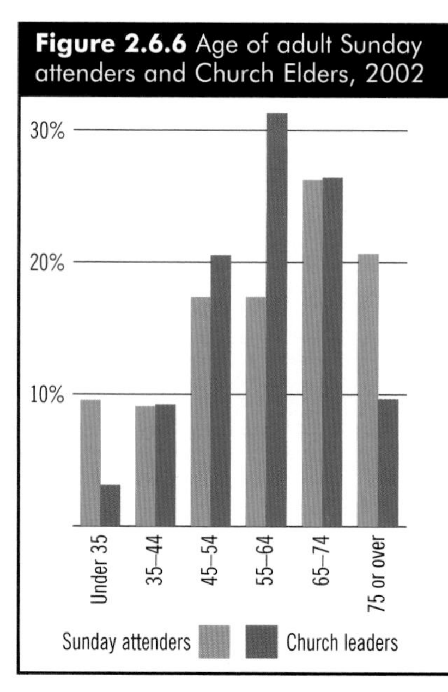

Figure 2.6.6 Age of adult Sunday attenders and Church Elders, 2002

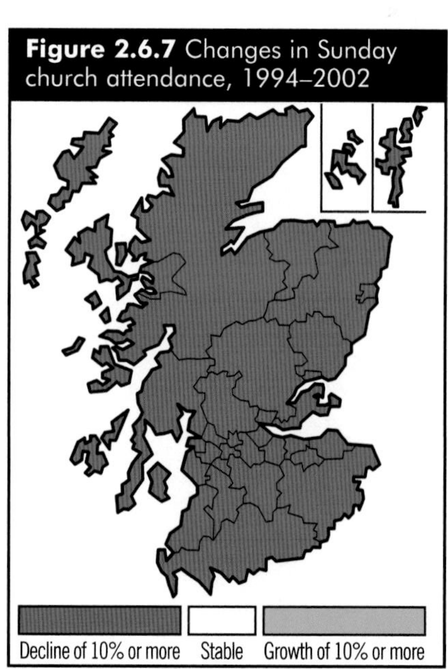

Figure 2.6.7 Changes in Sunday church attendance, 1994–2002

Figure 2.7.1 Sunday church attendance as % of population, 1984

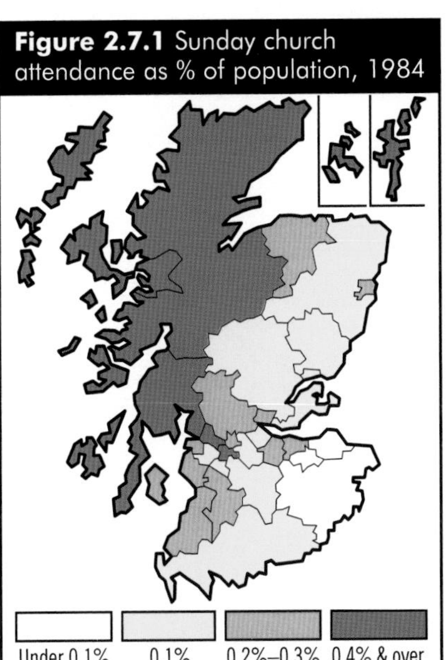

Figure 2.7.2 Sunday church attendance as % of population, 1994

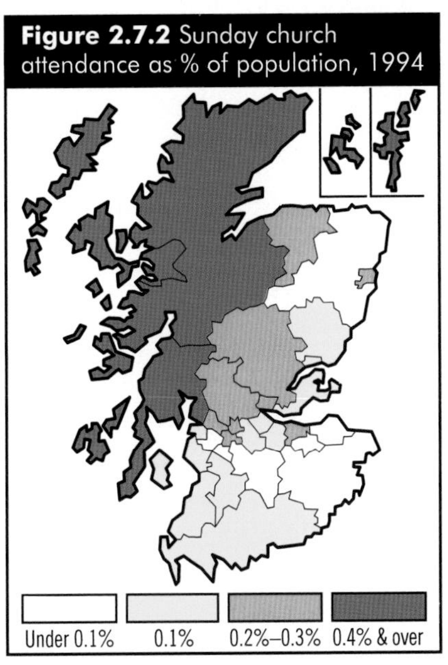

Figure 2.7.3 Sunday church attendance as % of population, 2002

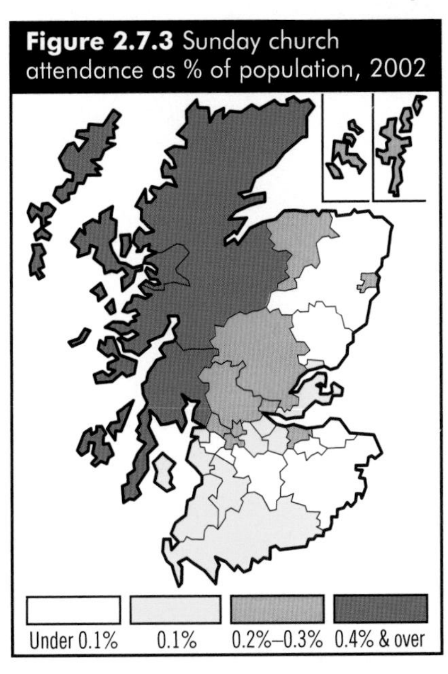

Figure 2.7.4 Changes in Sunday church attendance, 1984–1994

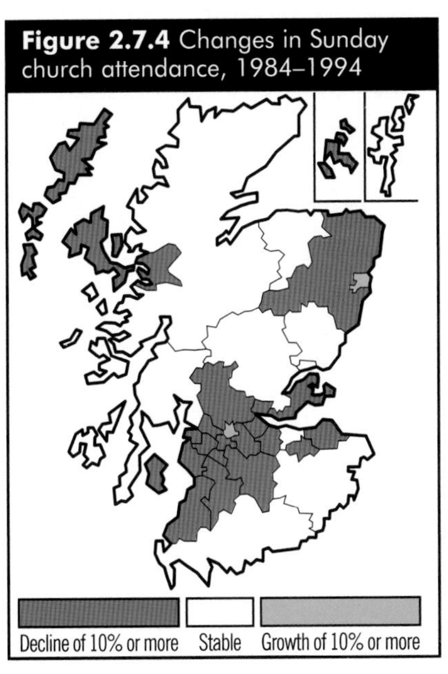

Figure 2.7.5 Sunday Church Attendance, by age, Other Presbyterian, 1984, 1994 and 2002

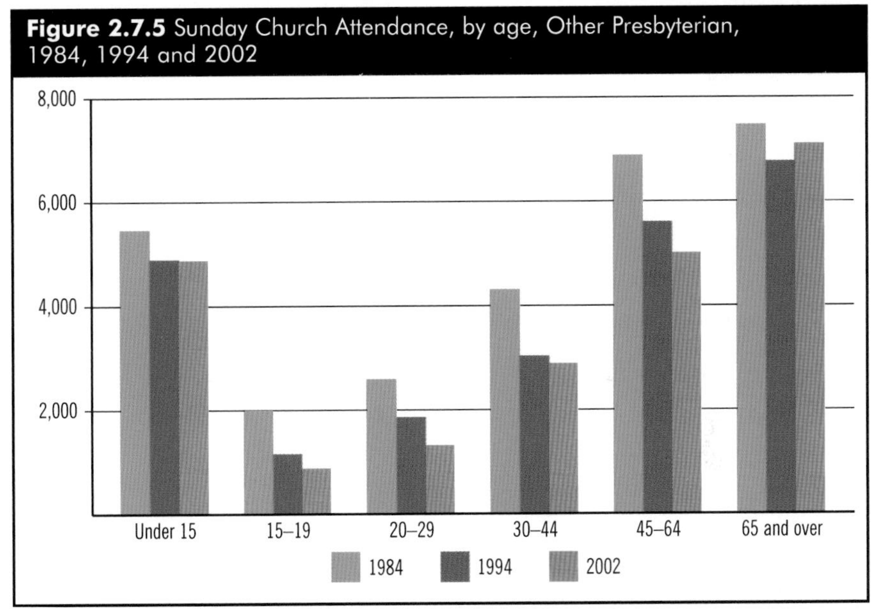

Figure 2.7.6 Changes in Sunday church attendance, 1994–2002

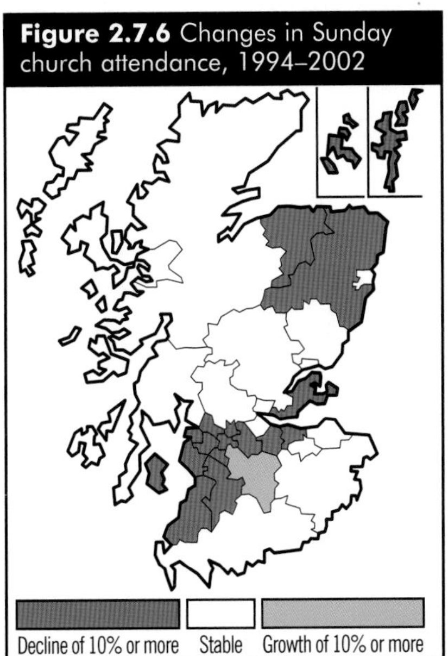

The Other Presbyterian Churches (including the Free Church of Scotland) collectively have declined proportionately less than the Church of Scotland. Their strength in the Western Isles changed in the period 1984 to 1994, as **Figure 2.7.4** shows, but the overall high level of attendance here and in the Highlands has been maintained. Although the highest level in **Figures 2.7.1–3** is shown as "0.4% or over" the reality in the Western Isles was 29% of the population went to Other Presbyterian churches in 1984, and was still 24% in 2002.

Their strength below the urban belt of Glasgow–Edinburgh is however much less, and hardly exists in the south-east corner of Scotland. The Western Isles remain the Celtic heartland.

Figure 2.7.5 indicates other features unique to the Other Presbyterians. In the 8 years to 2002, they have lost hardly any children, and very few parents in the 30 to 44 age-group (two facts which are undoubtedly linked), but this is in total contrast to the other denominations.

Figure 2.7.7 shows that the Eldership of Other Presbyterian congregations often has more people aged 55 to 74 than are in congregations as a whole, and far fewer under 35. The average age of these Elders is 62, slightly higher than the adult congregation.

Figure 2.7.7 Age of adult Sunday attenders and Church Elders, 2002

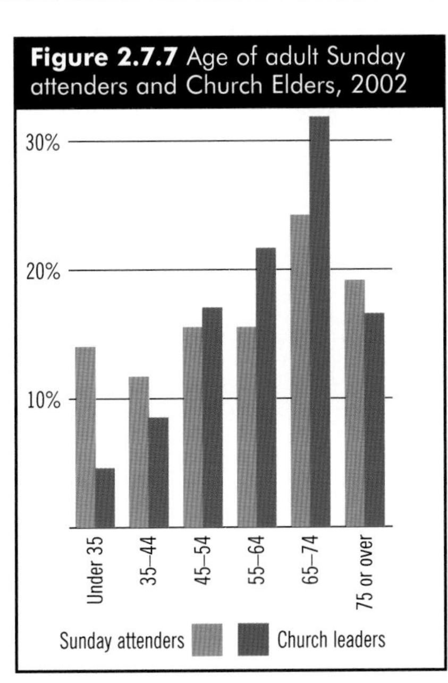

2.8 Scottish Church Census 2002: Episcopal

Figure 2.8.1 Sunday church attendance as % of population, 1984

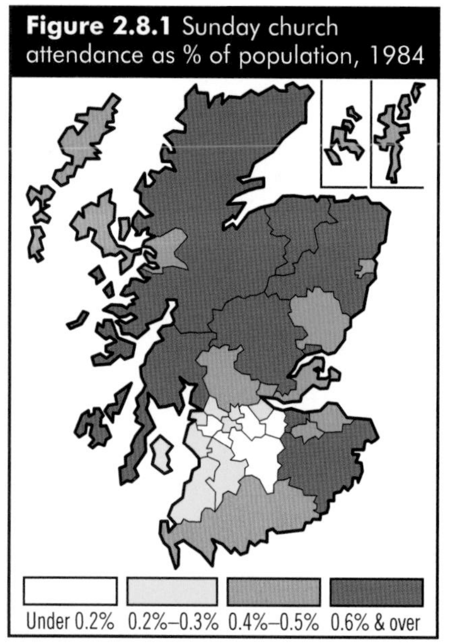

Figure 2.8.2 Sunday church attendance as % of population, 1994

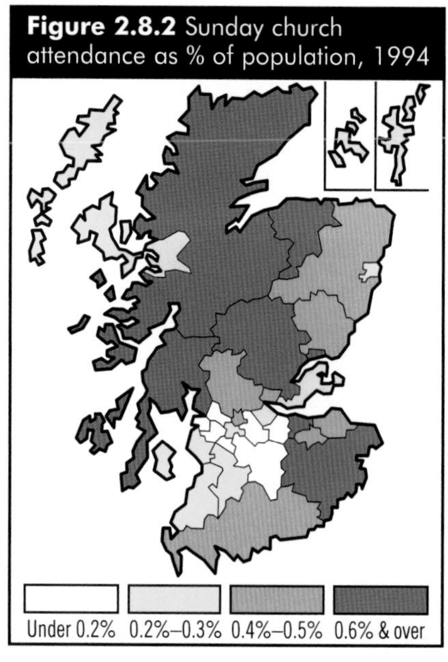

Figure 2.8.3 Sunday church attendance as % of population, 2002

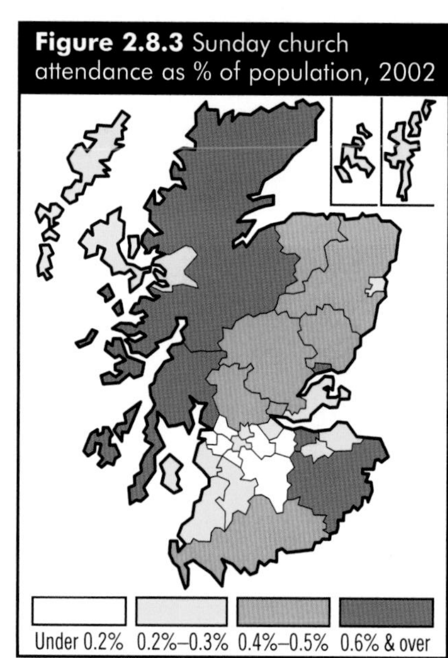

Figure 2.8.4 Sunday Church Attendance, by age, Episcopal, 1984, 1994 and 2002

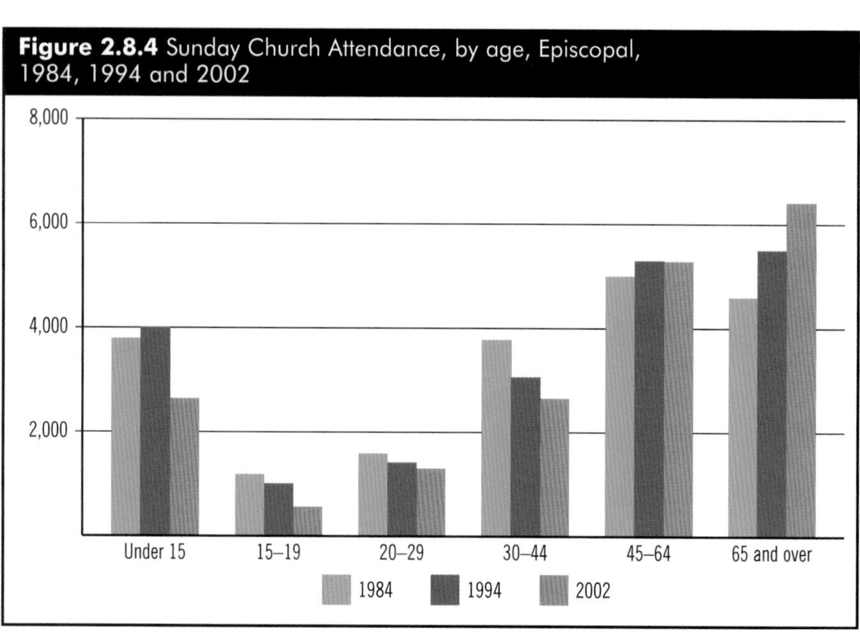

Figure 2.8.5 Changes in Sunday church attendance, 1984–1994

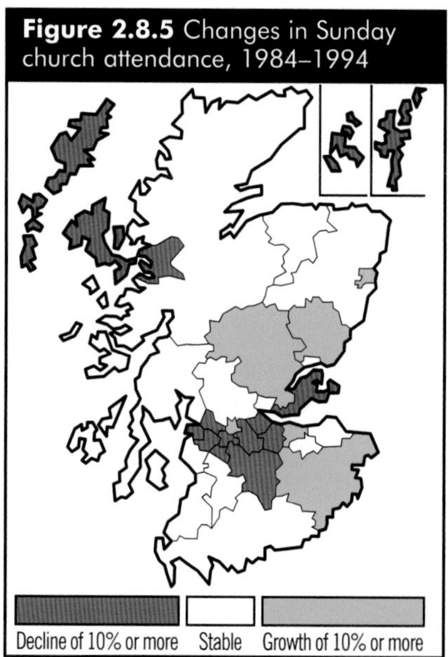

Between 1984 and 1994 the Episcopal Church grew largely because a number of independent Episcopal churches joined the main denomination. That growth, as **Figure 2.8.5** indicates was broadly in the south-east of Scotland, though it included the city of Aberdeen and East Dunbartonshire. In the next 8 years growth above 10% was only seen in West Dunbartonshire, though 6 other regions saw smaller growth, of which the largest was Edinburgh with 9%. Thus Episcopal growth has been both urban and rural.

Episcopal strength lies especially in the northern and central parts of Scotland, but with high attendances also in Edinburgh and the Borders, where in 1994 more than 1% of the population attended an Episcopal Church on Sunday.

The growth between 1984 and 1994 came largely through increased numbers of children under 15 and adults over 45. The decline between 1994 and 2002 is made up very largely of children, as **Figure 2.8.4** indicates, offset to some extent by growth amongst those over 65, following the same trend in England between 1989 and 1998.

The average age of Episcopal Leaders, at 54, is less than that of adults in their congregations. Nevertheless **Figure 2.8.6** shows they have twice the proportion aged 55 to 64 as normally attend on Sunday, though, of all denominations, they have most proportionately under 35.

Figure 2.8.6 Age of adult Sunday church attenders and leaders, 2002

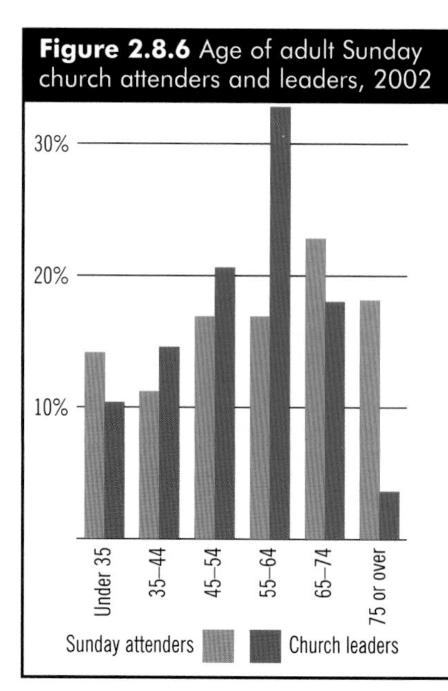

Figure 2.8.7 Changes in Sunday church attendance, 1994–2002

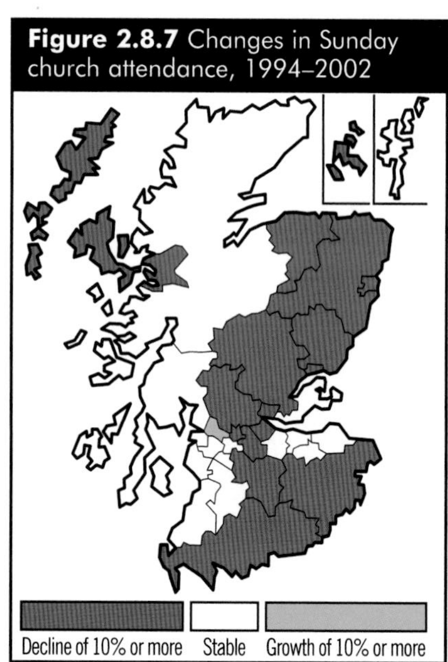

Figure 2.9.1 Sunday church attendance as % of population, 1984

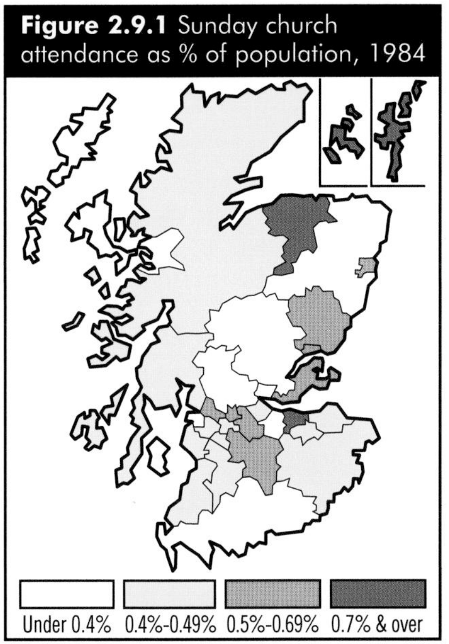

Figure 2.9.2 Sunday church attendance as % of population, 1994

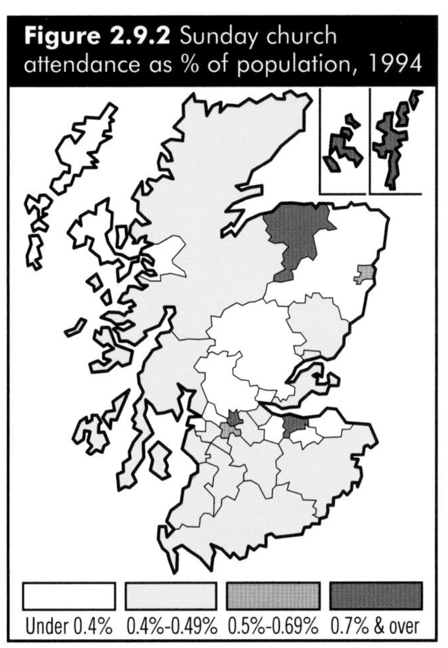

Figure 2.9.3 Sunday church attendance as % of population, 2002

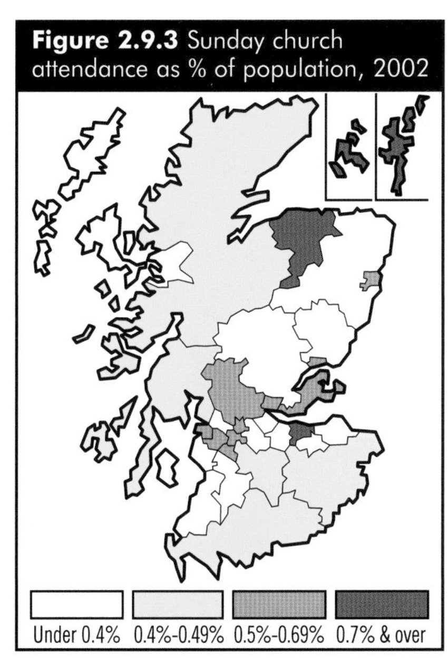

Figure 2.9.4 Changes in Sunday church attendance, 1984–1994

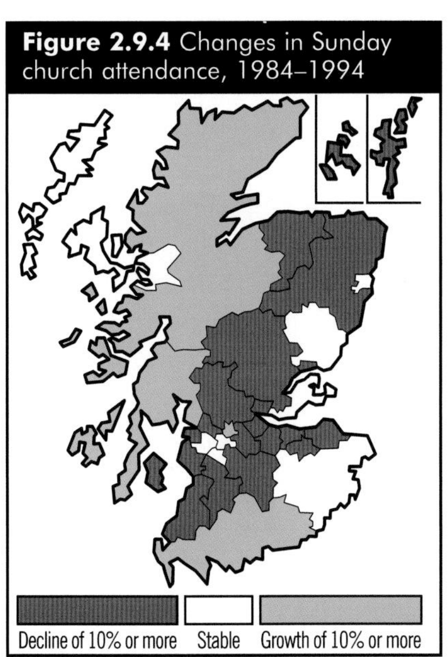

Figure 2.9.5 Sunday Church Attendance, by age, Baptist, 1984, 1994 and 2002

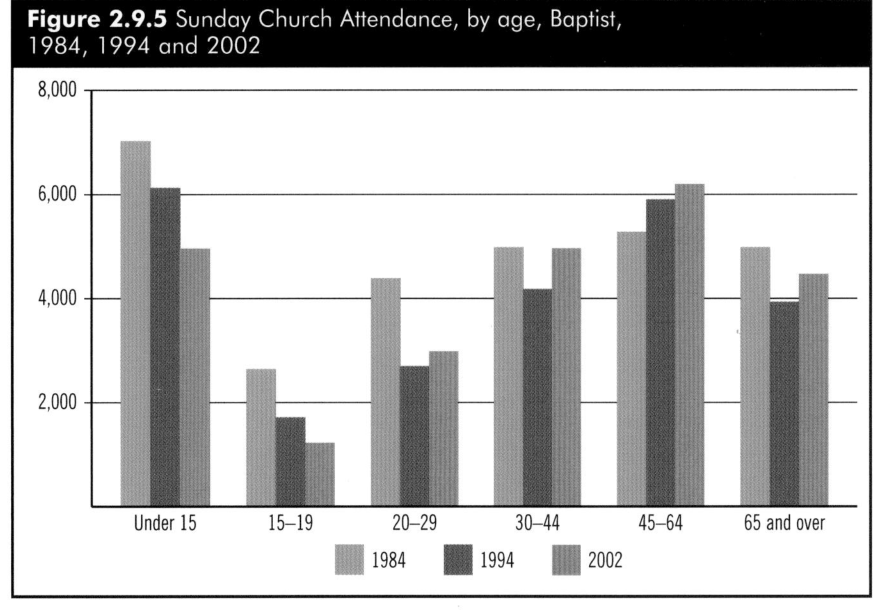

Figure 2.9.6 Changes in Sunday church attendance, 1994–2002

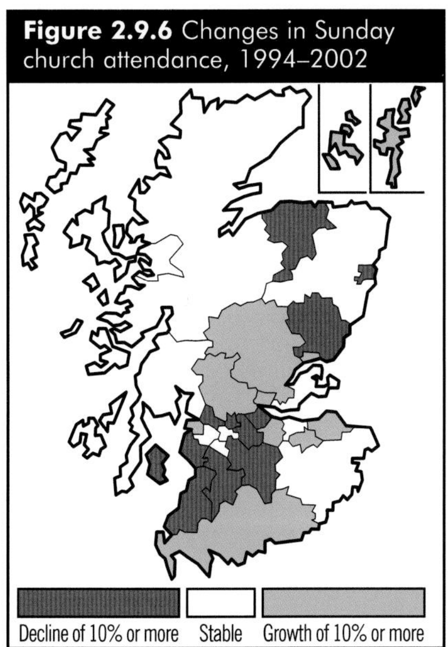

The Baptist churches in Scotland collectively declined between 1984 and 1994 but grew slightly (the only denominational group that did!) between 1994 and 2002. However during both these periods they grew in some areas and declined in others. **Figures 2.9.4** and **2.9.6** show they grew in the Highland and Argyll, East Dunbartonshire and Dumfries and Galloway Councils in the earlier period, and in the Orkneys, Shetlands, central Scotland and again in Dumfries and Galloway in the latter period.

The main Baptist strength is in the Orkneys, Shetlands, Moray and the City of Edinburgh, as **Figures 2.9.1–3** indicate. But Aberdeen City, Fife, and East Dunbartonshire are also proportionately strong. The Western Isles and parts of east Scotland are the weakest areas.

Figure 2.9.5 shows interesting variations in Sunday attendance by age-group. Declining numbers of children and young people have been consistent since 1984, but in the period 1994 to 2002, Baptists have seen increases in each of the age-groups from those in their 20s and upwards. When other denominations are seeing decreases between 20 and 64, this must be an encouragement, even if it means that the average age of a Baptist is increasing.

Figure 2.9.7 shows that the proportion of Deacons under 35 is much smaller than adults of this age.

Figure 2.9.7 Age of adult Sunday church attenders and Deacons, 2002

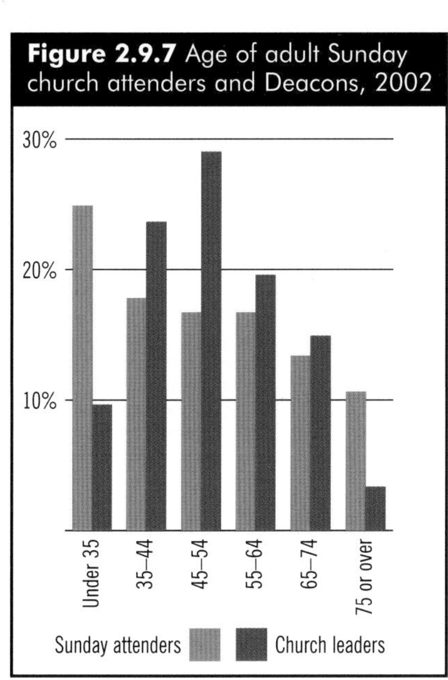

2.10 Scottish Church Census 2002: Independent

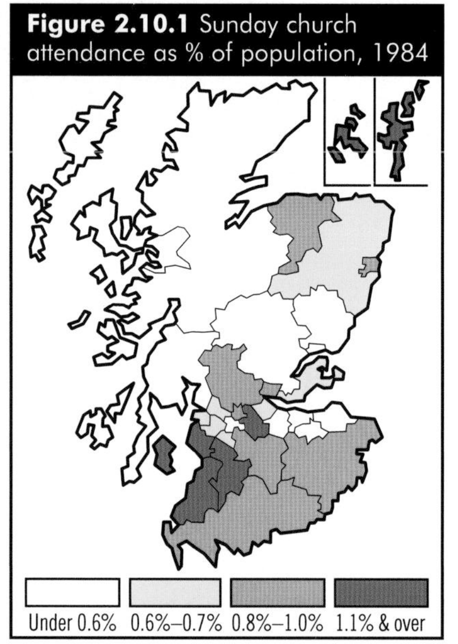

Figure 2.10.1 Sunday church attendance as % of population, 1984

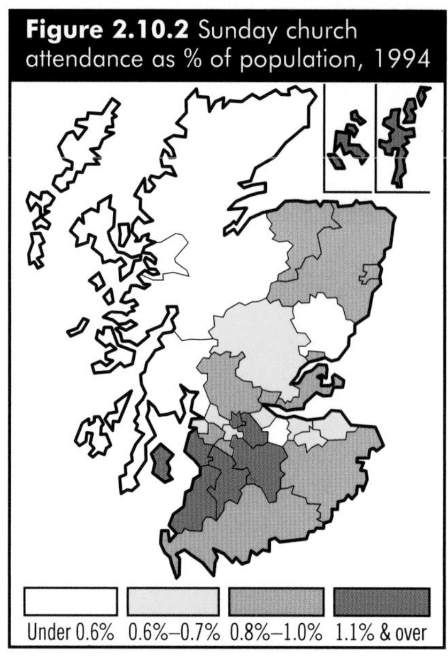

Figure 2.10.2 Sunday church attendance as % of population, 1994

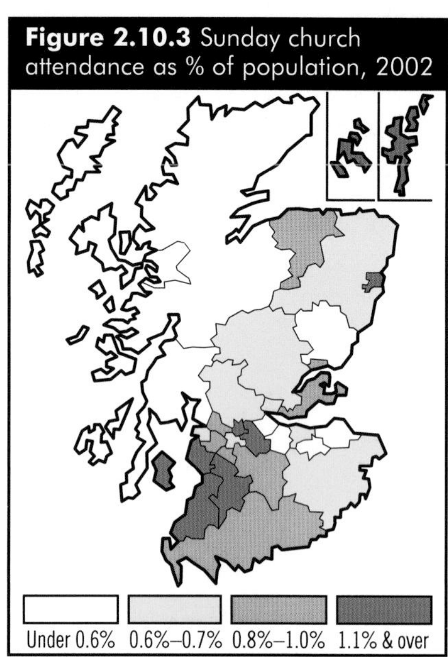

Figure 2.10.3 Sunday church attendance as % of population, 2002

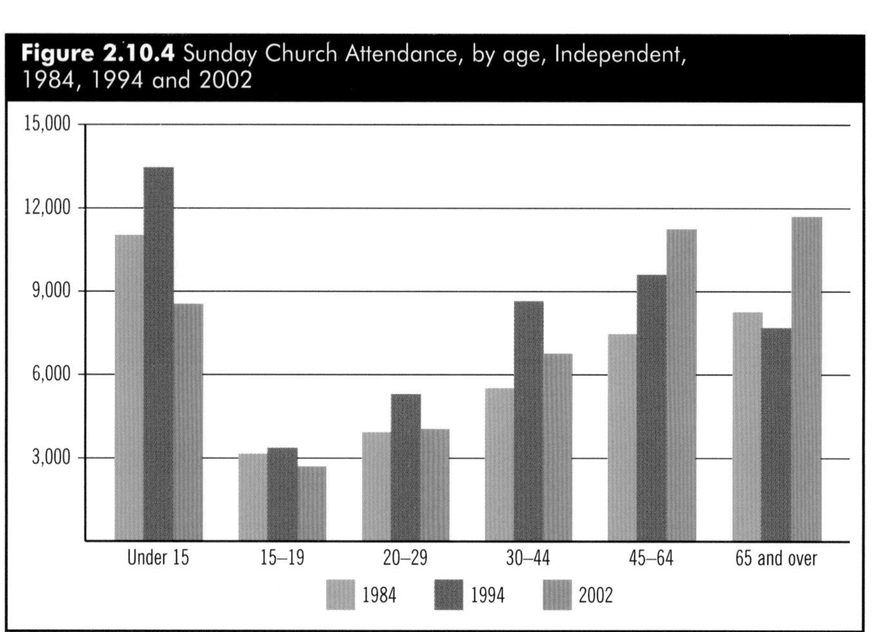

Figure 2.10.4 Sunday Church Attendance, by age, Independent, 1984, 1994 and 2002

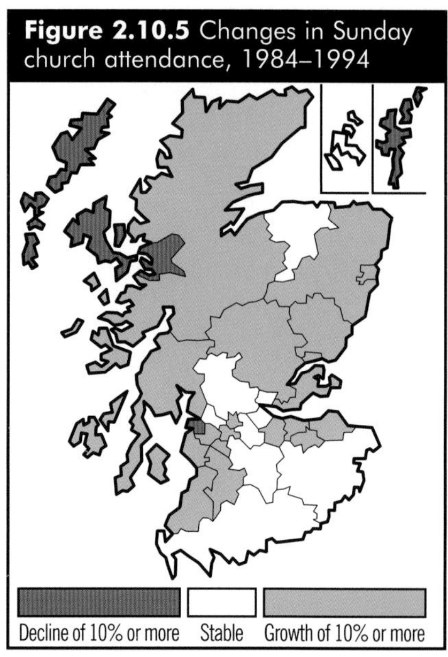

Figure 2.10.5 Changes in Sunday church attendance, 1984–1994

The Independent churches collectively grew between 1984 and 1994 but declined between 1994 and 2002. **Figure 2.10.5** shows that the growth took place across substantial parts of northern and eastern Scotland, Ayrshire and the urban areas of Glasgow and Edinburgh. Most of that growth did not continue in the years 1994 to 2002 as can be seen in **Figure 2.10.7**, although Aberdeen City continued to flourish, as did Perth and Kinross Council.

The strength of the Independents has been the Orkney and Shetland Islands, Ayrshire and North Lanarkshire, augmented in 1994 by East Dunbartonshire and South Lanarkshire, and by the City of Aberdeen in 2002. Independent churches are weak in the Highland and Argyll Councils and the Western Isles, and in Angus and West Lothian on the east.

Figure 2.10.4 shows that the Independent churches grew across all age-groups between 1984 and 1994 except the oldest, but only grew amongst the oldest (45 and over) between 1994 and 2002. In this latter period, parents and children seem to have left but those of grandparent age have stayed – and grown!

While the average age of Independent church leaders (55) is much the same as that of their adult congregations, they have many more aged 45 to 64 than might be expected, as **Figure 2.10.6** indicates.

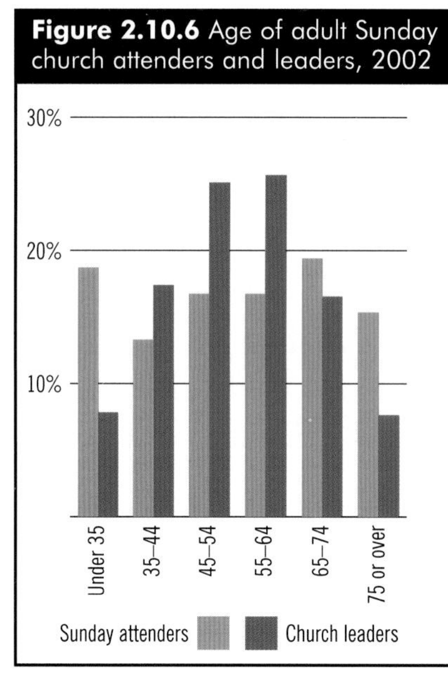

Figure 2.10.6 Age of adult Sunday church attenders and leaders, 2002

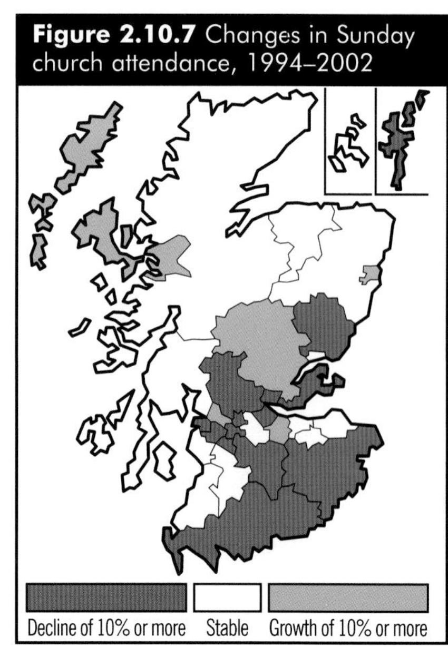

Figure 2.10.7 Changes in Sunday church attendance, 1994–2002

Figure 2.11.1 Sunday church attendance as % of population, 1984

Under 0.4% 0.4%–0.5% 0.6%–0.7% 0.8% & over

Figure 2.11.2 Sunday church attendance as % of population, 1994

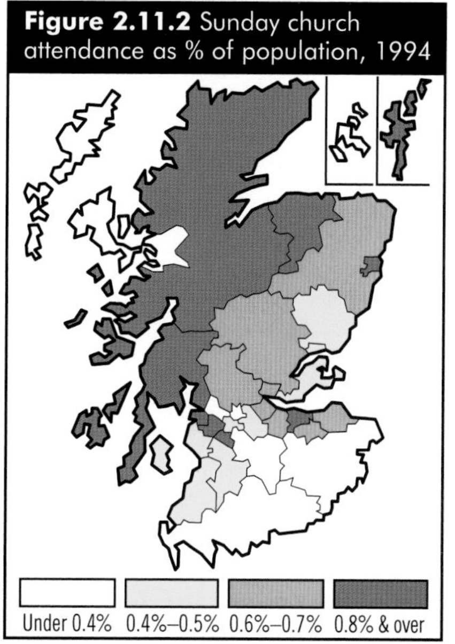

Figure 2.11.3 Sunday church attendance as % of population, 2002

Under 0.4% 0.4%–0.5% 0.6%–0.7% 0.8% & over

Figure 2.11.4 Changes in Sunday church attendance, 1984–1994

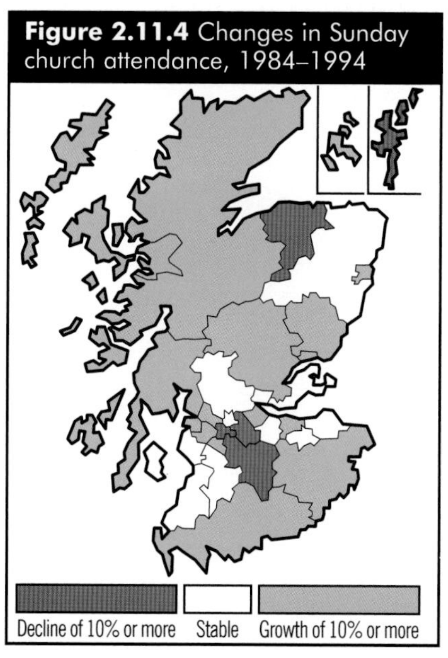

Figure 2.11.5 Sunday Church Attendance, by age, Smaller Denominations, 1984, 1994 and 2002

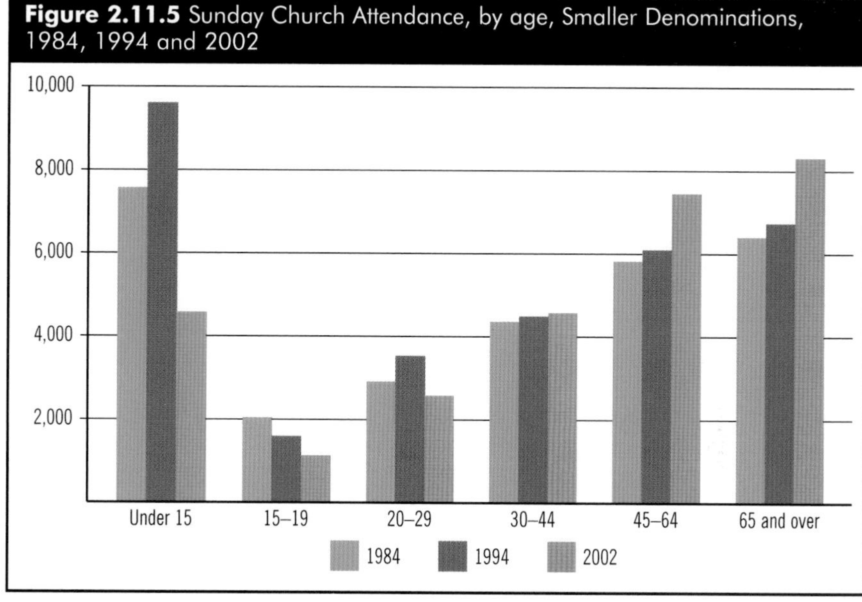

Figure 2.11.6 Changes in Sunday church attendance, 1994–2002

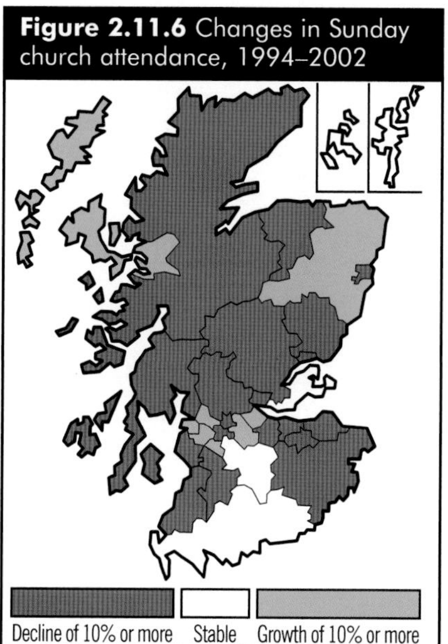

Like the Independent churches, the Smaller Denominations grew between 1984 and 1994 but declined between 1994 and 2002. **Figure 2.11.4** therefore shows a considerable amount of growth over most parts of Scotland, and **Figure 2.11.6** shows the opposite. But in both periods, growth took place in the Western Isles, Falkirk, West Dunbartonshire, Inverclyde and Renfrewshire, and in both there was decline in Moray and the City of Glasgow.

Notwithstanding this decline, Moray continues to be a bastion of strength for the Smaller Denominations as **Figures 2.11.1–3** indicate, together with the Shetland Islands (where the Methodists are strong) and Inverclyde. In 1984 4% of the Shetland Islands population went to a Smaller Denomination church on Sunday, reducing to 3% in 1994 and 2002, but still a high percentage. It is 1% in Inverclyde and Moray.

Figure 2.11.5 shows that the Smaller Denominations gained people across most age-groups between 1984 and 1994, and amongst the three oldest age-groups between 1994 and 2002, especially those 45 to 64 and 65 and over. But in the latter period they have lost more than half their children under 15 (down to 4,600 in 2002 from 9,600 in 1994).

The average age of Leaders is 58, higher than the average adult age of Smaller Denomination congregations. **Figure 2.11.7** shows this to be particularly true of those aged 45 to 64.

Figure 2.11.7 Age of adult Sunday church attenders and leaders, 2002

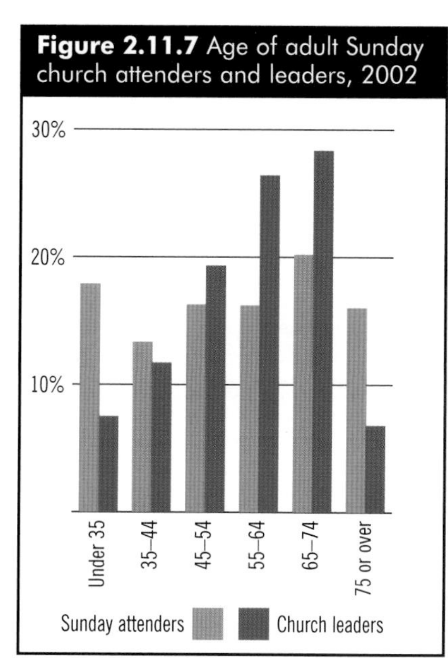

2.12 Scottish Church Census 2002: Roman Catholic

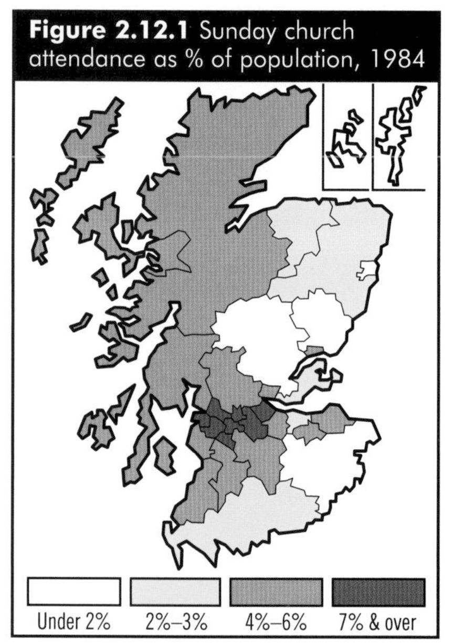

Figure 2.12.1 Sunday church attendance as % of population, 1984

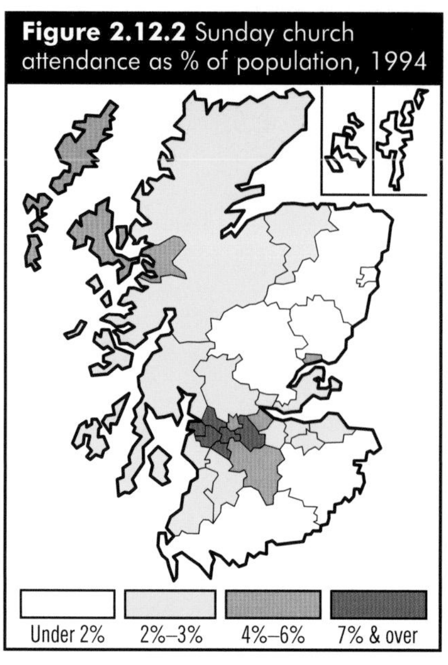

Figure 2.12.2 Sunday church attendance as % of population, 1994

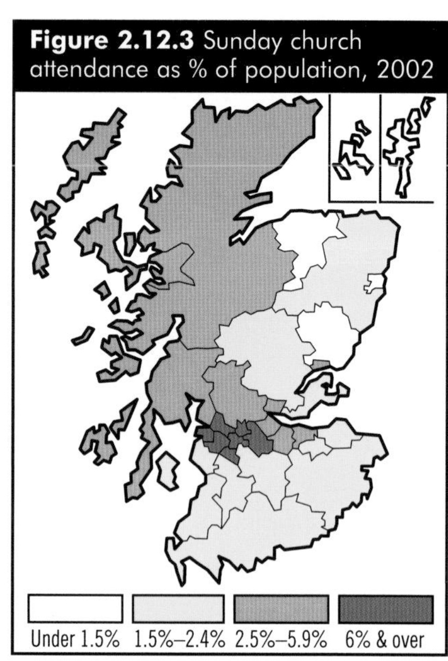

Figure 2.12.3 Sunday church attendance as % of population, 2002

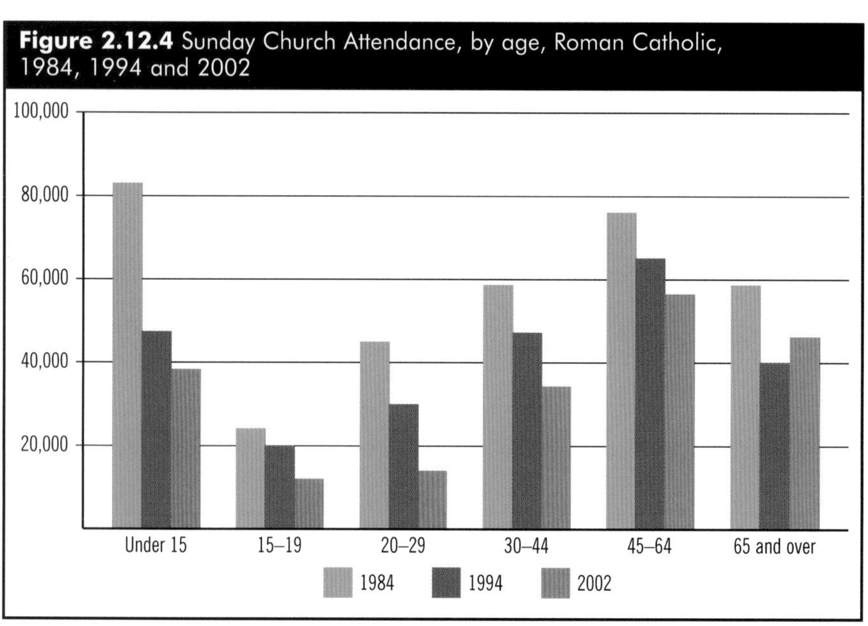

Figure 2.12.4 Sunday Church Attendance, by age, Roman Catholic, 1984, 1994 and 2002

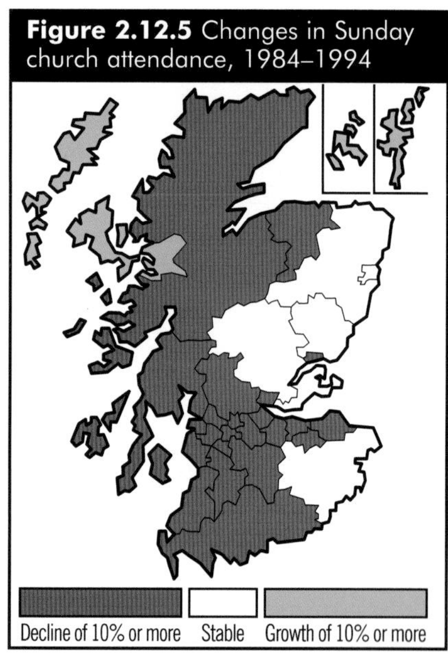

Figure 2.12.5 Changes in Sunday church attendance, 1984–1994

The decline in Sunday mass attendance in the Roman Catholic Church in Scotland is readily seen by the reduction in colour in **Figures 2.12.1–3.** The strength across the middle of Scotland on the Glasgow-Falkirk axis (in this case) gets weaker between 1984 and 2002. Whereas 15% of the North Lanarkshire population were practising Catholics in 1984, this had dropped to below 9% by 2002, and the 13% of Glasgow to under 8%.

The decline was less noticeable on the eastern side of Scotland between 1984 and 1994, as **Figure 2.12.5** indicates, and was offset by some growth in the outer Islands. But between 1994 and 2002 there was no growth, and as **Figure 2.12.7** indicates few stable areas apart from the outer Islands and Perth and Kinross.

Figure 2.12.4 shows that all age-groups have seen loss between 1984 and 1994, and with the exception of those 65 and over between 1994 and 2002 also. The high reduction in children under 15 in the first period was not repeated to the same extent in the second period, although the decline amongst those aged 20 to 44 was proportionately relatively high (53% of those in their 20s and 28% of those aged 30 to 44).

Unlike the Protestant denominations, the Roman Catholics Lay Ministries have an average age of 52, and are frequently much closer to the average age of their adult congregations, as **Figure 2.12.6** indicates.

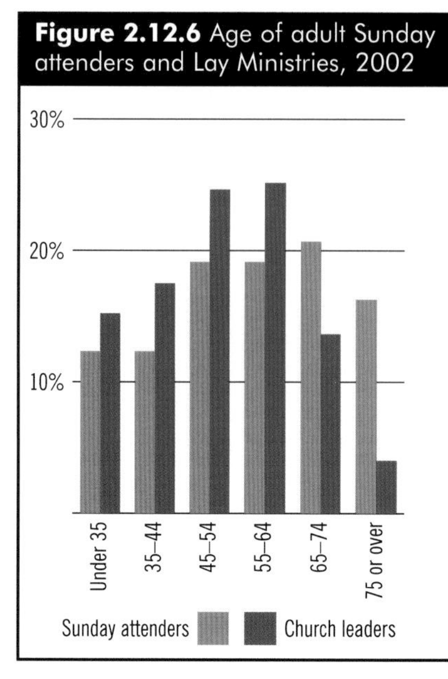

Figure 2.12.6 Age of adult Sunday attenders and Lay Ministries, 2002

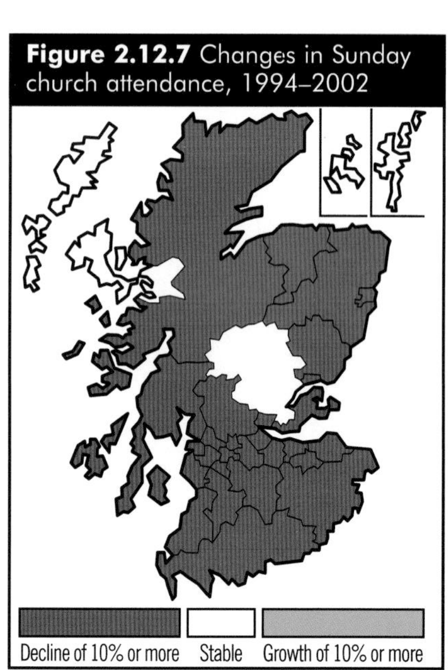

Figure 2.12.7 Changes in Sunday church attendance, 1994–2002

Scottish Church Census 2002: Churchmanships: All & Catholic

Pages 2.13–17 look at Sunday church attendance in Scotland by churchmanship. As this was only measured for the first time in 1994, the maps and diagrams simply show data and comparisons for the two years 1994 and 2002.

"Churchmanship" describes the system of belief in a particular church. The questionnaire invited the minister to describe the churchmanship of his/her congregation by ticking up to three of nine words – Broad, Catholic, Charismatic, Evangelical, High Church, Liberal, Low Church, Radical or Reformed, with an option to write in other descriptions of required. According to the mix of options chosen (described in detail on **Page 12.2**) one of six churchmanship types was selected for that church. It is assumed that at least two-thirds of all attending that church will agree with this description (a figure obtained from congregational surveys), and that those who don't will balance with others in other churches who are likewise different.

For each of these six groups a map has been drawn showing its strength (against the general population) in both 1994 and 2002, with a third map illustrating growth or decline. These three maps are accompanied by a chart illustrating the numbers attending church broken down by age-group. There are thus 6 sets of three maps + one chart on this and the following pages. **Figure 2.13.2** gives an overview of these six groups and their relative strength and the degree they have changed between 1994 and 2002. It should be noted that "Catholic" is one kind of churchmanship and should not be identified solely with the Roman Catholic Church. (See also **Table 12.3.3**)

It was also possible to break down the "Evangelical" category into three sub-categories: Broad, Mainstream and Charismatic Evangelicals, these emerging from the various ticks on the form. "Mainstream" Evangelicals are those ticking only the one box "Evangelical", and the word "Mainstream" has been added to distinguish this group from "Reformed" and "Charismatic" Evangelicals. These three Evangelical groups, together with the total Evangelical are given on **Pages 2.14** and **2.15.**

Figure 2.13.1 Sunday Church Attendance, by age, Catholic, 1994–2002

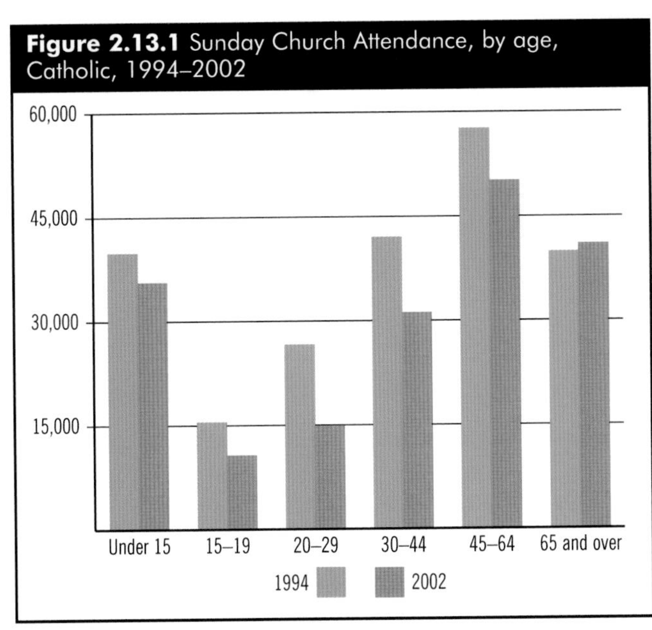

Figure 2.13.2 Sunday Church Attendance, by churchmanship, 1994–2002

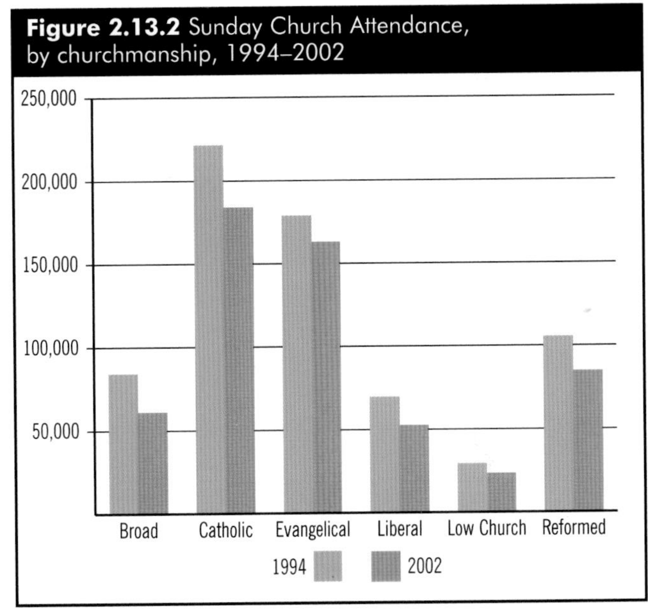

Figure 2.13.3 Catholic Sunday attendance as % of population, 1994

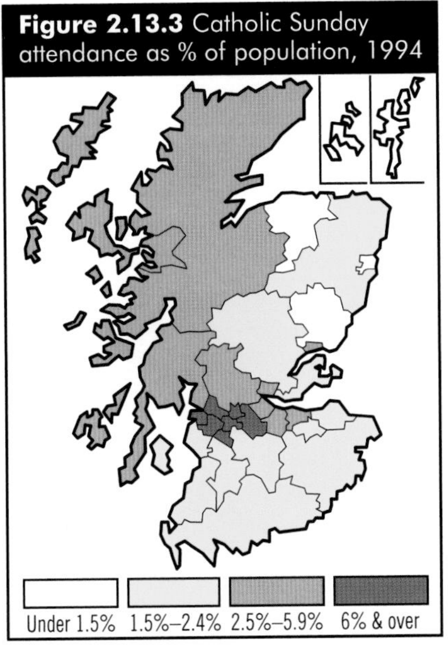

Figure 2.13.4 Catholic Sunday attendance as % of population, 2002

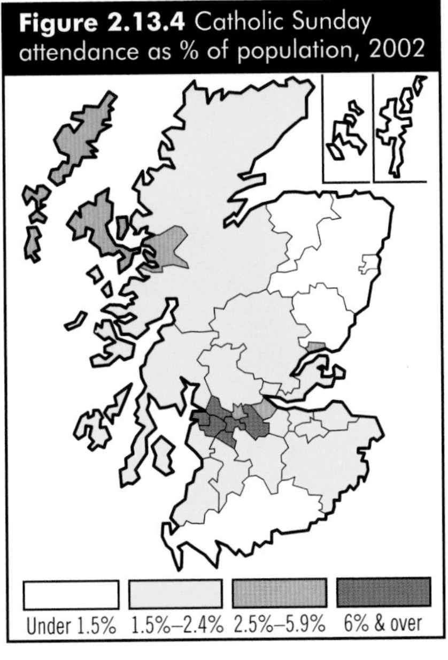

Figure 2.13.5 Changes in Catholic Sunday attendance, 1994–2002

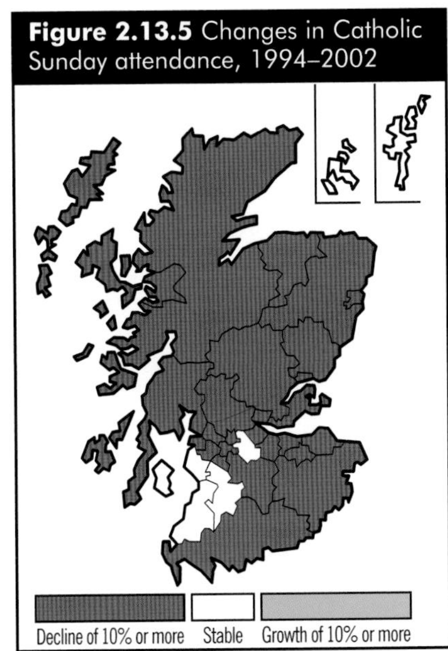

2.14 Scottish Church Census 2002: Reformed & Mainstream Evangelical

2

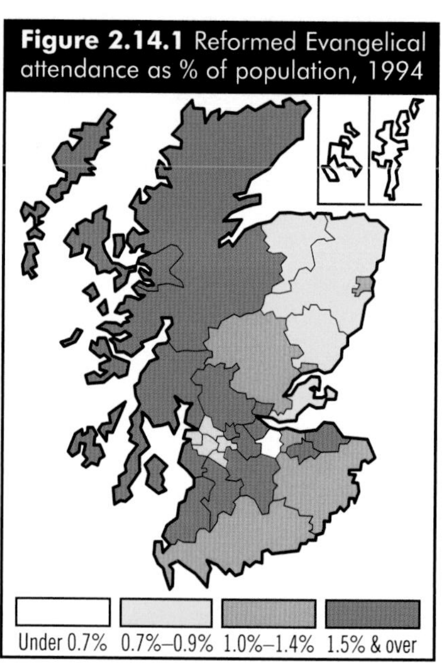

Figure 2.14.1 Reformed Evangelical attendance as % of population, 1994

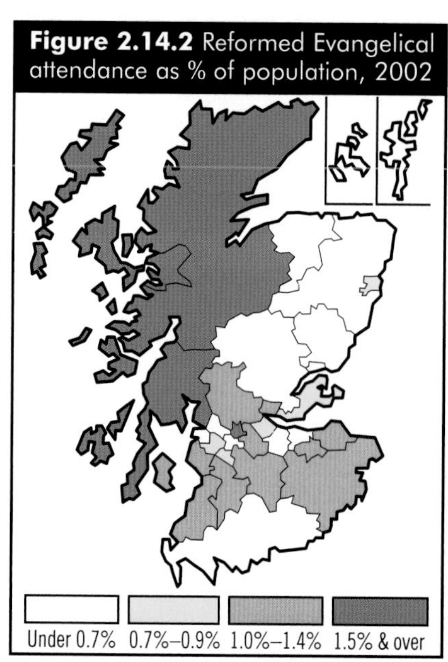

Figure 2.14.2 Reformed Evangelical attendance as % of population, 2002

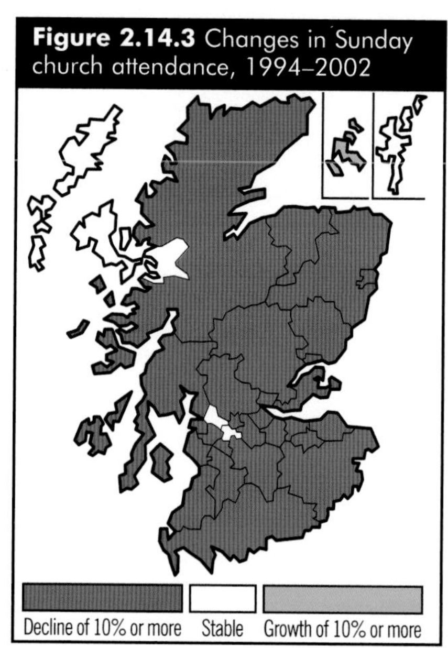

Figure 2.14.3 Changes in Sunday church attendance, 1994–2002

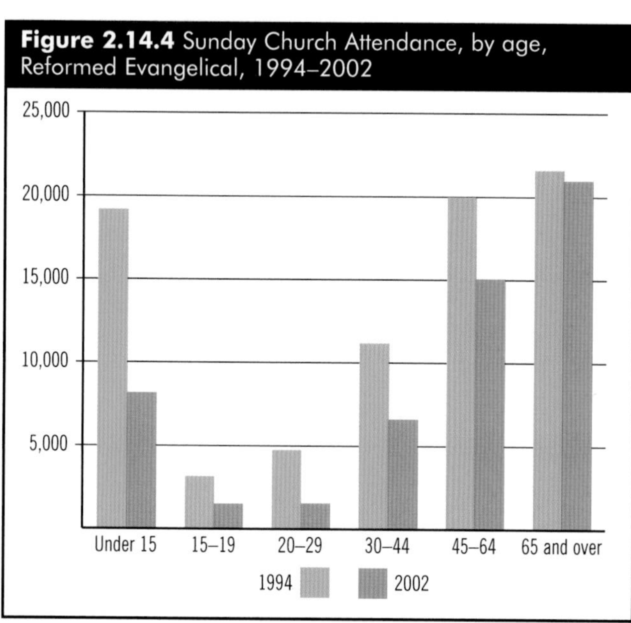

Figure 2.14.4 Sunday Church Attendance, by age, Reformed Evangelical, 1994–2002

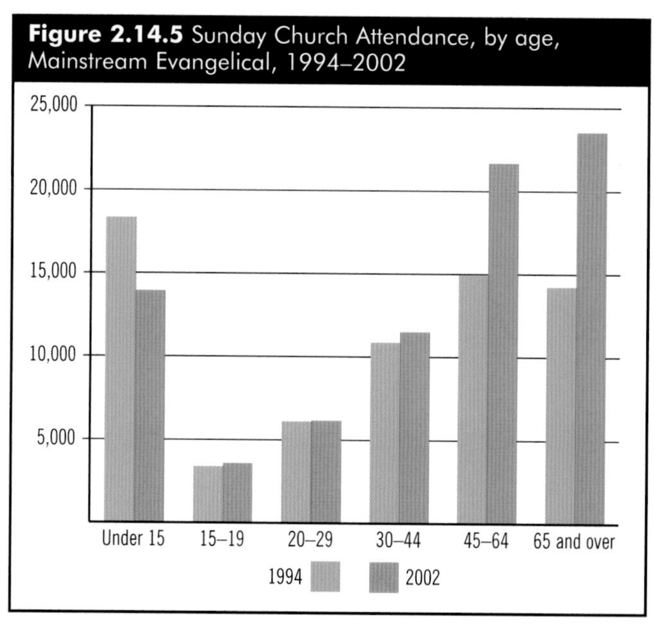

Figure 2.14.5 Sunday Church Attendance, by age, Mainstream Evangelical, 1994–2002

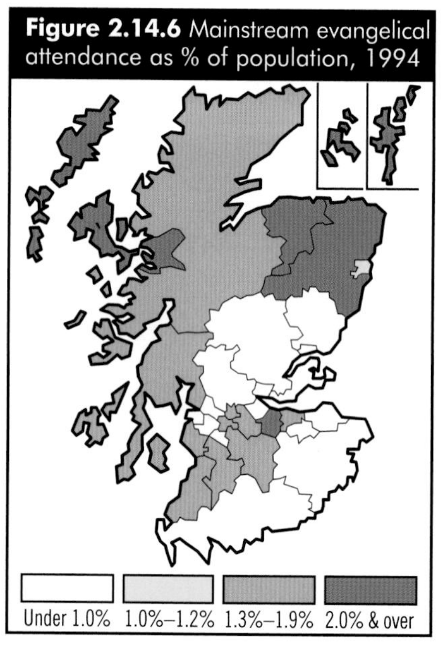

Figure 2.14.6 Mainstream evangelical attendance as % of population, 1994

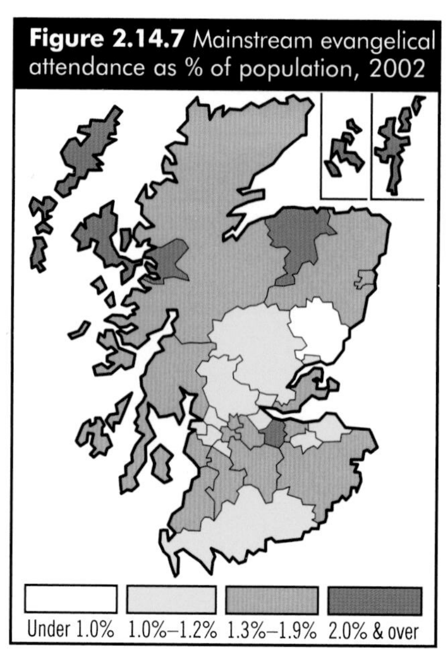

Figure 2.14.7 Mainstream evangelical attendance as % of population, 2002

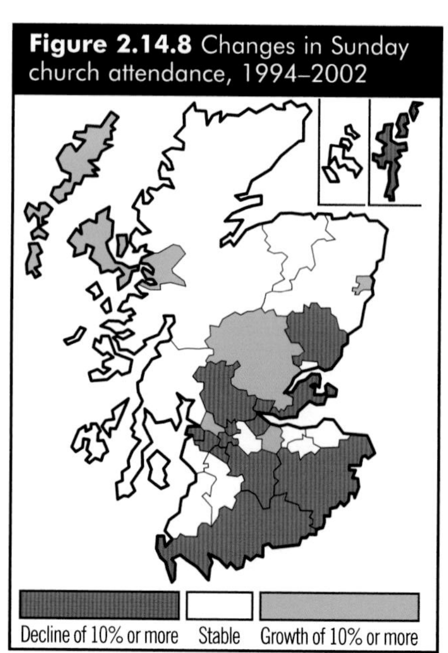

Figure 2.14.8 Changes in Sunday church attendance, 1994–2002

Scottish Church Census 2002: Charismatic & Total Evangelical 2.15

Figure 2.15.1 Charismatic evangelical attendance as % of population, 1994

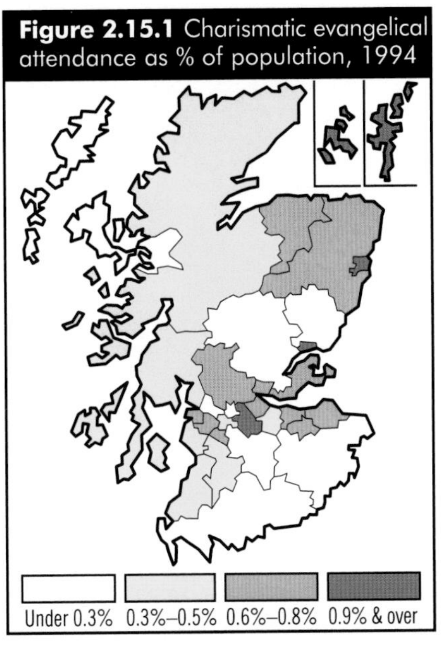

Figure 2.15.2 Charismatic evangelical attendance as % of population, 2002

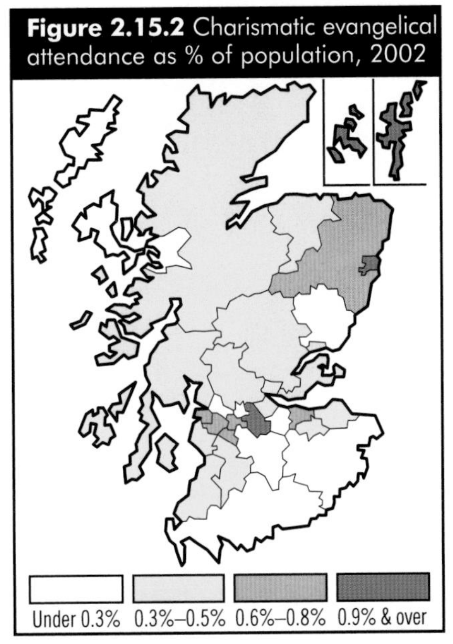

Figure 2.15.3 Changes in Sunday church attendance, 1994–2002

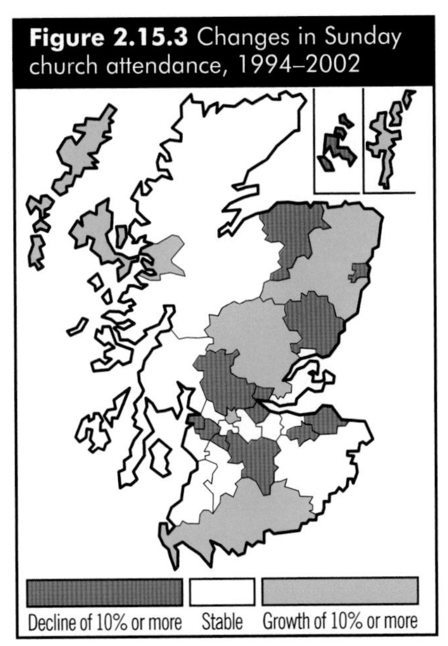

Figure 2.15.4 Sunday Church Attendance, by age, Charismatic Evangelical, 1994–2002

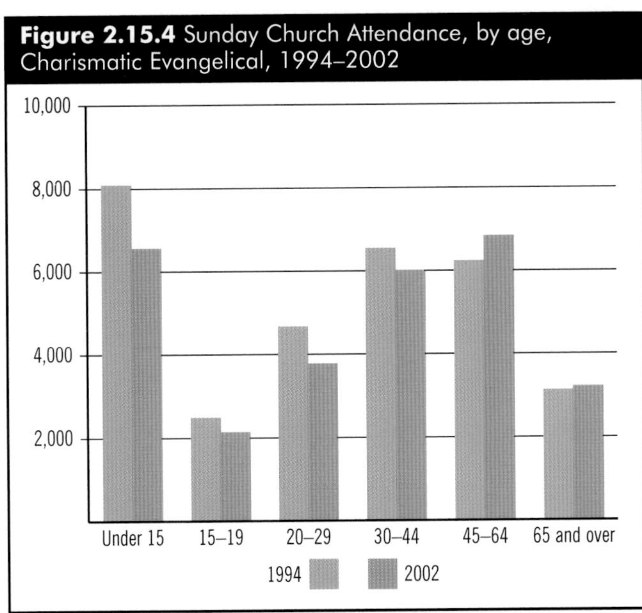

Figure 2.15.5 Sunday Church Attendance, by age, Total Evangelical, 1994–2002

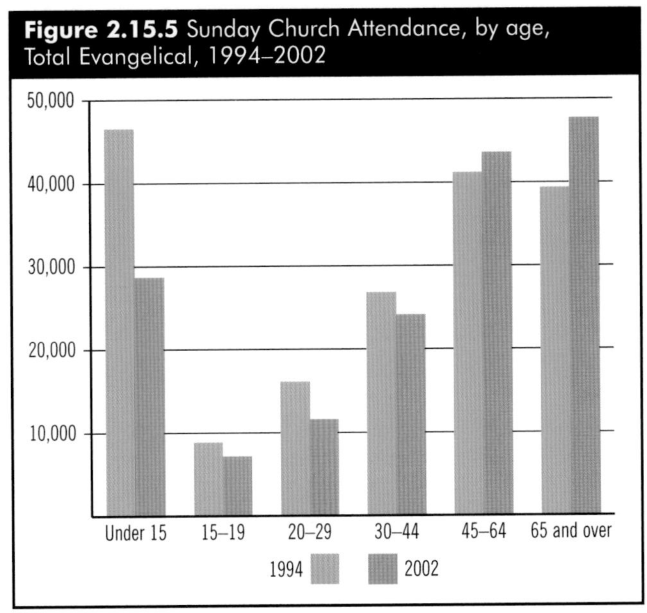

Figure 2.15.6 Total evangelical attendance as % of population, 1994

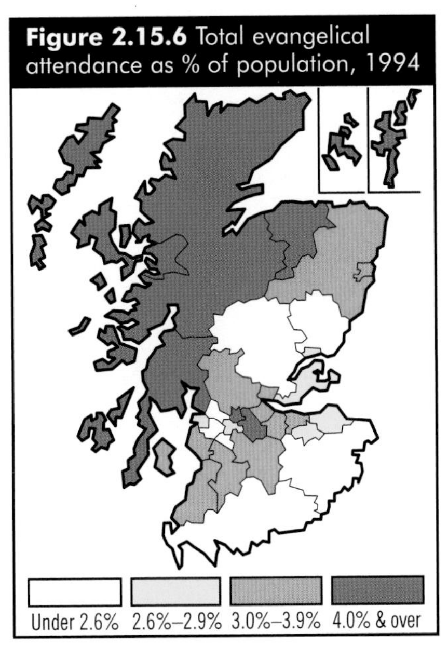

Figure 2.15.7 Total evangelical attendance as % of population, 2002

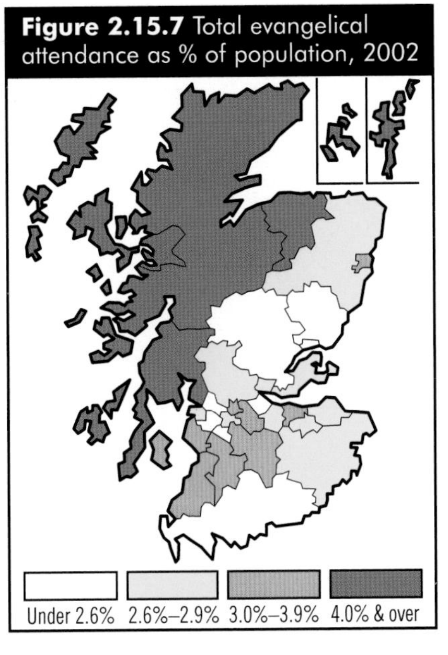

Figure 2.15.8 Changes in Sunday church attendance, 1994–2002

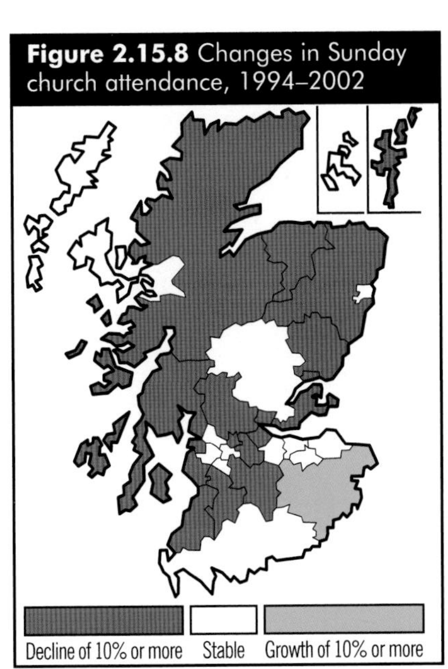

2.16 Scottish Church Census 2002: Reformed & Low Church

Figure 2.16.1 Reformed church attendance as % of population, 1994

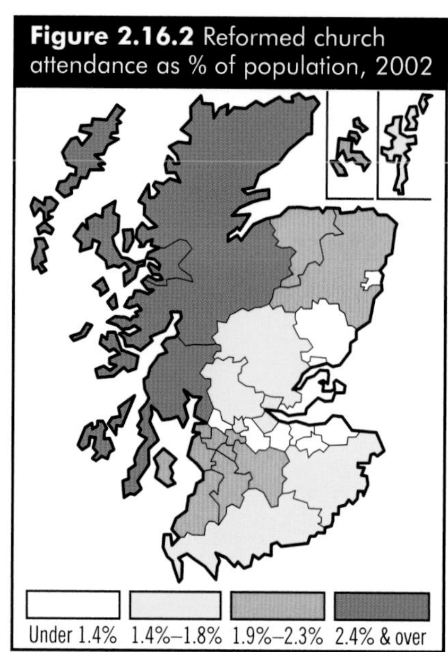

Figure 2.16.2 Reformed church attendance as % of population, 2002

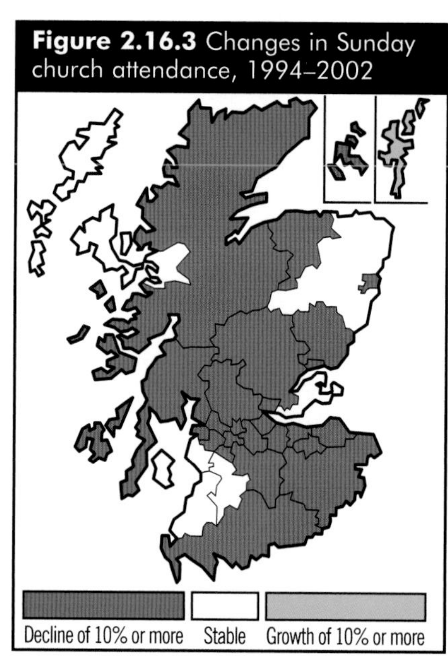

Figure 2.16.3 Changes in Sunday church attendance, 1994–2002

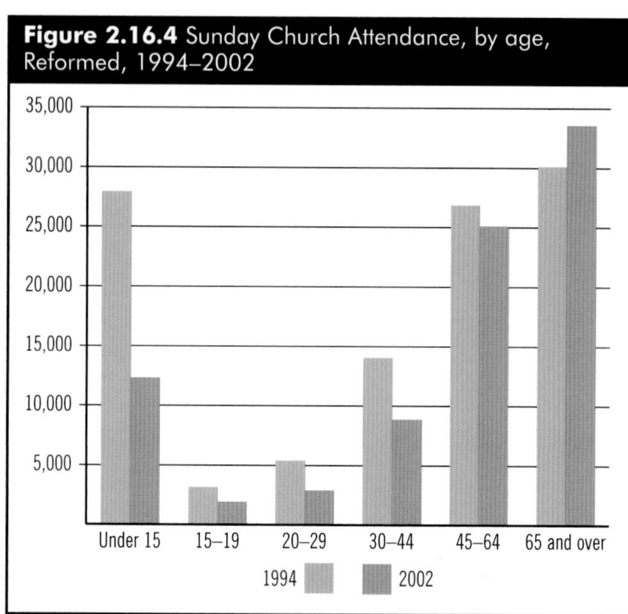

Figure 2.16.4 Sunday Church Attendance, by age, Reformed, 1994–2002

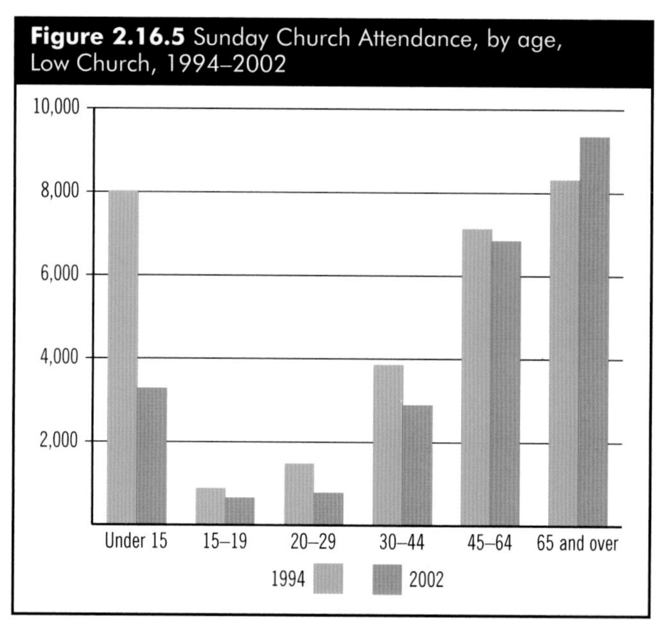

Figure 2.16.5 Sunday Church Attendance, by age, Low Church, 1994–2002

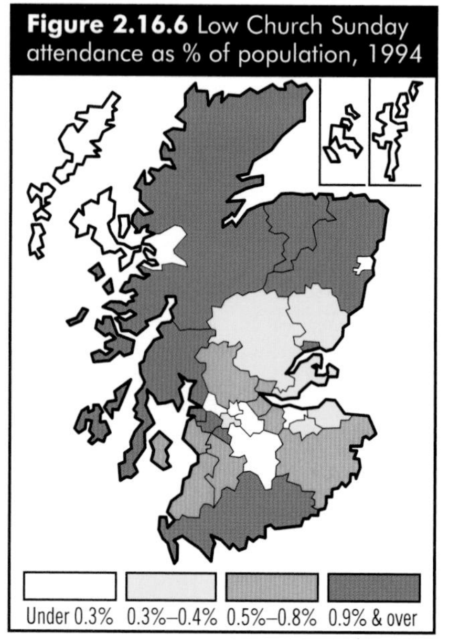

Figure 2.16.6 Low Church Sunday attendance as % of population, 1994

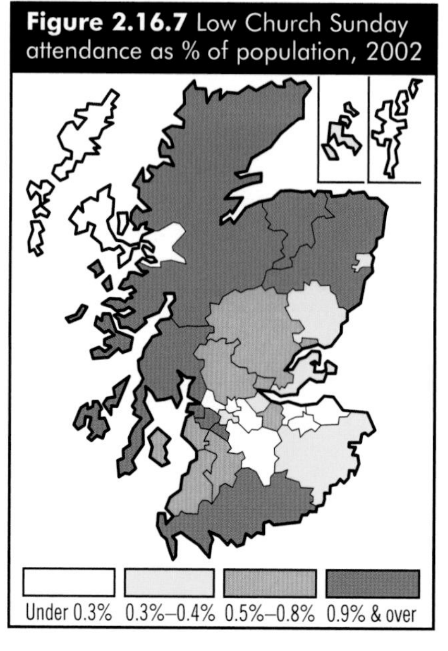

Figure 2.16.7 Low Church Sunday attendance as % of population, 2002

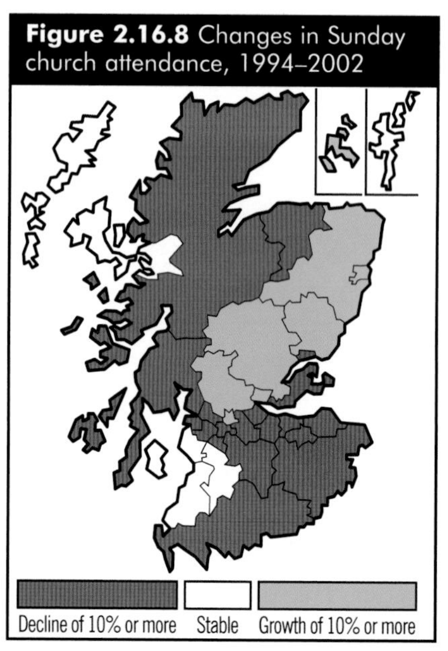

Figure 2.16.8 Changes in Sunday church attendance, 1994–2002

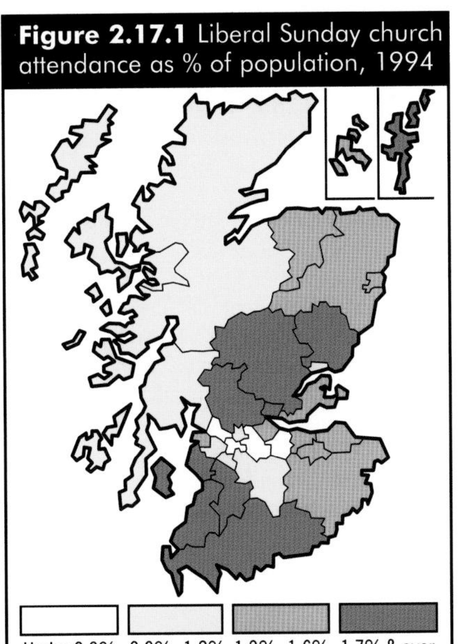

Figure 2.17.1 Liberal Sunday church attendance as % of population, 1994

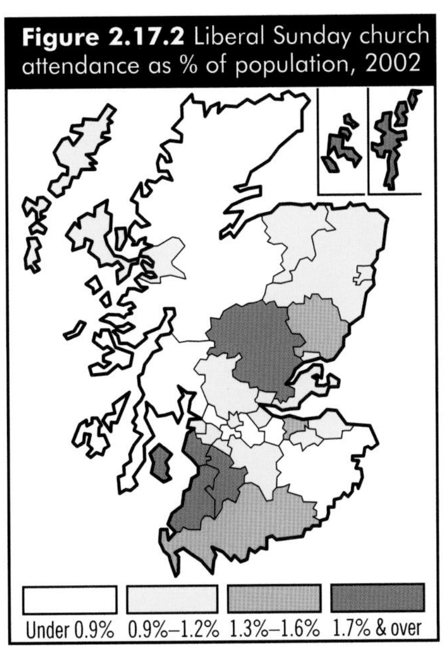

Figure 2.17.2 Liberal Sunday church attendance as % of population, 2002

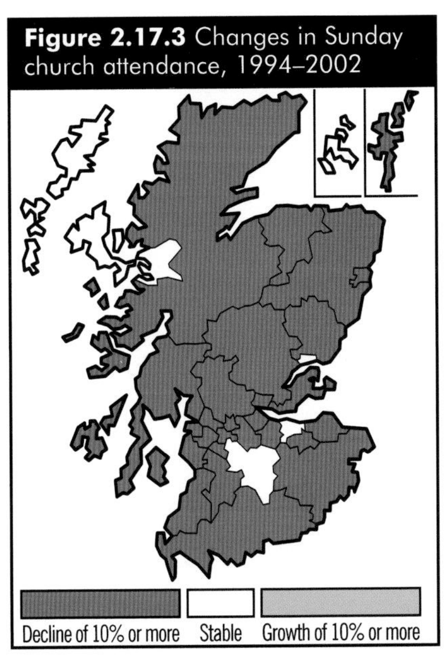

Figure 2.17.3 Changes in Sunday church attendance, 1994–2002

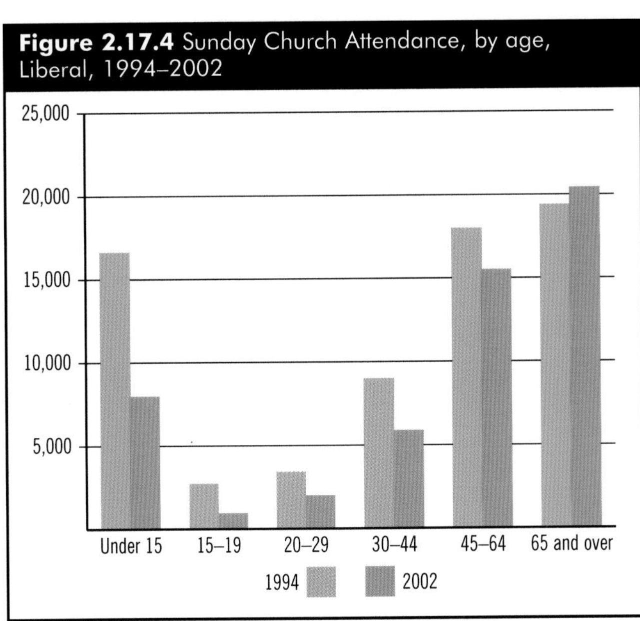

Figure 2.17.4 Sunday Church Attendance, by age, Liberal, 1994–2002

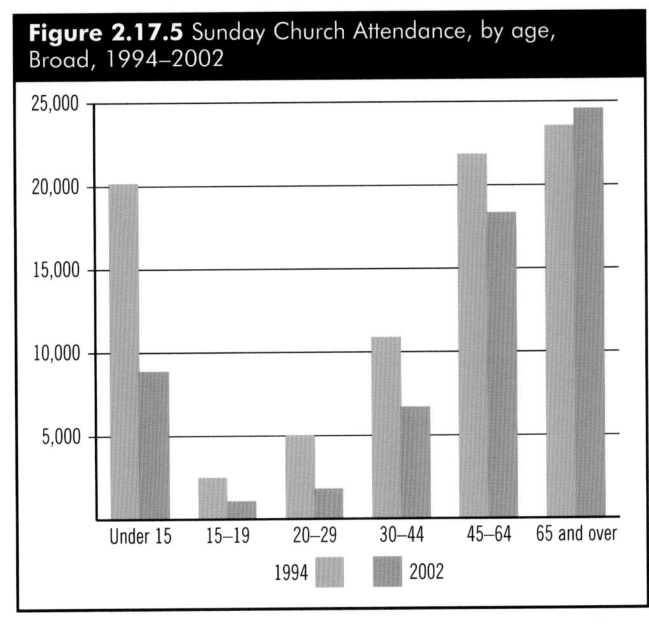

Figure 2.17.5 Sunday Church Attendance, by age, Broad, 1994–2002

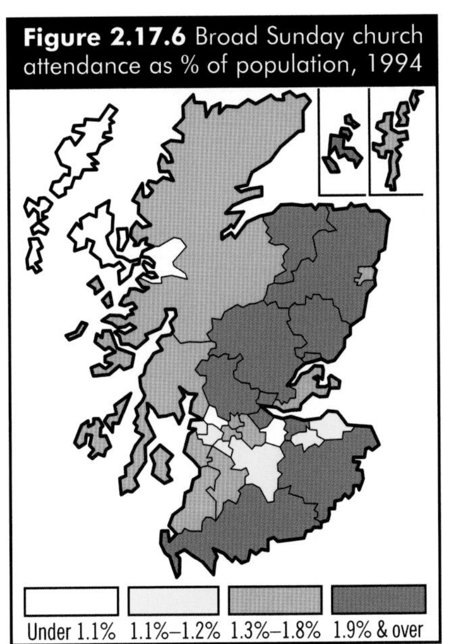

Figure 2.17.6 Broad Sunday church attendance as % of population, 1994

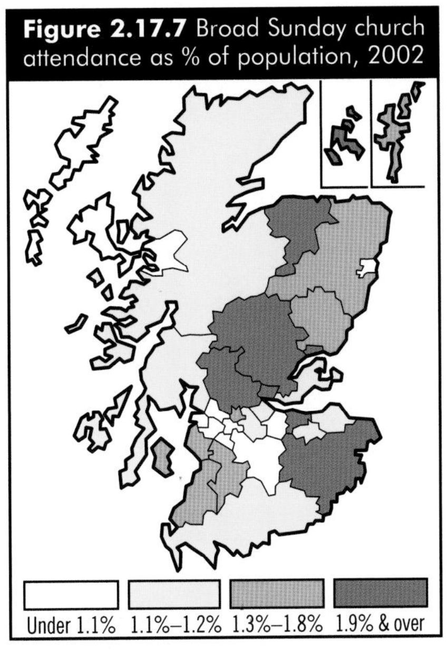

Figure 2.17.7 Broad Sunday church attendance as % of population, 2002

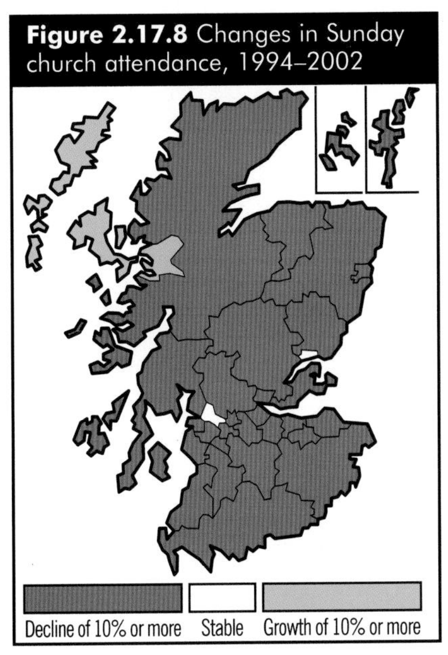

Figure 2.17.8 Changes in Sunday church attendance, 1994–2002

2

2.18 Scottish Church Census 2002: Churches by Environment

Figure 2.18.1 Total Sunday Church Attendance, by environment, 1994 and 2002

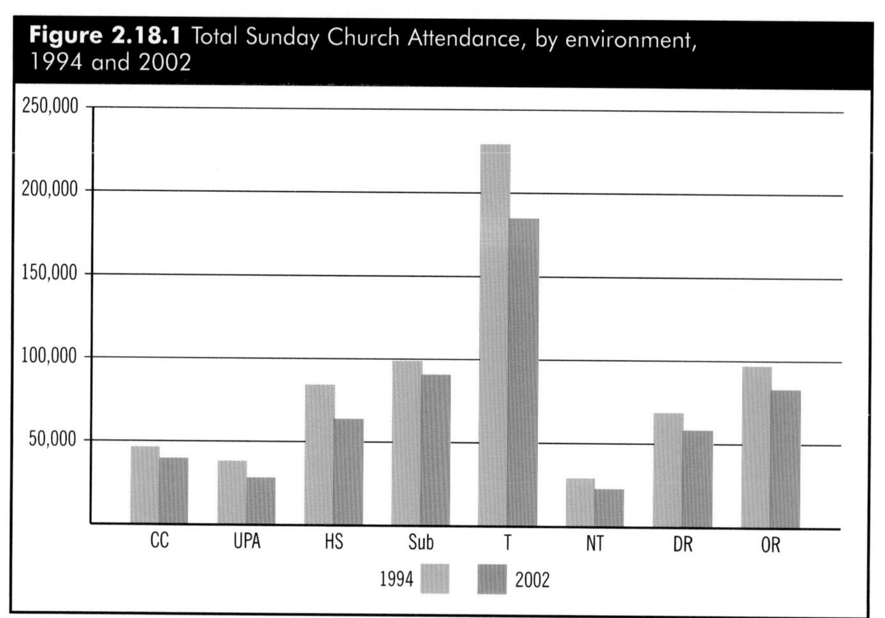

The environment in which a church is set changes slowly, if ever. Eight classifications were used, and **Figure 2.18.1** represents them in total. **Figures 2.18.2–4** then break down these total into three denominational groups, details of which are in **Tables 12.30–36.5.**

Church attendance in all environments has declined, but that in suburban areas proportionately less, and in UPA and Housing Scheme areas more. Note that in City Centres and Suburban areas there was very small growth in attendance amongst the non-Church of Scotland and Roman Catholic denominations.

KEY

CC	City Centre
UPA	Urban Priority Area
HS	Housing Scheme
Sub	Suburban
T	Town
NT	New Town
DR	Dormitory Rural
OR	Other Rural

Figure 2.18.2 Sunday Church Attendance by environment: Church of Scotland, 1994 and 2002

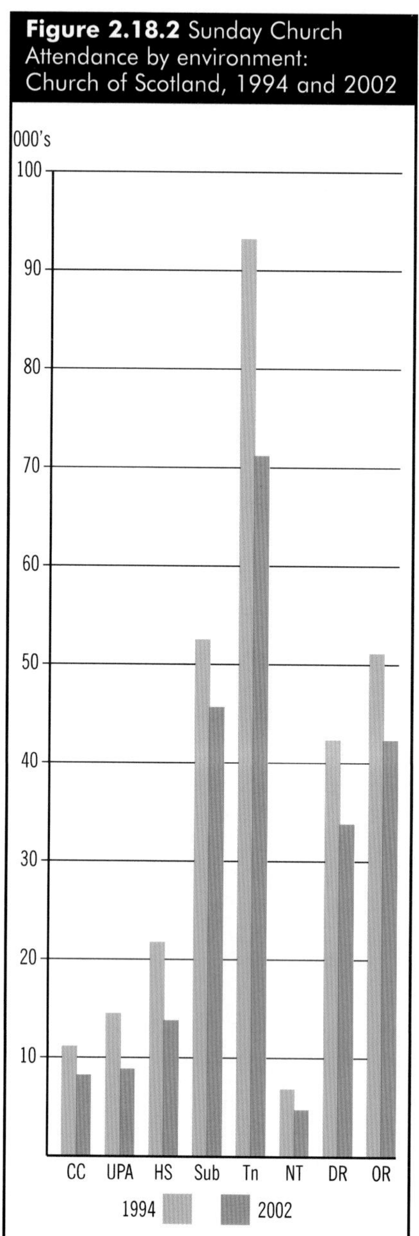

Figure 2.18.3 Sunday Church Attendance by environment: Roman Catholic, 1994 and 2002

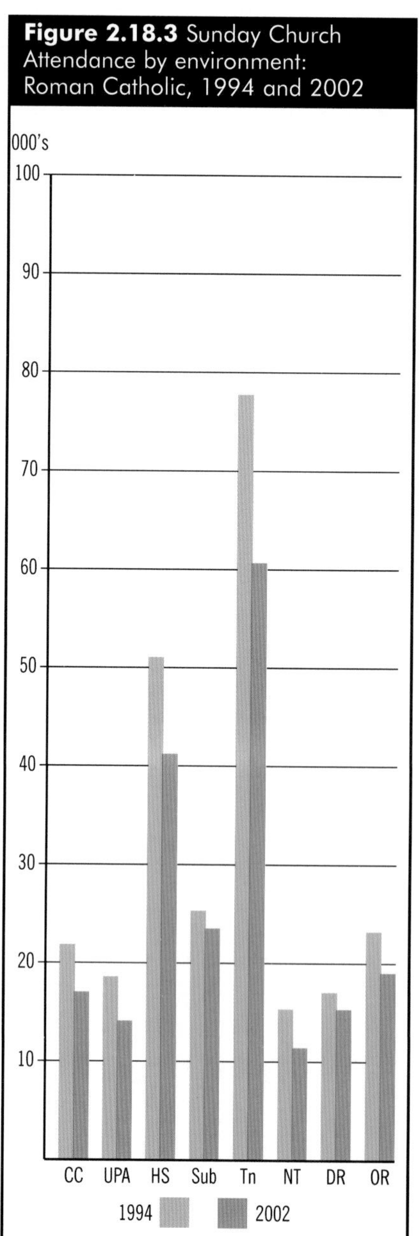

Figure 2.18.2 Sunday Church Attendance by environment: All other denominations, 1994 and 2002

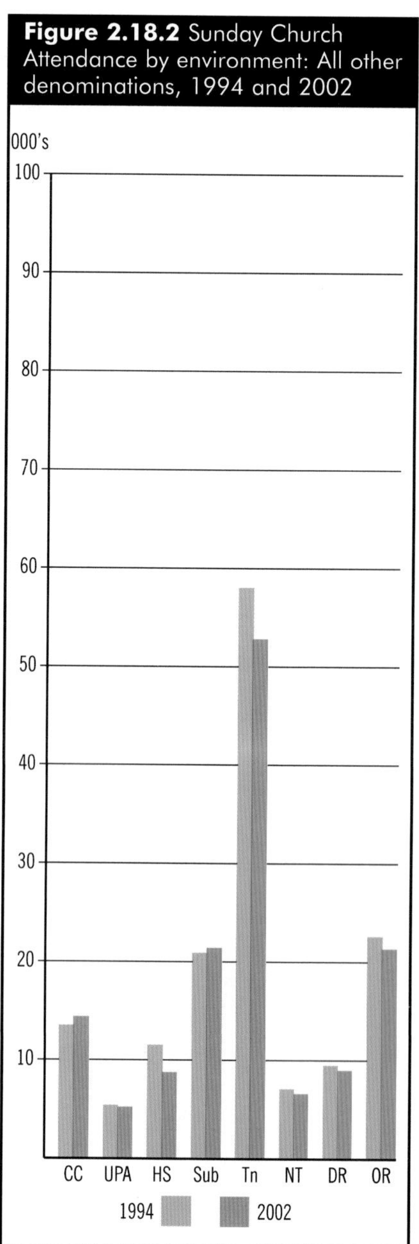

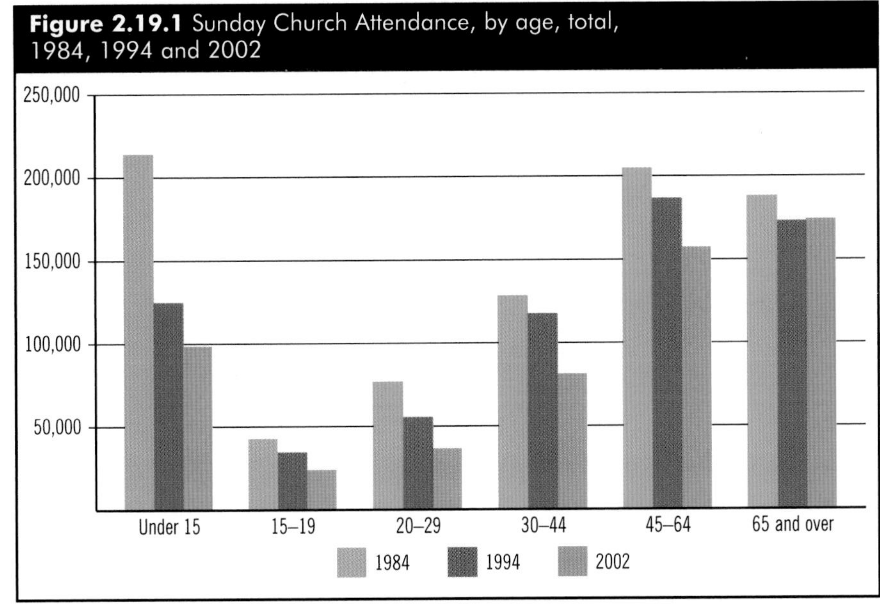

Figure 2.19.1 Sunday Church Attendance, by age, total, 1984, 1994 and 2002

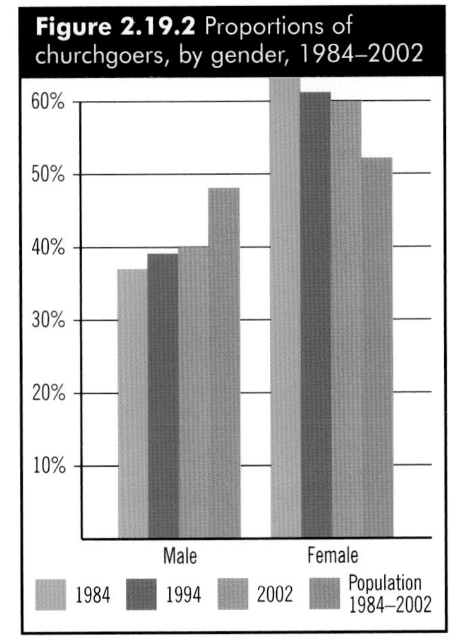

Figure 2.19.2 Proportions of churchgoers, by gender, 1984–2002

Figure 2.19.1 shows how Sunday churchgoers in Scotland have changed since 1984. Numbers of children fell especially between 1984 and 1994, but between 1994 and 2002 it is those of parent age, 30 to 44 and 45 to 64, who have left, with a small increase in overall numbers for those 65 and over.

Figure 2.19.2 shows that the percentage of men in church has increased since 1984, but this is due more to women leaving than men coming.

Figure 2.19.3 looks complicated! Each pair of bars represents a comparison between the proportion of churchgoers of a given age and the population of that age. Perhaps the easiest to follow is the group for 30 to 44. The right hand column of each pair shows that the proportion of this age-group in the population has been increasing since 1984, whereas the left-hand columns show that the proportion of churchgoers of this age-group rose between 1984 and 1994 but fell between 1994 and 2002, to below the 1984 level. The proportion of older people in the church has markedly increased between 1994 and 2002 (against a stable population trend), but this is due more to numbers leaving who are younger than large increases in numbers of older people.

Figure 2.19.4 breaks down the changes in the two periods 1984 to 1994 and 1994 to 2002 by age and gender. It is clear that in the latter period women have been leaving church at twice the rate of men – some 43,500 men leaving but 77,500 women leaving, almost a third of whom were in the 30 to 44 age-group.

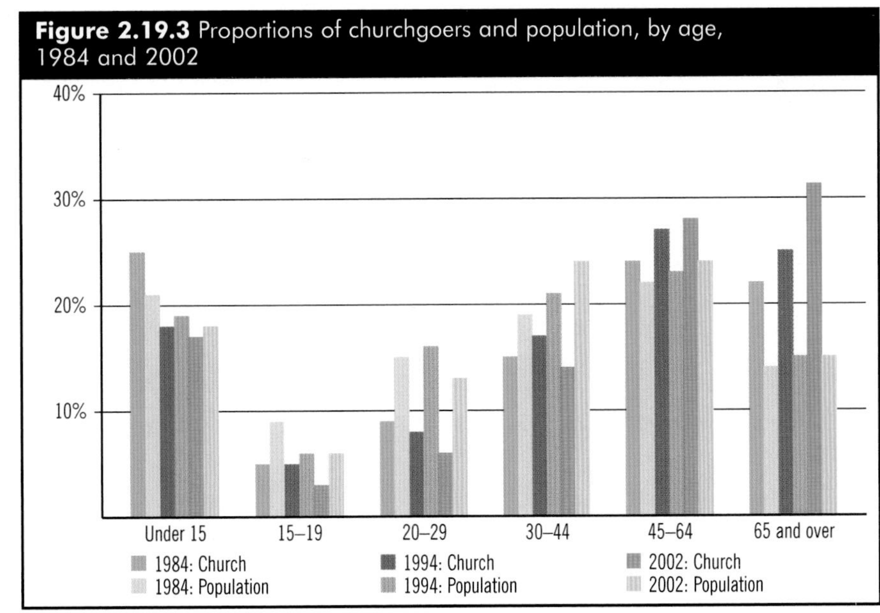

Figure 2.19.3 Proportions of churchgoers and population, by age, 1984 and 2002

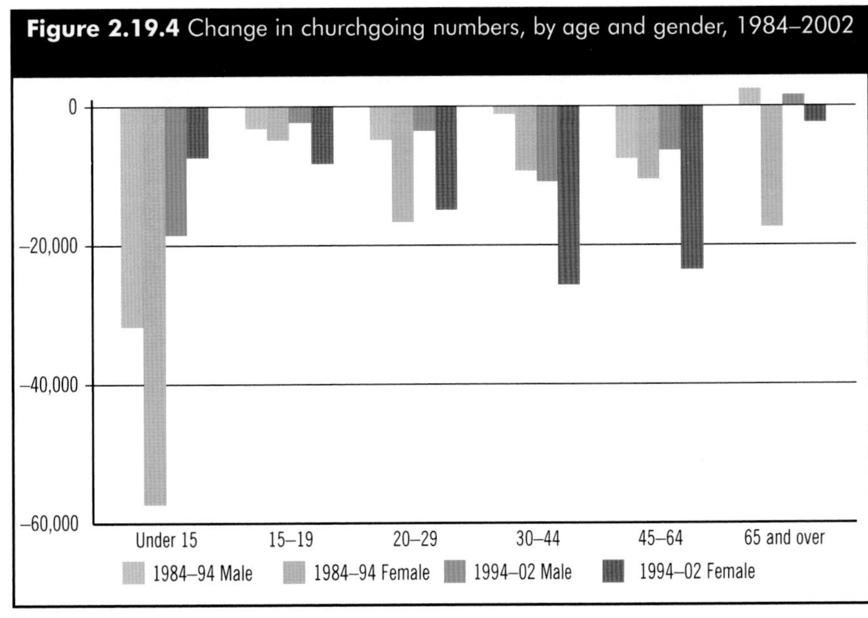

Figure 2.19.4 Change in churchgoing numbers, by age and gender, 1984–2002

2.20 Change in the Church of England by Diocese

Figure 2.20.1
Average Weekly Attendance as % of population, 2000, by Diocese

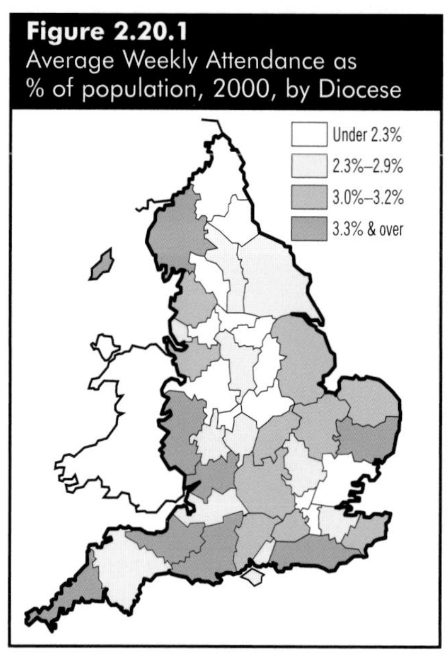

Figure 2.20.2
Dioceses of the Church of England

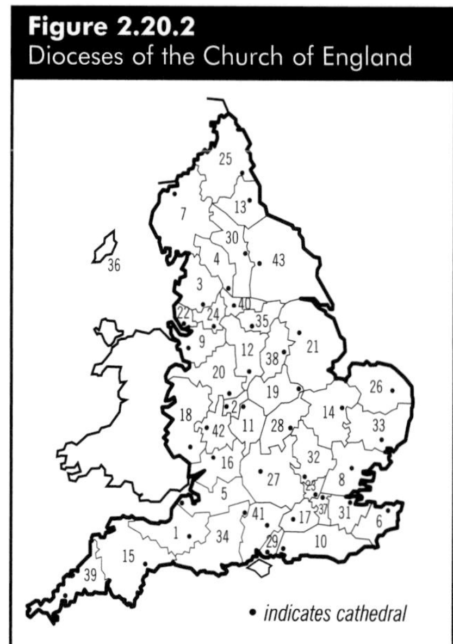

Table 2.20
Dioceses of the Church of England

1 Bath & Wells	16 Gloucester	31 Rochester
2 Birmingham	17 Guildford	32 St Albans
3 Blackburn*	18 Hereford	33 St Edmundsbury & Ipswich
4 Bradford*	19 Leicester	34 Salisbury
5 Bristol	20 Lichfield	35 Sheffield*
6 Canterbury	21 Lincoln	36 Sodor & Man*
7 Carlisle*	22 Liverpool*	37 Southwark
8 Chelmsford	23 London	38 Southwell
9 Chester*	24 Manchester*	39 Truro
10 Chichester	25 Newcastle*	40 Wakefield*
11 Coventry	26 Norwich	41 Winchester
12 Derby	27 Oxford	42 Worcester
13 Durham*	28 Peterborough	43 York*
14 Ely	29 Portsmouth	44 Europe *(not shown)*
15 Exeter	30 Ripon & Leeds*	

**indicates Northern Province*

Figure 2.20.3 % change in Average Weekly Attendance 2000–2001 by CofE Diocese

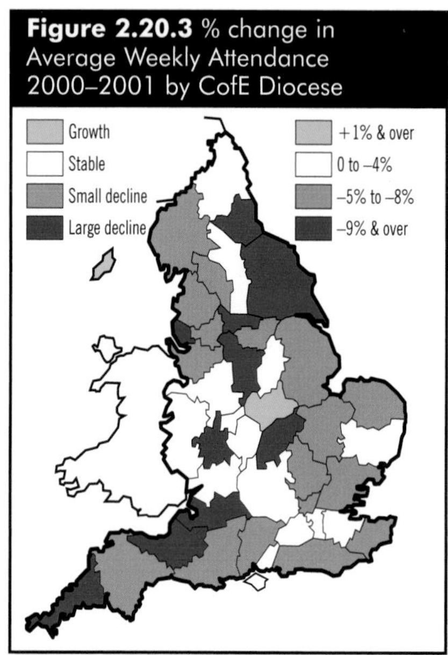

Figure 2.20.4
Population per church, 2000, by Diocese

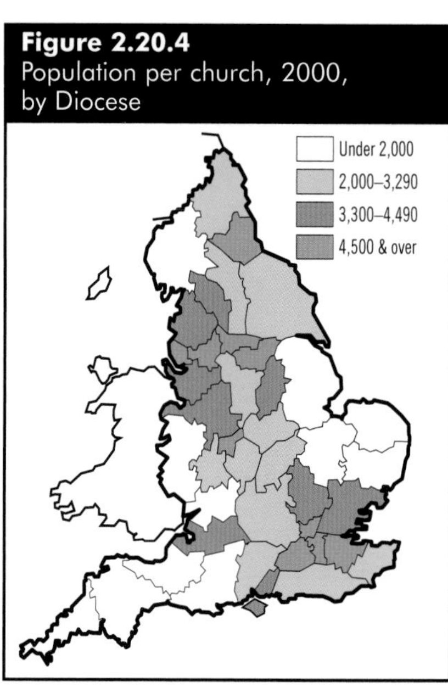
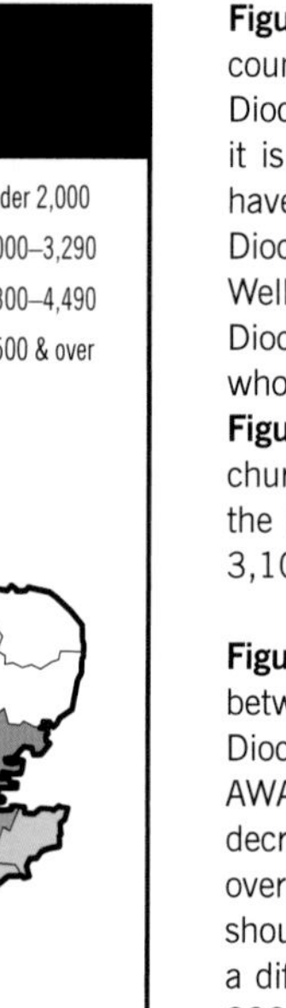

Figure 2.20.5 Average annual % change in Electoral Roll 1998–2000 by Church of England Diocese

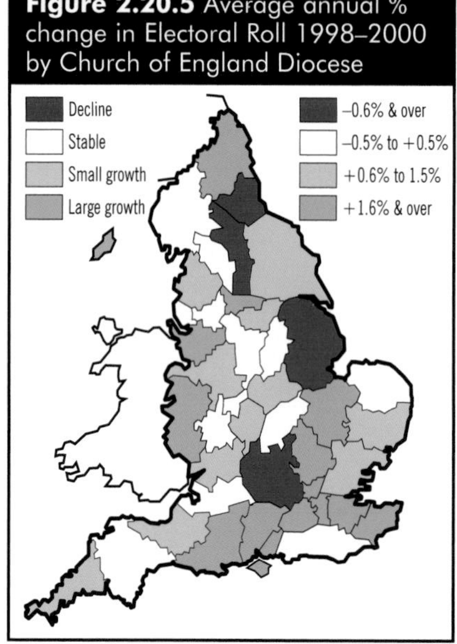

Figure 2.20.6 Percentage Average Weekly Attendance of Electoral Roll in 2000 by Diocese

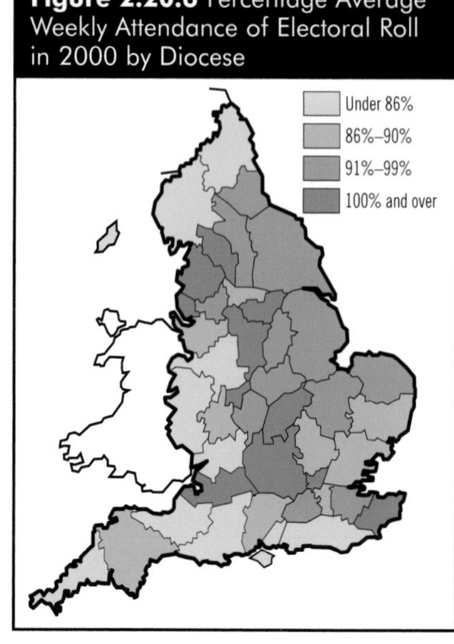

Figure 2.20.1 gives the proportion of the new count of Average Weekly Attendance (AWA) by Diocesan population. It is readily observed that it is the more rural parts of the country which have the higher attendance rates, with the Dioceses of Salisbury, Hereford and Bath & Wells all being 4% or over. The lowest is the Diocese of Birmingham at 1.4%. Over the whole country the percentage is 2.5%. Likewise **Figure 2.20.4**, which gives population per church, shows it is the urban areas which have the highest numbers (the overall average being 3,100 people per church).

Figure 2.20.3 shows how the AWA varied between 2000 and 2001 by Diocese. The Dioceses of Leicester and Sodor & Man saw the AWA increase, but 27 of the 43 Dioceses saw it decrease at least 5%, and 10 9% or more. The overall change was a decline of 5%. However, it should be noted that Leicester counts its AWA at a different time to other Dioceses, and that the 2001 AWA excluded attendance at mid-week wedding and funeral services which were included in 2000 AWA figures. This accounts for much of the decline.

Figures 2.20.5 and **6** look at the Electoral Roll (ER) – the average annual change between 1998 and 2000, when the large majority increased, as it always does between revisions, the last of which was 1996 and the next was in 2002. The movement here is totally different from that of the AWA! **Figure 2.20.6** gives the AWA as a percentage of the ER – in a quarter of Dioceses, it is greater.

The figures behind these maps are in **Table 8.3.2.**

Table 2.21.1
Total Churches

	Membership					Churches					Ministers				
	England	Wales	Scotland	N. Ireland	**Total UK**	England	Wales	Scotland	N. Ireland	**Total UK**	England	Wales	Scotland	N. Ireland	**Total UK**
1990	4,062,227	372,877	1,252,284	946,947	**6,634,335**	38,508	5,283	3,975	2,209	**49,975**	29,393	1,947	3,460	1,858	**36,658**
1995	3,904,942	330,395	1,120,165	948,224	**6,303,726**	38,513	5,045	3,822	2,203	**49,583**	29,322	1,916	3,290	1,746	**36,274**
2000	3,733,304	284,921	994,374	946,729	**5,959,328**	38,113	4,789	3,732	2,191	**48,825**	28,790	1,786	3,095	1,757	**35,428**
2001	3,716,816	276,168	965,343	944,940	**5,903,267**	38,413	4,738	3,706	2,200	**49,057**	28,922	1,786	3,069	1,762	**35,539**
2002	3,534,075	264,341	935,597	944,290	**5,678,303**	38,269	4,684	3,691	2,200	**48,844**	28,939	1,770	3,035	1,754	**35,498**
2005	3,557,583	241,162	861,713	937,799	**5,598,257**	38,237	4,534	3,641	2,186	**48,598**	28,977	1,737	2,936	1,751	**35,401**

Figure 2.21.1
Trends in UK church membership

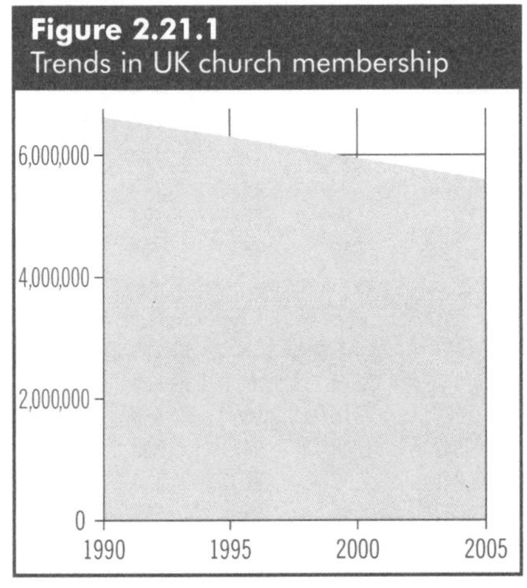

Figure 2.21.2
Trends in number of churches, UK

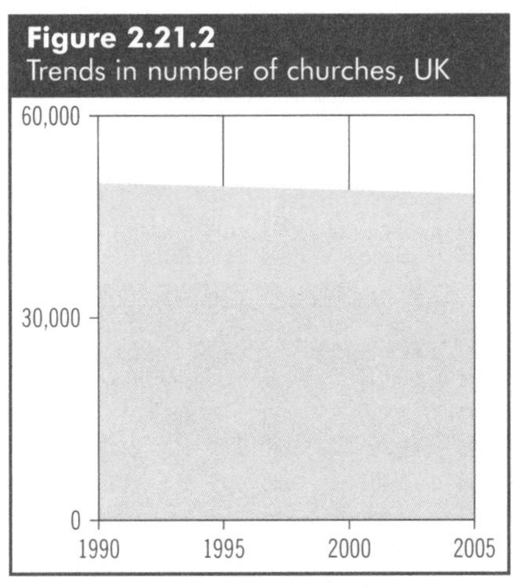

Figure 2.21.3
Trends in number of ministers, UK

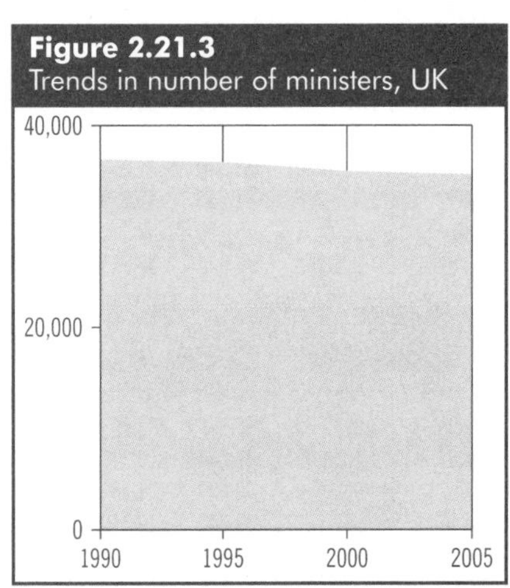

Figure 2.21.4 Proportions of membership by country, 2002

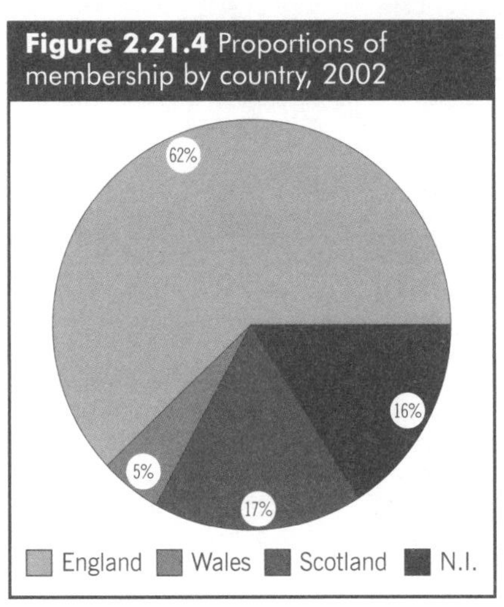

Figure 2.21.5 Proportions of churches by country, 2002

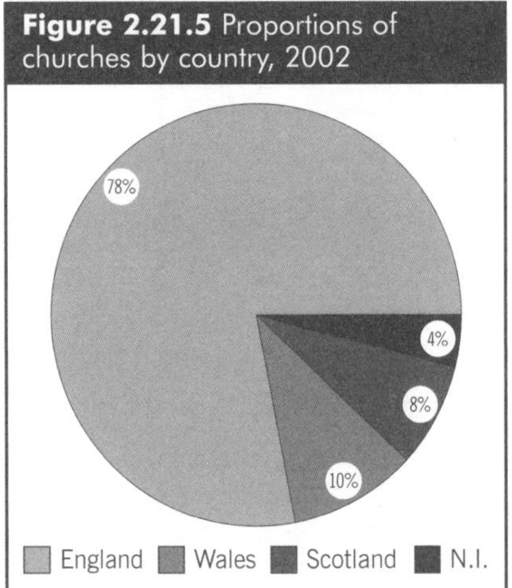

Figure 2.21.6 Proportions of ministers by country, 2002

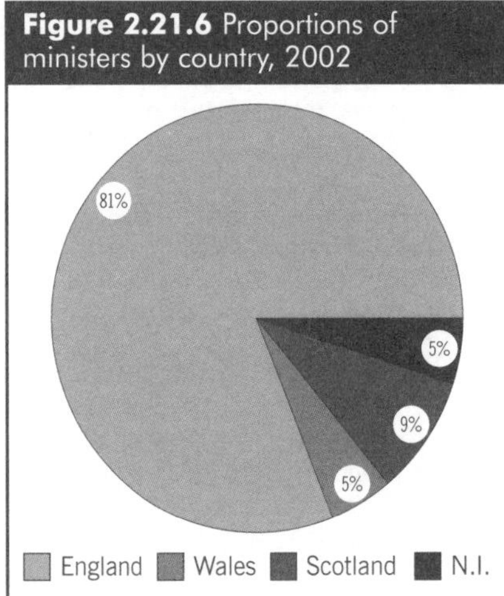

Figures 2.21.1–3 show that the rate of decline is not at the same rate for church members, buildings and ministers. Between 1990 and 2005, church membership is due to drop (if present trends continue) 16% or –1.1% a year. The number of church buildings declines only 3% in this period, or –0.2% a year. Ministers are closer to the buildings than members in terms of change, declining 4% in these 15 years, a rate of –0.3% a year.

In 1990, there were 133 members per church; by 2005 it will be 115. In 1990 there were 1.36 churches for every minister; by 2005 it will be 1.37.

Figures 2.21.4–6 show that the distribution between the countries of the UK is not evenly balanced. England has proportionately more ministers than churches, and more churches than members. In England in 2000 there were 98 members per church, but in Wales there were only 59 members per church. However Scotland could boast 266 members per church and Northern Ireland 432! Two countries with smaller churches and two with much larger. Members are however declining fast in Wales (at –2.9% per year between 1990 and 2005) and in Scotland (at –2.5% per annum, whereas the rate is slower in England (–0.9% per annum) and Northern Ireland (–0.06% per annum).

In 2000, England had 1.32 churches for every minister, but Wales 2.71, showing the relative paucity of ministers there (or too many churches). Scotland had 1.21 and Northern Ireland had 1.25 showing a more equable distribution.

Ministers in England are decreasing at the rate –0.1% per year (across the period 1990 to 2005), or 1 per thousand per year. In Wales, however, the rate of decline is –0.9% per year, nine times as fast. In Scotland, the rate is faster still, at –1.1% per year, but in Northern Ireland it is –0.4% per year. An analysis of the change by gender shows it is generally the male clergy who are leaving, at –0.8% per year, whereas the female clergy are growing at +3.0% per year.

Table 2.21.2 Membership as percentage of population

Year	England %	Wales %	Scotland %	N Ireland %	Overall UK %
1990	*8.5*	*13.2*	*24.5*	*59.4*	***11.6***
1995	*8.1*	*11.6*	*22.0*	*57.3*	***10.9***
2000	*7.6*	*9.8*	*19.6*	*56.4*	***10.2***
2001	*7.6*	*9.5*	*19.1*	*56.1*	***10.0***
2002	*7.2*	*9.1*	*18.6*	*55.9*	***9.6***
2005	*7.2*	*8.2*	*17.4*	*55.1*	***9.4***

2.22 Total Institutional Church Membership, UK

Table 2.22.1
Total Institutional Churches[5]

	MEMBERSHIP					CHURCHES					MINISTERS				
	England	Wales	Scotland	N. Ireland	**Total UK**	England	Wales	Scotland	N. Ireland	**Total UK**	England	Wales	Scotland	N. Ireland	**Total UK**
1990	3,033,044	237,809	1,170,721	892,784	**5,334,358**	21,846	2,995	2,867	1,540	**29,248**	18,050	1,205	2,748	1,453	**23,456**
1995	2,857,535	207,104	1,046,521	894,948	**5,006,108**	21,701	2,872	2,746	1,525	**28,844**	16,935	1,163	2,580	1,312	**21,990**
2000	2,678,109	178,058	930,478	895,020	**4,682,615**	21,591	2,751	2,757	1,516	**28,615**	15,915	1,063	2,375	1,329	**20,682**
2001	2,659,065	172,543	902,524	893,121	**4,627,253**	21,619	2,727	2,736	1,522	**28,604**	15,845	1,062	2,355	1,331	**20,593**
2002	2,474,985	163,485	872,732	892,343	**4,403,545**	21,613	2,702	2,720	1,521	**28,556**	15,745	1,048	2,322	1,318	**20,433**
2005	2,485,954	149,937	798,267	886,128	**4,320,286**	21,519	2,638	2,669	1,508	**28,334**	15,196	1,019	2,224	1,306	**19,745**

Table 2.22.2
Ttal Anglican Churches[1]

	England	Wales	Scotland	N. Ireland	**Total UK**	England	Wales	Scotland	N. Ireland	**Total UK**	England	Wales	Scotland	N. Ireland	**Total UK**
1990	1,398,863	108,365	58,619	162,130	**1,727,977**	16,440	1,595	319	476	**18,830**	11,130	700	240	304	**12,374**
1995	1,472,617	95,785	55,106	161,525	**1,785,033**	16,361	1,540	320	452	**18,673**	10,378	710	244	250	**11,582**
2000	1,381,930	83,840	49,853	160,827	**1,676,450**	16,350	1,514	315	447	**18,624**	9,754	657	174	295	**10,885**
2001	1,377,085	81,345	48,868	160,727	**1,668,025**	16,354	1,513	316	442	**18,625**	9,682	662	181	305	**10,830**
2002	1,211,455	75,470	47,992	160,528	**1,495,445**	16,371	1,515	320	442	**18,648**	9,611	659	178	304	**10,752**
2005	1,271,130	71,675	45,635	160,130	**1,548,570**	16,386	1,513	321	432	**18,652**	9,238	660	161	304	**10,363**

Table 2.22.3
Total Catholic Churches[2]

	England	Wales	Scotland	N. Ireland	**Total UK**	England	Wales	Scotland	N. Ireland	**Total UK**	England	Wales	Scotland	N. Ireland	**Total UK**
1990	1,351,342	54,659	283,793	515,700	**2,205,494**	3,535	213	485	467	**4,700**	5,789	316	1,050	643	**7,798**
1995	1,105,940	47,244	250,302	518,000	**1,921,486**	3,462	240	462	470	**4,634**	5,637	288	947	600	**7,472**
2000	989,440	40,630	223,186	521,100	**1,774,356**	3,401	238	463	470	**4,572**	5,246	253	869	554	**6,922**
2001	971,172	39,640	212,740	522,100	**1,745,652**	3,428	233	463	470	**4,594**	5,247	255	855	547	**6,904**
2002	947,845	38,650	202,365	523,150	**1,712,010**	3,423	230	464	470	**4,587**	5,225	249	840	540	**6,854**
2005	888,369	35,170	183,710	524,200	**1,631,449**	3,320	222	465	470	**4,475**	5,041	228	794	520	**6,583**

Table 2.22.4
Total Orthodox Churches[3]

	England	Wales	Scotland	N. Ireland	**Total UK**	England	Wales	Scotland	N. Ireland	**Total UK**	England	Wales	Scotland	N. Ireland	**Total UK**
1990	167,480	7,116	12,176	95	**186,867**	213	8	8	1	**230**	149	6	7	1	**163**
1995	177,486	7,252	15,868	220	**200,826**	242	7	13	2	**264**	174	6	9	1	**190**
2000	218,497	7,285	22,137	263	**248,182**	253	7	15	2	**277**	212	7	10	1	**230**
2001	225,503	7,285	22,247	273	**255,308**	253	7	15	2	**277**	217	6	11	1	**235**
2002	232,879	7,295	22,307	288	**262,769**	255	7	15	2	**279**	220	6	11	1	**238**
2005	252,101	7,322	24,537	338	**284,298**	266	8	16	2	**292**	234	7	13	1	**255**

Table 2.22.5
Total All Presbyterian Churches[4]

	England	Wales	Scotland	N. Ireland	**Total UK**	England	Wales	Scotland	N. Ireland	**Total UK**	England	Wales	Scotland	N. Ireland	**Total UK**
1990	115,359	67,669	816,133	214,859	**1,214,020**	1,658	1,180	2,055	596	**5,489**	982	183	1,451	505	**3,121**
1995	101,492	56,823	725,245	215,203	**1,098,763**	1,636	1,085	1,951	601	**5,273**	746	159	1,380	461	**2,746**
2000	88,242	46,303	635,302	212,830	**982,677**	1,587	992	1,964	597	**5,140**	698	146	1,322	479	**2,645**
2001	85,305	44,273	618,669	210,021	**958,268**	1,584	974	1,942	608	**5,108**	699	139	1,308	478	**2,624**
2002	82,806	42,070	600,068	208,377	**933,321**	1,564	950	1,921	607	**5,042**	689	134	1,293	473	**2,589**
2005	74,354	35,770	544,385	201,460	**855,969**	1,547	895	1,867	604	**4,913**	683	124	1,256	481	**2,544**

[1] Repeat of **Table 8.2.1**
[2] Repeat of **Table 8.5.1**
[3] Repeat of **Table 8.8.1**
[4] Repeat of **Table 8.12.1**
[5] Total of **Tables 2.22.2–5**

Total Free Church Membership, UK 2.23

Table 2.23.1
Total Free Churches[7]

	MEMBERSHIP					CHURCHES					MINISTERS				
	England	Wales	Scotland	N. Ireland	**Total UK**	England	Wales	Scotland	N. Ireland	**Total UK**	England	Wales	Scotland	N. Ireland	**Total UK**
1990	1,029,183	135,068	81,563	54,163	**1,299,977**	16,662	2,288	1,108	669	**20,727**	11,343	742	712	405	**13,202**
1995	1,047,407	123,291	73,644	53,276	**1,297,618**	16,812	2,173	1,076	678	**20,739**	12,387	753	710	434	**14,284**
2000	1,055,195	106,863	63,896	51,709	**1,277,663**	16,522	2,038	975	675	**20,210**	12,875	723	720	428	**14,746**
2001	1,057,751	103,625	62,819	51,819	**1,276,014**	16,794	2,011	970	678	**20,453**	13,077	724	714	431	**14,946**
2002	1,059,090	100,856	62,865	51,947	**1,274,758**	16,656	1,982	971	679	**20,288**	13,194	722	713	436	**15,065**
2005	1,071,629	91,225	63,446	51,671	**1,277,971**	16,718	1,896	972	678	**20,264**	13,781	718	712	445	**15,656**

Table 2.23.2
Total Baptist Churches[1]

	MEMBERSHIP					CHURCHES					MINISTERS				
	England	Wales	Scotland	N. Ireland	**Total UK**	England	Wales	Scotland	N. Ireland	**Total UK**	England	Wales	Scotland	N. Ireland	**Total UK**
1990	168,078	37,820	18,103	8,167	**232,168**	2,542	743	195	103	**3,583**	2,100	221	171	100	**2,592**
1995	163,784	34,169	18,068	8,208	**224,229**	2,574	714	203	112	**3,603**	2,210	229	175	105	**2,719**
2000	165,722	26,271	16,785	8,249	**217,027**	2,582	626	207	113	**3,528**	2,275	178	191	89	**2,733**
2001	164,771	25,506	16,464	8,321	**215,062**	2,586	616	206	116	**3,524**	2,382	180	190	94	**2,846**
2002	164,305	24,414	16,513	8,345	**213,577**	2,587	600	204	117	**3,508**	2,389	180	190	95	**2,854**
2005	163,441	20,790	16,842	8,406	**209,479**	2,593	556	203	117	**3,469**	2,418	175	185	95	**2,873**

Table 2.23.3
Total All Independent Churches[2]

	MEMBERSHIP					CHURCHES					MINISTERS				
	England	Wales	Scotland	N. Ireland	**Total UK**	England	Wales	Scotland	N. Ireland	**Total UK**	England	Wales	Scotland	N. Ireland	**Total UK**
1990	118,448	60,085	39,256	13,878	**231,667**	2,482	809	519	261	**4,071**	835	165	156	63	**1,219**
1995	112,393	53,132	31,501	13,380	**210,406**	2,403	768	470	253	**3,894**	857	173	150	67	**1,247**
2000	106,795	46,282	23,044	13,079	**189,200**	2,188	722	360	251	**3,521**	873	167	122	66	**1,228**
2001	106,964	44,841	22,561	13,131	**187,497**	2,174	705	357	250	**3,486**	873	166	125	68	**1,232**
2002	105,228	42,931	22,217	13,183	**183,559**	2,149	694	358	250	**3,451**	877	165	120	70	**1,232**
2005	106,258	37,719	21,473	12,933	**178,383**	2,113	651	352	248	**3,364**	867	159	116	70	**1,212**

Table 2.23.4
Total Methodist Churches[3]

	MEMBERSHIP					CHURCHES					MINISTERS				
	England	Wales	Scotland	N. Ireland	**Total UK**	England	Wales	Scotland	N. Ireland	**Total UK**	England	Wales	Scotland	N. Ireland	**Total UK**
1990	404,356	20,627	7,133	17,404	**449,520**	6,849	451	77	160	**7,537**	2,094	90	37	98	**2,319**
1995	362,273	18,293	6,312	15,868	**402,746**	6,433	402	75	157	**7,067**	2,187	81	41	103	**2,412**
2000	314,706	16,676	5,847	14,500	**351,729**	5,906	402	75	145	**6,528**	2,200	98	39	97	**2,434**
2001	308,319	15,261	5,693	14,423	**343,696**	6,119	402	75	145	**6,741**	2,205	98	35	95	**2,433**
2002	298,711	15,253	5,553	14,272	**333,789**	5,899	402	75	144	**6,520**	2,206	98	38	97	**2,439**
2005	272,905	13,920	5,190	13,856	**305,871**	5,671	401	76	141	**6,289**	2,236	100	38	99	**2,473**

Table 2.23.5
Total New Churches[4]

	MEMBERSHIP					CHURCHES					MINISTERS				
	England	Wales	Scotland	N. Ireland	**Total UK**	England	Wales	Scotland	N. Ireland	**Total UK**	England	Wales	Scotland	N. Ireland	**Total UK**
1990	74,838	1,690	2,935	1,200	**80,663**	1,131	27	32	12	**1,202**	1,142	22	30	12	**1,206**
1995	101,766	1,995	3,550	1,500	**108,811**	1,398	33	45	17	**1,493**	1,458	30	39	18	**1,545**
2000[1]	123,498	2,460	4,041	1,685	**131,684**	1,674	39	48	22	**1,783**	1,938	40	50	22	**2,050**
2001[1]	127,624	2,730	4,005	1,695	**136,054**	1,715	40	47	22	**1,824**	2,020	42	48	22	**2,132**
2002[1]	133,719	3,015	4,075	1,870	**142,679**	1,789	40	47	23	**1,899**	2,119	43	49	23	**2,234**
2005[1]	154,900	3,455	4,900	2,045	**165,300**	1,981	43	51	25	**2,100**	2,518	48	60	29	**2,655**

Table 2.23.6
Total Pentecostal Churches[5]

	MEMBERSHIP					CHURCHES					MINISTERS				
	England	Wales	Scotland	N. Ireland	**Total UK**	England	Wales	Scotland	N. Ireland	**Total UK**	England	Wales	Scotland	N. Ireland	**Total UK**
1990	142,806	10,017	4,412	9,771	**167,006**	1,948	163	75	70	**2,256**	3,161	153	73	73	**3,460**
1995	182,750	10,871	4,711	10,299	**208,631**	2,229	154	76	73	**2,532**	3,716	150	68	82	**4,016**
2000	218,788	10,926	6,292	10,468	**246,474**	2,376	145	87	74	**2,682**	3,781	146	86	90	**4,103**
2001	225,686	11,104	6,394	10,538	**253,722**	2,414	144	88	76	**2,722**	3,805	145	87	86	**4,123**
2002	233,065	11,030	6,765	10,555	**261,415**	2,440	142	89	76	**2,747**	3,828	145	88	86	**4,147**
2005	251,085	11,109	7,365	10,701	**280,260**	2,564	138	94	77	**2,873**	4,008	148	93	87	**4,336**

Table 2.23.7
Total Other Denominations[6]

	MEMBERSHIP					CHURCHES					MINISTERS				
	England	Wales	Scotland	N. Ireland	**Total UK**	England	Wales	Scotland	N. Ireland	**Total UK**	England	Wales	Scotland	N. Ireland	**Total UK**
1990	120,657	4,829	9,724	3,743	**138,953**	1,710	95	210	63	**2,078**	2,011	91	245	59	**2,406**
1995	124,441	4,831	9,502	4,021	**142,795**	1,775	102	207	66	**2,150**	1,959	90	237	59	**2,345**
2000	125,686	4,248	7,887	3,728	**141,549**	1,796	104	198	70	**2,168**	1,808	94	232	64	**2,198**
2001	124,387	4,183	7,702	3,711	**139,983**	1,786	104	197	69	**2,156**	1,792	93	229	66	**2,180**
2002	124,062	4,213	7,742	3,722	**139,739**	1,792	104	198	69	**2,163**	1,775	91	228	65	**2,159**
2005	123,040	4,232	7,676	3,730	**138,678**	1,796	107	196	70	**2,169**	1,734	88	220	65	**2,107**

[1]Repeat of **Table 9.2.1** [2]Repeat of **Table 9.6.1** [3]Repeat of **Table 9.8.1** [4]Repeat of **Table 9.9.1** [5]Repeat of **Table 9.12.1** [6]Repeat of **Table 9.16.1** [7]Total of **Tables 2.23.2–7**

2.24 Church Attendance in Great Britain

The figures in **Table 2.24.1** include the latest estimates by denomination for the year 2005. The 1980 and 1990 figures mostly come from the English Church Census, but the Catholic figures are as given in this and previous editions of *Religious Trends*. The 2000 figures are extrapolated from the 1998 English Church Attendance Survey, but the latest figures as also given in this volume have been used where appropriate. They show a drop of 1.4 million people attending church on Sunday in the 25 year period 1980 to 2005, an average decrease of 1,100 people per week.

Tables 2.24.2 and **2.24.3** give similar information for Wales and Scotland respectively, again based in the main on national church attendance surveys, as indicated in the sources. The English decrease 1980 to 2025 is 30%. In Wales it is more, 53%, and in Scotland it is between these two at 42%. The overall average decrease, shown from the total figures in **Table 2.24.4**, is a third, 33%. Equivalent figures are not available for Northern Ireland.

The total decrease in churchgoing numbers between 1980 and 2005, 2.0 million, is against a population increase in the same period of 2.8 million.

The percentage figures beneath each Table are graphed in **Figure 2.24** below.

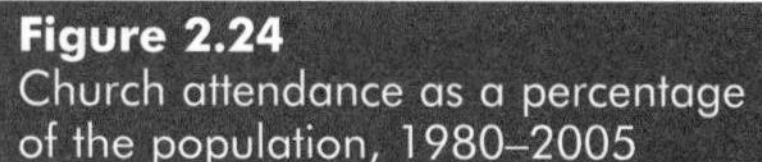

Figure 2.24
Church attendance as a percentage of the population, 1980–2005

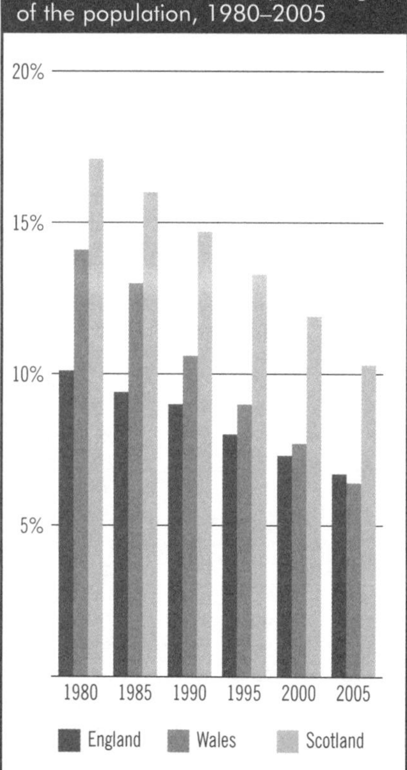

Table 2.24.1
Total Church Attendance in England 1980–2005

England	1980	1985	1990	1995	2000	2005
Anglican	1,370,400	1,301,500	1,259,800	1,161,400	1,063,300	964,800
Baptist	286,900	274,000	267,800	275,800	280,000	276,000
Catholic	1,601,400	1,424,200	1,351,300	1,105,900	990,400	889,000
Independent	239,200	252,900	258,100	198,900	150,200	138,000
Methodist	606,400	560,500	506,400	433,100	372,600	323,100
New Churches	75,000	124,700	174,600	213,100	248,400	292,000
Orthodox	10,200	11,300	12,700	20,500	25,600	29,800
Pentecostal	221,100	225,800	235,900	228,600	216,400	218,800
United Reformed	188,300	163,000	141,500	127,900	112,000	93,400
Other Churches	139,800	116,800	112,100	99,300	94,800	92,800
TOTAL	**4,738,700**	**4,454,700**	**4,320,200**	**3,864,500**	**3,553,700**	**3,317,700**
% of population	*10.1*	*9.4*	*9.0*	*8.0*	*7.3*	*6.7*

Sources: Figures taken from **Table 2.23.1** in *Religious Trends* No 3, 2002/2003. For Church of England this volume **Table 8.3.1** (average Sunday attendance), and United Reformed **Table 8.12.6.** Revised population figures have been used throughout.

Table 2.24.2
Total Church Attendance in Wales 1980–2005

Wales	1980	1985	1990	1995	2000	2005
Church in Wales	108,200	100,100	85,000	71,900	62,300	53,300
Baptist	47,900	42,500	34,700	27,300	22,500	17,800
Catholic	75,800	72,200	58,300	50,200	43,800	35,200
Methodist	27,000	23,900	19,500	17,200	15,600	13,000
Presbyterian Church of Wales	55,600	46,100	35,100	29,500	23,800	18,200
Union of Welsh Independents	34,800	31,000	24,400	19,900	16,300	12,400
Other Churches	46,500	48,000	43,500	40,400	39,500	37,900
TOTAL	**395,800**	**363,800**	**300,500**	**256,400**	**223,800**	**187,800**
% of population	*14.1*	*13.0*	*10.6*	*9.0*	*7.7*	*6.4*

Sources: Figures taken from **Table 2.23.2** in *Religious Trends* No 3, 2002/2003, but adjusted in the light of trends given in this volume. Revised population figures used throughout.

Table 2.24.3
Total Church Attendance in Scotland 1980–2005

Scotland	1980	1985	1990	1995	2000	2005
Episcopal	17,900	19,900	19,900	20,100	19,500	18,500
Baptist	30,200	29,100	25,900	24,500	24,800	24,000
Catholic	367,100	328,900	283,600	250,400	211,200	166,300
Church of Scotland	371,000	348,100	320,800	281,800	248,600	208,400
Independent	41,400	40,500	44,400	45,000	45,000	45,800
Other Presbyterian	32,300	28,600	26,000	23,100	22,600	20,300
Other Churches	27,200	29,600	30,500	31,600	30,700	27,600
TOTAL	**887,100**	**824,700**	**751,000**	**676,500**	**602,400**	**510,900**
% of population	*17.1*	*16.0*	*14.7*	*13.3*	*11.9*	*10.3*

Sources: Figures taken from **Table 2.23.3** in *Religious Trends* No 3, 2002/2003, but 1995, 2000 and 2005 have been completely revised in the light of 2002 figures given in this volume. 1980 figures are unchanged, and a few 1985 and 1990 figures have been adjusted to give more reasonable trends. Revised population figures used throughout.

Table 2.24.4
Total Church Attendance in Great Britain1980–2005

Great Britain	1980	1985	1990	1995	2000	2005
TOTAL	**6,021,600**	**5,643,200**	**5,371,700**	**4,797,400**	**4,379,900**	**4,016,400**
% of population	*11.0*	*10.2*	*9.6*	*8.5*	*7.7*	*7.0*

3

UK Mission Overseas

3

Sources: Statistics provided by UK mission agencies of all denominations in a special survey specifically designed for publication in this volume. Plus previous editions of *Religious Trends* and *UK Christian Handbook*

3.2 Changes to Mission Statistics

The type of statistics collected for this section has changed since the publication of *Religious Trends* No 3. These notes explain these changes.

Method of collection

Up to this edition of *Religious Trends,* the publication coincided with that of the *UK Christian Handbook.* This meant that some information could be collected simultaneously. The information about mission was part of the data supplied which was used in both publications.

With the two volumes now being published at separate times, the data about mission was collected by sending a form to all the Mission Agencies listed in the 2002/2003 edition of the *UK Christian Handbook.* The information supplied on these forms has been used as the basis for the data in this Section. Where, despite reminders, data was not forthcoming, the information previously supplied has been used.

More relevant data

Several suggestions by members of the mission community over the last few years about the type of data collected led to a meeting with Global Connections and the Council for World Mission. It was agreed to ask for some different data this time, the analysis of which would hopefully be more useful to the mission community. Some of the information requested was identical to that previously collected.

A draft questionnaire was produced and sent to mission agencies in 2002 asking for their comments. In the light of those comments further changes were made, and the final questionnaire sent to all mission agencies asked for data as at 31st December 2002. Previously information was collected as at 1st January in a particular year, so as the change between 31st December 2002 and 1st January 2003 will be minimal, the data is labelled here 2003 as this gives a more consistent comparison of periods between earlier data.

Different data

The key difference is a move away from asking whether mission workers are working in their own culture overseas or in a cross-cultural context to one of asking how many years workers had been with the mission. After a few years it will be possible to produce a time series of such information, but in this issue there is only the starting point. Those designated as working in a "short-term" capacity are now included with those working with an agency for "under 2 years".

However there was a continued request to have workers in the UK broken down by their type of ministry, and this has been repeated.

It was agreed that the categories of workers overseas and workers on home leave (or furlough) should be amalgamated, since there are many ways in which home leave is taken today.

It was requested that the number of new workers who joined and left in the past year be asked, and this is reported in **Tables 3.5.1** and **2,** together with the reasons for joining or leaving.

Unchanged data

Information has continued to be requested by country, so the total number of workers in a particular location can be known. That list is not however included in *Religious Trends,* but will be included in the 2004/2005 edition of the *UK Christian Handbook.* Likewise tables showing the largest societies or the countries with most mission workers.

Societies working totally within the UK are excluded from this section.

Virtually all numbers have been requested broken down by gender, as before.

Information on associates and secondments has not changed. Nor has the request for details of countries in which an agency is interested but has no current personnel serving in it; again this will be given in the next *UK Christian Handbook.*

Finance of societies is dependent on information collected for the Handbook, and hence no new information is given in this edition.

Purpose of changes

Naturally we hope that these changes will provide more relevant (and hence more useful) data for the mission community. At present the data collected for each edition of *Religious Trends* is the only regular statistical research across the mission community, so naturally it is important that it reflects the data that is wanted.

Further suggestions on what extra data could be collected, or modifications to the existing information are always welcome. Please contact the Editor at Christian Research (address on Page 0.2).

Definitions

Those working overseas have traditionally been termed "missionaries", but the phrase "mission workers" is now used instead.

Mission workers have traditionally been sent by missionary "societies". These are now called "agencies".

"Associates" are those linked to the Agency in some way (for prayer support perhaps) but are not financially supported nor under Agency leadership.

Mission workers given under the heading "Direct Sending Churches" are those who are sent overseas directly by their individual churches, rather than through any intermediary agency. Many of these are from (Open) Christian Brethren Assemblies or churches.

Total British mission workers were collected in even numbered years in the 1980s and odd numbered years in the 1990s, making evenly spaced trends difficult. In **Table 3.3.1** the 1985, 1990 and 2000 figures have been taken as a linear extrapolation between the years on either side of them (1988 and 1991 for 1990) to give regular intervals. This has the consequence of also smoothing some of the inevitable "blips" in any time series.

The consequent figures are graphed in **Figure 3.3.1**, and show:

- The number of mission workers generally increased up to 1995, but has been decreasing since.
- There were above normal declines in the number of Anglican mission workers in the early 1980s, and an above average increase in Interdenominational workers in the early 1990s.
- Catholic mission workers overseas have seen decline especially in the 1990s.
- The number of workers in other denominational agencies has been remarkably stable over the last 8 years, and this has helped the total non-Catholic mission workers to likewise stay at the 6,600 mark since 1995.

British mission workers are those serving overseas, mostly in cross-cultural situations, but they also include some working in the UK, often amongst ethnic minority groups.

Those serving with interdenominational societies have not relinquished their denomination, but prefer to serve with agencies where many different denominations are reflected in their membership. For a definition of "Direct Sending Churches", see **Page 3.2.**

The proportions of the total by denomination in 2003 are shown in **Figure 3.3.2.** Three out of every five British mission workers are in an interdenominational agency.

Figure 3.3.1 Total British Missionaries by Denomination, 1980–2003

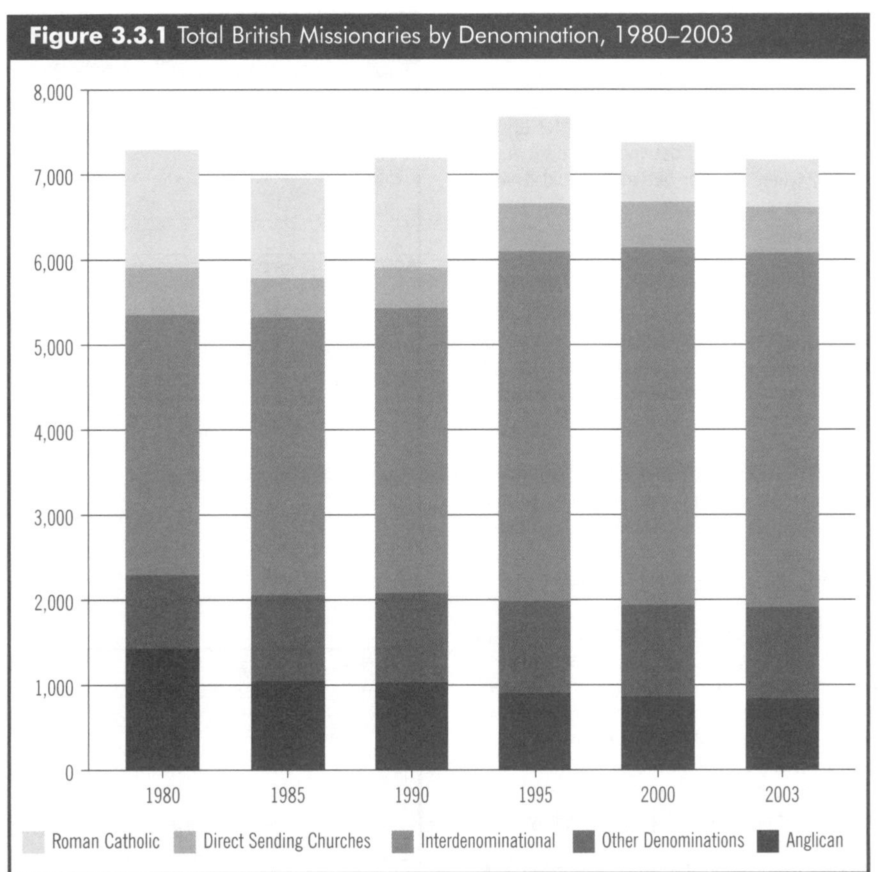

Table 3.3.1 Total British Mission Workers 1980–2003[1]

Denomination	1980	1985	1990	1995	2000	2003
Anglican	1,428	1,056	1,028	912	866	836
Roman Catholic[2]	1,386	1,172	1,293	1,018	700	562
Other Denominations[3]	867	1,001	1,050	1,079	1,078	1,078
Interdenominational	3,058	3,267	3,348	4,160	4,204	4,167
Direct Sending Churches	560	461	487	508	524	527
TOTAL	**7,299**	**6,957**	**7,206**	**7,677**	**7,372**	**7,170**
TOTAL (excluding Catholics)	5,913	5,785	5,913	6,659	6,672	6,608

[1] Includes estimates for missing data [2] Those serving overseas only [3] Excluding Salvation Army interchanged personnel

Table 3.3.2
Mission Workers by Type of Work, 1990–2003

Mission workers	1990	1995	2000	2003
Overseas	6,281	6,099	5,402	**4,876**[4]
Cross-culture UK	} 560	284	320	**278**
Own culture UK		799[6]	902	**1,008**
Secondments	135	185	172	**117**
UK Home staff[1, 2]	} 230	310[6]	576	**513**
UK Executive staff				**378**
Total: Serving Members	**7,206**	**7,677**	**7,372**	**7,170**
UK Office staff[1]	937	1,231	1,123	**960**
Associates	291	264	268	**409**
Retired personnel[5]	1,624	2,643	2,230	**1,431**
Total: Mission Workers	**10,058**	**11,815**	**10,993**	**9,970**
Number of Societies	211	224	230	232

[1] Some Home Staff were formerly classified as Executive staff and some as Office staff
[2] Defined as "not located at HQ"
[3] This total was previously split between cross-cultural and own-culture workers overseas and those on furlough or home leave
[4] This figure is not strictly comparable to earlier figures as it excludes some members of the Home staff, perhaps of the order of 300 in 2003.
[5] Not financially dependant on the Agency; the years 1995 and 2000 probably included some who were.
[6] Revised figure

Figure 3.3.2 Proportions of UK Mission Workers, 2003

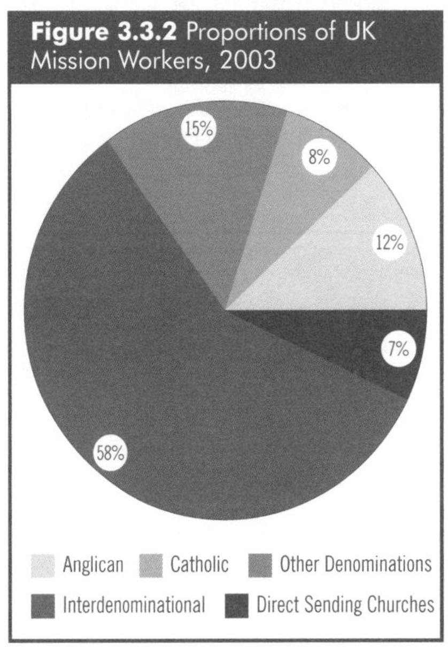

3.4 Length of Service and Workers Worldwide

Figure 3.4.1 and **Table 3.4.1** show that the proportion of mission workers serving for up to 4 years is double the number serving for 5 to 8 years, a period broadly equivalent to a "second term" of service, and those serving for up to 4 years are equally split between those serving for up to 2 years and for between 2 and 4 years. There are slightly more men serving 2 to 4 years than up to 2 years.

There are however twice as many serving for 13 years or more as serving between 9 and 12 years (the "third term") suggesting that as mission workers retire the proportion of longer serving people will decrease. There are slightly more men serving 13 years or more.

The 19% serving for under 2 years will include new "career" workers who have yet to serve more than 2 years. **Table 3.5.1** indicates 12% joined in 2002 in a short-term capacity, suggesting 7% were career workers.

The 42% who are male compares with 47% in 1997 and 49% in 2001, but these earlier figures included Home or Executive staff. In 1995 the percentage of mission workers alone who were male was 42.5%, rising to 44.6% in 1997 (**Table 3.10.1** in *Religious Trends* No 1) compared with 42.4% in 2003, indicating that the proportion of men fluctuates slightly.

The average length of service from **Table 3.4.1** is 7.3 years (taking 13 and over as 16 years).

Table 3.4.2 shows there has been very little change over the last few years in the location of British mission workers, from a continental viewpoint. There is more change from country to country year by year, and details of 2003 dispositions will be given in the next *UK Christian Handbook.*

Figure 3.4.1
Length of service

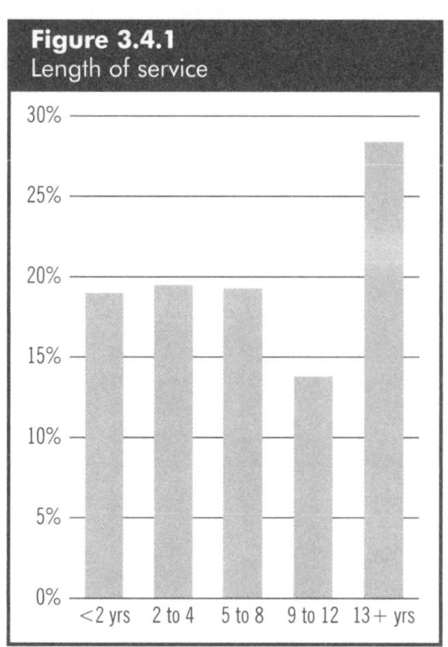

Figure 3.4.2 Mission Workers by Continent, 1995–2003

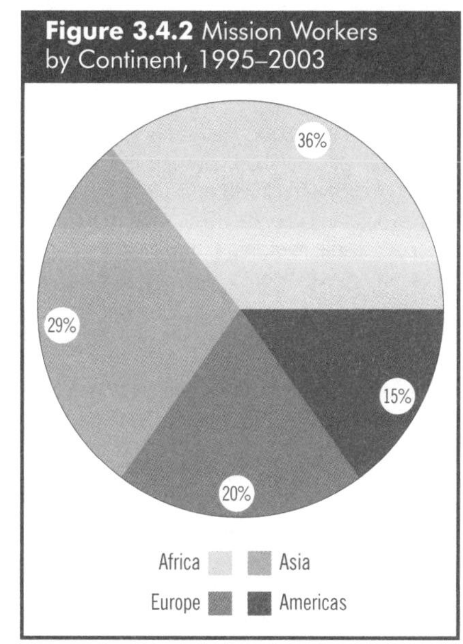

Table 3.4.1
Length of service by gender, 2003

Length in years	Male %	Female %	Overall %	Male proportion
Under 2	*17*	*20*	***19***	*39%*
2 to 4	*20*	*19*	***20***	*43%*
5 to 8	*19*	*20*	***19***	*41%*
9 to 12	*13*	*14*	***14***	*41%*
13 & over	*31*	*27*	***28***	*46%*
Base	1,047	1,421	2,468	***42%***

Table 3.4.2 Proportions of British Mission Workers by Continent, 1995–2003

Continent	1995 %	1997 %	1999 %	2003 %
Africa	*38*	*36*	*37*	*36*
Americas	*15*	*15*	*16*	*15*
Asia	*27*	*29*	*28*	*29*
Europe	*20*	*20*	*19*	*20*

In *Operation World* the worldwide percentages are Asia 49%, the Americas 25% (split equally between North and South), Africa 14% and Europe 12%. The dominance of Africa in British agency destinations reflects the days of Empire.

Table 3.4.3
Number of Mission Workers worldwide, 1991–2003

	Other denominations		Interdenominational		Roman Catholic		All denominations	
Year	Number	Agencies[2]	Number	Agencies[2]	Number	Agencies[2]	Number	Agencies[2]
1991	4,352[1]	31	42,645	65	80,511	55	**127,508**	151
1993	3,851[1]	31	42,449	66	84,544	54	**130,844**	151
1995	3,686	32	45,586	67	92,999	63	**144,372**	162
1997	3,674	33	49,121	74	89,000	59	**141,795**	166
1999	6,263	35	39,823	78	69,743	54	**115,829**	167
2003	5,725[1]	32[1]	36,404	80[3]	49,000[1]	54[1]	**91,130**	166

Other denominations includes Anglicans
[1] Estimate [2] Number of agencies giving details [3] Grossed up

The number of mission workers sent out by British Agencies is not always representative of their total strength worldwide. This is especially true for large international agencies which include a British sending operation. Hence in the *UK Christian Handbook* details are given of worldwide numbers to give a more balanced picture. These figures are accumulated in *Religious Trends*, although they were not published for 2001, and are shown in **Table 3.4.3.**

The total number worldwide of Protestant, Independent and Anglican missionaries as given by Patrick Johnstone in *Operation World* (Paternoster Lifestyle, 2001, Page 747) for the year 2001 is 97,732 foreign (or cross-culture) missionaries[1] and 104,271 national (or own-culture) missionaries, a total of 202,003. This total is less than half the figure of 434,000 "foreign missionaries" given by David Barrett for 2003 in the January 2003 issue of the *International Bulletin of Missionary Research* (which would however include national missionaries as defined by Patrick Johnstone).

Table 3.4.3 indicates that nearly half, 48%, of the world's total of non-Roman Catholic mission workers come from agencies with a British base, a percentage which would have been much higher say 50 years ago. This reduced proportion indirectly indicates the huge numbers of mission workers now being sent out by Third World countries.

[1] This is taking the totals as given, which are not however the sum of the constituent parts in the book. The missing numbers are presumably workers whose location is in sensitive areas.

Joining and Leaving Agencies, and Associates 3.5

Apart from sample surveys, or studies within a particular denomination or agency, an overview of from where people have joined agencies has not been available before. That almost half have come directly from secular employment is interesting, as it is not clear whether or not these will have had any training in mission work before going overseas. Just a fifth came straight from college. The 12% short-term workers compares with 11% designated "short-term" in 2001, and 16% in 1999.

A study for the Evangelical Missionary Alliance in 1991 suggested that 9% of mission workers "switched" agencies. The 11% shown in this analysis suggests that the percentage has probably been fairly constant around the 10% mark during the 1990s.

Relatively few mission workers returned after being back in the UK for some time – just 9 people in 2002.

Table 3.5.1
Joining Agencies, 2002

Where people had joined from	%
Secular employment	*47*
An accredited training agency	*20*
As short-term or gap year	*12*
Another agency	*11*
Return after medical absence	*1*
Return after absence for children's education	*1*
Return after looking after parents	$^1/_3$
Other reasons	*8*
Base (= 100%)	392

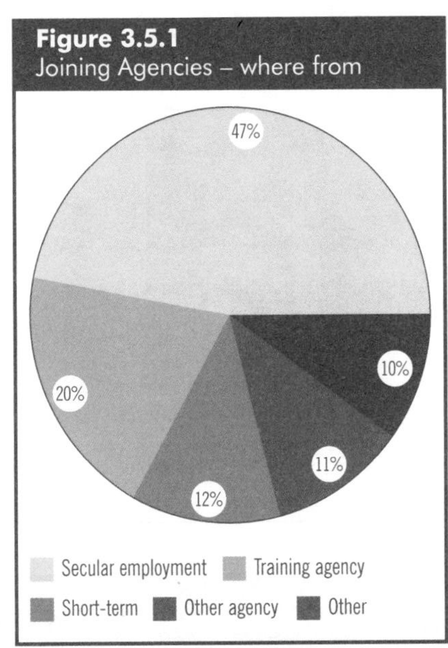

Figure 3.5.1
Joining Agencies – where from

Leaving because a person had come to the end of their contract was not explicitly given on the form agencies completed, so has been estimated based on the numbers joining for that reason. The reasons why people left fell into five virtually equal areas: resignation, retirement, end of contract, other specified reasons given in **Table 3.5.2** (all of which are positive except for the few who were asked to leave), and "other" reasons, which would include changes due to political crises and death in service.

While the number joining in 2002 comfortably exceeded those leaving, the numbers in these Tables were given by less than half the agencies approached. As the overall numbers in **Table 3.3.1** show an overall decrease in the number of mission workers, it is likely that those who did not answer the question had more people leaving than joining.

In a detailed worldwide survey of missionary attrition undertaken in 1995 under the auspices of the World Evangelical Alliance (formerly World Evangelical Fellowship) and reported in the book edited by Dr William Taylor *Too Valuable to Lose* (William Carey Library, 1997) the reasons UK missionaries left were:

- 14% Normal retirement
- 14% To look after their children
- 11% Change of job (probably including end of contract)
- 10% Heath problems
- 5% To look after parents
- 5% Marriage outside agency
- 41% Other reasons.

The number of Associate workers (for definition see **Page 3.2**) has always varied from year to year as **Figure 3.5.3** indicates, but the most recent figures suggest a significant increase in the last 2 years. Whether this is just a "blip" in the figures (albeit a large one) will not be known until data from future years is available.

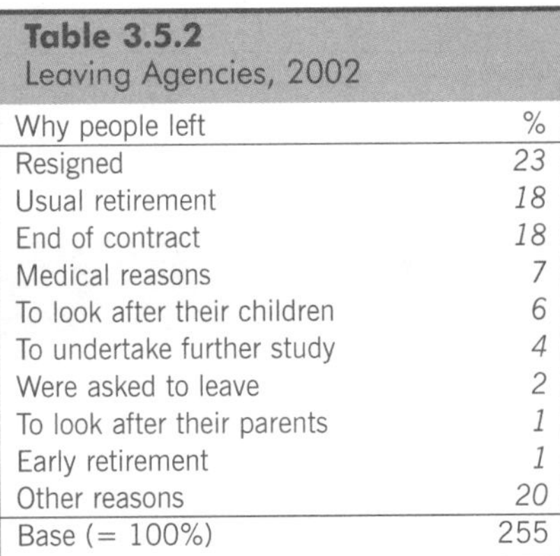
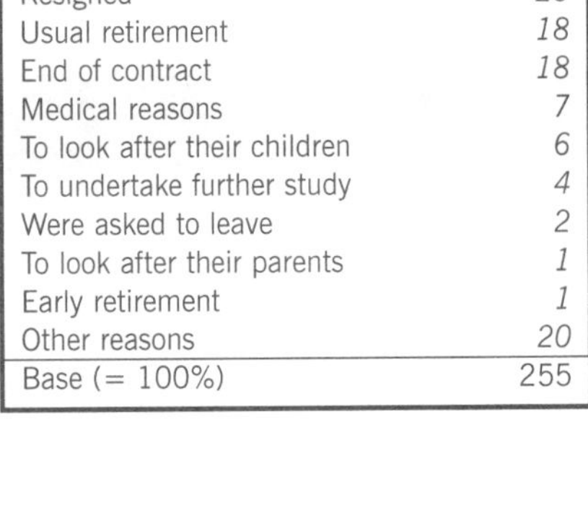
Table 3.5.2
Leaving Agencies, 2002

Why people left	%
Resigned	*23*
Usual retirement	*18*
End of contract	*18*
Medical reasons	*7*
To look after their children	*6*
To undertake further study	*4*
Were asked to leave	*2*
To look after their parents	*1*
Early retirement	*1*
Other reasons	*20*
Base (= 100%)	255

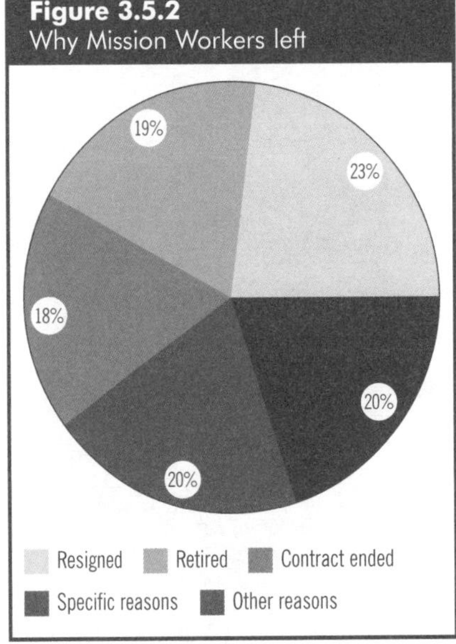

Figure 3.5.2
Why Mission Workers left

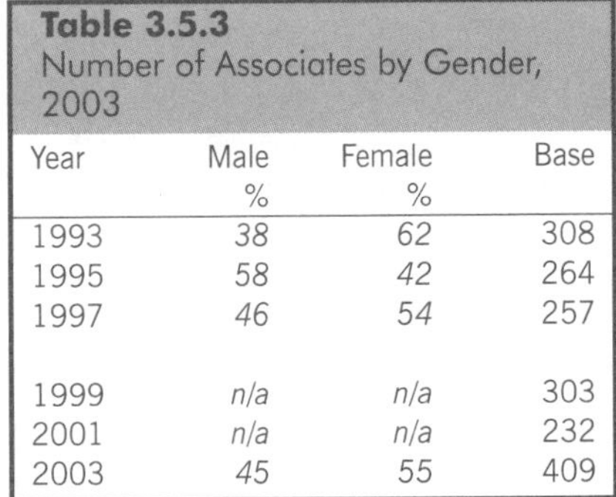
Table 3.5.3
Number of Associates by Gender, 2003

Year	Male %	Female %	Base
1993	*38*	*62*	308
1995	*58*	*42*	264
1997	*46*	*54*	257
1999	*n/a*	*n/a*	303
2001	*n/a*	*n/a*	232
2003	*45*	*55*	409

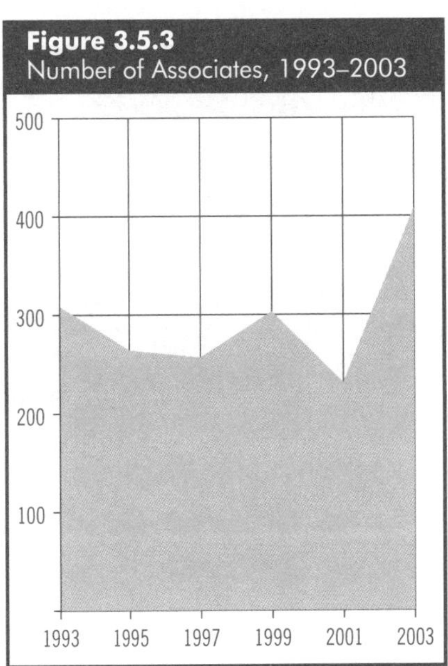

Figure 3.5.3
Number of Associates, 1993–2003

3.6 Other Mission Statistics

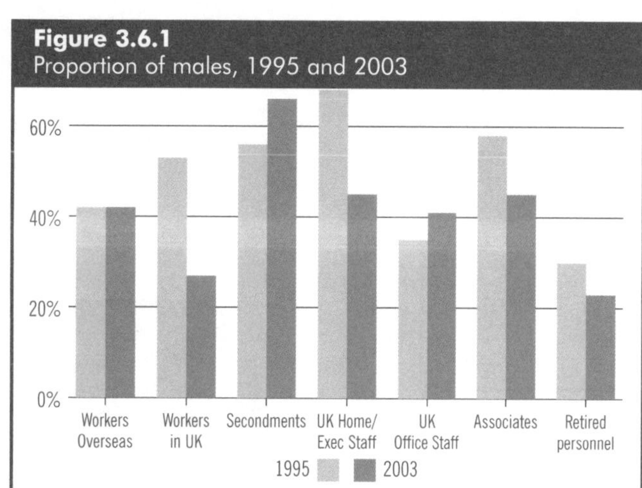

Figure 3.6.1
Proportion of males, 1995 and 2003

Table 3.6.1
Mission Workers by Gender, 1995 and 2003

	Male %	Female %	Total 1995	Male %	Female %	Total 2003
Overseas	*42*	*58*	6,099	*42*	*58*	**4,876**
Cross-culture Overseas	*49*	*51*	284	*38*	*62*	**278**
Own culture UK	*54*	*46*	799	*24*	*76*	**1,008**
Secondments	*56*	*44*	185	*66*	*34*	**117**
UK Home staff }	*68*	*68*	310	*30*	*70*	**513**
UK Executive staff }				*66*	*34*	**378**
Total: Serving Members	***45***	***55***	**7,677**	***40***	***60***	**7,170**
UK Office staff	*35*	*65*	1,231	*41*	*59*	960
Associates	*58*	*46*	264	*45*	*55*	409
Retired personnel	*30*	*70*	2,643	*23*	*77*	1,431
Total: Mission Workers	***41***	***59***	**11,815**	***38***	***62***	**9,970**

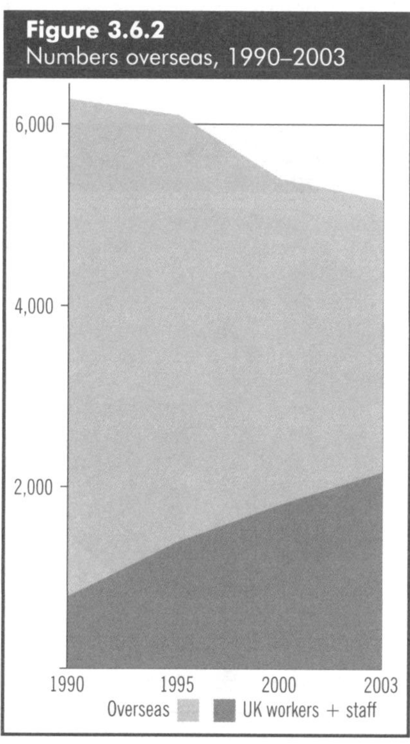

Figure 3.6.2
Numbers overseas, 1990–2003

Table 3.6.2
Number of overseas personnel working in the UK, 2001 and 2003

	2001	2003	% male in 2003	% female in 2003
Outreach	114	142	*45*	*55*
Admin	53	40	*50*	*50*
TOTAL	**167**	**182**	***46***	***54***

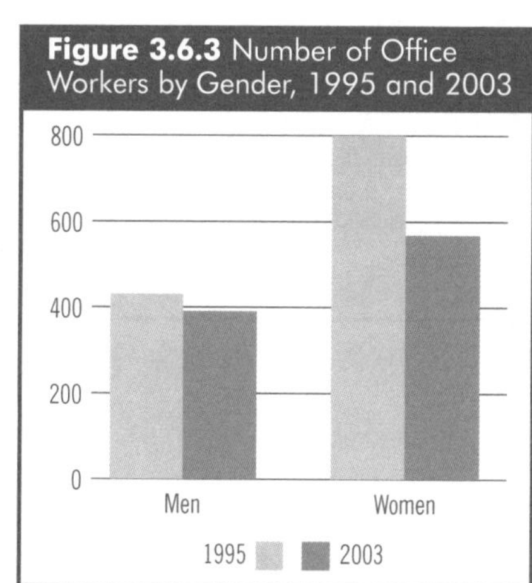

Figure 3.6.3 Number of Office Workers by Gender, 1995 and 2003

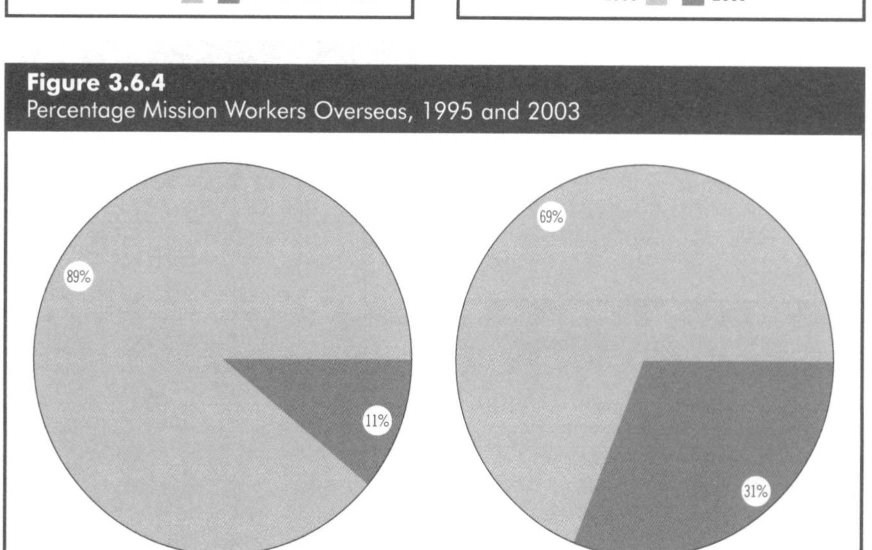

Figure 3.6.4
Percentage Mission Workers Overseas, 1995 and 2003

Table 3.6.1 indicates that the proportion of men working overseas remained unchanged between 1995 and 2003; for every three men there are four women. If marital status was available, this would perhaps be two married couples plus a single man and two single women.

However, both the Table and **Figure 3.6.1** show that the proportion of men who are working in the UK (either in cross-cultural or own-culture ministry) has drastically dropped. In 1995 there were 571 men and 512 women in UK ministry; 8 years later there were 348 men and 938 women. Why should this be?

Although the proportion of men working as office staff has increased, the actual number has decreased from 431 in 1995 to 394 in 2003. It is the number of female office staff which has dropped greatly, however – from 800 in 1995 to 566 in 2003, as shown in **Figure 3.6.3.** Is this because more of them are on contract, the growth of IT has made more of them redundant, or declining income has led to reduced numbers?

Figure 3.6.2 is based on the figures in **Table 3.3.2.** It shows a clear decline in the number of mission workers overseas, matched by an almost corresponding growth in the number of workers in the UK (adding ministry and staff together).

In 1995, 89% of mission workers (excluding secondments) served overseas; by 2003, it had declined to 69%, as shown in **Figure 3.6.4.** This is very large drop in just 8 years!

Table 3.6.2 shows that the number of non-UK personnel working with UK mission agencies has increased 9% since 2001. The number engaged in outreach activity has increased, the number in administration has reduced. Earlier figures are not available.

4

Population in the UK by Religion

4

Sources: Statistics giving population by Religion – England & Wales, Office for National Statistics (ONS) www.statistics.gov.uk/census2001/profiles; Scotland General Register Office for Scotland, *Scotland's Census 2001,* Key Statistics for Council Areas; Northern Ireland *Key Statistics Tables.* Population for 2001 from same sources. © Crown Copyright. Church Attendance data from English, Scottish and Welsh Churches Censuses and like studies; Welsh 1995 data from *Challenge to Change,* Bible Society, 1996; Northern Ireland data from *Irish Christian Handbook,* Christian Research, 1995/96.

Methodological note. ONS percentages have only been directly used when they added to exactly 100%; otherwise they have been appropriately changed. All church attendance data have been recalculated to new populations as given by ONS.

4.2 Population in UK by Religion: England

	Population 2001	Population 91–01 %	Churchgoers 1989	Churchgoers 1998	Churchgoers 89–98 %	% population 1989	% population 1998	Xian %	Buddhist %	Hindu %	Jew %	Muslim %	Sikh %	Other %	None %	n/a %
ALL ENGLAND	49,138,831	+2.5	4,742,800	3,714,700	–22	9.9	7.6	71.7	0.3	1.1	0.5	3.1	0.7	0.3	14.6	7.7
(AVON)	983,860	+2.8	99,300	77,500	–22	10.4	7.9	69.0	0.3	0.3	0.1	1.0	0.2	0.4	20.4	8.3
Bath and N E Somerset UA[1]	169,040	+3.6	21,300	16,800	–21	13.2	10.0	71.0	0.3	0.2	0.1	0.4	0.1	0.4	19.5	8.0
Bristol, City of UA	380,615	–2.9	39,700	26,700	–33	10.1	7.0	62.1	0.4	0.6	0.2	2.0	0.5	0.4	24.5	9.3
North Somerset UA[2]	188,564	+5.2	20,400	17,500	–14	11.5	9.4	75.0	0.2	0.1	0.1	0.2	0	0.3	16.6	7.5
South Gloucestershire UA[3]	245,641	+10.6	17,900	16,500	– 8	8.3	6.9	73.9	0.1	0.3	0.1	0.4	0.1	0.2	17.5	7.4
BEDFORDSHIRE	565,943	+6.9	52,200	45,800	–12	10.0	8.3	68.3	0.2	1.5	0.2	5.7	0.8	0.3	15.5	7.5
Bedford	147,911	+9.2	16,500	13,600	–18	12.5	9.5	68.8	0.2	1.7	0.1	3.3	1.9	0.3	14.9	8.8
Luton UA	184,371	+6.2	15,400	14,100	– 8	9.0	7.8	59.7	0.2	2.7	0.3	14.6	0.8	0.4	14.1	7.2
Mid Bedfordshire	121,024	+8.9	10,800	9,800	– 9	10.0	8.3	75.2	0.1	0.3	0.1	0.3	0.2	0.2	16.8	6.8
South Bedfordshire	112,637	+3.0	9,500	8,300	–13	8.7	7.4	74.5	0.1	0.5	0.2	0.3	0.2	0.2	17.1	6.9
(BERKSHIRE)	800,118	+6.4	59,700	51,800	–13	8.1	6.6	68.7	0.3	1.3	0.3	3.5	1.9	0.3	16.3	7.4
Bracknell Forest UA	109,617	+11.8	6,700	5,800	–13	7.1	5.5	72.0	0.3	1.0	0.2	0.7	0.2	0.3	17.9	7.4
Reading UA	143,096	+6.1	17,200	14,000	–19	13.0	10.0	62.6	0.5	1.0	0.3	4.0	0.5	0.4	22.0	8.7
Slough UA	119,067	+13.0	7,600	7,000	– 8	7.5	6.1	53.7	0.2	4.5	0.1	13.4	9.1	0.3	11.0	7.7
West Berkshire UA[4]	144,483	+4.1	9,300	8,200	–12	6.8	5.7	75.9	0.3	0.2	0.2	0.4	0.1	0.3	15.7	6.9
Windsor & Maidenhead UA	133,626	–0.1	9,900	8,800	–11	7.4	6.6	73.7	0.3	1.0	0.4	2.4	1.2	0.3	13.9	6.8
Wokingham UA	150,229	+6.4	9,000	8,000	–11	6.5	5.4	72.8	0.3	0.8	0.4	1.3	1.0	0.2	16.6	6.6
BUCKINGHAMSHIRE	686,083	+8.2	56,300	52,800	– 6	9.1	7.9	70.5	0.3	0.8	0.3	3.2	0.3	0.3	17.1	7.2
Aylesbury Vale	165,748	+12.6	12,300	12,400	+1	8.7	7.8	73.8	0.2	0.4	0.2	2.7	0.1	0.3	15.7	6.6
Chiltern	89,228	–0.2	9,000	7,400	–18	10.1	8.3	74.7	0.3	0.5	0.5	1.9	0.1	0.3	15.0	6.7
Milton Keynes UA	207,057	+16.1	14,000	13,800	– 1	8.3	7.0	65.5	0.4	1.3	0.2	2.3	0.4	0.4	21.6	7.9
South Buckinghamshire	61,945	+2.9	7,600	6,200	–19	12.7	10.1	75.6	0.3	1.2	0.5	1.1	1.6	0.3	12.5	6.9
Wycombe	162,105	+2.0	13,400	13,000	– 3	8.5	8.1	69.1	0.2	0.6	0.3	6.5	0.3	0.2	15.6	7.2
CAMBRIDGESHIRE	708,719	+6.6	68,600	51,700	–25	10.5	7.4	70.6	0.3	0.5	0.2	1.9	0.2	0.3	17.6	8.3
Cambridge	108,863	+2.0	19,600	14,000	–29	18.4	12.9	57.7	1.0	1.2	0.8	2.4	0.2	0.5	26.6	9.6
East Cambridgeshire	73,214	+20.3	5,400	5,700	+6	9.7	8.3	74.8	0.2	0.1	0.1	0.2	0.1	0.3	15.5	8.7
Fenland	83,519	+11.2	4,900	3,500	–29	6.8	4.3	77.7	0.1	0.1	0.1	0.3	0.1	0.1	13.0	8.5
Huntingdonshire	156,954	+7.5	14,000	10,100	–29	9.8	6.6	74.5	0.2	0.2	0.1	0.6	0.1	0.3	16.5	7.5
Peterborough UA	156,061	+1.2	13,200	10,000	–24	8.6	6.4	68.3	0.2	0.9	0.1	5.8	0.5	0.2	15.6	8.4
South Cambridgeshire	130,108	+6.7	11,500	8,400	–27	9.6	6.6	72.9	0.3	0.3	0.2	0.5	0.1	0.2	17.9	7.6
CHESHIRE	983,076	+2.1	110,400	85,300	–23	11.5	8.7	81.2	0.2	0.1	0.1	0.4	0	0.2	11.1	6.7
Chester	118,210	+0.7	16,800	13,400	–20	14.3	11.4	78.1	0.2	0.2	0.1	0.5	0.1	0.2	13.0	7.6
Congleton	90,655	+6.5	10,100	6,800	–33	12.1	7.7	81.4	0.1	0.1	0.1	0.2	0	0.2	11.5	6.4
Crewe & Nantwich	111,007	+6.0	10,500	8,200	–22	10.2	7.5	80.3	0.1	0.1	0	0.4	0	0.2	11.9	7.0
Ellesmere Point & Neston	81,672	+0.5	9,000	6,500	–28	11.1	8.0	82.5	0.1	0.1	0.1	0.3	0	0.1	10.2	6.6
Halton UA	118,208	–5.3	13,300	9,000	–32	10.6	7.5	83.8	0.1	0.1	0.1	0.1	0	0.1	8.7	7.0
Macclesfield	150,155	–0.4	23,000	18,600	–19	15.2	12.4	79.6	0.2	0.3	0.3	0.5	0.1	0.2	12.7	6.1
Vale Royal	122,089	+7.0	11,900	10,000	–16	10.6	8.4	82.1	0.2	0.1	0	0.2	0.1	0.1	10.9	6.3
Warrington UA	191,080	+3.4	15,800	12,800	–19	8.6	6.8	82.0	0.1	0.2	0.1	0.6	0.1	0.1	10.3	6.5
(CLEVELAND)	541,006	–2.8	52,000	32,300	–38	9.3	5.9	80.4	0.1	0.2	0	1.7	0.1	0.1	9.9	7.5
Hartlepool UA	88,611	–2.7	6,000	4,800	–20	6.6	5.4	80.7	0.1	0.2	0	0.4	0	0.1	9.4	9.0
Middlesborough UA	134,855	–6.8	14,200	7,500	–47	9.7	5.5	76.8	0.1	0.3	0.1	4.2	0.3	0.1	10.1	8.0
Redcar & Cleveland UA[5]	139,132	–4.6	14,100	7,400	–48	9.6	5.2	82.1	0.1	0.1	0	0.4	0	0.2	9.8	7.3
Stockton-on-Tees UA	178,408	+1.9	17,700	12,600	–29	10.2	7.1	81.6	0.1	0.2	0	1.4	0.2	0.1	10.0	6.4
CORNWALL	501,267	+6.3	53,900	42,000	–22	11.6	8.5	74.3	0.2	0	0.1	0.1	0	0.5	16.7	8.0
Caradon	79,649	+2.8	8,500	7,000	–18	11.0	8.9	75.5	0.2	0	0.1	0.1	0	0.4	16.2	7.5
Carrick	87,865	+5.4	10,600	7,800	–26	12.9	9.0	73.6	0.2	0.1	0.1	0.2	0	0.5	17.0	8.3
Kerrier	92,517	+4.9	9,400	7,800	–17	10.8	8.6	73.7	0.2	0	0.1	0.1	0	0.4	17.4	8.1
North Cornwall	80,509	+8.8	8,100	6,400	–21	11.2	8.2	75.4	0.1	0.1	0.1	0	0	0.5	15.6	8.2
Penwith	63,012	+5.7	8,000	5,400	–32	13.6	8.7	72.3	0.3	0	0.1	0.2	0	0.7	18.2	8.2
Restormel	95,562	+9.8	8,900	7,200	–19	10.5	7.8	75.2	0.2	0	0.1	0.2	0	0.4	16.0	7.9
Isles of Scilly	2,153	+7.2	400	400	– 6	20.3	19.0	70.5	0.3	0	0	0	0	0.3	20.2	8.7

[1]Formerly Bath and Wansdyke Local Authority Districts [2]Formerly Woodspring Local Authority District [3]Formerly Northavon and Kingswood Local Authority Districts [4]Formerly Newbury Local Authority District [5]Formerly Langbaurgh Local Authority District Xian: Christian; Other: Other Religions; None: No Religion; n/a: not answered.

Population in UK by Religion: England

	Population		Churchgoers			% population		Percentage in each religion, 2001								
	2001	91–01 %	1989	1998	89–98 %	1989	1998	Xian %	Buddhist %	Hindu %	Jew %	Muslim %	Sikh %	Other %	None %	n/a %
CUMBRIA	487,607	+0.3	67,900	46,200	-32	14.0	9.5	82.1	0.2	0	0	0.2	0	0.2	10.4	6.9
Allerdale	93,492	–2.7	12,700	8,000	–37	13.2	8.5	85.3	0.1	0	0	0.1	0	0.1	8.2	6.2
Barrow-in-Furness	71,980	–1.8	6,700	4,200	–37	9.1	5.8	81.0	0.1	0.1	0	0.3	0	0.1	10.8	7.6
Carlisle	100,739	–0.6	14,800	10,900	–26	14.6	10.8	80.7	0.1	0.1	0	0.2	0	0.1	11.0	7.8
Copeland	69,318	–3.0	11,300	8,600	–24	15.7	12.3	86.3	0.1	0.1	0	0.2	0	0.1	7.0	6.2
Eden	49,777	+8.8	7,600	5,400	–29	17.1	11.2	81.4	0.2	0	0	0.1	0	0.2	11.4	6.7
South Lakeland	102,301	+4.0	14,800	9,100	–39	15.2	9.0	79.1	0.4	0	0.1	0.1	0	0.2	13.3	6.8
DERBYSHIRE	956,293	+2.1	77,400	63,300	-18	8.3	6.7	74.8	0.1	0.2	0.1	1.2	0.9	0.2	14.9	7.6
Amber Valley	116,471	+3.8	7,200	7,400	+3	6.5	6.4	75.6	0.1	0.1	0	0.1	0.1	0.2	16.1	7.7
Bolsover	71,766	+1.1	4,000	3,000	–25	5.6	4.2	78.1	0.1	0.1	0	0.1	0.1	0.1	12.6	8.8
Chesterfield	98,845	–0.9	9,300	7,400	–20	9.3	7.5	77.9	0.1	0.1	0	0.4	0.1	0.2	13.3	7.9
Derby UA	221,708	–0.5	18,800	14,100	–25	8.4	6.4	67.4	0.2	0.6	0.1	4.5	3.2	0.2	15.9	7.9
Derbyshire Dales	69,469	+2.3	10,100	8,300	–18	15.0	12.0	79.4	0.2	0	0.1	0.2	0	0.2	12.9	7.0
Erewash	110,099	+3.2	8,100	7,200	–11	7.6	6.6	72.3	0.1	0.3	0.1	0.2	0.2	0.2	18.9	7.7
High Peak	89,433	+4.6	8,900	7,600	–15	10.5	8.6	76.5	0.2	0.1	0.1	0.2	0	0.3	15.8	6.8
North East Derbyshire	96,940	–0.9	6,700	5,000	–25	6.8	5.1	79.9	0.1	0.1	0.1	0.1	0.1	0.2	12.2	7.2
South Derbyshire	81,562	+12.2	4,300	3,300	–23	6.2	4.2	78.2	0.1	0.2	0	0.2	1.3	0.2	13.3	6.5
DEVON	1,074,919	+4.2	116,100	92,600	-20	11.4	8.7	74.7	0.2	0.1	0.1	0.3	0	0.4	16.5	7.7
East Devon	125,520	+6.7	16,300	12,000	–26	14.1	9.8	77.8	0.2	0	0.1	0.1	0	0.4	13.9	7.5
Exeter	111,076	+6.0	13,300	10,000	–25	12.9	9.2	69.1	0.3	0.1	0.1	0.8	0.1	0.4	20.5	8.6
Mid Devon	69,774	+7.9	8,400	8,100	– 4	13.3	11.9	75.4	0.2	0	0.1	0.1	0	0.4	16.0	7.8
North Devon	87,508	+2.9	13,400	9,200	–31	15.9	10.6	75.1	0.2	0.1	0.1	0.2	0	0.3	15.9	8.1
Plymouth UA	240,720	–4.2	17,500	15,300	–13	6.9	6.3	73.5	0.2	0.1	0.1	0.4	0	0.3	18.3	7.1
South Hams	81,849	+4.8	5,000	5,400	+8	6.5	6.7	74.7	0.4	0	0.1	0.1	0	0.5	16.5	7.7
Teignbridge	120,958	+10.5	11,600	8,800	–24	11.0	7.5	75.6	0.2	0	0.1	0.1	0	0.4	15.7	7.9
Torbay UA	129,706	+6.4	13,500	11,200	–17	11.3	8.8	76.2	0.1	0.1	0.1	0.3	0	0.4	14.9	7.9
Torridge	58,965	+11.7	7,500	5,400	–28	14.8	9.5	75.5	0.2	0	0.1	0.1	0	0.4	15.6	8.1
West Devon	48,843	+6.0	9,600	7,200	–25	21.2	15.0	76.4	0.2	0	0.1	0.2	0	0.4	15.4	7.3
DORSET	692,712	+5.5	75,000	54,800	-27	11.6	8.0	75.5	0.3	0.1	0.4	0.4	0	0.4	15.2	7.7
Bournemouth UA	163,444	+3.9	20,900	13,300	–36	13.4	8.2	70.9	0.4	0.2	1.0	0.9	0.1	0.5	17.9	8.1
Christchurch	44,865	+8.5	3,000	2,000	–33	7.4	4.6	79.1	0.2	0	0.3	0.2	0	0.3	13.2	6.7
East Dorset	83,786	+6.5	6,600	6,100	– 8	8.5	7.4	79.9	0.1	0.1	0.2	0.2	0	0.3	12.6	6.6
North Dorset	61,905	+15.5	8,500	6,000	–29	16.8	10.2	77.7	0.3	0.2	0.1	0.2	0	0.3	13.6	7.6
Poole UA	132,288	+3.2	11,300	8,300	–27	8.9	6.3	74.3	0.2	0.2	0.3	0.4	0.1	0.3	16.2	8.0
Purbeck	44,416	+2.7	4,800	3,700	–23	11.2	8.4	78.3	0.3	0	0.1	0.2	0	0.3	13.8	7.0
West Dorset	92,360	+7.1	15,300	11,700	–24	18.1	13.0	77.6	0.3	0	0.1	0.2	0	0.4	13.6	7.8
Weymouth & Portland	63,648	+2.7	4,600	3,700	–20	7.5	5.9	74.7	0.2	0.1	0.1	0.3	0	0.3	15.9	8.4
DURHAM	591,308	+1.6	66,800	47,100	-29	11.5	8.0	82.9	0.1	0.1	0	0.3	0.1	0.2	9.7	6.6
Chester-le-Street	53,692	+3.4	6,100	6,100	0	11.8	11.5	84.1	0.1	0.1	0	0.2	0.1	0.1	9.8	5.5
Darlington UA	97,838	–1.5	8,900	5,400	–39	8.9	5.5	79.8	0.1	0.1	0	0.6	0.3	0.2	11.4	7.5
Derwentside	85,074	–1.7	13,400	9,900	–26	15.4	11.6	84.3	0.1	0	0	0.1	0.1	0.2	9.4	5.8
Durham	87,709	+2.0	11,500	7,200	–37	13.4	8.3	79.7	0.3	0.2	0.1	0.6	0.1	0.2	12.5	6.3
Easington	93,993	–4.7	9,400	5,300	–44	9.5	5.6	85.2	0.1	0.1	0	0.2	0.2	0.1	7.1	7.0
Sedgefield	87,206	–4.3	9,400	6,200	–34	10.2	7.0	83.5	0.1	0	0	0.1	0.1	0.1	9.1	7.0
Teesdale	24,457	+0.7	2,700	2,800	+4	11.1	11.5	83.9	0.1	0.1	0	0.1	0	0.3	9.4	6.1
Wear Valley	61,339	–2.7	5,400	4,200	–22	8.5	6.8	84.7	0.1	0.1	0	0.1	0.1	0.2	7.9	6.8
EAST SUSSEX	740,141	+4.3	67,200	57,000	-15	9.6	7.8	68.8	0.4	0.3	0.6	0.9	0	0.6	20.0	8.4
Brighton and Hove UA	247,817	+3.0	18,700	14,800	–21	7.8	6.0	59.1	0.7	0.5	1.4	1.5	0.1	0.8	27.0	8.9
Eastbourne	89,667	+6.3	7,800	7,300	– 6	9.4	8.3	72.8	0.3	0.2	0.3	1.0	0.1	0.5	16.7	8.1
Hastings	85,029	+2.7	7,100	6,600	– 7	8.6	7.8	67.4	0.3	0.3	0.1	0.7	0	0.5	21.4	9.3
Lewes	92,177	+4.5	8,200	7,500	– 9	9.4	8.2	72.0	0.3	0.2	0.3	0.4	0	0.4	18.2	8.2
Rother	85,248	+3.2	8,100	7,700	– 5	9.9	9.1	76.5	0.2	0.1	0.2	0.6	0	0.4	13.9	8.1
Wealden	140,023	+7.0	17,300	13,100	–24	13.5	9.6	77.2	0.2	0.1	0.2	0.4	0	0.7	13.8	7.4
EAST YORKSHIRE	557,702	0	37,400	28,900	-23	6.7	5.2	76.2	0.1	0.2	0.1	0.5	0.1	0.2	14.7	7.9
East Riding UA[1]	314,113	+6.7	23,500	17,200	–27	8.1	5.6	79.7	0.1	0.2	0.1	0.3	0.1	0.1	11.9	7.5
Kingston upon Hull UA	243,589	–7.5	13,900	11,700	–16	5.2	4.7	71.7	0.2	0.1	0.1	0.9	0.1	0.2	18.3	8.4

[1]Including former Local Authority Districts of Beverley, East Yorkshire, Holderness and the northern half of Boothferry
Xian: Christian; Other: Other Religions; None: No Religion; n/a: not answered.

4.4 Population in UK by Religion: England

	Population		Churchgoers			% population		Percentage in each religion, 2001								
	2001	91–01 %	1989	1998	89–98 %	1989	1998	Xian %	Buddhist %	Hindu %	Jew %	Muslim %	Sikh %	Other %	None %	n/a %
ESSEX	1,614,220	+4.9	131,400	112,300	-15	8.6	7.1	73.7	0.2	0.4	0.6	0.7	0.1	0.3	16.6	7.4
Basildon	165,668	+2.3	11,500	10,100	-12	7.1	6.1	73.3	0.2	0.4	0.2	0.6	0.1	0.3	17.4	7.5
Braintree	132,179	+10.6	9,700	8,800	- 9	8.4	6.9	74.2	0.2	0.2	0.1	0.3	0	0.3	17.0	7.7
Brentwood	68,456	-3.1	8,600	7,500	-13	12.1	10.9	79.2	0.2	0.7	0.3	0.6	0.1	0.3	12.6	6.0
Castle Point	86,608	-0.3	5,500	4,300	-22	6.3	5.0	75.7	0.1	0.2	0.2	0.3	0.1	0.3	15.5	7.63
Chelmsford	157,072	+2.3	14,000	11,400	-19	9.2	7.3	74.7	0.2	0.4	0.2	0.7	0.1	0.3	16.4	7.0
Colchester	155,796	+6.4	11,200	11,400	+2	7.8	7.5	71.6	0.3	0.5	0.1	0.8	0.1	0.4	18.5	7.7
Epping Forest	120,896	+4.5	9,900	10,100	+2	8.7	8.5	72.4	0.2	0.9	3.1	1.2	0.6	0.3	14.1	7.2
Harlow	78,768	+5.0	4,800	4,000	-17	6.5	5.2	67.3	0.3	0.4	0.3	1.3	0.1	0.2	22.4	7.7
Maldon	59,418	+12.6	5,100	4,200	-18	10.1	7.4	75.8	0.1	0.1	0.2	0.3	0	0.2	16.5	6.8
Rochford	78,489	+3.9	9,800	7,000	-29	13.1	9.0	75.8	0.1	0.3	0.3	0.2	0	0.2	15.7	7.4
Southend on Sea UA	160,257	-0.6	15,800	13,700	-13	9.8	8.5	68.6	0.3	0.6	1.7	1.2	0.1	0.4	18.8	8.3
Tendring	138,539	+10.0	12,100	9,000	-26	9.9	6.7	76.0	0.1	0.1	0.2	0.2	0	0.3	15.0	8.1
Thurrock UA	143,128	+11.2	6,300	5,500	-13	5.1	4.0	75.1	0.2	0.5	0.2	1.1	0.7	0.2	15.5	6.5
Uttlesford	68,946	+5.5	7,100	5,300	-25	11.0	7.8	76.6	0.2	0.2	0.3	0.4	0	0.3	15.2	6.8
GLOUCESTERSHIRE	564,559	+5.3	52,000	36,700	-29	9.8	6.6	75.9	0.2	0.3	0.1	0.6	0.1	0.3	15.0	7.5
Cheltenham	110,013	+2.8	9,300	5,600	-40	8.7	5.1	72.4	0.3	0.7	0.1	0.5	0.1	0.3	18.2	7.4
Cotswold	80,376	+7.4	9,800	6,500	-34	13.4	8.3	80.1	0.2	0.1	0.1	0.1	0	0.3	12.9	6.2
Forest of Dean	79,982	+5.5	6,600	5,000	-24	8.8	6.4	77.1	0.1	0	0	0.1	0.1	0.3	13.9	8.4
Gloucester	109,885	+6.2	9,200	6,000	-35	9.0	5.6	74.3	0.1	0.4	0.1	2.3	0.1	0.3	14.3	8.1
Stroud	107,898	+3.6	10,100	7,900	-22	9.8	7.4	75.0	0.2	0.1	0.1	0.2	0	0.4	16.1	7.9
Tewkesbury	76,405	+8.0	7,000	5,700	-19	10.1	7.6	79.1	0.1	0.2	0.1	0.2	0.1	0.2	13.0	7.0
GREATER LONDON	7,172,091	+5.0	649,600	617,900	-5	9.6	8.7	58.2	0.7	4.1	2.1	8.5	1.4	0.5	15.8	8.7
INNER LONDON	2,766,114	+6.4	251,600	239,700	-5	9.8	8.8	54.6	1.0	1.9	1.8	11.7	0.5	0.4	18.3	9.8
OUTER LONDON	4,405,977	+4.2	398,000	378,200	-5	9.5	8.7	60.5	0.6	5.4	2.3	6.5	2.0	0.6	14.1	8.0
Barking & Dagenham	163,944	+5.4	10,200	8,500	-17	6.7	5.3	69.0	0.2	1.1	0.3	4.4	1.1	0.2	15.3	8.4
Barnet	314,564	+5.7	15,300	18,700	+22	5.2	6.1	47.3	1.1	6.7	14.8	6.2	0.4	1.0	12.8	9.7
Bexley	218,307	+0.1	16,200	12,400	-23	7.4	5.7	73.0	0.4	0.9	0.1	1.4	1.4	0.2	14.7	7.9
Brent	263,464	+9.4	35,000	39,700	+13	15.0	15.5	47.7	0.9	17.2	2.4	12.3	0.7	1.1	10.0	7.7
Bromley	295,532	+0.7	31,400	24,000	-24	10.7	8.1	72.0	0.3	1.1	0.4	1.7	0.2	0.3	16.3	7.7
Camden[1]	198,020	+9.6	15,700	15,600	- 1	8.9	8.1	47.1	1.3	1.5	5.6	11.6	0.2	0.6	22.0	10.1
Croydon	330,587	+4.7	44,000	34,600	-21	14.1	10.6	65.1	0.5	5.1	0.3	5.3	0.4	0.5	14.7	8.1
Ealing	300,948	+6.0	20,900	19,700	- 6	7.5	6.7	50.8	1.0	7.8	0.5	10.3	8.5	0.4	13.4	7.3
Enfield	273,559	+5.2	32,300	37,000	+15	12.6	13.7	63.2	0.5	3.4	2.0	9.6	0.3	0.6	12.3	8.1
Greenwich[2]	214,403	+1.7	17,400	14,500	-17	8.3	6.8	61.5	0.9	2.0	0.2	4.3	2.2	0.3	19.3	9.3
Hackney[1]	202,824	+9.7	9,700	11,700	+21	5.4	5.9	46.6	1.1	0.8	5.3	13.8	0.8	0.6	19.0	12.0
Hammersmith & Fulham[1]	165,242	+7.4	11,200	9,500	-15	7.4	5.9	63.6	0.8	1.1	0.8	6.9	0.2	0.4	17.6	8.6
Haringey[1,2]	216,507	+4.6	17,400	19,400	+11	8.5	9.1	50.1	1.1	2.0	2.6	11.3	0.3	0.5	20.0	12.1
Harrow	206,814	+1.9	26,400	27,000	+2	13.1	13.1	47.3	0.7	19.6	6.4	7.2	1.0	2.0	9.0	6.8
Havering	224,248	-2.9	19,400	18,500	- 5	8.4	8.2	76.1	0.2	0.8	0.5	0.8	0.4	0.2	13.2	7.8
Hillingdon	243,006	+3.7	19,600	23,200	+18	8.4	9.7	64.1	0.4	4.6	0.8	4.6	4.6	0.4	13.4	7.1
Hounslow	212,341	+4.1	10,700	12,500	+17	5.3	6.0	52.1	0.7	7.6	0.3	9.1	8.6	0.5	13.5	7.6
Islington[1]	175,797	+2.4	11,200	10,500	- 6	6.6	6.0	54.2	1.1	1.0	1.1	8.1	0.3	0.4	23.7	10.1
Kensington & Chelsea[1]	158,919	+10.6	23,500	25,000	+6	16.9	16.3	62.0	1.2	1.0	2.2	8.4	0.2	0.6	15.2	9.2
Kingston upon Thames	147,273	+8.2	15,800	15,600	- 1	11.9	10.9	64.6	0.8	3.6	0.7	3.9	0.6	0.4	18.0	7.4
Lambeth[1]	266,169	+4.4	21,600	16,800	-22	8.6	6.4	58.8	0.9	1.3	0.4	5.4	0.1	0.5	21.7	10.9
Lewisham[1]	248,922	+3.6	34,000	28,000	-18	14.3	11.4	61.2	1.1	1.7	0.3	4.6	0.2	0.5	20.4	10.0
London,City of[1]	7,185	+34.0	5,200	4,400	-15	119.2	69.4	55.0	0.6	1.5	3.1	5.6	0.3	0.7	24.6	8.6
Merton	187,908	+9.9	14,800	11,200	-24	8.9	6.1	63.3	0.8	4.6	0.5	5.8	0.3	0.3	16.5	7.9
Newham[1,2]	243,891	+12.8	9,400	10,100	+7	4.5	4.3	46.8	0.7	6.9	0.2	24.3	2.8	0.3	9.0	9.0
Redbridge	238,635	+7.5	22,800	18,400	-19	10.5	7.9	50.7	0.5	7.8	6.2	11.9	5.5	0.4	9.6	7.4
Richmond-upon-Thames	172,335	+3.4	17,500	14,500	-17	10.6	8.5	65.8	0.7	1.5	0.9	2.2	0.7	0.4	19.5	8.3
Southwark[1]	244,866	+7.8	23,700	23,900	+1	10.7	10.0	61.6	1.1	1.1	0.4	6.8	0.2	0.4	18.5	9.9
Sutton	179,768	+5.7	15,300	12,600	-18	9.1	7.1	70.5	0.4	2.1	0.3	2.3	0.1	0.3	16.7	7.3
Tower Hamlets[1]	196,106	+17.9	10,700	11,000	+3	6.9	6.0	38.6	1.0	0.8	0.9	36.4	0.4	0.3	14.2	7.4
Waltham Forest	218,341	+1.1	13,000	15,600	+20	6.0	7.2	56.8	0.4	1.8	0.6	15.1	0.6	0.4	15.4	8.9
Wandsworth[1]	260,380	-0.6	26,800	27,900	+4	10.2	10.7	61.8	0.7	2.3	0.6	5.2	0.2	0.4	20.0	8.8
Westminster[1]	181,286	-2.0	31,500	25,900	-15	17.0	14.2	55.0	1.3	1.9	4.3	11.8	0.2	0.5	16.2	8.8

[1]These are Boroughs of Inner London; so those not marked are Outer London [2]The old Inner London Education Authority excluded Haringey and Newham, but included Greenwich
Xian: Christian; Other: Other Religions; None: No Religion; n/a: not answered.

Population in UK by Religion: England

	Population		Churchgoers			% population		Percentage in each religion, 2001								
	2001	91–01 %	1989	1998	89–98 %	1989	1998	Xian %	Buddhist %	Hindu %	Jew %	Muslim %	Sikh %	Other %	None %	n/a %
GREATER MANCHESTER	2,482,328	–2.8	241,400	172,200	–29	9.4	6.9	74.2	0.2	0.7	0.9	5.0	0.1	0.2	11.3	7.4
Bolton	261,037	–0.1	24,400	20,700	–15	9.3	7.9	74.6	0.1	2.0	0.1	7.1	0	0.1	8.7	7.3
Bury	180,608	+1.3	15,900	9,500	–40	8.9	5.3	73.7	0.1	0.4	4.9	3.7	0.1	0.2	10.2	6.7
Manchester	392,819	–9.2	36,100	34,400	– 5	8.3	8.5	62.4	0.6	0.7	0.8	9.1	0.4	0.3	16.0	9.7
Oldham	217,273	–0.6	14,100	11,100	–21	6.4	5.1	72.6	0.1	0.6	0.1	11.1	0	0.1	8.9	6.5
Rochdale	205,357	+0.7	20,700	13,500	–35	10.2	6.6	72.1	0.1	0.3	0.1	9.4	0	0.1	10.8	7.1
Salford	216,103	–6.4	15,500	10,900	–30	6.7	5.0	76.5	0.2	0.3	2.4	1.2	0.1	0.2	11.0	8.1
Stockport	284,528	–1.4	26,800	20,300	–24	9.3	7.1	75.4	0.2	0.5	0.6	1.7	0.1	0.2	14.2	7.1
Tameside	213,043	–2.3	26,900	14,500	–46	12.3	6.8	75.5	0.1	1.4	0.1	2.5	0	0.2	12.1	8.1
Trafford	210,145	–2.6	23,300	14,800	–36	10.8	7.0	75.8	0.2	0.6	1.1	3.3	0.5	0.1	12.0	6.4
Wigan	301,415	–1.4	37,700	22,500	–40	12.3	7.4	86.9	0.1	0.2	0	0.3	0	0.1	6.9	5.5
HAMPSHIRE	1,644,249	+4.7	139,200	122,900	–12	9.0	7.6	73.9	0.2	0.3	0.1	0.8	0.3	0.3	16.9	7.2
Basingstoke & Deane	152,573	+5.0	15,100	15,100	0	10.5	10.1	74.0	0.2	0.5	0.1	0.5	0.2	0.3	17.0	7.2
East Hampshire	109,274	+5.1	7,700	7,200	– 6	7.5	6.7	77.0	0.2	0.1	0.2	0.3	0	0.3	15.4	6.5
Eastleigh	116,169	+9.0	6,900	7,100	+3	6.7	6.3	76.7	0.2	0.3	0.1	0.3	0.5	0.3	15.2	6.4
Fareham	107,977	+8.4	6,800	5,200	–24	7.0	4.9	78.0	0.1	0.2	0.1	0.3	0.1	0.4	14.2	6.6
Gosport	76,415	–0.1	6,200	4,500	–27	8.1	5.9	75.3	0.2	0.1	0.1	0.3	0	0.3	16.6	7.1
Hart	83,505	+3.7	6,300	5,100	–19	7.9	6.2	77.2	0.2	0.3	0.1	0.4	0.1	0.3	15.0	6.4
Havant	116,849	–2.5	8,100	8,100	0	6.7	6.9	73.6	0.1	0.1	0.1	0.3	0.1	0.3	17.4	8.0
New Forest	169,331	+5.2	18,100	15,000	–17	11.4	9.0	78.3	0.1	0.1	0.1	0.2	0	0.3	14.0	6.9
Portsmouth UA	186,701	0	13,900	10,100	–27	7.4	5.4	68.1	0.4	0.4	0.1	2.1	0.2	0.4	20.0	8.3
Rushmoor	90,987	+5.9	10,400	7,400	–29	12.3	8.3	73.0	0.4	0.6	0.1	0.7	0.1	0.3	16.8	8.0
Southampton UA	217,445	+6.2	18,800	16,100	–14	9.3	7.5	65.6	0.3	0.7	0.1	1.9	1.3	0.5	21.6	8.0
Test Valley	109,801	+8.4	9,500	10,000	+5	9.6	9.4	78.1	0.1	0.2	0.1	0.3	0.3	0.3	14.2	6.4
Winchester	107,222	+9.0	11,400	12,000	+5	11.9	11.5	76.2	0.2	0.2	0.2	0.3	0.1	0.3	15.9	6.5
HEREFORDSHIRE, County of, UA[1]	174,871	+9.0	15,000	9,700	–35	9.6	5.7	79.0	0.2	0.1	0.1	0.1	0	0.2	12.6	7.7
HERTFORDSHIRE	1,033,977	+5.0	90,100	76,500	–15	9.3	7.5	70.2	0.3	1.0	1.6	1.7	0.4	0.3	17.1	7.4
Broxbourne	87,054	+6.5	6,300	5,700	–10	7.8	6.7	76.4	0.2	0.5	0.3	1.2	0.1	0.2	13.9	7.2
Dacorum	137,709	+3.5	9,700	7,900	–19	7.6	6.0	70.7	0.2	0.8	0.4	1.2	0.1	0.2	18.4	8.0
East Hertfordshire	128,919	+9.9	10,000	8,500	–15	8.8	6.8	74.5	0.2	0.4	0.3	0.6	0.1	0.2	17.0	6.7
Hertsmere	94,450	+4.9	9,400	8,100	–14	10.6	8.7	63.0	0.3	2.0	11.3	1.4	0.2	0.5	13.4	7.9
North Hertfordshire	116,908	+4.1	12,400	10,300	–17	11.2	8.9	69.8	0.3	0.7	0.2	0.7	1.9	0.3	18.7	7.4
St Albans	129,005	+2.2	14,300	11,800	–17	11.4	9.2	71.0	0.3	0.7	0.9	2.6	0.1	0.3	17.5	6.6
Stevenage	79,715	+5.3	4,600	4,200	– 9	6.2	5.4	67.0	0.2	0.7	0.2	1.1	0.3	0.4	21.9	8.2
Three Rivers	82,848	+4.9	7,700	6,800	–12	9.9	8.3	70.8	0.2	2.6	2.1	1.5	0.3	0.4	14.9	7.2
Watford	79,726	+6.4	8,200	7,000	–15	11.1	9.0	66.5	0.3	1.7	1.1	6.1	0.5	0.4	16.1	7.3
Welwyn Hatfield	97,553	+4.0	7,500	6,200	–17	8.1	6.4	69.9	0.4	1.1	0.7	1.1	0.2	0.3	18.1	8.2
ISLE OF WIGHT UA[2]	132,731	+5.4	15,400	12,600	–18	12.4	9.7	73.7	0.2	0.1	0.1	0.3	0	0.4	17.3	7.9
KENT	1,579,206	+3.3	128,100	109,600	–14	8.4	7.0	74.7	0.2	0.4	0.1	0.6	0.7	0.3	15.2	7.8
Ashford	102,661	+10.2	9,000	9,100	+1	10.0	9.2	76.4	0.2	0.3	0.1	0.6	0.1	0.3	14.6	7.4
Canterbury	135,278	+4.4	12,000	12,200	+2	9.4	9.1	73.3	0.4	0.4	0.2	0.6	0.1	0.4	16.6	8.0
Dartford	85,911	+7.2	9,100	6,200	–32	11.6	7.4	73.3	0.2	0.8	0.1	0.7	1.1	0.2	15.0	8.6
Dover	104,566	+0.1	8,000	6,600	–17	7.7	6.3	76.6	0.2	0.1	0.1	0.3	0	0.3	14.2	8.2
Gravesham	95,717	+2.6	5,400	4,000	–24	5.8	4.2	72.3	0.2	0.6	0.1	0.8	6.7	0.3	12.0	7.0
Maidstone	138,948	+1.4	9,400	8,000	–15	6.9	5.8	76.3	0.2	0.5	0.1	0.5	0.1	0.5	14.4	7.4
Medway UA[3]	249,488	+2.9	16,300	12,000	–26	6.8	4.9	72.0	0.2	0.7	0.1	1.0	1.2	0.3	16.7	7.8
Sevenoaks	109,305	–0.1	12,200	10,600	–13	11.1	9.7	77.0	0.2	0.2	0.2	0.3	0.1	0.3	14.4	7.3
Shepway	96,238	+3.4	7,000	7,000	0	7.6	7.3	75.4	0.2	1.1	0.1	0.4	0	0.3	14.6	7.9
Swale	122,801	+5.7	5,700	5,600	– 2	5.0	4.6	75.9	0.1	0.2	0.1	0.3	0.1	0.3	15.4	7.6
Thanet	126,702	+0.5	12,000	10,200	–15	9.5	8.1	73.6	0.3	0.2	0.2	0.5	0.1	0.3	15.8	9.0
Tonbridge & Malling	107,561	+5.3	9,500	7,400	–22	9.4	7.0	76.1	0.2	0.2	0.1	0.3	0.1	0.2	15.0	7.8
Tunbridge Wells	104,030	+2.5	12,500	10,700	–14	12.4	10.4	75.0	0.3	0.2	0.2	0.6	0	0.3	16.0	7.4

[1]Formerly the Local Authority Districts of Hereford, Leominster and South Herefordshire [2]Including the former Local Authority Districts of Medina and South Wight
[3]Formerly the Local Authority Districts of Gillingham and Rochester-upon-Medway
Xian: Christian; Other: Other Religions; None: No Religion; n/a: not answered.

4.6 Population in UK by Religion: England

	Population 2001	Population 91–01 %	Churchgoers 1989	Churchgoers 1998	Churchgoers 89–98 %	% population 1989	% population 1998	Xian %	Buddhist %	Hindu %	Jew %	Muslim %	Sikh %	Other %	None %	n/a %
LANCASHIRE	1,414,727	+0.9	184,300	123,300	-33	13.2	8.7	76.8	0.1	0.5	0.1	4.7	0.1	0.2	10.3	7.2
Blackburn with Darwen UA	137,470	0	15,300	10,200	−33	11.1	7.4	63.3	0.1	0.3	0.1	19.4	0.1	0.1	8.0	8.6
Blackpool UA	142,283	−4.3	13,600	9,700	−29	9.1	6.7	78.6	0.2	0.1	0.2	0.5	0	0.2	11.4	8.8
Burnley	89,542	−2.6	8,900	6,600	−26	9.6	7.3	74.5	0.1	0.3	0	6.6	0	0.2	11.0	7.3
Chorley	100,449	+3.6	13,000	10,200	−22	13.5	10.3	84.0	0.2	0.2	0	0.7	0.1	0.1	9.1	5.6
Fylde	73,217	+1.8	8,300	6,100	−27	11.6	8.4	82.4	0.1	0.2	0.5	0.3	0	0.2	9.6	6.7
Hyndburn	81,496	+3.6	9,600	6,400	−33	12.3	7.9	76.3	0.1	0.1	0	7.2	0	0.1	9.2	7.0
Lancaster	133,914	+3.3	16,900	13,000	−23	13.1	9.8	76.3	0.3	0.1	0.1	0.6	0	0.3	13.6	8.7
Pendle	89,248	+4.3	11,100	6,500	−41	13.1	7.4	65.4	0.1	0.1	0.1	13.4	0	0.2	13.1	7.6
Preston	129,633	−0.3	22,500	14,400	−36	17.3	11.1	71.4	0.2	2.6	0	8.2	0.6	0.2	9.8	7.0
Ribble Valley	53,960	+4.2	10,300	8,400	−18	20.1	15.8	85.3	0.1	0.2	0.1	0.6	0	0.1	8.2	5.4
Rossendale	65,652	−0.2	11,700	7,000	−40	17.8	10.7	75.7	0.1	0.1	0.1	2.9	0	0.2	13.9	7.0
South Ribble	103,867	+1.3	12,000	7,500	−37	11.7	7.2	84.7	0.1	0.4	0	0.3	0.1	0.1	8.7	5.6
West Lancashire	108,378	−0.6	15,300	8,500	−44	14.0	7.8	83.8	0.1	0.2	0	0.2	0.1	0.1	8.9	6.6
Wyre	105,618	+3.0	15,800	8,800	−43	15.5	8.4	83.1	0.1	0.1	0.1	0.2	0.1	0.2	9.4	6.7
LEICESTERSHIRE	922,962	+4.1	70,600	52,500	-26	8.0	5.8	65.5	0.2	5.8	0.1	3.9	1.8	0.3	15.8	6.6
Blaby	90,252	+8.8	5,500	4,300	−22	6.8	4.9	73.7	0.1	1.9	0.1	0.4	1.4	0.2	15.9	6.3
Charnwood	153,462	+4.7	11,800	10,300	−13	8.1	6.8	69.5	0.2	4.0	0.1	1.6	0.5	0.3	17.3	6.5
Harborough	76,559	+12.7	6,000	4,800	−20	9.2	6.5	78.0	0.1	0.5	0.1	0.2	0.3	0.2	14.0	6.6
Hinckley & Bosworth	100,141	+3.6	5,500	4,800	−13	5.7	4.8	78.4	0.1	0.5	0.1	0.3	0.2	0.2	14.2	6.0
Leicester UA	279,921	−0.5	23,200	14,300	−38	8.2	5.1	44.7	0.2	14.8	0.2	11.0	4.2	0.4	17.4	7.1
Melton	47,866	+5.6	3,600	2,900	−19	8.1	6.2	79.2	0.1	0.3	0.1	0.1	0	0.2	13.4	6.6
North West Leicestershire	85,503	+5.6	8,200	5,900	−28	10.3	7.0	78.2	0.1	0.2	0.1	0.1	0.1	0.2	14.5	6.5
Oadby & Wigston	55,795	+5.5	4,100	3,200	−22	7.9	5.8	64.7	0.2	6.0	0.3	2.8	4.2	0.2	14.7	6.9
Rutland UA	34,563	+4.7	2,700	2,000	−26	8.3	5.9	79.8	0.2	0.1	0.1	0.3	0.1	0.2	13.1	6.1
LINCOLNSHIRE	957,473	+6.1	75,500	56,900	-25	8.5	6.1	79.4	0.1	0.1	0.1	0.4	0.1	0.2	12.3	7.3
Boston	55,750	+4.5	2,200	1,900	−14	4.2	3.5	80.2	0.1	0.2	0.1	0.4	0	0.2	11.4	7.4
East Lindsey	130,447	+10.8	9,800	7,700	−21	8.6	6.1	79.9	0.1	0.1	0.1	0.2	0.1	0.2	11.7	7.6
Lincoln	85,595	+1.9	9,000	6,600	−27	10.8	7.8	73.9	0.2	0.2	0.1	0.4	0.1	0.3	16.9	8.0
North East Lincolnshire UA[1]	157,979	−1.9	7,400	5,600	−24	4.6	3.5	75.7	0.1	0.2	0	0.5	0.1	0.1	14.6	8.6
North Kesteven	94,024	+17.5	7,900	5,400	−32	10.6	6.1	82.4	0.1	0.1	0	0.2	0	0.2	10.9	6.1
North Lincolnshire UA[2]	152,849	0	15,600	11,400	−27	10.2	7.5	79.5	0.1	0.2	0	1.2	0.3	0.1	11.4	7.2
South Holland	76,522	+13.4	5,800	3,900	−33	9.0	5.3	82.6	0.1	0	0.1	0.2	0.1	0.2	9.7	7.0
South Kesteven	124,792	+13.9	11,100	9,000	−19	10.6	7.5	81.3	0.2	0.2	0.1	0.2	0.1	0.2	11.5	6.2
West Lindsey	79,515	+3.9	6,700	5,400	−19	8.8	6.9	81.8	0.1	0.1	0	0.1	0.1	0.2	10.9	6.7
MERSEYSIDE	1,362,056	-5.3	248,700	169,500	-32	17.3	12.3	82.4	0.2	0.2	0.3	0.6	0	0.1	8.7	7.5
Knowsley	150,459	−3.0	37,700	19,500	−48	24.2	12.8	85.6	0.1	0.1	0	0.2	0	0.1	5.8	8.1
Liverpool	439,473	−7.6	80,900	55,500	−31	16.9	12.4	79.5	0.3	0.3	0.6	1.3	0.1	0.1	9.7	8.1
St Helens	176,843	−1.8	33,500	22,100	−34	18.5	12.4	86.9	0.1	0.2	0	0.2	0	0.1	6.3	6.2
Sefton	282,958	−3.4	47,900	34,500	−28	16.3	12.1	84.4	0.1	0.2	0.3	0.3	0	0.1	8.1	6.5
Wirral	312,293	−6.6	48,700	37,900	−22	14.4	11.9	80.6	0.2	0.1	0.1	0.3	0.1	0.1	10.5	8.0
NORFOLK	796,728	+5.6	73,700	53,500	-27	9.9	6.8	74.0	0.2	0.1	0.1	0.3	0	0.3	16.8	8.2
Breckland	121,418	+12.5	10,100	9,700	− 4	9.8	8.3	75.6	0.1	0	0.1	0.2	0	0.3	15.7	8.0
Broadland	118,513	+11.2	7,200	6,300	−12	7.0	5.5	76.6	0.2	0.1	0.1	0.2	0	0.2	14.9	7.7
Great Yarmouth	90,810	+2.5	5,500	4,500	−18	6.2	5.0	74.6	0.2	0.1	0.1	0.3	0	0.2	16.6	7.9
King's Lynn & West Norfolk	135,345	+3.2	10,100	7,500	−26	7.8	5.6	78.2	0.1	0.1	0.1	0.2	0.1	0.2	13.0	8.0
North Norfolk	98,382	+7.3	12,800	8,200	−36	14.2	8.5	77.5	0.2	0	0.1	0.1	0	0.3	13.9	7.9
Norwich	121,550	−2.8	17,000	10,300	−39	13.5	8.4	60.4	0.4	0.3	0.2	0.7	0.1	0.5	27.8	9.6
South Norfolk	110,710	+7.0	11,000	7,000	−36	10.8	6.5	75.8	0.2	0.1	0.1	0.1	0	0.3	15.4	8.0
NORTH YORKSHIRE	750,754	+5.1	90,600	55,000	-39	12.9	7.4	78.9	0.2	0.1	0.1	0.3	0	0.2	13.1	7.1
Craven	53,620	+6.6	6,900	3,600	−48	14.0	6.9	78.1	0.2	0	0.1	0.6	0	0.2	13.8	7.0
Hambleton	84,111	+6.3	10,800	6,900	−36	13.9	8.4	83.0	0.1	0.1	0	0.1	0	0.2	10.4	6.1
Harrogate	151,336	+7.9	22,200	14,100	−36	16.2	9.5	79.0	0.2	0.1	0.2	0.2	0	0.2	13.1	7.0
Richmondshire	47,010	+3.7	4,100	2,500	−39	9.1	5.4	82.0	0.3	0.7	0.1	0	0	0.1	10.4	6.4
Ryedale	50,872	+10.1	4,400	3,600	−19	9.8	7.3	82.3	0.1	0	0	0.1	0	0.2	10.7	6.6
Scarborough	106,243	−2.3	15,400	7,900	−49	14.1	7.4	78.8	0.2	0.1	0.1	0.2	0	0.2	12.5	7.9
Selby	76,468	+6.5	8,500	5,300	−38	12.0	7.1	81.1	0.1	0.1	0.1	0	0	0.2	11.2	7.2
York UA[3]	181,094	+5.1	18,300	11,100	−39	10.8	6.2	74.4	0.2	0.2	0.1	0.6	0.1	0.3	16.6	7.6

[1]Formerly Cleethorpes and Great Grimsby Local Authority Districts of Humberside [2]Formerly Glanford, Scunthorpe and southern half of Boothferry Local Authority Districts of Humberside [3]The new York Unitary Authority includes a substantial part of the former Ryedale Local Authority District; the 1989 figures are estimated to take account of this.

Population in UK by Religion: England 4.7

	Population		Churchgoers			% population		Percentage in each religion, 2001								
	2001	91–01 %	1989	1998	89–98 %	1989	1998	Xian %	Buddhist %	Hindu %	Jew %	Muslim %	Sikh %	Other %	None %	n/a %
NORTHAMPTONSHIRE	629,676	+7.8	49,400	42,400	–14	8.6	6.9	71.5	0.2	0.9	0.1	0.9	0.3	0.3	18.0	7.8
Corby	53,174	–0.1	2,700	2,500	–7	5.1	4.7	69.4	0.1	0.2	0	0.2	0.2	0.2	21.3	8.4
Daventry	71,838	+14.4	4,200	4,300	+2	7.0	6.3	76.1	0.2	0.3	0.1	0.3	0.1	0.2	15.8	6.9
East Northamptonshire	76,550	+12.0	8,000	7,400	–7	12.2	10.0	73.3	0.2	0.2	0.1	0.1	0.1	0.2	17.8	8.0
Kettering	81,844	+6.8	7,300	5,300	–27	9.7	6.6	71.6	0.2	0.5	0.1	0.5	0.8	0.3	18.3	7.7
Northampton	194,458	+5.7	15,800	12,400	–22	8.7	6.5	68.3	0.3	1.1	0.2	2.1	0.4	0.3	19.1	8.2
South Northamptonshire	79,293	+12.1	5,500	5,600	+2	8.1	7.3	77.8	0.1	0.2	0.1	0.2	0.1	0.2	14.5	6.8
Wellingborough	72,519	+6.1	5,900	4,900	–17	8.8	6.9	68.2	0.4	3.3	0.1	0.9	0.1	0.3	18.4	8.3
NORTHUMBERLAND	307,190	+0.5	29,300	24,100	–18	9.6	7.9	81.1	0.1	0.1	0	0.2	0.1	0.2	11.8	6.4
Alnwick	31,029	+2.6	3,600	3,200	–11	12.0	10.4	82.6	0.1	0	0	0.1	0	0.2	10.8	6.2
Berwick-upon-Tweed	25,949	–3.0	2,700	2,400	–11	10.0	9.2	82.4	0.2	0	0	0	0	0.2	10.8	6.4
Blyth Valley	81,265	+1.6	6,300	5,100	–19	7.9	6.3	79.5	0.1	0	0	0.3	0.1	0.2	13.2	6.6
Castle Morpeth	49,001	–2.1	4,200	3,400	–19	8.4	6.9	81.2	0.2	0.3	0.1	0.4	0.3	0.2	11.1	6.2
Tynedale	58,808	+2.7	7,500	6,300	–16	13.2	10.8	80.8	0.2	0.1	0.1	0.1	0	0.2	12.2	6.3
Wansbeck	61,138	–0.1	5,000	3,700	–26	8.2	6.1	81.8	0.1	0.1	0	0.3	0.2	0.2	10.9	6.4
NOTTINGHAMSHIRE	1,015,498	+0.1	78,700	62,700	–20	7.8	6.2	70.3	0.2	0.4	0.1	1.6	0.6	0.2	18.3	8.3
Ashfield	111,387	+2.3	5,700	4,300	–25	5.3	3.9	72.9	0.1	0.1	0	0.1	0.1	0.2	17.8	8.7
Bassetlaw	107,713	+2.7	8,500	6,300	–26	8.2	5.9	81.5	0.1	0.1	0.1	0.3	0.1	0.2	10.0	7.6
Broxtowe	107,570	–0.6	10,100	8,100	–20	9.3	7.5	70.6	0.3	0.6	0.1	0.9	0.6	0.2	19.0	7.7
Gedling	111,787	+1.2	7,700	5,900	–23	7.0	5.3	71.8	0.2	0.3	0.1	0.6	0.4	0.3	18.7	7.7
Mansfield	98,181	–2.8	6,000	4,200	–30	5.9	4.2	76.0	0.1	0.2	0	0.3	0.2	0.2	15.2	7.8
Newark & Sherwood	106,273	+3.0	7,800	6,700	–14	7.6	6.4	79.1	0.1	0.1	0	0.2	0.1	0.2	12.9	7.3
Nottingham UA	266,988	–4.5	22,800	20,000	–12	8.1	7.4	57.7	0.4	0.8	0.2	4.6	1.3	0.3	24.9	9.8
Rushcliffe	105,599	+7.2	10,100	6,800	–29	10.5	6.6	71.8	0.2	0.6	0.4	0.9	0.7	0.3	18.0	7.1
OXFORDSHIRE	605,488	+5.1	55,600	47,700	–14	9.8	8.0	72.5	0.3	0.3	0.3	1.3	0.2	0.3	17.5	7.3
Cherwell	131,785	+6.2	10,600	10,800	+2	8.7	8.4	75.6	0.2	0.2	0.1	1.2	0.2	0.3	15.0	7.2
Oxford	134,248	+4.1	16,900	14,500	–14	13.2	10.9	60.4	0.8	0.8	0.8	3.9	0.2	0.5	23.9	8.7
South Oxfordshire	128,188	+6.8	9,400	8,000	–15	8.0	6.4	75.5	0.2	0.2	0.2	0.3	0.1	0.2	16.5	6.8
Vale of White Horse	115,627	+3.2	10,400	8,500	–18	9.4	7.4	75.8	0.2	0.2	0.2	0.5	0.1	0.2	15.8	7.0
West Oxfordshire	95,640	+5.1	8,300	5,900	–29	9.2	6.3	77.4	0.2	0.1	0.2	0.2	0	0.3	15.1	6.5
SHROPSHIRE	441,498	+7.7	37,700	29,100	–23	9.4	6.8	77.9	0.2	0.2	0	0.6	0.5	0.2	13.2	7.2
Bridgnorth	52,497	+3.8	4,200	3,500	–17	8.4	6.7	81.6	0.1	0	0.1	0.1	0.1	0.2	11.3	6.5
North Shropshire	57,108	+6.8	6,300	4,700	–25	12.0	8.4	82.3	0.1	0.1	0	0.2	0	0.2	10.6	6.5
Oswestry	37,308	+8.8	3,000	3,200	+7	9.0	8.8	79.5	0.2	0.1	0	0.2	0	0.2	12.3	7.5
Shrewsbury and Atcham	95,850	+4.1	8,300	6,700	–19	9.1	7.1	77.9	0.2	0.1	0	0.3	0.1	0.2	13.7	7.5
South Shropshire	40,410	+5.4	3,900	3,000	–23	10.3	7.5	79.6	0.2	0	0.1	0.2	0	0.4	12.3	7.2
Telford and Wrekin UA	158,325	+12.1	12,000	8,000	–33	8.8	5.3	74.3	0.3	0.4	0	1.3	1.1	0.2	15.1	7.3
SOMERSET	498,093	+7.0	46,300	32,800	–29	10.1	6.7	76.7	0.2	0.1	0.1	0.2	0	0.4	14.8	74.5
Mendip	103,869	+6.7	11,000	6,500	–41	11.5	6.4	74.5	0.3	0.1	0.1	0.1	0	0.7	16.1	8.1
Sedgemoor	105,881	+7.4	10,000	6,400	–36	10.4	6.2	77.8	0.2	0	0.1	0.2	0	0.3	14.1	7.3
South Somerset	150,969	+5.9	13,400	10,100	–25	9.5	6.8	78.0	0.2	0.1	0.1	0.1	0	0.2	14.0	7.3
Taunton Deane	102,299	+7.4	7,600	6,400	–16	8.1	6.4	75.9	0.2	0.1	0.1	0.3	0	0.4	15.8	7.2
West Somerset	35,075	+9.9	4,300	3,400	–21	13.9	10.0	76.0	0.3	0	0.1	0.2	0	0.4	14.6	8.4
SOUTH YORKSHIRE	1,266,338	–1.7	78,800	58,600	–26	6.2	4.6	75.3	0.1	0.2	0.1	2.5	0.2	0.2	13.7	7.7
Barnsley	218,063	–2.3	10,400	9,400	–10	4.6	4.3	81.1	0.1	0.1	0	0.2	0.1	0.1	10.8	7.5
Doncaster	286,866	–1.6	18,400	12,900	–30	6.3	4.5	79.6	0.1	0.2	0	0.7	0.3	0.2	11.3	7.6
Rotherham	248,175	–2.2	14,000	8,700	–38	5.5	3.5	79.4	0.1	0.1	0	2.2	0.1	0.1	10.2	7.8
Sheffield	513,234	–1.3	36,000	27,600	–23	6.9	5.4	68.6	0.2	0.3	0.2	4.6	0.2	0.2	17.9	7.8
STAFFORDSHIRE	1,047,380	+0.6	93,500	65,800	–30	9.0	6.3	78.8	0.1	0.2	0.1	1.3	0.2	0.2	12.1	7.0
Cannock Chase	92,126	+3.1	4,300	3,200	–26	4.8	3.5	80.8	0.1	0.1	0	0.2	0.2	0.1	11.3	7.2
East Staffordshire	103,370	+5.9	7,900	6,300	–20	8.2	6.2	77.4	0.1	0.2	0.1	4.0	0.2	0.2	11.5	6.3
Lichfield	93,232	+0.1	7,800	6,000	–23	8.5	6.5	80.4	0.1	0.2	0.1	0.3	0.3	0.1	11.9	6.6
Newcastle-under-Lyme	122,030	+1.0	14,500	10,900	–25	12.0	9.0	78.5	0.1	0.2	0.1	0.5	0.1	0.2	13.1	7.2
South Staffordshire	105,896	+1.3	11,000	6,100	–45	10.6	5.8	83.5	0.1	0.2	0	0.2	0.5	0.1	9.3	6.1
Stafford	120,670	+1.0	8,500	6,300	–26	7.1	5.2	79.9	0.1	0.3	0.1	0.4	0.3	0.2	12.1	6.6
Staffordshire Moorlands	94,489	–1.3	9,100	6,600	–27	9.5	7.0	82.8	0.1	0	0	0.1	0	0.2	9.8	7.0
Stoke-on-Trent UA	240,636	–3.5	24,500	15,900	–35	9.8	6.5	74.7	0.1	0.2	0	3.2	0.2	0.2	13.4	8.0
Tamworth	74,531	+5.7	5,900	4,500	–24	8.5	6.1	76.8	0.1	0.2	0	0.2	0.1	0.2	15.5	6.9

Xian: Christian; Other: Other Religions; None: No Religion; n/a: not answered.

4

4.8 Population in UK by Religion: England

	Population		Churchgoers			% population		Percentage in each religion, 2001								
	2001	91–01 %	1989	1998	89–98 %	1989	1998	Xian %	Buddhist %	Hindu %	Jew %	Muslim %	Sikh %	Other %	None %	n/a %
SUFFOLK	668,553	+3.0	82,100	57,200	–30	12.7	8.6	74.0	0.2	0.1	0.1	0.4	0.1	0.3	16.6	8.2
Babergh	83,461	+4.1	8,800	5,700	–35	11.1	6.9	75.5	0.1	0.1	0.1	0.2	0	0.3	16.3	7.4
Forest Heath	55,510	–3.8	7,100	5,300	–25	12.2	9.4	74.7	0.2	0.1	0.2	0.2	0	0.3	14.1	10.2
Ipswich	117,069	–1.1	16,900	10,700	–37	14.2	9.1	68.1	0.2	0.4	0.1	1.3	0.2	0.3	20.3	9.1
Mid Suffolk	86,837	+9.9	8,500	7,000	–18	11.1	8.3	76.8	0.1	0	0.1	0.1	0	0.3	15.1	7.5
St Edmundsbury	98,193	+6.1	11,600	10,100	–13	12.7	10.5	74.3	0.2	0.1	0.1	0.3	0	0.2	16.8	8.0
Suffolk Coastal	115,141	+1.7	15,900	9,700	–39	14.1	8.5	75.8	0.2	0.1	0.1	0.3	0.1	0.3	15.6	7.5
Waveney	112,342	+4.0	13,300	8,700	–35	12.4	7.8	74.3	0.2	0.1	0.1	0.2	0	0.3	16.3	8.5
SURREY	1,059,015	+3.5	105,400	99,600	– 6	10.4	9.5	71.7	0.3	1.1	0.5	3.0	0.6	0.3	14.8	7.7
Elmbridge	121,936	+7.2	13,500	12,700	– 6	12.1	10.7	74.4	0.5	0.9	0.8	1.3	0.2	0.3	14.7	6.9
Epsom & Ewell	67,059	–0.4	6,900	7,300	+6	10.2	10.9	73.0	0.5	1.8	0.4	1.9	0.1	0.3	14.8	7.2
Guildford	129,701	+3.0	15,000	15,600	+4	12.0	12.1	73.6	0.3	0.5	0.2	0.9	0.1	0.3	16.9	7.2
Mole Valley	80,287	+1.4	7,400	6,200	–16	9.4	7.8	75.4	0.2	0.4	0.2	0.6	0	0.3	15.6	7.3
Reigate & Banstead	126,523	+7.0	10,800	10,300	– 5	9.3	8.3	73.8	0.2	0.8	0.3	1.3	0.1	0.3	16.1	7.1
Runnymede	78,033	+5.1	6,500	5,500	–15	8.9	7.2	74.9	0.4	0.6	0.3	1.0	0.3	0.3	14.3	7.9
Spelthorne	90,390	+2.3	6,300	6,500	+3	7.2	7.2	75.3	0.3	1.1	0.2	0.9	0.7	0.2	14.1	7.2
Surrey Heath	80,314	+1.0	5,400	5,700	+6	6.8	7.1	76.4	0.3	0.7	0.2	1.2	0.3	0.2	14.1	6.6
Tandridge	79,267	+5.9	8,300	7,500	–10	11.3	9.6	76.2	0.2	0.5	0.2	0.5	0	0.6	14.9	6.9
Waverley	115,665	+0.4	14,500	12,200	–16	12.6	10.6	76.3	0.3	0.2	0.2	0.5	0.1	0.3	15.4	6.7
Woking	89,840	+3.7	10,800	10,100	– 6	12.6	11.4	71.3	0.3	0.7	0.3	5.1	0.1	0.3	15.1	6.8
TYNE & WEAR	1,075,938	–4.3	96,500	75,400	–22	8.5	6.9	78.1	0.1	0.3	0.2	1.4	0.3	0.2	12.0	7.4
Gateshead	191,151	–5.2	16,600	12,200	–27	8.2	6.3	80.3	0.1	0.1	0.8	0.6	0.2	0.1	10.9	6.9
Newcastle upon Tyne	259,536	–5.6	23,600	18,900	–20	8.5	7.2	70.7	0.3	0.6	0.3	3.6	0.5	0.2	16.0	7.8
North Tyneside	191,659	–1.5	18,900	16,000	–15	9.7	8.3	78.2	0.1	0.2	0	0.5	0.2	0.2	13.7	6.9
South Tyneside	152,785	–2.5	13,400	10,600	–21	8.5	6.9	81.8	0.1	0.3	0	1.1	0.3	0.1	8.9	7.4
Sunderland	280,807	–5.1	24,000	17,700	–26	8.1	6.2	81.5	0.1	0.1	0	0.8	0.2	0.1	9.6	7.6
WARWICKSHIRE	505,860	+3.8	54,800	38,200	–30	11.3	7.6	76.6	0.2	0.7	0.1	0.7	1.3	0.2	13.1	7.1
North Warwickshire	61,680	+1.3	5,000	3,100	–38	8.2	5.0	81.1	0.1	0.2	0.1	0.1	0.2	0.1	11.2	6.9
Nuneaton and Bedworth	119,132	+1.4	10,300	6,000	–42	8.8	5.1	76.9	0.1	0.6	0	1.6	1.5	0.2	11.7	7.4
Rugby	87,453	+2.9	10,400	7,500	–28	12.3	8.7	74.8	0.2	2.0	0.1	0.6	0.6	0.2	13.8	7.7
Stratford-on-Avon	111,484	+5.7	11,600	8,500	–27	11.2	7.8	81.1	0.2	0.1	0.1	0.2	0.1	0.2	11.7	6.3
Warwick	125,931	+6.6	17,500	13,100	–25	15.1	10.6	71.3	0.3	0.7	0.1	0.5	3.3	0.3	16.3	7.2
WEST MIDLANDS	2,555,592	–2.4	266,700	187,800	–30	10.1	7.3	66.6	0.2	1.9	0.1	7.5	3.6	0.2	12.0	7.9
Birmingham	977,087	–2.7	117,300	87,200	–26	11.6	8.9	59.1	0.3	2.0	0.3	14.3	2.9	0.3	12.4	8.4
Coventry	300,848	–1.0	35,000	20,200	–42	11.5	6.7	65.3	0.3	2.6	0.1	3.9	4.6	0.3	15.1	8.0
Dudley	305,155	–0.8	27,100	18,100	–33	8.8	5.9	77.7	0.1	0.5	0	2.5	0.9	0.2	10.7	7.4
Sandwell	282,904	–3.3	19,900	15,200	–24	6.8	5.3	68.6	0.1	2.0	0	4.6	6.9	0.2	10.4	7.2
Solihull	199,517	–0.5	21,100	15,300	–27	10.5	7.7	78.2	0.2	0.9	0.2	0.8	0.8	0.2	12.0	6.7
Walsall	253,499	–3.0	22,000	16,600	–25	8.4	6.5	72.1	0.1	1.6	0	5.4	3.0	0.2	10.0	7.6
Wolverhampton	236,582	–4.8	24,300	15,200	–37	9.7	6.3	66.5	0.3	3.9	0	1.7	7.6	0.2	11.4	8.4
WEST SUSSEX	753,614	+6.1	71,800	61,700	–14	10.3	8.3	74.5	0.2	0.6	0.2	1.0	0.1	0.4	15.6	7.4
Adur	59,627	+1.8	6,700	4,400	–34	11.5	7.4	73.3	0.2	0.2	0.3	0.7	0.1	0.4	16.8	8.0
Arun	140,759	+7.9	10,300	9,400	– 9	8.1	6.8	76.6	0.2	0.1	0.2	0.4	0	0.3	14.7	7.5
Chichester	106,450	+4.6	9,000	9,200	+2	8.9	8.8	77.3	0.3	0.1	0.2	0.3	0	0.4	14.2	7.2
Crawley	99,744	+13.0	5,900	4,200	–29	7.0	4.4	67.3	0.2	3.4	0.1	4.4	0.7	0.3	16.8	6.8
Horsham	122,088	+11.3	12,000	12,100	+1	11.4	10.3	76.3	0.2	0.2	0.2	0.4	0.1	0.4	15.4	6.8
Mid Sussex	127,378	+2.8	16,400	13,700	–16	13.3	10.8	75.9	0.2	0.3	0.2	0.6	0.1	0.6	15.3	6.8
Worthing	97,568	+0.4	11,500	8,700	–24	11.8	8.9	72.1	0.3	0.2	0.3	0.8	0.1	0.5	17.0	8.7
WEST YORKSHIRE	2,079,211	+0.8	199,800	126,900	–36	9.7	6.1	68.1	0.2	0.5	0.4	7.2	0.7	0.2	14.7	8.0
Bradford	467,665	–0.2	46,200	32,400	–30	9.9	6.9	60.1	0.1	1.0	0.1	16.1	1.0	0.2	13.3	8.1
Calderdale	192,405	–0.2	21,300	13,200	–38	11.0	6.9	69.6	0.2	0.2	0.1	5.3	0.1	0.2	16.4	7.9
Kirklees	388,567	+2.5	35,500	19,500	–45	9.4	5.1	67.2	0.1	0.3	0.1	10.1	0.7	0.2	14.0	7.3
Leeds	715,402	+1.2	74,900	47,800	–36	10.6	6.7	68.9	0.2	0.6	1.1	3.0	1.1	0.2	16.8	8.1
Wakefield	315,172	+0.3	21,900	14,000	–36	7.0	4.4	78.2	0.1	0.2	0	1.1	0.1	0.2	11.8	8.3

Xian: Christian; Other: Other Religions; None: No Religion; n/a: not answered.

Population in UK by Religion: England & Wales

	Population		Churchgoers			% population		Percentage in each religion, 2001								
	2001	91–01 %	1989	1998	89–98 %	1989	1998	Xian %	Buddhist %	Hindu %	Jew %	Muslim %	Sikh %	Other %	None %	n/a %
WILTSHIRE	613,024	+7.5	56,700	40,000	-29	10.2	6.6	74.7	0.2	0.2	0.1	0.5	0.2	0.4	16.2	7.5
Kennet	74,838	+4.9	10,200	7,100	–30	15.1	9.0	77.9	0.2	0.1	0.1	0.2	0	0.4	14.3	6.8
North Wiltshire	125,372	+10.9	9,300	7,000	–25	8.4	5.7	75.9	0.2	0.1	0.1	0.3	0.1	0.3	15.6	7.4
Salisbury	114,613	+8.1	13,200	8,300	–37	12.7	7.3	78.3	0.2	0.1	0.1	0.2	0	0.3	13.6	7.2
Swindon UA[1]	180,051	+5.0	14,300	11,100	–22	8.5	6.2	70.1	0.3	0.5	0.1	1.0	0.6	0.4	19.1	7.9
West Wiltshire	118,150	+9.1	9,700	6,500	–33	9.1	6.0	74.9	0.2	0.1	0.1	0.4	0	0.4	16.3	7.6
WORCESTERSHIRE	542,107	+5.8	49,000	32,400	-34	9.7	6.1	78.7	0.1	0.1	0.1	0.9	0.1	0.2	12.7	7.1
Bromsgrove	87,837	+5.5	6,900	4,300	–38	8.4	5.0	80.1	0.1	0.2	0.1	0.3	0.3	0.2	11.8	6.9
Malvern Hills	72,172	+3.2	13,600	8,300	–39	19.6	11.6	78.3	0.2	0.1	0.1	0.2	0	0.3	13.5	7.3
Redditch	78,807	+0.1	4,600	3,400	–26	5.8	4.3	75.0	0.1	0.2	0.1	2.4	0.2	0.2	14.5	7.3
Worcester	93,353	+12.1	7,100	5,800	–18	8.9	6.5	76.7	0.2	0.1	0.1	1.8	0.1	0.2	13.6	7.2
Wychavon	112,957	+10.8	8,600	5,300	–38	8.7	4.9	81.3	0.1	0.1	0.1	0.2	0.1	0.2	11.4	6.5
Wyre Forest	96,981	+1.8	8,200	5,300	–35	8.6	5.5	79.4	0.1	0.1	0	0.6	0.1	0.2	11.7	7.7
CHANNEL ISLANDS	147,300[2]	+2.7	17,000	15,600	- 8	12.5	10.6	n/a[3]	n/a[3]	n/a[3]	n/a[3]	n/a[3]	n/a[3]	n/a[3]	n/a[3]	n/a[3]
Alderney & Sark	1,900[2]	0	600	500	–17	32.1	26.4	n/a	n/a	n/a	n/a	n/a	n/a	n/a	n/a	n/a
Guernsey	59,200[2]	+2.7	5,200	5,100	– 2	9.0	8.6	n/a	n/a	n/a	n/a	n/a	n/a	n/a	n/a	n/a
Jersey	86,200[2]	+2.7	11,200	10,000	–11	13.3	11.6	n/a	n/a	n/a	n/a	n/a	n/a	n/a	n/a	n/a
ISLE OF MAN	72,600[2]	+14.4	8,300	6,500	-22	12.9	9.0	n/a[3]	n/a[3]	n/a[3]	n/a[3]	n/a[3]	n/a[3]	n/a[3]	n/a[3]	n/a[3]

	Population		Churchgoers			% population		Percentage in each religion, 2001								
	2001	91–01 %	1982	1995	82–95 %	1982	1995	Xian %	Buddhist %	Hindu %	Jew %	Muslim %	Sikh %	Other %	None %	n/a %
WALES	2,903,085	+0.9	400,300	253,065	-37	14.6	8.7	71.9	0.7	0.2	0.1	0.1	0.2	0.2	18.5	8.1
(CLWYD) & GWYNEDD	663,403	+2.4	105,300	61,162	-42	17.3	9.3	77.6	0.1	0.1	0.1	0.2	0	0.2	14.2	7.5
Conwy	109,596	+1.5	n/a	n/a	n/a	n/a	n/a	77.7	0.2	0.1	0.1	0.3	0	0.2	14.0	7.4
Denbighshire	93,065	+4.1	n/a	n/a	n/a	n/a	n/a	77.8	0.2	0.1	0.1	0.3	0	0.2	13.4	7.9
Flintshire	148,594	+4.6	n/a	n/a	n/a	n/a	n/a	79.2	0.1	0.1	0.1	0.1	0	0.1	12.9	7.4
Gwynedd	116,843	+1.6	n/a	n/a	n/a	n/a	n/a	74.5	0.2	0.1	0.1	0.3	0	0.3	16.5	8.0
Isle of Anglesey	66,829	–3.3	n/a	n/a	n/a	n/a	n/a	79.4	0.1	0	0	0.1	0	0.3	13.6	6.5
Wrexham	128,476	+3.5	n/a	n/a	n/a	n/a	n/a	77.3	0.1	0.1	0.1	0.3	0	0.1	14.5	7.5
(DYFED)	361,914	+4.0	60,300	42,413	-30	18.7	12.0	74.1	0.2	0.1	0.1	0.2	0	0.4	17.0	7.9
Ceredigion	74,941	+13.7	n/a	n/a	n/a	n/a	n/a	70.8	0.4	0.1	0.1	0.3	0	0.6	19.7	8.0
Carmarthenshire	172,842	+1.8	n/a	n/a	n/a	n/a	n/a	74.6	0.2	0.1	0	0.2	0	0.3	16.5	8.1
Pembrokeshire	114,131	+1.5	n/a	n/a	n/a	n/a	n/a	75.6	0.2	0.1	0.1	0.1	0	0.3	16.0	7.6
(GWENT)	552,428	+0.5	52,900	35,629	-33	12.1	7.9	69.3	0.1	0.1	0.1	0.7	0.1	0.2	20.7	8.7
Blaenau Gwent UA	70,064	–3.6	n/a	n/a	n/a	n/a	n/a	64.2	0.1	0.1	0	0.2	0.1	0.2	25.1	10.0
Caerphilly UA	169,519	–0.6	n/a	n/a	n/a	n/a	n/a	65.8	0.1	0.1	0	0.1	0.1	0.2	24.2	9.4
Monmouthshire UA	84,885	+5.8	n/a	n/a	n/a	n/a	n/a	74.7	0.2	0.2	0	0.1	0.1	0.2	16.7	7.8
Newport UA	137,011	+1.1	n/a	n/a	n/a	n/a	n/a	71.9	0.2	0.2	0.1	2.5	0.1	0.2	16.7	8.1
Torfaen UA	90,949	0	n/a	n/a	n/a	n/a	n/a	70.8	0.1	0.1	0	0.2	0.1	0.2	20.4	8.1
(MID-GLAMORGAN)	416,572	-3.1	55,000	34,512	-37	10.3	6.3	67.2	0.1	0.2	0	0.2	0.1	0.2	23.5	8.5
Bridgend UA	128,645	–0.6	n/a	n/a	n/a	n/a	n/a	70.2	0.2	0.2	0	0.2	0	0.3	21.3	7.6
Merthyr Tydfil UA	55,981	–6.1	n/a	n/a	n/a	n/a	n/a	69.8	0.1	0.2	0	0.3	0	0.2	21.0	8.4
Rhondda Cynon Taff UA	231,946	–1.3	n/a	n/a	n/a	n/a	n/a	64.9	0.1	0.1	0	0.3	0.1	0.2	25.3	9.0
POWYS	126,354	+5.6	17,000	12,353	-27	15.7	10.3	74.8	0.3	0.2	0.1	0.1	0	0.3	16.5	7.7
(SOUTH GLAMORGAN)	424,645	+2.3	55,100	39,283	-29	14.6	9.5	68.6	0.3	0.6	0.3	2.8	0.2	0.2	18.8	8.2
Cardiff UA	305,353	+2.8	n/a	n/a	n/a	n/a	n/a	66.9	0.3	0.8	0.3	3.7	0.3	0.3	18.8	8.6
Vale of Glamorgan UA	119,292	+1.0	n/a	n/a	n/a	n/a	n/a	73.0	0.2	0.2	0.1	0.4	0.1	0.2	18.6	7.2
(WEST GLAMORGAN)	357,769	-2.9	54,700	27,713	-49	15.1	7.5	71.4	0.2	0.1	0.1	0.7	0.1	0.2	19.5	7.7
Neath Port Talbot UA	134,468	–3.2	n/a	n/a	n/a	n/a	n/a	72.1	0.1	0.1	0	0.3	0.1	0.2	19.0	8.1
Swansea UA	223,301	–2.8	n/a	n/a	n/a	n/a	n/a	71.0	0.2	0.1	0.1	1.0	0.1	0.2	19.8	7.5

[1]Formerly Local Authority District of Thamesdown
[2]1998 figure; rate of change estimated
[3]Religion question not included in their Census
[4]The 1991 population comparisons take no account of any retrospective adjustments that may be introduced.
Xian: Christian; Other: Other Religions; None: No Religion; n/a: not answered.

4.10 Population in UK by Religion: Scotland

	Population		Churchgoers			% population		Percentage in each religion, 2001										
	2001	91–01 %[2]	1994	2002	94–02 %	1994	2002	CofS %	RC %	OXian %	Buddhist %	Hindu %	Jew %	Muslim %	Sikh %	Other %	None %	n/a %
SCOTLAND	5,062,011	-0.8	691,120	570,130	-18	13.5	11.2	42.4	15.9	6.8	0.1	0.1	0.1	0.9	0.1	0.5	27.6	5.5
Aberdeen City	212,125	–4.4	19,260	16,180	–16	8.8	7.7	37.3	5.6	7.5	0.3	0.2	0.1	0.8	0.1	0.9	42.4	4.8
Aberdeenshire	226,871	+0.7	26,710	21,690	–19	11.8	9.6	48.2	3.7	9.6	0.1	0	0	0.1	0	0.4	33.5	4.4
Angus	108,400	+4.4	9,830	7,390	–25	8.8	6.8	53.9	5.9	6.9	0.1	0	0	0.2	0	0.4	28.0	4.6
Argyll & Bute	91,306	–0.5	13,210[1]	11,010[1]	–17	15.2	12.7	48.2	11.4	10.1	0.2	0	0.1	0.1	0	0.5	23.4	6.0
Clackmannanshire	48,077	+2.4	6,090[1]	5,080[1]	–17	12.9	10.6	44.8	9.5	6.0	0	0	0	0.4	0	0.5	33.1	5.7
Dumfries & Galloway	147,765	–0.1	16,570	12,800	–23	11.2	8.7	55.1	6.6	8.4	0.2	0	0	0.1	0	0.4	24.7	4.5
Dundee City	145,663	–1.9	17,750	14,030	–21	12.1	9.7	34.9	20.2	6.7	0.2	0.3	0	2.0	0.1	0.7	29.1	5.8
East Ayrshire	120,235	–2.8	16,190[1]	13,840[1]	–15	13.2	11.5	53.4	10.4	4.5	0.1	0	0	0.2	0	0.3	25.8	5.3
East Dunbartonshire	108,243	–5.3	18,830	14,260	–24	16.7	13.2	43.1	22.5	5.6	0.1	0.5	0.1	0.7	0.8	0.3	22.0	4.3
East Lothian	90,088	+4.4	8,650[1]	7,200[1]	–17	9.9	8.0	47.9	9.5	6.9	0.1	0	0.1	0.2	0	0.5	30.0	4.8
East Renfrewshire	89,311	–4.5	17,250[1]	13,920[1]	–19	18.6	15.6	41.5	20.7	5.3	0.1	0.2	3.5	2.1	0.5	0.4	21.0	4.7
Edinburgh, City of	448,624	+2.4	50,430	40,670	–19	11.4	9.0	35.3	10.8	8.6	0.3	0.3	0.2	1.5	0.2	1.3	36.5	5.0
Eilean Siar	26,502	–0.5	16,510	16,120	– 2	40.0	39.2	42.3	13.0	28.1	0.1	0	0	0.2	0	0.6	11.4	4.3
Falkirk	145,191	+3.3	17,790	14,100	–21	12.5	9.7	48.2	12.1	4.9	0.1	0	0	0.6	0	0.4	28.8	4.9
Fife	349,429	0	33,660	28,040	–17	9.6	8.0	42.9	8.5	7.2	0.1	0.1	0	0.4	0.1	0.5	35.4	4.8
Glasgow City	577,869	–6.4	98,960	82,750	–19	16.1	14.2	31.5	29.2	4.1	0.2	0.2	0.2	3.1	0.4	0.7	22.7	7.7
Highland	208,914	–0.5	30,220[1]	25,190[1]	–17	15.2	12.7	48.2	6.8	12.0	0.1	0	0	0.2	0	0.6	27.2	4.9
Inverclyde	84,203	–13.6	18,640	14,340	–23	19.8	17.1	38.2	35.8	5.3	0.1	0.1	0	0.2	0.1	0.3	13.4	6.5
Midlothian	80,941	+4.4	7,770[1]	6,470[1]	–17	9.9	8.0	44.7	10.2	5.3	0	0.1	0	0.3	0	0.4	33.5	5.5
Moray	86,940	+4.1	11,170	9,170	–18	13.2	10.5	44.3	6.1	13.3	0.1	0	0.1	0.2	0	0.6	30.6	4.7
North Ayrshire	135,817	–2.8	18,290[1]	15,640[1]	–15	13.2	11.5	49.5	15.0	5.2	0.1	0	0	0.1	0.1	0.3	23.5	6.2
North Lanarkshire	321,067	–3.1	60,400	52,360	–13	18.3	16.3	37.5	34.5	4.1	0.1	0.1	0	0.6	0.1	0.2	16.7	6.1
Orkney Islands	19,245	–3.8	2,920	2,480	–15	14.8	12.9	52.7	2.4	9.0	0.1	0.1	0.1	0	0	0.6	30.8	4.2
Perth & Kinross	134,949	–2.0	15,970	13,520	–15	11.7	10.0	49.7	7.7	8.8	0.1	0.1	0	0.2	0	0.5	28.2	4.7
Renfrewshire	172,867	–4.5	33,390[1]	26,940[1]	–19	18.6	15.6	41.5	23.2	4.7	0.1	0.1	0	0.4	0.2	0.3	23.8	5.7
Scottish Borders	106,764	+2.8	12,090	9,730	–20	11.5	9.0	51.1	5.5	9.8	0.2	0	0	0.1	0	0.5	28.5	4.3
Shetland Islands	21,988	–5.6	3,130	2,890	– 8	13.7	13.3	37.6	2.7	13.5	0.2	0	0	0.3	0	0.9	39.5	5.3
South Ayrshire	112,097	–2.8	15,100[1]	12,910[1]	–15	13.2	11.5	54.4	9.7	6.3	0.1	0.1	0.1	0.1	0.1	0.4	23.4	5.3
South Lanarkshire	302,216	–2.8	37,480	28,870	–23	12.1	9.5	43.7	22.1	4.6	0.1	0.1	0.1	0.4	0	0.3	22.5	6.1
Stirling	86,212	+2.4	10,930[1]	9,100[1]	–17	12.9	10.6	45.0	12.8	7.8	0.2	0.1	0.1	0.4	0.1	0.8	27.9	4.8
West Dunbartonshire	93,378	–1.8	12,300	10,470	–15	13.1	11.3	35.7	33.4	4.3	0.1	0	0	0.2	0.1	0.2	19.4	6.6
West Lothian	158,714	+4.4	13,630	10,970	–20	9.3	6.8	41.8	15.5	5.3	0.1	0.1	0	0.6	0	0.4	31.3	4.9

[1]Estimated by splitting combined areas pro rata to population in 2001
[2]Extrapolated from change 1994 to 2002
CofS = Church of Scotland; RC = Roman Catholic; OX = Other Christian Denominations; Other = Another religion; None = No Religion; n/a = Not answered.

Figure 4.10
Religious affiliation in Scotland, 2001[4]

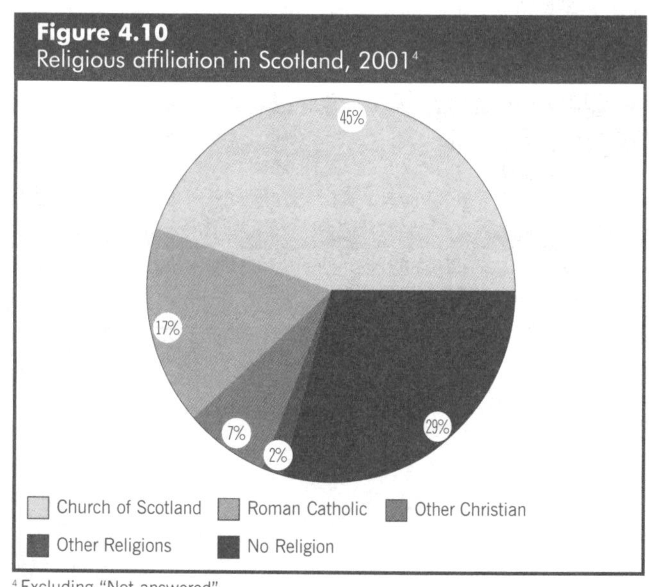

[4] Excluding "Not answered".

Table 4.10.2
Council with highest percentage

Group	Council	Percentage
Church of Scotland	Dumfries and Galloway	55.1
Roman Catholic	Inverclyde	35.8
Other Christian	Eilean Siar	28.1
Buddhist	Aberdeen City City of Edinburgh	0.3
Hindu	East Dunbartonshire	0.5
Jew	East Renfrewshire	3.5
Muslim	Glasgow City	3.1
Sikh	East Dunbartonshire	0.8
Other religions	City of Edinburgh	1.3
No religion	Aberdeen City	42.4
Not answered	Glasgow City	7.7

Population in UK by Religion: Northern Ireland

	Population		Percentage in each religion, 1991						Percentage in each religion, 2001						
	2001	91–01 %	RC %	Pres %	CofI %	Meth %	OXian %	None %	RC %	Pres %	CofI %	Meth %	OXian %	Other R %	No R %
NORTHERN IRELAND	1,685,267	+6.8	41	23	19	4	9	4	40	21	15	4	6	0	14
Antrim	48,366	+8.6	35	34	16	2	8	5	35	28	12	2	6	0	17
Ards	73,244	+13.1	12	43	21	6	11	7	10	38	17	5	9	0	21
Armagh	54,263	+4.7	48	18	22	3	7	2	46	17	20	2	6	0	9
Ballymena	58,610	+3.5	20	49	13	3	12	3	19	45	12	2	9	0	13
Ballymoney	26,894	+11.1	32	41	14	1	10	2	30	38	12	1	8	0	11
Banbridge	41,392	+23.6	30	31	21	2	13	3	29	30	18	2	9	0	12
Belfast	277,391	–0.7	42	19	20	6	7	6	42	16	14	5	5	1	17
Carrickfergus	37,659	+15.0	8	34	26	10	14	8	7	30	21	9	10	0	23
Castlereagh	66,488	+9.4	10	31	26	10	16	7	16	27	20	8	10	0	19
Coleraine	56,315	+11.7	24	34	27	2	9	4	24	30	23	2	6	0	15
Cookstown	32,581	+4.8	56	16	18	1	8	1	55	15	16	1	6	0	7
Craigavon	80,671	+7.6	43	11	27	6	10	3	42	11	23	5	8	0	11
Derry	105,066	+10.2	74	12	9	1	2	2	71	10	8	1	2	0	8
Down	63,828	+10.0	61	17	12	1	6	3	57	14	9	1	5	0	14
Dungannon	47,735	+5.1	59	14	19	2	5	1	57	12	17	2	4	0	8
Fermanagh	57,527	+6.5	58	3	28	5	5	1	55	3	25	5	4	0	8
Larne	30,832	+4.8	24	41	15	4	11	5	22	38	13	4	7	0	16
Limavady	32,422	+9.7	56	21	17	1	3	2	53	19	12	1	4	0	11
Lisburn	108,594	+9.3	29	23	29	4	10	5	30	21	21	4	8	0	16
Magherafelt	39,780	+9.6	62	16	13	0	8	1	62	14	11	1	6	0	6
Moyle	15,933	+7.7	56	20	19	0	3	2	57	17	15	0	2	0	9
Newry & Mourne	87,058	+5.0	77	12	5	0	5	1	76	10	4	0	2	0	8
Newtownabbey	79,995	+8.1	14	35	22	10	12	7	17	31	17	8	9	0	18
North Down	76,323	+6.3	10	36	25	8	12	9	10	31	19	6	9	0	25
Omagh	47,952	+4.7	68	12	13	2	4	1	65	11	11	1	3	0	9
Strabane	38,248	+5.8	64	18	12	1	4	1	63	17	11	1	2	0	6

RC = Catholic or Roman Catholic; Pres = Presbyterian Church of Ireland; CofI = Church of Ireland (Anglican); Meth = Methodist Church in Ireland; OXian = Other Christian Denominations; Other R = Other religions and philosophies (average across all N Ireland 0.3%); None (in 1991) = No Religion (those who did not answer the question have been excluded); No R (in 2001) = No Religion or Religion not stated.

4

Figure 4.11.1
Religious affiliation in Northern Ireland, 2001

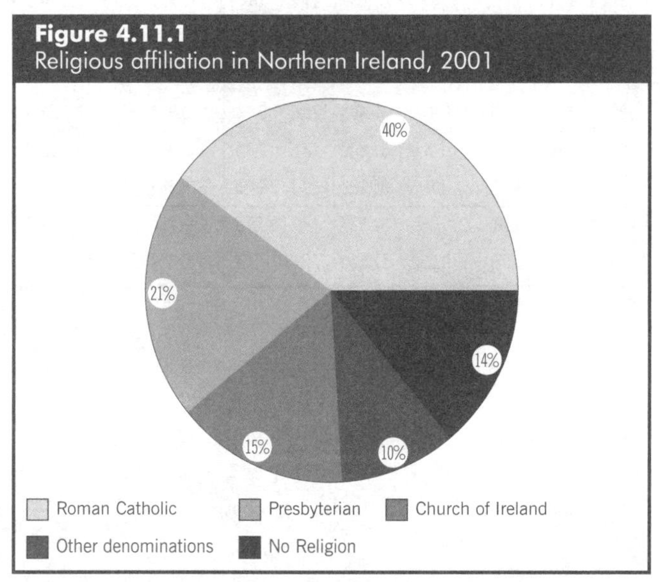

Figure 4.11.2
Change in numbers by denomination, 1991–2001

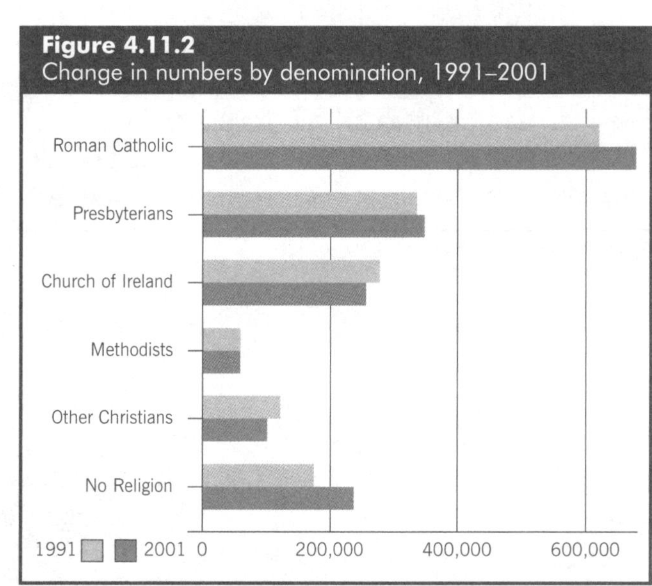

4.12 Church of Scotland and Catholic baptisms

Table 4.12
Presbyterian and Roman Catholic Baptisms, Scotland, 1929–2001

Year	CofS Baptisms Adult	CofS Baptisms Infant	Catholic Baptisms Infant	Births in Scotland	Infant baptisms as % of births CofS	Infant baptisms as % of births Cath	Church of Scotland Members	Population of Scotland	Mbrs as % pop.
1929	n/a	38,242	n/a	92,880	*41.2*	*n/a*	1,272,296	4,832,226	*26.3*
1930	1,248	37,109	18,057	94,549	*39.2*	*19.1*	1,271,095	4,828,004	*26.3*
1931	1,615	37,162	17,996	92,220	*40.3*	*19.5*	1,280,620	4,842,980	*26.4*
1932	1,610	36,084	17,847	91,000	*39.7*	*19.6*	1,287,438	4,883,069	*26.4*
1933	1,534	34,012	17,487	86,546	*39.3*	*20.2*	1,289,145	4,912,379	*26.2*
1934	1,684	34,533	17,427	88,836	*38.9*	*19.6*	1,290,271	4,934,291	*26.1*
1935	1,716	34,367	17,692	87,928	*39.1*	*20.1*	1,288,648	4,952,510	*26.0*
1936	1,732	34,499	17,461	88,928	*38.8*	*19.6*	1,288,571	4,966,302	*25.9*
1937	1,873	33,797	17,761	87,810	*38.5*	*20.2*	1,284,450	4,976,610	*25.8*
1938	1,941	34,674	17,516	88,627	*39.1*	*19.8*	1,286,509	4,993,126	*25.8*
1939	1,789	33,889	17,053	86,913	*39.0*	*19.6*	1,285,011	5,006,687	*25.7*
1940	1,655	33,350	15,342	86,392	*38.6*	*17.8*	1,278,297	4,841,241	*26.4*
1941	1,344	33,283	16,789	89,748	*37.1*	*18.7*	1,268,839	4,819,396	*26.3*
1942	1,281	34,265	17,241	90,703	*37.8*	*19.0*	1,261,890	4,750,995	*26.6*
1943	1,458	37,594	18,269	94,669	*39.7*	*19.3*	1,262,678	4,661,587	*27.1*
1944	1,718	39,522	17,826	95,920	*41.2*	*18.6*	1,264,125	4,653,645	*27.2*
1945	1,985	35,858	16,623	86,924	*41.3*	*19.1*	1,259,927	4,673,931	*27.0*
1946	2,610	41,001	18,527[2]	104,413	*39.3*	*17.7*	1,261,646	4,900,761	*25.7*
1947	2,697	48,406	20,911	113,147	*42.8*	*18.5*	1,256,167	5,072,254	*24.8*
1948	3,350	42,961	19,885	100,344	*42.8*	*19.8*	1,263,423	5,084,894	*24.8*
1949	3,874	40,914	20,391	95,674	*42.8*	*21.3*	1,268,315	5,098,922	*24.9*
1950	4,120	39,146	19,948	92,530	*42.3*	*21.6*	1,271,247	5,114,513	*24.9*
1951	4,574	38,756	19,809	90,639	*42.8*	*21.9*	1,273,027	5,102,458	*24.9*
1952	5,003	38,704	20,390	90,422	*42.8*	*22.5*	1,278,468	5,100,847	*25.1*
1953	5,212	39,792	20,678	90,913	*43.8*	*22.7*	1,283,305	5,099,809	*25.2*
1954	6,416	41,463	20,376	92,315	*44.9*	*22.1*	1,292,127	5,103,632	*25.3*
1955	7,490	42,636	22,215	92,539	*46.1*	*24.0*	1,307,573	5,111,338	*25.6*
1956	6,904	44,281	23,464	95,313	*46.5*	*24.6*	1,319,574	5,119,937	*25.8*
1957	5,803	43,804	24,552	97,977	*44.7*	*25.1*	1,315,630	5,124,688	*25.7*
1958	5,485	44,029	24,163	99,481	*44.3*	*24.3*	1,315,466	5,141,155	*25.6*
1959	5,640	45,743	23,929	99,251	*46.1*	*24.1*	1,306,661	5,162,622	*25.3*
1960	5,326	45,305	24,567	101,292	*44.7*	*24.3*	1,301,280	5,177,658	*25.1*
1961	5,118	45,269	25,825	101,169	*44.7*	*25.5*	1,292,617	5,183,836	*24.9*
1962	4,852	46,915	26,015	104,334	*45.0*	*24.9*	1,281,559	5,197,528	*24.7*
1963	4,404	43,806	25,230	102,691	*42.7*	*24.6*	1,268,887	5,205,100	*24.4*
1964	4,201	43,759	25,871	104,335	*41.9*	*24.8*	1,259,162	5,208,500	*24.2*

[1]Estimate [2]Adjusted figure (5,000 added)

Table 4.12 (continued)
Presbyterian and Roman Catholic Baptisms, Scotland, 1929–2001

Year	CofS Baptisms Adult	CofS Baptisms Infant	Catholic Baptisms Infant	Births in Scotland	Infant baptisms as % of births CofS	Infant baptisms as % of births Cath	Church of Scotland Members	Population of Scotland	Mbrs as % pop.
1965	4,024	40,950	24,311	100,660	*40.7*	*24.2*	1,247,972	5,209,900	*24.0*
1966	3,667	39,461	22,806	96,536	*40.9*	*23.6*	1,233,808	5,200,600	*23.7*
1967	3,456	39,264	23,769	96,211	*40.8*	*24.7*	1,220,023	5,198,300	*23.5*
1968	2,923	36,776	22,492	94,786	*38.8*	*23.7*	1,201,833	5,200,200	*23.1*
1969	2,580	35,097	21,277	90,290	*38.9*	*23.6*	1,178,334	5,208,500	*22.6*
1970	2,109	33,262	20,633	87,335	*38.1*	*23.6*	1,154,211	5,213,700	*22.1*
1971	2,026	32,054	19,002	86,738	*37.0*	*21.9*	1,133,515	5,235,600	*21.7*
1972	1,736	29,724	17,398	78,550	*37.8*	*22.1*	1,110,187	5,230,600	*21.2*
1973	1,599	27,721	16,159	74,392	*37.3*	*21.7*	1,088,873	5,233,900	*20.8*
1974	1,461	24,346	14,936	70,093	*34.7*	*21.3*	1,061,706	5,240,800	*20.3*
1975	1,542	23,435	14,467	67,943	*34.5*	*21.3*	1,041,772	5,232,400	*19.9*
1976	1,411	22,555	14,005	64,895	*34.8*	*21.6*	1,020,403	5,233,400	*19.5*
1977	1,626	21,525	13,030	62,342	*34.5*	*20.9*	1,002,945	5,226,200	*19.2*
1978	1,594	21,582	13,587	64,295	*33.6*	*21.1*	987,196	5,212,300	*18.9*
1979	1,650	22,373	14,204	68,366	*32.7*	*20.8*	970,741	5,203,600	*18.7*
1980	1,704	21,144	14,334	68,892	*30.7*	*20.8*	953,933	5,193,900	*18.4*
1981	1,773	21,566	14,612	69,054	*31.2*	*21.2*	938,930	5,180,200	*18.1*
1982	1,114	19,987	13,669	66,196	*30.2*	*20.6*	918,991	5,166,800	*17.8*
1983	1,769	19,507	13,536	65,078	*30.0*	*20.8*	902,714	5,152,600	*17.5*
1984	1,649	18,741	13,042	65,106	*28.8*	*20.0*	887,165	5,145,800	*17.2*
1985	1,582	18,736	13,238	66,676	*28.1*	*19.9*	870,527	5,136,900	*16.9*
1986	1,646	18,184	13,298	65,812	*27.6*	*20.2*	854,311	5,123,000	*16.7*
1987	1,547	17,247	12,891	66,241	*26.0*	*19.5*	838,659	5,112,600	*16.4*
1988	1,424	17,075	12,879	66,212	*25.8*	*19.5*	822,985	5,093,400	*16.2*
1989	1,454	16,588	12,282	63,480	*26.1*	*19.3*	804,468	5,096,600	*15.8*
1990	1,212	15,952	12,632	65,973	*24.2*	*19.1*	786,787	5,102,200	*15.4*
1991	1,200	15,541	12,309	67,024	*23.2*	*18.4*	770,217	5,107,100	*15.1*
1992	1,115	14,937	12,099	65,789	*22.7*	*18.4*	752,719	5,105,700[1]	*14.7*
1993	901	13,806	11,570	63,337	*21.8*	*18.3*	732,963	5,104,400[1]	*14.4*
1994	871	13,451	11,284	61,656	*21.8*	*18.3*	715,571	5,103,040	*14.0*
1995	747	12,737	11,214	60,051	*21.2*	*18.7*	698,552	5,095,500[1]	*13.7*
1996	753	11,971	10,718	59,300	*20.2*	*18.1*	680,082	5,088,000[1]	*13.4*
1997	610[1]	11,340[1]	10,344	59,400	*19.1*	*17.4*	660,954	5,080,600[1]	*13.0*
1998	520[1]	10,660[1]	10,000[1]	57,300	*18.6*	*17.5*	648,930	5,073,100[1]	*12.8*
1999	430[1]	9,980[1]	9,700[1]	55,100	*18.1*	*17.6*	626,665	5,065,600[1]	*12.4*
2000	340[1]	9,300[1]	9,360	52,687	*17.7*	*17.8*	607,714	5,058,200	*12.0*
2001	250[1]	8,620[1]	9,050[1]	52,500	*16.4*	*17.2*	590,824	5,064,200	*11.7*

5

Religious features in UK Society

5

Sources: Government statistics, specialist studies, daily newspapers, *Twentieth Century British Social Trends, Contemporary British Society, Lifestyle Pocket Book* and like resource volumes

5.2 The Salvation Army Church Growth Study

Figure 5.2.1
Average church income in England, 1990–2000

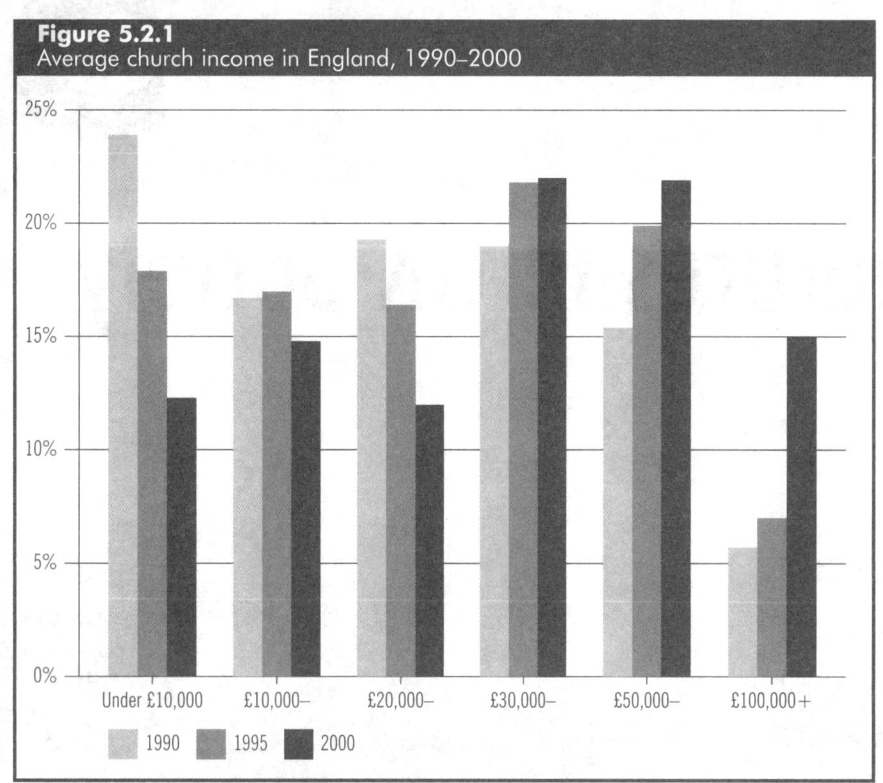

The source for the information on **Pages 5.2** and **5.3** are the same; the survey is described in detail on **Page 5.3**. As well as information about church growth, this study also yielded other information not readily available before, and this page gives some of that material.

Figure 5.2.1 shows the range of income received by churches in 1900, 1995 and 2000. In the first five years the income increased at the rate of inflation, from an average of £36,300 to £41,100, but in the second five years it increased at double the rate of inflation, from £41,000 to £57,000. The large jump in the second half of the 1990s in the most wealthy churches corresponds to the finding that larger churches tend to be the growing churches.

Figures 5.2.2 and **5.2.3** relate to the distance people have to travel to church, and how they might get there if going by bus. The average distance travelled, 1.5 miles, did not vary by whether a church was growing or declining. Nor did it vary by whether the church was well or poorly served by bus routes. "Have wheels, will travel" overrides distance and public transport; if people want to go to a certain church, they will get there!

Figure 5.2.2
Distance people travel to church

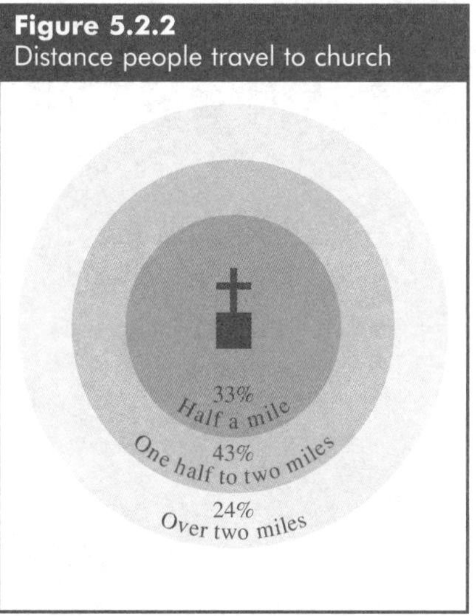

Figure 5.2.3
Churches served by bus routes

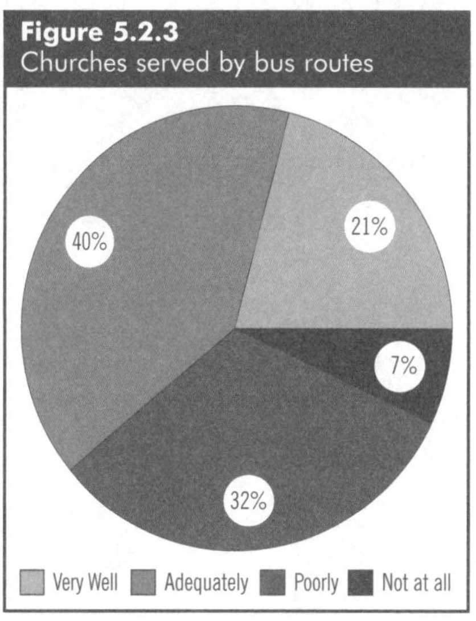

Table 5.2.1 Most important reasons for church growth

The warm *welcome* received	*81%*
The *ministry* of the church	*73%*
People *moving* into the area	*57%*
The relevance of the *teaching*	*55%*
Enjoyable *children's/youth programme*	*51%*
A personal liking for the *minister*	*47%*

Table 5.2.2
Age of minister, by denomination

Denomination	<30 %	35–39 %	40–44 %	45–49 %	50–54 %	55–59 %	60–64 %	65–69 %	70+ %	Average	Base
Catholic	*0*	*6*	*7*	*13*	*13*	*13*	*13*	*15*	*20*	**58**	46
Independent	*1*	*11*	*12*	*10*	*8*	*11*	*26*	*9*	*13*	**56**	92
United Reformed	*0*	*8*	*3*	*14*	*15*	*19*	*25*	*7*	*9*	**56**	59
Smaller denoms.	*0*	*9*	*7*	*14*	*24*	*13*	*23*	*5*	*5*	**54**	59
Pentecostal	*4*	*4*	*8*	*21*	*19*	*18*	*16*	*6*	*4*	**53**	51
Anglican	*1*	*7*	*12*	*18*	*18*	*18*	*19*	*5*	*2*	**52**	441
Methodist	*2*	*8*	*11*	*15*	*24*	*18*	*16*	*3*	*3*	**52**	152
Baptist	*1*	*12*	*16*	*19*	*16*	*13*	*14*	*4*	*5*	**51**	140
New Churches	*7*	*11*	*13*	*14*	*21*	*29*	*5*	*0*	*0*	**48**	62
Overall	***1***	***8***	***11***	***16***	***18***	***17***	***18***	***6***	***5***	**53**	**1,102**

Table 5.2.3
Number of years ministering in present church

Denomination	<5 %	5–7 %	8–10 %	11–14 %	15–19 %	20+ %	Avge
Independent	*12*	*8*	*12*	*18*	*14*	*36*	**15**
New Churches	*11*	*13*	*18*	*13*	*25*	*20*	**13**
Pentecostal	*12*	*20*	*14*	*24*	*10*	*20*	**12**
Catholic	*35*	*11*	*13*	*17*	*7*	*17*	**10**
Baptist	*22*	*16*	*24*	*18*	*10*	*10*	**10**
Smaller denoms.	*37*	*25*	*6*	*8*	*8*	*16*	**9**
Anglican	*32*	*24*	*16*	*13*	*7*	*8*	**8**
United Reformed	*31*	*22*	*23*	*14*	*3*	*7*	**8**
Methodist	*47*	*26*	*14*	*3*	*1*	*9*	7
Overall	***30***	***20***	***17***	***13***	***8***	***12***	10

Nearly 4,000 churches were approached in 2002 in a survey undertaken on behalf of The Salvation Army explicitly to ascertain what were the key reasons why churches grew. The importance of this study was that the churches to whom the forms were sent were already known to have grown or declined in the years between 1989 and 1998. Thus, 1,900 growing churches were approached and a matching sample of like number which had declined. In both groups churches were divided into two groups, fast and slow, that is, the growing group contained churches known to have grown quickly (60% or more over 9 years) and those who had grown, but not as fast.

A large number of factors were statistically evaluated, broken down by the growth or decline variable. Some factors (such as whether a minister had a team) were associated with growth or decline (in this case, the absence of a team went with decline) whereas the opposite was not necessarily true (so that the presence of a team was not necessarily associated with growth). **Table 5.3.1** lists the factors which proved to be significantly related to decline in order of importance, with the most important given first.

The detailed figures for four of these factors are given in **Table 5.3.2.** A fifth, on preaching base, is illustrated in **Figure 5.3.**

The survey was also important in ascertaining for the first time (as far as is known) the leadership gifting of the (senior) minister. One major factor emerged of key importance – there was only one factor associated significantly with growth. The leader must be a Shaper, the type of leader "driven by a vision – a vision of the role that the institution can play in a changing world – and by a desire to share this vision with others" (taken from *Strategic Church Leadership* by Prof Robin Gill and Derek Burke).

Table 5.3.1
Factors significantly related to decline

Churches were *more likely* to be Broad or Middle-of-the-Road
More likely not to have any ethnic minorities present
Churches are *less likely* to hold Alpha courses
Churches are *more likely* to have no other full-time staff
Churches *more likely* to follow Lectionary readings
The organ is *more likely* to be used for worship music
Visitors are *less likely* to receive something on their first visit
Churches are *less likely* to have a long term vision in place
Churches are *less likely* to consecutively expound the Scriptures
Fast declining churches *more likely* to have Task, Detail and Creative people as leaders
More likely to have above average amount of Council Housing in their area

Table 5.3.2
Importance of various factors in growth and decline

Factor		Overall %	Fast Growth %	Growth %	Decline %	Fast Decline %
Broad/Middle-of-the-Road	A	***44***	*37*	*36*	*45*	*61*
Evangelical/Charismatic	A	***44***	*49*	*53*	*46*	*25*
Anglo-Catholic/Catholic	A	***11***	*12*	*10*	*8*	*13*
Charismatic Catholic	A	***1***	*2*	*1*	*1*	*1*
Developing future plans for the church	B	***49***	*47*	*49*	*52*	*48*
Long term vision for the church already in place	B	***25***	*32*	*26*	*25*	*15*
Generally keep going as we are	B	***15***	*13*	*17*	*15*	*15*
Future is unclear; church has lost direction; likely this church will close	B	***11***	*8*	*8*	*8*	*22*
Church has held an Alpha course	C	***69***	*71*	*74*	*74*	*53*
0%	D	***44***	*38*	*38*	*48*	*61*
0.1% to 3%	D	***25***	*31*	*24*	*22*	*21*
4% to 20%	D	***22***	*22*	*27*	*20*	*14*
21% or over	D	***9***	*9*	*11*	*10*	*4*
Received something on first visit	E	***63***	*64*	*70*	*61*	*54*
Total (=100%)		**1,056**	**179**	**354**	**283**	**240**

A: Churchmanship B: Future direction of church C: Alpha D: Ethnic minority presence
E: Receive anything on first visit?
Source: Why do Churches grow? July 2002 research report by Christian Research for The Salvation Army Central North Division. Details from Major Chick Yuill, 80 Eccles New Road, Salford, M5 2RU; 0161 743 3900.

Figure 5.3
Preaching base

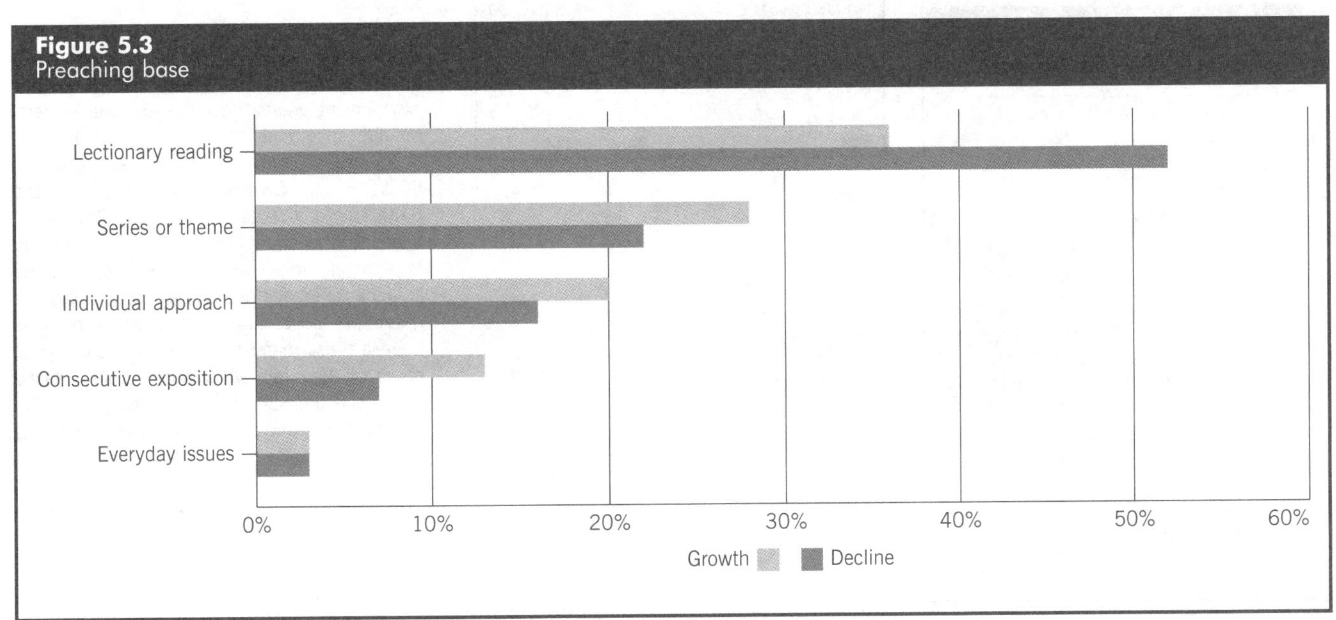

5.4

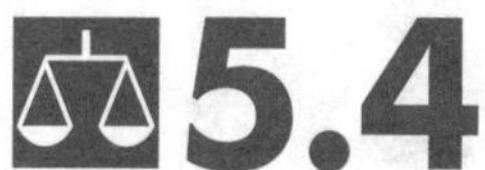

Figure 5.4.1 % Congregations which grew more than 10% 1994–2002

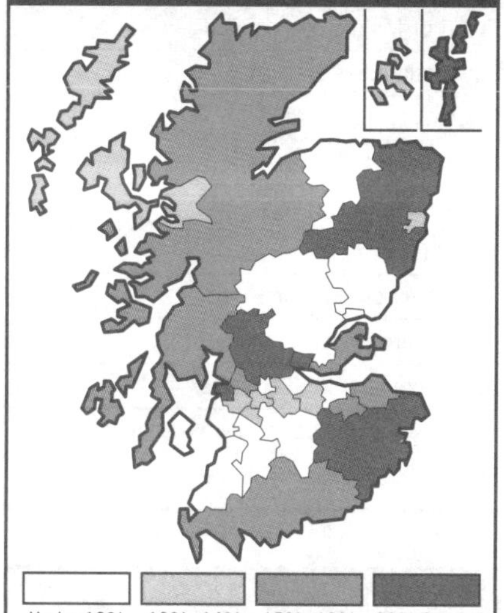

Figure 5.4.2 Growing, stable and declining churches in Scotland

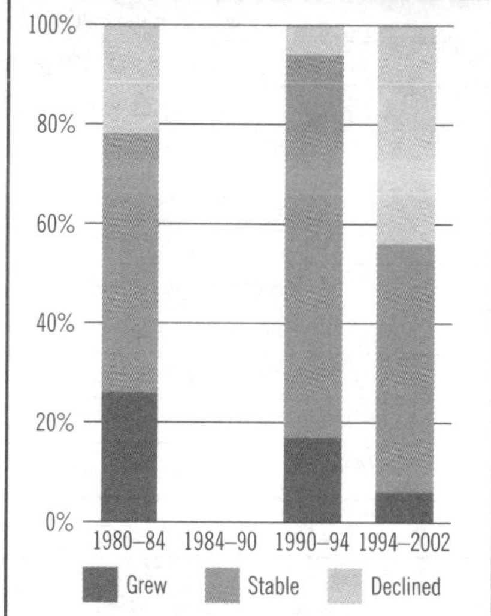

Figure 5.4.3 % Congregations which declined more than 40% 1994–2002

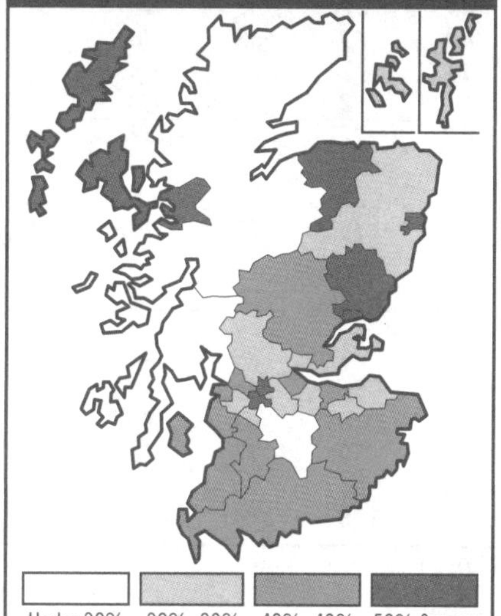

Figure 5.4.4 Average number of lay leaders per church, 2002

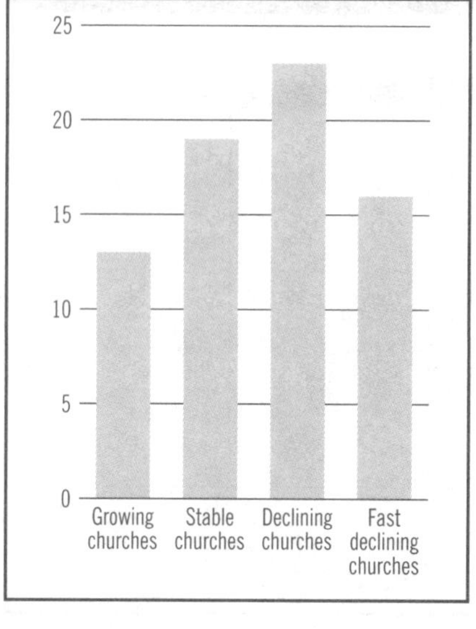

Table 5.4.1 Age distribution within growing and declining churches, 2002

Age-group	Growing churches (up 10% or more) %	Stable churches (up 9% to down 9%) %	Declining churches (down 10% to 39%) %	Declining churches (down 40% or more) %	Overall %
Under 12	*13*	*14*	*14*	*12*	***13***
12 – 14	*6*	*4*	*4*	*3*	***4***
15 – 19	*5*	*5*	*3*	*4*	***4***
20 – 29	*6*	*6*	*6*	*5*	***6***
30 – 44	*15*	*15*	*15*	*13*	***14***
45 – 64	*29*	*28*	*26*	*29*	***28***
65 & over	*26*	*28*	*32*	*34*	***31***
Base	**105**	**78**	**246**	**343**	**772**
Avge age	**45**	**46**	**48**	**49**	**47**

Table 5.4.2 Growth or decline by expectation of growth or decline

By 2010, we expect this church to have...	Growing churches (up 10% or more) %	Stable churches (up 9% to down 9%) %	Declining churches (down 10% to 39%) %	Declining churches (down 40% or more) %	Overall %
Grown a lot	*34*	*23*	*20*	*16*	***20***
Grown little	*24*	*42*	*41*	*34*	***37***
Stable	*30*	*22*	*25*	*19*	***22***
Declined	*12*	*13*	*12*	*28*	***19***
Closed	*0*	*0*	*2*	*3*	***2***
Base	**95**	**77**	**233**	**312**	**717**

Figure 5.4.2 shows the percentages of Scottish churches growing and declining since 1980. The proportions of churches which grew and declined were not calculated between 1984 and 1990. In this diagram a "growing" church is one which had grown 20% over a 4 year period (with a congregation of 50 or more) or 100% with a smaller congregation. A "declining" declined 20% over a 4 year period, or 100% if the present congregation was under 50 people. "Stable" congregations were those between these groups.

The number of stable churches has diminished, and the number of declining congregations has drastically increased, and the proportion of growing churches shrunk considerably. If it is true, as **Figure 5.4.2** might suggest, that the stable congregations of yesterday become the declining congregations of today, then with so many stable churches today the future for Scottish congregations is bleak. On the other hand, why can't the stable churches of yesterday become the growing congregations of today or tomorrow?

Table 5.4.1 shows that the younger the average age of a congregation the more likely it is to be growing, a result echoed in the 1998 English Church Attendance Survey. Older people move from being a quarter of the congregation, 26%, in growing churches, to a third, 34%, in the churches declining fastest.

Table 5.4.2 shows that churches which have been growing have the greatest expectation of continuing growth. This expectation, or vision or what the church might become, is in fact one of the most important features of a growing church, and is attested by other studies also. A third, 34%, of growing churches expect their church to have grown significantly by 2010. However, almost another third, 30%, expect their growing church to stabilise. A few expect it to decline, but none to close, whereas a third, 34%, of churches which have declined most expect that decline to continue or their church to close.

Growing churches have a smaller leadership team, as **Figure 5.4.4** indicates. Churches experiencing greater decline had fewer leaders, but almost certainly because they had great difficulty in finding enough leaders. As four-fifths, 80%, of all Scottish lay leaders in the Protestant churches are in the Church of Scotland, this strongly points to the desirability of reducing the number of Elders in these churches. Perhaps one of the reasons why the Church of Scotland has declined is because there are too many Elders. Appointed for life, many of these are older people, who maybe hold back their churches from progressing to new activities, and thereby limit the opportunity to grow.

Table 5.5.1 Proportion of Scottish churches which had held at least one Alpha or Emmaus Course by May 2002, by denomination

Course held	Church of Scotland	Roman Catholic	Independent	Smaller Denoms	Baptist	Other Presbyterian	Episcopal	Overall
Alpha	*29*	*8*	*31*	*32*	*58*	*11*	*16*	***27***
Emmaus	*1½*	*½*	*2*	*1*	*0*	*0*	*4*	***1⅓***

Table 5.5.2
Growth and decline by whether at least one Alpha or Emmaus Course held

Course held	Macro growth (+60% & over)	Micro growth (+10% to 59%)	Stable (+9% to 9%)	Micro decline (–10% to –24%)	Mini decline (–25% to –39%)	Medium decline (–40% to –59%)	Macro decline (–60% & over)	Overall
Alpha	*31*	*32*	*25*	*35*	*26*	*28*	*20*	***27***
Emmaus	*0*	*1⅔*	*0*	*0*	*4*	*1*	*1⅓*	***1⅓***

Table 5.5.3
Number of years over which courses have been held

Course held	Church of Scotland	Roman Catholic	Independent	Smaller Denoms	Baptist	Other Presbyterian	Episcopal	Overall
Alpha	*2.9*	*2.1*	*3.2*	*2.7*	*3.5*	*3.0*	*3.3*	***3.0***
Emmaus	*2*	*4*	*3*	*1*	*0*	*0*	*2*	***2.1***

Table 5.5.4
Average number attending per course

Course held	Church of Scotland	Roman Catholic	Independent	Smaller Denoms	Baptist	Other Presbyterian	Episcopal	Overall
Alpha	*13*	*10*	*14*	*11*	*11*	*9*	*12*	***11***
Emmaus	*9*	*10*	*5*	*5*	–	–	*6*	***8***

Figure 5.5.2
Whether a church has held an Alpha course by its 2001 expectations

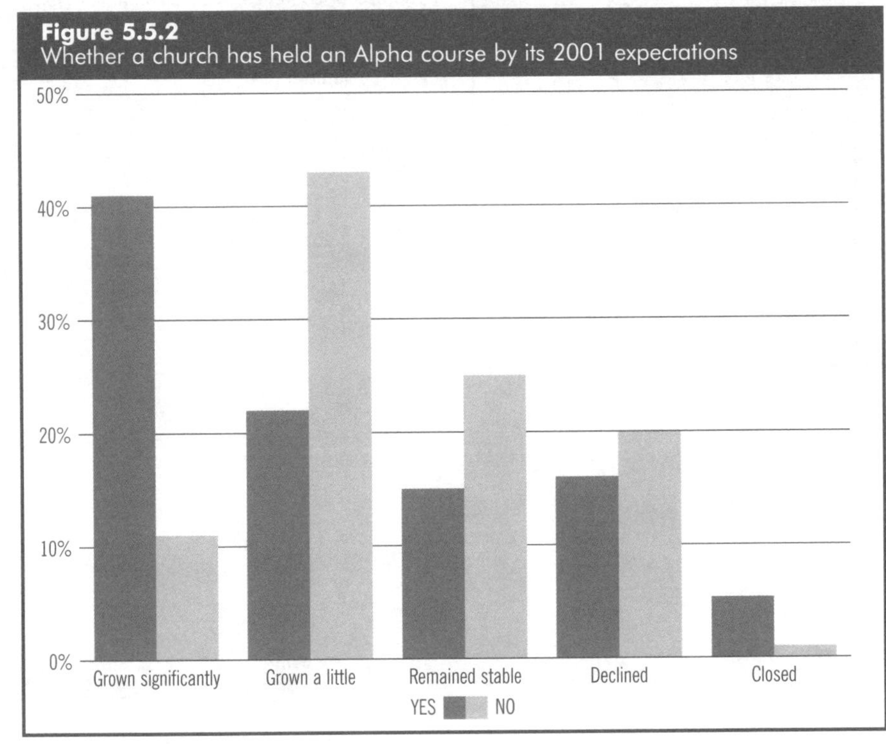

Figure 5.5.1

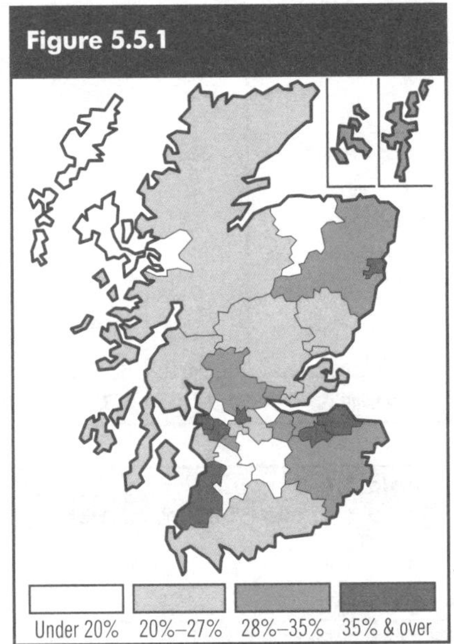

The information on this page about Alpha and Emmaus courses only reflects the data which emerged from the Scottish Church Census, which asked churches whether or not they had ever held one of these courses, and if so, how many, and total attendance. **Table 5.5.1** indicates the percentage of churches in each denomination which has held them, a total of about 1,100 who have used Alpha and just over 50 who have used Emmaus. It should be noted that the response rate to the Census was 52%; non-responding churches have been assumed to use these courses in the same proportions as responding churches.

Table 5.5.2 shows the percentage of churches which have used these courses according to their experience of growth or decline in the period 1994 to 2002.

It does not show any significant relationship between holding either of these courses and whether a church has seen growth or decline. In other words, growing churches are not more likely to hold these courses, nor are declining churches less likely to hold them. This is based on nearly one-fifth of Scottish churches. The numbers attending Alpha courses did not vary by whether a church was growing or declining.

Figure 5.5.2 indicates that churches with an expectation (or vision?) of significant growth by 2010 are more likely to have held an Alpha course.

Tables 5.5.3 and 4 show the number of courses held and average attendance at each by denomination.

5.6 Scottish Church Census 2002: Attendance by Churchmanship & Environment

Table 5.6.1 Proportions attending church on Sunday by denomination and churchmanship, 2002

	Broad %	Catholic %	Evangelical %	Liberal %	Low Church %	Reformed %	Base
Church of Scotland	22	1	24	11	8	34	228,500
Roman Catholic	2	88	2	7	1	0	202,110
Independent	2	0	89	5	1	3	45,010
Smaller denominations	9	1	66	14	7	3	28,640
Baptist	0	0	99	1	0	0	24,830
Other Presbyterian	1	0	78	0	1	20	22,170
Episcopal	15	19	22	31	7	6	18,870
All Scotland	**11**	**32**	**29**	**9**	**4**	**15**	**570,130**

Table 5.6.2 Proportions attending church on Sunday by denomination and environment, 2002

		City Centre	UPAs	Housing Scheme	Suburban	Town	New Town	Rural: Commuter dormitory	Rural: Other areas
Church of Scotland	%	4	4	6	20	31	2	15	18
Roman Catholic	%	8	7	20	12	30	6	8	9
Independent	%	7	3	9	16	43	4	8	10
Smaller denominations	%	12	8	9	10	39	7	6	9
Baptist	%	12	5	3	21	45	6	3	5
Other Presbyterian	%	7	1	5	10	26	2	7	42
Episcopal	%	18	1	2	19	29	3	9	19
All Scotland	**%**	**7**	**5**	**11**	**16**	**32**	**4**	**10**	**15**

Table 5.6.3
Proportions in each age-group by churchmanship, 2002

	Under 15 %	!5–19 %	20–29 %	30–44 %	45–64 %	65+ %	Base	Average Age
Broad	14	2	3	11	30	40	61,340	53
Catholic	20	6	9	18	26	21	183,900	41
Evangelical: Charismatic	23	8	13	21	24	11	28,560	36
Evangelical: Mainstream	17	5	8	14	27	29	80,580	46
Evangelical: Reformed	15	3	3	12	28	39	54,060	51
Liberal	15	2	4	11	29	39	52,760	52
Low Church	14	3	3	12	29	39	23,880	52
Reformed	15	2	4	10	29	40	85,050	52
All Scotland	**17**	**4**	**6**	**14**	**28**	**31**	**570,130**	**47**

Table 5.6.4 Average size of congregations by environment, 2002

Environment	*Average size*
City Centre	220
Urban Priority Area	130
Housing Scheme	170
Suburban	230
Town	165
New Town	200
Rural: Dormitory Area	125
Rural: Other Area	65
All Scotland	**140**

The percentages in **Tables 5.6.1** and **2** but put together in a convenient form the detail shown on **Pages 12.3, 30-36,** from where may be found both similar percentages for 1994 and a breakdown of the Evangelical percentage into its three main components. The base figures in **Table 5.6.2** are the same as in the first Table, but are omitted because this Table has more columns.

The shaded boxes in both Tables show where the particular strength of denominational allegiance or location lies, all the boxes shaded being well above the overall average for Scotland. The variations for environment are fewer than for churchmanship and tend to reflect where particular denominations are strong. For instance, the Free Church of Scotland (part of the Other Presbyterian group) is very strong in the Western Isles, Skye and Lochalsh which are part of the remoter rural areas of Scotland. The Scottish Episcopal Church has several Cathedrals, all located in the city centre.

The percentages in **Table 5.6.3** are not available elsewhere in this volume. It is readily seen that the age of charismatic churchgoers is quite different from those in other groups. They have by far the youngest profile, and by far the youngest average age. The Catholics, the next youngest group, are the only other churchmanship where the percentage attending 65 and over is less than the percentage of those who are 45 to 64.

The age of churchgoers by environment varies very little; it is the average size of congregations which is the main variant, and these figures are given in **Table 5.6.4.**

The Mind of Anglicans Survey, 2002

In 2002 a comprehensive survey of 4,000 Anglican clergy (46% of whom replied) and 2,500 laity (76% of whom replied) was undertaken by Cost of Conscience, a group linked with Forward in Faith, which campaigns against the possibility of women becoming bishops. The survey covered more aspects than just this issue however, and some of the key results are reflected in the Tables on this page.

The statements in **Table 5.7.1** are listed in the order of the size of difference between clergy and laity (taking "Strongly Agree" and "Agree" together, put in bold for convenience of identification). It may thus be seen that it is the statement of divorced people being ordained as priests which generates the greatest difference (clergy 76%, laity 59%), but there are similar size differences for the other three statements (respectively 52% and 39%, 67% and 55%, and 31% and 19%).

These percentages are very close to another survey, run by the *Church Times* in 2001 and reported in their 15th February 2002 issue, which, for the same questions, and in clergy/laity order, were, respectively, 68%/54%; 52%/43%; 62%/50%; and 30%/21%, each pair of percentages being the total of "Strongly Agree" and "Agree".

Table 5.7.2 is constructed in the same way, and shows that twice as many male clergy as female strongly believe that abortion should not be carried out. Gender differences are much less when it comes to some sexual issues and euthanasia.

Table 5.7.3 is also constructed similarly to the other Tables using the total of the "Strongly agree" and "Agree" columns. The laity feel more strongly than the clergy that bishops should have parochial experience, should be faithful to biblical teaching and that the bishop should respond to social issues. There were a number of other sections in this question, about which there was no significant difference in terms of agreement:

- 77% that the bishop is innovative in society initiatives
- 72% that the Church of England will have to accept female bishops eventually
- 46% would like to see bishops appointed by an open process
- 38% would like to see the bishop elected by vote
- 32% believe there are too many bishops for the dwindling number of churchgoers
- 29% are happy with the way bishops are appointed.

Figure 5.7 indicates the key pressures on clergy in the Church of England, as agreed by both clergy and laity.

Source: Christian Research survey for Cost of Conscience. To obtain more details please contact Rev Francis Gardom, Cost of Conscience, 020 8858 7052 or visit the website www.trushare.com

Table 5.7.1
Who should be ordained?

Statement		AS %	S %	NO %	D %	DS %	Base
Divorced people to be ordained as priests	C	***25***	***51***	*10*	*10*	*4*	1,707
	L	***14***	***45***	*16*	*17*	*8*	1,882
Divorced and re-married priests to be consecrated bishops	C	***18***	***34***	*12*	*20*	*16*	1,703
	L	***10***	***29***	*18*	*25*	*18*	1,876
Divorced and re-married people to be ordained as priests	C	***21***	***46***	*12*	*14*	*7*	1,708
	L	***13***	***42***	*15*	*20*	*10*	1,883
Practising homosexuals to be ordained as priests	C	***13***	***18***	*11*	*24*	*34*	1,710
	L	***6***	***13***	*12*	*26*	*43*	1,884

C: Clergy L: Laity AS: Agree strongly A: Agree NO: No opinion D: Disagree DS: Disagree strongly

Table 5.7.2
Clergy statements of moral belief, by gender

Statement		AS %	S %	NO %	D %	DS %	Base
Abortion should *not* be carried out, unless the mother's life is at risk	M	***32***	***36***	5	23	4	1,484
	F	***15***	***32***	7	41	5	165
Section 28 should *not* be repealed	M	***32***	***31***	9	16	12	1,483
	F	***18***	***40***	11	18	13	167
The morning after pill should *not* be widely available	M	***18***	***31***	15	29	7	1,484
	F	***9***	***33***	16	35	7	166
Some form of euthanasia should *[not]* be made legal*	M	***32***	***37***	8	20	3	1,482
	F	***24***	***38***	7	28	3	167

M: M F: F AS: Agree strongly A: Agree NO: No opinion D: Disagree DS: Disagree strongly
*This statement is reverse coded, so, for example, "strongly agree" is recorded in the "strongly disagree" column.

Figure 5.7
Pressures on Anglican clergy

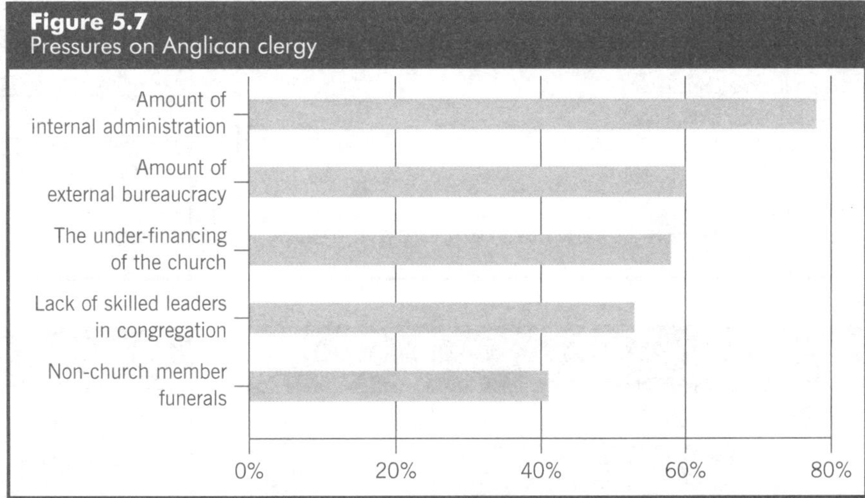

Table 5.7.3
Views on the episcopate, by clergy and laity

Statement		AS %	S %	NO %	D %	DS %	Base
Every bishop should have at least 10 years' parochial experience	C	***29***	***41***	*14*	*14*	*2*	1,701
	L	***30***	***49***	*11*	*9*	*1*	1,875
It is important that my bishop is faithful to biblical teaching	C	***43***	***41***	*10*	*5*	*1*	1,677
	L	***49***	***43***	*6*	*2*	*0*	1,869
I believe it is *[not]* the job of a bishop to respond to social issues*	C	***28***	***57***	*9*	*5*	*1*	1,704
	L	***23***	***55***	*12*	*8*	*2*	1,863

C: Clergy L: Laity AS: Agree strongly A: Agree NO: No opinion D: Disagree DS: Disagree strongly
*This statement is reverse coded, so, for example, "strongly agree" is recorded in the "strongly disagree" column.

5.8 The Woodlands Project Study, 2002

Table 5.8.1
Why respondents did not attend church

Reason	%
I never felt very committed to the church	*34%*
I grew up and started making decisions on my own	*27%*
I got out of habit of going to church	*23%*
I just gradually drifted away for no particular reason	*20%*
The church failed to connect with the rest of my life	*20%*
My church going was hypocritical	*18%*
Many of church's teachings were illogical or nonsensical	*16%*
I felt my lifestyle was not compatible with churchgoing	*16%*
Most of my friends were not churchgoers	*16%*

Table 5.8.2
Type of church which appeals, by generation

Generation	Traditional %	Modern %	Both %	None %
Parents	*75*	*6*	*2*	*17*
Self	*44*	*21*	*4*	*31*
Children	*25*	*26*	*4*	*45*

The Woodlands Project is an imaginative study in the north west and centre of England, focused around Manchester and Nottingham. The Research Fellow for the Project is Rev Chris Vermeulen (0161 929 6582) from whom details may be obtained.

The Project is seeking to ascertain some of the reasons why churches grow, and some of the reasons why they don't. It is also helping some of the churches linked to the Project to make an effective transition in becoming a missionary congregation in the future. It also holds conferences to help participants think through the issues involved with the process.

Some 2,000 questionnaires were distributed by volunteers through a small group of churches to different homes in the relevant areas in June 2002. 416 replies were received. **Table 5.8.1** gives the top reasons why respondents did not attend church, showing a wide range of personal factors few of which appear to be directly related to the church.

On the other hand, **Table 5.8.2** shows the type of church which appealed to different generations. It may be that this simply indicates the need for churches to become less traditional in order to reach today's generation, a finding seen in many other studies, but showing quite clearly across the generations in this study.

Tables 5.8.3 and **4** indicate on what kinds of issues people most agreed and disagreed, and **Figures 5.8.1** and **2** on what they felt was most important for themselves and for society.

Table 5.8.3
Issues where agreement is 60+ points above disagreement

Statement	AS %	S %	NO %	D %	DS %	~
Churches should give clear moral, ethical leadership	*34*	*45*	*13*	*5*	*3*	+71
What Jesus said is important today	*34*	*42*	*16*	*5*	*3*	+68
You don't have to go to church to be a Christian	*31*	*47*	*9*	*9*	*4*	+65
Churches should do more for young people	*24*	*45*	*24*	*5*	*2*	+62
Churches should do more for elderly and house bound	*24*	*43*	*26*	*6*	*1*	+60

AS: Agree strongly A: Agree NO: No opinion D: Disagree DS: Disagree strongly
~ = (AS+A) less (D+DS)

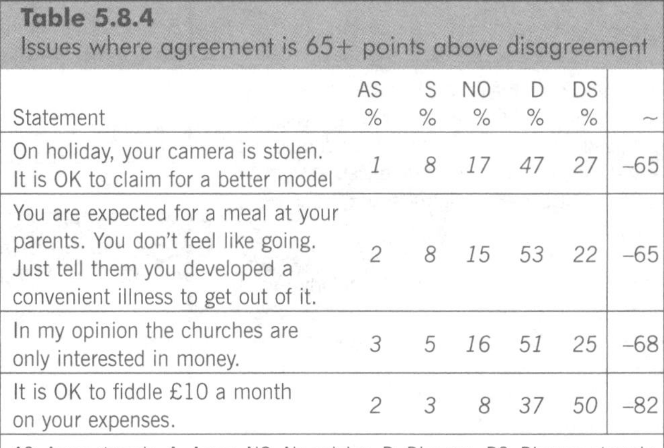

Table 5.8.4
Issues where agreement is 65+ points above disagreement

Statement	AS %	S %	NO %	D %	DS %	~
On holiday, your camera is stolen. It is OK to claim for a better model	*1*	*8*	*17*	*47*	*27*	–65
You are expected for a meal at your parents. You don't feel like going. Just tell them you developed a convenient illness to get out of it.	*2*	*8*	*15*	*53*	*22*	–65
In my opinion the churches are only interested in money.	*3*	*5*	*16*	*51*	*25*	–68
It is OK to fiddle £10 a month on your expenses.	*2*	*3*	*8*	*37*	*50*	–82

AS: Agree strongly A: Agree NO: No opinion D: Disagree DS: Disagree strongly
~ = (AS+A) less (D+DS)

Figure 5.8.1
Things most important to society

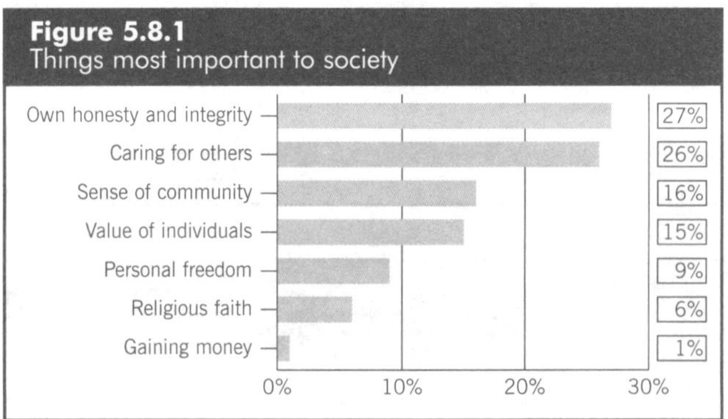

Figure 5.8.2
Things most important personally

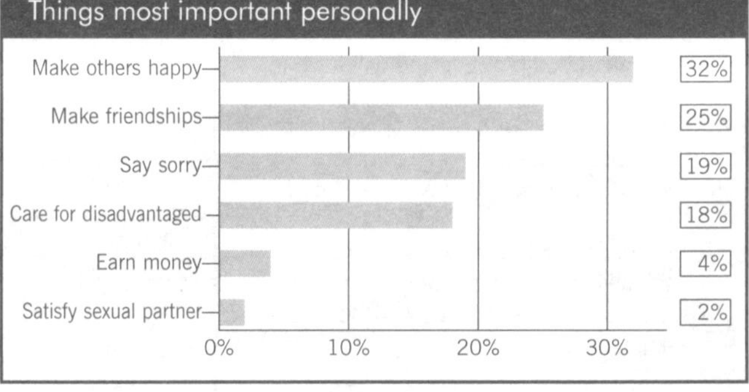

Section 6 is not included in this edition for space considerations; it will be restored in *Religious Trends* No. 5

7

Recent Research reports

This section of *Religious Trends* records recent, past (and in a few cases known forthcoming) research on Christian topics. The entries are listed alphabetically by author, and the address from which the book or report may be obtained is given underneath each entry. Where there is more than one entry from a particular author, the address is given under the first entry only.

The number after each name in the Subject index on Page 7.13 is the sequential number of the papers for a particular author. Thus Barna (2) is the second of the papers listed by George Barna.

Sources: Individual authors

7.2 Recent Research Reports

Above Bar Church
ABC Congregational Survey
Above Bar's seventh annual congregational survey showing further steady growth.
Above Bar Church, Above Bar Street, Southampton SO14 7FE
Published 2002

Adkins Peter
An investigation into the implementation of the Natural Church Development model of church growth in three churches, with particular reference to the identification of empowering leadership principles.
Postgraduate Administrative Assistant, Cliff College, Calver, Hope Valley, Derbyshire S32 3XG
Published 2001; c 20,000 words; MA in Evangelism studies; Price £30

Allen Rosemary
What does Paul really say about Women?
Cliff College Library, Calver, Hope Valley, Derbyshire S32 3XG
Published 2001; 10,000 words; BA

Almonte Katarina
The Link between Charismatic Experiences and Revelation in John's Gospel
London Bible College, Green Lane, Northwood, Middlesex HA6 2UW
Published 2001; MPhil

Anderson Kevin
The Resurrection of Jesus in Luke-Acts
London Bible College, Green Lane, Northwood, Middlesex HA6 2UW
Published 2001; PhD Thesis

Armstrong-MacDonnell Rev
Cuckoos in the Nest?
Critical thinking and competency as legitimisers of knowledge in Christian adult education.
Strand House, Woodbury, Exeter EX5 1LZ
Published 2002; MEd dissertation

Astley J & L J Francis (1)
Christian education and critical openness:
an empirical investigation among undergraduates.
The Welsh National Centre for Religious Education, University of Wales Bangor, Normal Site, Bangor, Gwynedd LL57 2PX
Published 2002; Religious Education, Vol 97, pp 4-22

Astley J & L J Francis, C Wilcox, L Burton (2)
How different is religious education in Catholic schools?
A study of teacher aims in RE.
Published 2000; International Journal of Education and Religion, Vol 1, pp 267-281

Austen N C
The church in the Community: St Michael's Church Blewbury.
Results of qualitative research into the relationship between the church and village in Blewbury, Oxon.
Navisys Business Development Ltd, Boston House, Grove Technology Park, Wantage OX12 9FF
Published 2002; 70 pages; Publisher Navisys Business Development Ltd; Price £20

Avege Caroline
The British Church in Decline.
What can the non-western church offer to the British church to help to arrest decline and stimulate growth?
Cliff College Library, Calver, Hope Valley, Derbyshire S32 3XG
Published 2001; 10,000 words; BA

Ayeebo Jacob Kofi
Community development projects of the Anglican Diocese of Tamale: understanding holistic development from a Christian perspective.
Postgraduate Administrative Assistant, Cliff College, Calver, Hope Valley, Derbyshire S32 3XG
Published 2002; c 20,000 words; MA in Evangelism studies; Price £30

Baban Octavian
Luke's on the road encounters as narrative MIMESIS
London Bible College, Green Lane, Northwood, Middlesex HA6 2UW
Published 1999; PhD Thesis

Bachmann Steve
Enigma Variations:
The 'Imago Dei' as the basis for personhood with special reference to C E Gunton, M Volf and J D Zizioulas.
London Bible College, Green Lane, Northwood, Middlesex HA6 2UW
Published 2001; PhD Thesis

Baek Kyung-A
An Investigation into Calvin and the Genevan Theocracy.
London Bible College, Green Lane, Northwood, Middlesex HA6 2UW
Published 1998; MTh

Baigent Avril
The Y Church Report.
A look at the faith experience of young Catholics with strategy for making our youth ministry more effective.
Northampton Youth Ministry Office, Icer Anna, Aylesbury Road, Princes Risborough HP27 0NU
Published 2002; 113 pages; Price £10; Publisher Roman Catholic Northampton Diocese

Baines Geoffrey
Making a habit of leadership.
Postgraduate Administrative Assistant, Cliff College, Calver, Hope Valley, Derbyshire S32 3XG
Published 2001; 15,000 words; Postgraduate Diploma in Leadership, Renewal & Mission Studies; Price £30

Baptist Union of Great Britain (1)
Voices from the Baptistry
– how people come to faith, and who they are.
Baptist Union of Great Britain, Baptist House, PO Box 44, 129 Broadway, Didcot OX11 8RT
Published 2002

Baptist Union of Great Britain (2)
Report on Youth Ministry within the Baptist Union of Great Britain
– ministry among 11-25 year olds.
Published 2002

Baptist Union of Great Britain (3)
Some recommendations about refining Home Mission.
Published 2002

Bardgett Rev Dr F
Devoted Service Rendered.
History of the lay missionaries of the Church of Scotland, the development of team ministry withing the Churches Home Mission (19th and 20th Century).
Saint Andrew Press, The Church of Scotland Offices, 121 George Street, Edinburgh EH2 4YN
Published 2002; 365 pages; Price £7.50; Publisher St Andrew Press

Barnes L P & Dr W Kay
Religious Education in England and Wales: Innovations and Reflections.
An account of the opportunities, difficulties, practicalities and theoretical background of RE in England and Wales.
Religious and Theological Studies Fellowship, 38 De Montfort Street, Leicester LE1 7GP
Published 2002; 75 pages; Price £4; Publisher Religious and Theological Studies Fellowship

Barton Francis
Children's perceptions of church:
a comparison of year 3 pupils at three Cheltenham primary schools.
Cliff College Library, Calver, Hope Valley, Derbyshire S32 3XG
Published 2001; 10-20,000 words; Dip CEN

Bekele Girma
Theodicy in the Context of Ethiopia.
London Bible College, Green Lane, Northwood, Middlesex HA6 2UW
Published 1998; MTh

Bennema Cor
The Power of Saving Wisdom:
An investigation of spirit and wisdom in relation to the Soteriology of the fourth Gospel.
London Bible College, Green Lane, Northwood, Middlesex HA6 2UW
Published 2001; PhD Thesis; Publisher J C B Mohr, forthcoming

Bennett D R
A Study of how Adults become Christians, with special reference to the personal involvement of individual Christians. A study of the stories of 383 adults who became Christians in the last 7 years.
Cliff College, Calver, Hope Valley, Nr Sheffield S32 3XG or a summary is available from *Pocket Testament League, 1st Floor, Vision Building, 4 Footscray Road, Eltham, London SE9 2TZ*
Published 2003; 20,000 words; Post Graduate Dissertation, Price £30

Bigg Howard C
A Study of the Q Hypothesis from Harnack to Vincent Taylor with special reference to English-speaking Scholarship.
London Bible College, Green Lane, Northwood, Middlesex HA6 2UW
Published 1985; MPhil

Blaney Rev D L Z
Anabaptist Mission for Today. The contribution of 16th century Anabaptism to the contemporary missionary congreagation movement.
Brisge House, 37 Medway Road, Gillingham, Kent ME7 1NL or darren_blaney@lineone.net
Published 2000; 20,000 words; MA Dissertation (All Nations Christian College); Price £1 on disc, free via email

Bottomley Steve
The Success in Business Survey 2001, British Chambers of Commerce.
14,000 businesses reveal their 15 steps to success.
HSBC Invoice, finance (UK) Ltd, Farncombe Road, Worthing BN11 2BW, or info@invoicefinance,hsbc.co.uk
Published 2002

Bourke R & L J Francis (1)
Comparing Cattell's personality factors and Eysenck's personality dimensions among adolescents.
The Welsh National Centre for Religious Education, University of Wales Bangor, Normal Site, Bangor, Gwynedd LL57 2PX
Published 2000; The Irish Journal of Psychology, Vol 21, No 1.2

Bourke R & L J Francis, M Robbins (2)
Personality and prayer among practising Quakers.
Published 2002; The Psychologist in Wales, Vol 13, pp 10-12

Bradley Alan R
Building Bridges as mission among church-community groups:
a study of a church's work with mothers of young children.
Postgraduate Administrative Assistant, Cliff College, Calver, Hope Valley, Derbyshire S32 3XG
Published 2001; c 20,000 words; MA in Evangelism studies; Price £30

Brady Stephen W
The Intermediate State in the Theology of Barth, Hick, Moltmann and Rahner.
London Bible College, Green Lane, Northwood, Middlesex HA6 2UW
Published 1992; PhD

Brierley Dr Peter W (1)
Springboard:
church growth in the 1990s.
Christian Research, Vision Building, 4 Footscray Road, Eltham, London SE9 2TZ
Published 2000

Brierley Dr Peter W (2)
Scunthorpe Group of Churches:
Congregational studies across 6 denominational groups.
Published 2000

Brierley Dr Peter W (3)
Public Prayer in Church.
A pilot study.
Published 2000

Brierley Dr Peter W (4)
Students at 3 Theological and Bible Colleges.
Evaluation of training today.
Completed 2000

Brierley Dr Peter W (5)
Edmonton Baptist Church.
Times of Services Survey.
Published 2000

Brierley Dr Peter W (6)
Quadrant Survey:
CRA Members' use of IT.
Published 2000

Brierley Dr Peter W (7)
Gen X Lifestyle.
Comprehensive and comparative study of Christians and non-Christians.
Published 2001

Brierley Dr Peter W (8)
Mind of Anglicans
on key issues in today's church; study for Cost of Conscience.
Published 2001

Brierley Dr Peter W (9)
Larger Churches Focus Groups.
Evaluation of Anglican, Baptist and Independent churches.
Published 2001

Brierley Dr Peter W (10)
Peniel Pentecostal Church, Brentwood
– Congregational Survey.
Published 2001

7

Brierley Dr Peter W (11)
Peniel Pentecostal Church, Brentwood – Seminar Evaluation.
Published 2001

Brierley Dr Peter W (12)
Premier Radio:
Greater London churchgoing 2003 and 2011.
Published 2001

Brierley Dr Peter W (13)
Alpha Supper Initiative.
Analysis of those attending in 2001.
Published 2002

Brierley Dr Peter W (14)
Numbers attending Alpha,
UK and Worldwide.
Published 2002

Brierley Dr Peter W (15)
YFC Audit.
Who are Youth for Christ reaching?
Published 2002 as special edition of Quadrant

Brierley Dr Peter W (16)
Northampton RC Diocese.
Analysis of 11-16 year olds in school and parish.
Published 2002

Brierley Dr Peter W (17)
Spring Harvest.
Analysis of attendees in 2002.
Published 2002

Brierley Dr Peter W (18)
RAKES (Reaching and Keeping Early Secondaries)
Detailed survey of 2000+ 10-14 year olds in and out of church.
Published 2003 as a book, price £9.99

Brierley Dr Peter W (19)
Woodlands Project.
Community project in Manchester and Nottingham.
Published 2003

Brierley Dr Peter W & Wraight, H (20)
Parish Education, Church of Scotland
Survey of 11-14 year olds.
Published 2000

Brierley Dr Peter W & Wraight, Heather (21)
Salvation Army Central North Division
Church growth in the 1990s.
Published 2002

Brierley Dr Peter W & Wraight, H (22)
Charlotte Chapel Baptist Church.
Congregational Survey and Focus Groups.
Published 2002

Bromley Richard
The Use of the Internet for Evangelism.
Draws conclusions about the factors which make evangelism on the Internet effective for young people.
Youth for Christ, PO Box 5254, Halesowen B63 3DG
Published 2002

Bronnert Dr John
Weston Way, from Water to Wine – to replace the Sunday School?
Tyndale, 15 Craig Avenue, Flixton, Urmston, Manchester M41 5RS
Published 1999

Brown Colin A
The Relationship between Concepts of God and Criteria for Meaning and Truth.
London Bible College, Green Lane, Northwood, Middlesex HA6 2UW
Published 1984; PhD

Brown David
Youth ministry stress, its causes, effects and management within the Diocese of Canterbury.
Diocesan House, Lady Wootton's Green, Canterbury CT1 1NQ or dbrown@diocant.clara.co.uk
Published 2001

Brown Graham
Whatever happened to the Brethren: survey of local churches in 1998-99. 322 respondent churches.
Paternoster Press, PO Box 300, Carlisle CA3 0QS
Published 2003; Publisher Paternoster for Partnership Publications; Price £7 for hard copy or free from www.partnershipuk.org

Brown Mark
Anglican Evangelical Approaches to Evangelism: 1800 to the present day
London Bible College, Green Lane, Northwood, Middlesex HA6 2UW
Published 1997; MTh

Buchanan Rt Rev Colin
Churchgoing in Woolwich.
Bishop of Woolwich, 37 South Road, Forest Hill, London SE23 2UJ
Published 2002

Bühler Markus
The Fulfiller of the Law and the Law of Islam.
London Bible College, Green Lane, Northwood, Middlesex HA6 2UW
Published 1998; MTh

Byass Richard J
A study of the Internet Church and its Role in the Future of the Church
Cliff College Library, Calver, Hope Valley, Derbyshire S32 3XG
Published 2001; 10,000 words; BA

Cairns E & C Lewis (1)
Memories for political violence and mental health.
School of Psychology, University of Ulster at Magee College, Londonderry, Northern Ireland BT48 7JL
Published 1999; British Journal of Psychology, Vol 90, pp 25-33

Cairns E
& C Lewis, O Mumcu, N Waddell (2)
Memories of recent ethnic conflict and their relationship to social identity.
Published 1998; Journal of Peace Psychology, Vol 4, pp 13-22

Carnegie David R
The Hymns in Revelation:
Their origin and function.
London Bible College, Green Lane, Northwood, Middlesex HA6 2UW
Published 1978; PhD

Chadwick Linda
Constructing Hope: Community development as a tool in alleviating poverty, global north and global south (a comparison of poverty in Nicaragua and Blackpool, UK).
Postgraduate Administrative Assistant, Cliff College, Calver, Hope Valley, Derbyshire S32 3XG
Published 2000; c 20,000 words; MA in Evangelism studies; Price £30

Chae Daniel Jong-Sang
Paul as Apostle to the Gentiles:
His apostolic self-awareness and its influence on the Soteriological Argument in Romans
London Bible College, Green Lane, Northwood, Middlesex HA6 2UW
Published 1995; PhD Thesis; Publisher Paternoster Press 1997

Cheesman Graham J
English Protestant Eucharistic Theology in the Reign of Henry VIII.
London Bible College, Green Lane, Northwood, Middlesex HA6 2UW
Published 1980; MPhil

Chojnacka Agnleszka
Prophecy as a Tool for Evangelism.
Cliff College Library, Calver, Hope Valley, Derbyshire S32 3XG
Published 2001; 10,000 words; BA

The Christian Institute (1)
The Morning-After Pill.
Promotion promiscuity.
Published 2001; 40 pages; Research Briefing; Publisher The Christian Institute

The Christian Institute (2)
A Manifesto for Marriage in Sex Education.
A Christian view of sex education.
Published 2001; 20 pages

The Christian Institute (3)
Sex lessons for kids.
An exposé of the Scottish Executive's recommended sex education classroom materials.
Published 2001; 40 pages, Price £1

The Christian Institute (4)
Cut the Clause (England).
An examination of the implications for Christian teachers of Clause 5 of the General Teaching Council for England's draft professional code.
Published 2001; 12 pages; Research Paper; Publisher The Christian Institute

The Christian Institute (5)
Cut the Clause (Wales).
An examination of the implications for Christian teachers of the general principles of the General Teaching Council for Wales' draft professional code.
Published 2001; 12 pages; Research Paper; Publisher The Christian Institute

The Christian Institute (6)
Locking Up Parents.
A response to the Northern Ireland Executive's consultation on the physical punishment of children.
26 Jesmond Road, Newcastle upon Tyne, NE2 4PQ
Published 2002; 28 pages; Briefing Paper; Publisher The Christian Institute

The Christian Institute (7)
Locking Up Parents.
A rebuttal of the Scottish Executive's proposals to change the law on smacking in Scotland.
Published 2002; 38 pages; Briefing Paper; Publisher The Christian Institute

The Christian Institute (8)
Going Soft on Cannabis.
Demolishing 15 key arguments for the decriminalisation of Cannabis.
Published 2002; 30 pages; Briefing Paper; Publisher The Christian Institute

The Christian Institute (9)
Counterfeit Marriage.
Examines how 'civil partnerships' devalue the currency of marriage.
Published 2002; 28 pages; Briefing Paper; Publisher The Christian Institute

The Christian Institute (10)
Sidelining Stability and Security.
The case against abandoning the current grounds for adoption.
Published 2002; 24 pages; Briefing Paper; Publisher The Christian Institute

The Christian Institute (11)
Transsexualism Mind over Matter.
An examination of transsexualism.
Published 2002; 4 pages; Briefing Paper; Publisher The Christian Institute

Christian Medical Fellowship
Members' Attitudes to Abortion
A survey of reported views and practice of CMF Members.
Christian Medical Fellowship, 157 Waterloo Road, London SE1 8XN
Published 1996; 19 pages; Price £3

Church Pastoral Aid Society
ECS Questionnaire Feedback
Church Pastoral Aid Society, Athena Drive, Tachbrook Park, Warwick CV34 6NG
Published 2002

Clark Andrew
Parallel Lives: the relation of Paul to the apostles in the Lucan Perspective.
London Bible College, Green Lane, Northwood, Middlesex HA6 2UW
Published 1997; PhD Thesis; Publisher Paternoster Press 2000

Clark Peter
How is the gospel more effectively communicated to lower sixth secondary school pupils in a North Tyneside School: when presented in a 'modernist' way as logical integrated themes or in a 'post-modernist' way as jumbled do-it-yourself blocks?
Postgraduate Administrative Assistant, Cliff College, Calver, Hope Valley, Derbyshire S32 3XG
Published 2000; c 20,000 words; MA in Evangelism studies; Price £30

Clark Philip
An assessment of 'Kidz Klubs' as an appropriate twenty-first century model of ministry among children.
Postgraduate Administrative Assistant, Cliff College, Calver, Hope Valley, Derbyshire S32 3XG
Published 2000; c 15,000 words; Postgraduate Diploma in Leadership, Renewal & Mission Studies; Price £30

Clegg Malcolm
Understanding the Times
– research into the impact and direction of Christian mission in post-Communist Central and Eastern Europe at the turn of the century.
Postgraduate Administrative Assistant, Cliff College, Calver, Hope Valley, Derbyshire S32 3XG
Published 2001; c 20,000 words; MA in Evangelism studies; Price £30

Coad Patrick
Reflections on the Journey.
Cliff College Library, Calver, Hope Valley, Derbyshire S32 3XG
Published 2002; 10,000 words; BA

Cockling Carl
Preaching in an age of Postmodernity:
What preachers need to know in order to share in the church's missions in the postmodern world.
Cliff College Library, Calver, Hope Valley, Derbyshire S32 3XG
Published 2002; 10,000 words; BA

7.4 Recent Research Reports

Coleman Prof Peter, F McKiernan, M Mills & P Speck
Spiritual Beliefs and Existential Meaning in Later Life: the experience of older bereaved spouses
ESRC Growing Older Programme, Dept of Sociological Studies, Elmfield, Northumberland Road, University of Sheffield, Sheffield S10 2TU
Published 2002; 4 pages; Publisher ESRC

Condy Mark
Pentecostalism: the study of the Holy Spirit and its impact on the church.
Cliff College Library, Calver, Hope Valley, Derbyshire S32 3XG
Published 2001; 10,000 words; BA

Cook Robert R
Representative Survey and Critical Analysis of Theological and Philosophical Discussions of Divine Foreknowledge in the English-Speaking World from 1970-1989.
London Bible College, Green Lane, Northwood, Middlesex HA6 2UW
Published 1990; PhD

Cooke Barrie G
An evaluation of a Model of consultancy to help Churches become Mission-Oriented Congregations
Postgraduate Administrative Assistant, Cliff College, Calver, Hope Valley, Derbyshire S32 3XG
Published 2001; c 40,000 words; MPhil; Price £30

Cope Thomas H
The Africa Inland Mission in Kenya: Aspects of its history 1895-1945.
London Bible College, Green Lane, Northwood, Middlesex HA6 2UW
Published 1979; MPhil

Cornell Geoff
Consultancy in change: a study of consultancy provision in Methodist Circuits.
Postgraduate Administrative Assistant, Cliff College, Calver, Hope Valley, Derbyshire S32 3XG
Published 2001; c 20,000 words; MA in Consultancy, Mission & Ministry Studies; Price £30

Cotton Robert
Has the Tearfund research project 'Church, Community and Change' enabled Arnold Methodist Church to become more effective in the local community?
Postgraduate Administrative Assistant, Cliff College, Calver, Hope Valley, Derbyshire S32 3XG
Published 2000; c 20,000 words; MA in Evangelism studies; Price £30

Cree Rev Dr J
My name is John. An affirmation of parish ministry.
Amazon.com or from author Chorley Rectory, Rectory Close, Chorley, Lancs PR7 1QW
Published 2000; 232 pages; Price £14.90

Crockett Alasdair
Variations in Churchgoing Rates in England in 1851: Supply-side deficiency or demand-led decline?
Nuffield College, Oxford OX1 1NF
Published 2000; 38 pages; University of Oxford Discussion Papers in Economic and Social History, No 36

Croton Dr Elizabeth
God and the Physician – Should treating Physicians enquire into the religious beliefs of their patients as part of their care?
A survey collecting general demographic details from patients and examining their attitudes toward enquiries into their religious beliefs.
Dr Liz Croton, 98 War Lane, Harborne, Birmingham B17 9RR
Submitted to Journal of Medical Ethics 2001; 2,831 words

Czech Evangelical Alliance & Alliance for Saturation Church Planting
Research Project among Czech evangelical denominations 1990-2000.
Czech Evangelical Alliance, Michelska 1/7, 140 00 Praha 4, Czech Republic
Published 2002; 28 pages

Daley Joseph
An examination of the relationship between attitudes to, and the maintenance of, church buildings and the mission of a church.
Postgraduate Administrative Assistant, Cliff College, Calver, Hope Valley, Derbyshire S32 3XG
Published 2001; 20,000 words; MA in Evangelism studies; Price £30

Dandelion P
Those who leave and those who left: The Complexity of Quaker Disaffiliation.
Research into patterns of disaffiliation amongst ex-Quakers.
Centre for Postgraduate Quaker Studies, Woodbrooke, 1046 Bristol Road, Birmingham B29 6LJ
Published 2002; Journal of Contemporary Religion 17/2 (May 2002); pp 213-228

Davies Rev Stanley L
Business and Mission or Business as Mission.
Research report.
Global Connections, Whitefield House, 186 Kennington Park Road, London SE11 4BT
Published 2001; 34 pages; Price £5

Davies Stephen
An Investigation into the Relationship between Church and 'Parachurch' Structures in Mission Strategy.
London Bible College, Green Lane, Northwood, Middlesex HA6 2UW
Published 1995; MTh

Davis E Ainsley
Reasons for Decline: a case study of Annotto Bay Methodist Circuit (St Ann, Jamaica).
Postgraduate Administrative Assistant, Cliff College, Calver, Hope Valley, Derbyshire S32 3XG
Published 2001; c 20,000 words; MA in Evangelism studies; Price £30

Dawson-Jones Garry A
Spiritual Mapping – What value, if any, does it have for the mission, evangelism, growth and renewal of Ipstones Methodist Church?
Postgraduate Administrative Assistant, Cliff College, Calver, Hope Valley, Derbyshire S32 3XG
Published 2001; c 20,000 words; MA in Evangelism studies; Price £30

Desbois Danny
Understanding the position of children in the Kingdom of God.
Cliff College Library, Calver, Hope Valley, Derbyshire S32 3XG
Published 2001; 10-20,000 words; Dip CEN

Dorahy M J & C A Lewis (1)
The relationship between dissociation and religiosity: an empirical evaluation of Schumaker's theory.
School of Psychology, University of Ulster at Magee College, Londonderry, Northern Ireland BT48 7JL
Published 2001; Journal for the Scientific Study of Religion, Vol 40, pp 317-324

Dorahy M J & C A Lewis, J Schumaker, R Akuamoah-Boateng, M Duze, T Sibiya (2)
A cross-cultural analysis of religion and life satisfaction.
Published 1998; Mental Health, Religion and Culture, Vol 1, pp 37-43

Duce Philip
Science and Hermeneutics.
London Bible College, Green Lane, Northwood, Middlesex HA6 2UW
Published 1995; MTh

Dudley Carl S & Nancy Ammerman
Congregations in Transition: a guide for analysing, assessing and adapting in Changing Communities. A workbook to help leaders steer their church through strategic change. Most of the models are American, but many translate to other contexts.
Jossey-Bass, San Francisco, California
Published 2002; 188 pages; Price £14.95; Publisher Jossey-Bass, California

Duffett Chris
Mission and the homeless on the streets of Chester.
Postgraduate Administrative Assistant, Cliff College, Calver, Hope Valley, Derbyshire S32 3XG
Published 1999; 20,000 words; MA in Evangelism studies; Price £30

Ebeling Julie
The Matthean Jesus: The One they did not expect.
London Bible College, Green Lane, Northwood, Middlesex HA6 2UW
Published 1997; MTh

Edwards Graham M
No Regrets? A Study in Ecclesiology. What has the church been and where is it going?
Cliff College Library, Calver, Hope Valley, Derbyshire S32 3XG
Published 2001; 10,000 words; BA

Edwards Simon C
What's the alternative? An introduction to alternative worship.
Cliff College Library, Calver, Hope Valley, Derbyshire S32 3XG
Published 2001; 10,000 words; BA

Ellis Kevin
Degrees of Divinity: The importance of the role of mediatorial figures for an understanding of Jewish Monotheism and the development of Christological beliefs.
London Bible College, Green Lane, Northwood, Middlesex HA6 2UW
Published 1996; PhD Thesis

Ellis Simon
Structuring for a mission – or decline? The grouping of churches in the URC.
Postgraduate Administrative Assistant, Cliff College, Calver, Hope Valley, Derbyshire S32 3XG
Published 2001; c 20,000 words; MA in Evangelism studies; Price £30

Erdmann Martin
Building the Kingdom of God on Earth
London Bible College, Green Lane, Northwood, Middlesex HA6 2UW
Published 1999; PhD Thesis

Evans Mary
The Place of Women in the New Testament Church
London Bible College, Green Lane, Northwood, Middlesex HA6 2UW
Published 1977; MPhil; Publisher Paternoster Press 1983

Eyles Rev Brian
Decline in Membership of Large and Small Churches.
18 Sumburgh Road, London SW12 8A2
Published 2001

Fatehi Medrdad
The Spirit's Relation to the Risen Lord in Paul: An examination of its Christological implications
London Bible College, Green Lane, Northwood, Middlesex HA6 2UW
Published 1998; PhD Thesis; Publisher J C B Mohr 2000

Fearn M & B B Booker, L J Francis (1)
Personality and church attendance among artists.
The Welsh National Centre for Religious Education, University of Wales Bangor, Normal Site, Bangor, Gwynedd LL57 2PX
Published 2001; Journal of Beliefs and Values, Vol 22, pp 225-228

Fearn M & L J Francis, C Wilcox (2)
Attitude toward Christianity and psychological type: A survey among religious studies students.
Published 2001; Pastoral Psychology, Vol 49, pp 341-348

Ferdinando Keith
Biblical concepts of Redemption and African Perspectives of the Demonic.
London Bible College, Green Lane, Northwood, Middlesex HA6 2UW
Published 1992; PhD; Paternoster Press 1999

Field Dr Clive (1)
'The Secularized Sabbath' Revisited: Opinion polls as sources for Sunday observance in contemporary Britain.
Librarian and Director of Information Services, The University of Birmingham, Edgbaston, Birmingham B15 2TT or C.D.Field@bham.ac.uk
Published 2001; Contemporary British History, Vol 15(1), pp 1-20

Field Dr Clive (2)
'The Haemorrhage of Faith?' Opinion polls as sources for religious practices, beliefs and attitudes in Scotland since the 1970s. Evidence that Scotland is now no more religious than much of Western Europe.
Published 2001; Journal of Contemporary Religion, Vol 16(2)

Field Dr Clive (3)
The Devil in Solution: How temperate were the Methodists?
Published 2000; The Epworth Review, Vol 27(3)

Filby Ivan L
The historical development of New churches in Dublin 1970-2001.
Postgraduate Administrative Assistant, Cliff College, Calver, Hope Valley, Derbyshire S32 3XG
Published 2001; c 20,000 words; MA in Evangelism studies; Price £30

Finch Matthew
Hidden Treasures – What can the early church teach the emerging church?
Cliff College Library, Calver, Hope Valley, Derbyshire S32 3XG
Published 2001; 10,000 words; BA

Finis Thomas
An Examination of the Weaknesses of German Evangelicalism around the time of the Berlin Declaration as Exemplified by the Gnadau Union
London Bible College, Green Lane, Northwood, Middlesex HA6 2UW
Published 1999; MTh

Fleming Diane
Alcoholism.
Cliff College Library, Calver, Hope Valley, Derbyshire S32 3XG
Published 2002; 10,000 words; BA

Flynn David
The Debate between Oneness Pentecostalism and its Trinitarian Opponents.
London Bible College, Green Lane, Northwood, Middlesex HA6 2UW
Published 1998; MTh

Forsaith Peter
Methodist Heritage and Contemporary Mission.
Report to the Methodist Council.
Wesley Centre, Westminster Institute of Education, Oxford Brookes University, Harcourt Hill, Oxford OX2 9AT
Published 2001; 42 pages; Available for cost of copying plus p&p; Publisher Wesley & Methodist Studies Centre

Francis Rev Prof Leslie (1)
The Values Debate: a voice from the pupils.
The Welsh National Centre for Religious Education, University of Wales Bangor, Normal Site, Bangor, Gwynedd LL57 2PX
Published 2001; pp x + 246; Publisher Woburn Press, London

Francis Rev Prof Leslie (2)
Religion and Values: a quantitative perspective.
Published 2001; in The Fourth R for the Third Millennium: education in religion and values for the global future *L J Francis, J Astley & M Robbins (eds); pp 47-78; Publisher Lindisfarne Books, Dublin*

Francis Rev Prof Leslie (3)
The social significance of religious affiliation among adolescents in England and Wales.
Published 2001; in Religious Individualisation and Christian Religious Semantics, H G Ziebertz (ed), pp 115-138; Publisher Lit Verlag, Münster

Francis Rev Prof Leslie (4)
God images, personal and well-being and moral values: a survey among 13-15 year olds in England and Wales.
Published 2001; in Imagining God: empirical explorations from an international perspective, H G Ziebertz (ed), pp 125-144; Publisher Lit Verlag, Münster

Francis Rev Prof Leslie (5)
Christianity and dogmatism revisited: a study among UK 15 & 16 year olds.
Published 2001; Religious Education, Vol 96, pp 211-226

Francis Rev Prof Leslie (6)
Church Times survey of Anglican values and life.
Published 2001

Francis Rev Prof Leslie (7)
Shaping Teacher's Interpretation of Spirituality.
Published 2001; Journal of Research on Christian Education, Vol 10, No 1

Francis Rev Prof Leslie (8)
Personality and the Desire to Exhibit: a study among artists.
Published 2001; The Psychologist in Wales, Issue 12

Francis Rev Prof Leslie (9)
Caring for Clergy in Crisis.
Published 2001; Parson and Parish, No 156

Francis Rev Prof Leslie (10)
The relationship between bible reading and attitude toward substance use among 13-15 year olds
Published 2002; Religious Education, Vol 97, pp 44-60

Francis Rev Prof Leslie (11)
Catholic schools and Catholic Values? A study of moral and religious values among 13-15 year old pupils attending non-denominational and Catholic schools in England and Wales.
Published 2002; International Journal of Education and Religion, Vol 3, pp 69-84

Francis Rev Prof Leslie (12)
The personality characteristics of male evangelical clergy: denominational differences in the UK.
Published 2002; Mental Health, Religion and Culture, Vol 5, pp 175-181

Francis Rev Prof Leslie (13)
Psychological type and mystical orientation: anticipating individual differences within congregational life.
Published 2002; Pastoral Sciences, Vol 21, pp 77-93

Francis Rev Prof Leslie (14)
Confirmatory Factor Analysis of the French Translation of the Abbreviated Form of the Revised Eysenck Personality Questionnaire.
Published 2002; European Journal of Psychological Assessment, Vol 18, Issue 2

Francis Rev Prof Leslie (15)
Personal and Social Correlates of Spiritual Well-Being among Primary School Teachers.
Published 2002; Pastoral Psychology, Vol 51, No 1

Francis Rev Prof Leslie (16)
Internal consistency reliability and construct validity of the German translation of the Oxford Happiness Inventory.
Published 2002; North American Journal of Psychology, Vol 4, No 2

Francis Rev Prof Leslie & J Astley, M Robbins (eds) (17)
The Fourth R for the Third Millenium: education in religion and values for the global future.
Published 2001; 254 pages; Publisher Lindisfarne Books, Dublin

Francis Rev Prof Leslie & M Fearn (18)
Assessing and interpreting learning preferences among A-level religious studies students: the Revised Index of Learning Styles.
Published 2001; British Journal of Religious Education, Vol 24, pp 41-51

Francis Rev Prof Leslie & H M Gibson (19)
Growing up Catholic in a Scottish city: the relationship between denominational identity, denominational schools, and attitude toward Christianity among eleven to fifteen year olds.
Published 2001; Catholic Education: a journal of inquiry and practice, Vol 5, pp 39-54

Francis Rev Prof Leslie & H M Gibson, M Robbins (20)
God images and self-worth among adolescents in Scotland.
Published 2001; Mental Health Religions and Culture, Vol 4, pp 103-108

Francis Ref Prof Leslie & J D Greer (21)
Shaping adolescents' attitudes toward science and religion in Northern Ireland: the role of scientism, creationism and denominational schools.
Published 2001; Research in Science and Technological Education, Vol 19, pp 39-53

Francis Rev Prof Leslie & Z Grindle (22)
The changing ethos of church schools: a survey of teachers attitudes in 1982 and 1996.
Published 2001; Research in Education, Vol 65, pp 1-9

Francis Rev Prof Leslie & S H Jones (23)
Psychological type and happiness: a study among adult churchgoers.
Published 2000; Journal of Psychological Type, Vol 54, pp 36-41

Francis Rev Prof Leslie & S H Jones, C J Jackson, M Robbins (24)
The feminine personality profile of male Anglican clergy in Britain and Ireland: a study employing the Eysenck Personality Profiler.
Published 2001; Review of Religious Research, Vol 43, pp 14-23

Francis Rev Prof Leslie & S H Jones, C Wilcox (25)
Religiosity and happiness: during adolescence, young adulthood and later life.
Published 2000; Journal of Psychology and Christianity, Vol 19, pp 245-257

Francis Rev Prof Leslie & P Kaldor (26)
The relationship between religion and purpose in life in an Australian population sample.
Published 2001; Research in the Social Scientific Study of Religion, Vol 12, pp 53-63

Francis Rev Prof Leslie & P Kaldor (27)
The scale properties of the abbreviated Revised Eysenck personality Questionnaire in an Australian population study.
Published 2001; Irish Journal of Psychology, Vol 22, No 2

Francis Rev Prof Leslie & P Kaldor (28)
The relationship between psychological well-being and Christian faith and practice in an Australian population sample.
Published 2002; Journal for the Scientific Study of Religion, Vol 41, pp 179-184

Francis Rev Prof Leslie & P Kaldor (29)
The relationship between religion and Rosenberg's measure of self esteem in an Australian population sample.
Published 2002; Transpersonal Psychology Review, Vol 6(1), pp 53-59

Francis Rev Prof Leslie & D W Lankshear (30)
The relationship between church schools and local church life: distinguishing between aided and controlled status.
Published 2001; Educational Studies, Vol 27, pp 425-438

Francis Rev Prof Leslie & K T Littler (32)
Personality and preference for rural ministry among Church in Wales clergymen.
Published 2001; The Psychologist in Wales, Vol 11, pp 3-5

Francis Rev Prof Leslie & K T Littler, T H Thomas (33)
Fenced fonts or open doors? Implicit religion and baptismal policy among clergy in the Church in Wales.
Published 2000; Implicit Religion, Vol 3, pp 73-86

Francis Rev Prof Leslie & S H Louden (34)
Parish ministry and Roman Catholic regular clergy: applying Eysenck's dimensional model of personality.
Published 2001; International Journal of Practical Theology; Vol 5, pp 215-226

Francis Rev Prof Leslie & S H Louden, M Robbins, C F J Rutledge (35)
Unmasking the clerical persona: interpreting the correlation between neuroticism and lie scale scores among Roman Catholic and male and female Anglican clergy.
Published 2000; Mental Health, Religion and Culture, Vol 3, pp 133-141

Francis Rev Prof Leslie & J Martineau (36)
Rural Visitors
Published 2001; pp viii + 116; Publisher Acora Publishing, Stoneleigh Park

Francis Rev Prof Leslie & J Martineau (37)
Rural Youth
Published 2001; pp viii + 124; Publisher Acora Publishing, Stoneleigh Park

Francis Rev Prof Leslie & J Martineau (38)
Rural Mission
Published 2002; Publisher Acora Publishing, Stoneleigh Park

Francis Rev Prof Leslie & V J Payne, S H Jones (39)
Psychological types of male Anglican clergy in Wales.
Published 2001; Journal of Psychological Type, Vol 56, pp 19-23

Francis Rev Prof Leslie A W Pension, S H Jones (40)
Psychological types of male and female Bible college students in England.
Published 2001; Mental Health, Religion and Culture, Vol 4, pp 23-32

Francis Rev Prof Leslie & M Robbins (41)
The influence of religion on undergraduates attending an Anglican college: church attendance, personality and wellbeing.
Published 2000; Prologue, Vol 2, pp 11-19

Francis Rev Prof Leslie & M Robbins (42)
Psychological types of male evangelical church leaders.
Published 2002; Journal of Belief and Values, Vol 23, pp 217-220

7

7.6 Recent Research Reports

Francis Rev Prof Leslie & M Robbins, C J Jackson, S H Jones (43)
Personality theory and male Anglican clergy: the EPP.
Published 2000; Contact, Vol 113, pp 27-36

Francis Rev Prof Leslie & M Robbins, J Johnson (44)
Shaping teachers' interpretation of spirituality: the contribution of Anglican and Free Church Colleges in England and Wales.
Published 2001; Journal of Research on Christian Education, Vol 10, pp 39-51

Francis Rev Prof Leslie & M Robbins, S H Louden, J M Haley (45)
A revised psychoticism scale for the Revised Eysenck Personality Questionnaire:
a study among clergy.
Published 2001; Psychological reports, Vol 88, pp 1,131-4

Francis Rev Prof Leslie & R Rodger (46)
The personality profile of Anglican clergymen.
Published 2000; in Spiritual Dimensions of Pastoral Care: practical theology in a multi disciplinary context, D Willows & J Swinton (eds), pp 66-71; Publisher Jessica Kingsley, London

Francis Rev Prof Leslie & C F J Ross (47)
Personality type and quest orientation of religiosity
Published 2000; Journal of Psychological Type, Vol 55, pp 22-25

Francis Rev Prof Leslie & D Turton (48)
Are charismatic clergy more satisfied with their ministry?
A study among male parochial clergy in the Church of England.
Published 2002; Mental Health, Religion and Culture, Vol 5, pp 1,235-42

Francis Rev Prof Leslie & C Wilcox (49)
Personality and sex role orientation among 17-19 year old females in England.
Published 1999; Irish Journal of Psychology, Vol 20, pp 172-178

Francis Ray
The History and Spirituality of Labyrinths.
Cliff College Library, Calver, Hope Valley, Derbyshire S32 3XG
Published 2002; 10,000 words; BA

Freebury Charles
Alpha or Emmaus? Assessing today's top evangelistic courses.
In-depth comparative evaluation of the Alphas and Emmaus courses, drawing from all 11 available surveys and other sources.
C A Freebury MA FIEx, 89 Hermitage Street, Crewkerne, Somerset TA18 8EX
Published 2002; 89 pages; £11.50; Post Graduate dissertation Cliff College

Fuller Lois
The Image of Babylon in Revelation 17-18 and Implications for the Church Today.
London Bible College, Green Lane, Northwood, Middlesex HA6 2UW
Published 2001; MTh

Garnes Sarah
Christian Development Work in Islamic Contexts with special reference to Bangladesh.
London Bible College, Green Lane, Northwood, Middlesex HA6 2UW
Published 2001; MTh

Gerloff Rev Dr Roswith (1)
An African Continuum in Variation:
The African Christian Diaspora in Britain
Reprint of article in Black Theology in Britain, (A Journal of Contextual Praxis), issue 4, May 2000, (Sheffield Academic Press), pp 84-112.
39 West Park Road, Roundhay, Leeds LS8 2HA
Published July 2002; 12-44 Pages; Journal of Constructive Theology 8/2, pp 12-44

Gerloff Rev Dr Roswith (2)
Religion, Culture and Resistance: The Significance of the African Christian Diaspora in Europe
On development of African churches in S European countries.
Published 2001; 14 pages; Exchange 30/3 (Brill, Leiden NL), pp 276-289

Gerloff Rev Dr Roswith (3)
Open Space: The African Christian Diaspora in Europe and the Quest for Human Community
Publication of material gathered at the Partnership of African Christian Communities in Europe Conference, Westminster College, Cambridge 1999.
Published July 2000; International Review of Mission, Vol. LXXXIX No 354, pp 269-510

Golding Kellis
How can Christians be Effective Witnesses to Prisoners?
Cliff College Library, Calver, Hope Valley, Derbyshire S32 3XG
Published 2002; 10,000 words; BA

Goncalves de Lima Maristela
Evaluating the concepts of 'Liberation' as a holistic example of evangelism in 20th and 21st Centuries.
Cliff College Library, Calver, Hope Valley, Derbyshire S32 3XG
Published 2001; 10,000 words; BA

Goodwin Robert
A Critique of the Functional Foundations of Contemporary Mission and the Proposal of an Ontological Alternative
London Bible College, Green Lane, Northwood, Middlesex HA6 2UW
Published 1998; PhD Thesis

Goodwin Victor
The Decline of the Mainline Churches in Britain and has the Church a Future?
Cliff College Library, Calver, Hope Valley, Derbyshire S32 3XG
Published 2001; 10,000 words; BA

Gordon Rev K
What Impact does September 11th have on the mission of the church?
A review and analysis of the response of Christ's Church to the September 11th 2001 terrorist attacks.
United College of the Ascension, Wesley Park Road, Selly Oak, Birmingham B29 6RD
Published 2002; 12,000 words; MA Dissertation, University of Birmingham

Graham Anthony
An Investigation into the Challenge of Faith and Discipleship in John's Gospel.
London Bible College, Green Lane, Northwood, Middlesex HA6 2UW
Published 1997; MTh

Grainger Rev Peter (1)
Challenges Facing the Church in Britain in the 21st Century.
Sabbatical Report – Whitefield Institute, Oxford
www.charlottechapel.org
Published 2001; 18 pages

Grainger Rev Peter (2)
A Study in Biblical Identity and Core Values as a Basis for Women's Ministry
Personal Sabbatical study.
Published 2002; 23 pages

Greenslade Philip
Integrated Worship: An exploration of the Polarities inherent in Biblical worship as a base for integrated worship with special reference to the work of Walter Brueggemann.
London Bible College, Green Lane, Northwood, Middlesex HA6 2UW
Published 2002; MTh

Griffiths Tudor & N Hawkins
A New People for a New Millennium.
Report of a visit to the Diocese of Sabah, July 2000.
6 Old Barn Court, Undy, Caldicot NP26 3TE
Published 2001

Grimshaw Nicola
How can we learn from the women in Luke's Gospel using feminist theology as a tool for interpretation?
Cliff College Library, Calver, Hope Valley, Derbyshire S32 3XG
Published 2001; 10,000 words; BA

The Guide Association
Today's Girl, Tomorrow's Women.
Commonwealth Headquarters, 17 Buckingham Palace Road, London SW1W 0PT
Published 2000

Hall Carla Saraid
A study of the Role of Women in Ministry using Pauline Texts as the Primary Source.
Cliff College Library, Calver, Hope Valley, Derbyshire S32 3XG
Published 2002; 10,000 words; BA

Hamilton Norman & D Welch
Reconnecting with a Missing Generation.
A study on those aged 18-35 (Gen X).
Presbyterian Church in Ireland, Church House, fisherwick Place, Belfast BT1 6DW or info@presbyterianireland.org
Published 2001

Harrington Andy
Implications of cultural change in the evangelism and discipleship of young people.
An investigation into the appropriateness of various methodologies as used by Greater Vancouver Youth for Christ.
Postgraduate Administrative Assistant, Cliff College, Calver, Hope Valley, Derbyshire S32 3XG
Published 2001; c 20,000 words; MA in Evangelism studies; Price £30

Harris Jonathan
Transitioning to cell church structure:
an assessment.
Postgraduate Administrative Assistant, Cliff College, Calver, Hope Valley, Derbyshire S32 3XG
Published 2000; c 20,000 words; MA in Evangelism studies; Price £30

Hartford Institute for Religion Research
Congregational Life in America.
www.fact.hartsem.edu
Published 2001

Hartley Stewart
The establishment and evaluation of an alternative mid-week service at the New Church of St John, Nelson.
Postgraduate Administrative Assistant, Cliff College, Calver, Hope Valley, Derbyshire S32 3XG
Published 2001; c 20,000 words; MA in Evangelism studies; Price £30

Hastings Raymond
Non-attendance of the Church in High Wycombe.
4 Redhouse Close, Cressex, High Wycombe HP11 1TT
Published 2001

Hawkins Michael
Prologue, Baptism and Spirit:
A narrative-critical approach to a problem of Johannine Definition.
London Bible College, Green Lane, Northwood, Middlesex HA6 2UW
Published 1996; MTh

Heald Gordon
Belief in the Existence of Jesus.
Opinion Research Business, 9-13 Cursitor Street, London EC4A 1LL
Published 2001

Heliso Desta
Spirit and Resurrection:
A comparative study of 1 (Ethiopic) Enoch and Paul (1 Corinthians).
London Bible College, Green Lane, Northwood, Middlesex HA6 2UW
Published 1998; MTh

Henzel Jan
An Evangelical View of the Perseverance of the Believer within a Revised Order of Salvation.
London Bible College, Green Lane, Northwood, Middlesex HA6 2UW
Published 2001; PhD Thesis

Higgins John
Belief and Conduct:
The relationship of Christology and ethics in Colossians with special reference to Colossians 1:3-2:7.
London Bible College, Green Lane, Northwood, Middlesex HA6 2UW
Published 1998; MTh

Hill Clifford & Philip Boydell
Does Your Mother Know?
Underage sexual behaviour and parental responsibility.
Family Matters Institute, The Park, Moggerhanger, Bedford MK44 3RW
Published 2001

Hill Gareth
How does the Gospel become good news?
(A comparison of *The Times* 1971 and 2001).
Postgraduate Administrative Assistant, Cliff College, Calver, Hope Valley, Derbyshire S32 3XG
Published 2001; c 20,000 words; MA in Evangelism studies; Price £30

Hilton Julie-Ann
Trinitarian Theology, Old and New, in Light of Feminist Thought:
An attempt at a relevant Biblical theology of God on the eve of the New Millennium.
London Bible College, Green Lane, Northwood, Middlesex HA6 2UW
Published 1997; MTh

Hitching Roger
The Church and Deaf People:
A study of identity, communication and relationships with special reference to the ecclesiology of Jürgen Moltmann.
London Bible College, Green Lane, Northwood, Middlesex HA6 2UW
Published 2002; PhD Thesis

Holden John
An Appraisal of 'Orientation to Industrial Life':
a course to relate theology to experience.
Postgraduate Administrative Assistant, Cliff College, Calver, Hope Valley, Derbyshire S32 3XG
Published 2001; c 20,000 words; MA in Evangelism studies; Price £30

Holloway Rev S A (1)
The Gospel Breaks Down Barriers.
An exloration of mono-cultural and multi-cultrual chruches with case studies in Birmingham, England; Sierra Leone and Pakistan.
Horley Parish Office, St Bartholemew's Church, Church Road, Horley, Surrey RH6 8AB
Published 2003; 20,000 words; MA dissertation; Price £10 hard copy, free via email from holloway.horley@virgin.net

Holloway Rev S A (2)
A Bridge and a Plough.
Reflections on 18 years in a multi-faith, inner-city parish in Birmingham, UK.
Published 2002; 20 pages; Price £3

Holwell Liz
Four Methodist Women.
Morton House, 32 Hollow Lane, Cheddleton, Nr Leek, Staffs ST13 7HP
Published 2002

Hong Young Gi
The Impact of Charismatic Pastoral Leadership on Religious Commitment and Church Growth in the Korean Mega-churches.
iams@missionstudies.org
Published 2001; Journal of the International Association for Mission Studies, Vol XV111-2, 36

Hopkins Neil
An Analysis of the Idea of "Church in Youth Culture" within the United Kingdom.
London Bible College, Green Lane, Northwood, Middlesex HA6 2UW
Published 2002; MTh

Horrocks Don
The Soteriological Eclecticism of Thomas Erskine of Linathen:
Perceptions of theological innovation in an age of reconstruction.
London Bible College, Green Lane, Northwood, Middlesex HA6 2UW
Published 2001; PhD Thesis; Publisher Paternoster Press, forthcoming

Hotonu Dr O E O
Sexually transmitted diseases:
The facts.
The Christian Institute, 26 Jesmond Road, Newcastle upon Tyne, NE2 4PQ
Published 2001; 8 pages; Research Briefing; Publisher The Christian Institute

Hout Michael & Claude Fischer (1)
Explaining the rise of Americans with no religious preference:
politics and generations.
Survey Research Centre, 2538 Channing Way, Berkeley, CA 94720-5100
Published 2001; GSS Social Change Report, No 46

Hout Michael & A Greeley, M Wilde (2)
Demographic imperative in religious change in the United States.
Published 2001; GSS Social Change Report, No 45

Hovenden Gerald
An Evaluation of Early Christian Speaking in Tongues in the Light of Pre-Christian and Para-Christian 'Inspired Speech'.
London Bible College, Green Lane, Northwood, Middlesex HA6 2UW
Published 1998; MTh

Howse Kenneth
Religion, Spirituality and Older People.
Centre for Policy on Ageing, 25-31 Ironmonger Row, London EC1V 3QP
Published 1999

Hudson Mary
Evangelicalism Past, Present, Future?
Cliff College Library, Calver, Hope Valley, Derbyshire S32 3XG
Published 2002; 10,000 words; BA

Hughes Philip & Sharon Bond
Youth Spirituality.
Summary of published research.
Christian Research Association, 2 King Street, Ringwood East, Victoria 3135 Australia
Published 2001

Hurr Eun-Ah
Evolving Terminology in Interfaith Relations: Paradigm Shifts and the World Council of Churches
London Bible College, Green Lane, Northwood, Middlesex HA6 2UW
Published 2001; MTh

Idler Ellen
Measuring multiple dimensions of religion and spirituality for health research:
conceptual findings from 1998.
Institute for Health, Health Care Policy & Ageing Research, Rutges, State University of New Jersey, 30 College Avenue, New Brunswick, NJ 08901-1293
Published 2001; GSS Topical Report, No 33

Ilyes Brigitta
What is the Relationship between our Personality Preferences and the way we Receive and Communicate the Gospel?
Cliff College Library, Calver, Hope Valley, Derbyshire S32 3XG
Published 2002; 10,000 words; BA

Ireland Mark
A study of the effectiveness of process evangelism courses in the Diocese of Lichfield, with special reference to Alpha.
Postgraduate Administrative Assistant, Cliff College, Calver, Hope Valley, Derbyshire S32 3XG
Published 2000; 20,000 words; MA in Evangelism studies; Price £30

Irish Council of Churches
Annual Report of the Irish Council of Churches, including statistics on church attendance from 1998 Life & Times Survey for Northern Ireland.
Irish Council of Churches, Inter-Church Centre, 48 Elmwood Avenue, Belfast BT9 6AZ or icpep@email.com
Published 2001

Ives Keith
William Robertson Nicoll and the Great Decline.
London Bible College, Green Lane, Northwood, Middlesex HA6 2UW
Published 2000; MTh

Ives Sharon
An exploration into new lay worker positions with regards to job descriptions, management groups and support groups.
Postgraduate Administrative Assistant, Cliff College, Calver, Hope Valley, Derbyshire S32 3XG
Published 2001; c 15,000 words; Postgraduate Diploma in Leadership, Renewal & Mission Studies; Price £30

Jenkins Garry
Good News on the estate?
An investigation into opportunities for Christian outreach into an 'outer' housing estate.
Postgraduate Administrative Assistant, Cliff College, Calver, Hope Valley, Derbyshire S32 3XG
Published 2001; c 20,000 words; MA in Evangelism studies; Price £30

Johnson Rev I D
Nourishing Roots as well as Shoots?
Research into current ministry and mission grant programme.
The Methodist Church, Resourcing Mission Office, Central Buildings, Oldham Street, Manchester M1 1JQ
Published 2002; 43 pages; Price £5

Johnson Ian D
Consultancy to Circuit leadership teams by members of the Connexional Team as a means of developing mission policy in Methodist Circuits in the UK.
Postgraduate Administrative Assistant, Cliff College, Calver, Hope Valley, Derbyshire S32 3XG
Published 2001; c 20,000 words; MA in Consultancy, Mission & Ministry Studies; Price £30

Joseph S & C Lewis
The Francis Scale of Attitude towards Christianity: Intrinsic or extrinsic religion?
School of Psychology, University of Ulster at Magee College, Londonderry, Northern Ireland BT48 7JL
Published 1997; Psychological Reports, Vol 80, pp 609-610

Joseph Rowntree Foundation
Monitoring poverty and social exclusion 2000. Indicators of poverty and social exclusion.
Joseph Rowntree Foundation, The Homestead, 40 Water End, York YO30 6WP
Published 2001

Jump Phil
Community Regeneration and Neighbourhood Renewal
– Towards a Baptist Response.
Department of Research and Training in Mission, Baptist Union of Great Britain, Baptist House, 129 Broadway, Didcot OX11 8RT
Published 2001; 40 pages; Price £3

Kaldor P & L J Francis, J W Fisher (1)
Personality and Spirituality:
Christian prayer and Eastern meditation are not the same.
The Welsh National Centre for Religious Education, University of Wales Bangor, Normal Site, Bangor, Gwynedd LL57 2PX
Published 2002; Pastoral Psychology, Vol 50, pp 165-172

Kaldor P & L J Francis, P Hughes (2)
Personality and Community involvement:
is churchgoing different?
Published 2002; Journal of Beliefs and Values, Vol 23, pp 101-105

Kay Dr William (1)
Personality and Renewal.
An account of the role of personality in the renewal of Christianity.
Grove Books Ltd, Ridley Hall Road, Cambridge CB3 9HU
Published 2001; 24 pages; Price £3.50; Publisher Grove Books

Kay Dr William (2)
Pentecostal and Charismatic Movements in the British Isles.
Dictionary article in the *New International Dictionary of Pentcostal and Charismatic Movements* (eds) S Burgess and E V Der Maas.
Zondervan, PO Box 749, Harrow HA1 1DP
Published 2002; 42-46 pages; Price £35; Publisher Zondervan

Kay Dr William (3)
Rethinking Primary Religious Education.
A systematic rather than thematic approach to religious education is advocated and justified.
University libraries
Published 2002; Publisher Journal of Beliefs and Values, pp 203-216

Kay Dr William (4)
Pentecostals in Britain.
An account of the history and beliefs of the main Pentecostal groups in the UK.
Paternoster Publishing, PO Box 300, Carlisle CA3 0QS
Published 2000; 372 pages; Price £18; Publisher Paternoster

Kay Dr William & L J Francis (5)
Religious education and school assembly in England and Wales: what do religious minorities think?
The Welsh National Centre for Religious Education, University of Wales Bangor, Normal Site, Bangor, Gwynedd LL57 2PX
Published 2002; Towards Religious Competence: diversity as a challenge for education in Europe, H G Heimbrock, C Th Scheilke & P Schreiner (eds), pp 117-128; Publisher Lit Verlag, Münster

Kay Dr William & M Robbins (6)
A woman's place is on her knees:
the pastor's view of the role of women in the Assemblies of God.
Published 2000

Kay Dr William & Dr L Smith (7)
Classroom factors and attitude toward six world religions.
Research showing that the use of the Bible in RE results in more positive attitudes to Christianity and, unexpectedly, to Hinduism and Islam.
Christian Education Movement, Royal Buildings, Derby DE1 1GW
Published 2002l; Publisher British Journal of Religious Education, pp 111-122

Kelly Gerard
Mission Impossible?
Christian mission in 21st century France.
Postgraduate Administrative Assistant, Cliff College, Calver, Hope Valley, Derbyshire S32 3XG
Published 2001; c 20,000 words; MA in Evangelism studies; Price £30

Kim Dae Jo
Preaching on Romans:
A critical comparison of the expository preaching of John Stott (UK) and Han Hum Oak (Korea).
London Bible College, Green Lane, Northwood, Middlesex HA6 2UW
Published 2002; PhD Thesis

7.8 Recent Research Reports

Kim K J
Mission Pneumatology.
The Holy Spirit and Mission with special reference to the Indian theologies of Stanley Samartha, Vandana and Samuel Rayan.
United College of the Ascension, Wesley Park Road, Selly Oak, Birmingham B29 6RD
Published 2002; 80,000 words; PhD Dissertation, University of Birmingham

Kimber Geoffrey
An investigation into the Attitude of a Warwickshire Mining Community to Church and Spirituality.
An in depth study drawing on the author's ministry.
Christian Research, Vision Building, 4 Footscray Road, Eltham, London SE9 2TZ
Published 2001; Leaders Briefing No 17; Price £9

Kimberlee Joyce
Can Healing be a Useful Evangelistic Tool?
Cliff College Library, Calver, Hope Valley, Derbyshire S32 3XG
Published 2001; 10,000 words; BA

Kirk Dorothy M E
Church for the unchurched under-thirteens.
Postgraduate Administrative Assistant, Cliff College, Calver, Hope Valley, Derbyshire S32 3XG
Published 2001; c 20,000 words;
MA in Evangelism studies; Price £30

Kirschner Estevan F
The Place of the Exorcism Motif in Mark's Christology with special reference to Mark 3:22-30
London Bible College, Green Lane, Northwood, Middlesex HA6 2UW
Published 1988; PhD

Kwon Soonbok
Growth of the Korean Church:
its causes and problems, the importance of youth ministry.
Postgraduate Administrative Assistant, Cliff College, Calver, Hope Valley, Derbyshire S32 3XG
Published 2001; c 20,000 words; MA in Evangelism studies; Price £30

Lacy Allan John
Parish mission and the Church school.
Postgraduate Administrative Assistant, Cliff College, Calver, Hope Valley, Derbyshire S32 3XG
Published 2001; c 20,000 words; MA in Evangelism studies; Price £30

Laing Mark
A Study of Indian Mass Movements: Mass conversion movements to Protestantism from 1850.
London Bible College, Green Lane, Northwood, Middlesex HA6 2UW
Published 2001; MTh

Lane Nigel
Why young people leave the church.
Postgraduate Administrative Assistant, Cliff College, Calver, Hope Valley, Derbyshire S32 3XG
Published 2001; c 20,000 words; MA in Evangelism studies; Price £30

Laudert Carsten
Peter Stuhlmacher: Four Decades of New Testament Scholarship in Germany.
An investigation into Stuhlmacher's contribution to academic theology in the fields of New Testament exegesis, hermeneutics and Biblical theology.
London Bible College, Green Lane, Northwood, Middlesex HA6 2UW
Published 1997; MTh

Lee Hyoun-Kyoung
Sainthood and Modern Java:
A window into the world of Muhammad Zuhri.
London Bible College, Green Lane, Northwood, Middlesex HA6 2UW
Published 2000; MTh

Lewis Dr C A (1)
Obsessionality and religiosity:
The relationship between Freud's 'religious practices'.
Published 1994; Journal of Psychology, Vol 128, pp 189-196

Lewis Dr C A (2)
Towards a clarification of the association between religiosity and life satisfaction.
Published 1998; Journal of Beliefs and Values, Vol 19, pp 107-110

Lewis Dr C A (3)
Cleanliness is next to Godliness:
Religiosity and obsessiveness.
Published 1998; Journal of Religion and Health, Vol 37, pp 49-61

Lewis Dr C A (4)
Is the relationship between religiosity and personality 'contaminated' by social desirability as assessed by the Lie Scale?:
a methodological response to Michael W Eysenck (1998).
Published 1999; Mental Health, Religion and Culture, Vol 2, pp 105-114

Lewis Dr C A (5)
The religiosity-psychoticism relationship and the two factors of social desirability: a response to Michael W Eysenck (1999).
Published 2000; Mental Health, Religion and Culture, Vol 3, pp 39-45

Lewis Dr C A (6)
Cultural stereotype of the effects of religion on mental health.
Published 2001; British Journal of Medical Psychology, Vol 74, pp 359-367

Lewis Dr C A (7)
Church attendance and happiness among Northern Irish undergraduates:
No association.
School of Psychology, University of Ulster at Magee College, Londonderry, Northern Ireland BT48 7JL
Published 2002; Pastoral Psychology, Vol 50

Lewis Dr C A & M Dorahy, J Schumaker, R Akuamoah-Boateng, M Duze, T Subiya (8)
Reliability of the Maranell Theism Scale among Ghanaian, Nigerian, Northern Irish, and Swaziland university students.
Published 1998; Personality and Individual Differences, Vol 24, pp 443-446

Lewis Dr C A & L J Francis (9)
Personality and religion among female university students in France
Published 2000; International Journal of Psychology, Vol 35 p 229

Lewis Dr C A & S Joseph (10)
Obsessive actions and religious practices.
Published 1994; Journal of Psychology, Vol 128, pp 699-700

Lewis Dr C A & S Joseph (11)
Religiosity:
Psychoticism and obsessionality in Northern Irish students.
Published 1994; Personality and Individual Differences, Vol 17, pp 685-687

Lewis Dr C A & S Joseph, K Noble (12)
Is religiosity associated with life satisfaction?
Published 1996; Psychological Reports, Vol 79, pp 429-430

Lewis Dr C A
& C Lanigan, S Joseph, J de Fockert (13)
Religiosity and happiness:
Intrinsic or extrinsic religion?
Published 1997; Personality and Individual Differences, Vol 22, pp 119-121

Lewis Dr C A & J Maltby (14)
Religiosity and preoedipal fixation:
A refinement.
Published 1992; Journal of Psychology, Vol 126, pp 687-688

Lewis Dr C A & J Maltby (15)
Religious attitudes and obsessional personality traits among UK adults.
Published 1994; Psychological Reports, Vol 75, pp 353-354

Lewis Dr C A & J Maltby (16)
The reliability and validity of the Francis Scale of Attitude Towards Christianity among US Adults.
Published 1995; Psychological Reports, Vol 76, pp 1243-1247

Lewis Dr C A & J Maltby (17)
Religious Attitude and practice:
the relationship with obsessionality.
Published 1995; Personality and Individual Differences, Vol 19, pp 105-108

Lewis Dr C A & J Maltby (18)
Religiosity and personality among US Adults.
Published 1995; Personality and Individual Differences, Vol 18, pp 293-295

Lewis Dr C A & J Maltby (19)
Personality, prayer and church attendance in a sample of male college students in the USA.
Published 1996; Psychological Reports, Vol 78, pp 976-978

Lewis Dr C A & J Maltby (20)
Reliability and validity of the Francis Scale of Attitude Towards Christianity (adult) among Northern Irish university students.
Published 1997; Irish Journal of Psychology, Vol 18, pp 349-354

Lewis Dr C A & J Maltby (21)
Conservatism and attitude towards Christianity.
Published 2000; Personality and Individual Differences, Vol 29, pp 793-798

Lewis Dr C A
& J Maltby, S Burkinshaw (22)
Religion and Happiness:
Still no association.
Published 2000; Journal of Beliefs and Values, Vol 21, pp 233-236

Lewis Dr C A & J Maltby, A Hersey (23)
The reliability and validity of the 'Rejection of Christianity' Scale among Northern Irish students
Published 1999, Journal of Beliefs and Values, Vol 20, pp 231-238

Lewis Dr C A
& M Shevlin, N Lloyd, G Adamson (24)
The Francis Scale of Attitude Towards Christianity (short-scale):
Exploratory and confirmatory factor analysis among English students.
Published 1998; Journal of Social Behaviour and Personality, Vol 13, pp 167-175

Lewis Dr C A & M Shevlin, C McGuckin, M Navrátil (25)
The Santa Clara Strength of Religious Faith Questionnaire: Confirmatory factor analysis.
Published 2001; Pastoral Psychology, Vol 49, pp 379-384

Lewis Mike
Why not the Dove?
A study of the teaching and practice of the Holy Spirit as experienced in the Alpha Courses in the Dove Valley Methodist Circuit 1997-2000
Postgraduate Assistant, Cliff College, Calver, Hope Vally, Derbyshire S32 3XG.
Published 2001; c. 20,000 words; MA in Evangelism Studies; Price £30

Littler K T & L J Francis (1)
Do villages remain Christian Communities?
The Welsh National Centre for Religious Education, University of Wales Bangor, Normal Site, Bangor, Gwynedd LL57 2PX
Published 2002; Journal of Beliefs and Values, Vol 23, pp 221-224

Littler K T
& L J Francis, J Martineau (2)
The acceptability of lay liturgical ministry: a survey among rural Anglican churchgoers.
Published 2000; Journal of Empirical Theology, Vol 13(1), pp 42-54

Littler K T
& L J Francis, T H Thomas (3)
Guarded gateway or wider witness?
An empirical survey of confirmation policy and practice among clergy in the Church in Wales.
Published 2001; Theology Wales, pp 36-54

London Churches Group for Social Action and Greater London Enterprise
Neighbourhood renewal in London, the Role of the Faith Communities.
Shows that thousands of projects are funded and run by faith communities in the 20 boroughs surveyed.
London Churches Groups, Central Hall, Westminster, Storey's Gate, London SW1H 8NH
Published 2002

London Churches Group for Social Action
Regenerating London:
Faith communities and social action. Report of survey produced jointly with Greater London Enterprise on the scale of faith-organised social action projects in London.
Laurie Anderson, Greater London Enterprise 020 7940 1554 or laurie.a@gle.co.uk
Published 2002; 47 pages

Louden S H & L J Francis
Are Catholic priests in England and Wales attracted to the charismatic movement emotionally less stable?
The Welsh National Centre for Religious Education, University of Wales Bangor, Normal Site, Bangor, Gwynedd LL57 2PX
Published 2001; British Journal of Theological Education, Vol 11(2), pp 65-76

Lovejoy Tim
The Comparative analysis of three forms of consultancy (an assessment of their effectiveness in terms of consultancy method and the consultant's use of them).
Postgraduate Administrative Assistant, Cliff College, Calver, Hope Valley, Derbyshire S32 3XG
Published 2001; c 20,000 words; MA in Consultancy, Mission & Ministry Studies; Price £30

MacDonald Rev Fergus
Towards engaging postmodern young people and the holy Scriptures.
113 St Albans Road, Edinburgh EH9 2PQ
Started 2002

Mackey F Elizabeth
A pearl of great price for the golden years:
a study of why over 50's begin/resume church attendance – and why they do not.
Postgraduate Administrative Assistant, Cliff College, Calver, Hope Valley, Derbyshire S32 3XG
Published 2001; c 20,000 words; MA in Evangelism studies; Price £30

Maltby J & I Garner, C Lewis, L Day (1)
Religious orientation and schizotypal traits.
School of Psychology, University of Ulster at Magee College, Londonderry, Northern Ireland BT48 7JL
Published 2000; Personality and Individual Differences, Vol 28, pp 143-152

Maltby J & C Lewis (2)
Measuring intrinsic and extrinsic orientation to religion: amendments for its use among religious and non-religious samples.
Published 1996; Personality and Individual Differences, Vol 21, pp 937-946

Maltby J & C Lewis (3)
The reliability and validity of a short scale of attitude towards Christianity among USA, English, Republic of Ireland and Northern Ireland adults.
Published 1997; Personality and Individual Differences, Vol 22, pp 649-654

Maltby J & C Lewis, L Day (4)
Religious orientation and psychological well-being: the role of the frequency of personal prayer.
Published 1999; British Journal of Health Psychology, Vol 4, pp 363-378

Mantyjarvi Marjut
The Validity of the Concepts and Methods of Strategic Level Spiritual Warfare in the Theology of Peter Wagner.
London Bible College, Green Lane, Northwood, Middlesex HA6 2UW
Published 2000; MTh

Martin Glanville J
Redemptive healing: an integrated ministry for growth and effective evangelism?
Postgraduate Administrative Assistant, Cliff College, Calver, Hope Valley, Derbyshire S32 3XG
Published 2001; c 20,000 words; MA in Evangelism studies; Price £30

Martin Nicola & David Watts
Two Community Profiles
for the Metropolitan Boroughs of Dudley and Sandwell, considered by ward and intended to provide a "state of the churches" review.
Churches Millennium Community Profile Office, 24 Sandhurst Avenue, Stourbridge DY9 OXL
Published 2001

Martola Yngvill
Worship Renewal.
Research into the particular experience of their denomination.
Research Institute of the Evangelical Lutheran Church of Finland, Box 239, FIN-33101, Tampere, Finland or ktk@evl.fi
Published 2001; No 50; 174 pages

Mashiter Andrew
The effectiveness of contemporary circuit structures within the Manchester and Stockport District of the Methodist Church.
Postgraduate Administrative Assistant, Cliff College, Calver, Hope Valley, Derbyshire S32 3XG
Published 2000; 15,000 words; Postgraduate Diploma in Leadership, Renewal & Mission Studies; Price £30

Mason Jem
Humbled under the Mighty Hand:
An exposition of the pastoral theology of First Peter.
London Bible College, Green Lane, Northwood, Middlesex HA6 2UW
Published 2001; MTh

Masood Steven
Naskh: Al-Nasikh wa al-Mansukh:
A study of the Islamic Theory of Abrogation, its formulation, development and use today.
London Bible College, Green Lane, Northwood, Middlesex HA6 2UW
Published 2001; MTh

Mazuru Marius
Experiencing God:
Towards an epistemology of the charismatic experience.
London Bible College, Green Lane, Northwood, Middlesex HA6 2UW
Published 1997; Mth

Mbui Michael
Some Contemporary Issues behind the Eschatological Motifs of Matthew 24: 1-14.
London Bible College, Green Lane, Northwood, Middlesex HA6 2UW
Published 1997; MTh

McCartney Dr H
Effectiveness in Ministry.
A random sample of J Frazer's people. J Frazer was an effective Presbyterian Minister whose congregation grew conspicuously.
23 Ballyhome Road, Coleraine, N Ireland BT52 2LU
Published 2001; 8,000 words; Undergraduate dissertation

McCormack Jenna
Reaching and Keeping the postmodern generation.
Developing a principle-based mission strategy for 15–19 year olds.
stu_jen25@hotmail.com
Published 2002

McIntosh Gary L
Staff your Church for Growth.
Looks at team ministry in churches.
www.bakerbooks.com
Published 2000; 208 pages

McRoy Anthony
Rushdie's Legacy:
The emergence of a radical British Muslim identity.
London Bible College, Green Lane, Northwood, Middlesex HA6 2UW
Published 2002; PhD Thesis

Mear Donna Marie
Listening as an Avenue for Evangelism.
Cliff College Library, Calver, Hope Valley, Derbyshire S32 3XG
Published 2002; 10,000 words; BA

Medley Roger
Why didn't they come?
An investigation into the unchurched spirituality of those who financially support a Cornish Parish Church, but never attend it.
Postgraduate Administrative Assistant, Cliff College, Calver, Hope Valley, Derbyshire S32 3XG
Published 2000; 20,000 words; MA in Evangelism studies; Price £30

Mengistu Yoseph
The Christology of the Ethiopian Orthodox Church
London Bible College, Green Lane, Northwood, Middlesex HA6 2UW
Published 2000; MTh

Mercer Nicholas S
A Critical Evaluation of Contemporary Hermeneutical Approaches to Genesis 1
London Bible College, Green Lane, Northwood, Middlesex HA6 2UW
Published 1987; MPhil

Mills Carol
'Faith in the Family':
The parental role in faith development.
Cliff College Library, Calver, Hope Valley, Derbyshire S32 3XG
Published 2001; 10-20,000 words; Dip CEN

Mitchel Patrick
Distance and Belonging: Evangelicalism and national identity in Ulster 1921-1998.
London Bible College, Green Lane, Northwood, Middlesex HA6 2UW
Published 2001 and OUP, 2003; PhD Thesis

Morgan P (1)
Adoption by Homosexuals.
Examining the Department of Health's claims about the evidence.
The Christian Institute, 26 Jesmond Road, Newcastle upon Tyne, NE2 4PQ
Published 2002; 12 pages; Briefing Paper; Publisher The Christian Institute

Morgan P (2)
Placing Children with Lesbian and Gay Couples.
A response to the Barnardo's research briefing "The Impact on Children of having Lesbian or Gay parents".
Published 2002; 14 pages' Briefing Paper; Publisher The Christian Institute

Morgan P (3)
Children as Trophies.
Examines the evidence on same-sex parenting.
Published 2002, 160 pages; Price £6.99; Publisher The Christian Institute

MORI (1)
Awareness of Alpha 2000 Pre Advertising and Post Advertising.
Research conducted for Alpha - Holy Trinity Brompton.
MORI, Published 2000; 14 pages

MORI (2)
Awareness of Alpha 2001 Pre Advertising.
Research conducted for Alpha - Holy Trinity Brompton.
MORI, 79-81 Borough Road, London SE7 1FU
Published 2001; 5 pages

Morrison Rujon Wilson
Clergy identity and role in a changing church.
Postgraduate Administrative Assistant, Cliff College, Calver, Hope Valley, Derbyshire S32 3XG
Published 2001; c 20,000 words; MA in Evangelism studies; Price £30

Mounstephen Philip
Children's Ministry Survey,
looking at children's groups affiliated to the CY Network run by CPAS.
Church Pastoral Aid Society, Athena Drive, Tachbrook Park, Warwick CV34 6NG or mail@cpas.org.uk
Published 2002

Moxon Nicholas
Evangelism within the Deaf Community.
Postgraduate Administrative Assistant, Cliff College, Calver, Hope Valley, Derbyshire S32 3XG
Published 2000; c 20,000 words; MA in Evangelism studies; Price £30

Mruka-Mgoye Johana N V
Christology in the Black Theology of Liberation.
London Bible College, Green Lane, Northwood, Middlesex HA6 2UW
Published 1990; PhD

Musson Rev Dr D J (1)
Personality of Male Anglican Clergy in England: revisited using the 16PF.
Comparison of clergy profile using old and new version of Catell's 16PF personality questionnaire.
Taylor & Francis, 4 Park Square, Milton Park, Abingdon OX14 4RN
Published 2002; 12 pages; Journal of Mental Health, Religion and Culture; Publisher Brunner Routledge

Musson Rev Dr D J (2)
Male and Female Anglican Clergy: gender reversal of the 16PF5.
Study of how male and female gender characteristics are partly reversed in clergy population.
Review of Religion Research, Department of Sociology, Box 1811 Station B, Vanderbilt University, Nashville, USA TN37235
Published 2001; Review of Religious Research

Musson Rev Dr D J & L J Francis (3)
A comparison of the psychometric properties of the 16PF4 and 16PF5 among male Anglican clergy
The Welsh National Centre for Religious Education, University of Wales Bangor, Normal Site, Bangor, Gwynedd LL57 2PX
Published 2002; Pastoral Psychology, Vol 54, pp 281-289

Neagoe Alexandru
The Trial and Confirmation of the Gospel: An apologetic reading of Luke's trial narratives.
London Bible College, Green Lane, Northwood, Middlesex HA6 2UW
Published 1998; PhD Thesis; Publisher CUP 2002

Neale Rev Canon Dr Eddie
Reinhold Niebuhr and the Issues of our Time.
Reflections on relations between the Church and the City of Nottingham.
St Mary's Parish Office, Standard Hill, Nottingham NG1 6GA
Published 2001; 16 pages(A5); Price of photocopying and postage

7

7.10 Recent Research Reports

Negrut Paul
The Development of the Concept of Authority Within the Romanian Orthodox Church During the Twentieth Century
London Bible College, Green Lane, Northwood, Middlesex HA6 2UW
Published 1994; PhD Thesis

Ng Edmund
A Survey of NECF-affiliated Evangelical churches in Peninsual Malaysia. Statistical data about churches and the work and ministry of pastors and Christians.
National Evangelical Christian Fellowship Malaysia 32-A, Jalan SS2/103, 47300 Petaling Jaya, Selangor Darul Ehsan, Malaysia
Published 2002

North Mark
Culture, Religion and Christianity:
A search for a universal mission strategy.
Cliff College Library, Calver, Hope Valley, Derbyshire S32 3XG
Published 2002; 10,000 words; BA

Obwa Samson O
A Study of Concepts of Poverty in Old and New Testaments and their Relevance for Contemporary Expressions of Poverty in Nairobi
London Bible College, Green Lane, Northwood, Middlesex HA6 2UW
Published 1994; PhD Thesis

Office of National Statistics
60 Years of Social Survey 1941-2001.
A miscellany of information to celebrate the 60th Anniversary of the founding of the Government Social Survey.
From HMSO outlets, or info@statistics.gov.uk
Published 2002

Okunola Sunday
Servant Leadership:
A trajectory study from Jesus to Ignatius.
London Bible College, Green Lane, Northwood, Middlesex HA6 2UW
Published 2001; MPhil

7

Oldroyd Richard
Church Buildings: opportunities for mission or misdirected energies?
Postgraduate Administrative Assistant, Cliff College, Calver, Hope Valley, Derbyshire S32 3XG
Published 2000; c 20,000 words; MA in Evangelism studies; Price £30

Oliver Robert W
The Emergence of a Strict and Particular Baptist Community among the English Calvinistic Baptists, 1770-1850.
London Bible College, Green Lane, Northwood, Middlesex HA6 2UW
Published 1986; PhD

Ormston Richard
The Diversity of Post-Keele Evangelicalism within the Church of England.
London Bible College, Green Lane, Northwood, Middlesex HA6 2UW
Published 1997; MTh

Pain Alan A
The Relation of the Sermon on the Mount to the Gospel.
London Bible College, Green Lane, Northwood, Middlesex HA6 2UW
Published 1978; MPhil

Park Wan-Chull
The Interpretation of Paul and the Law
Some crucial issues in the Pauline Theology of the Law and 'Works of the Law' in recent scholarship.
London Bible College, Green Lane, Northwood, Middlesex HA6 2UW
Published 1996; MTh

Parnell Susan
An examination of the way in which consultancy can contribute to handling conflict situations in Christian Agencies
Postgraduate Administrative Assistant, Cliff College, Calver, Hope Valley, Derbyshire S32 3XG
Published 2001; c 20,000 words; MA in Consultancy, Mission & Ministry Studies; Price £30

Parsons Michael
The connection between Eschatology and Ethics in Paul's Theology.
London Bible College, Green Lane, Northwood, Middlesex HA6 2UW
Published 1985; MPhil

Pearson Robert
Can working unity among evangelicals in the Wolverhampton area become a practical reality?
Postgraduate Administrative Assistant, Cliff College, Calver, Hope Valley, Derbyshire S32 3XG
Published 2000; c 20,000 words; MA in Evangelism studies; Price £30

Pegg Glenis Susan
Can baptism families be integrated into the life of the church?
Postgraduate Administrative Assistant, Cliff College, Calver, Hope Valley, Derbyshire S32 3XG
Published 2001; c 20,000 words; MA in Evangelism studies; Price £30

Peppiatt Elizabeth
Visiting children in their family context:
How effective is this as a means of outreach in inner city Salford?
Cliff College Library, Calver, Hope Valley, Derbyshire S32 3XG
Published 2001; 10-20,000 words; Dip CEN

Perriman Andrew (1)
The Interpretation of Metaphor in the New Testament with special reference to the Corinthian Correspondence.
Published 1987; MPhil

Perriman Andrew (2)
Church and Body in 1 Corinthians:
A study in exegesis and the poetics of argumentation
London Bible College, Green Lane, Northwood, Middlesex HA6 2UW
Published 1999; PhD Thesis

Petrenko Victor
Theology of Icons:
A Protestant perspective.
London Bible College, Green Lane, Northwood, Middlesex HA6 2UW
Published 1997; MTh

Pettifer Rev Bryan G E (1)
Management and Spiritual Energy.
Research identified conditions which facilitated the release of spiritual energy in managers and noted the importance of good human resource management in creating these conditions.
Peter Bates, Carselands, Woodmancote, Henfield, West Sussex BN5 9SS or www.modem.uk.com under "Project"
Published 2002; 32 pages; Price £3; Report of Modem Research Project The Hope of the Managers

Pettifer Rev Bryan G E (2)
Spiritual Energy in Managers.
Summary report of Modem Research Project The Hope of the Managers.
Published 2002; 8 pages; Price A4 sae

Philip Charles
Outreach to families in Rural Contemporary Society.
Cliff College Library, Calver, Hope Valley, Derbyshire S32 3XG
Published 2002; 10,000 words; BA

Pittis Stephen
An evaluation and critique of the 'Walk of 1000 Men' in the context of changes in understanding and practice of evangelism during the Decade of Evangelism
(Jan 1991 to Jan 2001).
Postgraduate Administrative Assistant, Cliff College, Calver, Hope Valley, Derbyshire S32 3XG
Published 2000; c 20,000 words; MA in Evangelism studies; Price £30

Plenderleith Adam
Christian Ministry and the older person
Published 2002; Thesis

Porter Matthew
The Missiological Influence of David Watson on Evangelicalism in the Church of England.
Postgraduate Administrative Assistant, Cliff College, Calver, Hope Valley, Derbyshire S32 3XG
Published 2000; c 20,000 words; MA in Evangelism studies; Price £30

Powell Roger
Contemporary Cessationism circa 1980-1997. Some cessationist arguments in a charismatic age.
London Bible College, Green Lane, Northwood, Middlesex HA6 2UW
Published 1999; MTh

Presbyterian Church (USA)
Alpha Course Survey - 2000.
Summary of findings.
Research Services, A Ministry of the General Assembly Council, Presbyterian Church, 100 Witherspoon Street, Louisville, KY 40202
Published 2000; 16 pages

Punch Aidan & D L Pearce (eds)
Europe's population and labour Market beyond 2000.
Council of Europe Publishing, F-67075 Strasbourg
Published 2000; Vol 1

Pye Avril
Open to All?
Is it a necessity for children to have an academic understanding of Communion before taking it?
Cliff College Library, Calver, Hope Valley, Derbyshire S32 3XG
Published 2001; 15,000 words; Dip CEN

Randall Ian M
The Career of F B Meyer.
London Bible College, Green Lane, Northwood, Middlesex HA6 2UW
Published 1992; MPhil

Randall K J & L J Francis
Are evangelical Anglican clergy as happy as they could be?
A quantitative perspective in empirical theology.
The Welsh National Centre for Religious Education, University of Wales Bangor, Normal Site, Bangor, Gwynedd LL57 2PX
Published 2002; British Journal of Theological Education, Vol 13(1), pp 57-73

Reddie Dr Anthony (1)
Pentecost – Dreams and Visions
The Queen's Foundation, Somerset Road, Edgbaston, Birmingham B15 2QH
Published 2001; Discovering Christ: Ascension and Pentecost Maureen Edwards (ed), pp 27-42; Publisher Birmingham: International Bible Reading Association

Reddie Dr Anthony (2)
Dread and Pentecostal:
A political Theology for the Black Church in Britain.
A book review
Published 2001; Epworth Review of Robert Beckford, pp 82-83

Reddie Dr Anthony (3)
Faith, Stories and the Experience of Black Elders.
Published 2001; Publisher Jessica Kingsley, London ISBN 1 85302 993 9

Reddie Dr Anthony (4)
Peace and Justice through Black Christian Education
Published 2001; Black Theology in Britain (a journal of Contextual Praxis), Issue 6, pp 73-85

Reed Bruce, J Bazalgette et al
Becoming Fit For Purpose.
Report of a study of how 3 church schools were transformed from being at risk of closure, focussing particularly on how the Christian beliefs of the headteachers shaped the way they worked.
The Grubb Institute, Cloudesley Street, London N1 0HU
Published: 2003; 100 pages; Price: not yet available

Rees Craig
The Relation of Faith and the Miracles of Jesus in the Gospel of Matthew.
London Bible College, Green Lane, Northwood, Middlesex HA6 2UW
Published 1997; MTh

Reeves Rev John
Male Spirituality Then and Now.
The Rectory, 14 The Green, Aldridge, Walsall WS9 8NH
Published 2002

Reid Dr M S B
Strategic Level Spiritual Warfare:
A Modern Mythology? A detailed evaluation of the Biblical, theological and historical basis of spiritual warfare in contemporary thought.
Alive UK, 49 Coxtie Green Road, Pilgrims Hatch, Brentwood, Essex CM14 5PS
Published 2002; 348 pages; Price £11.95; Publisher Xulon Press

Reid Dr Norman
Pentecostal Contributions of Mission in Scotland.
An analysis of Pentecostal mission and growth in Scotland set in the context of a review of worldwide Pentecostal Mission, with recommendations and suggestions for action.
Hazelbank, 83 Marjoribanks Street, Bathgate, Scotland EH48 1QH
Published 2000; 50 pages; MA dissertation (Mattersey College); Price £3

Reynolds Ruth
The Way Forward for the Church.
Is it improved styles of Worship? Is blended worship a better model for the future?
Cliff College Library, Calver, Hope Valley, Derbyshire S32 3XG
Published 2002; 10,000 words; BA

Richards Wesley

An Examination of the Growth of the Global Holy Spirit Movement.
London Bible College, Green Lane, Northwood, Middlesex HA6 2UW
Published 2002; Mth

Robbins Dr Mandy (1)
Clergywomen in the Church of England and the Gender Inclusive Language Debate.
Research amongst 1,139 clergywomen in the Church of England.
University of Wales at Bangor, Normal Site, Bangor LL57 2PX
Published 2001; Publisher Review of Religious Research, Vol 42, No 4, pp 405-414

Robbins Dr Mandy & L J Francis (2)
Religion, personality and well-being: the relationship between church attendance and purpose in life among undergraduates attending an Anglican College in Wales.
Published 2000; Journal of Research on Christian Education, Vol 9, pp 223-238

Robbins Dr Mandy
& L J Francis, J M Haley, W K Kay (3)
The personality characteristics of Methodist ministers: feminine men and masculine women?
Published 2001; Journal for the Scientific Study of Religion, Vol 40, pp 123-128

Rogobete Silviu
Subject and Supreme Personal Reality in the Theological thought of Fr Dumitru Staniloae.
An ontology of love.
London Bible College, Green Lane, Northwood, Middlesex HA6 2UW
Published 1998; PhD Thesis

Roof Wade Clark
Spiritual seeking in the US: report on a Panel Study.
Published 2000; Arch.de Sc. Soc. Des. Rel, No 109

Rourke Jonathan
What does it mean to them?
A study into children's understanding of religious language.
Cliff College Library, Calver, Hope Valley, Derbyshire S32 3XG
Published 2001; 10-20,000 words; Dip CEN

Rowden Harold
Church Leaders Handbook.
51 chapters by 44 authors addressing a wide range of church leadership, management and activities issues. Mostly relevant to Free Churches.
Partnership Publications, c/o 3 Longlands Road, Carlisle CA3 9AD
Published 2002, Price £19.99 hardback, £14.99 paperback; Publisher Partnership and Paternoster Press

Rowe Robert D
God's Kingdom and God's Son:
A study in the background to Mark's Christology with special reference to concepts of kingship in the Psalms.
London Bible College, Green Lane, Northwood, Middlesex HA6 2UW
Published 1990; PhD; Publisher Brill 2002

Saarinen Jorma
An Investigation of the Placement and Authenticity of 2 Corinthians 6:14-7:1
London Bible College, Green Lane, Northwood, Middlesex HA6 2UW
Published 1999; MTh

Sabu Sorin
Between Horror and Hope:
Paul's metaphorical language of death in Romans 6: 1-11.
London Bible College, Green Lane, Northwood, Middlesex HA6 2UW
Published 2001: PhD Thesis

Salonen Kari
& K Kääriäinen, K Niemelä
The Church at the Turn of the Millennium.
The Denomination's position in the Finnish context.
Research Institute of the Evangelical Lutheran Church of Finland, Bos 239, FIN-33101, Tampere, Finland
Published 2001; No 51; 80 pages

Salvation Army
The Burden of Youth.
A report on the major social issues facing young people today.
External Relations Officer, Salvation Army Territorial Headquarters, 101 Newington Causeway, London SE1 6BN
Published 2002

Sanderson Robin
The Aims of Jesus in Recent Historical Quests.
London Bible College, Green Lane, Northwood, Middlesex HA6 2UW
Published 1997; MTh

Sauer Dr Christof
Spreading the Word of God among Muslims in South Africa: some considerations on Scripture distribution.
PO Box 23273, 7735 Claremont, Cape Town, Rep. South Africa
Published 2002; 17 pages

Savina Anna
God's Prosperity Facing Christians
– Philosophic reflections to be or not to be for money at God's service. What is the Christian attitude towards the use of money in the 'blessed purposes'?
Cliff College Library, Calver, Hope Valley, Derbyshire S32 3XG
Published 2001; 10,000 words; BA

Scott J Martin
The Theology of the so-called 'New Churches Movement':
An analysis of eschatology.
London Bible College, Green Lane, Northwood, Middlesex HA6 2UW
Published 1997; MTh

Sedgwick Colin
Predestination in the Letter to the Ephesians.
London Bible College, Green Lane, Northwood, Middlesex HA6 2UW
Published 1996; MTh

Selvanagam Rev Dr I (ed)
Moving Forms of Theology Faith Talk's changing contexts.
Compilation of scholarly articles.
United College of the Ascension, Wesley Park Road, Selly Oak, Birmingham B29 6RD
Published 2002; 196 pages; Price £5

Siewart John & D Welliver (eds)
Mission Handbook, US And Canadian Ministries Overseas, 2001-2003.
This 18th edition lists 814 agencies and has four chapters of interpretation.
Evangelism and Missions Information Service, Billy Graham Centre, Wheaton, Illinois 60187-5593 USA
Published 2001; 504 pages

Silber Heinrich
Aspects of the Righteous and the Wicked in Psalms 7 and 137:
Exegetical and hermeneutical considerations.
London Bible College, Green Lane, Northwood, Middlesex HA6 2UW
Published 2000; PhD Thesis

Simon Elizabeth
Church-sponsored social action and community regeneration projects in London.
Executive Officer, London Churches Group for Social Action, Central Hall Westminster, Storey's Gate, London SW1H 9NH
Published 2002

Skinner Shaun
Christianity and Politics.
Cliff College Library, Calver, Hope Valley, Derbyshire S32 3XG
Published 2001; 10,000 words; BA

Smith Colin S
Calvin's doctrine of Justification in Relation to the Sense of Sin and the Dialogue with Rome.
London Bible College, Green Lane, Northwood, Middlesex HA6 2UW
Published 1994; MPhil

Smith G & L J Francis, M Robbins
Establishment or disestablishment?
A survey among Church of England clergy.
The Welsh National Centre for Religious Education, University of Wales Bangor, Normal Site, Bangor, Gwynedd LL57 2PX
Published 2002; Implicit Religion, Vol 5, pp 105-120

Smith Greg (1)
Community Research:
A practitioner's perspective on methods and values.
Greg@maister-smith.fsnet.co.uk
Published 2002; Journal of Community Work and Development; Vol 1, No 3

Smith Greg (2)
Religion and the Rise of Social Capitalism.
Published 2002; Community Development Journal, April 2002 edition, OUP

Smith Greg (3)
Mapping and Tracing:
Directories and Databases of the voluntary and community Sector. Is it worth it?
Published 2002; PowerPoint presentation at NCVO Research Conference

Smith Greg (4)
The State and the Faith:
Involving religious organisations in the delivery of urban policy in England.
Published 2002; PowerPoint presentation at BASR Conference

Smith Greg (5)
The Faith Sector
– Part of the voluntary sector or a distinct sector in itself?
Published 2002; PowerPoint presentation at Voluntary Sector Studies Network meeting in Manchester

Smith Greg (6)
Faith in Local Politics:
A case study from an inner London borough.
www.homepages.uel.ac.uk/G.Smith/faithandpolitics.rtf
Published 2002; Presented at a BSA Sociology of Religion Study Group Conference

Smith Tom
Religious Diversity in America:
Emergence of Muslims, Buddhists, Hindus and Others.
NOP Centre, Chicago, USA
Published 2002; GSS Social Change Report

Stackhouse Ian
The Problem of Immediacy in Charismatic Worship and Experience.
London Bible College, Green Lane, Northwood, Middlesex HA6 2UW
Published 1997; MTh

Stafford Maurice
Church Growth Theory and the Small Church.
A study of small and large churches within British Methodism.
British Church Growth Association, The Park, Moggerhanger, Bedford MK44 3RW
Published 2002

Stevens Dr David & F Olayisade
Black Immigrant Churches in the Republic of Ireland
Research project into aspects of the religious life of refugees, asylum seekers and immigrants in the Republic of Ireland.
Inter Church Centre, 48 Elmwood Avenue, Belfast BT9 6AZ or via ccpep@email.com
Published 2002; 18 pages

Strange Rev Alan
Windsor Project.
What do church leaders think they are doing?
Holy Trinity Church, 17 Essex Street, Norwich NR2 2BL
Published 2002; 40 pages

Strange Dr Daniel
Filling the Gaps, Church Planting:
New ways of being church in post-Christian Britain.
RTSF, 38 De Montfort Street, Leicester LE1 7GP
Published 2002

Sykes Rev Ken
Manse Children:
Some indicators towards their adult faith.
Vencroft, Venn Road, Barnstaple EX32 0HT
Published 2000

Tanner Mark S
The Southwell Cluster
– A 'missional church'?
Postgraduate Administrative Assistant, Cliff College, Calver, Hope Valley, Derbyshire S32 3XG
Published 2001; c 20,000 words; MA in Evangelism studies; Price £30

The Theological Research Exchange Network
Online listing of over 10,000 theological thesis and dissertation titles.
Also included are over 1,000 papers read at annual and regional meetings of the Evangelical Theological Society.
http://www.tren.com/search.cfm

Thomas Janet
Methodism, mission and money: how the availability of money impacts three very small congregations in British Methodism.
Postgraduate Administrative Assistant, Cliff College, Calver, Hope Valley, Derbyshire S32 3XG
Published 2001; c 20,000 words; MA in Evangelism studies; Price £30

7.12 Recent Research Reports

Thomas Michael G
The Extent of the Atonement:
A Dilemma for Reformed Theology from Calvin to the Consensus (1536-1675)
London Bible College, Green Lane, Northwood, Middlesex HA6 2UW
Published 1993; PhD Thesis; Publisher Paternoster Press 1997

Tomkins Stephen
The Quicksands of Anabaptistry:
The covenant theology of the English Separatists and the origins of the Baptists.
London Bible College, Green Lane, Northwood, Middlesex HA6 2UW
Published 2000; PhD Thesis

Tregale John
Youth Church explored.
Postgraduate Administrative Assistant, Cliff College, Calver, Hope Valley, Derbyshire S32 3XG
Published 2001; c 20,000 words; MA in Evangelism studies; Price £30

Tsang Nai Ming
The Use of Paradox in the Gospel of Mark.
London Bible College, Green Lane, Northwood, Middlesex HA6 2UW
Published 1997; MTh

Turner Philip Stanley
Can we have faith in undergraduates: university as a place of finding and losing faith.
Postgraduate Administrative Assistant, Cliff College, Calver, Hope Valley, Derbyshire S32 3XG
Published 2001; c 20,000 words; MA in Evangelism studies; Price £30

Uddin Mohan
Paul and the Jews:
Causal agency in unbelief and the question of coherence (with special reference to 2 Corinthians 3-4 and Romans 9-11).
London Bible College, Green Lane, Northwood, Middlesex HA6 2UW
Published 1998; PhD Thesis

7

Ventom Joy
Ministry among children in the Wheatley area of Doncaster.
Cliff College Library, Calver, Hope Valley, Derbyshire S32 3XG
Published 2001; 10-20,000 words; Dip CEN

Vermulen Rev Chris
Woodlands Community Project.
Working with churches and community in Manchester and Nottingham.
22 Woodlands Parkway, Timperley, Altrincham WA15 7QU
Published 2002

Walker Etleva
Mother Teresa and Mission to the Poor.
Cliff College Library, Calver, Hope Valley, Derbyshire S32 3XG
Published 2002; 10,000 words; BA

Walker Rev Canon Geoffrey (1)
Folk Religion:
Is churchmanship really an attitude predictor?
This research suggests that attitudes to folk religion are less a matter of churchmanship than of other factors.
Principal, Local Ministry Training Scheme, Diocesan House, Lady Wootton's Green, Canterbury, Kent CY1 1NQ
Published 2002; 8pp; Modern Believing, *Vol 43, No 2; Price £1.50*

Walker Rev Canon Geoffrey (2)
Contemporary Clerical Constructions of a Spiritual Rural Idyll. Highlights the role of Anglican clergy in the creation of a spiritual variant of the (imaginary) rural idyll.
Published 2002; 11 pages; Sociologia Ruralis, Vol 42(2), pp 131-142; Price £1.50

Walker Rev Canon Geoffrey (3)
The Changed Meanings of the Occasional Officer (officeS?): some recent clerical observations.
Published 2001; 6 pages; Conference Paper: XXIVth Denton Consultation on Implicit Religion; Price £1.50

Walker Rev Canon Geoffrey (4)
Clergy Attitudes to Folk-Religion:
new light on an uneasy alliance.
Published 2003; 7 pages; Conference paper from Vernacular Religious to Contemporary Spirituality; Price £1.50

Walker Michael Brian
Ecumenism and Evangelism:
the need to be together to spread the 'Good News'?
Cliff College Library, Calver, Hope Valley, Derbyshire S32 3XG
Published 2001; 10,000 words; BA

Walker Yasmin
'Truth' Bane or Blessing of Christianity in the West today?
Cliff College Library, Calver, Hope Valley, Derbyshire S32 3XG
Published 2001; 10,000 words; BA

Walton Rachel
Who is the Church for?
An investigation into self perception of members of a local Methodist church.
Postgraduate Administrative Assistant, Cliff College, Calver, Hope Valley, Derbyshire S32 3XG
Published 2000; c 20,000 words; MA in Evangelism studies; Price £30

Warren Alison M
The Bible as Story
– As we move from a literate culture to a non-literate culture.
Cliff College Library, Calver, Hope Valley, Derbyshire S32 3XG
Published 2001; 10,000 words; BA

Warrington Keith
An Exegesis of James 5:13-18.
London Bible College, Green Lane, Northwood, Middlesex HA6 2UW
Published 1991; MPhil

The Welcome Trust
Public Perspectives on Human Cloning.
A Social Research Study.
The Wellcome Trust, 183 Euston Road, London NW1 2BE or contact@wellcome.ac.uk
Published 1998; reprinted 2001. Free.

Wenk Matthias
The Holy Spirit and the Ethical/Religious Life of the People of God in Luke-Acts.
London Bible College, Green Lane, Northwood, Middlesex HA6 2UW
Published 1998; PhD Thesis; Publisher Sheffield Academic Press 2000

Weston Ann
Church Growth amongst Indigenous East Anglican Churches in Greater London.
11 Kings Court, Kings Drive, Wembley, Middlesex HA9 9ES
Published 2002; LBC Dissertation

Whittaker Clare
A review of the children's work at Woodley Baptist Church in relation to the needs of children and families in the local community.
Cliff College Library, Calver, Hope Valley, Derbyshire S32 3XG
Published 2001; 10-20,000 words; Dip CEN

Wiarda Timothy
Peter in the Gospels:
pattern, personality and relationship
London Bible College, Green Lane, Northwood, Middlesex HA6 2UW
Published 1999; PhD Thesis; Publisher J C B Mohr 2000

Wibberley John
Created Stewards for God's Husbandry.
London Bible College, Green Lane, Northwood, Middlesex HA6 2UW
Published 2002; MTh

Widmer Michael
Approaches to Re-reading the Psalms of Lament as Christian Scripture.
London Bible College, Green Lane, Northwood, Middlesex HA6 2UW
Published 1998; MTh

Wilkinson-Hayes Anne
Respecting Communities:
Intentional community as a model for the local church.
London Bible College, Green Lane, Northwood, Middlesex HA6 2UW
Published 1997; MTh

Williams Edward S
The Great Divorce Controversy
The theological and practical history of divorce.
Belmont House Publishing, 36 The Crescent, Sutton SM2 6BJ
Published 2002; 468 pages, Price £25

Womersley Eric
The Role of Shoeburyness and Thorpe Bay Baptist Church.
Cliff College Library, Calver, Hope Valley, Derbyshire S32 3XG
Published 2001; 10-20,000 words; Dip CEN

Woodall David
Can my Church Grow?
An evaluation of various church growth models in relation to a 'stagnant' and declining Urban Priority Area Church in Northern England.
Postgraduate Administrative Assistant, Cliff College, Calver, Hope Valley, Derbyshire S32 3XG
Published 2000; c 15,000 words; Postgraduate Diploma in Leadership, Renewal & Mission Studies; Price £30

Woodhouse B
Aspects of the Evangelical Metanarrative
– a deconstructive critique.
Cliff College Library, Calver, Hope Valley, Derbyshire S32 3XG
Published 2002; 10,000 words; BA

Worcestershire Historical Society
1851 Census of Religious Worship, returns for Worcestershire.
Worcestershire Historical Society
Published 2000; edited John Aitken; ISSN 0141-4577

Wraight, Heather (1)
World Vision. Focus Groups.
Christian Research, Vision Building, 4 Footscray Road, Eltham, SE9 2TZ
Published 2000

Wraight, Heather (2)
Church of England Newspaper:
Focus Groups.
Published 2000

Zinomuhangi Medad
Coexistence between Traditionalism and Charismaticism in the Anglican Church Today.
London Bible College, Green Lane, Northwood, Middlesex HA6 2UW
Published 1998; MTh

7

7.14 Recent Research Reports: Subject Index

7

7.16 Recent Research Reports: Subject Index

7

8

Institutional Church Statistics

8

See notes and definitions on Page 0.6

Sources: Individual denominations and previous editions of *Religious Trends*

8.2 Institutional Church Statistics: Anglican Churches

Table 8.2.1
Total Anglican Churches[8]

	MEMBERSHIP					CHURCHES					MINISTERS				
	England	Wales	Scotland	N. Ireland	**Total UK**	England	Wales	Scotland	N. Ireland	**Total UK**	England	Wales	Scotland	N. Ireland	**Total UK**
1990	1,398,863	108,365	58,619	162,130	**1,727,977**	16,440	1,595	319	476	**18,830**	11,130	700	240	304	**12,374**
1995	1,472,617	95,785	55,106	161,525	**1,785,033**	16,361	1,540	320	452	**18,673**	10,378	710	244	250	**11,582**
2000	1,381,930	83,840	49,853	160,827	**1,676,450**	16,350	1,514	315	447	**18,624**	9,754	657	174	295	**10,885**
2001	1,377,085	81,345	48,868	160,727	**1,668,025**	16,354	1,513	316	442	**18,625**	9,682	662	181	305	**10,830**
2002	1,211,455	75,470	47,992	160,528	**1,495,445**	16,371	1,515	320	442	**18,648**	9,611	659	178	304	**10,752**
2005	1,271,130	71,675	45,635	160,130	**1,548,570**	16,386	1,513	321	432	**18,652**	9,238	660	161	304	**10,363**

Table 8.2.2
Church of England[2]

	MEMBERSHIP					CHURCHES					MINISTERS				
	England	Wales	Scotland	N. Ireland	**Total UK**	England	Wales	Scotland	N. Ireland	**Total UK**	England[4]	Wales	Scotland	N. Ireland	**Total UK**
1990	1,396,000	0	0	0	**1,396,000**	16,380	0	0	0	**16,380**	11,072	0	0	0	**11,072**
1995	1,468,000	0	0	0	**1,468,000**	16,255	0	0	0	**16,255**	10,260	0	0	0	**10,260**
2000	1,377,000	0	0	0	**1,377,000**	16,222	0	0	0	**16,222**	9,600[5]	0	0	0	**9,600**
2001	1,372,000	0	0	0	**1,372,000**	16,220	0	0	0	**16,220**	9,500	0	0	0	**9,500**
2002[1]	1,206,000	0	0	0	**1,206,000**	16,217	0	0	0	**16,217**	9,400	0	0	0	**9,400**
2005[1]	1,265,000	0	0	0	**1,265,000**	16,205	0	0	0	**16,205**	9,000	0	0	0	**9,000**

Table 8.2.3
Church in Wales

	MEMBERSHIP					CHURCHES					MINISTERS				
	England	Wales	Scotland	N. Ireland	**Total UK**	England	Wales	Scotland	N. Ireland	**Total UK**	England	Wales	Scotland	N. Ireland	**Total UK**
1990	0	108,200	0	0	**108,200**	0	1,593	0	0	**1,593**	0	696	0	0	**696**
1995	0	95,400	0	0	**95,400**	0	1,537	0	0	**1,537**	0	702	0	0	**702**
2000	0	83,400	0	0	**83,400**	0	1,511	0	0	**1,511**	0	648	0	0	**648**
2001	0	80,900	0	0	**80,900**	0	1,510	0	0	**1,510**	0	653	0	0	**653**
2002	0	75,000	0	0	**75,000**	0	1,511	0	0	**1,511**	0	646	0	0	**646**
2005	0	71,000	0	0	**71,000**	0	1,500	0	0	**1,500**	0	635	0	0	**635**

Table 8.2.4
Scottish Episcopal Church

	MEMBERSHIP					CHURCHES					MINISTERS				
	England	Wales	Scotland	N. Ireland	**Total UK**	England	Wales	Scotland[6]	N. Ireland	**Total UK**	England	Wales	Scotland	N. Ireland	**Total UK**
1990	0	0	58,299	0	**58,299**	0	0	316	0	**316**	0	0	233	0	**233**
1995	0	0	54,352	0	**54,352**	0	0	316	0	**316**	0	0	230	0	**230**
2000[1]	0	0	49,000	0	**49,000**	0	0	310	0	**310**	0	0	167	0	**167**
2001[1]	0	0	48,000	0	**48,000**	0	0	310	0	**310**	0	0	158	0	**158**
2002[1]	0	0	47,000	0	**47,000**	0	0	309	0	**309**	0	0	149	0	**149**
2005[1]	0	0	44,500	0	**44,500**	0	0	305	0	**305**	0	0	120	0	**120**

Table 8.2.5
Church of Ireland (Northern Ireland)

	MEMBERSHIP					CHURCHES					MINISTERS				
	England	Wales	Scotland	N. Ireland	**Total UK**	England	Wales	Scotland	N. Ireland	**Total UK**	England	Wales	Scotland	N. Ireland	**Total UK**
1990	0	0	0	162,110	**162,110**	0	0	0	475	**475**	0	0	0	300	**300**
1995	0	0	0	161,500	**161,500**	0	0	0	450	**450**	0	0	0	245	**245**
2000	0	0	0	160,800[1]	**160,800**	0	0	0	445[5]	**445**	0	0	0	290	**290**
2001	0	0	0	160,700[1]	**160,700**	0	0	0	440	**440**	0	0	0	300	**300**
2002	0	0	0	160,500[1]	**160,500**	0	0	0	440	**440**	0	0	0	300	**300**
2005[1]	0	0	0	160,100	**160,100**	0	0	0	430	**430**	0	0	0	300	**300**

Table 8.2.6
Free Church of England

	MEMBERSHIP					CHURCHES					MINISTERS				
	England	Wales	Scotland	N. Ireland	**Total UK**	England	Wales	Scotland	N. Ireland	**Total UK**	England	Wales	Scotland	N. Ireland	**Total UK**
1990	1,850	0	0	0	**1,850**	30	0	0	0	**30**	27	0	0	0	**27**
1995	1,510	0	0	0	**1,510**	30	0	0	0	**30**	40	0	0	0	**40**
2000[1]	1,410	0	0	0	**1,410**	30	0	0	0	**30**	45	0	0	0	**45**
2001[1]	1,400	0	0	0	**1,400**	30	0	0	0	**30**	45	0	0	0	**45**
2002[1]	1,380	0	0	0	**1,380**	30	0	0	0	**30**	45	0	0	0	**45**
2005[1]	1,300	0	0	0	**1,300**	30	0	0	0	**30**	45	0	0	0	**45**

Table 8.2.7
Protestant Evangelical Church of England[7]

	MEMBERSHIP					CHURCHES					MINISTERS				
	England	Wales	Scotland	N. Ireland	**Total UK**	England	Wales	Scotland	N. Ireland	**Total UK**	England	Wales	Scotland	N. Ireland	**Total UK**
1990	70	0	0	10	**80**	3	0	0	0	**3**	6	0	0	2	**8**
1995	90	0	0	10	**100**	3	0	0	0	**3**	5	0	0	2	**7**
2000	80	0	0	10	**90**	3	0	0	0	**3**	5	0	0	2	**7**
2001	80	0	0	10	**90**	3	0	0	0	**3**	5	0	0	2	**7**
2002	85	0	0	10	**95**	3	0	0	0	**3**	5	0	0	1	**6**
2005	90	0	0	10	**100**	4	0	0	0	**4**	6	0	0	1	**7**

[1] Estimate. *For other footnotes, see* **Page 8.4**

Table 8.3.1
Other Church of England Statistics

	Baptisms [2]	Confirmations	Marriages	Sunday Attendance Total	of which Children [3]	Easter Attendance Communicants	All Ages	Christmas Attendance Communicants	All Ages
1990	229,000	60,000	109,369	1,142,300[4]	226,300	1,376,000	n/a	1,556,000	n/a
1995	194,000	44,000	79,616	1,045,300[4]	192,000	1,365,000	n/a	1,393,000	n/a
1999	179,040	37,469	63,371	968,800[4]	169,700	1,180,100	n/a	1,225,400	n/a
2000	161,110	36,469	61,519	1,058,000[5]	180,000	1,163,100	1,626,300	1,366,000	2,851,600
2001	153,300	33,400	58,100[1]	1,041,000[5]	173,000	1,156,000	1,616,000	1,228,000	2,608,000
2005[1]	133,000	25,800	48,900	960,000[5]	163,000	1,064,000	1,490,000	1,154,000	2,410,000

[1] Estimate [2] Adult and infant [3] Aged 15 and under [4] Usual Sunday Attendance [5] Average Sunday Attendance

Table 8.3.2 Average Weekly Attendance (AWA) 2000 and 2001 and Electoral Roll (ER) 1998–2000 by Church of England Diocese

Diocese	Average Weekly Attendance 2000	2001	% change	Electoral Roll 1998	1999	2000	% average annual change	AWA as % in 2000 of ER	Pop
Bath and Wells	34,100	29,000	*–15*	42,500	43,000	43,500	*+1.2*	*78*	*4.0*
Birmingham	20,200	20,200	*0*	19,500	19,300	19,700	*+0.5*	*103*	*1.4*
Blackburn	40,000	37,000	*–7*	38,300	38,600	38,900	*+0.8*	*103*	*3.1*
Bradford	14,300	13,200	*–8*	13,300	13,100	13,300	*0*	*108*	*2.2*
Bristol	21,500	19,000	*–12*	20,200	20,400	20,300	*+0.2*	*106*	*2.4*
Canterbury	26,300	24,200	*–8*	21,800	22,300	22,700	*+2.0*	*116*	*3.1*
Carlisle	18,900	17,400	*–8*	25,200	25,000	25,300	*+0.2*	*75*	*3.9*
Chelmsford	47,200	44,700	*–5*	53,200	54,200	54,100	*+0.8*	*87*	*1.7*
Chester	46,700	43,700	*–6*	50,900	52,100	54,100	*+3.1*	*86*	*3.0*
Chichester	51,900	48,700	*–6*	61,400	61,300	60,800	*–0.5*	*85*	*3.4*
Coventry	17,900	17,100	*–4*	17,700	18,200	18,200	*+1.4*	*98*	*2.3*
Derby	23,800	19,500	*–18*	21,900	21,900	22,000	*+0.2*	*108*	*2.4*
Durham	26,800	24,100	*–10*	28,900	27,700	28,100	*–1.4*	*95*	*1.8*
Ely	20,000	19,000	*–5*	21,200	21,500	22,000	*+1.9*	*91*	*3.1*
Exeter	30,000	28,600	*–5*	35,000	34,600	34,700	*–0.4*	*86*	*2.8*
Gloucester	22,900[1]	22,400	*–2*	26,900	26,900	27,200	*+0.6*	*84*	*3.8*
Guildford	31,500	30,600	*–3*	31,500	31,900	32,800	*+2.0*	*96*	*3.2*
Hereford	12,700	12,700	*0*	19,400	20,100	20,300	*+2.3*	*63*	*4.1*
Leicester	16,800	17,600	*+5*	16,600	16,700	17,100	*+1.5*	*98*	*1.9*
Lichfield	42,100	41,500	*–1*	54,300	54,800	55,400	*+1.0*	*76*	*2.1*
Lincoln	28,600	26,400	*–8*	32,300	30,700	31,600	*–1.1*	*91*	*3.0*
Liverpool	37,800	34,500	*–9*	33,300	33,300	33,200	*–0.2*	*114*	*2.4*
London	77,200	71,400	*–8*	57,800	59,900	62,400	*+3.9*	*124*	*2.1*
Manchester	37,700	34,700	*–8*	39,500	39,800	39,700	*+0.3*	*95*	*1.9*
Newcastle	15,000	15,000	*0*	17,800	18,300	18,600	*+2.2*	*81*	*1.9*
Norwich	26,500	25,000	*–6*	26,700	26,800	26,700	*0*	*99*	*3.2*
Oxford	64,700	62,300	*–4*	64,600	63,200	63,800	*+0.6*	*101*	*3.0*
Peterborough	24,800	22,000	*–11*	19,800	19,600	20,000	*+0.5*	*124*	*3.2*
Portsmouth	17,300[1]	16,900	*–2*	19,200	19,300	20,300	*+2.8*	*85*	*2.4*
Ripon & Leeds	17,800	17,300	*–3*	20,100	20,000	19,000	*–2.8*	*94*	*2.3*
Rochester	32,500	32,400	*0*	32,200	32,800	33,600	*+2.2*	*97*	*2.7*
St Albans	42,300	39,400	*–7*	45,500	46,100	47,500	*+2.2*	*89*	*2.5*
St Edmundsbury & Ipswich	23,300	22,400	*–4*	26,100	26,500	26,900	*+1.5*	*87*	*3.8*
Salisbury	38,000	35,800	*–6*	47,100	47,500	48,700	*+1.7*	*78*	*4.4*
Sheffield	23,800	22,200	*–7*	21,500	21,800	22,000	*+1.2*	*119*	*2.0*
Sodor & Man	2,900	3,000	*+3*	3,000	2,900	3,100	*+1.7*	*94*	*3.8*
Southwark	43,200[1]	42,200	*–2*	46,400	47,200	48,900	*+2.7*	*88*	*1.8*
Southwell	18,900	18,900	*0*	18,900	18,600	19,000	*+0.3*	*99*	*1.8*
Truro	17,200	15,400	*–10*	17,700	18,100	18,000	*+0.8*	*96*	*3.4*
Wakefield	22,400	19,100	*–15*	24,100	24,700	25,400	*+2.7*	*88*	*2.1*
Winchester	38,900	35,600	*–8*	43,500	43,500	45,200	*+1.9*	*86*	*3.1*
Worcester	20,800	18,300	*–12*	23,200	23,400	23,300	*+0.2*	*89*	*2.5*
York	36,800	32,400	*–12*	39,500	39,800	40,400	*+1.1*	*91*	*2.7*
TOTAL	**1,262,000**	**1,192,800**	***–5***	**1,338,300**	**1,347,400**	**1,367,700**	***+1.1***	***93***	***2.5***

[1] Estimate.

Table 8.3.3 Total Church of England Clergy and Church Army Officers

	SC	N-SC	Chaps	Total[2]	CAO	RetdC
1990	11,100	1,300	1,000	**13,400**	400	5,974
1995	10,300	1,900	1,100	**13,300**	400	6,745
1999	9,648	2,050[1]	1,250[1]	**12,948**	375[1]	7,531
2000	9,538	2,083	1,258	**12,879**	350[1]	7,670[1]
2001	9,487	2,000	1,100	**12,587**	323	7,840[1]
2005[1]	9,217	1,800	1,000	**12,017**	250	8,530

SC: Stipendiary Clergy
NSC: Non-stipendiary Clergy
Chaps: Chaplains[3]
CAO: Church Army Officers
RetdC: All retired Clergy
[1] Estimate
[2] Excluding Lay Church Army Officers and other lay workers
[3] Armed Services, Prison, School and Hospital Chaplains, including 30 for deaf people

Five maps on **Page 2.20** illustrate some of the data in **Table 8.3.2**. They show considerable disparity between Dioceses, often related to whether they are in a rural or urban area. The Church of England is generally stronger in rural areas than urban.

Table 8.3.3 indicates a decline in the number of clergy at an average rate of 1.4% per annum during the 1990s, a rate expected to almost halve in the immediate years ahead. This is a much smaller rate than the decline in Average Weekly Attendance – lay people are leaving the church faster than the clergy. The number of other leaders shown in this Table reflects the continued widespread ministry of the church, in all areas of society.

Sources: Research & Statistics Dept., Archbishops' Council; *Ministry Issues,* Gordon Kuhrt, Church House Publishing, 2001; *UK Christian Handbook,* Christian Research, 1994/95 and 1996/97 editions; *Church Statistics 2000,* Church House Publishing, 2002; *Religious Trends No 3* 2002/2003, Table 8.8.2; *Church Times* 5th May 2000.

8.4 Institutional Church Statistics: Anglican Churches (continued)

Table 8.4.1
Anglian Apostolic Episcopal Free Church

	MEMBERSHIP					CHURCHES					MINISTERS				
	England	Wales	Scotland	N. Ireland	**Total UK**	England	Wales	Scotland	N. Ireland	**Total UK**	England	Wales	Scotland	N. Ireland	**Total UK[2]**
1990	505	165	320	10	**1,000**	12	2	3	1	**18**	15	4	7	2	**28**
1995	1,182	385	754	15	**2,336**	19	3	4	2	**28**	28	8	14	3	**53**
2000[1]	1,340	440	853	17	**2,650**	22	3	5	2	**32**	33	9	17	3	**62**
2001[1]	1,370	445	868	17	**2,700**	22	3	6	2	**33**	33	9	18	3	**63**
2002[1]	1,390	450	892	18	**2,750**	23	3	6	2	**34**	34	10	18	3	**65**
2005[1]	1,470	475	935	20	**2,900**	24	3	6	2	**35**	37	10	20	3	**70**

Table 8.4.2
Anglican Orthodox Free Church[3]

	MEMBERSHIP					CHURCHES					MINISTERS				
	England	Wales	Scotland	N. Ireland	**Total UK**	England	Wales	Scotland	N. Ireland	**Total UK**	England	Wales	Scotland	N. Ireland	**Total UK[2]**
1990	438	0	0	0	**438**	15	0	0	0	**15**	10	0	0	0	**10**
1995	1,000	0	0	0	**1,000**	20	0	0	0	**20**	10	0	0	0	**10**
2000[1]	1,000	0	0	0	**1,000**	20	0	0	0	**20**	10	0	0	0	**10**
2001[1]	1,000	0	0	0	**1,000**	20	0	0	0	**20**	10	0	0	0	**10**
2002[1]	1,000	0	0	0	**1,000**	20	0	0	0	**20**	10	0	0	0	**10**
2005[1]	1,200	0	0	0	**1,200**	22	0	0	0	**22**	11	0	0	0	**11**

Table 8.4.3
Anglican Catholic Church[5]

	MEMBERSHIP					CHURCHES					MINISTERS				
	England	Wales	Scotland	N. Ireland	**Total UK**	England	Wales	Scotland	N. Ireland	**Total UK**	England	Wales	Scotland	N. Ireland	**Total UK**
1990	–	–	–	–	–	–	–	–	–	–	–	–	–	–	–
1995	650	0	0	0	**650**	27	0	0	0	**27**	25	0	0	0	**25**
2000[1]	650	0	0	0	**650**	27	0	0	0	**27**	25	0	0	0	**25**
2001[1]	650	0	0	0	**650**	27	0	0	0	**27**	25	0	0	0	**25**
2002[1]	650	0	0	0	**650**	27	0	0	0	**27**	25	0	0	0	**25**
2005[1]	650	0	0	0	**650**	27	0	0	0	**27**	25	0	0	0	**25**

Table 8.4.4
Other Anglican Churches[6]

	MEMBERSHIP					CHURCHES					MINISTERS				
	England	Wales	Scotland	N. Ireland	**Total UK**	England	Wales	Scotland	N. Ireland	**Total UK**	England	Wales	Scotland	N. Ireland	**Total UK**
1990	–	–	–	–	–	–	–	–	–	–	–	–	–	–	–
1995	185	0	0	0	**185**	7	0	0	0	**7**	10	0	0	0	**10**
2000[1]	380	0	0	0	**380**	23	0	0	0	**23**	33	0	0	0	**33**
2001[1]	385	0	0	0	**385**	23	0	0	0	**23**	33	0	0	0	**33**
2002[1]	390	0	0	0	**390**	23	0	0	0	**23**	33	0	0	0	**33**
2005[1]	400	0	0	0	**400**	23	0	0	0	**23**	33	0	0	0	**33**

Table 8.4.5
St Thomas-à-Becket Episcopal Synod[7]

	MEMBERSHIP					CHURCHES					MINISTERS				
	England	Wales	Scotland	N. Ireland	**Total UK**	England	Wales	Scotland	N. Ireland	**Total UK**	England	Wales	Scotland	N. Ireland	**Total UK**
1990	–	–	–	–	–	–	–	–	–	–	–	–	–	–	–
1995	–	–	–	–	–	–	–	–	–	–	–	–	–	–	–
2000	20	0	0	0	**20**	1[1]	0	0	0	**1**	1[1]	0	0	0	**1**
2001[1]	20	0	0	0	**20**	1	0	0	0	**1**	1	0	0	0	**1**
2002[1]	20	0	0	0	**20**	1	0	0	0	**1**	1	0	0	0	**1**
2005[1]	20	0	0	0	**20**	1	0	0	0	**1**	1	0	0	0	**1**

Page 8.2

[2] Major revisions of the Electoral Roll took place in 1990, 1996 and 2002. Numbers exclude Diocese of Europe
[3] Electoral Roll
[4] Full-time stipendiary within the Diocesan framework up to 1997. 1998 and onwards includes the full-time equivalent of part-time stipendiary Diocesan clergy. Numbers exclude Lay Church Army Officers and other lay workers. For non-stipendiary numbers and Chaplains see Table 8.3.3
[5] Revised figure
[6] Excluding preaching points
[7] Began in 1990
[8] Total of Tables 8.2.2–6 and 8.4.1–5.

Page 8.4

[1] Estimate
[2] All unpaid
[3] Includes breakaway Church of England Homechurches Union
[4] Services largely held in homes
[5] Began in 1992
[6] Includes the Traditional Church of England, Church of England (Continuing), Traditional Anglican Church and the Continuing Church of England.
[7] Started in UK in 1996; Head Office in Canterbury, Kent. Worldwide there are 800 churches, 1,200 members but 100,000 in attendance. Strong in Nigeria where new church is being built, and 4 Bishops in United States.

Page 8.5

[1] Estimate
[2] As measured on the first Sunday in October each year
[3] Taken as the full number of church buildings and all other buildings open to the public for mass
[4] Revised figure
[5] Parishes not churches
[6] In 2002 there were 594 churches in these 461 parishes
[7] The Northern Ireland proportion is based on the following percentages of the 4 Dioceses that straddle the border: 95% of Derry, 75% of Armagh, 60% of Clogher and 5% of Kilmore, plus 100% of the 2 Dioceses wholly within Northern Ireland – Down and Connor & Dromere
[8] Founded in 1992
[9] Not a *Roman* Catholic Church
[10] Total of **Tables 8.5.2–7, 8.6.1–7** and **8.7.1** and **2.**

Institutional Church Statistics: Roman Catholic Churches

Table 8.5.1
Total Catholic Churches[10]

	Mass Attendance					Churches					Priests				
	England	Wales	Scotland	N. Ireland	**Total UK**	England	Wales	Scotland	N. Ireland	**Total UK**	England	Wales	Scotland	N. Ireland	**Total UK**
1990	1,351,342	54,659	283,793	515,700	**2,205,494**	3,535	213	485	467	**4,700**	5,789	316	1,050	643	**7,798**
1995	1,105,940	47,244	250,302	518,000	**1,921,486**	3,462	240	462	470	**4,634**	5,637	288	947	600	**7,472**
2000	989,440	40,630	223,186	521,100	**1,774,356**	3,401	238	463	470	**4,572**	5,246	253	869	554	**6,922**
2001	971,172	39,640	212,740	522,100	**1,745,652**	3,428	233	463	470	**4,594**	5,247	255	855	547	**6,904**
2002	947,845	38,650	202,365	523,150	**1,712,010**	3,423	230	464	470	**4,587**	5,225	249	840	540	**6,854**
2005	888,369	35,170	183,710	524,200	**1,631,449**	3,320	222	465	470	**4,475**	5,041	228	794	520	**6,583**

Table 8.5.2
Roman Catholic Church in England

	Mass Attendance					Churches					Priests				
	England[2]	Wales	Scotland	N. Ireland	**Total UK**	England[3]	Wales	Scotland	N. Ireland	**Total UK**	England	Wales	Scotland	N. Ireland	**Total UK**
1990	1,332,826	0	0	0	**1,332,826**	3,473	0[4]	0	0	**3,473**	5,712	0	0	0	**5,712**
1995	1,087,890	0	0	0	**1,087,890**	3,399	0[4]	0	0	**3,399**	5,555	0	0	0	**5,555**
2000	973,000	0	0	0	**973,000**	3,359[1]	0	0	0	**3,359**	5,145	0	0	0	**5,145**
2001	954,132	0	0	0	**954,132**	3,351	0	0	0	**3,351**	5,144	0	0	0	**5,144**
2002[1]	930,000	0	0	0	**930,000**	3,345	0	0	0	**3,345**	5,120	0	0	0	**5,120**
2005[1]	870,000	0	0	0	**870,000**	3,230	0	0	0	**3,230**	4,930	0	0	0	**4,930**

Table 8.5.3
Roman Catholic Church in Wales

	Mass Attendance					Churches					Priests				
	England	Wales[2]	Scotland	N. Ireland	**Total UK**	England	Wales[3]	Scotland	N. Ireland	**Total UK**	England	Wales	Scotland	N. Ireland	**Total UK**
1990	0	54,609	0	0	**54,609**	0	211	0	0	**211**	0	316	0	0	**316**
1995	0	47,154	0	0	**47,154**	0	238	0	0	**238**	0	288	0	0	**288**
2000	0	40,500	0	0	**40,500**	0	236	0	0	**236**	0	253	0	0	**253**
2001	0	39,500[1]	0	0	**39,500**	0	231	0	0	**231**	0	255	0	0	**255**
2002[1]	0	38,500	0	0	**38,500**	0	228	0	0	**228**	0	249	0	0	**249**
2005[1]	0	35,000	0	0	**35,000**	0	220	0	0	**220**	0	228	0	0	**228**

Table 8.5.4
Roman Catholic Church in Scotland

	Mass Attendance					Churches					Priests				
	England	Wales	Scotland[2]	N. Ireland	**Total UK**	England	Wales	Scotland[5]	N. Ireland	**Total UK**	England	Wales	Scotland	N. Ireland	**Total UK**
1990	0	0	283,633	0	**283,633**	0	0	484	0	**484**	0	0	1,049	0	**1,049**
1995	0	0	250,142	0	**250,142**	0	0	461	0	**461**	0	0	946	0	**946**
2000	0	0	222,956	0	**222,956**	0	0	461	0	**461**	0	0	866	0	**866**
2001[1]	0	0	212,500	0	**212,500**	0	0	461	0	**461**	0	0	851	0	**851**
2002	0	0	202,110	0	**202,110**	0	0	461[6]	0	**461**	0	0	835[1]	0	**835**
2005[1]	0	0	183,400[4]	0	**183,400**	0	0	461	0	**461**	0	0	789	0	**789**

Table 8.5.5
Roman Catholic Church in Northern Ireland[7]

	Mass Attendance					Churches					Priests				
	England	Wales	Scotland	N. Ireland	**Total UK**	England	Wales	Scotland	N. Ireland	**Total UK**	England	Wales	Scotland	N. Ireland	**Total UK**
1990	0	0	0	515,700	**515,700**	0	0	0	467	**467**	0	0	0	643	**643**
1995	0	0	0	518,000	**518,000**	0	0	0	470	**470**	0	0	0	600	**600**
2000	0	0	0	521,000	**521,000**	0	0	0	470	**470**	0	0	0	554	**554**
2001[1]	0	0	0	522,000	**522,000**	0	0	0	470	**470**	0	0	0	547	**547**
2002[1]	0	0	0	523,000	**523,000**	0	0	0	470	**470**	0	0	0	540	**540**
2005[1]	0	0	0	524,000	**524,000**	0	0	0	470	**470**	0	0	0	520	**520**

Table 8.5.6
Independent Catholic Church of Great Britain[8, 9]

	Mass Attendance					Churches					Priests				
	England	Wales	Scotland	N. Ireland	**Total UK**	England	Wales	Scotland	N. Ireland	**Total UK**	England	Wales	Scotland	N. Ireland	**Total UK**
1990	–	–	–	–	–	–	–	–	–	–	–	–	–	–	–
1995	100[1]	0	0	0	**100[4]**	2[1]	0	0	0	**2[4]**	2[1]	0	0	0	**2[4]**
2000[1]	480	0	20	0	**500[4]**	9	0	1	0	**10[4]**	19	0	1	0	**20[4]**
2001[1]	540	0	30	0	**570**	11	0	1	0	**12**	21	0	2	0	**23**
2002	600	0	40	0	**640**	12	0	2	0	**14**	23	0	3	0	**26**
2005	800	0	100	0	**900**	25	0	3	0	**28**	28	0	3	0	**31**

Table 8.5.7
Old Roman Catholic Church of Great Britain[9]

	Mass Attendance					Churches					Priests				
	England	Wales	Scotland	N. Ireland	**Total UK**	England	Wales	Scotland	N. Ireland	**Total UK**	England	Wales	Scotland	N. Ireland	**Total UK**
1990	70	0	0	0	**70**	4	0	0	0	**4**	5	0	0	0	**5**
1995	50	0	0	0	**50**	4	0	0	0	**4**	9[4]	0	0	0	**9**
2000	50	0	0	0	**50**	4	0	0	0	**4**	10	0	0	0	**10**
2001	50	0	0	0	**50**	4	0	0	0	**4**	10	0	0	0	**10**
2002	55	0	0	0	**55**	4	0	0	0	**4**	10	0	0	0	**10**
2005	59	0	0	0	**59**	3	0	0	0	**3**	9	0	0	0	**9**

[1] Estimate. *For other footnotes, see* **Page 8.4**

8.6 Institutional Churches: Catholic Churches for Overseas Nationals

Table 8.6.1
Croatian Catholic Church

	MASS ATTENDANCE					CHURCHES					PRIESTS				
	England	Wales	Scotland	N. Ireland	**Total UK**	England	Wales	Scotland	N. Ireland	**Total UK**	England	Wales	Scotland	N. Ireland	**Total UK**
1990	1,206	0	0	0	**1,206**	1	0	0	0	**1**	1	0	0	0	**1**
1995	1,550	0	0	0	**1,550**	1	0	0	0	**1**	1	0	0	0	**1**
2000	160[2]	0	0	0	**160**	1	0	0	0	**1**	1	0	0	0	**1**
2001[1]	160	0	0	0	**160**	1	0	0	0	**1**	1	0	0	0	**1**
2002[1]	160	0	0	0	**160**	1	0	0	0	**1**	1	0	0	0	**1**
2005[1]	160	0	0	0	**160**	1	0	0	0	**1**	1	0	0	0	**1**

Table 8.6.2
German Catholic Church

	England	Wales	Scotland	N. Ireland	**Total UK**	England	Wales	Scotland	N. Ireland	**Total UK**	England	Wales	Scotland	N. Ireland	**Total UK**
1990	1,400	0	0	0	**1,400**	1	0	0	0	**1**	1	0	0	0	**1**
1995	1,400	0	0	0	**1,400**	1	0	0	0	**1**	1	0	0	0	**1**
2000	1,400	0	0	0	**1,400**	1	0	0	0	**1**	1	0	0	0	**1**
2001[1]	1,400	0	0	0	**1,400**	1	0	0	0	**1**	1	0	0	0	**1**
2002[1]	1,400	0	0	0	**1,400**	1	0	0	0	**1**	1	0	0	0	**1**
2005[1]	1,400	0	0	0	**1,400**	1	0	0	0	**1**	1	0	0	0	**1**

Table 8.6.3
Hungarian Catholic Church

	England	Wales	Scotland	N. Ireland	**Total UK**	England	Wales	Scotland	N. Ireland	**Total UK**[5]	England	Wales	Scotland	N. Ireland	**Total UK**
1990	3,000[3]	0	100[3]	0	**3,100**	0	0	0	0	**0**	2	0	0	0	**2**
1995	3,000[3]	0	100[3]	0	**3,100**	0	0	0	0	**0**	2	0	0	0	**2**
2000	3,000[3]	0	100[3]	0	**3,100**	0	0	0	0	**0**	1[1]	0	0	0	**1**
2001[1]	3,000	0	100	0	**3,100**	0	0	0	0	**0**	1	0	0	0	**1**
2002	3,000	0	100	0	**3,100**[4]	0	0	0	0	**0**	1	0	0	0	**1**
2005[1]	3,000	0	100	0	**3,100**	0	0	0	0	**0**	2	0	0	0	**2**

Table 8.6.4
Latvian Catholic Church

	England[7]	Wales	Scotland	N. Ireland	**Total UK**	England	Wales	Scotland	N. Ireland	**Total UK**	England	Wales	Scotland	N. Ireland	**Total UK**
1990	500	0	0	0	**500**	1	0	0	0	**1**	1	0	0	0	**1**
1995	500	0	0	0	**500**	1	0	0	0	**1**	1	0	0	0	**1**
2000	500	0	0	0	**500**	0[6]	0	0	0	**0**	0	0	0	0	**0**
2001	500	0	0	0	**500**	0	0	0	0	**0**	0	0	0	0	**0**
2002	500	0	0	0	**500**	0	0	0	0	**0**	0	0	0	0	**0**
2005[1]	500	0	0	0	**500**	0	0	0	0	**0**	0	0	0	0	**0**

Table 8.6.5
Lithuanian St Casimir Catholic Church

	England	Wales	Scotland	N. Ireland	**Total UK**	England	Wales	Scotland	N. Ireland	**Total UK**	England	Wales	Scotland	N. Ireland	**Total UK**
1990	1,000	0	0	0	**1,000**	1	0	0	0	**1**	1	0	0	0	**1**
1995	350	0	0	0	**350**	1	0	0	0	**1**	1	0	0	0	**1**
2000	800	0	50	100	**950**	1	0	0	0	**1**	4	0	1	0	**5**
2001	1,300	0	50	100	**1,450**	1	0	0	0	**1**	4	0	1	0	**5**
2002	2,000	0	50	150	**2,200**	1	0	0	0	**1**	4	0	1	0	**5**
2005[1]	2,200	0	50	200	**2,450**	1	0	0	0	**1**	4	0	1	0	**5**

Table 8.6.6
Slovene Catholic Church

	England[3,7]	Wales	Scotland	N. Ireland	**Total UK**	England	Wales	Scotland	N. Ireland	**Total UK**	England	Wales	Scotland	N. Ireland	**Total UK**
1990	400	50	0	0	**450**	7	2	0	0	**9**	1	0	0	0	**1**
1995	600	90	10	0	**700**	7	2	0	0	**9**	1	0	0	0	**1**
2000[1]	800	130	20	0	**950**	7	2	0	0	**9**	1	0	0	0	**1**
2001[1]	840	140	40	0	**1,000**	7	2	0	0	**9**	1	0	0	0	**1**
2002[1]	880	150	25	0	**1,055**	7	2	0	0	**9**	1	0	0	0	**1**
2005[1]	1,000	170	30	0	**1,200**	7	2	0	0	**9**	2	0	0	0	**2**

[1] Estimate.
[2] The reduction in numbers is partly because people have returned to Croatia after the end of the war and partly because they have joined the main Catholic churches
[3] Revised figure
[4] Approximate figure
[5] There are no church buildings
[6] Now just meet twice a year in London
[7] Community figure

[8] Previously called the Tridentine Institute of our Lady of Walsingham, but are untraced since they left Walsingham in 1995, although still believed to be active. A *Daily Telegraph* article 22nd July 1997 gave their numbers as 330 total celebrants of the Tridentine Mass in 5 churches. These numbers are assumed included in the above, presuming they were followers of Archbishop Lefebvre, who is no longer in communion with Rome. Tridentine Masses are also celebrated by the Latin Mass Society, with a membership of 3,000 including 80 priests; these Masses are celebrated in official Roman Catholic churches, and are assumed to be included within the relevant Mass figures for each country.
[9] Based on letter from Peter Robbins, April 2002.

Institutional Church Statistics: Catholic Churches (continued) 8.7

Table 8.7.1
The Society of St Pius X[8]

	MASS ATTENDANCE					CHURCHES					PRIESTS				
	England	Wales	Scotland	N. Ireland	**Total UK**	England	Wales	Scotland	N. Ireland	**Total UK**	England	Wales	Scotland	N. Ireland	**Total UK**
1990[1]	8,000	0	0	0	**8,000**	30[9]	0	0	0	**30**	50	0	0	0	**50**
1995[1]	8,000	0	0	0	**8,000**	30	0	0	0	**30**	50	0	0	0	**50**
2000[1]	8,000	0	0	0	**8,000**	30	0	0	0	**30**	50	0	0	0	**50**
2001[1]	8,000	0	0	0	**8,000**	30	0	0	0	**30**	50	0	0	0	**50**
2002[1]	8,000	0	0	0	**8,000**	30	0	0	0	**30**	50	0	0	0	**50**
2005[1]	8,000	0	0	0	**8,000**	30	0	0	0	**30**	50	0	0	0	**50**

Table 8.7.2
Ukrainian Catholic Churches

	MASS ATTENDANCE					CHURCHES					PRIESTS				
	England	Wales	Scotland	N. Ireland	**Total UK**	England	Wales	Scotland	N. Ireland	**Total UK**	England	Wales	Scotland	N. Ireland	**Total UK**
1990	2,440	0	60	0	**2,500**	13	0	1	0	**14**	11	0	1	0	**12**
1995	2,000[1]	0	50	0	**2,050**	12	0	1	0	**13**	10	0	1	0	**11**
2000	750	0	40	0	**1,740**	15	0	1	0	**15**	10	0	1	0	**11**
2001	750	0	40	0	**1,640**	18	0	1	0	**18**	10	0	1	0	**11**
2002[1]	750	0	40	0	**1,540**	18	0	1	0	**18**	10	0	1	0	**11**
2005[1]	750	0	30	0	**1,430**	18	0	1	0	**18**	10	0	1	0	**11**

Table 8.7.3
Other Catholic Churches[2]

	MASS ATTENDANCE					CHURCHES					PRIESTS				
	England	Wales	Scotland	N. Ireland	**Total UK**	England	Wales	Scotland	N. Ireland	**Total UK**	England	Wales	Scotland	N. Ireland	**Total UK**
1990[1]	500	0	0	0	**500**	4	0	0	0	**4**	4	0	0	0	**4**
1995[1]	500	0	0	0	**500**	4	0	0	0	**4**	4	0	0	0	**4**
2000[1]	500	0	0	0	**500**	4	0	0	0	**4**	4	0	0	0	**4**
2001[1]	500	0	0	0	**500**	4	0	0	0	**4**	4	0	0	0	**4**
2002[1]	500	0	0	0	**500**	4	0	0	0	**4**	4	0	0	0	**4**
2005[1]	500	0	0	0	**500**	4	0	0	0	**4**	4	0	0	0	**4**

Table 8.7.4
Other Roman Catholic statistics

	Infant Baptisms			Confirmations (England & Wales)	Adult Conversions (Great Britain)	First Communions	Marriages (England & Wales)				Marriages (Elsewhere)	
	England & Wales	Scotland	% of births				Both Catholic	Other marriages	% all marriages	% of religious	Scotland	Northern Ireland
1996	67,412	10,718	*11.0*	39,921	5,180	59,069	5,290	10,492	*5.7*	*13.5*	2,500	3,074
1997	67,384	10,344	*11.1*	38,558	5,089	59,931	5,193	9,601	*5.4*	*13.6*	2,488	3,058
1998[1]	65,200	10,000	*10.8*	38,300	5,050	60,400	5,080	9,100	*5.3*	*13.6*	2,260	2,960
1999[1]	64,600	9,700	*11.0*	38,100	5,000	61,000	4,970	8,600	*5.1*	*13.5*	2,050	2,860
2000[1]	64,032	9,360	*11.2*	37,800	4,960	61,500	4,861[3]	8,178[3]	*4.9*	*13.4*	1,858	2,770
2001[1]	58,716	9,050	*10.5*	37,600	4,920	62,000	4,565	7,680[3]	*4.7*	*13.2*	1,690	2,680

Figure 8.7.1 Rate of change in Mass Attendance, by country, 1990–2005

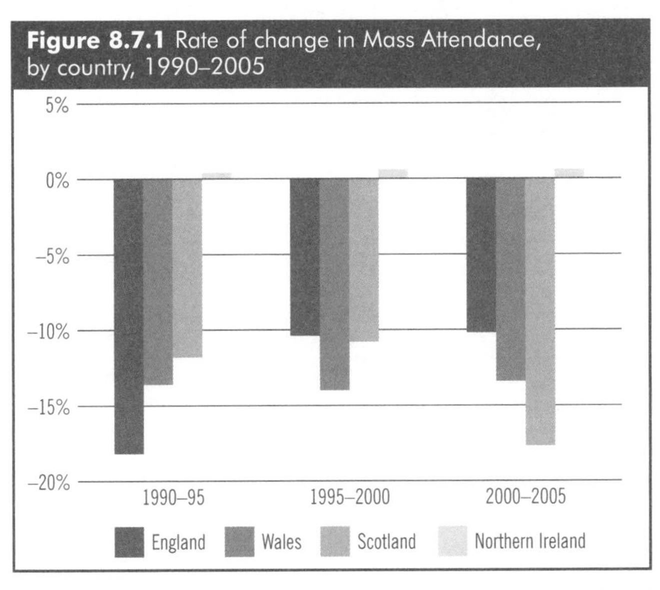

Figure 8.7.2 Rate of change in Priests, by country, 1990–2005

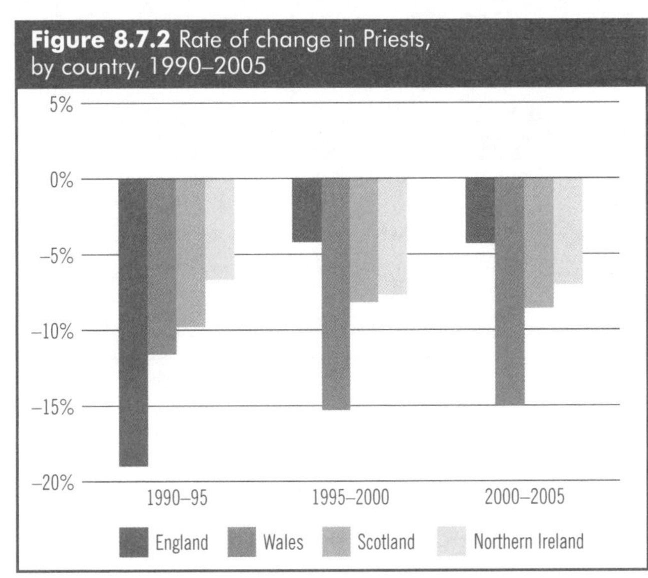

[1] Estimate [2] Including the Ecumenical Old Catholic Church (not in communion with Rome), meeting infrequently in the Parish of St Anselm and St Aelred in south east London. 3 Split estimated.
For Footnotes 8 and 9 please see Page 8.6

8

8.8 Institutional Church Statistics: Orthodox Churches: Eastern

Table 8.8.1
Total Orthodox Churches

	MEMBERSHIP					CONGREGATIONS					PRIESTS				
	England	Wales	Scotland	N. Ireland	**Total UK**	England	Wales	Scotland	N. Ireland	**Total UK**	England	Wales	Scotland	N. Ireland	**Total UK**
1990	167,480	7,116	12,176	95	**186,867**	213	8	8	1	**230**	149	6	7	1	**163**
1995	177,486	7,252	15,868	220	**200,826**	242	7	13	2	**264**	174	6	9	1	**190**
2000	218,497	7,285	22,137	263	**248,182**	253	7	15	2	**277**	212	7	10	1	**230**
2001	225,503	7,285	22,247	273	**255,308**	253	7	15	2	**277**	217	6	11	1	**235**
2002	232,879	7,295	22,307	288	**262,769**	255	7	15	2	**279**	220	6	11	1	**238**
2005	252,101	7,322	24,537	338	**284,298**	266	8	16	2	**292**	234	7	13	1	**255**

Table 8.8.2
Eastern Orthodox: Greek Orthodox[2]

	England	Wales	Scotland	N. Ireland	**Total UK**[3]	England	Wales	Scotland	N. Ireland	**Total UK**	England	Wales	Scotland	N. Ireland	**Total UK**[6]
1990	152,928	5,000	12,000	72[4]	**170,000**[5]	81	3	6	0	**90**	59	3	6	0	**68**[5]
1995	159,420	5,000	15,500	80	**180,000**	83	2	8	0	**93**	64	3	6	0	**73**
2000	188,200	5,000	21,700	100	**215,000**	87	2	10	0	**99**	74	3	7	0	**84**
2001[1]	193,100	5,000	21,800	100	**220,000**	89	2	10	0	**101**	75	3	7	0	**85**
2002[1]	198,045	5,000	21,850	105	**225,000**	91	2	10	0	**103**	76	3	7	0	**86**
2005[1]	210,880	5,000	24,000	120	**240,000**	97	2	11	0	**110**	79	3	8	0	**90**

Table 8.8.3
Eastern Orthodox: Russian Orthodox; Patriarchate of Moscow[7]

	England	Wales	Scotland	N. Ireland	**Total UK**	England	Wales	Scotland	N. Ireland	**Total UK**	England	Wales	Scotland	N. Ireland	**Total UK**
1990	2,115	0	85	0	**2,200**	23	0	1	0	**24**	13	0	0	0	**13**[5]
1995	2,130	85	85	0	**2,300**	27	0	1	0	**28**	13	0	0	0	**13**
2000	2,420	100	100	0	**2,620**	27	0	1	0	**28**	19	0	0	0	**19**
2001[1]	2,450	100	100	0	**2,650**	27	0	1	0	**28**	19	0	0	0	**19**
2002[1]	2,500	100	100	0	**2,700**	27	0	1	0	**28**	19	0	0	0	**19**
2005[1]	2,570	105	125	0	**2,800**	27	0	1	0	**28**	19	0	0	0	**19**

Table 8.8.4
Eastern Orthodox: Russian Orthodox Church Outside Russia[8]

	England	Wales	Scotland	N. Ireland	**Total UK**	England	Wales	Scotland	N. Ireland	**Total UK**	England	Wales	Scotland	N. Ireland	**Total UK**
1990	800	0	0	0	**800**[5]	2	0	0	0	**2**[5]	4	0	0	0	**4**[5]
1995	800	0	0	0	**800**	2	0	0	0	**2**	4	0	0	0	**4**
2000	1,050	0	0	0	**1,050**	10	0	0	0	**10**	11	0	0	0	**11**
2001[1]	1,100	0	0	0	**1,100**	10	0	0	0	**10**	11	0	0	0	**11**
2002[1]	1,100	0	0	0	**1,100**	10	0	0	0	**10**	12	0	0	0	**12**
2005[1]	1,200	0	0	0	**1,200**	11	0	0	0	**11**	13	0	0	0	**13**

Table 8.8.5
Eastern Orthodox: Serbian Orthodox Church; Diocese of Western Europe

	England	Wales	Scotland	N. Ireland	**Total UK**	England	Wales	Scotland	N. Ireland	**Total UK**	England	Wales	Scotland	N. Ireland	**Total UK**
1990	2,900	100	0	0	**3,000**	35	1	0	0	**36**	10	0	0	0	**10**
1995	3,195	105	0	0	**3,300**	35	1	0	0	**36**	9	0	0	0	**9**
2000	3,690	110	0	0	**3,800**	35	1	0	0	**36**	9	0	0	0	**9**
2001[1]	3,740	110	0	0	**3,850**	35	1	0	0	**36**	9	0	0	0	**9**
2002[1]	3,790	110	0	0	**3,900**	35	1	0	0	**36**	9	0	0	0	**9**
2005[1]	3,880	120	0	0	**4,000**	35	1	0	0	**36**	9	0	0	0	**9**

Table 8.8.6
Eastern Orthodox: Patriarchate of Antioch[4]

	England	Wales	Scotland	N. Ireland	**Total UK**	England	Wales	Scotland	N. Ireland	**Total UK**	England	Wales	Scotland	N. Ireland	**Total UK**
1990	200	0	0	0	**200**	5	0	0	0	**5**[1]	2	0	0	0	**2**[1]
1995	200	0	0	0	**200**	10	0	0	0	**10**	7	0	0	0	**7**
2000[1]	800	0	0	0	**800**	14	0	0	0	**14**	13	0	0	0	**13**
2001[1]	900	0	0	0	**900**	14	0	0	0	**14**	14	0	0	0	**14**
2002[1]	1,000	0	0	0	**1,000**	14	0	0	0	**14**	15	0	0	0	**15**
2005[1]	1,200	0	0	0	**1,200**	15	0	0	0	**15**	18	0	0	0	**18**

[1] Estimate

[2] The Œcumenical Patriarchate of Constantinople, Diocese of Thyateira and Great Britain, an international Jurisdiction composed 99% of Greek and Cypriot members in the British Isles. Membership taken as approximately two-thirds community.

[3] Figures proportioned to number of churches

[4] Northern Ireland Census 1991

[5] Revised figure

[6] All male

[7] Diocese of Sourozh

[8] Diocese of Great Britain and Ireland; made up of Russian immigrant churches and the English Orthodox Deanery

[9] Meeting in six churches

[10] Made up of the Antiochian Arab Orthodox Church and the British Orthodox Deanery

[11] Patriarchate's own estimate

Institutional Church Statistics: Orthodox Churches: Eastern (contd.) 8.9

Table 8.9.1
Eastern Orthodox: Patriarchate of Bulgaria; Diocese of Western Europe

	MEMBERSHIP					CONGREGATIONS					PRIESTS				
	England	Wales	Scotland	N. Ireland	**Total UK**	England	Wales	Scotland	N. Ireland	**Total UK**	England	Wales	Scotland	N. Ireland	**Total UK**
1990	30	0	0	0	**30**	1	0	0	0	**1**	1	0	0	0	**1**
1995	80	0	0	0	**80**[6]	1	0	0	0	**1**	1	0	0	0	**1**
2000	82	0	0	0	**82**[6]	1	0	0	0	**1**	1	0	0	0	**1**
2001[1]	83	0	0	0	**83**	1	0	0	0	**1**	1	0	0	0	**1**
2002[1]	84	0	0	0	**84**	1	0	0	0	**1**	1	0	0	0	**1**
2005[1]	86	0	0	0	**86**	1	0	0	0	**1**	1	0	0	0	**1**

Table 8.9.2
Eastern Orthodox: Latvian Orthodox Church; Patriarchate of Constantinople

	MEMBERSHIP					CONGREGATIONS					PRIESTS				
	England	Wales	Scotland	N. Ireland	**Total UK**[5]	England	Wales	Scotland	N. Ireland	**Total UK**	England	Wales	Scotland	N. Ireland	**Total UK**
1990	500	0	0	0	**500**	1	0	0	0	**1**	1	0	0	0	**1**
1995	200	0	0	0	**200**	1	0	0	0	**1**	1	0	0	0	**1**
2000[1]	160	0	0	0	**160**	1	0	0	0	**1**	1	0	0	0	**1**
2001[1]	150	0	0	0	**150**	1	0	0	0	**1**	1	0	0	0	**1**
2002	140	0	0	0	**140**	1	0	0	0	**1**	1	0	0	0	**1**
2005[1]	110	0	0	0	**110**	1	0	0	0	**1**	1	0	0	0	**1**

Table 8.9.3
Eastern Orthodox: Patriarchate of Romania

	MEMBERSHIP					CONGREGATIONS					PRIESTS				
	England	Wales	Scotland	N. Ireland	**Total UK**	England	Wales	Scotland	N. Ireland	**Total UK**	England	Wales	Scotland	N. Ireland	**Total UK**
1990	35	0	0	0	**35**	1	0	0	0	**1**	1	0	0	0	**1**
1995	60	0	0	0	**60**	2	0	0	0	**2**	2	0	0	0	**2**
2000	800	0	0	0	**800**[3]	2	0	0	0	**2**	2	0	0	0	**2**
2001[1]	900	0	0	0	**900**	1	0	0	0	**1**	2	0	0	0	**2**
2002	1,000	0	0	0	**1,000**[2]	1	0	0	0	**1**[2]	2	0	0	0	**2**[2]
2005[1]	1,200	0	0	0	**1,200**	1	0	0	0	**1**	2	0	0	0	**2**

Table 8.9.4
Eastern Orthodox: Byelorussian Orthodox Church; Patriarchate of Constantinople[4]

	MEMBERSHIP					CONGREGATIONS					PRIESTS				
	England	Wales	Scotland	N. Ireland	**Total UK**	England	Wales	Scotland	N. Ireland	**Total UK**	England	Wales	Scotland	N. Ireland	**Total UK**
1990	1,500	0	0	0	**1,500**	17	0	0	0	**17**[3]	7	0	0	0	**7**
1995	1,800	0	0	0	**1,800**	17	0	0	0	**17**	9	0	0	0	**9**
2000	2,100	0	0	0	**2,100**	17	0	0	0	**17**	9	0	0	0	**9**
2001[1]	2,150	0	0	0	**2,150**	17	0	0	0	**17**	9	0	0	0	**9**
2002[1]	2,200	0	0	0	**2,200**	17	0	0	0	**17**	9	0	0	0	**9**
2005[1]	2,300	0	0	0	**2,300**	17	0	0	0	**17**	9	0	0	0	**9**

Page 8.9
[1] Estimate
[2] Priest-in-charge's own estimate
[3] Revised figure
[4] Ukrainian Diocese of Great Britain and Ireland
[5] When the Soviet occupation ended and Latvia became a free republic again, many returned to their birthplace, so numbers of worshippers in the UK dropped. Hence the reduced numbers in the 1990s.
[6] Patriarch's own estimate.

Page 8.10
[1] Estimate
[2] Revised figure
[3] Formerly listed as the Indian (Syrian) Church
[4] Figures for 1996
[5] Comprising the four Dioceses: (a) Diocese of Birmingham; (b) Diocese of Ireland, Scotland, North-East England and its affiliated territories; (c) The British Orthodox Church [listed separately in the following Table]; and (d) The Churches directly under Pope Shenouda III
[6] Church in County Wicklow, Republic of Ireland
[7] Part of the Coptic Orthodox Patriarchate (see Footnote 5)
[8] Includes full deacons
[9] Estimates pro rata to British Orthodox Church
[10] This is the longest established Orthodox community in Britain
[11] Began in 1996

Page 8.11
[1] Estimate
[2] Not in communion with any Orthodox Church
[3] Began in 1995
[4] Archimandrite's own estimates

Page 8.12
[1] Estimate.
[2] Excludes adherents.
[3] Figures for communicant members only.
[4] Revised figure.
[5] Began 1996
[6] Non-stipendiary ministry only
[7] Started by Rev Jonathan Blake, who resigned Anglican orders after a year in 1993. Dr Elizabeth Stuart, a controversial Catholic theologian who is Professor of Theology and Religious Studies at King Alfred's College, Winchester, was consecrated a Bishop in the church in the autumn of 2002 (report in *The Tablet* 10th August 2002).
[8] These figures were not collected in 1990

Table 8.9.5 Proportions across the four countries, 2002

	Members %	Congregns %	Priests %
England	89	91	92
Wales	3	3	3
Scotland	8	5	5
N. Ireland	0	1	0

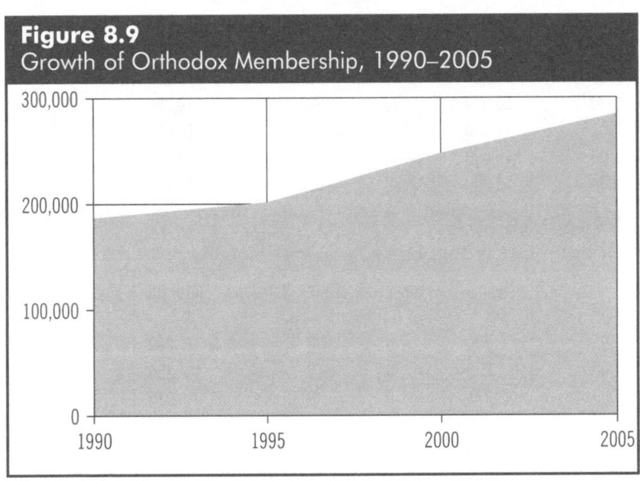

Figure 8.9
Growth of Orthodox Membership, 1990–2005

8.10 Institutional Church Statistics: Orthodox Churches: Oriental

Table 8.10.1
Oriental Orthodox: Ethiopian Orthodox Tewahido Church

	MEMBERSHIP					CONGREGATIONS					PRIESTS				
	England	Wales	Scotland	N. Ireland	**Total UK**	England	Wales	Scotland	N. Ireland	**Total UK**	England	Wales	Scotland	N. Ireland	**Total UK**
1990	600	0	0	0	**600**	5	0	0	0	**5**	5	0	0	0	**5**
1995	400	0	0	0	**400**[2]	4	0	0	0	**4**[2]	5	0	0	0	**5**
2000[1]	300	0	0	0	**300**	3	0	0	0	**3**	5	0	0	0	**5**
2001[1]	250	0	0	0	**250**	2	0	0	0	**2**	4	0	0	0	**4**
2002	250	0	0	0	**250**[1]	2	0	0	0	**2**	4	0	0	0	**4**
2005[1]	250	0	0	0	**250**	2	0	0	0	**2**	4	0	0	0	**4**

Table 8.10.2
Oriental Orthodox: Malankara Orthodox Syrian Church[3]

	MEMBERSHIP					CONGREGATIONS					PRIESTS				
	England	Wales	Scotland	N. Ireland	**Total UK**	England	Wales	Scotland	N. Ireland	**Total UK**	England	Wales	Scotland	N. Ireland	**Total UK**
1990	400	0	0	0	**400**	3	1	0	0	**4**	3	0	0	0	**3**
1995	250	0	0	0	**250**[2]	3	0	0	0	**3**[2]	2	0	0	0	**2**[2]
2000	100	0	0	0	**100**	2	0	0	0	**2**[2]	1	0	0	0	**1**[2]
2001[1]	100	0	0	0	**100**	1	0	0	0	**1**	1	0	0	0	**1**
2002	100	0	0	0	**100**[1]	1	0	0	0	**1**	1	0	0	0	**1**[1]
2005[1]	100	0	0	0	**100**	1	0	0	0	**1**	1	0	0	0	**1**

Table 8.10.3
Oriental Orthodox: Syrian Orthodox Church

	MEMBERSHIP					CONGREGATIONS					PRIESTS				
	England	Wales	Scotland	N. Ireland	**Total UK**	England	Wales	Scotland	N. Ireland	**Total UK**	England	Wales	Scotland	N. Ireland	**Total UK**
1990[1]	200	0	0	0	**200**	2	0	0	0	**2**	2	0	0	0	**2**
1995[1]	200	0	0	0	**200**	2	0	0	0	**2**	2	0	0	0	**2**
2000[1]	200	0	0	0	**200**	2	0	0	0	**2**	2	0	0	0	**2**
2001[1]	200	0	0	0	**200**	2	0	0	0	**2**	2	0	0	0	**2**
2002	200	0	0	0	**200**[1]	2	0	0	0	**2**	2	0	0	0	**2**[1]
2005[1]	200	0	0	0	**200**	2	0	0	0	**2**	2	0	0	0	**2**

Table 8.10.4
Oriental Orthodox: Coptic Orthodox Patriarchate[5]

	MEMBERSHIP					CONGREGATIONS					PRIESTS				
	England	Wales	Scotland	N. Ireland	**Total UK**[9]	England	Wales	Scotland	N. Ireland	**Total UK**	England	Wales	Scotland	N. Ireland	**Total UK**
1990[1]	1,400	0	80	20	**1,500**	6	0	1	1	**8**	8	0	1	1	**10**
1995[1]	3,840	0	235	125	**4,200**	12	0	1	1	**14**	17	0	1	1	**19**
2000[1]	4,300	0	260	140	**4,700**	14	0	1	1	**16**	19	0	1	1	**21**
2001[1]	4,340	0	265	145	**4,750**	14	0	1	1	**16**	19	0	1	1	**21**
2002	4,400	0	270	145[6]	**4,815**	14	0	1	1[6]	**16**	19	0	1	1[6]	**21**
2005[1]	4,650	0	285	165	**5,100**	14	0	1	1	**16**	19	0	1	1	**21**

Table 8.10.5
Oriental Orthodox: British Orthodox Church[7]

	MEMBERSHIP					CONGREGATIONS					PRIESTS				
	England	Wales	Scotland	N. Ireland	**Total UK**	England	Wales	Scotland	N. Ireland	**Total UK**	England	Wales	Scotland	N. Ireland	**Total UK**[8]
1990	258	0	0	0	**258**	6	0	0	0	**6**	13	0	0	0	**13**
1995	735	0	15	0	**750**	13	0	1	0	**14**	16	0	1	0	**17**
2000	825	0	0	0	**825**	10	0	0	0	**10**	15	0	0	0	**15**
2001	835	0	0	0	**835**	11	0	0	0	**11**	15	0	0	0	**15**
2002	850	0	0	0	**850**	11	0	0	0	**11**	16	0	0	0	**16**
2005[1]	900	0	0	0	**900**	12	0	0	0	**12**	17	0	0	0	**17**

Table 8.10.6
Oriental Orthodox: Armenian Orthodox Church[10]

	MEMBERSHIP					CONGREGATIONS					PRIESTS				
	England	Wales	Scotland	N. Ireland	**Total UK**	England	Wales	Scotland	N. Ireland	**Total UK**	England	Wales	Scotland	N. Ireland	**Total UK**
1990	1,000	0	0	0	**1,000**	3	0	0	0	**3**	4	0	0	0	**4**
1995	1,200	0	0	0	**1,200**	3	0	0	0	**3**	3	0	0	0	**3**
2000	10,000	50	30	10	**10,090**	3	0	0	0	**3**	4	0	0	0	**4**
2001	11,000	50	30	10	**11,090**	3	0	0	0	**3**	7	0	0	0	**7**
2002	12,000	50	30	20	**12,100**	3	0	0	0	**3**	6	0	0	0	**6**
2005[1]	15,000	60	35	25	**15,120**	3	0	0	0	**3**	7	0	0	0	**7**

Table 8.10.7
Oriental Orthodox: Eritrean Orthodox Church[11]

	MEMBERSHIP					CONGREGATIONS					PRIESTS				
	England	Wales	Scotland	N. Ireland	**Total UK**	England	Wales	Scotland	N. Ireland	**Total UK**	England	Wales	Scotland	N. Ireland	**Total UK**
1990	–	–	–	–	**–**	–	–	–	–	**–**	–	–	–	–	**–**
1995[4]	200	0	0	0	**200**	1	0	0	0	**1**	1	0	0	0	**1**
2000	250	0	0	0	**250**	2	0	0	0	**2**	1	0	0	0	**1**[1]
2000	275	0	0	0	**275**	2	0	0	0	**2**	1	0	0	0	**1**[1]
2002	300	0	0	0	**300**	2	0	0	0	**2**	1	0	0	0	**1**[1]
2005	350	0	0	0	**350**	2	0	0	0	**2**[1]	1	0	0	0	**1**[1]

[1] Estimate. *For other footnotes, see* **Page 8.9**

8

Table 8.11.1
Other Orthodox Churches: Ukrainian Orthodox Church; Patriarchate of Kiev in Great Britain and Ireland[2, 3]

	MEMBERSHIP					CONGREGATIONS					PRIESTS				
	England	Wales	Scotland	N. Ireland	**Total UK**	England	Wales	Scotland	N. Ireland	**Total UK**	England	Wales	Scotland	N. Ireland	**Total UK**
1990	–	–	–	–	–	–	–	–	–	–	–	–	–	–	–
1995	177	9	7	12	**205**	4	1	1	1	**7**	3	0	0	0	**3**
2000[1]	85	5	5	5	**100**	4	1	1	1	**7**	3	0	0	0	**3**
2001[1]	85	5	5	5	**100**	4	1	1	1	**7**	3	0	0	0	**3**
2002[1]	85	5	5	5	**100**	4	1	1	1	**7**	3	0	0	0	**3**
2005[1]	85	5	5	5	**100**	4	1	1	1	**7**	3	0	0	0	**3**

Table 8.11.2
Other Orthodox Churches: Ukrainian Autocephalous Patriarchate

	England	Wales	Scotland	N. Ireland	**Total UK**	England	Wales	Scotland	N. Ireland	**Total UK**	England	Wales	Scotland	N. Ireland	**Total UK**
1990	1,250	0	0	0	**1,250**	15	0	0	0	**15**	10	0	0	0	**10**
1995	1,200	0	0	0	**1,200**	12	0	0	0	**12**	7	0	0	0	**7**
2000	1,150	0	0	0	**1,150**	12	0	0	0	**12**	7	0	0	0	**7**
2001	1,150	0	0	0	**1,150**	12	0	0	0	**12**	7	0	0	0	**7**
2002	1,130	0	0	0	**1,130**	12	0	0	0	**12**	7	0	0	0	**7**
2005	1,000	0	0	0	**1,000**	12	0	0	0	**12**	7	0	0	0	**7**

Table 8.11.3
Other Orthodox Churches: Orthodox Church in Wales[2]

	England	Wales	Scotland	N. Ireland	**Total UK**	England	Wales	Scotland	N. Ireland	**Total UK**	England	Wales	Scotland	N. Ireland	**Total UK**
1990	0	2,000	0	0	**2,000**[4]	0	3	0	0	**3**	0	3	0	0	**3**
1995	0	2,000	0	0	**2,000**	0	3	0	0	**3**	0	3	0	0	**3**
2000	0	2,000	0	0	**2,000**	0	3	0	0	**3**	0	3	0	0	**3**
2001	0	2,000	0	0	**2,000**	0	3	0	0	**3**	0	3	0	0	**3**
2002	0	2,000	0	0	**2,000**	0	3	0	0	**3**	0	3	0	0	**3**
2005	0	2,000	0	0	**2,000**	0	3	0	0	**3**	0	3	0	0	**3**

Table 8.11.4
Other Orthodox Churches: Ancient Orthodox Church

	England	Wales	Scotland	N. Ireland	**Total UK**	England	Wales	Scotland	N. Ireland	**Total UK**	England	Wales	Scotland	N. Ireland	**Total UK**
1990	104	7	11	3	**125**	2	0	0	0	**2**	1	0	0	0	**1**
1995[1]	104	7	11	3	**125**	2	0	0	0	**2**	1	0	0	0	**1**
2000[1]	105	10	12	3	**130**	2	0	0	0	**2**	1	0	0	0	**1**
2001[1]	105	10	12	3	**130**	2	0	0	0	**2**	1	0	0	0	**1**
2002[1]	105	10	12	3	**130**	2	0	0	0	**2**	1	0	0	0	**1**
2005[1]	110	10	12	3	**135**	2	0	0	0	**2**	1	0	0	0	**1**

Table 8.11.5
Other Orthodox Churches: Assyrian Church of the East (Nestorian)

	England	Wales	Scotland	N. Ireland	**Total UK**	England	Wales	Scotland	N. Ireland	**Total UK**	England	Wales	Scotland	N. Ireland	**Total UK**
1990	1,000	0	0	0	**1,000**	1	0	0	0	**1**	3	0	0	0	**3**
1995	1,000	0	0	0	**1,000**	1	0	0	0	**1**	2	0	0	0	**2**
2000	1,800	10	15	5	**1,830**	1	0	0	0	**1**	5	0	0	0	**5**
2001	2,500	10	15	10	**2,535**	1	0	0	0	**1**	7	0	0	0	**7**
2002	3,500	10	20	10	**3,540**	1	0	0	0	**1**	7	0	0	0	**7**
2005[1]	5,910	20	50	20	**6,000**	2	0	0	0	**2**	10	0	0	0	**10**

Table 8.11.6
Other Orthodox Churches: Byelorussian Autocephalous Church

	England	Wales	Scotland	N. Ireland	**Total UK**	England	Wales	Scotland	N. Ireland	**Total UK**	England	Wales	Scotland	N. Ireland	**Total UK**
1990	260	0	0	0	**260**	4	0	0	0	**4**	2	0	0	0	**2**
1995	250	0	0	0	**250**	4	0	0	0	**4**	2	0	0	0	**2**
2000	20	0	0	0	**20**	1	0	0	0	**1**	1	0	0	0	**1**
2001	20	0	0	0	**20**	1	0	0	0	**1**	1	0	0	0	**1**
2002	20	0	0	0	**20**	1	0	0	0	**1**	1	0	0	0	**1**
2005[1]	20	0	0	0	**20**	1	0	0	0	**1**	1	0	0	0	**1**

Table 8.11.7
Other Orthodox Churches: Celtic Orthodox Church, British Eparchy[3]

	England	Wales	Scotland	N. Ireland	**Total UK**	England	Wales	Scotland	N. Ireland	**Total UK**	England	Wales	Scotland	N. Ireland	**Total UK**
1990	–	–	–	–	–	–	–	–	–	–	–	–	–	–	–
1995	45	0	15	0	**60**	3	0	1	0	**4**	3	0	1	0	**4**
2000	60	0	15	0	**75**	3	0	2	0	**5**	9	1	2	0	**12**
2001	70	0	20	0	**90**	3	0	2	0	**5**	8	0	3	0	**11**
2002[1]	80	0	20	0	**100**	3	0	2	0	**5**	8	0	3	0	**11**
2005[4]	100	2	25	0	**127**	4	1	2	0	**7**	10	1	4	0	**15**

[1] Estimate. *For other footnotes, see* **Page 8.9**

8.12 Institutional Church Statistics: Presbyterian: English and Welsh

Table 8.12.1
Total All Presbyterian Churches

	MEMBERSHIP					CONGREGATIONS					MINISTERS				
	England	Wales	Scotland	N. Ireland	**Total UK**	England	Wales	Scotland	N. Ireland	**Total UK**	England	Wales	Scotland	N. Ireland	**Total UK**
1990	115,359	67,669	816,133	214,859	**1,214,020**	1,658	1,180	2,055	596	**5,489**	982	183	1,451	505	**3,121**
1995	101,492	56,823	725,245	215,203	**1,098,763**	1,636	1,085	1,951	601	**5,273**	746	159	1,380	461	**2,746**
2000	88,242	46,303	635,302	212,830	**982,677**	1,587	992	1,964	597	**5,140**	698	146	1,322	479	**2,645**
2001	85,305	44,273	618,669	210,021	**958,268**	1,584	974	1,942	608	**5,108**	699	139	1,308	478	**2,624**
2002	82,806	42,070	600,068	208,377	**933,321**	1,564	950	1,921	607	**5,042**	689	134	1,293	473	**2,589**
2005	74,354	35,770	544,385	201,460	**855,969**	1,547	895	1,867	604	**4,913**	683	124	1,256	481	**2,544**

Table 8.12.2
United Reformed Church[2, 3]

	England	Wales	Scotland	N. Ireland	**Total UK**	England	Wales	Scotland[2]	N. Ireland	**Total UK**	England	Wales	Scotland[2]	N. Ireland	**Total UK**
1990	110,317	6,053	300	0	**116,670**	1,639	155	6	0	**1,800**	966	46	4	0	**1,016**
1995	97,249	5,103	255	0	**102,582**	1,616	146	6	0	**1,768**	731	40	3	0	**774**
2000	84,101	4,275	4,411	0	**92,787**	1,558	139	56	0	**1,753**	674	42	34	0	**750**
2001	80,940	4,168	5,206	0	**90,314**	1,552	138	55	0	**1,745**	673	40	36	0	**749**
2002	78,574	3,950	5,208	0	**87,732**	1,533	131	55	0	**1,719**	666	38	38	0	**742**
2005[1]	70,500	3,450	5,230	0	**79,180**	1,514	129	55	0	**1,698**	655	38	44	0	**737**

Table 8.12.3
Presbyterian Church of Wales[4]

	England	Wales	Scotland	N. Ireland	**Total UK**	England	Wales	Scotland	N. Ireland	**Total UK**	England	Wales	Scotland	N. Ireland	**Total UK**
1990	0	61,616	0	0	**61,616**	0	1,025	0	0	**1,025**	0	137	0	0	**137**
1995	0	51,720	0	0	**51,720**	0	939	0	0	**939**	0	119	0	0	**119**
2000	0	41,778	0	0	**41,778**	0	850[1]	0	0	**850**	0	101	0	0	**101**
2001	0	39,805	0	0	**39,805**	0	832	0	0	**832**	0	97	0	0	**97**
2002[1]	0	37,820	0	0	**37,820**	0	815	0	0	**815**	0	94	0	0	**94**
2005[1]	0	31,970	0	0	**31,970**	0	762	0	0	**762**	0	83	0	0	**93**

Table 8.12.4
Evangelical Presbyterian Church in England and Wales

	England	Wales	Scotland	N. Ireland	**Total UK**	England	Wales	Scotland	N. Ireland	**Total UK**	England	Wales	Scotland	N. Ireland	**Total UK**
1990	60	0	0	0	**60**	3	0	0	0	**3**	3	0	0	0	**3**
1995	80	0	0	0	**80**	4	0	0	0	**4**	3	0	0	0	**3**
2000	170	0	0	0	**170**	7	0	0	0	**7**	6	0	0	0	**6**
2001[1]	185	0	0	0	**185**	8	0	0	0	**8**	6	0	0	0	**6**
2002[1]	200	0	0	0	**200**	8	0	0	0	**8**	6	0	0	0	**6**
2005[1]	240	0	0	0	**240**	10	0	0	0	**10**	8	0	0	0	**8**

Table 8.12.5
Adherents of the United Reformed Church

	England	Wales	Scotland	N. Ireland	**Total UK**
1990	–	–	–	–	–
1995	–	–	–	–	–
2000	31,456	1,025	311	0	**32,792**
2001	29,549	949	362	0	**30,860**
2002	28,318	972	608	0	**29,898**
2005[1]	23,500	875	830	0	**25,205**

Table 8.12.6 Other statistics of the United Reformed Church

	Average Congregation at Main Service					Children at Worship				
	England	Wales	Scotland	N. Ireland	**Total UK**	England	Wales	Scotland	N. Ireland	**Total UK**
1991[8]	98,487	5,613	0	0	**104,100**	37,933	1,737	0	0	**39,670**
1995	96,121	4,248	0	0	**100,369**	31,828	1,527	0	0	**33,355**
2000	86,515	4,070	0	0	**90,585**	25,489	1,277	0	0	**26,766**
2001	81,228	3,885	2,685	0	**87,798**	23,586	1,204	769	0	**25,559**
2002	79,473	3,763	3,100	0	**86,336**	21,918	1,125	675	0	**23,718**
2005[1]	75,525	3,250	3,250	0	**82,025**	17,910	985	515	0	**19,410**

Table 8.12.7
Anglican Independent Communion in Great Britain[5, 7]

	England	Wales	Scotland	N. Ireland	**Total UK**	England	Wales	Scotland	N. Ireland	**Total UK**	England	Wales	Scotland	N. Ireland	**Total UK**[6]
1990	–	–	–	–	–	–	–	–	–	–	–	–	–	–	–
1995	–	–	–	–	–	–	–	–	–	–	–	–	–	–	–
2000[1]	25	0	0	0	**25**	1	0	0	0	**1**	2	0	0	0	**2**
2001[1]	100	0	0	0	**100**	5	0	0	0	**5**	10	0	5	0	**15**
2002	300[1]	20[1]	100[1]	0	**420**	15	1	5	0	**21**	25	1	10	0	**36**
2005	600[1]	200[1]	200[1]	0	**1,000**	30	10	10	0	**50**	40	10	20	0	**70**

Table 8.12.8
Open Episcopal Church

	England	Wales	Scotland	N. Ireland	**Total UK**	England	Wales	Scotland	N. Ireland	**Total UK**	England	Wales	Scotland	N. Ireland	**Total UK**[6]
1990	–	–	–	–	–	–	–	–	–	–	–	–	–	–	–
1995	–	–	–	–	–	–	–	–	–	–	–	–	–	–	–
2000[1]	25	0	0	0	**25**	1	0	0	0	**1**	5	0	0	0	**5**
2001[1]	80	0	0	0	**80**	4	0	0	0	**4**	20	0	0	0	**20**
2002	240[1]	0	0	0	**240**	12	0	0	0	**12**	33	2	1	0	**36**
2005	400[1]	0	0	0	**400**	20	0	0	0	**20**	40	5	1	0	**46**

[1] Estimate. *For other footnotes, see* **Page 8.9**

Table 8.31.1
Church of Scotland

	MEMBERSHIP					CONGREGATIONS					MINISTERS				
	England	Wales	Scotland	N. Ireland	**Total UK**	England	Wales	Scotland	N. Ireland	**Total UK**	England	Wales	Scotland	N. Ireland	**Total UK**
1990	4,810	0	781,977	0	**786,787**	12	0	1,673	0	**1,685**	10	0	1,248	0	**1,258**
1995	3,993	0	694,559	0	**698,552**	12	0	1,604	0	**1,616**	10	0	1,197	0	**1,207**
2000	3,175	0	604,539	0	**607,714**	12	0	1,555	0	**1,567**	10	0	1,101	0	**1,111**
2001	3,140	0	587,684	0	**590,824**	12	0	1,543	0	**1,555**	10	0	1,090	0	**1,100**
2002[1]	2,922	0	569,745	0	**572,667**	12	0	1,530	0	**1,542**	10	0	1,077	0	**1,087**
2005	2,358	0	515,820	0	**518,178**	12	0	1,496	0	**1,508**	10	0	1,028	0	**1,038**

Table 8.13.2
Free Church of Scotland

	MEMBERSHIP					CONGREGATIONS					MINISTERS				
	England	Wales	Scotland	N. Ireland	**Total UK**	England	Wales	Scotland	N. Ireland	**Total UK**	England	Wales	Scotland	N. Ireland	**Total UK**
1990	100	0	19,900	0	**20,000**	1	0	199	0	**200**	1	0	114	0	**115**
1995	90	0	18,310	0	**18,400**	1	0	181	0	**182**	1	0	102	0	**103**
2000	95	0	13,505	0	**13,600**	1	0	180	0	**181**	1	0	76	0	**77**
2001	120	0	13,060	0	**13,180**[1]	2	0	174	0	**176**	2	0	75	0	**77**
2002[1]	120	0	12,640	0	**12,760**[1]	2	0	170	0	**172**	0	0	73	0	**73**
2005	135	0	11,365	0	**11,500**[1]	2	0	160	0	**162**	2	0	80	0	**82**

Table 8.13.3
Free Church of Scotland (Continuing)[2]

	MEMBERSHIP					CONGREGATIONS					MINISTERS				
	England	Wales	Scotland	N. Ireland	**Total UK**	England	Wales	Scotland	N. Ireland	**Total UK**	England	Wales	Scotland	N. Ireland	**Total UK**
1990	–	–	–	–	–	–	–	–	–	–	–	–	–	–	–
1995	–	–	–	–	–	–	–	–	–	–	–	–	–	–	–
2000	0	0	2,000	0	**2,000**	0	0	30	0	**30**	0	0	38	1	**39**
2001	0	0	2,000	2	**2,002**	0	0	30	0	**30**	0	0	38	1	**39**
2002	0	0	2,000	2	**2,002**	0	0	30	0	**30**	0	0	38	1	**39**
2005	0	0	2,000	2	**2,002**	0	0	30	0	**30**	0	0	40	1	**41**

Table 8.13.4
Free Presbyterian Church of Scotland

	MEMBERSHIP					CONGREGATIONS					MINISTERS				
	England	Wales	Scotland	N. Ireland	**Total UK**	England	Wales	Scotland	N. Ireland	**Total UK**	England	Wales	Scotland	N. Ireland	**Total UK**[4]
1990	60	0	4,440	0	**4,500**	2	0	64	0	**66**[3]	1	0	21	0	**22**
1995	60	0	4,220	20	**4,300**[3]	2	0	55	1	**58**[3]	0	0	16	0	**16**
2000	80[3]	0	4,000	20	**4,100**[3]	2	0	48	1	**51**[3]	0	0	15	0	**15**
2001[1]	100	0	3,925	25	**4,050**	2	0	47	1	**50**	0	0	15	0	**15**
2002	120	0	3,850	30	**4,000**	2	0	45	1	**48**	0	0	14	0	**14**[1]
2005[1]	150	0	3,700	50	**3,900**	2	0	41	1	**44**	1	0	13	0	**14**

Table 8.13.5
Reformed Presbyterian Church of Scotland

	MEMBERSHIP					CONGREGATIONS					MINISTERS				
	England	Wales	Scotland	N. Ireland	**Total UK**	England	Wales	Scotland	N. Ireland	**Total UK**	England	Wales	Scotland	N. Ireland	**Total UK**
1990	0	0	190	0	**190**	0	0	5	0	**5**	0	0	4	0	**4**
1995	0	0	100	0	**100**	0	0	4	0	**4**	0	0	4	0	**4**
2000	0	0	80	0	**80**	0	0	3	0	**3**	0	0	3	0	**3**
2001	0	0	75	0	**75**	0	0	3	0	**3**	0	0	3	0	**3**
2002	0	0	75	0	**75**	0	0	3	0	**3**	0	0	3	0	**3**
2005	0	0	70[1]	0	**70**	0	0	2	0	**2**	0	0	2	0	**2**

Table 8.13.6
United Free Church of Scotland

	MEMBERSHIP					CONGREGATIONS					MINISTERS				
	England	Wales	Scotland	N. Ireland	**Total UK**	England	Wales	Scotland	N. Ireland	**Total UK**	England	Wales	Scotland	N. Ireland	**Total UK**
1990	0	0	8,076	0	**8,076**	0	0	75	0	**75**	0	0	47	0	**47**
1995	0	0	6,551	0	**6,551**	0	0	71	0	**71**	0	0	43	0	**43**
2000	0	0	5,217	0	**5,217**	0	0	69	0	**69**	0	0	40	0	**40**
2001	0	0	5,119	0	**5,119**	0	0	68	0	**68**	0	0	38	0	**38**
2002	0	0	5,000	0	**5,000**	0	0	67	0	**67**	0	0	38	0	**38**
2005	0	0	4,600	0	**4,600**	0	0	63	0	**63**	0	0	35	0	**35**

Table 8.13.7
Associated Presbyterian Churches

	MEMBERSHIP					CONGREGATIONS					MINISTERS				
	England	Wales	Scotland	N. Ireland	**Total UK**	England	Wales	Scotland	N. Ireland	**Total UK**	England	Wales	Scotland	N. Ireland	**Total UK**
1990	0	0	1,250	0	**1,250**	0	0	33	0	**33**	0	0	13	0	**13**
1995	0	0	1,250	0	**1,250**	0	0	30	0	**30**	0	0	15	0	**15**
2000	0	0	1,200	0	**1,200**	0	0	20	0	**20**	0	0	12	0	**12**
2001	0	0	1,100	0	**1,100**	0	0	18	0	**18**	0	0	10	0	**10**
2002	0	0	1,000	0	**1,000**	0	0	17	0	**17**	0	0	8	0	**8**
2005	0	0	900	0	**900**	0	0	16	0	**16**	0	0	9	0	**9**

[1] Estimate. [2] Separated from the Free Church of Scotland in January 2000. [3] Revised figure. [4] All male.

8.14 Institutional Church Statistics: Presbyterian: Irish Churches

8

Table 8.14.1
Evangelical Presbyterian Church in Ireland[2]

	MEMBERSHIP					CONGREGATIONS					MINISTERS				
	England	Wales	Scotland	N. Ireland	**Total UK**	England	Wales	Scotland	N. Ireland	**Total UK**	England	Wales	Scotland	N. Ireland	**Total UK**
1990	12	0	0	418	**430**	1	0	0	10	**11**	1	0	0	9	**10**
1995	20[4]	0	0	420[4]	**440**	1	0	0	11	**12**	1	0	0	9	**10**
2000	21	0	0	413	**434**	1	0	0	11	**12**	1	0	0	10	**11**
2001	20	0	0	410	**430**	1	0	0	11	**12**	1	0	0	10	**11**
2002	20[1]	0	0	410[1]	**430**	0	0	0	11	**11**	0	0	0	9	**9**
2005[1]	21	0	0	409	**430**	0	0	0	11	**11**	0	0	0	9	**9**

Table 8.14.2
Free Presbyterian Church of Ulster

	England	Wales	Scotland	N. Ireland	**Total UK**	England	Wales	Scotland	N. Ireland	**Total UK**	England	Wales	Scotland	N. Ireland	**Total UK**
1990	0	0	0	12,550	**12,550**	0	0	0	60	**60**	0	0	0	50	**50**
1995	0	0	0	14,100	**14,100**	0	0	0	66	**66**	0	0	0	54	**54**
2000	600[1]	250[1]	350[1]	15,000	**16,200**[4]	6	3	3	63	**75**	6	3	3	58	**70**
2001	800[1]	300[1]	500[1]	15,200	**16,800**	7	4	4	63	**78**	7	2	3	58	**70**
2002	850[1]	300[1]	550[1]	15,400	**17,100**	7	4	4	63	**78**	7	2	4	59	**72**
2005[1]	950	350	700	16,000[4]	**18,000**	7	4	4	63	**78**	7	3	5	60	**75**

Table 8.14.3
Non-Subscribing Presbyterian Church of Ireland

	England	Wales	Scotland	N. Ireland	**Total UK**	England	Wales	Scotland	N. Ireland	**Total UK**	England	Wales	Scotland	N. Ireland	**Total UK**
1990	0	0	0	3,815	**3,815**	0	0	0	34	**34**	0	0	0	16	**16**
1995	0	0	0	3,640	**3,640**	0	0	0	34	**34**	0	0	0	13	**13**
2000	0	0	0	3,561	**3,561**	0	0	0	34	**34**	0	0	0	14	**14**
2001	0	0	0	3,431	**3,431**	0	0	0	34	**34**	0	0	0	12	**12**
2002	0	0	0	3,529	**3,529**	0	0	0	33	**33**	0	0	0	12	**12**
2005	0	0	0	3,600	**3,600**	0	0	0	33	**33**	0	0	0	14	**14**

Table 8.14.4
Presbyterian Church in Ireland (Northern Ireland)

	England	Wales	Scotland	N. Ireland	**Total UK**	England	Wales	Scotland	N. Ireland	**Total UK**	England	Wales	Scotland	N. Ireland	**Total UK**
1990	0	0	0	195,576	**195,576**	0	0	0	456	**456**	0	0	0	398	**398**
1995	0	0	0	194,718	**194,718**	0	0	0	455	**455**	0	0	0	360	**360**
2000	0	0	0	191,797	**191,797**	0	0	0	452	**452**	0	0	0	370	**370**
2001	0	0	0	188,920	**188,920**	0	0	0	463	**463**	0	0	0	370	**370**
2002	0	0	0	187,031	**187,031**	0	0	0	463	**463**	0	0	0	365	**365**
2005	0	0	0	179,549	**179,549**	0	0	0	460	**460**	0	0	0	370	**370**

Table 8.14.5
Reformed Presbyterian Church of Ireland

	England	Wales	Scotland	N. Ireland	**Total UK**	England	Wales	Scotland	N. Ireland	**Total UK**	England	Wales	Scotland	N. Ireland	**Total UK**
1990	0	0	0	2,500	**2,500**	0	0	0	36	**36**	0	0	0	32	**32**
1995	0	0	0	2,305	**2,305**	0	0	0	34	**34**	0	0	0	25	**25**
2000	0	0	0	2,039	**2,039**	0	0	0	36	**36**	0	0	0	26	**26**
2001	0	0	0	2,033	**2,033**	0	0	0	36	**36**	0	0	0	27	**27**
2002	0	0	0	1,975[1]	**1,975**	0	0	0	36	**36**	0	0	0	27	**27**
2005	0	0	0	1,850[1]	**1,850**	0	0	0	36	**36**	0	0	0	27	**27**

[1] Estimate. [2] Excludes adherents. [3] For communicant members only. [4] Revised figure.

9

Free Church Statistics

9

See notes and definitions on Page 0.6

Sources: Individual denominations and previous editions of *Religious Trends*

9.2 Free Church Statistics: Baptist Churches

Table 9.2.1
Total Baptist Churches

	MEMBERSHIP					CHURCHES					MINISTERS				
	England	Wales	Scotland	N. Ireland	**Total UK**	England	Wales	Scotland	N. Ireland	**Total UK**	England	Wales	Scotland	N. Ireland	**Total UK**
1990	168,078	37,820	18,103	8,167	**232,168**	2,542	743	195	103	**3,583**	2,100	221	171	100	**2,592**
1995	163,784	34,169	18,068	8,208	**224,229**	2,574	714	203	112	**3,603**	2,210	229	175	105	**2,719**
2000	165,722	26,271	16,785	8,249	**217,027**	2,582	626	207	113	**3,528**	2,275	178	191	89	**2,733**
2001	164,771	25,506	16,464	8,321	**215,062**	2,586	616	206	116	**3,524**	2,382	180	190	94	**2,846**
2002	164,305	24,414	16,513	8,345	**213,577**	2,587	600	204	117	**3,508**	2,389	180	190	95	**2,854**
2005	163,441	20,790	16,842	8,406	**209,479**	2,593	556	203	117	**3,469**	2,418	175	185	95	**2,873**

Table 9.2.2
Baptist Union of Great Britain

	MEMBERSHIP					CHURCHES					MINISTERS				
	England[3]	Wales	Scotland	N. Ireland	**Total UK**	England	Wales	Scotland	N. Ireland	**Total UK**	England	Wales	Scotland	N. Ireland	**Total UK**
1990	138,370	10,892	0	0	**149,262**	1,970	180	0	0	**2,150**	1,569	100	0	0	**1,669**
1995	133,619	10,284	256	0	**144,159**	1,982[2]	171	3	0	**2,156**	1,657	104	3	0	**1,764**
2000	135,759	6,661	216	0	**142,636**	1,993	126	3	0	**2,122**	1,709	62	2	0	**1,773**
2001	134,815	6,493	207	0	**141,515**	1,996	126	3	0	**2,125**	1,816	65	2	0	**1,883**
2002[1]	134,354	6,176	200	0	**140,730**	1,995	121	3	0	**2,119**	1,823	65	2	0	**1,890**
2005[1]	133,653	5,200	175	0	**139,028**	1,991	105	3	0	**2,099**	1,850	65	2	0	**1,917**

Table 9.2.3
Baptist Union of Ireland

	MEMBERSHIP					CHURCHES					MINISTERS				
	England	Wales	Eire[4]	N. Ireland	**Total UK**	England	Wales	Scotland	N. Ireland	**Total UK**	England	Wales	Scotland	N. Ireland	**Total UK**
1990	0	0	8,500	8,022	**8,022**	0	0	0	101	**101**	0	0	0	98	**98**
1995	0	0	8,475	7,998	**7,998**	0	0	0	109	**109**	0	0	0	102	**102**
2000	0	0	8,444	7,969	**7,969**	0	0	0	109	**109**	0	0	0	85	**85**
2001	0	0	8,446	7,971	**7,971**	0	0	0	111	**111**	0	0	0	89	**89**
2002[1]	0	0	8,440	7,965	**7,965**	0	0	0	111	**111**	0	0	0	89	**89**
2005[1]	0	0	8,420	7,946	**7,946**	0	0	0	111	**111**	0	0	0	89	**89**

Table 9.2.4
Baptist Union of Scotland

	MEMBERSHIP					CHURCHES					MINISTERS				
	England	Wales	Scotland	N. Ireland	**Total UK**	England	Wales	Scotland	N. Ireland	**Total UK**	England	Wales	Scotland	N. Ireland	**Total UK**
1990	0	0	16,212	0	**16,212**	0	0	166	0	**166**	0	0	137	0	**137**
1995	0	0	15,781	0	**15,781**	0	0	172	0	**172**	0	0	139	0	**139**
2000	0	0	14,384	0	**14,384**	0	0	176	0	**176**	0	0	158	0	**158**
2000	0	0	14,002	0	**14,002**	0	0	176	0	**176**	0	0	159	0	**159**
2002	0	0	14,001	0	**14,001**	0	0	174	0	**174**	0	0	159	0	**159**
2005	0	0	14,250	0	**14,250**	0	0	174	0	**174**	0	0	155	0	**155**

Table 9.2.5
Baptist Union of Wales

	MEMBERSHIP					CHURCHES					MINISTERS				
	England	Wales	Scotland	N. Ireland	**Total UK**	England	Wales	Scotland	N. Ireland	**Total UK**	England	Wales	Scotland	N. Ireland	**Total UK**
1990	200	26,563	0	0	**26,763**	4	556	0	0	**560**	2	115	0	0	**117**
1995	150[2]	23,450	0	0	**23,600**	3[2]	535	0	0	**538**	2[2]	118	0	0	**120**
2000	103	19,125	0	0	**19,228**	3	491	0	0	**494**	2	107	0	0	**109**
2001	95	18,483	0	0	**18,578**	3	481	0	0	**484**	2	105	0	0	**107**
2002	91	17,683	0	0	**17,774**	3	470	0	0	**473**	2	104	0	0	**106**
2005	73	15,000	0	0	**15,073**	3	440	0	0	**443**	2	98	0	0	**100**

Table 9.2.6
Old Baptist Union

	MEMBERSHIP					CHURCHES					MINISTERS				
	England	Wales	Scotland	N. Ireland	**Total UK**	England	Wales	Scotland	N. Ireland	**Total UK**	England	Wales	Scotland	N. Ireland	**Total UK**
1990	456[1]	25[1]	0	0	**481**	12	1	0	0	**13**	8	1	0	0	**9**
1995	475	25	0	0	**500**	14	1	0	0	**15**	8	1	0	0	**9**
2000	485	30	0	0	**515**	14	1	0	0	**15**	9	1	0	0	**10**
2001	501	60	0	0	**561**	14	1	0	0	**15**	9	1	0	0	**10**
2002	510	55	0	0	**565**	14	1	0	0	**15**	10	2	0	0	**12**
2005	550	50	0	0	**600**	15	2	0	0	**17**	12	2	0	0	**14**

[1] Estimate
[2] Revised figure
[3] Churches in Wales may be members of either the Baptist Union of Wales or the Baptist Union of Great Britain (BUGB) or both. If they are members of both, their membership will be doubly counted. This column gives an estimate of the membership of the churches belonging only to the BUGB. Likewise this column excludes members of churches which are members of BUGB and the Baptist Union of Scotland.
[4] The Baptist Union of Ireland includes the whole of Ireland, and this column gives the total membership for the Union. The next column gives estimates for the proportion in Northern Ireland which is used for the overall totals (taken as 94.4% of the Union membership).
[5] These figures include non-Baptist Union figures, some of which are or were listed in the Baptist Union of Great Britain Directory.
[6] Taken as pro rata to the Baptist Union of Great Britain 1990-2005.
[7] Based on the 1994 Scottish Church Census.
[8] Based on the 2002 Scottish Church Census.
[9] Attendance can be 50% more than membership.

Free Church Statistics: Baptist Churches (continued)

Table 9.3.1
Gospel Standard Strict Baptist

	MEMBERSHIP					CHURCHES					MINISTERS				
	England	Wales	Scotland	N. Ireland	**Total UK**	England	Wales	Scotland	N. Ireland	**Total UK**	England	Wales	Scotland	N. Ireland	**Total UK**
1990	6,000[2]	0[2]	0[2]	0	**6,000**	151[2]	0[2]	0[2]	0	**151**	141[2]	0[2]	0[2]	0	**141**
1995	5,600[2]	0[2]	0[2]	0	**5,600**	139[2]	0[2]	0[2]	0	**139**	140[2]	0[2]	0[2]	0	**140**
2000	5,200[2]	0	0	0	**5,200**	126[2]	0	0	0	**126**	141[2]	0	0	0	**141**
2001	5,100	0	0	0	**5,100**	124	0	0	0	**124**	140	0	0	0	**140**
2002	5,000	0	0	0	**5,000**	122	0	0	0	**122**	138	0	0	0	**138**
2005	4,500	0	0	0	**4,500**	120	0	0	0	**120**	135	0	0	0	**135**

Table 9.3.2
Grace Baptist Churches

	MEMBERSHIP					CHURCHES					MINISTERS				
	England	Wales	Scotland	N. Ireland	**Total UK**	England	Wales	Scotland	N. Ireland	**Total UK**	England	Wales	Scotland	N. Ireland	**Total UK**
1990	11,920[2]	115	190	0	**12,225**	252	3	5	0	**260**	203[2]	3	7	0	**213**
1995[1]	11,130	125	250	0	**11,505**	252	3	6	0	**261**	201	3	7	0	**211**
2000[1]	10,340	165	290	0	**10,795**	251	4	7	0	**262**	199	4	6	0	**209**
2001[1]	10,185	170	295	40	**10,690**	251	4	7	1	**263**	198	5	5	1	**209**
2002	10,025[1]	175[1]	295[1]	40[1]	**10,535**	251	4	7	1	**263**	197	5	5	1	**208**
2005[1]	9,555	190	305	40	**10,090**	250	4	7	1	**262**	194	5	5	1	**205**

Table 9.3.3
Biblical Ministries Worldwide

	MEMBERSHIP					CHURCHES					MINISTERS				
	England	Wales	Scotland	N. Ireland	**Total UK**	England	Wales	Scotland	N. Ireland	**Total UK**	England	Wales	Scotland	N. Ireland	**Total UK**
1990	57	0	6	0	**63**	3	0	1	0	**4**	3	0	2	0	**5**
1995	75	0	11	0	**86**	4	0	1	0	**5**	6	0	3	0	**9**
2000	85	0	15	0	**100**	2	0	1	0	**3**	5	0	3	0	**8**
2001	75	0	15	0	**90**	2	0	1	0	**3**	5	0	3	0	**8**
2002	75	0	7	0	**82**	2	0	1	0	**3**	5	0	3	0	**8**
2005	80	0	12	0	**92**	3	0	1	0	**4**	5	0	3	0	**8**

Table 9.3.4
Other Baptist Churches[5]

	MEMBERSHIP					CHURCHES					MINISTERS				
	England[6]	Wales	Scotland	N. Ireland	**Total UK**	England	Wales	Scotland	N. Ireland	**Total UK**	England	Wales	Scotland	N. Ireland	**Total UK**
1990[1]	11,075	225	1,695	145	**13,140**	150	3	23	2	**178**	174	2	25	2	**203**
1995[1]	12,735	285	1,770	210	**15,000**	180	4	21[7]	3	**208**	196	3	23[2]	3	**225**
2000[1]	13,750[2]	290	1,880[2]	280	**16,200**	193[2]	4	20	4	**221**	210[2]	4	22	4	**240**
2001[1]	14,000	300	1,945	310	**16,555**	196	4	19	4	**223**	212	4	21	4	**241**
2002[1]	14,250	325	2,010[8]	340	**16,925**	200	4	19[8]	5	**228**	214	4	21	5	**244**
2005[1]	15,030	350	2,100	420	**17,900**	211	5	18	5	**239**	220	5	20	5	**250**

[1] Estimate. *For other footnotes, see* **Page 9.2**

Table 9.3.5 Baptist Union of Great Britain, 2000 and 2001

		England	Wales	Scot	**Total**
Children up to 12	2000	103,792	1,911	46	**105,749**
	2001	102,913	1,965	50	**104,928**
Young People (13–19)	2000	34,943	644	7	**35,594**
	2001	34,768	661	6	**35,435**
Baptisms	2000	4,049	31	7	**4,087**
	2001	3,991	36	0	**4,027**

Source: Baptist Union of Great Britain

Table 9.3.6
Patterns of believing and belonging

Believing and belonging	In the past there was a requirement that everyone within European society believed what the church taught and belonged to this church
Belonging but no longer believing	As the era of Christendom fades, some continue to belong out of loyalty or social convention but no longer believe – the phenomenon of nominality
Belonging but only partly believing	The influence of postmodernity is seen in a tendency to pick and mix, as some who belong do not feel the need to assent to all that the church teaches
Believing but no longer belonging	Some continue to believe but choose no longer to belong – a different form of nominality that raises the question of how long belief is sustainable without community
Belonging but not yet believing	Growing numbers of churches, regardless of their theology, are discovering and acknowledging that many today need to belong before they believe
Believing but belonging less intensely	It is clear from recent research that belonging no longer implies the same level of personal participation as before
Believing and belonging intermittently	Recent research has also indicated that believing and belonging are dynamic rather than static categories – many who continue to believe after they stop belonging choose to belong again later
Believing but not yet belonging	In a postmodern culture where spirituality is in vogue, some will come to Christian faith outside the church and will not assume that belonging is an important expression of their faith

Source: Baptist Union paper "Church membership: Setting the Scene, Raising the Questions" by Rev Stuart Murray-Williams, September 2002

9.4 Free Church Statistics: Independents: Christian Brethren

Table 9.4.1
Total Brethren

	MEMBERSHIP					ASSEMBLIES					FULL-TIME WORKERS				
	England	Wales	Scotland	N. Ireland	**Total UK**	England	Wales	Scotland	N. Ireland	**Total UK**	England	Wales	Scotland	N. Ireland	**Total UK**
1990	62,268	4,694	17,787	9,180	**93,929**	1,451	124	368	214	**2,157**	143	8	32	24	**207**
1995	58,077	4,766	17,110	8,910	**88,863**	1,368	112	323	208	**2,011**	173	10	42	27	**252**
2000	53,991	4,568	17,511	8,804	**84,874**	1,134	101	267	204	**1,706**	160	11	48	23	**242**
2001	53,456	4,500	17,221	8,811	**83,988**	1,126	99	264	204	**1,693**	159	11	47	23	**240**
2002	51,400	4,497	16,926	8,815	**81,638**	1,112	99	262	204	**1,677**	154	11	45	23	**233**
2005	51,130	4,237	16,175	8,668	**80,210**	1,076	91	253	203	**1,623**	155	10	43	23	**231**

Table 9.4.2
Christian Brethren (Open)

	MEMBERSHIP					ASSEMBLIES					FULL-TIME WORKERS				
	England	Wales	Scotland	N. Ireland	**Total UK**	England	Wales	Scotland	N. Ireland	**Total UK**	England	Wales	Scotland	N. Ireland	**Total UK**[6]
1990	48,850[2]	3,978[2]	16,066[2]	8,145	**77,039**	977	102	277	181	**1,537**	105	8	30	22	**165**
1995	44,523[2]	4,050	15,474[2]	7,875	**71,922**	898	90	234	175	**1,397**	135	10	40	25	**210**
2000[1]	42,276	3,855	16,060	7,697	**69,888**	729[5]	79	215	171	**1,194**	123	11	47	22	**203**
2001[1]	41,991	3,790	15,800	7,696	**69,277**	726	77	212	171	**1,186**	123	11	46	22	**202**
2002	40,419	3,789	15,540	7,695	**67,443**	719	77	210	171	**1,177**	118	11	45	22	**196**
2005[1]	40,350	3,530	14,760	7,502	**66,142**	700	69	201	170	**1,140**	119	10	43	22	**194**

Table 9.4.3
Churches of God (International) Brethren

	MEMBERSHIP					ASSEMBLIES					FULL-TIME WORKERS				
	England	Wales	Scotland	N. Ireland	**Total UK**	England	Wales	Scotland	N. Ireland	**Total UK**	England	Wales	Scotland	N. Ireland	**Total UK**
1990	200[2]	0[2]	200[2]	0[2]	**400**	36	0[2]	40	0[2]	**76**	–	–	–	–	**0**[2]
1995	190[2]	0[2]	190[2]	0[2]	**380**	34	0[2]	36	0[2]	**70**	–	–	–	–	**0**[2]
2000[1]	150[1]	0[1]	150[2]	0[1]	**300**[4]	0	0	0	0	**0**[3]	–	–	–	–	–
2001[1]	150	0	150	0	**300**	0	0	0	0	**0**	–	–	–	–	–
2002[1]	150	0	150	0	**300**	0	0	0	0	**0**	–	–	–	–	–
2005[1]	125	0	125	0	**250**	0	0	0	0	**0**	–	–	–	–	–

Table 9.4.4
Plymouth Brethren No 4

	MEMBERSHIP					ASSEMBLIES					FULL-TIME WORKERS				
	England	Wales	Scotland	N. Ireland	**Total UK**	England	Wales	Scotland	N. Ireland	**Total UK**	England	Wales	Scotland	N. Ireland	**Total UK**
1990	9,300	700	1,018	1,000	**12,018**	310	20	40	30	**400**	30	0	0	0	**30**
1995	9,500	700	944	1,000	**12,144**	312	20	43	30	**405**	30	0	0	0	**30**
2000[1]	9,700	700	1,050	1,080	**12,530**	312	20	43	30	**405**	30	0	0	0	**30**
2001[1]	9,750	700	1,075	1,090	**12,615**	312	20	43	30	**405**	30	0	0	0	**30**
2002	9,800	700	1,100	1,100	**12,700**	312	20	43	30	**405**	30	0	0	0	**30**
2005[1]	9,950	700	1,200	1,150	**13,000**	312	20	43	30	**405**	30	0	0	0	**30**

Table 9.4.5
Kelly Brethren

	MEMBERSHIP					ASSEMBLIES					FULL-TIME WORKERS				
	England	Wales	Scotland	N. Ireland	**Total UK**	England	Wales	Scotland	N. Ireland	**Total UK**	England	Wales	Scotland	N. Ireland	**Total UK**
1990	62	0	3	0	**65**	4	0	0	0	**4**	–	–	–	–	–
1995	58	0	2	0	**60**	4	0	0	0	**4**	–	–	–	–	–
2000[1]	35	0	1	0	**36**	3	0	0	0	**3**	–	–	–	–	–
2001[1]	30	0	1	0	**31**	3	0	0	0	**3**	–	–	–	–	–
2002	26	0	1	0	**27**	2[1]	0	0	0	**2**	–	–	–	–	–
2005	15	0	0	0	**15**	2[1]	0	0	0	**2**	–	–	–	–	–

Table 9.4.6
Reunited Brethren[7]

	MEMBERSHIP					ASSEMBLIES					FULL-TIME WORKERS				
	England	Wales	Scotland	N. Ireland	**Total UK**	England	Wales	Scotland	N. Ireland	**Total UK**	England	Wales	Scotland	N. Ireland	**Total UK**
1990	3,460	10	500	30	**4,000**	101	1	11	2	**115**	8	0	2	2	**12**
1995	3,460	10	500	30	**4,000**	99	1	10	2	**112**	8	0	2	2	**12**
2000[1]	1,640	8	250	22	**1,920**	74	1	9	2	**86**	7	0	1	1	**9**
2001[1]	1,420	5	195	20	**1,640**	69	1	9	2	**81**	6	0	1	1	**8**
2002	900	3	135	15	**1,053**	64	1	9	2	**76**	6	0	0	1	**7**
2005[1]	600	3	90	12	**705**	50	1	9	2	**62**	6	0	0	1	**7**

Table 9.4.7
Tunbridge Wells Brethren[8]

	MEMBERSHIP					ASSEMBLIES					FULL-TIME WORKERS				
	England	Wales	Scotland	N. Ireland	**Total UK**	England	Wales	Scotland	N. Ireland	**Total UK**	England	Wales	Scotland	N. Ireland	**Total UK**
1990	396	6	0	5	**407**	23	1	0	1	**25**	–	–	–	–	–
1995	346	6	0	5	**357**	21	1	0	1	**23**	–	–	–	–	–
2000[1]	190	5	0	5	**200**	16	1	0	1	**18**	–	–	–	–	–
2001[1]	165	5	0	5	**175**	16	1	0	1	**18**	–	–	–	–	–
2002	105	5	0	5	**115**	15	1	0	1	**17**	–	–	–	–	–
2005	90	4	0	4	**98**	12	1	0	1	**14**	–	–	–	–	–

[1] Estimate. *For other footnotes, see* **Page 9.5**

Free Church Statistics: Independents: Congregational Churches

Table 9.5.1
Total Congregational Churches

	MEMBERSHIP					CHURCHES					MINISTERS				
	England	Wales	Scotland	N. Ireland	**Total UK**	England	Wales	Scotland	N. Ireland	**Total UK**	England	Wales	Scotland	N. Ireland	**Total UK**
1990	13,312	53,789	18,566	4,118	**89,785**	379	662	96	34	**1,171**	117	134	82	33	**366**
1995	12,464	46,716	12,085	3,980	**75,245**	376	632	94	36	**1,138**	106	140	65	36	**347**
2000	11,482	39,939	3,503	3,825	**58,749**	366	591	38	36	**1,031**	123	133	30	37	**323**
2001	11,266	38,531	3,350	3,850	**56,997**	352	575	38	35	**1,000**	121	132	33	38	**324**
2002	11,073	36,543	3,300	3,875	**54,791**	354	561	40	35	**990**	127	130	28	38	**323**
2005	10,473	31,497	3,218	3,760	**48,948**	344	525	41	34	**944**	129	127	27	38	**321**

Table 9.5.2
Congregational Federation

	MEMBERSHIP					CHURCHES					MINISTERS				
	England	Wales	Scotland	N. Ireland	**Total UK**	England	Wales	Scotland	N. Ireland	**Total UK**	England	Wales	Scotland	N. Ireland	**Total UK**
1990	8,061	1,133	81	0	**9,275**	252	33	1	0	**286**	61	6	1	0	**68**
1995	7,692	988	3,247	0	**11,927**[3]	252	33	31	0	**316**	52	4	13	0	**69**
2000	7,111	968	3,353	0	**11,432**	242	33	37	0	**312**	61	2	15	0	**78**
2001	6,960	950	3,200	0	**11,110**	240	33	37	0	**310**	57	2	15	0	**74**
2002	6,818	915	3,150	0	**10,883**	241	33	39	0	**313**	63	2	10	0	**75**
2005[1]	6,558	874	3,078	0	**10,510**	237	33	40	0	**310**	67	2	10	0	**79**

Table 9.5.3
Evangelical Fellowship of Congregational Churches

	MEMBERSHIP					CHURCHES					MINISTERS				
	England	Wales	Scotland	N. Ireland	**Total UK**[4]	England	Wales	Scotland	N. Ireland	**Total UK**[4]	England	Wales	Scotland	N. Ireland	**Total UK**[4]
1990	4,510	370	145	1,175	**6,200**	114	8	1	9	**132**	54	4	0	7	**65**
1995	4,250	365	165	1,120	**5,900**	113	10	1	10	**134**	52	4	13	6	**75**
2000[1]	3,900	335	150	1,015	**5,400**	113	10	1	10	**134**	60	4	15	7	**86**
2001[1]	3,880	330	150	1,040	**5,400**	101	9	1	9	**120**	62	5	18	8	**93**
2002[1]	3,860	325	150	1,065	**5,400**	102	8	1	9	**120**	62	5	18	8	**93**
2005[1]	3,600	300	140	960	**5,000**	96	7	1	8	**112**	60	5	17	8	**90**

Table 9.5.4
Congregational Union of Ireland

	MEMBERSHIP					CHURCHES					MINISTERS				
	England	Wales	Scotland	N. Ireland	**Total UK**	England	Wales	Scotland	N. Ireland	**Total UK**	England	Wales	Scotland	N. Ireland	**Total UK**
1990	0	0	0	2,943[5]	**2,943**	0	0	0	25	**25**	0	0	0	26	**26**
1995[1]	0	0	0	2,860	**2,860**	0	0	0	26	**26**	0	0	0	30	**30**
2000[1]	0	0	0	2,810	**2,810**	0	0	0	26	**26**	0	0	0	30	**30**
2001[1]	0	0	0	2,810	**2,810**	0	0	0	26	**26**	0	0	0	30	**30**
2002[1]	0	0	0	2,810	**2,810**	0	0	0	26	**26**	0	0	0	30	**30**
2005[1]	0	0	0	2,800	**2,800**	0	0	0	26	**26**	0	0	0	30	**30**

Table 9.5.5
Union of Welsh Independents[6]

	MEMBERSHIP					CHURCHES					MINISTERS				
	England	Wales	Scotland	N. Ireland	**Total UK**	England	Wales	Scotland	N. Ireland	**Total UK**	England	Wales	Scotland	N. Ireland	**Total UK**
1990	741[2]	51,286[2]	0	0	**52,027**[7]	13[2]	621[2]	0	0	**634**	2[2]	124[2]	0	0	**126**
1995	522	41,920	0	0	**42,442**[8]	11	544	0	0	**555**	2	122[2]	0	0	**124**
2000	471	34,414	0	0	**34,885**[9]	11	503	0	0	**514**	2	117	0	0	**119**
2001	426	33,026	0	0	**33,452**[9]	11	488	0	0	**499**	2	115	0	0	**117**
2002[1]	395	31,078	0	0	**31,473**[9]	11	475	0	0	**486**	2	113	0	0	**115**
2005[1]	315	26,123	0	0	**26,438**[10]	11	440	0	0	**451**	2	110	0	0	**112**

Table 9.5.6
Scottish Congregational Church

	MEMBERSHIP					CHURCHES					MINISTERS				
	England	Wales	Scotland	N. Ireland	**Total UK**	England	Wales	Scotland	N. Ireland	**Total UK**	England	Wales	Scotland	N. Ireland	**Total UK**
1990	0	0	18,340	0	**18,340**	0	0	94	0	**94**	0	0	81	0	**81**
1995	0	0	8,673	0	**8,673**	0	0	62	0	**62**	0	0	39	0	**39**
2000	Joined the United Reformed Church on 1st April 2000; figures included with URC in Table 8.12.2 2000 onwards.														

Page 9.4
[1] Estimate
[2] Revised figure
[3] Since 1996 have closed all Assembly Halls and only rent one occasionally as needed.
[4] "Active" addresses out of a mailing list of 2,000. Outreach now undertaken by literature only (bi-monthly magazine *New Horizons*).
[5] Actual figure, not estimated.
[6] Taken pro rata to number of members, 2000 and onwards.
[7] Combining the Kelly, Lowe, Glanton, Stuart and one Tunbridge Wells Group.
[8] Four Groups of the Tunbridge Wells Brethren exist in the UK.

Page 9.5
[1] Estimate
[2] Revised figure
[3] Excludes 4,500 Adherents.
[4] Totals for 2000 to 2002 given; country distribution estimated.
[5] 36% of the 8,176 in the 1991 N Ireland Census.
[6] Or Welsh Congregational Union.
[7] Excluding 1,000 who are members of associated churches, which are included in **Table 9.5.1.**
[8] Excluding an estimated 3,443 Welsh members of 45 associated churches with 10 pastors, which are included in **Table 9.5.1.**
[9] Excluding an estimated 4,225 Welsh members of 45 associated churches with 10 pastors, which are included in **Table 9.5.1.**
[10] Excluding an estimated 4,200 Welsh members of 45 associated churches with 10 pastors, which are included in **Table 9.5.1.**

9

9.6 Free Churches: Independents: FIEC/UEC, Churches of Christ, CMA

Table 9.6.1
Total All Independent Churches[7]

	MEMBERSHIP					CHURCHES					MINISTERS				
	England	Wales	Scotland	N. Ireland	**Total UK**	England	Wales	Scotland	N. Ireland	**Total UK**	England	Wales	Scotland	N. Ireland	**Total UK**
1990	118,448	60,085	39,256	13,878	**231,667**	2,482	809	519	261	**4,071**	835	165	156	63	**1,219**
1995	112,393	53,132	31,501	13,380	**210,406**	2,403	768	470	253	**3,894**	857	173	150	67	**1,247**
2000	106,795	46,282	23,044	13,079	**189,200**	2,188	722	360	251	**3,521**	873	167	122	66	**1,228**
2001	106,964	44,841	22,561	13,131	**187,497**	2,174	705	357	250	**3,486**	873	166	125	68	**1,232**
2002	105,228	42,931	22,217	13,183	**183,559**	2,149	694	358	250	**3,451**	877	165	120	70	**1,232**
2005	106,258	37,719	21,473	12,933	**178,383**	2,113	651	352	248	**3,364**	867	159	116	70	**1,212**

Table 9.6.2
Fellowship of Independent Evangelical Churches (FIEC)

	MEMBERSHIP					CHURCHES					MINISTERS				
	England	Wales	Scotland	N. Ireland	**Total UK**	England	Wales	Scotland	N. Ireland	**Total UK**	England	Wales	Scotland	N. Ireland	**Total UK**
1990	30,200	1,250	1,450	150	**33,050**	387	16	18	2	**423**	312	18	16	1	**347**
1995	28,740	1,300	820	140	**31,000**	397	17	15	1	**430**	316	18	15	1	**350**
2000[1]	27,977	1,420	500	40	**29,937**	424	22	16	1	**463**	303	18	14	1	**336**
2001	28,794	1,450	450	40	**30,734**	433	23	16	1	**473**	299	18	12	1	**330**
2002	29,257	1,496	433	38	**31,224**	421	25	17	1	**464**	294	18	11	1	**324**
2005	30,880	1,580	500	40	**33,000**	433	26	20	1	**480**	275	16	9	1	**301**

Table 9.6.3
Union of Evangelical Churches (UEC)

	MEMBERSHIP					CHURCHES					MINISTERS				
	England	Wales	Scotland	N. Ireland	**Total UK**	England	Wales	Scotland	N. Ireland	**Total UK**	England	Wales	Scotland	N. Ireland	**Total UK**
1990	554	0	0	0	**554**	20	0	0	0	**20**	32	0	0	0	**32**
1995	575	0	0	0	**575**	20	0	0	0	**20**	29	0	0	0	**29**
2000[1]	510	0	0	0	**510**	20	0	0	0	**20**	22	0	0	0	**22**
2001	503	0	0	0	**503**	20	0	0	0	**20**	22	0	0	0	**22**
2002	493	0	0	0	**493**	20	0	0	0	**20**	24	0	0	0	**24**
2005	475	0	0	0	**475**	18	0	0	0	**18**	23	0	0	0	**23**

Table 9.6.4
Fellowship of Churches of Christ

	MEMBERSHIP					CHURCHES					MINISTERS				
	England	Wales	Scotland	N. Ireland	**Total UK**	England	Wales	Scotland	N. Ireland	**Total UK**	England	Wales	Scotland	N. Ireland	**Total UK**
1990	1,129[5]	12	63	0	**1,204**	33	1	3	0	**37**	18	0	0	0	**18**
1995	1,132[5]	5	31	0	**1,168**	32[5]	1	2	0	**35**	22[5]	0	0	0	**22**
2000[1]	965	5	30	0	**1,000**	32	1	2	0	**33**	21	0	0	0	**21**
2001[1]	985	5	30	0	**1,020**	32	1	2	0	**33**	21	0	0	0	**21**
2002[1]	1,005	5	30	0	**1,040**	32	1	2	0	**33**	21	0	0	0	**21**
2005[1]	1,055	5	40	0	**1,100**	32	1	2	0	**33**	20	0	0	0	**20**

Table 9.6.5
Non-Instrumental Churches of Christ[2]

	MEMBERSHIP					CHURCHES					MINISTERS				
	England	Wales	Scotland	N. Ireland	**Total UK**	England	Wales	Scotland	N. Ireland	**Total UK**	England	Wales	Scotland	N. Ireland	**Total UK**
1990	1,400[5]	50[1]	740[1]	280[3]	**2,470**	49[5]	2	25	9	**85**	31[5]	1	17	3	**52**
1995	1,240	50	760	200	**2,250**[4]	43	2	26	6[1]	**77**	23	1	18	1	**43**
2000	1,225[1]	50[1]	750[1]	200[1]	**2,225**	41[1]	2[1]	25[1]	6[1]	**74**	20[1]	1[1]	18[1]	1[1]	**40**
2001[1]	1,200	45	730	195	**2,170**	41	2	25	6	**74**	20	1	18	1	**40**
2002[1]	1,185	45	720	190	**2,140**	41	2	25	6	**74**	20	1	18	1	**40**
2005[1]	1,150	45	700	185	**2,080**	40	2	24	6	**72**	19	1	18	1	**39**

Table 9.6.6
Christian Missionary Alliance

	MEMBERSHIP					CHURCHES					MINISTERS				
	England	Wales	Scotland	N. Ireland	**Total UK**	England	Wales	Scotland	N. Ireland	**Total UK**	England	Wales	Scotland	N. Ireland	**Total UK**
1990	130	0	0	0	**130**	5	0	0	0	**5**	4	0	0	0	**4**
1995	350	0	0	0	**350**	7	0	0	0	**7**	8	0	0	0	**8**
2000[1]	350	0	0	0	**350**	7	0	0	0	**7**	4	0	0	0	**4**
2001[1]	350	0	0	0	**350**	7	0	0	0	**7**	4	0	0	0	**4**
2002	350	0	0	0	**350**	7	0	0	0	**7**	4	0	0	0	**4**
2005[1]	350	0	0	0	**350**	7	0	0	0	**7**	4	0	0	0	**4**

Table 9.6.7
Bruderhof Communities in the UK[6]

	MEMBERSHIP					CHURCHES					MINISTERS				
	England	Wales	Scotland	N. Ireland	**Total UK**	England	Wales	Scotland	N. Ireland	**Total UK**	England	Wales	Scotland	N. Ireland	**Total UK**
1990	350	0	0	0	**350**	1	0	0	0	**1**	5	0	0	0	**5**
1995	350	0	0	0	**350**	1	0	0	0	**1**	5	0	0	0	**5**
2000	500	0	0	0	**500**	2	0	0	0	**2**	7	0	0	0	**7**
2001	500	0	0	0	**500**	2	0	0	0	**2**	7	0	0	0	**7**
2002	500	0	0	0	**500**	2	0	0	0	**2**	7	0	0	0	**7**
2005	600	0	0	0	**600**	3	0	0	0	**3**	9	0	0	0	**9**

[1] Estimate. *For other footnotes, see* **Page 9.7**

Free Church Statistics: Independent Churches: Others

Table 9.7.1
London City Mission

	MEMBERSHIP					CONGREGATIONS					MINISTERS				
	England	Wales	Scotland	N. Ireland	**Total UK**	England[2]	Wales	Scotland	N. Ireland	**Total UK**	England	Wales	Scotland	N. Ireland	**Total UK**
1990	1,400	0	0	0	**1,400**	31	0	0	0	**31**	31	0	0	0	**31**
1995	1,250	0	0	0	**1,250**	28	0	0	0	**28**	28	0	0	0	**28**
2000	950	0	0	0	**950**	28	0	0	0	**28**	28	0	0	0	**28**
2001[1]	950	0	0	0	**950**	28	0	0	0	**28**	28	0	0	0	**28**
2002[1]	900	0	0	0	**900**	28	0	0	0	**28**	28	0	0	0	**28**
2005[1]	800	0	0	0	**800**	28	0	0	0	**28**	28	0	0	0	**28**

Table 9.7.2
New Apostolic Church (UK)[3]

	England	Wales	Scotland	N. Ireland	**Total UK**	England	Wales	Scotland	N. Ireland	**Total UK**	England	Wales	Scotland	N. Ireland	**Total UK**
1990	1,950	0	0	0	**1,950**	37	0	0	0	**37**	56	0	0	0	**56**
1995	2,040	0	0	0	**2,040**	35	0	0	0	**35**	57	0	0	0	**57**
2000[1]	2,250	0	30	50	**2,330**	30	0	1	1	**32**	83	0	1	2	**86**
2001[1]	2,300	0	50	75	**2,425**	28	0	1	1	**30**	89	0	4	3	**96**
2002	2,340	25	68	105	**2,538**	26	1	1	1	**29**	94	1	7	5	**107**
2005[1]	2,420	25	70	110	**2,625**	25	1	1	1	**28**	99	1	8	5	**113**

Table 9.7.3
Catholic Apostolic Church

	England	Wales	Scotland	N. Ireland	**Total UK**	England	Wales	Scotland	N. Ireland	**Total UK**	England	Wales	Scotland	N. Ireland	**Total UK**
1990[1]	25	0	0	0	**25**	3	0	0	0	**3**	0	0	0	0	**0**
1995[1]	15	0	0	0	**15**	3	0	0	0	**3**	0	0	0	0	**0**
2000[1]	10	0	0	0	**10**	2	0	0	0	**2**	0	0	0	0	**0**
2001[1]	10	0	0	0	**10**	2	0	0	0	**2**	0	0	0	0	**0**
2002[1]	10	0	0	0	**10**	2	0	0	0	**2**	0	0	0	0	**0**
2005[1]	5	0	0	0	**5**	1	0	0	0	**1**	0	0	0	0	**0**

Table 9.7.4
Universal Fellowship of Metropolitan Community Churches[4]

	England	Wales	Scotland	N. Ireland	**Total UK**	England	Wales	Scotland	N. Ireland	**Total UK**	England	Wales	Scotland	N. Ireland	**Total UK**
1990	200	0	0	0	**200**	8	0	0	0	**8**	12	0	0	0	**12**
1995	380	0	20	0	**400**[1]	11[5]	0	1	0	**12**[1]	14	0	1	0	**15**[1]
2000[1]	480	0	20	0	**500**	13	0	1	0	**14**	17	0	1	0	**18**
2001[1]	500	0	20	0	**520**	13	0	1	0	**14**	17	0	1	0	**18**
2002[1]	520	0	20	0	**540**	13	0	1	0	**14**	17	0	1	0	**18**
2005[1]	570	0	30	0	**600**[6]	14	0	1	0	**15**	18	0	1	0	**19**

Table 9.7.5
Reformed Liberal Catholic Church (Old Catholic)[7]

	England	Wales	Scotland	N. Ireland	**Total UK**	England	Wales	Scotland	N. Ireland	**Total UK**	England	Wales	Scotland	N. Ireland	**Total UK**
1990	–	–	–	–	–	–	–	–	–	–	–	–	–	–	–
1995	–	–	–	–	–	–	–	–	–	–	–	–	–	–	–
2000	65	0	0	0	**65**	5	0	0	0	**5**	6	0	0	0	**6**
2001[1]	70	0	0	0	**70**	5	0	0	0	**5**	6	0	0	0	**6**
2002[1]	75	0	0	0	**75**	5	0	0	0	**5**	6	0	0	0	**6**
2005[1]	90	0	0	0	**90**	5	0	0	0	**5**	6	0	0	0	**6**

Table 9.7.6
Other Independent Churches[8]

	England	Wales	Scotland	N. Ireland	**Total UK**	England	Wales	Scotland	N. Ireland	**Total UK**	England	Wales	Scotland	N. Ireland	**Total UK**
1990	5,510	290	650	150	**6,600**	77	4	9	2	**92**	73	4	9	2	**88**
1995	5,780	295	675	150	**6,900**	82	4	9	2	**97**	76	4	9	2	**91**
2000	6,040	300	700	160	**7,200**	84	5	10	3	**102**	79	4	10	2	**95**
2001	6,080	310	710	160	**7,260**	85	5	10	3	**103**	80	4	10	2	**96**
2002	6,120	320	720	160	**7,320**	86	5	10	3	**104**	81	4	10	2	**97**
2005	6,260	330	740	170	**7,500**	87	5	10	3	**105**	82	4	10	2	**98**

Page 9.6

[1] Estimate

[2] Includes groups called "Two by Two"; "Cooneyites"; "People of the Way".

[3] Taken from the 1991 Northern Ireland Census

[4] The 1995 Christian Worker Directory gives a membership of 1,719 for 57 of the 75 listed congregations giving details.

[5] Revised figure

[6] The Community started in Germany in 1920, coming to England in 1937 to flee the Nazis. Choosing unity rather than internment of their German members, the Community fled to Paraguay. They now have 7 communities in the United States, 2 in the UK and 2 in Australia.

[7] Total of **Tables 9.4.1** (Brethren), **9.5.1** (Congregational), **9.6.2–7** and **9.7.1–6.** It also includes 20 English (1 church, 1 minister) of the Independent Old Catholic Orthodox Church which closed in 1994.

Page 9.7

[1] Estimate

[2] These are preaching centres, whose attenders are encouraged to attend worship at other local churches. There is no formal membership.

[3] Emerged from the Catholic Apostolic Church in 1861. Their brochure indicated that in 1990 worldwide membership was 6 million in 40,000 congregations in 170 countries.

[4] Part of the European and North Sea District which covers Scandinavia, Germany and the UK. One of 13 Districts globally.

[5] One in Bath, Birmingham, Bournemouth, Brighton, Bristol, Exeter and Manchester, with 3 in London, and one in Glasgow in 1992.

[6] Revised figure

[7] Church started 23rd May 1999 and has broken all ties with the Liberal Catholic Church. It affirms "Christ as Lord and Saviour in His death and resurrection in accordance with spiritual truth."

[8] All estimated; membership figures proportional to population.

9.8 Free Church Statistics: Methodist Churches

Table 9.8.1
Total Methodist[6]

	MEMBERSHIP England	Wales	Scotland	N. Ireland	Total UK	CHURCHES England	Wales	Scotland	N. Ireland	Total UK	MINISTERS England	Wales	Scotland	N. Ireland	Total UK
1990	404,356	20,627	7,133	17,404	**449,520**	6,849	451	77	160	**7,537**	2,094	90	37	98	**2,319**
1995	362,273	18,293	6,312	15,868	**402,746**	6,433	402	75	157	**7,067**	2,187	81	41	103	**2,412**
2000	314,706	16,676	5,847	14,500	**351,729**	5,906	402	75	145	**6,528**	2,200	98	39	97	**2,434**
2001	308,319	15,261	5,693	14,423	**343,696**	6,119	402	75	145	**6,741**	2,205	98	35	95	**2,433**
2002	298,711	15,253	5,553	14,272	**333,789**	5,899	402	75	144	**6,520**	2,206	98	38	97	**2,439**
2005	272,905	13,920	5,190	13,856	**305,871**	5,671	401	76	141	**6,289**	2,236	100	38	99	**2,473**

Table 9.8.2
Methodist Church in Great Britain

	MEMBERSHIP England	Wales	Scotland	N. Ireland	Total UK	CHURCHES England	Wales	Scotland	N. Ireland	Total UK	MINISTERS England	Wales	Scotland	N. Ireland	Total UK
1990	396,860	20,620	7,060	0	**424,540**	6,604	450	75	0	**7,129**	1,931	90	35	0	**2,056**
1995	355,714	18,293	6,262	0	**380,269**[2]	6,202	402	74	0	**6,678**	2,041	81	40	0	**2,162**
2000	309,075	16,676	5,809	0	**331,560**	5,685	402	74	0	**6,161**	2,067	98	39	0	**2,204**
2001	302,903	15,261	5,657	0	**323,821**	5,902	402	74	0	**6,378**	2,071	98	35	0	**2,204**
2002[1]	293,400	15,253	5,519	0	**314,172**	5,686	402	74	0	**6,162**	2,075	98	38	0	**2,211**
2005[1]	267,360	13,910	5,150	0	**286,420**	5,461	400	74	0	**5,935**	2,111	100	38	0	**2,249**

Table 9.8.3
Methodist Church in Ireland

	MEMBERSHIP England	Community[4]	Eire[1]	N. Ireland[5]	Total UK[3]	CHURCHES England	Wales	Eire[1]	N. Ireland[5]	Total UK	MINISTERS England	Wales	Eire[1]	N. Ireland[5]	Total UK
1990	0	45,150	2,187	17,130	**19,317**	0	0	19	152	**171**	0	0	12	93	**105**
1995	0	47,360[5]	2,004	15,696	**17,700**	0	0	19	151	**170**	0	0	12	97	**109**
2000	0	47,148	1,833	14,358	**16,191**	0	0	18	139	**157**	0	0	12	93	**105**
2001	0	47,038[1]	1,824	14,280	**16,104**	0	0	18	139	**157**	0	0	12	93	**105**
2002[1]	0	46,929	1,804	14,121	**15,925**	0	0	18	138	**156**	0	0	12	93	**105**
2005[1]	0	46,600	1,744	13,656	**15,400**	0	0	18	134	**152**	0	0	12	93	**105**

Table 9.8.4
Wesleyan Reform Union

	MEMBERSHIP England	Wales	Scotland	N. Ireland	Total UK	CHURCHES England	Wales	Scotland	N. Ireland	Total UK	MINISTERS England	Wales	Scotland	N. Ireland	Total UK
1990	2,946	0	50	0	**2,996**	130	0	1	0	**131**	21	0	1	0	**22**
1995	2,473	0	50	0	**2,523**	117	0	1	0	**118**	20	0	1	0	**21**
2000	2,108	0	38	0	**2,146**	111	0	1	0	**112**	16	0	0	0	**16**
2001	2,036	0	36	0	**2,072**	109	0	1	0	**110**	15	0	0	0	**15**
2002[1]	1,941	0	34	0	**1,975**	106	0	1	0	**107**	15	0	0	0	**15**
2005[1]	1,695	0	30	0	**1,725**	100	0	1	0	**101**	14	0	0	0	**14**

Table 9.8.5
Free Methodist Church in the UK

	MEMBERSHIP England	Wales	Scotland	N. Ireland	Total UK	CHURCHES England	Wales	Scotland	N. Ireland	Total UK	MINISTERS England	Wales	Scotland	N. Ireland	Total UK
1990	710	0	23	274	**1,007**	11	0	1	8	**20**	13	0	1	5	**19**
1995	808	0	0	172	**980**	14	0	0	6	**20**	16	0	0	6	**22**
2000	750	0	0	142	**892**	14	0	0	6	**20**	16	0	0	4	**20**
2001	726	0	0	143	**869**	14	0	0	6	**20**	17	0	0	2	**19**
2002	786	0	0	151	**937**	15	0	0	6	**21**	19	0	0	4	**23**
2005	1,500	10	10	200	**1,720**	20	1	1	7	**29**	24	0	0	6	**30**

Table 9.8.6
Independent Methodist Churches

	MEMBERSHIP England	Wales	Scotland	N. Ireland	Total UK	CHURCHES England	Wales	Scotland	N. Ireland	Total UK	MINISTERS England	Wales	Scotland	N. Ireland	Total UK
1990	3,540	7	0	0	**3,547**	104	1	0	0	**105**	129	0	0	0	**129**
1995	2,978	0	0	0	**2,978**	100	0	0	0	**100**	110	0	0	0	**110**
2000	2,473	0	0	0	**2,473**	96	0	0	0	**96**	101	0	0	0	**101**
2001	2,354	0	0	0	**2,354**	94	0	0	0	**94**	102	0	0	0	**102**
2002	2,284	0	0	0	**2,284**	92	0	0	0	**92**	97	0	0	0	**97**
2005	2,050	0	0	0	**2,050**	90	0	0	0	**90**	87	0	0	0	**87**

Page 9.8

[1] Estimate

[2] In 1995, the Community Roll was 1,239,476.

[3] Taken as adult members plus one-quarter of junior membership.

[4] Figures include the Republic of Ireland.

[5] In 1995, the Community Roll in Northern Ireland was 41,997, or 88.7% of the total, and this percentage has been used to estimate the Northern Ireland proportion of the total.

[6] These totals include throughout for England 300 members, 6 churches and 6 ministers as an estimate for other Methodist churches not listed here.

Page 9.9

[1] Estimate

[2] Revised figure

[3] Abundant Life Ministries was part of Covenant Ministries until 1998.

[4] Based on the 1994 Scottish Church Census

[5] Based on the 2002 Scottish Church Census

[6] Based on the 7th edition of the *Body Book* which showed 15 congregations in 1996 and 11 in 1998 of average size 175 and 190 respectively.

[7] Based on the 8th edition of the *Body Book* which showed 13 congregations in 2000 of average size 228.

[8] Based on the 9th edition of the *Body Book* which showed 10 congregations in 2002 of average size 194.

Free Church Statistics: New Churches

9.9

Table 9.9.1
Total New Churches

	ATTENDANCE					CONGREGATIONS					LEADERS				
	England	Wales	Scotland	N. Ireland	**Total UK**	England	Wales	Scotland	N. Ireland	**Total UK**	England	Wales	Scotland	N. Ireland	**Total UK**
1990	74,838	1,690	2,935	1,200	**80,663**	1,131	27	32	12	**1,202**	1,142	22	30	12	**1,206**
1995	101,766	1,995	3,550	1,500	**108,811**	1,398	33	45	17	**1,493**	1,458	30	39	18	**1,545**
2000	123,498	2,460	4,041	1,685	**131,684**	1,674	39	48	22	**1,783**	1,938	40	50	22	**2,050**
2001	127,624	2,730	4,005	1,695	**136,054**	1,715	40	47	22	**1,824**	2,020	42	48	22	**2,132**
2002	133,719	3,015	4,075	1,870	**142,679**	1,789	40	47	23	**1,899**	2,119	43	49	23	**2,234**
2005	154,900	3,455	4,900	2,045	**165,300**	1,981	43	51	25	**2,100**	2,518	48	60	29	**2,655**

Table 9.9.2
Abundant Life Ministries[3]

	ATTENDANCE					CONGREGATIONS					LEADERS				
	England	Wales	Scotland	N. Ireland	**Total UK**	England	Wales	Scotland	N. Ireland	**Total UK**	England	Wales	Scotland	N. Ireland	**Total UK**
1990	–	–	–	–	**–**	–	–	–	–	**–**	–	–	–	–	**–**
1995	–	–	–	–	**–**	–	–	–	–	**–**	–	–	–	–	**–**
2000	700	0	0	0	**700**	1	0	0	0	**1**	3	0	0	0	**3**
2001	800	0	0	0	**800**	1	0	0	0	**1**	5	0	0	0	**5**
2002	1,000	0	0	0	**1,000**	1	0	0	0	**1**	6	0	0	0	**6**
2005	1,800	0	0	0	**1,800**	1	0	0	0	**1**	10	0	0	0	**10**

Table 9.9.3
Association of Vineyard Churches

	ATTENDANCE					CONGREGATIONS					LEADERS				
	England	Wales	Scotland	N. Ireland	**Total UK**	England	Wales	Scotland	N. Ireland	**Total UK**	England	Wales	Scotland	N. Ireland	**Total UK**
1990	2,000	0	25[4]	0	**2,025**	4	0	1	0	**5**	2	0	1	0	**3**
1995	4,300	0	55[4]	0	**4,355**	24	0	1	0	**25**	11	0	1	0	**14**
2000	8,000	0	85[2]	0	**8,085**	74	0	1	0	**75**	180	0	1	0	**181**
2001[1]	8,800	0	95	0	**8,895**	75	0	1	0	**76**	182	0	1	0	**183**
2002[1]	9,600	0	100[5]	0	**9,700**	76	0	1	0	**77**	184	0	1	0	**185**
2005[1]	11,000	0	120	0	**11,120**	96	0	1	0	**97**	220	0	1	0	**221**

Table 9.9.4
Bristol Christian Fellowship

	ATTENDANCE					CONGREGATIONS					LEADERS				
	England	Wales	Scotland	N. Ireland	**Total UK**	England	Wales	Scotland	N. Ireland	**Total UK**	England	Wales	Scotland	N. Ireland	**Total UK**
1990	400	0	0	0	**400**	8	0	0	0	**8**	5	0	0	0	**5**
1995	600	0	0	0	**600**	9	0	0	0	**9**	3	0	0	0	**3**
2000	400	0	0	0	**400**	3	0	0	0	**3**	1[1]	0	0	0	**1**
2001	350	0	0	0	**350**	3	0	0	0	**3**	1[1]	0	0	0	**1**
2002	350	0	0	0	**350**	3	0	0	0	**3**	1[1]	0	0	0	**1**
2005	400	0	0	0	**400**	1	0	0	0	**1**	1[1]	0	0	0	**1**

Table 9.9.5
Christian Outreach Centre

	ATTENDANCE					CONGREGATIONS					LEADERS				
	England	Wales	Scotland	N. Ireland	**Total UK**	England	Wales	Scotland	N. Ireland	**Total UK**	England	Wales	Scotland	N. Ireland	**Total UK**
1990	240[1]	0	60[1]	0	**300**	2	0	2	0	**4**	4	0	4	0	**8**
1995	400[1]	0	100[1]	0	**500**	4	0	3	0	**7**	8	0	6	0	**14**
2000	850[1]	0	200[1]	0	**1,050**	11	0	3	0	**14**	18	0	8	0	**26**
2001	1,000	0	200	0	**1,200**	13	0	3	0	**16**	26	0	8	0	**34**
2002	1,300	0	230	0	**1,530**	18	0	3	0	**21**	40	0	8	0	**48**
2005	3,500	0	500	0	**4,000**	30	0	5	0	**35**	74	0	16	0	**90**

Table 9.6.6
Cornerstone (c.net)

	ATTENDANCE					CONGREGATIONS					LEADERS				
	England	Wales	Scotland	N. Ireland	**Total UK**	England	Wales	Scotland	N. Ireland	**Total UK**	England	Wales	Scotland	N. Ireland	**Total UK**
1990	3,750	0	0	0	**3,750**	30	0	0	0	**30**	30	0	0	0	**30**
1995	4,415	0	0	0	**4,415**	36	0	0	0	**36**	33	0	0	0	**33**
2000	5,000	0	100	0	**5,100**	40	0	1	0	**41**	45[1]	0	4	0	**49**
2001	5,750	0	100	0	**5,850**	45	0	1	0	**46**	48[1]	0	4	0	**52**
2002	6,500	0	100	0	**6,600**	55	0	1	0	**56**	50	0	4	0	**54**
2005	8,500	0	100	0	**8,600**	70	0	1	0	**71**	70	0	4	0	**74**

Table 9.9.7
Covenant Ministries

	ATTENDANCE					CONGREGATIONS					LEADERS				
	England	Wales	Scotland	N. Ireland	**Total UK**	England	Wales	Scotland	N. Ireland	**Total UK**	England	Wales	Scotland	N. Ireland	**Total UK**
1990[1]	4,000	500	500	0	**5,000**	40	5	5	0	**50**	40	5	5	0	**50**
1995	2,040[1]	200[1]	300[1]	0	**2,540**[2]	11	2	3	0	**16**[6]	15[1]	2[1]	3[1]	0	**20**
2000	2,604[1]	260[1]	100[1]	0	**2,964**	10	2	1	0	**13**[7]	12[1]	3[1]	1[1]	0	**16**
2001[1]	2,100	410	0	0	**2,510**	9	2	0	0	**11**	11	3	0	0	**14**
2002	1,370	570	0	0	**1,940**	8	2	0	0	**10**[8]	9[1]	3[1]	0	0	**12**
2005[1]	1,000	800	0	0	**1,800**	6	2	0	0	**8**	7	3	0	0	**10**

[1] Estimate. *For other footnotes, see* **Page 9.8**

9.10 Free Church Statistics: New Churches (continued)

Table 9.10.1
Ground Level

	ATTENDANCE					CONGREGATIONS					LEADERS				
	England	Wales	Scotland	N. Ireland	**Total UK**	England	Wales	Scotland	N. Ireland	**Total UK**	England	Wales	Scotland	N. Ireland	**Total UK**
1990	1,000	0	0	0	**1,000**	25	0	0	0	**25**	18	0	0	0	**18**
1995	1,800	100	0	0	**1,900**[2]	25	1	0	0	**26**[2]	30	1	0	1	**32**
2000	2,808	100	0	0	**2,908**	25	1	0	0	**26**	62[1]	2[1]	0	0	**64**
2001[1]	3,890	110	0	0	**4,000**	40	1	0	0	**41**	68	2	0	0	**70**
2002	6,500	120	0	0	**6,620**	65	1	0	0	**66**	75	2	0	0	**77**
2005[1]	10,000	150	0	0	**10,150**	100	1	0	0	**101**	120	2	0	0	**122**

Table 9.10.2
Ichthus Christian Fellowship

	ATTENDANCE					CONGREGATIONS					LEADERS				
	England[3]	England[4]	Scotland[1]	N. Ireland	**Total UK**	England[3]	England[4]	Scotland[1]	N. Ireland	**Total UK**	England[3]	England[4]	Scotland[1]	N. Ireland	**Total UK**
1990	1,701	830	150	0	**2,681**	33	8	2	0	**43**	43	21	3	0	**67**
1995	2,200	1,640	365	0	**4,205**	21	11	5	0	**37**	30	22	5	0	**57**
2000	1,700	2,444	376	0	**4,520**	21	12	4[5]	0	**37**	33[1]	47	7	0	**87**
2001	1,750	2,605	360	0	**4,715**	21	12	4	0	**37**	33[1]	49	7	0	**89**
2002	1,800	2,766	345	0	**4,911**	24	18	3[5]	0	**45**	34	52	7	0	**93**
2005[1]	2,200	3,300	350	0	**5,850**	28	22	3	0	**53**	36	54	7	0	**97**

Table 9.10.3
Jesus Fellowship and Multiply Network

	ATTENDANCE					CONGREGATIONS					LEADERS				
	England	Wales	Scotland	N. Ireland	**Total UK**	England	Wales	Scotland	N. Ireland	**Total UK**[6]	England	Wales	Scotland	N. Ireland	**Total UK**[7]
1990	1,260	0	0	0	**1,260**	45	0	0	0	**45**	99	0	0	0	**99**
1995	2,540	30	30	0	**2,600**	46[1]	1	0	0	**46**	127	2	1	0	**130**
2000	3,875	75	20	5	**3,975**	47	1	0	0	**48**	145	3	1	0	**149**
2001[1]	4,000	75	20	10	**4,105**	48[1]	1	0	0	**49**	148	3	1	0	**152**
2002	4,130	75	20	15	**4,240**	49	1	0	0	**50**	152	2	0	0	**154**
2005	4,800	120	30	50	**5,000**	59	3	1	2	**65**	164	5	2	4	**175**

Table 9.10.4
Kingdom Faith Ministries[8]

	ATTENDANCE					CONGREGATIONS					LEADERS				
	England	Wales	Scotland	N. Ireland	**Total UK**	England	Wales	Scotland	N. Ireland	**Total UK**	England	Wales	Scotland	N. Ireland	**Total UK**
1990	–	–	–	–	**–**	–	–	–	–	**–**	–	–	–	–	**–**
1995	750	0	0	0	**750**	3	0	0	0	**3**	7	0	0	0	**7**
2000	1,000	0	0	0	**1,000**	3	0	0	0	**3**	12[1]	0	0	0	**12**
2001[1]	1,000	0	0	0	**1,000**	4	0	0	0	**4**	12	0	0	0	**12**
2002	1,000	0	0	0	**1,000**	6	0	0	0	**6**	13	0	0	0	**13**
2005[1]	1,100	0	0	0	**1,000**	7	0	0	0	**7**	14	0	0	0	**14**

Table 9.10.5
Kings Church[9]

	ATTENDANCE					CONGREGATIONS					LEADERS				
	England	Wales	Scotland	N. Ireland	**Total UK**	England	Wales	Scotland	N. Ireland	**Total UK**	England	Wales	Scotland	N. Ireland	**Total UK**
1990	1,750	0	0	0	**1,750**	15	0	0	0	**15**	20	0	0	0	**20**
1995	600	0	0	0	**600**	5	0	0	0	**5**	10	0	0	0	**10**
2000	550	0	0	0	**550**	5	0	0	0	**5**	9	0	0	0	**9**
2001	550	0	0	0	**550**	5	0	0	0	**5**	9	0	0	0	**9**
2002	550	0	0	0	**550**	5	0	0	0	**5**	8	0	0	0	**8**
2005[1]	800	0	0	0	**800**	5	0	0	0	**5**	8	0	0	0	**8**

Table 9.10.6
Lifeline Community Church

	ATTENDANCE					CONGREGATIONS					LEADERS				
	England	Wales	Scotland	N. Ireland	**Total UK**	England	Wales	Scotland	N. Ireland	**Total UK**	England	Wales	Scotland	N. Ireland	**Total UK**
1990	500	0	0	0	**500**	4	0	0	0	**4**	8	0	0	0	**8**
1995	298	0	0	0	**298**	2	0	0	0	**2**	4	0	0	0	**4**
2000	190	0	0	0	**190**	2	0	0	0	**2**	2	0	0	0	**2**
2001	194	0	0	0	**194**	2	0	0	0	**2**	2	0	0	0	**2**
2002	192	0	0	0	**192**	2	0	0	0	**2**	2	0	0	0	**2**
2005	200[1]	0	0	0	**200**	2	0	0	0	**2**	2[1]	0	0	0	**2**

Table 9.10.7
New Frontiers International

	ATTENDANCE					CONGREGATIONS					LEADERS				
	England	Wales	Scotland	N. Ireland	**Total UK**	England	Wales	Scotland	N. Ireland	**Total UK**	England	Wales	Scotland	N. Ireland	**Total UK**
1990	9,000	0	0	0	**9,000**	60	0	0	0	**60**	150	0	0	0	**150**
1995[10]	19,850	150	0	0	**20,000**	134	1	0	0	**135**	304	2	0	0	**306**
2000	20,600	150	0	0	**20,750**	140	1	0	0	**141**	357	2	0	0	**359**
2001	20,900	150	0	0	**21,050**	142	1	0	0	**143**	362	2	0	0	**364**
2002	22,000	150	0	75	**22,225**	149	1	0	1	**151**[11]	380	2	0	1	**383**
2005[1]	25,700	150	0	100	**25,950**	199	1	0	1	**201**[11]	508	2	0	2	**512**

[1] Estimate. *For other footnotes, see* **Page 9.11**

9

Free Church Statistics: New Churches (continued)

Table 9.11.1
Pioneer

	ATTENDANCE					CONGREGATIONS					LEADERS				
	England	Wales	Scotland	N. Ireland	**Total UK**	England	Wales	Scotland	N. Ireland	**Total UK**	England	Wales	Scotland	N. Ireland	**Total UK**[3]
1990	3,114[2]	90	0	0	**3,204**	31[2]	1	0	0	**32**	60[2]	1	0	0	**61**
1995	5,621	195	0	0	**5,816**	57	2	0	0	**59**	112	2	0	0	**114**
2000[1]	9,460	235	0	0	**9,695**	77	3	0	0	**80**	164	4	0	0	**168**
2001[1]	10,230	240	0	0	**10,470**	81	3	0	0	**84**	174	5	0	0	**179**
2002	11,000	250	80	0	**11,330**	85	3	1	0	**89**	185	7	2	0	**194**
2005[1]	12,500	270	100	0	**12,870**	97	3	1	0	**101**	217	8	2	0	**227**

Table 9.11.1
Plumbline Ministries

	England	Wales	Scotland	N. Ireland	**Total UK**	England	Wales	Scotland	N. Ireland	**Total UK**	England	Wales	Scotland	N. Ireland	**Total UK**
1990	124	0	0	0	**124**	4	0	0	0	**4**	4	0	0	0	**4**
1995	440	0	0	0	**440**	7	0	0	0	**7**	14	0	0	0	**14**
2000	690	0	0	0	**690**	8	0	0	0	**8**	17	0	0	0	**17**
2001	755	0	0	20	**775**	7	0	0	1	**8**	17	0	0	0	**17**
2002	381	0	0	30	**411**	6	0	0	1	**7**	12	0	0	0	**12**
2005	770	0	0	50	**820**	7[1]	0	0	1	**8**	16	0	0	1	**17**

Table 9.11.3
Rainbow Churches

	England	Wales	Scotland	N. Ireland	**Total UK**	England	Wales	Scotland	N. Ireland	**Total UK**	England	Wales	Scotland	N. Ireland	**Total UK**
1990	399	0	0	0	**399**	3	0	0	0	**3**	8	0	0	0	**8**
1995	317	0	0	0	**317**	5	0	0	0	**5**	11	0	0	0	**11**
2000	75	0	0	0	**75**	2	0	0	0	**2**	2	0	0	0	**2**
2001[1]	80	0	0	0	**80**	1	0	0	0	**1**	1	0	0	0	**1**
2002	90	0	0	0	**90**	1	0	0	0	**1**	1	0	0	0	**1**
2005[1]	110	0	0	0	**110**	1	0	0	0	**1**	1	0	0	0	**1**

Table 9.11.4
Salt & Light Ministries

	England	Wales	Scotland	N. Ireland	**Total UK**	England	Wales	Scotland	N. Ireland	**Total UK**	England	Wales	Scotland	N. Ireland	**Total UK**[3]
1990	4,500	100	200	200	**5,000**	46	1	2	2	**51**	55	1	2	2	**60**
1995[2]	5,230	120	200	200	**5,750**	48	1	3	2	**54**	58	1	3	2	**64**
2000	6,520[1]	140[1]	160[1]	180[1]	**7,000**	56	1	3	2	**62**	84	1	3	2	**90**
2001	5,760	145	130	165	**6,200**	58	2	3	1	**64**	117	2	2	2	**123**
2002	5,000	150	100	150	**5,400**	60	2	3	1	**66**	150	2	2	2	**156**
2005	5,800	165	200	145	**6,310**	70	3	4	1	**78**	200	3	3	2	**208**

Table 9.11.5
Other New Churches[4]

	England	Wales	Scotland	N. Ireland	**Total UK**	England	Wales	Scotland	N. Ireland	**Total UK**	England	Wales	Scotland	N. Ireland	**Total UK**
1990[1]	4,270	0	0	0	**4,270**	23	0	0	0	**23**	15	0	0	0	**15**
1995[1]	3,725	0	0	0	**3,725**	20	0	0	0	**20**	14	0	0	0	**14**
2000[1]	2,032	0	0	0	**2,032**	22	0	0	0	**22**	15	0	0	0	**15**
2001[1]	2,110	0	0	0	**2,110**	23	0	0	0	**23**	15	0	0	0	**15**
2002[1]	2,190	0	0	0	**2,190**	23	0	0	0	**23**	15	0	0	0	**15**
2005[1]	2,420	0	0	0	**2,420**	25	0	0	0	**25**	16	0	0	0	**16**

Table 9.11.6
Other Non-Denominational Churches[5]

	England	Wales	Scotland	N. Ireland	**Total UK**	England	Wales	Scotland	N. Ireland	**Total UK**	England	Wales	Scotland	N. Ireland	**Total UK**
1990[1]	36,000	1,000	2,000	1,000	**40,000**	750	20	20	10	**800**	560	15	15	10	**600**
1995[1]	45,000	1,200	2,500	1,300	**50,000**	930	25	30	15	**1,000**	645	20	20	15	**700**
2000[1]	54,000	1,500	3,000	1,500	**60,000**	1,115	30	35	20	**1,200**	730	25	25	20	**800**
2001[1]	55,000	1,600	3,100	1,500	**61,200**	1,125	30	35	20	**1,210**	740	25	25	20	**810**
2002[1]	56,000	1,700	3,100	1,600	**62,400**	1,135	30	35	20	**1,220**	750	25	25	20	**820**
2005[1]	59,000	1,800	3,500	1,700	**66,000**	1,155	30	35	20	**1,240**	780	25	25	20	**850**

Page 9.10

[1] Estimate
[2] Revised figure
[3] London based Ichthus Linked Churches only.
[4] English Ichthus Linked Churches outside London area, all estimated but based on respective editions of the *Body Book*.
[5] Actual figure, not estimated.
[6] Church households.
[7] Nearly all part-time.
[8] Founded in 1992.
[9] Formerly Antioch Ministries.
[10] 1996 figures.
[11] 79 churches were in the process of being planted in 2002. The 2005 estimates assume 50 of these are successful by then.

Page 9.11

[1] Estimate
[2] Revised figure
[3] Nearly all part-time.
[4] Estimated from successive editions of the *Body Book*.
[5] All figures estimated.

9.12 Free Church Statistics: Pentecostal Churches

Table 9.12.1
Total Pentecostal Churches

	MEMBERSHIP					CONGREGATIONS					MINISTERS				
	England	Wales	Scotland	N. Ireland	**Total UK**	England	Wales	Scotland	N. Ireland	**Total UK**	England	Wales	Scotland	N. Ireland	**Total UK**
1990	142,806	10,017	4,412	9,771	**167,006**	1,948	163	75	70	**2,256**	3,161	153	73	73	**3,460**
1995	182,750	10,871	4,711	10,299	**208,631**	2,229	154	76	73	**2,532**	3,716	150	68	82	**4,016**
2000	218,788	10,926	6,292	10,468	**246,474**	2,376	145	87	74	**2,682**	3,781	146	86	90	**4,103**
2001	225,686	11,104	6,394	10,538	**253,722**	2,414	144	88	76	**2,722**	3,805	145	87	86	**4,123**
2002	233,065	11,030	6,765	10,555	**261,415**	2,440	142	89	76	**2,747**	3,828	145	88	86	**4,147**
2005	251,085	11,109	7,365	10,701	**280,260**	2,564	138	94	77	**2,873**	4,008	148	93	87	**4,336**

Table 9.12.2
Apostolic Church

	MEMBERSHIP					CONGREGATIONS					MINISTERS				
	England	Wales	Scotland	N. Ireland	**Total UK**	England	Wales	Scotland	N. Ireland	**Total UK**	England	Wales	Scotland	N. Ireland	**Total UK**[3]
1990	2,500[1]	2,182[1]	977	441	**6,100**	58[1]	56[1]	20	11	**145**	35	27	13	6	**81**
1995	2,252	1,988	760	376	**5,386**	45	43	17	10	**115**	36[1]	29[1]	13[1]	7[1]	**85**
2000	2,555	1,799	657	291	**5,302**	47	38	16	9	**110**	36	31	12	9	**88**
2001	2,198	1,944	503	315	**4,960**	47	37	16	10[2]	**110**	36	30	10	6	**82**
2002	2,135[1]	1,827[1]	500[1]	285[1]	**4,747**	47	36	15	10[2]	**108**	36[1]	29[1]	9[1]	6[1]	**80**
2005[1]	2,091	1,744	400	246	**4,481**	47	35	14	10	**106**	36	27	8	6	**77**

Table 9.12.3
Apostolic Faith Church

	MEMBERSHIP					CONGREGATIONS					MINISTERS				
	England	Wales	Scotland	N. Ireland	**Total UK**	England	Wales	Scotland	N. Ireland	**Total UK**	England	Wales	Scotland	N. Ireland	**Total UK**
1990	180	0	0	0	**180**	1	0	0	0	**1**	5	0	0	0	**5**
1995	245	5	0	0	**250**	3	0	0	0	**3**	4	1	0	0	**5**
2000[1]	310	20	0	0	**330**	3	1	0	0	**4**	6	1	0	0	**7**
2001[1]	330	24	0	0	**354**	3	1	0	0	**4**	6	1	0	0	**7**
2002[1]	350	28	0	0	**378**	4	1	0	0	**5**	7	1	0	0	**8**
2005[1]	400	40	0	0	**440**	4	1	0	0	**5**	8	2	0	0	**10**

Table 9.12.4
Assemblies of God

	MEMBERSHIP					CONGREGATIONS					MINISTERS				
	England	Wales	Scotland	N. Ireland	**Total UK**	England	Wales	Scotland	N. Ireland	**Total UK**	England	Wales	Scotland	N. Ireland	**Total UK**
1990	39,400	5,900	1,900	800	**48,000**	501	71	23	10	**605**	576	82	25	12	**695**
1995	44,818	6,558	2,186	1,093	**54,655**	535	73	27	11	**646**	717	69	20	12	**818**
2000[4]	50,520	6,532	3,520	1,027	**61,599**	515	68	37	10	**630**	572	59	35	10	**676**
2001[1]	51,627	6,516	3,706	1,013	**62,862**	512	68	38	10	**628**	543	58	38	9	**648**
2002	53,500	6,500	4,000	1,000	**65,000**	508	67	40	10	**625**	514	57	40	9	**620**
2005	55,500	6,500	4,500	1,000	**67,500**	525	65	45	10	**645**	530	60	45	9	**644**

Table 9.12.5
Church of God of Prophecy

	MEMBERSHIP					CONGREGATIONS					MINISTERS				
	England	Wales	Scotland	N. Ireland	**Total UK**	England	Wales	Scotland	N. Ireland	**Total UK**	England	Wales	Scotland	N. Ireland	**Total UK**
1990	5,007	20	0	0	**5,027**	90	1	0	0	**91**	426[1]	5[1]	0	0	**431**
1995	4,745	40	0	0	**4,785**	83	2	0	0	**85**[5]	423[4]	7[1]	0	0	**430**
2000	4,520[1]	40[1]	0	0	**4,560**[4]	82[1]	2[1]	0	0	**84**	421[1]	7[1]	0	0	**428**
2001[1]	4,470	40	0	0	**4,510**	80	2	0	0	**82**	420	7	0	0	**427**
2002[1]	4,424	40	0	0	**4,464**	80	2	0	0	**82**	420	7	0	0	**427**
2005[1]	4,284	40	0	0	**4,324**	78	2	0	0	**80**	419	7	0	0	**426**

Table 9.12.6
Elim Pentecostal Church

	MEMBERSHIP					CONGREGATIONS					MINISTERS				
	England	Wales	Scotland	N. Ireland	**Total UK**	England	Wales	Scotland	N. Ireland	**Total UK**	England	Wales	Scotland	N. Ireland	**Total UK**
1990	24,640[4]	1,810[4]	1,180[4]	8,470[4]	**36,100**	332	33	24	48	**437**	365	37	27	54	**483**
1995[4]	31,320	1,990	1,470	8,770	**43,550**	357	32	24	51	**464**	409	40	28	62	**539**
2000[4]	38,010	2,180	1,750	9,080	**51,020**	382	31	23	54	**490**	453	43	29	70	**595**
2001[1]	39,340	2,210	1,810	9,140	**52,500**	387	31	23	55	**496**	461	44	30	70	**605**
2002	40,680	2,250	1,870	9,200	**54,000**	393	31	23	55	**502**	470	45	30	70	**615**
2005[1]	44,690	2,360	2,040	9,380	**58,470**	418	30	23	56	**527**	514	46	30	71	**661**

Table 9.12.7
Foursquare Gospel Church of Great Britain

	MEMBERSHIP					CONGREGATIONS					MINISTERS				
	England	Wales	Scotland	N. Ireland	**Total UK**	England	Wales	Scotland	N. Ireland	**Total UK**	England	Wales	Scotland	N. Ireland	**Total UK**
1990	562	0	25	0	**587**	8	0	1	0	**9**	6[4]	0	3	0	**9**
1995	495[1]	0	25	0	**520**	10	0	1	0	**11**	7	0	2	0	**9**[4]
2000[1]	785	0	25	0	**810**	12	0	1	0	**13**	7	0	2	0	**9**
2001[1]	835	0	25	0	**860**	12	0	1	0	**13**	7	0	1	0	**8**
2002	900	0	25	0	**925**	12	0	1	0	**13**	7	0	1	0	**8**
2005[1]	960	0	25	0	**985**	12	0	1	0	**13**	7	0	1	0	**8**

[1] Estimate. *For other footnotes, see* **Page 9.13**

9

Free Church Statistics: Pentecostal Churches (continued)

Table 9.13.1
Life-Changing Ministries[2]

	MEMBERSHIP					CONGREGATIONS					MINISTERS				
	England	Wales	Scotland	N. Ireland	**Total UK**	England	Wales	Scotland	N. Ireland	**Total UK**	England	Wales	Scotland	N. Ireland	**Total UK**
1990	–	–	–	–	–	–	–	–	–	–	–	–	–	–	–
1995	55[1]	20[1]	0	0	**75**	1	1	0	0	**2**	1	0	0	0	**1**
2000[1]	70	50	0	0	**120**	3	2	0	0	**5**	2	1	0	0	**3**
2001[1]	75	55	0	0	**130**	4	2	0	0	**6**	3	1	0	0	**4**
2002	80	60	0	0	**140**	4	2	0	0	**6**	3	2	0	0	**5**
2005[1]	95	75	0	0	**170**	4	2	0	0	**6**	3	2	0	0	**5**

Table 9.13.2
New Testament Church of God

	England	Wales	Scotland	N. Ireland	**Total UK**	England	Wales	Scotland	N. Ireland	**Total UK**	England	Wales	Scotland	N. Ireland	**Total UK**
1990[3]	9,000	0	0	0	**9,000**	60	0	0	0	**60**	150	0	0	0	**150**
1995[3,4]	19,850	150	0	0	**20,000**	134	1	0	0	**135**	304	2	0	0	**306**
2000	19,368	160	0	0	**19,528**	107	1	0	0	**108**	273	2	0	0	**275**
2001	19,750	165	0	0	**19,915**	117	1	0	0	**118**	273	2	0	0	**275**
2002[1]	20,140	170	0	0	**20,310**	118	1	0	0	**119**	275	2	0	0	**277**
2005[1]	21,355	185	0	0	**21,540**	119	1	0	0	**120**	278	2	0	0	**280**

Table 9.13.3
Peniel Church

	England	Wales	Scotland	N. Ireland	**Total UK**	England	Wales	Scotland	N. Ireland	**Total UK**	England	Wales	Scotland	N. Ireland	**Total UK**
1990	326	0	0	0	**326**	1	0	0	0	**1**	7[1]	0	0	0	**7**
1995	556	0	0	0	**556**	1	0	0	0	**1**	9	0	0	0	**9**
2000	700	0	0	0	**700**	1	0	0	0	**1**	9	0	0	0	**9**
2001	725[1]	0	0	0	**725**	1	0	0	0	**1**	9	0	0	0	**9**
2002	750	0	0	0	**750**	1	0	0	0	**1**	9	0	0	0	**9**
2005[1]	825	0	0	0	**825**	1	0	0	0	**1**	10	0	0	0	**10**

Table 9.13.4
United Pentecostal Church of Great Britain[5]

	England	Wales	Scotland	N. Ireland	**Total UK**	England	Wales	Scotland	N. Ireland	**Total UK**	England	Wales	Scotland	N. Ireland	**Total UK**
1990	1,825	45	110	0	**1,980**	18	1	3	0	**22**	22	1	3	0	**26**
1995	2,790[1]	60[1]	150[1]	0	**3,000**	34	1	3	0	**38**	50[1]	1[1]	3[1]	0	**54**
2000[1]	3,330	75	200	0	**3,605**	39	1	5	0	**45**	50	1	5	0	**56**
2001[1]	3,440	80	210	0	**3,730**	39	1	5	0	**45**	50	1	5	0	**56**
2002[1]	3,550	85	220	0	**3,855**	39	1	5	0	**45**	50	1	5	0	**56**
2005[1]	3,870	90	250	0	**4,210**	40	1	5	0	**46**	52	1	5	0	**58**

Table 9.13.5
Other Pentecostal Churches[6]

	England	Wales	Scotland	N. Ireland	**Total UK**	England	Wales	Scotland	N. Ireland	**Total UK**	England	Wales	Scotland	N. Ireland	**Total UK**
1990	360	60	120	60	**600**	8	1	4	1	**14**	6	1	2	1	**10**
1995	360	60	120	60	**600**	9	1	4	1	**15**	6	1	2	1	**10**
2000	420	70	140	70	**700**	11	1	5	1	**18**	7	1	3	1	**12**
2001	440	70	140	70	**720**	11	1	5	1	**18**	7	1	3	1	**12**
2002	450	70	150	70	**740**	11	1	5	1	**18**	7	1	3	1	**12**
2005	500	75	150	75	**800**	12	1	6	1	**20**	8	1	4	1	**14**

Table 9.13.6
Summary of English African and Caribbean Churches

	Total African & Caribbean Churches[7]			Total Oneness Apostolic Churches[8]			Other African & Caribbean Churches[9]			**Total African & Caribbean Churches**		
	Membership	Congregations	Ministers	Membership	Congregations	Ministers	Membership	Congregations	Ministers	Membership	Congregations	Ministers
1990	9,726	112	188	8,430	89	134	40,850	670	1,243	**59,006**	**871**	**1,565**
1995	13,255	148	210	11,624	103	169	50,385	766	1,371	**75,264**	**1,017**	**1,750**
2000	18,908	177	256	17,145	124	177	62,147	873	1,512	**98,200**	**1,174**	**1,945**
2001	20,264	182	276	18,814	129	186	63,378	890	1,528	**102,456**	**1,201**	**1,990**
2002	21,458	185	290	20,040	131	197	64,608	907	1,543	**106,106**	**1,223**	**2,030**
2005	24,040	194	320	24,175	150	233	68,300	960	1,590	**116,515**	**1,304**	**2,143**

Page 9.12
[1] Estimate
[2] Including one in Dublin.
[3] Includes unpaid ministers, of which there were 47 in 1995 and 51 in 2000.
[4] Revised figures.
[5] In 39 buildings.

Page 9.13
[1] Estimate
[2] Began 1991
[3] Revised figures
[4] 1996 figures
[5] A Oneness Apostolic Church
[6] All estimated; includes Struthers Memorial Church and other independent Pentecostal churches which are not African or Caribbean.
[7] From **Table 9.14**
[8] From **Table 9.15.1**
[9] Includes African and Caribbean Churches previously included in *Religious Trends* but which could not be traced for this edition: Beulah United Church of God, Chalvey Community Church, Christian Care Ministries, The Christ Family, Church of God Assembly, Leghorn Baptist Church of God and the True Vine Church. It also includes similar Oneness Apostolic Churches: Church of God in Christ United, First United Church of Jesus Christ, The Immaculate Conception Spiritual Baptist Church, United Pentecostal Church of Great Britain and Ireland, Universal Pentecostal Church and the Well of Living Water Ministries. It also includes churches never listed separately: Apostolic Faith and Acts Church, Church of God Church, United Apostolic Church and other independent Pentecostal churches.

9.14 Pentecostal Church Statistics: African and Caribbean Churches

Table 9.14
Pentecostal Churches: African and Caribbean Churches in England only

	MEMBERSHIP						CHURCHES						MINISTERS					
	1990	1995	2000	2001	2002	2005[1]	1990	1995	2000	2001	2002	2005[1]	1990	1995	2000	2001	2002	2005[1]
Aladura International Church	500	750	750	750	750	750	3	3	3	3[1]	3[1]	3	7	7	0	0[1]	0[1]	2
All Saints Pentecostal Assembly	20	20	50	55[1]	60[1]	75	1	1	1	1[1]	1[1]	1	4	4	5	5[1]	5[1]	5
Beneficial Veracious Christ Church	100	980	1,000	1,000[1]	1,000[1]	1,000	1	6	6	6[1]	6[1]	6	1	6	12	12[1]	12[1]	12
Bethany Church of God Faith Temple	45	48	40	33	47	60	1	2	2	2	2	2	4	3	4	4	4	4
Born Again Christ Healing Church	60	70	160	160	160	160	1	1	2	2	2	2	4	4	5	5	5	5
Cherubim & Seraphim Church Council	1,300	2,400	5,000	5,500[1]	6,000[1]	7,500	9	18	30	32[1]	34[1]	37	6	13	22	24[1]	26[1]	30
Christ Apostolic Church Mount Bethel	300	500	800	850[1]	900[1]	1,000	1	7	10	8	8	8	9	15	9	8	8	8
Christ the King Pentecostal Church	100	150	200	210[1]	220[1]	250	1	1	1	1[1]	1[1]	1	2	2	2	2[1]	2[1]	2
Church of God Ground of Truth	60	60	50	48[1]	46[1]	40	2	2	2	2[1]	2[1]	2	5	5	5	5[1]	5[1]	5
Church of God Reformation Movement	300	200	160	150[1]	145[1]	120	5	5	4	4[1]	4[1]	4	6	5	4	4[1]	4[1]	4
Church of God Worldwide Mission	40	60	80	100	200	250	1	1	1	1	1	1	1	1	1	2	2	2
Church of the Lord (Brotherhood)	42[1]	45	47	48[1]	50	55	1[1]	1	2	2	2	2	1[1]	1	1	1[1]	1	1
Deeper Christian Life Ministry	400	570	1,000	1,100[1]	1,150[1]	1,250	9	12	16	17[1]	17[1]	18	5	7	7	7[1]	7[1]	7
Deeper Life Bible Church	20	40	50	52[1]	55[1]	60	1	1	1	1[1]	1[1]	1	1	1	1	1[1]	1[1]	1
Forest Gate Brethren in Christ	60	45	65	70[1]	75[1]	90	2	1	1	1[1]	1[1]	1	1	1	1	1[1]	1[1]	1
Full Gospel Revival Centre	120	150	150	150[1]	150[1]	150	1	1	2	2[1]	2[1]	2	3	3	2	2[1]	2[1]	2
The Gospel Faith Mission International	180	310	460	490[1]	520[1]	600	2	2	4	4[1]	4[1]	4	7	3	7	7[1]	7[1]	7
Gospel Tabernacle Assembly	120	90	45[1]	40[1]	30	20	3	3	1	1	1	1	4	4	4	3[1]	2	2
Healing Church of God in Christ	80	65	60	59[1]	58[1]	55	2	2	2	2[1]	2[1]	2	3	3	3	3[1]	3[1]	3
The Latter-Rain Outpouring Revival	170	260	290	295[1]	300[1]	315	6	8	9	9[1]	9[1]	9	8	8	10	10[1]	10[1]	10
Miracle Church of God in Christ	94	200	81	75	75	70	3	5	4	3	3	3	5	5	4	3	3	3
Mustard Seed Church	60[2]	110	140	145[1]	150[1]	165	1	1	1	1[1]	1[1]	1	1	1	1	1[1]	1[1]	1
New Covenant Church	300	1,120	1,350	1,500	1,650	1,800	14	17	20	22	23	25	4	8	34[4]	51[4]	57[4]	70
New Testament Assembly (Pentecostal)	3,500	2,200	2,200	2,200[1]	2,200[1]	2,200	18	18	16	16[1]	16[1]	16	42	45	45[1]	45[1]	45[1]	45
Pentecostal Assembly of Mount Calvary	60	60	50	48[1]	45[1]	40	4	4	4	4[1]	4[1]	4	5	5	5	5[1]	5[1]	5
Pentecostal Gospel Church	100[3]	250	300[1]	310[1]	320[1]	350	1	1	1	1[1]	1[1]	1	1	2	3	3[1]	3[1]	3
Pentecostal Revival Church of Christ	200	250[5]	50	50[1]	50[1]	50	1	1[5]	1	1[1]	1[1]	1	6	6[5]	8	8[1]	8[1]	8
Progressive National Baptist Convention[6]	–	95	1,375	1,700	1,800	1,900	–	3	9	12	12	15	–	3	11	14	21	30
The People's Christian Fellowship	50	65	120	130[1]	145[1]	175	1	1	1	1[1]	1[1]	1	1	1	2	2[1]	2[1]	2
Ransom Church of God Universal Fellowship	100	100	100	100[1]	100[1]	100	2	1	1	1[1]	1[1]	1	12	3	3	3[1]	3[1]	3
Redemption Church of God	40	37	35	35[1]	35[1]	35	1	1	1	1[1]	1[1]	1	4	3	3	3[1]	3[1]	3
Redemption Ministries, London	175	175	175	175[1]	175[1]	175	1	1	1	1[1]	1[1]	1	2	2	2	2[1]	2[1]	2
Shiloh Pentecostal Church	400	450	500[1]	510[1]	520[1]	550	6	6[1]	6[1]	6[1]	6[1]	6	6[1]	6[1]	6[1]	6[1]	6[1]	6
Triumphant Church of God in Christ	50	60	65	66[1]	67[1]	70	2	2	2[1]	2[1]	2[1]	2	4	4	4	4[1]	4[1]	4
Universal Prayer Ministries	300	500	800	850[1]	900[1]	1,000	1	3	3[1]	3[1]	3[1]	3	5	10	13	13[1]	14[1]	15
Victory Bible Church International	200	400[1]	600[1]	650[1]	700[1]	800	1[1]	1[1]	1	1[1]	1[1]	1	5	5	5	5[1]	4[1]	5
Victory Pentecostal Church of God in Christ	30	70	10	10	10	10	1	2	1	1	1	1	2	4	1	1	1	1
Vision International Ministries	50	300	500	550[1]	600[1]	750	1	2	4	4[1]	4[1]	4	1	1	1[1]	1[1]	1[1]	1
Total	**9,726**	**13,255**	**18,908**	**20,264**	**21,458**	**24,040**	**112**	**148**	**177**	**182**	**185**	**194**	**188**	**210**	**256**	**276**	**290**	**320**

[1] Estimate
[2] Membership of 80 in 1992
[3] Membership of 200 in 1992
[4] Includes 9 full-time
[5] 1994 figure
[6] Began in 1995

Table 9.15.1
Pentecostal Churches: Oneness Apostolic Churches in England only

	MEMBERSHIP						CHURCHES						MINISTERS					
	1990	1995	2000	2001	2002	2005[1]	1990	1995	2000	2001	2002	2005[1]	1990	1995	2000	2001	2002	2005[1]
Assembly of the First Born	2,000	2,400	2,650	2,700[1]	2,750[1]	2,900	18	21	21	21[1]	21[1]	21	25	31	35	35[1]	36[1]	40
Bethany Fellowship of Great Britain	2,000	2,100	2,000	2,000[1]	2,000[1]	2,000	4	4	4	4[1]	4[1]	4	5	7	9	9[1]	9[1]	10
Bible Truth Church of God	200	220[2]	220	220[1]	220[1]	220	7	4[2]	4	4[1]	4[1]	4	18	5[2]	5	5[1]	5[1]	5
Bibleway Church of our Lord Jesus Christ	1,004	1,750	1,750	1,750[1]	1,750[1]	1,750	28	30	30	30[1]	30[1]	30	40	60	51	51[1]	51[1]	51
Christ Apostolic Church in Great Britain	2,100	3,200	3,700	3,800[1]	3,850[1]	4,200	11	19	23	24[1]	24[1]	27	10	16	20	21[1]	21[1]	24
Church of God in Christ Congregational Independent	106	130	150	155[1]	160[1]	170	6	7	7	7[1]	7[1]	7	7	8	8	8[1]	8[1]	8
Church of Jesus Christ of the Apostolic Faith	20	21	25	22[1]	20	15	1	1	1	1	1	1	1	1	1	1[1]	2	2
Eagles Nest Community Church	150	300	300	300[1]	300[1]	300	1	4	4	4[1]	4[1]	4	2	6	6	6[1]	6[1]	6
Elijah Tabernacle	30	28	40	42[1]	44[1]	50	1	1	2	2[1]	2[1]	2	3	2	3	3[1]	3[1]	3
Hackney Pentecostal Apostolic Church	100	210	230	235[1]	240[1]	250	1	1	1	1[1]	1[1]	1	7	10	10	10[1]	10[1]	10
Mount Zion Pentecostal Apostolic Church	200	300	1,600	1,600[1]	1,600[1]	1,600	1	2	15	15[1]	15[1]	15	3	6	7	7[1]	7[1]	7
Shiloh United Church of Christ Apostolic	400	275	300	300	406	500	8	6	5	5	4	4	10	10	4	4	4	4
United Church of God[3]	120	190	180[2]	190	200	220	2[2]	2[2]	2[2]	2[1]	2[1]	2	3[2]	3[2]	3[2]	3	3	3
Universal Church of the Kingdom of God[4]	–	500	4,000	5,500	6,500	10,000	–	1	5	9	12	28	–	4	15	23	32	60
Total	**8,430**	**11,624**	**17,145**	**18,814**	**20,040**	**24,175**	**89**	**103**	**124**	**129**	**131**	**150**	**134**	**169**	**177**	**186**	**197**	**233**

Table 9.15.2
Liberal Catholic Churches

	MEMBERSHIP						CHURCHES						MINISTERS					
	1990	1995	2000	2001	2002	2005[1]	1990	1995	2000	2001	2002	2005[1]	1990	1995	2000	2001	2002	2005[1]
Gnostic Church of Sofia[3]	–	35	35	35[1]	35[1]	35	–	3	3	3[1]	3[1]	3	–	5	5	5[1]	5[1]	5
Liberal Catholic Church (Grail Community)[2,4,5,6]	70[1]	70[1]	70[1]	70[1]	70	70	1	4	5	5	5	5	3	5	6	7	7	7
Liberal Catholic Church (Theosophia Synod)[6]	100[1]	100[1]	100[1]	100[1]	100[1]	100	2[1]	2[1]	2[1]	2[1]	2[1]	2	14[1]	14[1]	14[1]	14[1]	14[1]	14
Total	**170**	**205**	**205**	**205**	**205**	**205**	**3**	**9**	**10**	**10**	**10**	**10**	**17**	**24**	**25**	**26**	**26**	**26**

Table 9.15.1
[1] Estimate
[2] Revised figure
[3] All ministers are part-time
[4] Began in 1995 and is linked to the Rainbow Theatre

Table 9.15.2
[1] Estimate
[2] Revised figures
[3] An independent church in the Catholic tradition which claims to be Trinitarian. All figures are estimated
[4] All churches are House Churches.
[5] All clergy are non-stipendiary as a matter of policy.
[6] A breakaway group from the Liberal Catholic Church but with different theology.

9

9.16 Free Church Statistics: Other Denominations

Table 9.16.1
Total Other Denominations[5]

	MEMBERSHIP					CHURCHES					MINISTERS				
	England	Wales	Scotland	N. Ireland	**Total UK**	England	Wales	Scotland	N. Ireland	**Total UK**	England	Wales	Scotland	N. Ireland	**Total UK**
1990	120,657	4,829	9,724	3,743	**138,953**	1,710	95	210	63	**2,078**	2,011	91	245	59	**2,406**
1995	124,441	4,831	9,502	4,021	**142,795**	1,775	102	207	66	**2,150**	1,959	90	237	59	**2,345**
2000	125,686	4,248	7,887	3,728	**141,549**	1,796	104	198	70	**2,168**	1,808	94	232	64	**2,198**
2001	124,387	4,183	7,702	3,711	**139,983**	1,786	104	197	69	**2,156**	1,792	93	229	66	**2,180**
2002	124,062	4,213	7,742	3,722	**139,739**	1,792	104	198	69	**2,163**	1,775	91	228	65	**2,159**
2005	123,040	4,232	7,676	3,730	**138,678**	1,796	107	196	70	**2,169**	1,734	88	220	65	**2,107**

Table 9.16.2
Conference of British Mennonites[2]

	MEMBERSHIP					CHURCHES					MINISTERS				
	England	Wales	Scotland	N. Ireland	**Total UK**	England	Wales	Scotland	N. Ireland	**Total UK**	England	Wales	Scotland	N. Ireland	**Total UK**
1990	30	0	0	0	**30**	1	0	0	0	**1**	0	0	0	0	**0**
1995	30	0	0	0	**30**	1	0	0	0	**1**	1	0	0	0	**1**
2000	30	0	0	0	**30**	1	0	0	0	**1**	1	0	0	0	**1**
2001	35	0	0	0	**35**	1	0	0	0	**1**	1	0	0	0	**1**
2002	40	0	0	0	**40**	1	0	0	0	**1**	1	0	0	0	**1**
2005	40	0	0	0	**40**	1	0	0	0	**1**	1	0	0	0	**1**

Table 9.16.3
Countess of Huntingdon's Connexion

	MEMBERSHIP					CHURCHES					MINISTERS				
	England	Wales	Scotland	N. Ireland	**Total UK**	England	Wales	Scotland	N. Ireland	**Total UK**	England	Wales	Scotland	N. Ireland	**Total UK**
1990	853	0	0	0	**853**	24	0	0	0	**24**	14	0	0	0	**14**
1995	970	0	0	0	**970**	24	0	0	0	**24**	19	0	0	0	**19**
2000	700	0	0	0	**700**	23	0	0	0	**23**	20	0	0	0	**20**
2001[1]	680	0	0	0	**680**	23	0	0	0	**23**	20	0	0	0	**20**
2002[1]	660	0	0	0	**660**	23	0	0	0	**23**	20	0	0	0	**20**
2005[1]	600	0	0	0	**600**	23	0	0	0	**23**	20	0	0	0	**20**

Table 9.16.4
Emmanuel Holiness Church[3]

	MEMBERSHIP					CHURCHES					MINISTERS				
	England	Wales	Scotland	N. Ireland	**Total UK**	England	Wales	Scotland	N. Ireland	**Total UK**	England	Wales	Scotland	N. Ireland	**Total UK**
1990	299	140	0	0	**439**	5	2	0	0	**7**	2	0	0	0	**2**
1995	285	145	0	0	**430**	3	2	0	0	**5**	4	2	0	0	**6**
2000	200	150	0	0	**350**	3	1	0	0	**4**	3	2	0	0	**5**
2001[1]	185	155	0	0	**340**	3	1	0	0	**4**	3	2	0	0	**5**
2002[1]	170	160	0	0	**330**	3	1	0	0	**4**	3	2	0	0	**5**
2005[1]	160	160	0	0	**320**	3	1	0	0	**4**	3	2	0	0	**5**

Table 9.16.5
Moravian Church in Great Britain and Ireland[2]

	MEMBERSHIP					CHURCHES					MINISTERS				
	England	Wales	Scotland	N. Ireland	**Total UK**	England	Wales	Scotland	N. Ireland	**Total UK**	England	Wales	Scotland	N. Ireland	**Total UK**
1990	2,195	0	0	384	**2,579**	35	0	0	5	**40**	24	0	0	3	**27**
1995	1,952	0	0	374	**2,326**	31	0	0	5	**36**	21	0	0	4	**25**
2000	1,544	0	0	320[1]	**1,864**	30	0	0	5	**35**	15	0	0	4[1]	**19**
2001	1,580	0	0	320[1]	**1,900**	30	0	0	5	**35**	16	0	0	4[1]	**20**
2002[1]	1,500	0	0	300	**1,800**	30	0	0	5	**35**	16	0	0	4	**20**
2005[1]	1,330	0	0	270	**1,600**[4]	29	0	0	5	**34**	16	0	0	4	**20**

Table 9.16.6
Church of the Nazarene[3]

	MEMBERSHIP					CHURCHES					MINISTERS				
	England	Wales	Scotland	N. Ireland	**Total UK**	England	Wales	Scotland	N. Ireland	**Total UK**	England	Wales	Scotland	N. Ireland	**Total UK**
1990	2,418[1]	135[1]	1,455[1]	728	**4,736**	57	3	25	11	**96**	67	5	38	8	**118**
1995	2,527	145	1,462	816	**4,950**	55	3	24	13	**95**	57	3	39	12	**111**
2000[1]	2,660[4]	140	1,480	920	**5,200**	54	3	24	14	**95**	56	4	40	12	**112**
2001[1]	2,690	145	1,490	925	**5,250**	54	3	24	14	**95**	56	4	40	12	**112**
2002[1]	2,720	150	1,500	930	**5,300**	54	3	24	14	**95**	56	4	40	12	**112**
2005[1]	2,770	170	1,540	950	**5,430**	54	3	24	14	**95**	55	4	40	13	**112**

Table 9.16.7
Religious Society of Friends

	MEMBERSHIP					CHURCHES					MINISTERS				
	England	Wales	Scotland	N. Ireland	**Total UK**	England	Wales	Scotland	N. Ireland	**Total UK**	England	Wales	Scotland	N. Ireland	**Total UK**
1990	16,052	514	598	920	**18,084**	408	23	26	15	**472**	–	–	–	–	–
1995	16,202	611	705	922	**18,440**	431	31	31	15	**508**	–	–	–	–	–
2000	15,195	579	694	874	**17,342**	424	32	30	14	**500**	–	–	–	–	–
2001	14,974	575	694	873	**17,116**	423	33	31	13	**500**	–	–	–	–	–
2002	14,884[1]	571[1]	693	870	**17,018**	423[1]	33[1]	31	13	**500**	–	–	–	–	–
2005[1]	14,794	580	690	856	**16,920**	424	34	31	13	**502**	–	–	–	–	–

[1] Estimate [2] Including adherents [3] This is a Holiness church [4] Revised figure [5] Total of **Tables 9.16.2-7, 9.17.1-7, 9.18.1 and 9.20.1-3,5.**

Free Church Statistics: Other Denominations (continued) 9.17

Table 9.17.1
Salvation Army[3]

	MEMBERSHIP					CHURCHES					MINISTERS				
	England	Wales	Scotland	N. Ireland	**Total UK**	England	Wales	Scotland	N. Ireland	**Total UK**	England	Wales	Scotland	N. Ireland	**Total UK**
1990	51,215	2,322	5,638	1,110	**60,285**	673	44	125	20	**862**	1,500	70	187	36	**1,793**
1995	48,395	2,218	5,187	1,324	**57,124**	672[1]	42[1]	117[1]	22[1]	**853**[2]	1,425	66	178	34	**1,703**
2000	46,323	1,754	3,638	1,025	**52,740**	671	40	110	23	**844**	1,253	66	170	40	**1,529**
2001[1]	43,600	1,650	3,420	970	**49,640**	657	39	108	22	**826**	1,239	65	168	40	**1,512**
2002[1]	42,690	1,620	3,350	940	**48,600**	654	39	107	22	**822**	1,216	64	165	39	**1,484**
2005[1]	39,520	1,500	3,100	880	**45,000**	636	38	104	22	**800**	1,147	60	156	37	**1,400**

Table 9.17.2
Seventh Day Adventists

	MEMBERSHIP					CHURCHES					MINISTERS				
	England	Wales	Scotland	N. Ireland	**Total UK**	England	Wales	Scotland	N. Ireland	**Total UK**	England	Wales	Scotland	N. Ireland	**Total UK**
1990	16,641	529	270	299	**17,739**	204	11	10	7	**232**	121	8	6	9	**144**
1995	17,642	481	281	330	**18,734**	206[2]	12	9	7	**234**	130	7	6	7	**150**
2000	19,573	449	281	334	**20,637**	207	15	9	10	**241**	142	9	6	6	**163**
2001	20,048	459	277	353	**21,137**	212	15	9	10	**246**	144	9	6	7	**166**
2002[1]	20,197	442	281	352	**21,272**	212	15	9	10	**246**	146	9	6	7	**168**
2005[1]	21,136	422	283	364	**22,205**	212	17	9	11	**249**	152	9	6	7	**174**

Table 9.17.3
Worldwide Church of God

	MEMBERSHIP					CHURCHES					MINISTERS				
	England	Wales	Scotland	N. Ireland	**Total UK**	England	Wales	Scotland	N. Ireland	**Total UK**	England	Wales	Scotland	N. Ireland	**Total UK**
1990	2,476	51	260	210	**2,997**	33	2	6	3	**44**	25	0	2	1	**28**
1995	2,099	39	220	178	**2,536**	33	2	7	3	**45**	13	2	1	1	**17**
2000	1,921	37	210	165	**2,333**	33	2	7	3	**45**	13	2	1	1	**17**
2001	1,785	31	210	150	**2,176**	33	2	7	3	**45**	10	2	0	1	**13**
2002	1,685	30	207	150	**2,072**	34	2	7	3	**46**	9	1	0	1	**11**
2005[1]	1,510	25	193	135	**1,863**	34	2	7	3	**46**	9	1	0	1	**11**

Table 9.17.4
The Christian Community

	MEMBERSHIP					CHURCHES					MINISTERS				
	England	Wales	Scotland	N. Ireland	**Total UK**	England	Wales	Scotland	N. Ireland	**Total UK**	England	Wales	Scotland	N. Ireland	**Total UK**
1990	800	0	0	0	**800**	18	0	0	0	**18**	25	0	0	0	**25**
1995	600	0	0	0	**600**	12	0	0	0	**12**	18	0	0	0	**18**
2000[1]	530	0	50	0	**580**	12	0	1	0	**13**	15	0	1	0	**16**
2001[1]	515	0	75	25	**615**	12	0	1	1	**14**	14	0	1	1	**16**
2002	500	0	100	50	**650**	12	0	2	1	**15**	14	0	2	1	**17**
2005[1]	450	0	125	75	**650**	12	0	2	1	**15**	14	0	2	1	**17**

Table 9.17.5
Chinese Churches

	MEMBERSHIP					CHURCHES					MINISTERS				
	England	Wales	Scotland	N. Ireland	**Total UK**	England	Wales	Scotland	N. Ireland	**Total UK**	England	Wales	Scotland	N. Ireland	**Total UK**
1990[1]	3,850	150	450	50	**4,500**	36	3	5	1	**45**	11	3	5	1	**20**
1995[1]	4,370	160	510	60	**5,100**	57	3	7	1	**68**	21	3	5	1	**30**
2000[1]	5,190	170	570	70	**6,000**	59	3	8	1	**71**	23	4	7	1	**35**
2001[1]	5,270	175	580	75	**6,100**	60	3	8	1	**72**	23	4	7	1	**35**
2002[1]	5,340	180	600	80	**6,200**	61	3	8	1	**73**	24	4	7	1	**36**
2005[1]	5,550	200	650	100	**6,500**	64	3	9	1	**77**	26	4	7	1	**38**

Table 9.17.6
Hungarian Reformed Church

	MEMBERSHIP					CHURCHES					MINISTERS				
	England	Wales	Scotland	N. Ireland	**Total UK**	England[4]	Wales	Scotland	N. Ireland	**Total UK**	England	Wales	Scotland	N. Ireland	**Total UK**
1990	52	3	3	2	**60**	2[2]	0	0	0	**2**	3	0	0	0	**3**
1995	42	2	2	2	**48**	2[2]	0	0	0	**2**	1	0	0	0	**1**
2000[1]	32	1	1	0	**34**	2	0	0	0	**2**	1	0	0	0	**1**
2001[1]	31	0	1	0	**32**	2	0	0	0	**2**	1	0	0	0	**1**
2002	30	0	1	0	**31**	2	0	0	0	**2**	1	0	0	0	**1**
2005[1]	29	0	0	0	**29**	2	0	0	0	**2**	1	0	0	0	**1**

Table 9.17.7
Mar Thoma Syrian Church UK

	MEMBERSHIP					CHURCHES					MINISTERS				
	England	Wales	Scotland	N. Ireland	**Total UK**	England	Wales	Scotland	N. Ireland	**Total UK**	England	Wales	Scotland	N. Ireland	**Total UK**
1990	545	25	15	15	**600**	1	0	0	0	**1**	2	0	0	0	**2**
1995	695	25	15	15	**750**	1	0	0	0	**1**	2	0	0	0	**2**
2000	725	35	20	20	**800**	2	0	0	0	**2**	3	0	1	0	**4**
2001	910	50	20	20	**1,000**	2	0	0	0	**2**	3	0	1	0	**4**
2002	1,300	100	50	50	**1,500**	2	0	0	0	**2**	3	0	1	0	**4**
2005	2,100	200	100	100	**2,500**	4	1	0	0	**5**	4	1	1	1	**7**

[1] Estimate [2] Revised figure [3] Includes adherents [4] Consisting of 1 church in London and 1 church in Manchester.

9.18 Free Church Statistics: Other Denominations: Lutheran

MEMBERSHIP | CHURCHES | MINISTERS

Table 9.18.1
Total Lutheran

	England	Wales	Scotland	N. Ireland	Total UK	England	Wales	Scotland	N. Ireland	Total UK	England	Wales	Scotland	N. Ireland	Total UK
1990	15,470	890	925	25	**17,310**	92	6	10	1	**109**	48	3	5	1	**57**
1995	19,390	935	940	0	**21,265**	92	6	8	0	**106**	47	4	5	0	**56**
2000	20,843	853	733	0	**22,429**	88	7	5	0	**100**	50	4	3	0	**57**
2001	21,772	853	715	0	**23,340**	88	7	5	0	**100**	51	4	3	0	**58**
2002	21,715	860	695	0	**23,270**	89	7	5	0	**101**	52	4	3	0	**59**
2005	20,855	855	685	0	**22,395**	88	7	5	0	**100**	52	4	3	0	**59**

Table 9.18.2
Evangelical Lutheran Church of England

	England	Wales	Scotland	N. Ireland	Total UK	England	Wales	Scotland	N. Ireland	Total UK	England	Wales	Scotland	N. Ireland	Total UK
1990	744	55	55	0	**854**	14[1]	1[1]	1[1]	0	**16**	14[1]	1[1]	1[1]	0	**16**
1995	760	60	60	0	**880**	13	1	1	0	**15**	14	1	1	0	**16**
2000[1]	780	55	55	0	**890**	13	1	1	0	**15**	14	1	1	0	**16**
2001[1]	785	55	55	0	**895**	13	1	1	0	**15**	14	1	1	0	**16**
2002[1]	790	55	55	0	**900**	13	1	1	0	**15**	14	1	1	0	**16**
2005[1]	810	55	55	0	**920**	13	1	1	0	**15**	14	1	1	0	**16**

Table 9.18.3
German Evangelical Lutheran Synod

	England	Wales	Scotland	N. Ireland	Total UK	England	Wales	Scotland	N. Ireland	Total UK	England	Wales	Scotland	N. Ireland	Total UK
1990	2,000	250	275	25	**2,550**	22	3	5	1	**31**	7	1	2	1	**11**
1995	2,000	250	250	0	**2,500**	23	3	4	0	**30**	7	2	2	0	**11**
2000	1,468	193	98	0	**1,759**	17	3	2	0	**22**	5	1	1	0	**7**
2001	1,450	185	100	0	**1,735**	17	3	2	0	**22**	5	1	1	0	**7**
2002[1]	1,420	185	85	0	**1,690**	17	3	2	0	**22**	5	1	1	0	**7**
2005[1]	1,250	165	60	0	**1,475**	15	3	2	0	**20**	5	1	1	0	**7**

Table 9.18.4
Latvian Evangelical Lutheran Synod

	England	Wales	Scotland	N. Ireland	Total UK	England	Wales	Scotland	N. Ireland	Total UK	England	Wales	Scotland	N. Ireland	Total UK
1990	2,050	50	50	0	**2,150**	7	0	0	0	**7**	7	0	0	0	**7**
1995	1,920	40	40	0	**2,000**	7	0	0	0	**7**	7	0	0	0	**7**
2000	1,850	35	30	0	**1,915**	7	1	0	0	**8**	7	1	0	0	**8**
2001	1,830	35	30	0	**1,895**	7	1	0	0	**8**	7	1	0	0	**8**
2002	1,810	35	30	0	**1,875**	7	1	0	0	**8**	7	1	0	0	**8**
2005	1,740	30	30	0	**1,800**	7	1	0	0	**8**	7	1	0	0	**8**

Table 9.18.5
Lutheran Church in Great Britain

	England	Wales	Scotland	N. Ireland	Total UK[4]	England	Wales	Scotland	N. Ireland	Total UK[4]	England	Wales	Scotland	N. Ireland	Total UK[4]
1990	2,170	160	170	0	**2,500**	9	1	1	0	**11**	10	1	1	0	**12**
1995[2]	2,185	160	165	0	**2,510**	10	1	1	0	**12**	10	1	1	0	**12**
2000	2,040	140	120	0	**2,300**	10	1	1	0	**12**	13	1	1	0	**15**
2001	2,250	150	100	0	**2,500**	10	1	1	0	**12**	14	1	1	0	**16**
2002	2,250	155	95	0	**2,500**	11	1	1	0	**13**	15	1	1	0	**17**
2005	2,355	155	90	0	**2,600**	13	1	1	0	**15**	16	1	1	0	**18**

Table 9.18.6
Polish Evangelical Church of the Augsburg Confession Abroad

	England	Wales	Scotland	N. Ireland	Total UK	England	Wales	Scotland	N. Ireland	Total UK	England	Wales	Scotland	N. Ireland	Total UK
1990	2,650	50	50	0	**2,750**	25	0	2	0	**27**	4	0	1	0	**5**
1995	2,650	25	25	0	**2,700**[1]	25[1]	0	1[5]	0	**26**	4	0	1	0	**5**
2000[1]	2,700	0	0	0	**2,700**	25[6]	0	0	0	**25**	4	0	0	0	**4**
2001[1]	2,700	0	0	0	**2,700**	25	0	0	0	**25**	4	0	0	0	**4**
2002[1]	2,700	0	0	0	**2,700**	25	0	0	0	**25**	4	0	0	0	**4**
2005[1]	2,700	0	0	0	**2,700**	25	0	0	0	**25**	4	0	0	0	**4**

Table 9.18.7
Swedish Lutheran Church

	England[3]	Wales	Scotland	N. Ireland	Total UK	England	Wales	Scotland	N. Ireland	Total UK	England	Wales	Scotland	N. Ireland	Total UK
1990	2,300	0	0	0	**2,300**	4	0	0	0	**4**	5	0	0	0	**5**
1995	5,425	0	0	0	**5,424**	4	0	0	0	**4**	4	0	0	0	**4**
2000	7,065	0	0	0	**7,065**	4	0	0	0	**4**	4	0	0	0	**4**
2001	7,797	0	0	0	**7,797**	4	0	0	0	**4**	4	0	0	0	**4**
2002	7,765	0	0	0	**7,765**	4	0	0	0	**4**	4	0	0	0	**4**
2005	7,000	0	0	0	**7,000**	3	0	0	0	**3**	3	0	0	0	**3**

[1] Estimate. *For other footnotes, see* **Page 9.20**

Table 9.19.1
Overseas National Churches in England only

	MEMBERSHIP						CHURCHES						PRIESTS					
	1990	1995	2000	2001	2002	2005[1]	1990	1995	2000	2001	2002	2005[1]	1990	1995	2000	2001	2002	2005[1]
American Church in London	591[3]	480	468	460[1]	450[1]	450	1	1	1	1[1]	1[1]	1	3	1	2	2[1]	2[1]	2
Danish Church[5]	80	100[1]	100	100[1]	100[1]	100	2	2	2	2	2	2	2	2	2	3	3	3
Dutch Church	270	270	230	230	230	230	1	1	1	1	1	1	1	1	1	1	1	1
Estonian Evangelical Lutheran Synod	710	640	550	530[1]	520[1]	500	5	5	5	5[1]	5[1]	5	3	3	3	3[1]	3[1]	3
Finnish Church and Seaman's Mission	50	50	100[2]	200	300	300	1	1	1	1	1	1	2	2	2	2	2	2
French Protestant Church in the UK[6]	200	260	300	259	230[1]	200	3	3	3	3	3	3	3	3	3	3	3	3
Greek Christian Fellowship	12	16	19	20[1]	21[1]	24	1	1	1	1[1]	1[1]	1	0	0	0	0[1]	0[1]	0
Icelandic Lutheran Church in England[7,8]	100[1]	100[1]	100[1]	100[1]	100	100	1[1]	1[1]	1[1]	1[1]	1	1	1[1]	1	1[1]	1[1]	1	1
International Presbyterian Church[4]	500	700	800	800[1]	800[1]	800	6	7	9	9[1]	9[1]	9	4	5	0	0[1]	0[1]	0
Iranian Christian Fellowship	50	90	120	150	180[1]	300	1	1	1	2	2[1]	3	2	3	3	3	3	4
Italian Pentecostal Church	75	100	150	150	150	170	4	6	5	5	5	5	4	4	5	5	5	5
Japanese Churches[9]	0	77	65	60[1]	55[1]	50	0	1	2	2[1]	2[1]	2	0	5	5	5[1]	5[1]	5
Bread of Life (Portuguese)[10,11]	100	300	520	300	350	1,000	1	5	10	3	1	1	2	6	12	6	6	10
Scottish Asian Christian Fellowship[12]	–	–	23	25	27[1]	30	–	–	1	1	1[1]	1	–	–	0	0	0[1]	0
Spanish Evangelical Church	60	120	120	200	200	250	1	2	7	8	10	13	3	3	2	2	1	2
Swahili Churches[13]	90	95	105	108[1]	110[1]	115	1	1	1	1[1]	1[1]	1	1	1	1	1[1]	1[1]	1
Swiss Church in London[14]	550[2]	350[1]	150	150	150	250	1	1	1	1	1	1	2	2	2	2	2	3
Swiss Evangelical Brotherhood	30	25[1]	20[1]	18[1]	15	12	1	1	1	1	1	1	1	1	1	1	1	1
Tamil Language Churches	220	920	1,400	1,500[1]	1,600[1]	1,900	3	14	24	26[1]	28[1]	34	4	15	17	17[1]	18[1]	19
Turkish Christian Fellowship[15]	–	3	4	5	3	5	–	0	1	1	1	1	–	0	0	0	0	0
Urdu and Punjabi	50	50	50	50[1]	50[1]	50	1	1	1	1[1]	1[1]	1	1	1	1	1[1]	1[1]	1
Other Language Groups[16]	600	750	850	875	900	1,000	12	15	17	17	18	20	6	8	9	9	9	10
Total	**4,338**	**5,496**	**6,244**	**6,290**	**6,541**	**7,836**	**47**	**70**	**96**	**93**	**96**	**108**	**45**	**67**	**72**	**67**	**67**	**76**

Table 9.19.2
Other Churches: Holiness in England only

	MEMBERSHIP						CHURCHES						MINISTERS					
	1990	1995	2000	2001	2002	2005[1]	1990	1995	2000	2001	2002	2005[1]	1990	1995	2000	2001	2002	2005[1]
African Methodist Episcopal Church	300	300	200	200	200	200	8	8	4	4	4	4	10	10	4	4	4	4
African Methodist Episcopal Zion Church	450	470	500	505[1]	510[1]	530	12	12	12	12[1]	12[1]	12	15	15	15	15[1]	15[1]	15
Cherubim & Seraphim Oke-Ayo Movement No 2 UK Church	–	105	150	160[1]	170[1]	200	–	3	8	9[1]	10[1]	13	–	3	8	9[1]	10[1]	15
Pentecostal Holiness Church[4]	220	280	280	280[1]	280[1]	280	6	7	7	7[1]	7[1]	7	16	20	20	20[1]	20[1]	20
Pillar of Fire Church	20	26	25[2]	25[2]	25[3]	25[3]	1	1	1	1	1	1	3	3	3	2	2	2
Wesleyan Holiness Church	653	540	496	485[1]	475[1]	450	20	18	17	17[1]	17[1]	16	26	16	17	17[1]	17[1]	18
Other Holiness Churches[5]	150	150	150	150	150	150	4	4	4	4	4	4	5	5	5	5	5	5
Totals for Holiness Churches	**1,793**	**1,871**	**1,801**	**1,805**	**1,810**	**1,835**	**51**	**53**	**53**	**54**	**55**	**57**	**75**	**72**	**72**	**72**	**73**	**79**

Table 9.19.1
[1] Estimate
[2] Revised figures.
[3] Includes regular attenders and children
[4] Includes 5 Korean and 2 English congregations.
[5] Includes 1 church in London, and 1 in Hull. Membership figures are estimated as the church sees itself more as a community than a congregation.
[6] Includes churches in London, Brighton and Canterbury.
[7] Have a community of 500, with twice monthly services in London, and less frequent but regular services in Hull and Grimsby.
[8] Regular attendance in London is between 90-110 including 25 choir members. Figures rise to approximately 300 for special services during the year.
[9] Closed in 1986 and reopened in 1993.
[10] In 2000 autonomy was given to 9 churches.
[11] In fellowship with Elim Pentecostal Church.
[12] Began in 1998.
[13] Part of St Anne's Lutheran Church.
[14] In the 1980's the Swiss Reformed Church amalgamated with the Swiss Church in London.
[15] Set up in 1994 and run by London City Mission.
[16] All estimated.

Table 9.19.2
[1] Estimate
[2] Total attendance of 45.
[3] Total attendance of 50.
[4] The full title is "Fellowship of Pentecostal Holiness Churches in Great Britain".
[5] All estimated.

9.20 Free Church Statistics: Other Denominations: Other Churches

Table 9.20.1 Korean Churches[2]

	MEMBERSHIP					CONGREGATIONS					MINISTERS				
	England	Wales	Scotland	N. Ireland	**Total UK**	England	Wales	Scotland	N. Ireland	**Total UK**	England	Wales	Scotland	N. Ireland	**Total UK**
1990[1]	960	70	70	0	**1,100**	14	1	1	0	**16**	26	2	2	0	**30**
1995[1]	1,090	70	140	0	**1,300**	15	1	2	0	**18**	30	2	3	0	**35**
2000[1]	1,300	80	170	0	**1,550**	19	1	2	0	**22**	35	2	3	0	**40**
2001[1]	1,330	90	180	0	**1,600**	20	1	2	0	**23**	36	2	3	0	**41**
2002[1]	1,380	100	200	0	**1,680**	21	1	2	0	**24**	37	2	3	0	**42**
2005[1]	1,510	120	220	0	**1,850**	23	1	2	0	**26**	40	2	3	0	**45**

Table 9.20.2 Norwegian Church and Seaman's Mission[3]

	England	Wales	Scotland	N. Ireland	**Total UK[10]**	England	Wales	Scotland	N. Ireland	**Total UK**	England	Wales	Scotland	N. Ireland	**Total UK**
1990	400[1]	0	40	0	**440**	4	0	2	0	**6**	3	0	0	0	**3**
1995	430[1]	0	40	0	**470**	5	0	2	0	**7**	4	0	0	0	**4**
2000	500[1]	0	40	0	**540**	5	0	2	0	**7**	4	0	0	0	**4**
2001	510[1]	0	40	0	**550**	5	0	2	0	**7**	4[1]	0	0	0	**4**
2002	520[1]	0	40	0	**560**	5	0	2	0	**7**	3	0	0	0	**3**
2005	560[1]	0	40	0	**600**	5	0	2	0	**7**	3	0	0	0	**3**

Table 9.20.3 Union of British Messianic Jewish Congregations[4]

	England	Wales	Scotland	N. Ireland	**Total UK**	England	Wales	Scotland	N. Ireland	**Total UK**	England	Wales	Scotland	N. Ireland	**Total UK**
1990	100	0	0	0	**100**	2	0	0	0	**2**	2	0	0	0	**2**
1995	150	0	0	0	**150**	3	0	0	0	**3**	3	0	0	0	**3**
2000	170[1]	0	0	0	**170**	4	0	0	0	**4**	5	0	0	0	**5**
2001	172[1]	0	0	0	**172**	4	0	0	0	**4**	6	0	0	0	**6**
2002	175	0	25	0	**200**	5	0	1	0	**6**	8	0	1	0	**9**
2005	250	0	50	0	**300**	7	0	1	0	**8**	10	0	2	0	**12**

Table 9.20.4 Other Lutheran Churches[5]

	England	Wales	Scotland	N. Ireland	**Total UK**	England	Wales	Scotland	N. Ireland	**Total UK**	England	Wales	Scotland	N. Ireland	**Total UK**
1990	3,556	325	325	0	**4,206[6]**	11[1]	1[1]	1[1]	0	**13**	1	0	0	0	**1**
1995	4,450	400	400	0	**5,250[1]**	10[1]	1[1]	1[1]	0	**12[1]**	1	0	0	0	**1[1]**
2000[1]	4,940	430	430	0	**5,800**	12	1	1	0	**14**	3	0	0	0	**3**
2001[1]	4,960	430	430	0	**5,820**	12	1	1	0	**14**	3	0	0	0	**3**
2002[1]	4,980	430	430	0	**5,840**	12	1	1	0	**14**	3	0	0	0	**3**
2005[1]	5,000	450	450	0	**5,900**	12	1	1	0	**14**	3	0	0	0	**3**

Table 9.20.5 Summary of English Overseas, Holiness and Liberal Catholic Churches

	Overseas National Churches[7]			Holiness Churches[8]			Liberal Catholic Churches[9]			**Total of these 3 streams of Churches**		
	Members	Congregations	Ministers	Members	Congregations	Ministers	Members	Congregations	Ministers	Members	Congregations	Ministers
1990	4,338	47	45	1,793	51	75	170	3	17	**6,301**	**101**	**137**
1995	5,496	70	67	1,871	53	72	205	9	24	**7,572**	**132**	**163**
2000	6,244	96	72	1,801	53	72	205	10	25	**8,250**	**159**	**169**
2001	6,290	93	67	1,805	54	72	205	10	26	**8,300**	**157**	**165**
2002	6,541	96	67	1,810	55	73	205	10	26	**8,556**	**161**	**166**
2005	7,836	108	76	1,835	57	79	205	10	26	**9,876**	**175**	**181**

Page 9.18

[1] Estimate

[2] Figures are for 1996

[3] Members are counted as number of households on the address list.

[4] Totals given by Lutheran Church; distribution by country pro rata to other Lutheran churches.

[5] Scottish Church Census 1994; the church had closed by 2002.

[6] Revised figure

Page 9.20

[1] Estimate

[2] Excludes 2 Korean in the International Presbyterian Church.

[3] Full title "Norwegian and Seaman's Mission: St Olav's Church".

[4] Previously these figures were reported for the "London Messianic Congregation", who are now known as the B'Nai Maccabim (The Children of the Maccabees) Messianic Synagogue, and are part of the Union of British Messianic Jewish Congregations (UBMJC).

[5] Includes the London Chinese Lutheran Church which began in 1994 with 50 members, 1 church and 1 minister, but excludes the Estonian Evangelical Lutheran Synod and the Icelandic Lutheran Church which are in **Table 9.19.1**.

[6] Estimate derived by subtracting the constituent churches from Lutheran Council of Great Britain figures.

[7] See **Table 9.19.1.**

[8] See **Table 9.19.2.**

[9] See **Table 9.15.2.**

[10] Mailing list to supporters consists of 1,400 names; about two-fifths taken as active members.

10

Other Religions and Non-Trinitarian Church Statistics

10

Sources: Individual religions and non-Trinitarian churches and previous editions of *Religious Trends*

10.2 Non-Trinitarian Churches

MEMBERSHIP — CHURCHES — MINISTERS

Table 10.2.1
Total Non-Trinitarian Churches

	Membership					Churches					Ministers				
	England	Wales	Scotland	N. Ireland	**Total UK**	England	Wales	Scotland	N. Ireland	**Total UK**	England	Wales	Scotland	N. Ireland	**Total UK**
1990	397,282	20,108	34,919	5,363	**457,672**	2,898	193	199	71	**3,361**	13,246	871	986	335	**15,438**
1995	452,763	21,257	37,828	6,040	**517,888**	2,837	190	206	84	**3,317**	14,317	950	1,061	366	**16,694**
2000	472,849	21,532	39,799	6,650	**540,830**	2,902	195	210	96	**3,403**	12,531	832	933	396	**14,692**
2001	475,571	21,459	40,153	6,720	**543,903**	2,911	196	212	95	**3,414**	12,599	837	941	401	**14,778**
2002	480,275	21,419	40,598	6,775	**549,067**	2,921	196	212	96	**3,425**	12,554	834	940	407	**14,736**
2005	491,590	21,767	42,168	7,210	**562,735**	2,922	193	216	98	**3,429**	12,649	838	949	436	**14,872**

Table 10.2.2
Christadelphians

	England	Wales	Scotland	N. Ireland	**Total UK**	England	Wales	Scotland	N. Ireland	**Total UK**[3]	England	Wales	Scotland	N. Ireland	**Total UK**[4]
1990	17,880	1,150	900	70	**20,000**[1]	278	23	18	1	**320**	–	–	–	–	–
1995	17,130[2]	1,120	880	70	**19,200**[1]	257[1]	22[1]	17[1]	1[1]	**297**	–	–	–	–	–
2000	16,450[2]	1,060	830	60[2]	**18,400**[1]	240	21	16	1	**292**	–	–	–	–	–
2001[1]	16,350	1,000	800	50	**18,200**	239	21	16	1	**291**	–	–	–	–	–
2002[1]	16,300	900	760	40	**18,000**	238	21	16	1	**290**	–	–	–	–	–
2005[1]	16,060	800	700	40	**17,600**	234	20	16	1	**285**	–	–	–	–	–

Table 10.2.3
Church of Christ, Scientist (Christian Science Church)[5]

	England	Wales	Scotland	N. Ireland	**Total UK**	England	Wales	Scotland	N. Ireland	**Total UK**	England	Wales	Scotland	N. Ireland	**Total UK**[6]
1990[1]	12,300	300	600	100	**13,300**	297	6	14	3	**320**	462	11	23	4	**500**[1]
1995	8,780	200	430	90	**9,500**	185	4	9	2	**200**	282	6	14	3	**305**
2000	6,500	150	300	50	**7,000**	145	3	6	2	**156**	104	2	5	1	**112**
2001[1]	6,000	150	300	50	**6,500**	140	3	5	2	**150**	98	2	4	1	**105**[1]
2002[1]	5,740	120	250	40	**6,150**	135	2	4	2	**143**	88	2	4	1	**95**[1]
2005[1]	3,920	80	170	30	**4,200**	115	1	3	1	**120**	61	1	3	0	**65**[1]

Table 10.2.4
Church of God International[7]

	England	Wales	Scotland	N. Ireland	**Total UK**	England	Wales	Scotland	N. Ireland	**Total UK**	England	Wales	Scotland	N. Ireland	**Total UK**
1990[1]	1,500	0	0	0	**1,500**	12	0	0	0	**12**	6	0	0	0	**6**
1995	1,500	0	0	0	**1,500**	12[1]	0	0	0	**12**	6[1]	0	0	0	**6**
2000[1]	2,000	0	0	0	**2,000**	15[1]	0	0	0	**15**	8[1]	0	0	0	**8**
2001[1]	2,000	0	0	0	**2,000**	15	0	0	0	**15**	8	0	0	0	**8**
2002[1]	2,000	0	0	0	**2,000**	15	0	0	0	**15**	8	0	0	0	**8**
2005[1]	2,200	0	0	0	**2,200**	16	0	0	0	**16**	9	0	0	0	**9**

Table 10.2.5
Church of God Sabbath-Keeping

	England	Wales	Scotland	N. Ireland	**Total UK**	England	Wales	Scotland	N. Ireland	**Total UK**	England	Wales	Scotland	N. Ireland	**Total UK**
1990[1]	20	0	0	0	**20**	1	0	0	0	**1**	1	0	0	0	**1**
1995	30	0	0	0	**30**	1	0	0	0	**1**	1	0	0	0	**1**
2000	55	0	0	0	**55**	2	0	0	0	**2**	1	0	0	0	**1**
2001[1]	60	0	0	0	**60**	2	0	0	0	**2**	1	0	0	0	**1**
2002[1]	65	0	0	0	**65**	2	0	0	0	**2**	1	0	0	0	**1**
2005[1]	75	0	0	0	**75**	2	0	0	0	**2**	1	0	0	0	**1**

Table 10.2.6
Church of Jesus Christ of Latter-Day Saints (LDS Church or Mormons)[8]

	England	Wales	Scotland	N. Ireland	**Total UK**	England	Wales	Scotland	N. Ireland	**Total UK**	England	Wales	Scotland	N. Ireland	**Total UK**[10]
1990	132,382	7,600	18,370	1,437	**159,789**	267	15	37	10	**329**	267	15	37	10	**329**
1995	140,835[2]	8,130	19,650	1,585	**170,200**	306[2]	18	45	12	**381**	306	18	45	12	**381**
2000[9]	147,470	8,470	20,460	1,600	**178,000**[2]	320	18	45	12	**395**	320	18	45	12	**395**
2001[9]	148,310	8,510	20,570	1,610	**179,000**	337	19	47	12	**415**	337	19	47	12	**415**
2002[9]	149,130	8,560	20,690	1,620	**180,000**	349	20	48	13	**430**	349	20	48	13	**430**
2005[9]	155,750	8,950	21,600	1,700	**188,000**	357	20	50	13	**440**	357	20	50	13	**440**

Table 10.2.7
Community of Christ[11]

	England	Wales	Scotland	N. Ireland	**Total UK**	England	Wales	Scotland	N. Ireland	**Total UK**	England	Wales	Scotland	N. Ireland	**Total UK**
1990	1,547	273	4	0	**1,824**	17	4	0	0	**21**	115	28	0	0	**143**
1995	1,216	217	3	0	**1,446**	17	4	0	0	**21**	125	30	0	0	**155**
2000	1,100	200	3	0	**1,303**	17	4	0	0	**21**	127	30	0	0	**157**
2001[1]	1,070	197	3	0	**1,270**	17	4	0	0	**21**	127	30	0	0	**157**
2002[1]	1,035	192	3	0	**1,230**	17	4	0	0	**21**	128	30	0	0	**158**
2005[1]	925	172	3	0	**1,100**	17	4	0	0	**21**	130	32	0	0	**162**

[1] Estimate. *For other footnotes, see* **Page 10.3**

MEMBERSHIP | CHURCHES | MINISTERS

Table 10.3.1
The Family[3]

	Membership					Churches					Ministers				
	England	Wales	Scotland	N. Ireland	**Total UK**	England	Wales	Scotland	N. Ireland	**Total UK**	England	Wales	Scotland	N. Ireland	**Total UK**
1990	170	0	0	0	**170**[2]	5	0	0	0	**5**	10	0	0	0	**10**
1995	170	0	0	0	**170**	5	0	0	0	**5**	10	0	0	0	**10**
2000	170	0	0	0	**170**	5	0	0	0	**5**	10	0	0	0	**10**
2001	170	0	0	0	**170**	5	0	0	0	**5**	10	0	0	0	**10**
2002	170	0	0	0	**170**	5	0	0	0	**5**	10	0	0	0	**10**
2005	170	0	0	0	**170**	5	0	0	0	**5**	10	0	0	0	**10**

Table 10.3.2
Global Church of God[4]

	Membership					Churches					Ministers				
	England	Wales	Scotland	N. Ireland	**Total UK**	England	Wales	Scotland	N. Ireland	**Total UK**	England	Wales	Scotland	N. Ireland	**Total UK**
1990	–	–	–	–	–	–	–	–	–	–	–	–	–	–	–
1995	35	0	10	5	**50**	3	0	1	1	**5**	2	0	0	0	**2**
2000[1]	25	0	10	5	**40**[2]	2	0	1	1	**4**	1	0	0	0	**1**
2001[1]	25	0	10	5	**40**	2	0	1	1	**4**	1	0	0	0	**1**
2002	25	0	10	5	**40**	2	0	1	1	**4**	1	0	0	0	**1**
2005[1]	25	0	10	5	**40**	2	0	1	1	**4**	1	0	0	0	**1**

Table 10.3.3
International Churches of Christ[5]

	Membership					Churches					Ministers				
	England	Wales	Scotland	N. Ireland	**Total UK**	England	Wales	Scotland	N. Ireland	**Total UK**	England	Wales	Scotland	N. Ireland	**Total UK**
1990	950	0	50	0	**1,100**	7	0	1	0	**8**	3	0	1	0	**4**
1995	1,420	0	80	0	**1,500**	11	0	1	0	**12**	5	0	1	0	**6**
2000	2,800[1]	0	100[1]	0	**2,900**	11	0	1	0	**12**	45	0	5	0	**50**
2001[1]	3,000	0	200	0	**3,200**	11	0	1	0	**12**	48	0	6	0	**54**
2002[1]	3,200	0	300	0	**3,500**	11	0	1	0	**12**	50	0	8	0	**58**
2005[1]	3,500	0	500	0	**4,300**	11	0	2	0	**13**	60	0	10	0	**70**

Table 10.3.4
Jehovah's Witnesses

	Membership					Churches					Ministers				
	England	Wales	Scotland	N. Ireland	**Total UK**[11]	England	Wales	Scotland	N. Ireland	**Total UK**	England	Wales	Scotland	N. Ireland	**Total UK**[8]
1990	100,412	6,800	7,400	2,000[7]	**116,612**	1,112	77	84	45	**1,318**	10.900	745	808	280	**12,733**
1995	112.425	7,675	8,400	2,500	**131,000**	1,173	82	90	55	**1,400**	12,160	830	900	310	**14,200**
2000[6]	110,567	7,520	8,210	2,700[2]	**128,997**	1,275	89	97	65[2]	**1,526**	10,476	715	775	340[2]	**12,308**
2001[6]	109,288	7,430	8,110	2,700[1]	**127,528**	1,281	89	98	65[1]	**1,533**	10,523	719	780	345[1]	**12,367**
2002[6]	109,778	7,470	8,150	2,700[1]	**128,098**	1,287	90	98	65[1]	**1,540**	10,462	715	775	350[1]	**12,302**
2005[6]	111,620	7,590	8,290	2,900[1]	**130,400**	1,309	91	100	68[1]	**1,568**[2]	10,504	718	778	380[1]	**12,380**

Table 10.3.5
The Lord's Witnesses[9]

	Membership					Churches					Ministers				
	England	Wales	Scotland	N. Ireland	**Total UK**	England	Wales	Scotland	N. Ireland	**Total UK**	England	Wales	Scotland	N. Ireland	**Total UK**
1990	–	–	–	–	–	–	–	–	–	–	–	–	–	–	–
1995	–	–	–	–	–	–	–	–	–	–	–	–	–	–	–
2000	3	0	0	0	**3**[2]	–	–	–	–	–	1	0	0	0	**1**
2001	9[1]	0	0	0	**9**	–	–	–	–	–	1	0	0	0	**1**
2002	15	0	0	0	**15**	–	–	–	–	–	1	0	0	0	**1**
2005[1]	30	0	0	0	**30**	–	–	–	–	–	1	0	0	0	**1**

Table 10.3.6
Philadelphia Church of God[10]

	Membership					Churches					Ministers				
	England	Wales	Scotland	N. Ireland	**Total UK**	England	Wales	Scotland	N. Ireland	**Total UK**	England	Wales	Scotland	N. Ireland	**Total UK**
1990	–	–	–	–	–	–	–	–	–	–	–	–	–	–	–
1995[1]	50	0	0	0	**50**	3	0	0	0	**3**	3	0	0	0	**3**
2000[1]	30	0	0	0	**30**	3	0	0	0	**3**	3	0	0	0	**3**
2001[1]	28	0	0	0	**28**	3	0	0	0	**3**	3	0	0	0	**3**
2002[1]	26	0	0	0	**26**	3	0	0	0	**3**	3	0	0	0	**3**
2005[1]	20	0	0	0	**20**	3	0	0	0	**3**	3	0	0	0	**3**

Page 10.2

1 Estimate

2 Revised figure

3 Christadelphian churches are known as Ecclesias

4 No full-time ministers

5 As the Christian Science Church has a bye-law forbidding publication of membership numbers, the membership figures are all estimated. Members and churches are pro rata to Practitioners.

6 The leaders are known as Practitioners, the majority of whom are women.

7 An offshoot of the Worldwide Church of God; they believe the Holy Spirit is divine but not part of the Godhead.

8 While the Church "firmly holds to a trinity of God, Christ and the Holy Spirit", it is included here because the book of Mormon is regarded as containing inspired writings which provide an added testimony to the divinity of Christ.

9 Country split pro rata to 1990 figures.

10 Leaders are called Bishops, one per congregation. 2002 figure excludes 44 State Presidents (one each in charge of a Diocese).

11 Formerly The Re-organised Church of Latter Day Saints.

Page 10.3

1 Estimate

2 Revised figure

3 Previously called the Children of God which officially disbanded in 1978. The Family is Trinitarian but is included here because of its close association with the writings of its founder, David Berg (who died in the late 1990s), and its former controversial outreach methods such as "Flirty Fishing". Worldwide in 2002 they had 8,048 Charter (full-time) members of 91 nationalities and 3,249 Fellow (part-time) members *(continues overleaf)*

10.4 Non-Trinitarian Churches (continued)

Table 10.4.1
Scientology, Church of[11]

	MEMBERSHIP England	Wales	Scotland	N. Ireland	Total UK	CHURCHES England	Wales	Scotland	N. Ireland	Total UK	MINISTERS England	Wales	Scotland	N. Ireland	Total UK
1990	68,000	1,000	5,000	1,000	**75,000**	11	0	1	1	**13**	647	1	50	2	**700**
1995	113,500	1,300	6,000	1,000	**121,800**	14	1	1	1	**17**	700	1	36	2	**739**
2000[1]	134,000	1,600	7,500	1,300	**144,400**	14	1	1	1	**17**	719	2	37	2	**760**
2001[1]	139,200	1,650	7,800	1,350	**150,000**	14	1	1	1	**17**	733	2	38	2	**775**
2002[1]	143,800	1,700	8,100	1,400	**155,000**	14	1	1	1	**17**	747	2	39	2	**790**
2005[1]	153,100	1,800	8,600	1,500	**165,000**	14	1	1	1	**17**	804	2	42	2	**850**

Table 10.4.2
Spiritualists[3]

	MEMBERSHIP England	Wales	Scotland	N. Ireland	Total UK	CHURCHES England	Wales	Scotland	N. Ireland	Total UK	MINISTERS England	Wales	Scotland	N. Ireland	Total UK
1990	43,469[1]	460[1]	925[1]	146[4]	**45,000**	505	22	21	2	**550**	289	9	9	3	**310**
1995	38,630	400	800	170	**40,000**[1]	491	21	20	3	**535**	250	8	8	4	**270**
2000[1]	35,000	370	745	200	**36,315**	478[2]	20	19	3	**520**[2]	239[2]	8	8	5	**260**
2001[1]	33,710	350	740	200	**35,000**	474	20	19	3	**516**	237	8	8	5	**258**
2002[1]	32,740	330	730	200	**34,000**	470	20	19	3	**512**	235	8	8	5	**256**
2005[1]	28,780	300	700	220	**30,000**[2]	461	18	18	3	**500**[2]	231	7	7	5	**250**

Table 10.4.3
Swedenborgian New Church[5]

	MEMBERSHIP England	Wales	Scotland	N. Ireland	Total UK	CHURCHES England	Wales	Scotland	N. Ireland	Total UK	MINISTERS England	Wales	Scotland	N. Ireland	Total UK
1990	1,597	15	100	0	**1,712**	34	1	1	0	**36**	15	0	1	0	**16**
1995	1,382	15[1]	100[1]	0	**1,497**	30[1]	1	1	0	**32**	14	0	1	0	**15**
2000	1,180	12[1]	100[1]	0	**1,292**	26[1]	1	1	0	**28**	14[1]	0	1	0	**15**
2001	1,091[1]	12[1]	95[1]	0	**1,198**	25[1]	1	1	0	**27**	10[1]	0	1	0	**11**
2002	1,046[1]	12[1]	90[1]	0	**1,148**	25[1]	1	1	0	**27**	9[1]	0	1	0	**10**
2005[1]	970	10	70	0	**1,050**	24	1	1	0	**26**	10	0	1	0	**11**

Table 10.4.4
Theosophists[6]

	MEMBERSHIP England	Wales	Scotland	N. Ireland	Total UK	CHURCHES England	Wales	Scotland	N. Ireland	Total UK	MINISTERS England	Wales	Scotland	N. Ireland	Total UK[7]
1990[2]	2,000	80[2]	120[2]	50	**2,250**	52[2]	1[2]	2[2]	1	**56**	–	–	–	–	–
1995	1,940	50[2]	100[2]	50	**2,140**	50[2]	1[2]	2[2]	1	**54**	–	–	–	–	–
2000[1]	1,800	50	95	55	**2,000**	47	1	2	1	**51**	–	–	–	–	–
2001[1]	1,750	50	90	60	**1,950**	46	1	2	1	**50**	–	–	–	–	–
2002[1]	1,710	45	85	60	**1,900**	45	1	2	1	**49**	–	–	–	–	–
2005[1]	1,640	30	70	60	**1,800**	41	1	2	1	**45**[2]	–	–	–	–	–

Table 10.4.5
Unification Church[8]

	MEMBERSHIP England	Wales	Scotland	N. Ireland	Total UK	CHURCHES England	Wales	Scotland	N. Ireland	Total UK	MINISTERS England	Wales	Scotland	N. Ireland	Total UK
1990	300	20	30	35[4]	**385**[9]	7[2]	1	1[2]	1	**10**	22[2]	2	2	1[2]	**27**
1995[1]	300	20	30	40	**390**	7[2]	1	1[2]	1	**10**	22[2]	2	2	1[2]	**27**
2000[2]	750	50	75	125	**1,000**	12	1	2	2	**17**	22	2	2	1	**27**
2001[1]	830	50	80	140	**1,100**	12	1	2	1	**17**	22	2	2	1	**27**
2002[1]	900	50	100	150	**1,200**	12	1	2	1	**17**	22	2	2	1	**27**
2005[1]	1,230	60	130	180	**1,600**	14	1	3	1	**20**	23	3	3	1	**30**

Table 10.4.6
Unitarian and Free Christian Churches[8]

	MEMBERSHIP England	Wales	Scotland	N. Ireland	Total UK	CHURCHES England	Wales	Scotland	N. Ireland	Total UK	MINISTERS England	Wales	Scotland	N. Ireland	Total UK
1990	6,775[1]	1,370[1]	355[1]	0	**8,500**	182	30	4	0	**216**	129[1]	10[1]	4[1]	10[1]	**153**
1995	5,340	1,080	280	0	**6,700**	158	22	4	0	**184**	50	5	3	9	**67**
2000	4,589	1,000	271	0	**5,860**	158	23	4	0	**185**	53[1]	5	3	9	**70**
2001	4,350	1,000[1]	250[1]	0	**5,550**	155	23	4	0	**182**	53[1]	5[1]	3[1]	9[1]	**70**
2002	4,200	975[1]	225[1]	0	**5,300**	157	22	4	0	**183**	53[1]	5[1]	3[1]	9[1]	**70**
2005	3,300	900	200	0	**4,400**[1]	158	22	4	0	**184**	55	5	3	9	**72**

living in 1,045 homes, with 79,060 Active (congregational) members. See www.thefamilyeurope.org

[4] Began in 1995 as a breakaway group of the Worldwide Church of God.

[5] Formerly known as the London Church of Christ. Although Trinitarian the International Church of Christ is included here because it teaches that salvation is only through their church, as well as through Christ.

[6] Country division in Great Britain pro rata to average to estimates of 1990 and 1995.

[7] Northern Ireland Census figure.

[8] Jehovah's Witnesses do not have paid clergy; these figures represent the number of congregational elders.

[9] The Lord's Witnesses were established separately from the Jehovah's Witnesses in 1998. Their ministry is mainly via their website, though they meet once a week for research purposes.

[10] Began in 1994 as a breakaway group of the Worldwide Church of God.

[11] Membership is the number of Witnesses who have submitted reports regarding their preaching activities.

Page 10.4

[1] Estimate

[2] Revised figure

[3] A summation of the figures of the Greater World Christian Spiritual Association (670 members in 1990 but with total attendance of 9,000), the Spiritual Association of Great Britain (of which there is 1 assembly in London with approximately 65 mediums), and other groups.

[4] Northern Ireland Census figure.

[5] Also known as the General Conference of the New Church. Although Trinitarian, it is included because members worship the Lord Jesus Christ as One God in whom is a trinity of Father, Son and Holy Spirit rather than the God in three persons of the traditional creeds.

	MEMBERSHIP					CHURCHES					MINISTERS				
Table 10.5.1 United Church of God															
	England	Wales	Scotland	N. Ireland	**Total UK**	England	Wales	Scotland	N. Ireland	**Total UK**	England	Wales	Scotland	N. Ireland	**Total UK**
1990	–	–	–	–	–	–	–	–	–	–	–	–	–	–	–
1995	–	–	–	–	–	–	–	–	–	–	–	–	–	–	–
2000[1]	160	0	20	20	**200**	8	0	1	1	**10**	6	0	1	1	**8**
2001[1]	160	0	20	20	**200**	8	0	1	1	**10**	6	0	1	1	**8**
2002[1]	160	0	20	20	**200**	8	0	1	1	**10**	6	0	1	1	**8**
2005[1]	200	0	25	25	**250**	8	0	1	1	**10**	6	0	1	1	**8**
Table 9.5.2 The Way															
	England	Wales	Scotland	N. Ireland	**Total UK**	England	Wales	Scotland	N. Ireland	**Total UK**	England	Wales	Scotland	N. Ireland	**Total UK**
1990	480	40	55	25	**600**	36	3	4	2	**25**	5	0	1	0	**6**
1995	580	50	65	30	**725**	39	3	4	2	**48**	6	0	1	0	**7**
2000[1]	700	60	80	35	**875**	49	3	4	2	**58**	7	0	1	0	**8**
2001[1]	720	60	85	35	**900**	50	3	4	2	**59**	7	0	1	0	**8**
2002[1]	735	65	85	40	**925**	51	3	4	2	**60**	7	0	1	0	**8**
2005[1]	775	75	100	50	**1,000**	56	3	4	2	**65**	8	0	1	0	**9**
Table 10.5.3 Other Non-Trinitarian Churches[4]															
	England	Wales	Scotland	N. Ireland	**Total UK**	England	Wales	Scotland	N. Ireland	**Total UK**	England	Wales	Scotland	N. Ireland	**Total UK**
1990	7,500	1,000	1,000	500	**10,000**	75	10	10	5	**100**	375	50	50	25	**500**
1995	7,500	1,000	1,000	500	**10,000**	75	10	10	5	**100**	375	50	50	25	**500**
2000	7,500	1,000	1,000	500	**10,000**	75	10	10	5	**100**	375	50	50	25	**500**
2001	7,500	1,000	1,000	500	**10,000**	75	10	10	5	**100**	375	50	50	25	**500**
2002	7,500	1,000	1,000	500	**10,000**	75	10	10	5	**100**	375	50	50	25	**500**
2005	7,500	1,000	1,000	500	**10,000**	75	10	10	5	**100**	375	50	50	25	**500**

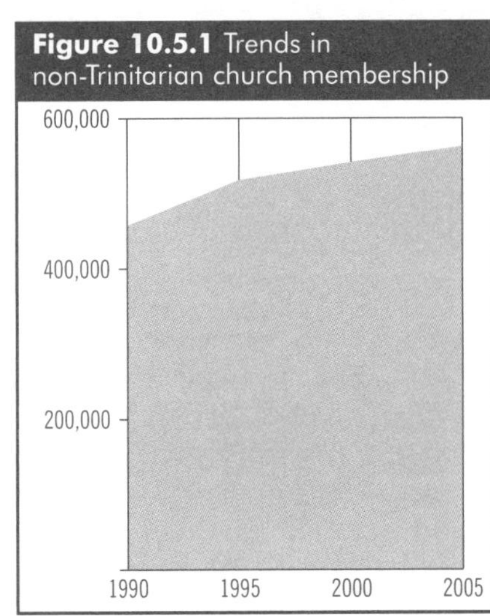

Figure 10.5.1 Trends in non-Trinitarian church membership

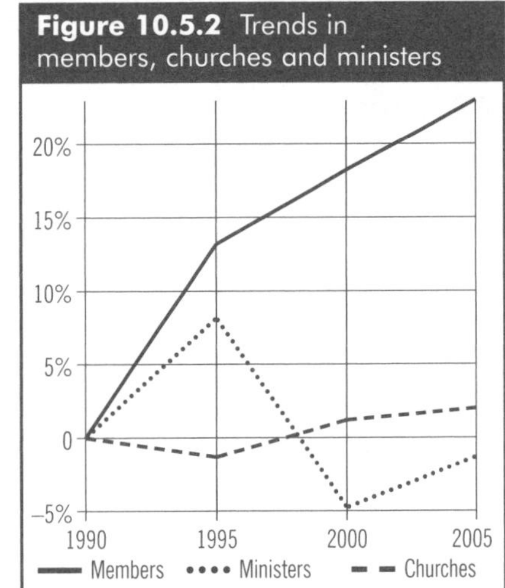

Figure 10.5.2 Trends in members, churches and ministers

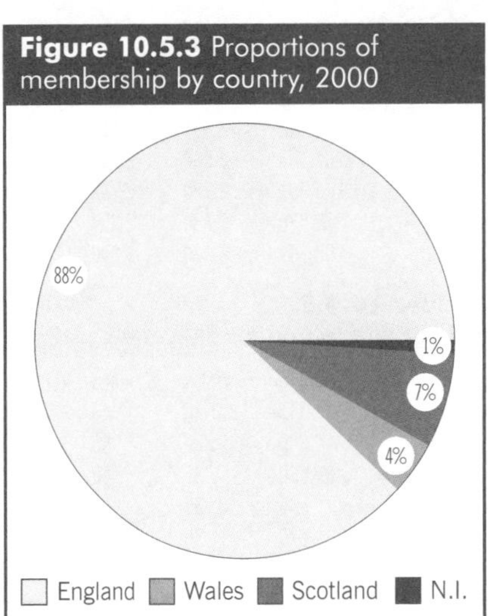

Figure 10.5.3 Proportions of membership by country, 2000

[6] These figures cover the United Lodge of Theosophists (with 35 members in 1990), plus the Theosophical Societies of England (1,500 members in 1990), Wales and Scotland, with estimates for N. Ireland.
[7] No full-time ministers.
[8] Full title is the Family Federation for World Peace and Unification (FFWPU), sometimes known as the "Moonies" after their founder, Rev S M Moon.
[9] Excluding an estimated 8,000 "associate" members and 100 "practicising" members given in *New Religious Movements* by Dr Eileen Barker, HMSO 1989.
[10] Unitarians have strong links with the Non-Subscribing Presbyterian Church of Ireland in which some of their members serve.
[11] Since 10th December 1996 Scientology has been officially recognised as a religion by the Home Office replacing its previous status as a cult.

Page 10.5
[1] Estimate
[2] Revised figure
[3] Began in 1996 as a breakaway group of the Worldwide Church of God with 150 members, 10 churches and 8 ministers.
[4] All estimated but includes the Local Church Movement and the True Jesus Church.

David Barrett defines "Non-Trinitarian" (or "Marginal") church members as "affiliated to bodies holding mainstream Christian doctrines except on the nature of Christ, and existence of the Trinity; also professing a second source of revelation in addition to the Bible".

The number of Non-Trinitarian members is increasing – up 23% in the 15 years 1990 to 2005, or +1.4% a year **(Figure 10.5.1)**, against a decline of –1.1% a year in the Trinitarian churches **(Figure 2.21.1)**. If the two were added together, non-Trinitarian church members would be 9% of the total in 2002.

The number of non-Trinitarian churches is also increasing, albeit at a relatively slow rate **(Figure 10.5.2)**. This contrasts with the decline in the number of Trinitarian churches. Between 1990 and 2005 the number of non-Trinitarian churches grew 2% against a 3% drop in Trinitarian **(Table 2.21)**.

The number of non-Trinitarian ministers however is decreasing, at the rate of –0.25% a year, virtually identical to the –0.26% decline a year in Trinitarian leadership (both measured 1990 to 2005).

Figure 10.5.3 shows that their spread over the UK is much more proportional to the general population than the Trinitarian churches (see **Figure 2.21.4**), showing scant regard for church history!

10.6 Other Religions

Table 10.6.1
Total Other Religions and New Religious Movements

	ACTIVE MEMBERS					GROUPS					LEADERS				
	England	Wales	Scotland	N. Ireland	**Total UK**	England	Wales	Scotland	N. Ireland	**Total UK**	England	Wales	Scotland	N. Ireland	**Total UK**
1990	984,162	14,306	32,312	2,114	**1,032,894**	1,759	66	100	19	**1,944**	4,438	115	203	29	**4,785**
1995	1,192,987	17,891	39,082	2,408	**1,252,368**	2,295	87	142	28	**2,552**	5,124	141	242	34	**5,541**
2000	1,402,826	21,461	46,364	2,702	**1,473,353**	2,667	105	176	38	**2,986**	5,790	163	280	39	**6,272**
2001	1,444,697	22,217	47,877	2,846	**1,517,637**	2,748	107	181	42	**3,078**	5,925	165	289	41	**6,420**
2002	1,485,141	22,931	49,251	2,959	**1,560,282**	2,835	110	188	46	**3,179**	6,071	172	299	42	**6,584**
2005	1,610,638	25,320	53,889	3,253	**1,693,100**	2,979	118	201	49	**3,347**	6,508	186	315	49	**7,058**

Table 10.6.2
Bahá'ís

	England	Wales	Scotland	N. Ireland	**Total UK**	England	Wales	Scotland	N. Ireland	**Total UK**[5]	England	Wales	Scotland	N. Ireland	**Total UK**
1990	4,025	235	421	319[3]	**5,000**	98[7]	11[7]	15[7]	6[7]	**130**[7]	–	–	–	–	–
1995	4,360	280	510	350	**5,500**	232	23[7]	38[7]	13[7]	**306**[6]	–	–	–	–	–
2000[1]	4,800	300	550	350	**6,000**	285	35	61	20	**401**[18]	–	–	–	–	–
2001[1]	4,850	300	550	350	**6,050**	337	37	65	24	**463**	–	–	–	–	–
2002	4,900	300	550	350	**6,100**[1]	390	39	69	28	**526**	–	–	–	–	–
2005[1]	4,950	350	600	400	**6,300**	427	43	75	31	**576**	–	–	–	–	–

Table 10.6.3
Buddhists

	England	Wales	Scotland	N. Ireland	**Total UK**	England	Wales	Scotland	N. Ireland	**Total UK**	England	Wales	Scotland	N. Ireland	**Total UK**
1990[12]	28,715	1,120	1,410	255[3]	**31,500**[9]	216[7]	20[7]	20[7]	2[7]	**258**[10]	320[7]	12[7]	16[7]	2[7]	**350**
1995[1]	47,265	1,840	2,320	260	**51,685**	239	19	18	2	**278**[11]	366	14	18	2	**400**
2000[1]	65,575	2,550	3,220	265	**71,610**	261	18	17	2	**298**[18]	421	16	21	2	**460**[7]
2001[8]	69,523	2,704	3,415	266	**75,908**	265	18	17	2	**302**	430	17	21	2	**470**
2002[1]	73,283	2,850	3,600	267	**80,000**	269	18	17	2	**306**	449	17	22	2	**490**
2005[1]	84,310	3,280	4,140	270	**92,000**	280	18	18	2	**318**	485	19	24	2	**530**[7]

Table 10.6.4
Hindus

	England	Wales	Scotland	N. Ireland	**Total UK**	England	Wales	Scotland	N. Ireland	**Total UK**	England	Wales	Scotland	N. Ireland	**Total UK**
1990[13]	205,484	2,045	2,100	371[3]	**210,000**	137[7]	1[7]	2[7]	0[7]	**140**	147[7]	1[7]	2[7]	0[7]	**150**
1995[1]	236,341	2,350	2,415	394	**241,500**	158	1	2	0	**161**[14]	147	1	2	0	**150**
2000[1]	267,193	2,660	2,730	417	**273,000**	315[16]	5	3	2	**325**[18]	157	1	2	0	**160**[7]
2001[8]	273,491	2,720	2,782	422	**279,405**	320	5	3	2	**330**	157	1	2	0	**160**
2002[1]	279,636	2,780	2,857	427	**285,700**	325	5	3	2	**335**	157	1	2	0	**160**
2005[1]	298,540	2,970	3,050	440	**305,000**	340	5	3	2	**350**	167	1	2	0	**170**[7]

Table 10.6.5
ISKCON (International Society of Krishna Consciousness)[15]

	England	Wales	Scotland	N. Ireland	**Total UK**	England	Wales	Scotland	N. Ireland	**Total UK**	England	Wales	Scotland	N. Ireland	**Total UK**
1990	335	20	40	10	**425**	3	0	0	0	**3**	338	18	36	8	**400**
1995[1]	505	30	55	10	**600**	5	1	1	0	**7**	421	25	45	9	**500**
2000[1]	560	35	60	15	**670**	8	2	1	1	**12**	480	28	51	11	**570**
2001[1]	565	35	60	15	**675**	9	2	1	1	**13**	484	28	52	11	**575**
2002[1]	570	35	60	15	**680**	10	2	2	1	**15**	488	28	53	11	**580**
2005[1]	570	40	70	20	**700**	15	2	2	1	**20**	505	29	54	12	**600**

[1] Estimate

[2] The National Spiritual Assembly of the Bahá'ís of the United Kingdom has no clergy and no individuals in positions of personal leadership. The administration of the community lies in the hands of elected bodies at local, national and international levels.

[3] Northern Ireland Census figure 1991.

[4] Based on Religion: Aspects of Britain, HMSO, 1992.

[5] Includes both Local Spiritual Assemblies (comprising a community of at least 9 members 21 and over) and Local Groups (where there are insufficient numbers to form a Spiritual Assembly).

[6] Including 41 Dharma Centres, all assumed to be in England. Religions in the UK: A Multi-Faith Directory, 1993 gives 135 Groups in England, 16 in Wales, 23 in Scotland and 8 in N Ireland.

[7] Revised figure

[8] Active members are taken as half the Community figure given in the 2001 Population Census, with earlier figures and country proportions revised as appropriate.

[9] Based on survey of all Buddhist groups in 1985.

[10] M Baumann states there were 213 Buddhist centres and groups in Great Britain in 1991 in Journal of Contemporary Religion, Vol 10, No 1, 1995, but *Religions in the UK: A Multi-Faith Directory,* 1993 lists 301.

[11] Chris Forster in Planting for a Harvest (Challenge 2000, 1995) gives a total of 509 groups of "Buddhist type religions" in 1994 but the 1997 *Religions in the UK: A Multi-Faith Directory* lists only 117 centres, viharas, monasteries and other publicly accessible buildings for worship.

[12] Including approximately 5,000 Soka Gakkai (Nichiren Shoshu) members, 5,000 lay and 300 ordained members of Friends of the Western Buddhist Order and 15,000 practitioners of Tibetan Buddhism (so the Office of Tibet) given in *Religion Today,* Volume 8, Number 2, Spring 1993.

[13] Including perhaps 10,000 followers of Satya Sai Baba (from *The Spirit of Hinduism,* Dr David Burnett, Monarch, 1992).

[14] *Religions in the UK: A Multi-Faith Directory,* 1997.

[15] The "Hare Krishna" Movement.

[16] Of which 121 are places of worship (*Religions in the UK,* 2001).

[17] If the 2000 figures are typical, these groups are about double the number of places of worship. In 2000 there were 129 worship centres in England, 10 in Wales, 8 in Scotland, and 1 in Northern Ireland (Religions in the UK, 2001).

[18] *Religions in the UK, Directory 2001–03* lists all these Groups.

[19] Total of **Tables 10.6.2–5, 10.7.1–5** and **10.8.1–4.**

ACTIVE MEMBERS | GROUPS | LEADERS

Table 10.7.1
Jains

	Active members					Groups					Leaders				
	England	Wales	Scotland	N. Ireland	**Total UK[4]**	England	Wales	Scotland	N. Ireland	**Total UK**	England	Wales	Scotland	N. Ireland	**Total UK**
1990	10,000	0	0	0	**10,000[2]**	12	0	0	0	**12**	–	–	–	–	–
1995[3]	14,000	0	0	0	**14,000[5]**	15	0	0	0	**15**	–	–	–	–	–
2000[1]	15,000	0	0	0	**15,000**	16	0	0	0	**16**	–	–	–	–	–
2001[1]	15,000	0	0	0	**15,000**	16	0	0	0	**16**	–	–	–	–	–
2002[1]	15,000	0	0	0	**15,000**	16	0	0	0	**16**	–	–	–	–	–
2005[1]	17,000	0	0	0	**17,000**	18	0	0	0	**18**	–	–	–	–	–

Table 10.7.2
Jews

	Active members					Groups					Leaders				
	England	Wales	Scotland	N. Ireland	**Total UK[6]**	England	Wales	Scotland	N. Ireland	**Total UK**	England	Wales	Scotland	N. Ireland	**Total UK**
1990	97,000	745	3,274	220	**101,239**	339[1]	6[1]	10[1]	1	**356**	424[1]	5[1]	10[1]	1[1]	**440**
1995	90,561	653	2,341	129	**93,684**	349	5	10	1	**365**	424[1]	5[1]	10[1]	1[1]	**440**
2000[1]	86,092	580	2,000	128	**88,800**	345	5	11	1	**362**	414	5	10[1]	1	**430**
2001	85,149	561	1,952	128	**87,790**	345	5	11	1	**362**	414[1]	5[1]	10[1]	1[1]	**430**
2002[1]	83,661	550	1,918	126	**86,255**	345	5	11	1	**362**	414	5	10	1	**430**
2005[1]	80,150	530	1,840	120	**82,640**	343	5	11	1	**360**	405	5	9	1	**430**

Table 10.7.3
Muslims[7, 11]

	Active members					Groups					Leaders				
	England	Wales	Scotland	N. Ireland	**Total UK**	England	Wales	Scotland	N. Ireland	**Total UK[12]**	England	Wales	Scotland	N. Ireland	**Total UK[13]**
1990[8]	474,507	6,765	13,242	489[9]	**495,000**	322	10	16	2	**350**	2,370	45	80	5	**2,500**
1995	605,387[1]	8,631[1]	16,895[1]	706[1]	**631,619**	546	16	23	2	**587**	2,750[1]	50[1]	95[1]	5[1]	**2,900**
2000[1]	736,267	10,497	20,547	927	**768,238**	567[18]	17[18]	26	2	**612**	3,150	60	110	5	**3,325**
2001[4]	762,444	10,870	21,278	971	**795,563**	571[1]	17[1]	26[1]	2[1]	**616**	3,230	60	115	5	**3,410**
2002[1]	788,621	11,243	22,009	1,015	**822,888**	575	18	27	2	**622**	3,310	65	120	5	**3,500**
2005[1]	867,300	12,400	24,200	1,100	**905,000**	590	18	27	2	**640**	3,550	70	125	5	**3,750**

Table 10.7.4
Satanists[14, 15, 16, 17]

	Active members					Groups					Leaders				
	England	Wales	Scotland	N. Ireland	**Total UK**	England	Wales	Scotland	N. Ireland	**Total UK**	England	Wales	Scotland	N. Ireland	**Total UK**
1990[1]	235	14	25	6	**280**	30	2	3	1	**35**	8	1	1	0	**10**
1995[1]	275	17	30	8	**330**	32	2	3	1	**38**	12	1	1	0	**14**
2000[5]	315	20	35	10	**380**	34	2	4	1	**41**	14	1	1	0	**16**
2001[1]	322	21	37	10	**390**	35	2	4	1	**42**	15	1	1	0	**17**
2002[1]	330	22	38	10	**400**	37	2	4	1	**44**	16	1	1	1	**18**
2005[1]	350	25	40	10	**425**	40	3	5	1	**49**	16	1	2	1	**20**

Table 10.7.5
School of Meditation

	Active members					Groups					Leaders				
	England	Wales	Scotland	N. Ireland	**Total UK[19]**	England	Wales	Scotland	N. Ireland	**Total UK**	England	Wales	Scotland	N. Ireland	**Total UK**
1990[1]	6,275	80	155	40	**7,000**	2	0	0	0	**2**	97	1	2	0	**100**
1995[1]	8,650	100	200	50	**9,000**	2	0	0	0	**2**	114	2	3	1	**120**
2000[1]	10,570	125	250	55	**11,000**	2	0	0	0	**2**	114	2	3	1	**120**
2001[1]	10,770	125	250	55	**11,200**	2	0	0	0	**2**	116	2	3	1	**122**
2002[1]	10,940	130	270	60	**11,400**	2	0	0	0	**2**	118	2	3	1	**124**
2005[1]	11,480	150	300	70	**12,000**	2	0	0	0	**2**	121	3	4	2	**130**

[1] Estimate
[2] Based on *Religion: Aspects in Britain,* HMSO, 1992.
[3] *Religions in the UK: A Multi-Faith Directory,* 1997 gives a community figure of 25-30,000 and lists 3 temples and 12 local groups where worship takes place. The 2001 Directory gives 4 temples.
[4] Active members are taken as half the Community figure given in the 2001 Population Census, with earlier figures and country proportions revised as appropriate.
[5] Revised figure
[6] Heads of Households.
[7] Including non-South Asians.
[8] Attendance at one of the main Muslim festivals in Great Britain was 50% of the community, according to a survey by Dr Jim Holway, reported in the 1987/88 edition of the *UK Christian Handbook.*
[9] Half the figure given in the 1991 Northern Ireland Population census.
[10] Community taken as 990,000, but country figures pro rata to 2001, except Northern Ireland.
[11] Assumed to include approximately 8,000 members of the Ahmadiyya Movement, with 40 groups and up to 230 leaders.
[12] Registered mosques, but many other buildings are used for worship. In 1990, there 1,020 groups meeting; in 1995 some 800 buildings were used, of which 200 were houses.
[13] Imams.
[14] Taken as 10% of the community, based on the estimated 4,000 in 2002 according to Vexen Crabtree (www.dpjs.co.uk).
[15] Including members of the Temple of Set, Northern Order of the Prince, Society of the Dark Lily and Order of the Nine Angels. The Church of Satan website is ChurchOfSatan.com.
[16] Country breakdown pro rata to general population.
[17] A University of Newcastle survey suggested there were 50,000 witches in the UK (*Church Times* article 7th July 2000).
[18] 1999 figure, from *Religions in the UK,* 2001.
[19] Estimates of Continuing Practitioners, not numbers enrolling.

10.8 Other Religions (continued)

Table 10.8.1
Sikhs

	ACTIVE MEMBERS					GROUPS					LEADERS				
	England	Wales	Scotland	N. Ireland	**Total UK**	England	Wales	Scotland	N. Ireland	**Total UK**[7]	England	Wales	Scotland	N. Ireland	**Total UK**
1990[3]	121,727	750	2,444	79[4]	**125,000**[5]	142	2	5	0[1]	**149**	171[1]	3[1]	6[1]	0[1]	**180**
1995[1]	140,793	867	2,827	93	**144,580**[6]	160[3]	2[3]	11	1	**174**[3]	185	4	10	1	**200**
2000[1]	159,860	985	3,208	107	**164,160**	177[8]	3[8]	11	1	**192**	202	5	12	1	**220**
2001[2]	163,672	1,008	3,286	109	**168,075**	180[1]	3[1]	11[1]	1[1]	**195**	205[1]	5[1]	12[1]	1[1]	**223**
2002[1]	167,500	1,030	3,359	111	**172,000**	183	3	11	1	**198**	207	5	13	1	**226**
2005[1]	179,185	1,100	3,600	115	**184,000**	192	3	12	1	**208**	215	5	14	1	**235**

Table 10.8.2
Zoroastrians

	ACTIVE MEMBERS					GROUPS					LEADERS				
	England	Wales	Scotland	N. Ireland	**Total UK**[2]	England	Wales	Scotland	N. Ireland	**Total UK**[11]	England	Wales	Scotland	N. Ireland	**Total UK**
1990[1]	2,145	125	225	5[4]	**2,500**[9]	1	0	0	0	**1**	–	–	–	–	–
1995[3]	2,575	150	270	5	**3,000**[10]	1	0	0	0	**1**	–	–	–	–	–
2000[1]	2,730	165	300	5	**3,200**	1	0	0	0	**1**	–	–	–	–	–
2001[1]	2,730	165	300	5	**3,200**	1	0	0	0	**1**	–	–	–	–	–
2002[1]	2,730	165	300	5	**3,200**	1	0	0	0	**1**	–	–	–	–	–
2005[1]	2,800	175	320	5	**3,300**	1	0	0	0	**1**	–	–	–	–	–

Table 10.8.3
Other Religions

	ACTIVE MEMBERS					GROUPS					LEADERS				
	England	Wales	Scotland	N. Ireland	**Total UK**	England	Wales	Scotland	N. Ireland	**Total UK**	England	Wales	Scotland	N. Ireland	**Total UK**
1990[3]	24,920	1,860	8,130	90	**35,000**	219[1]	3[1]	11[1]	1[1]	**234**	202[1]	12[1]	22[1]	4[1]	**240**
1995[1]	30,600	2,300	10,000	100	**43,000**	269	4	13	1	**287**	235	15	25	5	**280**
2000[1]	36,300	2,700	11,900	100	**51,000**	320[8]	4[8]	16[1]	1[1]	**341**	270	16	29	5	**320**
2001[2]	37,669	2,808	12,290	137	**52,904**	330	4	17	1	**352**	279	16	30	5	**330**
2002[1]	38,500	2,860	12,500	140	**54,000**	340	4	18	1	**363**	287	17	31	5	**340**
2005[1]	42,000	3,150	13,700	150	**59,000**	370	4	20	1	**395**	304	18	33	5	**360**

Table 10.8.4
Total New Religious Movements[12]

	ACTIVE MEMBERS					GROUPS					LEADERS				
	England	Wales	Scotland	N. Ireland	**Total UK**	England	Wales	Scotland	N. Ireland	**Total UK**	England	Wales	Scotland	N. Ireland	**Total UK**
1990	8,794	547	846	233	**10,420**	238	11	19	6	**274**	361	17	28	9	**415**
1995	11,675	673	1,219	303	**13,870**	287	14	23	7	**331**	470	24	33	10	**537**
2000	17,564	844	1,564	323	**20,295**	336	14	26	7	**383**	568	29	41	13	**651**
2001	18,512	900	1,677	378	**21,467**	337	14	26	7	**384**	595	30	43	15	**683**
2002	19,470	966	1,790	433	**22,659**	342	14	26	7	**389**	625	31	44	15	**715**
2005	22,003	1,150	2,029	553	**25,735**	361	17	26	6	**410**	740	35	48	20	**843**

Figure 10.8.1 Trends in Other Religions active members

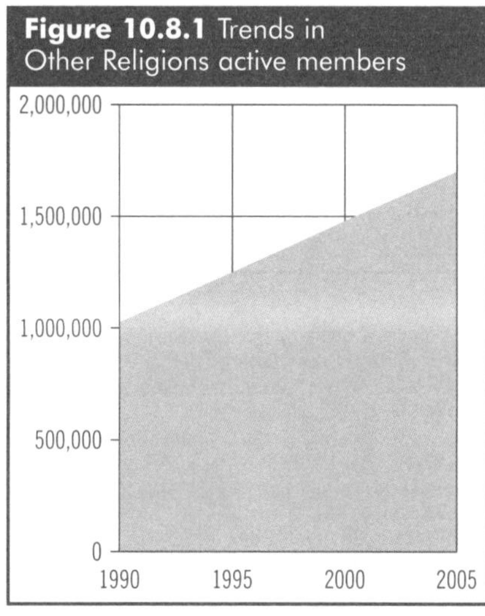

Figure 10.8.2 Trends in active members, groups and leaders

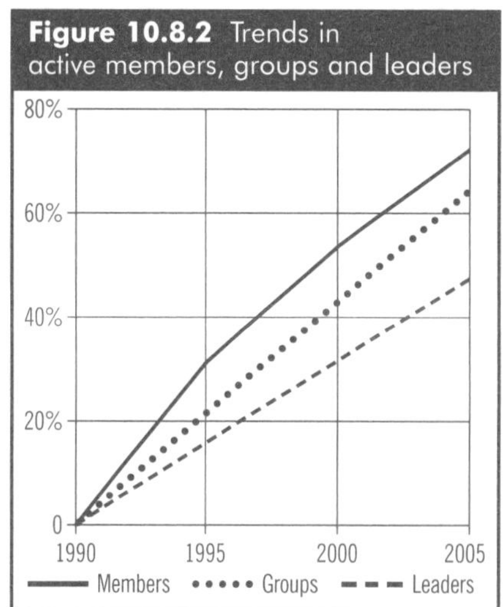

Figure 10.8.3 Proportions of active members by country, 2001

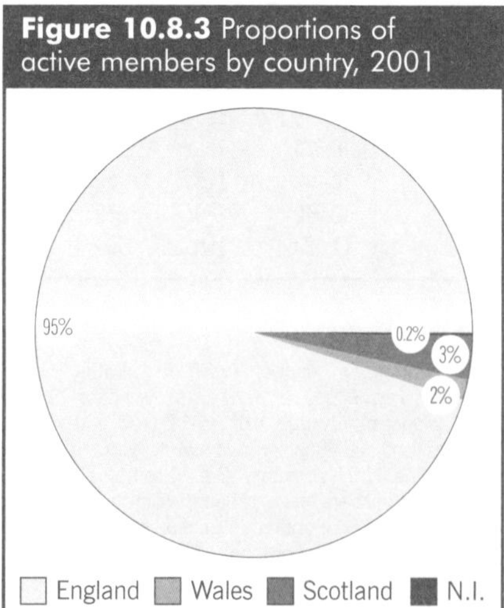

The religions in the UK other than Christianity are collectively growing much faster than Christianity (which is declining) whether this is measured by membership, groups or churches, leaders or ministers. Compare **Figures 2.21.1** and **10.8.1**.

At the same time, however, Christianity is much more widely spread across the UK than are the other religions, largely owing to the dominance of Muslims and Hindus in certain cities of England. Compare **Figures 2.21.4** and **10.8.3.**

Active membership for the other religions together has grown 64% in the period 1990 to 2005, a rate of 3.3% a year, which is fast. In 2001, their active members were 2.7% of the population, marginally more than half the total 5.24% their community forms of the UK population **(Table 2.3.2).**

(For footnotes, please see **Page 10.10**)

Table 10.9.1 Brahma Kumanis[5]	ACTIVE MEMBERS					GROUPS					LEADERS				
	England	Wales	Scotland	N. Ireland	**Total UK**	England	Wales	Scotland	N. Ireland	**Total UK**	England	Wales	Scotland	N. Ireland	**Total UK**
1990[1]	755	45	80	20	**900**	32	2	3	1	**38**	50	3	6	1	**60**
1995[1]	840	50	90	20	**1,000**	38	2	4	1	**45**	59	4	6	1	**70**
2000[1]	925	55	100	20	**1,100**	43	2	4	1	**50**	67	4	8	1	**80**
2001[1]	930	55	100	25	**1,110**	44	2	4	1	**51**	68	4	9	1	**82**
2002[1]	940	60	100	30	**1,130**	45	2	4	1	**52**	70	4	9	1	**84**
2005[1]	990	65	110	35	**1,200**	48	2	4	1	**55**	74	5	10	1	**90**

Table 10.9.2 Creme[7]	ACTIVE MEMBERS					GROUPS					LEADERS				
	England	Wales	Scotland	N. Ireland	**Total UK**	England	Wales	Scotland	N. Ireland	**Total UK**	England	Wales	Scotland	N. Ireland	**Total UK**
1990[1]	315	20	35	5	**375**	21	1	2	1	**25**	15	1	2	0	**18**
1995[1]	380	20	40	10	**450**	29	2	3	1	**35**	21	1	2	1	**25**
2000[3]	350	20	40	10	**420**	27	2	3	1	**33**	20	1	2	1	**24**
2001[1]	350	20	40	10	**420**	25	2	3	1	**31**	20	1	2	1	**24**
2002[1]	350	20	40	10	**420**	25	2	3	1	**31**	20	1	2	1	**24**
2005[1]	300	10	30	10	**350**	22	2	2	0	**26**	18	1	1	1	**21**

Table 10.9.3 Eckankar[9]	ACTIVE MEMBERS					GROUPS					LEADERS				
	England	Wales	Scotland	N. Ireland	**Total UK**	England	Wales	Scotland	N. Ireland	**Total UK**	England	Wales	Scotland	N. Ireland	**Total UK**
1990[1]	295	20	30	5	**350**	22	1	2	1	**26**	88	5	10	2	**105**
1995[1]	335	20	35	10	**400**	23	1	2	1	**27**	92	6	10	2	**110**
2000[3]	350	20	40	10	**420**	24	1	2	1	**28**	94	6	11	2	**113**
2001[1]	350	20	40	10	**420**	24	1	2	1	**28**	94	6	11	2	**113**
2002[1]	350	20	40	10	**420**	24	1	2	1	**28**	94	6	11	2	**113**
2005[1]	365	20	45	10	**440**	25	1	2	1	**29**	95	6	12	2	**115**

Table 10.9.4 Elan Vital[10]	ACTIVE MEMBERS					GROUPS					LEADERS				
	England	Wales	Scotland	N. Ireland	**Total UK**	England	Wales	Scotland	N. Ireland	**Total UK**	England	Wales	Scotland	N. Ireland	**Total UK**
1990[1]	1,500	90	160	50	**1,800**	–	–	–	–	–	1	0	0	0	**1**
1995[1]	1,760	100	190	50	**2,100**	–	–	–	–	–	1	0	0	0	**1**
2000[1]	2,000	115	225	60	**2,400**	–	–	–	–	–	1	0	0	0	**1**
2001[1]	2,040	120	230	60	**2,450**	–	–	–	–	–	1	0	0	0	**1**
2002[1]	2,080	125	235	60	**2,500**	–	–	–	–	–	1	0	0	0	**1**
2005[1]	2,230	145	250	75	**2,700**	–	–	–	–	–	1	0	0	0	**1**

Table 10.9.5 Fellowship of Isis[12]	ACTIVE MEMBERS					GROUPS					LEADERS				
	England	Wales	Scotland	N. Ireland	**Total UK**	England	Wales	Scotland	N. Ireland	**Total UK**	England	Wales	Scotland	N. Ireland	**Total UK**[13]
1990[1]	210	10	25	5	**250**	29	2	3	1	**35**	29	2	3	1	**35**
1995[1]	250	15	30	5	**300**	25[3]	2	2[3]	1	**30**	29[3]	2	3	1	**35**
2000[1]	330	25	40	5	**400**	16[3]	1	2[3]	1	**20**	29[3]	2	3[3]	1	**35**
2001[1]	345	25	45	5	**420**	16	1	2	1	**20**	29	2	3	1	**35**
2002[1]	355	30	50	5	**440**	16	1	2	1	**20**	29	2	3	1	**35**
2005[1]	400	40	55	5	**500**	15	1	1	1	**18**	29	2	3	1	**35**

Table 10.9.6 Pagan Federation[20]	ACTIVE MEMBERS					GROUPS					LEADERS				
	England	Wales	Scotland	N. Ireland	**Total UK**	England	Wales	Scotland	N. Ireland	**Total UK**	England	Wales	Scotland	N. Ireland	**Total UK**
1990[3]	3,180	300	400	120	**4,000**	67	4	7	2	**80**	65	5	5	5	**80**
1995[1]	4,720	400	700	180	**6,000**	92	6	10	2	**110**	125	10	10	5	**150**
2000[1]	9,250	550	1,000	200	**11,000**	110	7	13	2	**132**	182	15	15	8	**220**
2001[1]	10,050	600	1,100	250	**12,000**	112	7	13	2	**134**	188	16	16	10	**230**
2002[1]	10,850	650	1,200	300	**13,000**	114	7	13	2	**136**	196	17	17	10	**240**
2005[1]	12,400	800	1,400	400	**15,000**	123	10	15	2	**150**	245	20	20	15	**300**

Table 10.9.7 Sahaja Yoga[24]	ACTIVE MEMBERS					GROUPS					LEADERS				
	England	Wales	Scotland	N. Ireland	**Total UK**	England	Wales	Scotland	N. Ireland	**Total UK**	England	Wales	Scotland	N. Ireland	**Total UK**
1990[1]	235	15	25	5	**280**	19	1	2	0	**22**	8	1	1	0	**10**
1995[1]	280	15	30	5	**330**	21	1	2	1	**25**	8	1	1	0	**10**
2000[1]	305	20	35	5	**365**	23	1	2	1	**27**	8	1	1	0	**10**
2001[1]	310	20	35	5	**370**	23	1	2	1	**27**	8	1	1	0	**10**
2002[1]	315	20	35	5	**375**	23	1	2	1	**27**	8	1	1	0	**10**
2005[1]	330	40	40	5	**400**	25	1	2	1	**29**	8	1	1	0	**10**

[1] Estimate. *For other footnotes, see* **Page 10.10**

Table 10.10
New Religious Movements mostly only in England[18]

	Active Membership						Groups						Leaders					
	1990	1995	2000	2001	2002	2005[1]	1990	1995	2000	2001	2002	2005[1]	1990	1995	2000	2001	2002	2005[1]
The Atherius Society[4]	100[1]	120[1]	140[1]	140[1]	140[1]	150	7[1]	8[1]	9[1]	9[1]	9[1]	9	8[1]	9[1]	10[1]	10[1]	10[1]	10
Chrisemma[6]	5[1]	20[1]	50[1]	50[1]	50[1]	60	1[1]	1[1]	1[1]	1[1]	1[1]	1	2[1]	3[1]	4[1]	4[1]	4[1]	4
Da Free John[8]	50[1]	55[1]	60[1]	60[1]	60[1]	60	2[1]	2[1]	3[1]	3[1]	3[1]	4	14[1]	16[1]	18[1]	18[1]	18[1]	20
Falun Gong[11]	–	–	160[1]	162[1]	164[1]	170	–	–	20[1]	20[1]	20[1]	20	–	–	–	–	–	–
Life Training[15,25]	250[1]	300[1]	350[1]	360[1]	370[1]	400	1[1]	1[1]	1[1]	1[1]	1[1]	1	3[1]	3[1]	4[1]	4[1]	4[1]	4
Barry Long Foundation[14, 25]	400[1]	400[1]	0	0	0	0	–	–	–	–	–	–	1[1]	1[1]	0	0	0	0
Mahikari[16,25]	220[1]	250[1]	280[1]	280[1]	280[1]	300	1[1]	1[1]	1[1]	1[1]	1[1]	1	3[1]	3[1]	4[1]	4[1]	4[1]	4
Mazdaznam Association[2]	25[1]	25[1]	25[1]	25[1]	25[1]	25	2[1]	2[1]	2[1]	2[1]	2[1]	2	3[1]	3[1]	3[1]	3[1]	3[1]	3
New Age Movement, Centre of[17]	–	50	525[1]	530[1]	545[1]	600	1[1]	1[1]	1[1]	1[1]	1[1]	1	3[1]	3[1]	3[1]	3[1]	3[1]	3
Outlook Seminar Training[19]	75[1]	200[1]	300[1]	320[1]	340[1]	400	2[1]	2[1]	2[1]	2[1]	2[1]	2	3[1]	3[1]	3[1]	3[1]	3[1]	3
Raelian Movement[21, 25]	100[1]	100[1]	100[1]	100[1]	100[1]	150	–	–	–	–	–	–	–	–	–	–	–	–
Shinnyeon UK[22, 25]	40[1]	50[1]	60[1]	60[1]	60[1]	70	1[1]	1[1]	1[1]	1[1]	1[1]	1	2[1]	3[1]	4[1]	4[1]	4[1]	5
Solara[23]	140[1]	160[1]	180[1]	180[1]	180[1]	200	–	–	–	–	–	–	–	–	–	–	–	–
3HO[3, 25]	60[1]	60[1]	60[1]	60[1]	60[1]	60	–	–	–	–	–	–	15[1]	15[1]	15[1]	15[1]	15[1]	15
Other New Religious Movements[1]	1,000	1,500	1,900	1,950	2,000	2,500	30[1]	40[1]	50[1]	52[1]	54[1]	60	50[1]	75[1]	100[1]	120[1]	140[1]	200
Total	**2,465**	**3,290**	**4,190**	**4,277**	**4,374**	**5,145**	**48**	**59**	**91**	**93**	**95**	**103**	**107**	**137**	**168**	**188**	**208**	**271**

[1] Estimate

[2] Members taken as 10% of community

[3] 3HO stands for 'Healthy, Happy, Holy' and is made up of teachers and followers of Kundalini Yoga as taught by Yogi Bahjan. They came to the UK in the early 1970's, and have two annual events. Six of their Kundalini teachers are in London, three in the Midlands, and one in Scotland.

[4] The Atherius Society have had contact with perhaps 900 people in the UK, between 50 and 80 people attend their Sunday Service, frequently including newcomers. Branches are located in Bristol, Derby, Hull, London, Manchester, Merseyside and Sheffield, with 12 further unofficial locations with representatives.

[5] The number of actual members is about 10 times the numbers given, who are regular attenders. One fifth of these are in London, as are a third of their full time workers.

[6] The full name is 'The Chrisemma Foundation', founded by Chris Orchard and Emma Lea in November 1990. About 60 people have tried their teachings, and many were Sannyasins, or members of the Rajneesh. Figures given are for the committed who all live near Totnes in Devon.

[7] Benjamin Creme. There is no organisation as such but its sphere of influence could be 10,000. All workers are voluntary.

[8] Da Free John teach a combination of Tibetan Buddhism, Hinduism, and elements of Zen, est and Rajneesh. Their mailing list numbers only 110, including 60 friends. Of the 52 regular attenders, 40 are practitioners and 12 are novices. 16 members live in the Ashram in Norwich, of whom 8 are priests doing pujas every day, and the others work voluntarily. Also called Adi Dam.

[9] There are no full time workers, but each of the 27 local Directors has three helpers. Each major centre has a building, including Birmingham, London and Nottingham.

[10] The group has renounced its Hindu connections, but is included here for usefulness. Presentations take place to give Knowledge.

[11] The Falun Dafa (also known as Falun Gong) is a non-political, health-inducing set of exercises based on the ancient insights into the human mind, body and spirit. There are strict moral principles underlying Falun Gong, which encourage practitioners to be truthful, compassionate and tolerant. The movement originated in China and was introduced to the UK in 1996. There is no set membership, but the numbers are for practitioners. All workers are voluntary.

[12] The UK mailing list numbers 5,000.

[13] Taken as 10% of total priests and priestesses.

[14] The Barry Long Foundation is now based in Holland.

[15] 2,500 people in the UK have undertaken one course. Of the active members, 100 teach. One of the leaders is part-time.

[16] About 1,600 have attended during the 1990s, with a further 600 in 1989 when it began in the UK.

[17] The Centre for the New Age Movement is based at St James Church, Piccadilly, London to provide talks and lectures in Holistic Education, the membership figure being 'friends' who support the centre financially.

[18] The large majority of numbers in this Table are estimated. For the history of many see footnotes in *Religious Trends* No 2 Pages 10.9 and 10.10.

[19] Previously called 'I am Grove' after its founder, Pat Grove, with Tony Weisman. 7 courses are held every year with an average of 23 people at each. There are 2,300 graduates; 100 have done all three courses.

[20] The leadership claim a following of around 225,000; others suggest a figure of between 100,000 and 120,000 is more realistic. About 10% of these are taken as active members.

[21] There were 35,000 Raelians in 67 countries in 1999 (*Religion Watch*, 12/99, Page 6) but 55,000 in 84 countries in 2001, according to an article in *Cape Times*, South Africa, 5th July 2001. They are particularly strong in Belgium, Canada (Quebec), France, Italy, Japan and Switzerland.

[22] *Journal of Contemporary Religion* Vol 10 No 2, 1995 estimate. Shinnyeon UK claimed a following of 100 in 1995.

[23] Solara is also called Star-Borne Unlimited, with a membership of about 800. They started in 1986.

[24] Sahaja Yoga started in the early 1970s.

[25] These Movements have a small number of members in countries other than England (given in *Religious Trends* No 1, Pages 10-6-8). For reasons of space these are not given here, but have been correctly added into the overall totals for New Religious Movements given in **Table 10.8.4.**

Page 10.8

[1] Estimate

[2] Active members are taken as half the Community figure given in the 2001 Population Census, with earlier figures and country proportions revised as appropriate.

[3] Revised figure(s).

[4] Half the figure given in the 1991 Northern Ireland Population census.

[5] Equivalent to a community of 250,000, the Sikh's Society own estimate.

[6] Includes 10,000 Namdhari Sikhs (*Religions in the UK: A Multi-Faith Directory,* 1997).

[7] Gurdwaras.

[8] 1999 figure, from *Religions in the UK,* 2001.

[9] In *Zoroastrians,* (Routledge and Kegan Paul, 1976) Mary Boyce put the community in the UK at 3,000. A tribute to the rock musician Freddie Mercury in the *Independent* of 27th November 1991 put it that year at 6,000. An article by Harriot Crout-Tree in *Inter-Faith Network* on 17th February 1992 put it as 5,000 in 1990. Half this latter figure has been taken.

[10] *Religions in the UK: A Multi-Faith Directory,* 1997 gave a community figure of 5-10,000. It has been assumed to be 6,000.

[11] The Zoroastrians do not have any Fire Temples (places of worship) in the UK, but Zoroastrian House in London has a room which is used for worship.

[12] Total of **Tables 10.9.1-7** and **10.10.**

Section 11 is not included in this edition for space considerations; it will be restored in *Religious Trends* No. 5

12

Scottish Church Census 2002

Sources: 52% of Scotland's 4,144 churches in 2002, with comparative figures taken from *Prospects for the Nineties,* National Bible Society of Scotland and Christian Research, 1995; Office of National Statistics for population figures.

12

Abbreviations

* Fewer than 50 attenders/members
12 Figures in *italics* are percentages
12 Upright figures are actual numbers
▶ Percentages sum to 100% horizontally
▼ Percentages sum to 100% vertically
– There are none in this category
n/a Not applicable

Introduction On Sunday, 12th May 2002 the third Scottish Church Census was undertaken under the auspices of Christian Research, supported by a Scottish Census Steering Committee representing all the major denominations in Scotland. The full report of the study was published under the title *The Scottish Tide is Running Out,* providing a commentary on the results as well as highlighting the key results. It contains a description of the reasons for the study, how it was prepared, the pilot study and a copy of the questionnaire used.

The figures given for comparison for 1984 and 1994 come from the previous Scottish Church Censuses conducted in those years, full details of which were published in 1995 in the book *Prospects for Scotland 2000* which included detailed county tables.

The response There were an estimated 4,144 churches at the time of the Survey, and usable replies were received from 2,160, over half, 52.1%.

The Survey covered all Christian denominations, including all Free, Protestant, Anglican, Catholic and Orthodox churches, that is, all those accepting the Trinitarian formula of belief in God the Father, God the Son, and God the Holy Spirit in one Essence.

We separately identified and counted churches with two or more places of worship in distinct communities, such as linked Church of Scotland parishes where the parish churches were still in use. In team ministries each congregation counted as a unit, unless they all met unitedly together when they were treated as a single congregation.

Details collected The basic unit of the Survey was a *congregation,* which was defined as a "body of people meeting on a Sunday in the same premises primarily for public worship at regular intervals". A more precise description of what this definition means was given in *Religious Trends,* No 2, Page 12.2.

Sunday Church attendance was collected for Sunday 12th May 2002, broken down by adults and children. The number of adults attending twice was requested and subtracted from the total to give a count of the number of attenders, not attendances. Children were broken down between those in church services and those attending Sunday School, etc but not in church.

Frequency. A similar question to that used in the 1998 English survey asked for the frequency with which the adults in the congregation attended church on Sunday. Answers to this question are given in **Figure 1** and **Table 3** on each of the Denominational pages, **Pages 12.30-36.**

Age and sex of attenders. These were generally estimated by the person completing the questionnaire. They are given in **Table 5** on each page for the years 1984, 1994 and 2002, with population comparisons. These are illustrated in **Figure 1** on each of **Pages 12.3-29.** The 2002 Census broke the "Under 15" category previously used into two categories of "Under 12" and "12 to 14".

Size of church. The total numbers coming allow analysis of size, and this is given for each denomination in **Table 2** on **Pages 30-36.**

A denomination code was given to each congregation. The different denominations were grouped into 7 categories for ease of analysis:
1 The ***Church of Scotland***
2 The ***Other Presbyterian*** churches (including the Free Church of Scotland, the Continuing Free Church, the United Free Church, the Reformed Presbyterian, the Free Presbyterian & Associated Presbyterian churches)
3 The ***Episcopal*** Church of Scotland
4 The ***Baptist*** churches (Baptist Union, Grace Baptist and Independent Baptists)
5 The ***Independent Churches*** (the New/ "House" Churches and their various streams, the Christian Brethren, Congregational churches, FIEC, Churches of Christ, and churches for overseas nationals or immigrants)
6 The ***Smaller Denominations*** (Methodists, Salvation Army, Lutheran, Orthodox, Nazarenes, Pentecostal denominations, Quakers, Local Ecumenical Projects (LEPs), United Reformed Church, Seventh-Day Adventist, Worldwide Church of God, and Military chaplaincies)
7 The ***Roman Catholic Church*** (including a few immigrant Catholic churches).

The number attending church on Sunday in each of these denominational groups is given in **Table 2** on the Council pages in this Section. The proportion of attenders that each denomination is of the total is also given for 1984, 1994 and 2002, as is the number of churches by denomination in 1994 and 2002.

The population per church, across all denominations, is given for 1984, 1994 and 2002 in **Table 1** on each page.

Churchmanship. Respondents were invited to tick up to three boxes in a list of nine categories, and were able to use an "other, please specify" category as well. The nine categories used were the same as in the 1994 Scottish Church Census to allow comparisons. The information was completed by the minister, or leader, to describe his/her congregation not their own personal position.

The combinations of boxes ticked were used to derive six groups: Broad, Catholic, Evangelical, Liberal, Low Church and Reformed. The Evangelical category is further broken down into: Reformed, Mainstream and Charismatic Evangelicals.

Details of the numbers by each churchmanship are given in **Table 3** on each page, with a comparison for 1994 both in attendance terms and in the number of churches.

Environment. The 8 point classification used in the 1994 Census was carried through unchanged into 2002 and used to analyse attendance and church numbers for each Council, given in **Table 4** on each page.

Geographical area. Scotland is divided up by *geographical area* into 32 Councils. The 1984 Census was analysed by 21 area units, mostly counties, and the 1994 into 24 units. These have all been reworked in the light of the changes made by the Boundary Commission, some of which required very extensive and detailed work, and the results have been analysed into 26 areas. These have followed the earlier studies as much as possible, but are completely contiguous with the borders of the 32 Councils. The one exception is the Districts of Skye and Lochalsh which have been left with the Western Isles as in previous studies, and are therefore not part of Highland. In this process details of some Councils have been added together; these are:
1) North, East and South Ayrshire are taken together as "Ayrshire"
2) Renfrewshire and East Renfrewshire
3) Mid and East Lothian
4) Stirling and Clackmannanshire
5) Highland and Argyll & Bute.
Church attendance for each Council is given on **Pages 12.4-29.**

Arrows
To help the reader more easily understand the numbers in the following pages arrows have been used to indicate the direction in which the percentages have been taken. Thus a horizontal arrow ▶ indicates that the percentages sum to 100% horizontally; the number on which the percentages are based is given in the final column. A vertical arrow ▼ indicates that the percentages sum to 100% vertically, although the number on which these percentages are based is not usually given since they can be easily derived from the horizontal percentage figures.

Rates of change have been calculated over the 6, 4, or 8 year periods 1984 to 1990, 1990 to 1994 and 1994 to 2002 to give an historical perspective whenever possible.

Financial giving. Answers to this question are illustrated in **Figure 2** on each of the following pages. This question was not asked in the English survey.

Expectation of change. This question was asked in the English survey. The answers are illustrated in **Figure 3** on each of the following pages.

Other questions. Not all the Census questions have their answers in *Religious Trends.* Detailed answers to the following questions are given in the main Report in the above-mentioned book:
1) Mid-week activity,
2) Community work,
3) The Alpha and Emmaus programmes, and
4) Numbers and ages of lay leaders.

However, please see **Pages 2.5-19** for coloured maps and diagrams illustrating the results of the 2002 Census. Some additional information is also given on **Pages 5.4,5** and **5.6.**

For more details please contact Dr Peter Brierley at the address on Page 0.2.

Table 12.3.1

OVERALL FIGURES	1980	1984	1990	1994	**2002**
Total population	5,193,900	5,145,780	5,102,200	5,103,040	5,069,710
Usual Sunday church attendance	887,070	853,700	751,040	691,120	570,130
% attending on Sunday	*17·1*	*16·6*	*14·7*	*13·5*	*11·2*
Number of churches	4,108	4,063	4,123	4,164	4,144
Population per church	1,260	1,240	1,240	1,230	1,220
% churches responding	*75*	*75*	*81*	*81*	*52*

Table 12.3.2 Sunday attendance by denomination

	Church of Scotland	Other Presbyterian	Episcopal	Baptist	Independent	Smaller Denoms.	Total Protestant	Roman Catholic	**Total Christian**
1984	361,340	28,680	20,000	29,240	39,370	29,120	507,750	345,950	853,700
%▼	*–11*	*–9*	*0*	*–11*	*+13*	*+5*	*–8*	*–18*	*–12*
1990	320,770	26,000	19,900	25,920	44,400	30,500	467,490	283,550	751,040
%▼	*–9*	*–10*	*+2*	*–5*	*+8*	*+5*	*–6*	*–12*	*–8*
1994	293,170	23,310	20,350	24,530	48,020	32,020	441,400	249,720	691,120
%▼	*–22*	*–5*	*–7*	*+1*	*–6*	*–11*	*–17*	*–19*	*–18*
2002	**228,500**	**22,170**	**18,870**	**24,830**	**45,010**	**28,640**	**368,020**	**202,110**	**570,130**
1984▶	*42*	*3*	*2*	*4*	*5*	*3*	*59*	*41*	*100%*
1994▶	*42*	*3*	*3*	*4*	*7*	*5*	*64*	*36*	*100%*
2002▶	***40***	***4***	***3***	***5***	***8***	***5***	***65***	***35***	***100%***
Number of churches									
1984	1,790	375	306	186	438	362	3,457	606	4,063
1994	1,691	352	311	203	577	432	3,566	598	4,164
2002	**1,666**	**342**	**309**	**204**	**559**	**470**	**3,550**	**594**	**4,144**

Table 12.3.3 Sunday attendance by churchmanship

	Reformed Evangelical	Mainstream Evangelical	Charismatic Evangelical	TOTAL Evangelical	Reformed	Low church	Liberal	Broad	Catholic*	**ALL Churches**
1994	79,930	67,840	31,190	178,960	107,570	29,700	69,300	84,100	221,490	691,120
%▼	*–32*	*+19*	*–8*	*–9*	*–21*	*–20*	*–24*	*–27*	*–17*	*–18*
2002	**54,060**	**80,580**	**28,560**	**163,200**	**85,050**	**23,880**	**52,760**	**61,340**	**183,900**	**570,130**
1994▶	*11*	*10*	*5*	*26*	*16*	*4*	*10*	*12*	*32*	*100%*
2002▶	***10***	***14***	***5***	***29***	***15***	***4***	***9***	***11***	***32***	***100%***
Number of churches										
1994	618	670	281	1,569	668	239	486	576	626	4,164
2002	**594**	**684**	**286**	**1,564**	**667**	**239**	**484**	**573**	**617**	**4,144**

Table 12.3.4 Sunday attendance by environment

	City Centre	Urban Priority Area	Housing Scheme	Suburban	Town	New Town	Rural Area: Dormitory	Rural: Other Areas	**ALL Churches**
1994	46,330	38,340	84,150	98,530	228,940	29,220	68,860	96,750	691,120
%▼	*–15*	*–26*	*–24*	*–8*	*–19*	*–22*	*–16*	*–15*	*–18*
2002	**39,610**	**28,200**	**63,750**	**90,500**	**184,510**	**22,800**	**58,080**	**82,680**	**570,130**
1994▶	*7*	*6*	*12*	*14*	*33*	*4*	*10*	*14*	*100%*
2002▶	***7***	***5***	***11***	***16***	***32***	***4***	***10***	***15***	***100%***
Number of churches									
1994	182	212	383	394	1,121	113	458	1,301	4,164
2002	**184**	**212**	**380**	**399**	**1,121**	**113**	**462**	**1,273**	**4,144**

**Catholic: One kind of churchmanship, not to be identified solely with the Roman Catholic church.*

Table 12.3.5 Age and gender of churchgoers 1984, 1994 and 2002

Age Group	Population 1984			Churchgoers in 1984			Population 1994			Churchgoers in 1994			Population 2002			Churchgoers in 2002		
	Male %	Female %	Total %	Male %	Female %	Total %	Male %	Female %	Total %	Male %	Female %	Total %	Male %	Female %	Total %	Male %	Female %	Total %
<12 } 12–14 (combined 1984, 1994)	*11*	*10*	***21***	*11*	*14*	***25***	*10*	*9*	***19***	*9*	*9*	***18***						
<12													*7*	*7*	***14***	*6*	*7*	***13***
12–14													*2*	*2*	***4***	*2*	*2*	***4***
15–19	*5*	*4*	***9***	*2*	*3*	***5***	*3*	*3*	***6***	*2*	*3*	***5***	*3*	*3*	***6***	*2*	*2*	***4***
20–29	*7*	*8*	***15***	*3*	*6*	***9***	*8*	*8*	***16***	*3*	*5*	***8***	*7*	*6*	***13***	*3*	*3*	***6***
30–44	*9*	*10*	***19***	*5*	*10*	***15***	*10*	*11*	***21***	*6*	*11*	***17***	*12*	*12*	***24***	*5*	*9*	***14***
45–64	*11*	*11*	***22***	*9*	*15*	***24***	*11*	*12*	***23***	*10*	*17*	***27***	*12*	*12*	***24***	*11*	*17*	***28***
65/65+	*5*	*9*	***14***	*7*	*15*	***22***	*6*	*9*	***15***	*9*	*16*	***25***	*6*	*9*	***15***	*11*	*20*	***31***
All ages	*48*	*52*	***100***	*37*	*63*	***100***	*48*	*52*	***100***	*39*	*61*	***100***	*48*	*52*	***100***	*40*	*60*	***100***

Figure 12.3.1 Percentage of population in church by age-group

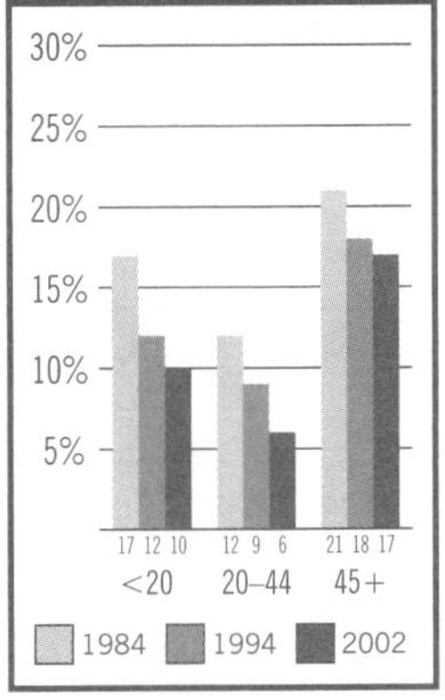

Figure 12.3.2 Financial giving in the past year

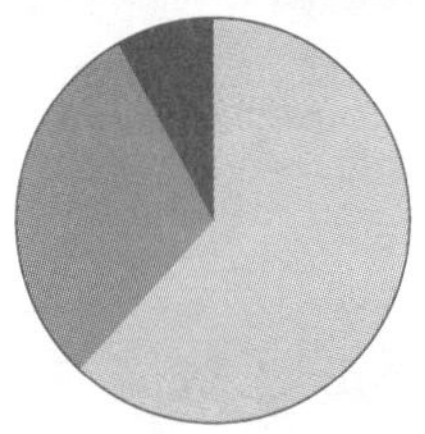

Figure 12.3.3 By 2010, our church will have...

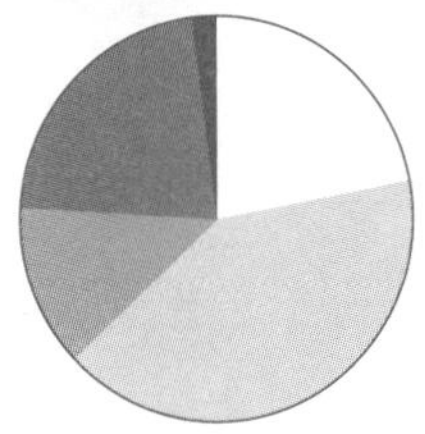

12.4 Aberdeen City

Table 12.4.1

OVERALL FIGURES	1984	1994	**2002**
Total population	204,210	218,220	210,490
Usual Sunday church attendance	19,750	19,260	16,180
% attending on Sunday	*9·7*	*8·8*	*7·7*
Number of churches	109	118	119
Population per church	1,870	1,850	1,770

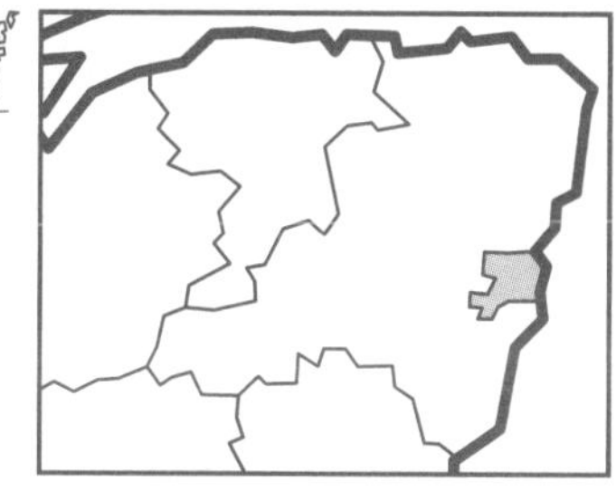

Figure 12.4.1 Percentage of population in church by age-group

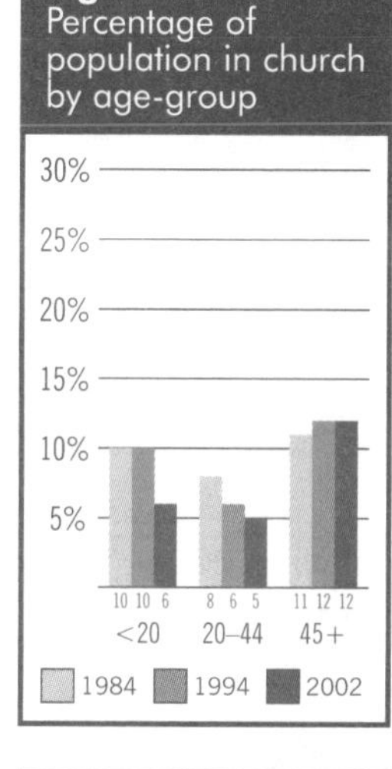

Table 12.4.2 Sunday attendance by denomination

	Church of Scotland	Other Presbyterian	Episcopal	Baptist	Independent	Smaller Denoms.	Total Protestant	Roman Catholic	**Total Christian**
1984	12,670	450	450	1,160	1,930	690	17,350	2,400	19,750
%▼	*–15*	*+16*	*+69*	*–4*	*+1*	*+113*	*–4*	*–6*	*–5*
1990	10,800	520	760	1,110	1,940	1,470	16,600	2,250	18,850
%▼	*–6*	*–4*	*+11*	*+10*	*+15*	*+35*	*+2*	*+5*	*+2*
1994	10,110	500	840	1,220	2,230	1,990	16,890	2,370	19,260
%▼	*–24*	*+6*	*–29*	*–10*	*+24*	*–21*	*–15*	*–21*	*–16*
2002	**7,730**	**530**	**600**	**1,100**	**2,770**	**1,570**	**14,300**	**1,880**	**16,180**
1984►	*64*	*2*	*2*	*6*	*10*	*4*	*88*	*12*	*100%*
1994►	*53*	*3*	*4*	*6*	*12*	*10*	*88*	*12*	*100%*
2002►	***48***	***3***	***4***	***7***	***17***	***9***	***88***	***12***	***100%***
Number of churches									
1984	54	4	11	5	14	12	100	9	109
1994	47	5	11	6	18	21	108	10	118
2002	**47**	**5**	**11**	**6**	**18**	**22**	**109**	**10**	**119**

Figure 12.4.2 Financial giving in the past year

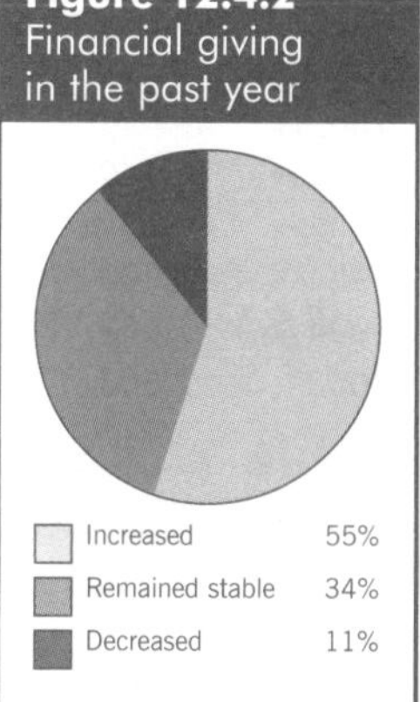

Table 12.4.3 Sunday attendance by churchmanship

	Reformed Evangelical	Mainstream Evangelical	Charismatic Evangelical	TOTAL Evangelical	Reformed	Low church	Liberal	Broad	Catholic*	**ALL Churches**
1994	2,250	2,380	2,830	7,460	2,510	620	3,460	2,990	2,220	19,260
%▼	*–8*	*+32*	*–19*	*0*	*–19*	*+13*	*–41*	*–24*	*–26*	*–16*
2002	**2,060**	**3,150**	**2,280**	**7,490**	**2,040**	**700**	**2,030**	**2,270**	**1,650**	**16,180**
1994►	*12*	*12*	*15*	*39*	*13*	*3*	*18*	*16*	*11*	*100%*
2002►	***13***	***19***	***14***	***46***	***13***	***4***	***13***	***14***	***10***	***100%***
Number of churches										
1994	18	16	17	51	11	5	27	14	10	118
2002	**18**	**18**	**17**	**53**	**11**	**5**	**26**	**14**	**10**	**119**

Table 12.4.4 Sunday attendance by environment

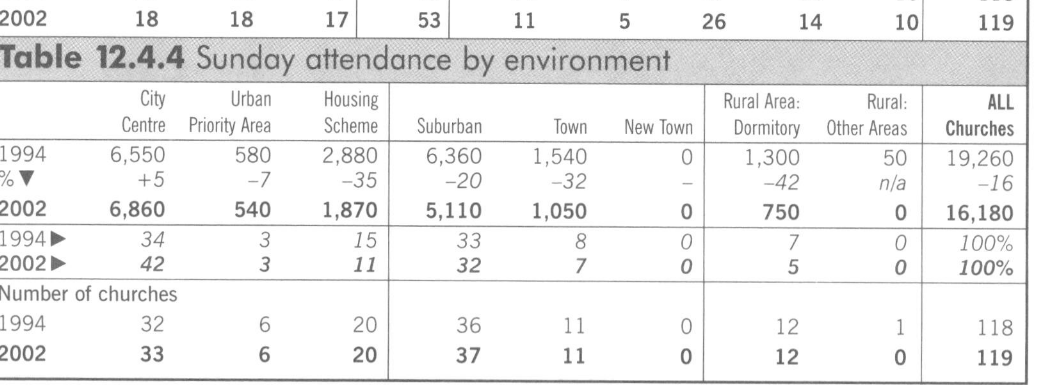

	City Centre	Urban Priority Area	Housing Scheme	Suburban	Town	New Town	Rural Area: Dormitory	Rural: Other Areas	**ALL Churches**
1994	6,550	580	2,880	6,360	1,540	0	1,300	50	19,260
%▼	*+5*	*–7*	*–35*	*–20*	*–32*	–	*–42*	*n/a*	*–16*
2002	**6,860**	**540**	**1,870**	**5,110**	**1,050**	**0**	**750**	**0**	**16,180**
1994►	*34*	*3*	*15*	*33*	*8*	*0*	*7*	*0*	*100%*
2002►	***42***	***3***	***11***	***32***	***7***	***0***	***5***	***0***	***100%***
Number of churches									
1994	32	6	20	36	11	0	12	1	118
2002	**33**	**6**	**20**	**37**	**11**	**0**	**12**	**0**	**119**

**Catholic: One kind of churchmanship, not to be identified solely with the Roman Catholic church.*

Figure 12.4.3 By 2010, our church will have...

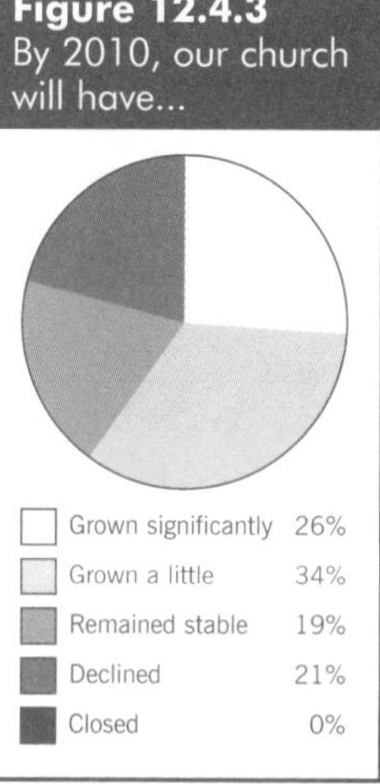

Table 12.4.5 Age and gender of churchgoers 1984, 1994 and 2002

Age Group	Population 1984			Churchgoers in 1984			Population 1994			Churchgoers in 1994			Population 2002			Churchgoers in 2002		
	Male %	Female %	Total %	Male %	Female %	Total %	Male %	Female %	Total %	Male %	Female %	Total %	Male %	Female %	Total %	Male %	Female %	Total %
<12 } 12–14	*10*	*9*	***19***	*10*	*12*	***22***	*9*	*8*	***17***	*10*	*11*	***21***						
<12													*7*	*7*	***14***	*6*	*7*	***13***
12–14													*2*	*2*	***4***	*1*	*2*	***3***
15–19	*4*	*5*	***9***	*3*	*4*	***7***	*3*	*3*	***6***	*2*	*2*	***4***	*3*	*3*	***6***	*2*	*2*	***4***
20–29	*8*	*8*	***16***	*4*	*7*	***11***	*10*	*10*	***20***	*5*	*7*	***12***	*7*	*7*	***14***	*4*	*5*	***9***
30–44	*9*	*9*	***18***	*6*	*10*	***16***	*11*	*11*	***22***	*6*	*10*	***16***	*13*	*12*	***25***	*6*	*8*	***14***
45–64	*11*	*12*	***23***	*8*	*15*	***23***	*10*	*11*	***21***	*9*	*14*	***23***	*11*	*12*	***23***	*9*	*16*	***25***
65/65+	*6*	*9*	***15***	*7*	*14*	***21***	*5*	*9*	***14***	*7*	*17*	***24***	*5*	*9*	***14***	*11*	*21*	***32***
All ages	*48*	*52*	***100***	*38*	*62*	***100***	*48*	*52*	***100***	*39*	*61*	***100***	*48*	*52*	***100***	*39*	*61*	***100***

Aberdeenshire[1] 12.5

[1] *Formerly part of Grampian: Other Region*

Table 12.5.1

OVERALL FIGURES	1984	1994	**2002**
Total population	195,680	225,550	226,860
Usual Sunday church attendance	29,190	26,710	21,690
% attending on Sunday	*14·9*	*11·8*	*9·6*
Number of churches	201	201	196
Population per church	970	1,120	1,160

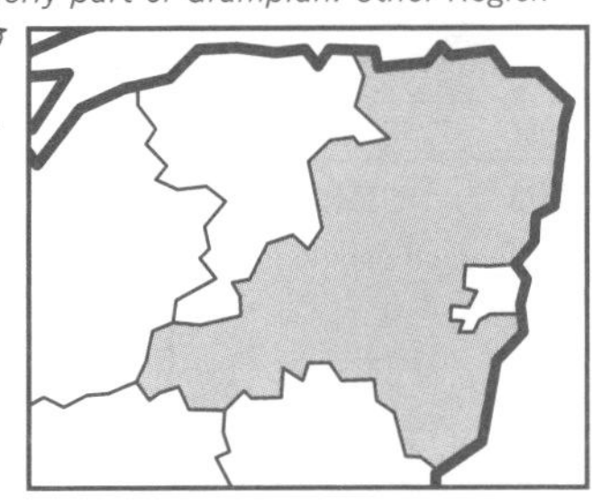

Figure 12.5.1 Percentage of population in church by age-group

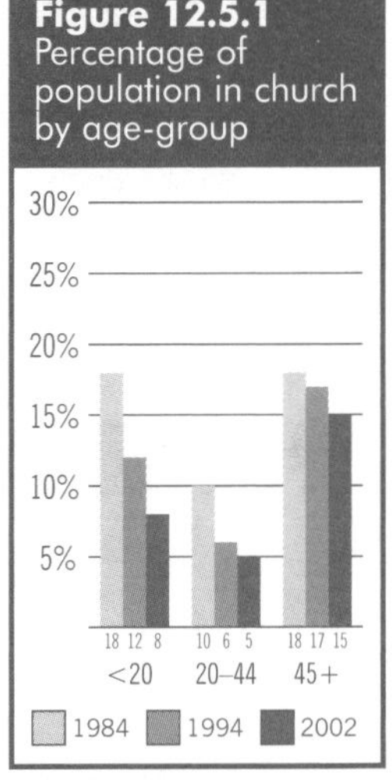

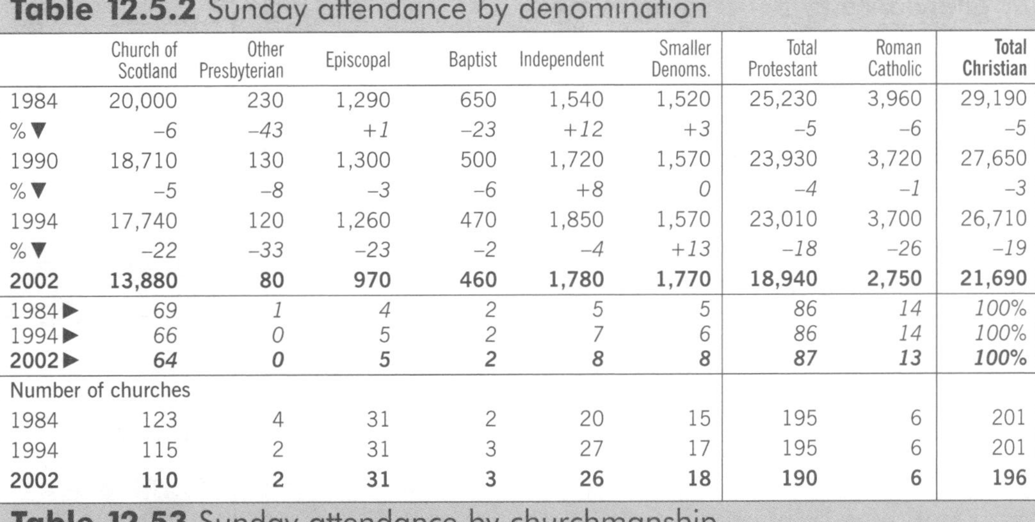

Table 12.5.2 Sunday attendance by denomination

	Church of Scotland	Other Presbyterian	Episcopal	Baptist	Independent	Smaller Denoms.	Total Protestant	Roman Catholic	**Total Christian**
1984	20,000	230	1,290	650	1,540	1,520	25,230	3,960	29,190
%▼	*–6*	*–43*	*+1*	*–23*	*+12*	*+3*	*–5*	*–6*	*–5*
1990	18,710	130	1,300	500	1,720	1,570	23,930	3,720	27,650
%▼	*–5*	*–8*	*–3*	*–6*	*+8*	*0*	*–4*	*–1*	*–3*
1994	17,740	120	1,260	470	1,850	1,570	23,010	3,700	26,710
%▼	*–22*	*–33*	*–23*	*–2*	*–4*	*+13*	*–18*	*–26*	*–19*
2002	**13,880**	**80**	**970**	**460**	**1,780**	**1,770**	**18,940**	**2,750**	**21,690**
1984▶	*69*	*1*	*4*	*2*	*5*	*5*	*86*	*14*	*100%*
1994▶	*66*	*0*	*5*	*2*	*7*	*6*	*86*	*14*	*100%*
2002▶	***64***	***0***	***5***	***2***	***8***	***8***	***87***	***13***	***100%***
Number of churches									
1984	123	4	31	2	20	15	195	6	201
1994	115	2	31	3	27	17	195	6	201
2002	**110**	**2**	**31**	**3**	**26**	**18**	**190**	**6**	**196**

Figure 12.5.2 Financial giving in the past year

Increased	63%
Remained stable	30%
Decreased	7%

Table 12.53 Sunday attendance by churchmanship

	Reformed Evangelical	Mainstream Evangelical	Charismatic Evangelical	TOTAL Evangelical	Reformed	Low church	Liberal	Broad	Catholic*	**ALL Churches**
1994	1,870	4,810	1,600	8,280	4,540	2,140	3,210	5,070	3,470	26,710
%▼	*–57*	*–19*	*+11*	*–22*	*–3*	*+17*	*–31*	*–26*	*–33*	*–19*
2002	**810**	**3,910**	**1,770**	**6,490**	**4,390**	**2,500**	**2,230**	**3,740**	**2,340**	**21,690**
1994▶	*7*	*18*	*6*	*31*	*17*	*8*	*12*	*19*	*13*	*100%*
2002▶	***4***	***18***	***8***	***30***	***20***	***12***	***10***	***17***	***11***	***100%***
Number of churches										
1994	14	36	12	62	34	16	24	39	26	201
2002	**12**	**34**	**13**	**59**	**34**	**17**	**22**	**39**	**25**	**196**

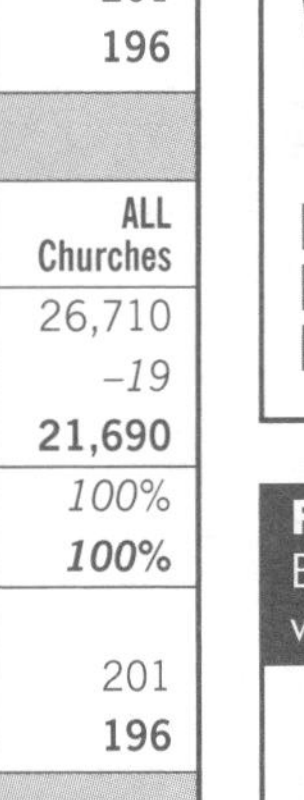

Table 12.5.4 Sunday attendance by environment

	City Centre	Urban Priority Area	Housing Scheme	Suburban	Town	New Town	Rural Area: Dormitory	Rural: Other Areas	**ALL Churches**
1994	0	270	530	0	8,010	0	5,070	12,830	26,710
%▼	–	*–19*	*+2*	–	*–13*	–	*–16*	*–24*	*–19*
2002	**0**	**220**	**540**	**0**	**6,950**	**0**	**4,250**	**9,730**	**21,690**
1994▶	*0*	*1*	*2*	*0*	*30*	*0*	*19*	*48*	*100%*
2002▶	***0***	***1***	***2***	***0***	***32***	***0***	***20***	***45***	***100%***
Number of churches									
1994	0	2	4	0	60	0	38	97	201
2002	**0**	**2**	**4**	**0**	**59**	**0**	**38**	**93**	**196**

**Catholic: One kind of churchmanship, not to be identified solely with the Roman Catholic church.*

Figure 12.5.3 By 2010, our church will have...

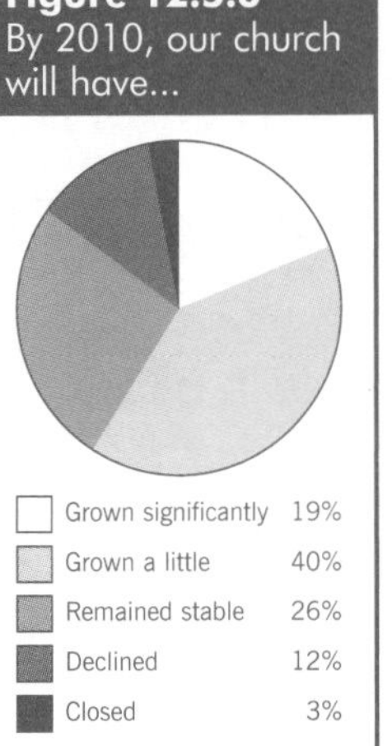

Grown significantly	19%
Grown a little	40%
Remained stable	26%
Declined	12%
Closed	3%

Table 12.5.5 Age and gender of churchgoers 1984, 1994 and 2002

Age Group	Population 1984			Churchgoers in 1984			Population 1994			Churchgoers in 1994			Population 2002			Churchgoers in 2002		
	Male %	Female %	Total %	Male %	Female %	Total %	Male %	Female %	Total %	Male %	Female %	Total %	Male %	Female %	Total %	Male %	Female %	Total %
<12 / 12–14	*12*	*11*	***23***	*13*	*18*	***31***	*11*	*10*	***21***	*12*	*13*	***25***	*8* *2*	*7* *2*	***15*** ***4***	*5* *2*	*8* *2*	***13*** ***4***
15–19	*4*	*4*	***8***	*2*	*4*	***6***	*3*	*3*	***6***	*1*	*2*	***3***	*3*	*3*	***6***	*1*	*2*	***3***
20–29	*7*	*7*	***14***	*3*	*5*	***8***	*7*	*7*	***14***	*2*	*4*	***6***	*6*	*6*	***12***	*1*	*2*	***3***
30–44	*11*	*10*	***21***	*6*	*9*	***15***	*12*	*11*	***23***	*5*	*9*	***14***	*12*	*12*	***24***	*6*	*10*	***16***
45–64	*10*	*10*	***20***	*8*	*13*	***21***	*11*	*11*	***22***	*10*	*18*	***28***	*13*	*13*	***26***	*12*	*18*	***30***
65/65+	*6*	*8*	***14***	*7*	*12*	***19***	*6*	*8*	***14***	*9*	*15*	***24***	*6*	*7*	***13***	*12*	*19*	***31***
All ages	*50*	*50*	***100***	*39*	*61*	***100***	*50*	*50*	***100***	*39*	*61*	***100***	*50*	*50*	***100***	*39*	*61*	***100***

12.6 Angus

[1] Formerly part of Tayside: Other Region, and including twelve churches formerly part of City of Dundee

Table 12.6.1

OVERALL FIGURES	1984	1994	**2002**
Total population	109,770	111,930	107,980
Usual Sunday church attendance	10,680	9,830	7,390
% attending on Sunday	*9·7*	*8·8*	*6·8*
Number of churches	96	101	100
Population per church	1,140	1,110	1,080

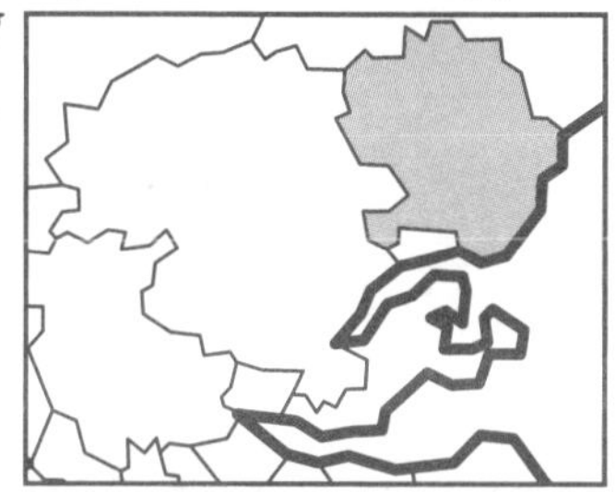

Figure 12.6.1 Percentage of population in church by age-group

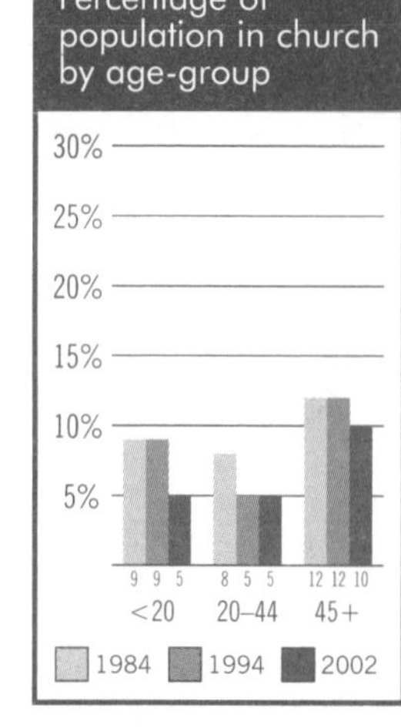

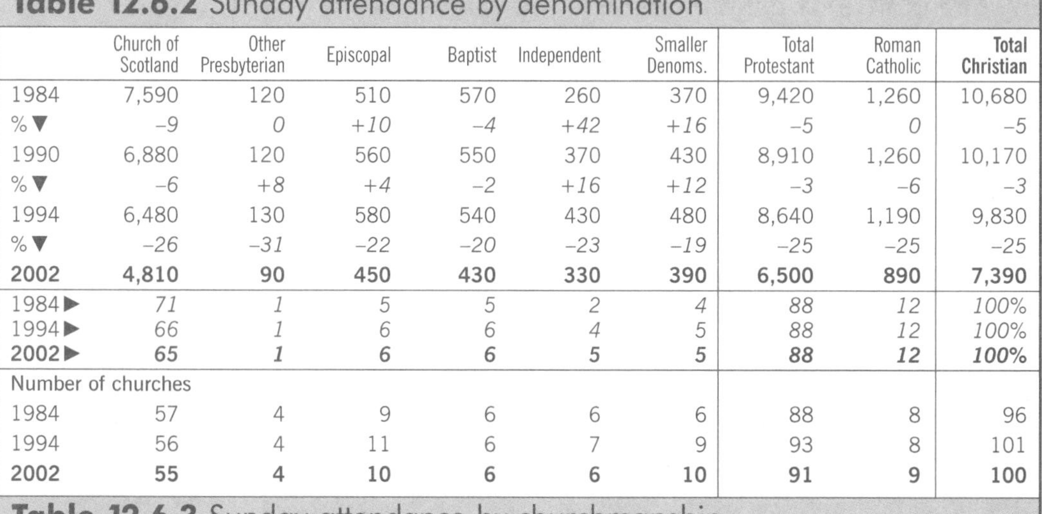

Table 12.6.2 Sunday attendance by denomination

	Church of Scotland	Other Presbyterian	Episcopal	Baptist	Independent	Smaller Denoms.	Total Protestant	Roman Catholic	**Total Christian**
1984	7,590	120	510	570	260	370	9,420	1,260	10,680
%▼	*–9*	*0*	*+10*	*–4*	*+42*	*+16*	*–5*	*0*	*–5*
1990	6,880	120	560	550	370	430	8,910	1,260	10,170
%▼	*–6*	*+8*	*+4*	*–2*	*+16*	*+12*	*–3*	*–6*	*–3*
1994	6,480	130	580	540	430	480	8,640	1,190	9,830
%▼	*–26*	*–31*	*–22*	*–20*	*–23*	*–19*	*–25*	*–25*	*–25*
2002	**4,810**	**90**	**450**	**430**	**330**	**390**	**6,500**	**890**	**7,390**
1984►	*71*	*1*	*5*	*5*	*2*	*4*	*88*	*12*	*100%*
1994►	*66*	*1*	*6*	*6*	*4*	*5*	*88*	*12*	*100%*
2002►	***65***	***1***	***6***	***6***	***5***	***5***	***88***	***12***	***100%***
Number of churches									
1984	57	4	9	6	6	6	88	8	96
1994	56	4	11	6	7	9	93	8	101
2002	**55**	**4**	**10**	**6**	**6**	**10**	**91**	**9**	**100**

Table 12.6.3 Sunday attendance by churchmanship

	Reformed Evangelical	Mainstream Evangelical	Charismatic Evangelical	TOTAL Evangelical	Reformed	Low church	Liberal	Broad	Catholic*	**ALL Churches**
1994	890	740	250	1,880	1,650	380	2,100	2,210	1,610	9,830
%▼	*–19*	*–30*	*–28*	*–26*	*–11*	*+34*	*–28*	*–32*	*–40*	*–25*
2002	**720**	**520**	**180**	**1,420**	**1,470**	**510**	**1,520**	**1,510**	**960**	**7,390**
1994►	*9*	*7*	*3*	*19*	*17*	*4*	*21*	*23*	*16*	*100%*
2002►	***10***	***7***	***2***	***19***	***20***	***7***	***21***	***20***	***13***	***100%***
Number of churches										
1994	7	9	5	21	20	6	20	23	11	101
2002	**7**	**8**	**5**	**20**	**20**	**7**	**20**	**22**	**11**	**100**

Table 12.6.4 Sunday attendance by environment

	City Centre	Urban Priority Area	Housing Scheme	Suburban	Town	New Town	Rural Area: Dormitory	Rural: Other Areas	**ALL Churches**
1994	200	40	520	280	4,460	0	1,910	2,420	9,830
%▼	*–25*	*–25*	*–23*	*–29*	*–19*	–	*–35*	*–28*	*–25*
2002	**150**	**30**	**400**	**200**	**3,630**	**0**	**1,240**	**1,740**	**7,390**
1994►	*2*	*0*	*5*	*3*	*45*	*0*	*20*	*25*	*100%*
2002►	***2***	***0***	***5***	***3***	***49***	***0***	***17***	***24***	***100%***
Number of churches									
1994	2	1	4	2	30	0	16	46	101
2002	**2**	**1**	**4**	**2**	**30**	**0**	**16**	**45**	**100**

Catholic: One kind of churchmanship, not to be identified solely with the Roman Catholic church.

Figure 12.6.2 Financial giving in the past year

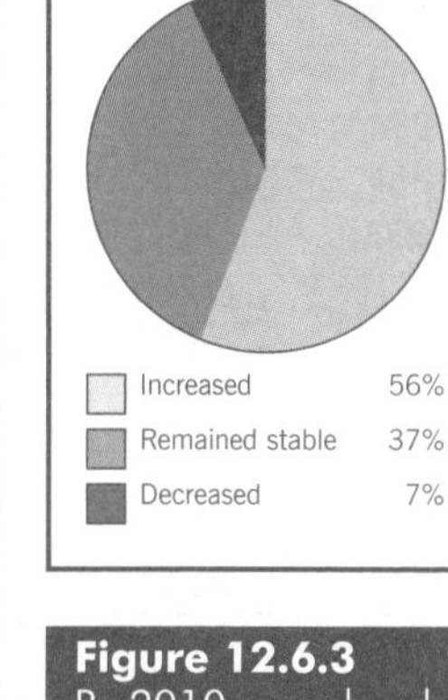

Figure 12.6.3 By 2010, our church will have...

Grown significantly	7%
Grown a little	43%
Remained stable	25%
Declined	25%
Closed	0%

Table 12.6.5 Age and gender of churchgoers 1984, 1994 and 2002

Age Group	Population 1984 Male %	Population 1984 Female %	Population 1984 Total %	Churchgoers in 1984 Male %	Churchgoers in 1984 Female %	Churchgoers in 1984 Total %	Population 1994 Male %	Population 1994 Female %	Population 1994 Total %	Churchgoers in 1994 Male %	Churchgoers in 1994 Female %	Churchgoers in 1994 Total %	Population 2002 Male %	Population 2002 Female %	Population 2002 Total %	Churchgoers in 2002 Male %	Churchgoers in 2002 Female %	Churchgoers in 2002 Total %
<12	*10*	*10*	**20**	*10*	*12*	**22**	*10*	*9*	**19**	*9*	*11*	**20**	*7*	*7*	**14**	*4*	*7*	**11**
12–14													*2*	*2*	**4**	*1*	*2*	**3**
15–19	*4*	*4*	**8**	*2*	*3*	**5**	*3*	*3*	**6**	*2*	*3*	**5**	*3*	*3*	**6**	*1*	*1*	**2**
20–29	*7*	*6*	**13**	*3*	*6*	**9**	*7*	*7*	**14**	*2*	*4*	**6**	*6*	*6*	**12**	*2*	*3*	**5**
30–44	*9*	*10*	**19**	*6*	*10*	**16**	*10*	*10*	**20**	*5*	*10*	**15**	*10*	*11*	**21**	*8*	*9*	**17**
45–64	*11*	*12*	**23**	*9*	*15*	**24**	*11*	*12*	**23**	*10*	*17*	**27**	*13*	*13*	**26**	*11*	*17*	**28**
65/65+	*7*	*10*	**17**	*8*	*16*	**24**	*7*	*11*	**18**	*10*	*17*	**27**	*8*	*9*	**17**	*13*	*21*	**34**
All ages	*48*	*52*	***100***	*38*	*62*	***100***	*48*	*52*	***100***	*38*	*62*	***100***	*49*	*51*	***100***	*40*	*60*	***100***

Ayrshire: North, South and East[1] 12.7

[1] *Formerly the Cumnock & Doon Valley, Cunninghame, Kilmarnock & London and Kyle & Carrick Districts of Strathclyde*

Table 12.7.1

OVERALL FIGURES	1984	1994	**2002**
Total population	383,280	376,800	368,370
Usual Sunday church attendance	63,360	49,580	42,390
% attending on Sunday	*16·5*	*13·2*	*11·5*
Number of churches	272	279	276
Population per church	1,410	1,350	1,330

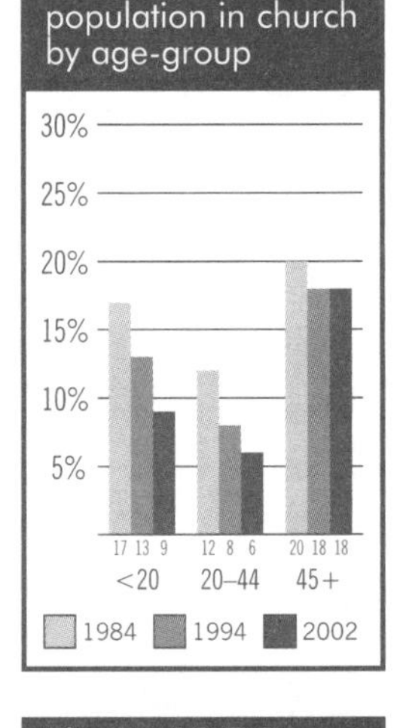

Figure 12.7.1 Percentage of population in church by age-group

Table 12.7.2 Sunday attendance by denomination

	Church of Scotland	Other Presbyterian	Episcopal	Baptist	Independent	Smaller Denoms.	Total Protestant	Roman Catholic	**Total Christian**
1984	33,910	940	850	1,920	4,990	1,760	44,370	18,990	63,360
%▼	*−14*	*−13*	*−4*	*−19*	*+12*	*−7*	*−11*	*−21*	*−14*
1990	29,270	820	820	1,550	5,580	1,640	39,680	15,020	54,700
%▼	*−8*	*−17*	*−2*	*+3*	*+4*	*−2*	*−5*	*−20*	*−9*
1994	27,020	680	800	1,600	5,830	1,610	37,540	12,040	49,580
%▼	*−17*	*−29*	*0*	*−10*	*−7*	*−24*	*−16*	*−11*	*−15*
2002	**22,300**	**480**	**800**	**1,440**	**5,450**	**1,220**	**31,690**	**10,700**	**42,390**
1984▶	*54*	*1*	*1*	*3*	*8*	*3*	*70*	*30*	*100%*
1994▶	*55*	*1*	*2*	*3*	*12*	*3*	*76*	*24*	*100%*
2002▶	***53***	***1***	***2***	***3***	***13***	***3***	***75***	***25***	***100%***
Number of churches									
1984	123	15	12	11	49	22	232	40	272
1994	119	12	12	13	61	24	241	38[1]	279
2002	**117**	**11**	**12**	**13**	**59**	**26**	**238**	**38**	**276**

Table 12.7.3 Sunday attendance by churchmanship

	Reformed Evangelical	Mainstream Evangelical	Charismatic Evangelical	TOTAL Evangelical	Reformed	Low church	Liberal	Broad	Catholic*	**ALL Churches**
1994	7,100	5,210	1,470	13,780	7,310	3,280	9,660	6,260	9,290	49,580
%▼	*−31*	*+2*	*0*	*−15*	*+3*	*−27*	*−30*	*−11*	*−9*	*−15*
2002	**4,870**	**5,320**	**1,470**	**11,660**	**7,530**	**2,390**	**6,780**	**5,570**	**8,460**	**42,390**
1994▶	*14*	*11*	*3*	*28*	*15*	*6*	*19*	*13*	*19*	*100%*
2002▶	***11***	***13***	***3***	***27***	***18***	***6***	***16***	***13***	***20***	***100%***
Number of churches										
1994	39	54	19	112	42	16	42	28	39	279
2002	**37**	**56**	**20**	**113**	**41**	**15**	**41**	**27**	**39**	**276**

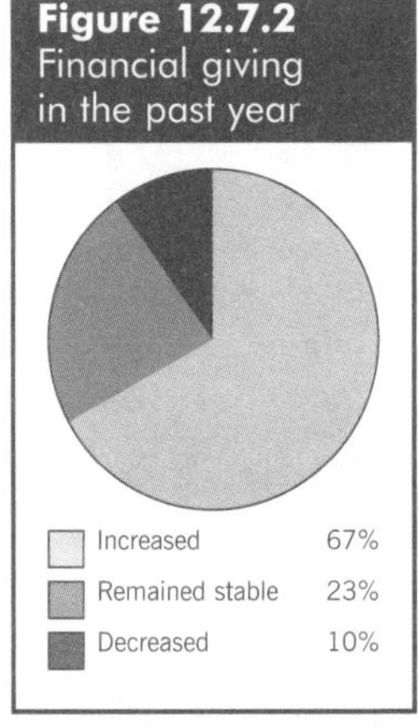

Figure 12.7.2 Financial giving in the past year

Table 12.7.4 Sunday attendance by environment

	City Centre	Urban Priority Area	Housing Scheme	Suburban	Town	New Town	Rural Area: Dormitory	Rural: Other Areas	**ALL Churches**
1994	0	2,410	3,470	1,490	26,840	3,970	4,460	6,940	49,580
%▼	–	*−24*	*−33*	*+7*	*−16*	*−15*	*−6*	*−4*	*−15*
2002	**0**	**1,840**	**2,310**	**1,590**	**22,460**	**3,370**	**4,190**	**6,630**	**42,390**
1994▶	*0*	*5*	*7*	*3*	*54*	*8*	*9*	*14*	*100%*
2002▶	***0***	***4***	***6***	***4***	***53***	***8***	***10***	***15***	***100%***
Number of churches									
1994	0	11	22	8	129	17	31	61	279
2002	**0**	**11**	**22**	**8**	**128**	**17**	**31**	**59**	**276**

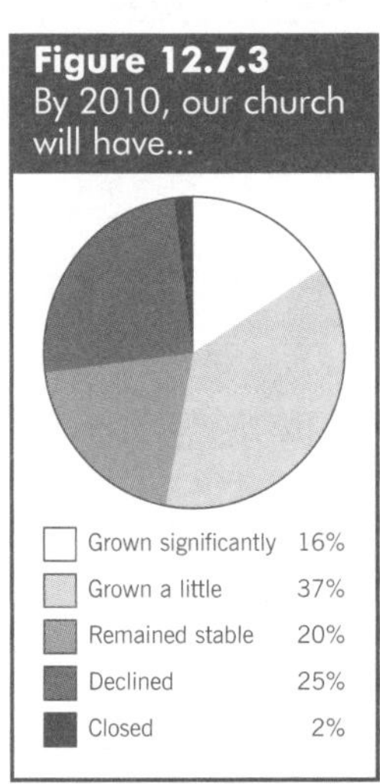

Figure 12.7.3 By 2010, our church will have...

*Catholic: One kind of churchmanship, not to be identified solely with the Roman Catholic church. [1] Revised figure

Table 12.7.5 Age and gender of churchgoers 1984, 1994 and 2002

Age Group	Population 1984			Churchgoers in 1984			Population 1994			Churchgoers in 1994			Population 2002			Churchgoers in 2002		
	Male %	Female %	Total %	Male %	Female %	Total %	Male %	Female %	Total %	Male %	Female %	Total %	Male %	Female %	Total %	Male %	Female %	Total %
<12	*11*	*11*	**22**	*12*	*14*	**26**	*10*	*9*	**19**	*9*	*12*	**21**	*7*	*7*	**14**	*5*	*6*	**11**
12–14													*2*	*2*	**4**	*2*	*2*	**4**
15–19	*5*	*4*	**9**	*2*	*4*	**6**	*3*	*3*	**6**	*2*	*2*	**4**	*3*	*3*	**6**	*2*	*1*	**3**
20–29	*7*	*7*	**14**	*3*	*6*	**9**	*7*	*7*	**14**	*2*	*4*	**6**	*6*	*6*	**12**	*3*	*2*	**5**
30–44	*9*	*10*	**19**	*5*	*10*	**15**	*10*	*11*	**21**	*5*	*9*	**14**	*11*	*11*	**22**	*5*	*8*	**13**
45–64	*10*	*12*	**22**	*8*	*14*	**22**	*12*	*12*	**24**	*10*	*18*	**28**	*12*	*13*	**25**	*12*	*17*	**24**
65/65+	*6*	*8*	**14**	*8*	*14*	**22**	*6*	*10*	**16**	*9*	*18*	**27**	*7*	*10*	**17**	*13*	*22*	**35**
All ages	*48*	*52*	**100**	*38*	*62*	**100**	*48*	*52*	**100**	*37*	*63*	**100**	*48*	*52*	**100**	*42*	*58*	**100**

(For 1984 and 1994, the <12 and 12–14 age groups are bracketed together.)

12.8 Borders, Scottish

Table 12.8.1

OVERALL FIGURES	1984	1994	**2002**
Total population	99,350	105,300	107,650
Usual Sunday church attendance	13,250	12,090	9,730
% attending on Sunday	*13·3*	*11·5*	*9·0*
Number of churches	147	151	149
Population per church	680	700	720

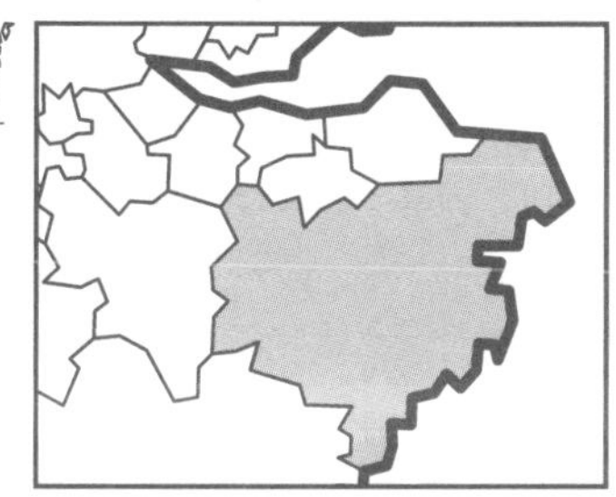

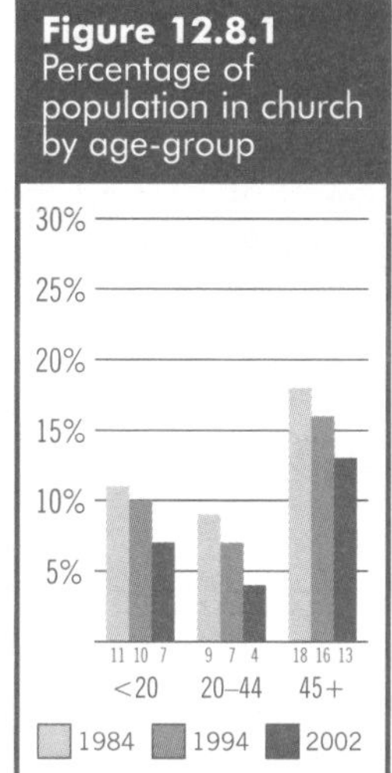

Figure 12.8.1 Percentage of population in church by age-group

Table 12.8.2 Sunday attendance by denomination

	Church of Scotland	Other Presbyterian	Episcopal	Baptist	Independent	Smaller Denoms.	Total Protestant	Roman Catholic	**Total Christian**
1984	8,960	40[1]	860	430	840	210	11,340	1,910	13,250
%▼	*–13*	*0*	*+6*	*+2*	*–10*	*–19*	*–10*	*–12*	*–11*
1990	7,830	40[1]	910	440	760	170	10,150	1,690	11,840
%▼	*–3*	*0*	*+22*	*+2*	*+20*	*+47*	*+2*	*+4*	*+2*
1994	7,580	40[1]	1,110	450	910	250	10,340	1,750	12,090
%▼	*–20*	*0*	*–17*	*0*	*–12*	*–32*	*–18*	*–28*	*–20*
2002	**6,090**	**40**	**920**	**450**	**800**	**170**	**8,470**	**1,260**	**9,730**
1984▶	*68*	*0*	*7*	*3*	*6*	*2*	*86*	*14*	*100%*
1994▶	*63*	*0*	*9*	*4*	*8*	*2*	*86*	*14*	*100%*
2002▶	***63***	***0***	***9***	***5***	***8***	***2***	***87***	***13***	***100%***
Number of churches									
1984	96	3	12	7	11	5	134	13	147
1994	88[1]	3	12	8[1]	19	7[1]	137	14	151
2002	**88**	**3**	**12**	**8**	**18**	**6**	**135**	**14**	**149**

Table 12.8.3 Sunday attendance by churchmanship

	Reformed Evangelical	Mainstream Evangelical	Charismatic Evangelical	TOTAL Evangelical	Reformed	Low church	Liberal	Broad	Catholic*	**ALL Churches**
1994	1,570	850	190	2,610	2,130	660	1,600	2,680	2,410	12,090
%▼	*–23*	*+104*	*+5*	*+20*	*–19*	*–41*	*–54*	*–22*	*–32*	*–20*
2002	**1,210**	**1,730**	**200**	**3,140**	**1,720**	**390**	**730**	**2,090**	**1,660**	**9,730**
1994▶	*13*	*7*	*2*	*22*	*18*	*5*	*13*	*22*	*20*	*100%*
2002▶	***12***	***18***	***2***	***32***	***18***	***4***	***8***	***21***	***17***	***100%***
Number of churches										
1994	16	15	6	37	24	12	23	32	23	151
2002	**16**	**16**	**6**	**38**	**24**	**11**	**22**	**32**	**22**	**149**

Table 12.8.4 Sunday attendance by environment

	City Centre	Urban Priority Area	Housing Scheme	Suburban	Town	New Town	Rural Area: Dormitory	Rural: Other Areas	**ALL Churches**
1994	0	0	600	0	4,720	0	600	6,170	12,090
%▼	–	–	*–30*	–	*–13*	–	*–13*	*–24*	*–20*
2002	**0**	**0**	**420**	**0**	**4,090**	**0**	**520**	**4,700**	**9,730**
1994▶	*0*	*0*	*5*	*0*	*38*	*0*	*6*	*51*	*100%*
2002▶	***0***	***0***	***4***	***0***	***42***	***0***	***6***	***48***	***100%***
Number of churches									
1994	0	0	4	0	38	0	7	102	151
2002	**0**	**0**	**4**	**0**	**38**	**0**	**7**	**100**	**149**

**Catholic: One kind of churchmanship, not to be identified solely with the Roman Catholic church.* *[1] Revised figure*

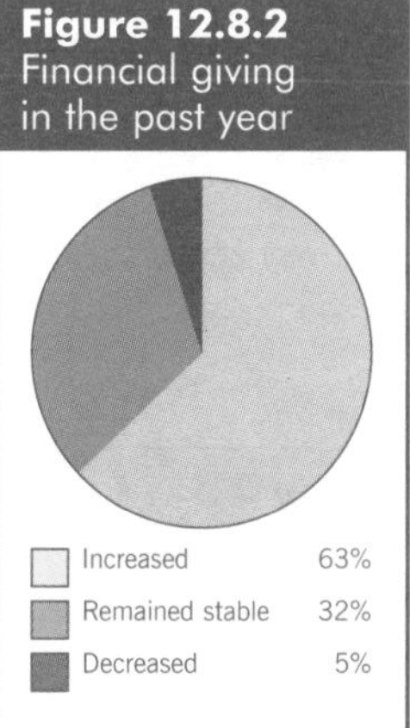

Figure 12.8.2 Financial giving in the past year

Increased	63%
Remained stable	32%
Decreased	5%

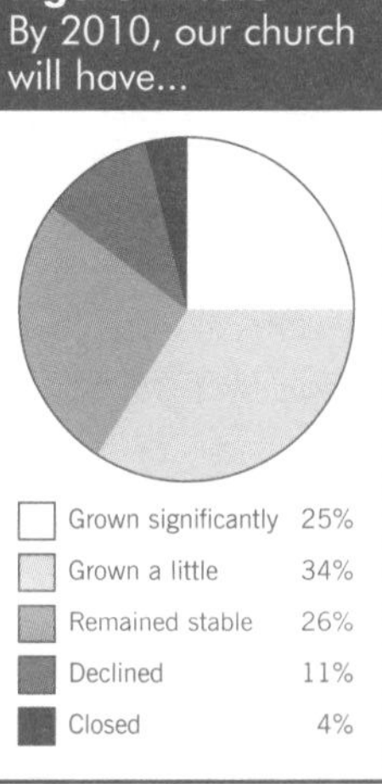

Figure 12.8.3 By 2010, our church will have...

Grown significantly	25%
Grown a little	34%
Remained stable	26%
Declined	11%
Closed	4%

Table 12.8.5 Age and gender of churchgoers 1984, 1994 and 2002

Age Group	Population 1984 Male %	Female %	Total %	Churchgoers in 1984 Male %	Female %	Total %	Population 1994 Male %	Female %	Total %	Churchgoers in 1994 Male %	Female %	Total %	Population 2002 Male %	Female %	Total %	Churchgoers in 2002 Male %	Female %	Total %
<12 }	*10*	*10*	***20***	*8*	*12*	***20***	*9*	*9*	***18***	*8*	*10*	***18***	*7*	*7*	***14***	*6*	*8*	***14***
12–14 }													*2*	*2*	***4***	*1*	*1*	***2***
15–19	*4*	*4*	***8***	*2*	*2*	***4***	*3*	*3*	***6***	*1*	*2*	***3***	*3*	*2*	***5***	*1*	*1*	***2***
20–29	*7*	*6*	***13***	*2*	*5*	***7***	*6*	*7*	***13***	*3*	*4*	***7***	*4*	*5*	***9***	*1*	*2*	***3***
30–44	*9*	*9*	***18***	*5*	*10*	***15***	*10*	*10*	***20***	*5*	*8*	***13***	*11*	*11*	***22***	*5*	*7*	***12***
45–64	*11*	*12*	***23***	*9*	*17*	***26***	*12*	*12*	***24***	*11*	*17*	***28***	*13*	*14*	***27***	*11*	*17*	***28***
65/65+	*7*	*11*	***18***	*10*	*18*	***28***	*8*	*11*	***19***	*11*	*20*	***31***	*8*	*11*	***19***	*15*	*24*	***39***
All ages	*48*	*52*	***100***	*36*	*64*	***100***	*48*	*52*	***100***	*39*	*61*	***100***	*48*	*52*	***100***	*40*	*60*	***100***

12

Table 12.9.1

OVERALL FIGURES	1984	1994	**2002**
Total population	145,000	147,900	147,730
Usual Sunday church attendance	20,230	16,570	12,800
% attending on Sunday	*14·0*	*11·2*	*8·7*
Number of churches	175	178	172
Population per church	830	830	860

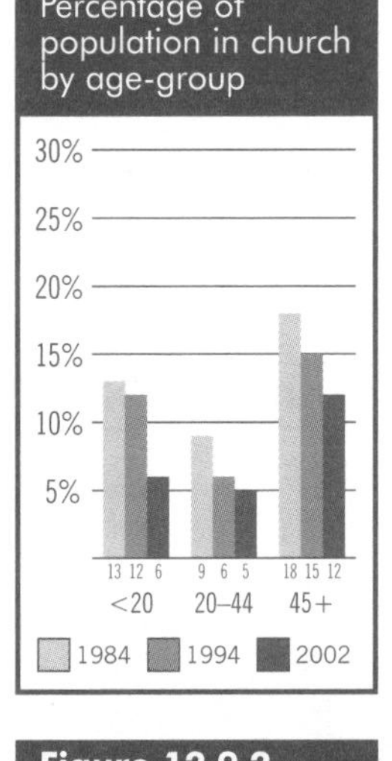

Figure 12.9.1 Percentage of population in church by age-group

Table 12.9.2 Sunday attendance by denomination

	Church of Scotland	Other Presbyterian	Episcopal	Baptist	Independent	Smaller Denoms.	Total Protestant	Roman Catholic	**Total Christian**
1984	13,480	150	830	400	1,320	230	16,410	3,820	20,230
%▼	*–11*	*–7*	*–6*	*+15*	*–15*	*+17*	*–10*	*–30*	*–14*
1990	11,960	140	780	460	1,120	270	14,730	2,670	17,400
%▼	*–9*	*+7*	*+4*	*+28*	*+14*	*+33*	*–4*	*–8*	*–5*
1994	10,920	150	810	590	1,280	360	14,110	2,460	16,570
%▼	*–26*	*–7*	*–26*	*+25*	*–15*	*–6*	*–22*	*–26*	*–23*
2002	**8,070**	**140**	**600**	**740**	**1,090**	**340**	**10,980**	**1,820**	**12,800**
1984▶	*67*	*1*	*4*	*2*	*6*	*1*	*81*	*19*	*100%*
1994▶	*66*	*1*	*5*	*3*	*8*	*2*	*85*	*15*	*100%*
2002▶	***63***	***1***	***5***	***6***	***8***	***3***	***86***	***14***	***100%***
Number of churches									
1984	104	4	17	3	21	7	156	19	175
1994	97[1]	4	15	7	21	12	156	22[1]	178
2002	**94**	**4**	**15**	**6**	**21**	**13**	**153**	**19**	**172**

Table 12.9.3 Sunday attendance by churchmanship

	Reformed Evangelical	Mainstream Evangelical	Charismatic Evangelical	TOTAL Evangelical	Reformed	Low church	Liberal	Broad	Catholic*	**ALL Churches**
1994	1,590	1,100	200	2,890	3,530	1,660	2,850	2,990	2,650	16,570
%▼	*–52*	*+62*	*+50*	*–1*	*–25*	*–14*	*–31*	*–38*	*–22*	*–23*
2002	**770**	**1,780**	**300**	**2,850**	**2,650**	**1,420**	**1,980**	**1,840**	**2,060**	**12,800**
1994▶	*10*	*7*	*1*	*18*	*21*	*10*	*17*	*18*	*16*	*100%*
2002▶	***6***	***14***	***2***	***22***	***21***	***11***	***16***	***14***	***16***	***100%***
Number of churches										
1994	20	16	5	41	39	16	27	30	25	178
2002	**17**	**15**	**6**	**38**	**39**	**16**	**27**	**30**	**22**	**172**

Table 12.9.4 Sunday attendance by environment

	City Centre	Urban Priority Area	Housing Scheme	Suburban	Town	New Town	Rural Area: Dormitory	Rural: Other Areas	**ALL Churches**
1994	330	0	330	170	7,290	0	980	7,470	16,570
%▼	*–21*	–	*–12*	*–24*	*–18*	–	*–33*	*–27*	*–23*
2002	**260**	**0**	**290**	**130**	**5,990**	**0**	**660**	**5,470**	**12,800**
1994▶	*2*	*0*	*2*	*1*	*44*	*0*	*6*	*45*	*100%*
2002▶	***2***	***0***	***2***	***1***	***47***	***0***	***5***	***43***	***100%***
Number of churches									
1994	2	0	7	2	47	0	14	106	178
2002	**2**	**0**	**7**	**2**	**46**	**0**	**14**	**101**	**172**

Catholic: One kind of churchmanship, not to be identified solely with the Roman Catholic church. [1] Revised figure

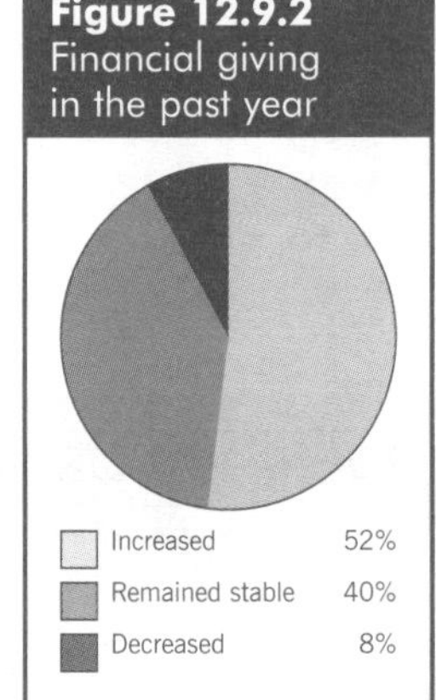

Figure 12.9.2 Financial giving in the past year

Figure 12.9.3 By 2010, our church will have...

Grown significantly	10%
Grown a little	31%
Remained stable	24%
Declined	26%
Closed	9%

Table 12.9.5 Age and gender of churchgoers 1984, 1994 and 2002

Age Group	Population 1984 Male %	Female %	Total %	Churchgoers in 1984 Male %	Female %	Total %	Population 1994 Male %	Female %	Total %	Churchgoers in 1994 Male %	Female %	Total %	Population 2002 Male %	Female %	Total %	Churchgoers in 2002 Male %	Female %	Total %
<12 }	*11*	*10*	*21*	*10*	*13*	*23*	*10*	*9*	*19*	*10*	*13*	*23*	*7*	*7*	*14*	*6*	*7*	*13*
12–14 }													*2*	*2*	*4*	*1*	*1*	*2*
15–19	*5*	*4*	*9*	*2*	*3*	*5*	*3*	*3*	*6*	*1*	*2*	*3*	*3*	*3*	*6*	*1*	*1*	*2*
20–29	*7*	*6*	*13*	*3*	*4*	*7*	*7*	*6*	*13*	*1*	*4*	*5*	*5*	*4*	*9*	*2*	*3*	*5*
30–44	*9*	*9*	*18*	*5*	*9*	*14*	*10*	*10*	*20*	*5*	*8*	*13*	*10*	*11*	*21*	*4*	*8*	*12*
45–64	*11*	*12*	*23*	*11*	*16*	*27*	*12*	*13*	*25*	*11*	*17*	*28*	*13*	*14*	*27*	*10*	*17*	*27*
65/65+	*6*	*10*	*16*	*8*	*16*	*24*	*7*	*10*	*17*	*9*	*19*	*28*	*9*	*10*	*19*	*14*	*25*	*39*
All ages	*49*	*51*	*100*	*39*	*61*	*100*	*49*	*51*	*100*	*37*	*63*	*100*	*49*	*51*	*100*	*38*	*62*	***100***

12.10 Dunbartonshire: East[1]

[1] *Formerly the Bearsden & Milngavie and Strathkelvin Districts of Strathclyde*

Table 12.10.1

OVERALL FIGURES	1984	1994	**2002**
Total population	111,250	112,850	108,010
Usual Sunday church attendance	23,870	18,830	14,260
% attending on Sunday	*21·5*	*16·7*	*13·2*
Number of churches	55	56	57
Population per church	2,020	2,020	1,890

Figure 12.10.1 Percentage of population in church by age-group

Table 12.10.2 Sunday attendance by denomination

	Church of Scotland	Other Presbyterian	Episcopal	Baptist	Independent	Smaller Denoms.	Total Protestant	Roman Catholic	**Total Christian**
1984	11,130	290	390	660	990	170	13,630	10,240	23,870
%▼	*–11*	*+7*	*+31*	*+41*	*+98*	*+6*	*+1*	*–28*	*–11*
1990	9,900	310	510	930	1,960	180	13,790	7,390	21,180
%▼	*–14*	*+13*	*+10*	*–9*	*+4*	*–11*	*–9*	*–14*	*–11*
1994	8,550	350	560	850	2,040	160	12,510	6,320	18,830
%▼	*–29*	*–31*	*–39*	*–20*	*–14*	*–19*	*–26*	*–20*	*–24*
2002	**6,060**	**240**	**340**	**680**	**1,750**	**130**	**9,200**	**5,060**	**14,260**
1984►	*46*	*1*	*2*	*3*	*4*	*1*	*57*	*43*	*100%*
1994►	*45*	*2*	*3*	*4*	*11*	*1*	*66*	*34*	*100%*
2002►	***43***	***2***	***2***	***5***	***12***	***1***	***65***	***35***	***100%***
Number of churches									
1984	25	3	4	3	6	1	42	13	55
1994	18	3	4	4	11	3	43	13	56
2002	**18**	**3**	**4**	**4**	**11**	**4**	**44**	**13**	**57**

Figure 12.10.2 Financial giving in the past year

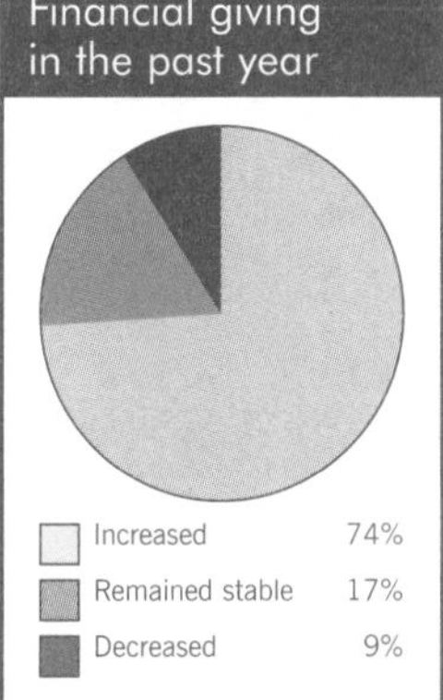

Table 12.10.3 Sunday attendance by churchmanship

	Reformed Evangelical	Mainstream Evangelical	Charismatic Evangelical	TOTAL Evangelical	Reformed	Low church	Liberal	Broad	Catholic*	**ALL Churches**
1994	3,520	2,040	130	5,690	2,550	50	1,090	2,090	7,360	18,830
%▼	*–43*	*+2*	*+62*	*–25*	*–30*	*+80*	*–38*	*–27*	*–20*	*–24*
2002	**2,000**	**2,080**	**210**	**4,290**	**1,780**	**90**	**680**	**1,530**	**5,890**	**14,260**
1994►	*18*	*11*	*1*	*30*	*14*	*0*	*6*	*11*	*39*	*100%*
2002►	***14***	***15***	***1***	***30***	***12***	***1***	***5***	***11***	***41***	***100%***
Number of churches										
1994	10	13	1	24	7	1	5	8	11	56
2002	**10**	**13**	**1**	**24**	**7**	**2**	**5**	**8**	**11**	**57**

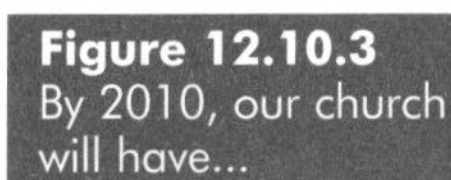

Figure 12.10.3 By 2010, our church will have...

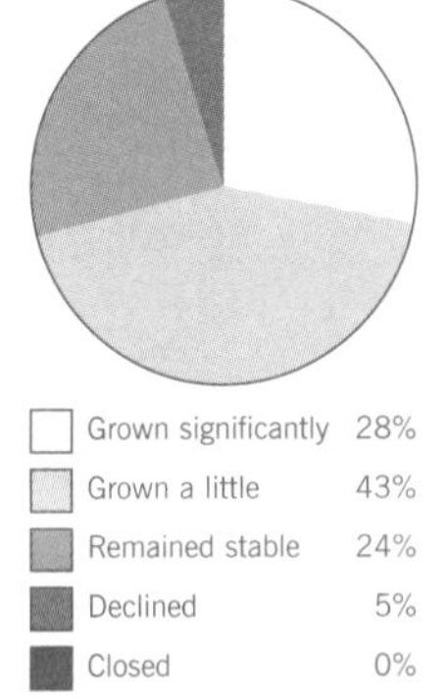

Table 12.10.4 Sunday attendance by environment

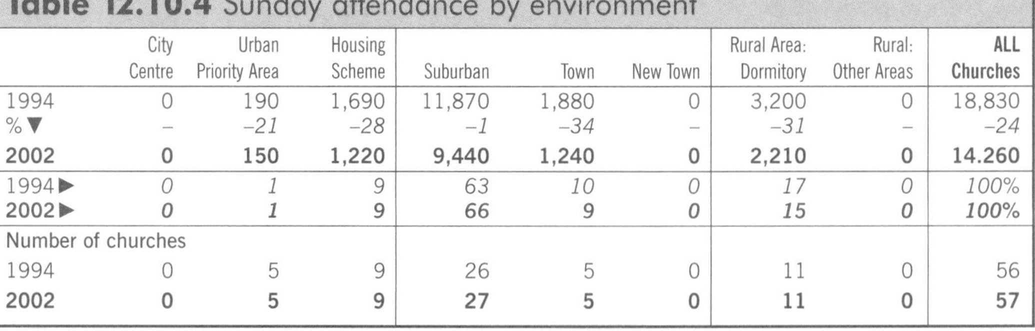

	City Centre	Urban Priority Area	Housing Scheme	Suburban	Town	New Town	Rural Area: Dormitory	Rural: Other Areas	**ALL Churches**
1994	0	190	1,690	11,870	1,880	0	3,200	0	18,830
%▼	–	*–21*	*–28*	*–1*	*–34*	–	*–31*	–	*–24*
2002	**0**	**150**	**1,220**	**9,440**	**1,240**	**0**	**2,210**	**0**	**14.260**
1994►	*0*	*1*	*9*	*63*	*10*	*0*	*17*	*0*	*100%*
2002►	***0***	***1***	***9***	***66***	***9***	***0***	***15***	***0***	***100%***
Number of churches									
1994	0	5	9	26	5	0	11	0	56
2002	**0**	**5**	**9**	**27**	**5**	**0**	**11**	**0**	**57**

*Catholic: One kind of churchmanship, not to be identified solely with the Roman Catholic church.

Table 12.10.5 Age and gender of churchgoers 1984, 1994 and 2002

Age Group	Population 1984			Churchgoers in 1984			Population 1994			Churchgoers in 1994			Population 2002			Churchgoers in 2002		
	Male %	Female %	Total %	Male %	Female %	Total %	Male %	Female %	Total %	Male %	Female %	Total %	Male %	Female %	Total %	Male %	Female %	Total %
<12 } 12–14	*12*	*11*	**23**	*15*	*17*	**32**	*10*	*10*	**20**	*7*	*9*	**16**						
<12													*7*	*7*	**14**	*5*	*7*	**12**
12–14													*2*	*2*	**4**	*2*	*2*	**4**
15–19	*5*	*4*	**9**	*3*	*5*	**8**	*3*	*3*	**6**	*3*	*3*	**6**	*3*	*3*	**6**	*2*	*2*	**4**
20–29	*6*	*7*	**13**	*3*	*6*	**9**	*7*	*6*	**13**	*4*	*5*	**9**	*6*	*7*	**13**	*3*	*3*	**6**
30–44	*11*	*11*	**22**	*7*	*11*	**18**	*11*	*12*	**23**	*8*	*12*	**20**	*11*	*11*	**22**	*5*	*11*	**16**
45–64	*10*	*12*	**22**	*9*	*12*	**21**	*12*	*13*	**25**	*11*	*19*	**30**	*13*	*13*	**26**	*13*	*18*	**31**
65/65+	*4*	*7*	**11**	*4*	*8*	**12**	*5*	*8*	**13**	*7*	*12*	**19**	*7*	*8*	**15**	*10*	*17*	**27**
All ages	*48*	*52*	***100***	*41*	*59*	***100***	*48*	*52*	***100***	*40*	*60*	***100***	*49*	*51*	***100***	*40*	*60*	***100***

[1] *Excluding 19 churches now part of Argyll & Bute, and 4 churches now in the city of Glasgow.*

Table 12.11.1

OVERALL FIGURES	1984	1994	**2002**
Total population	93,740	94,230	92,850
Usual Sunday church attendance	19,380	12,300	10,470
% attending on Sunday	*20·7*	*13·1*	*11·3*
Number of churches	57	62	62
Population per church	1,640	1,520	1,500

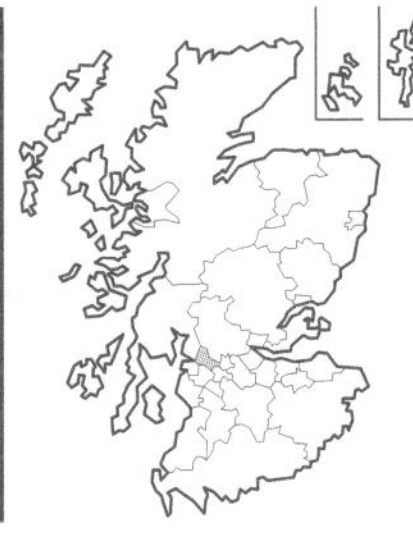

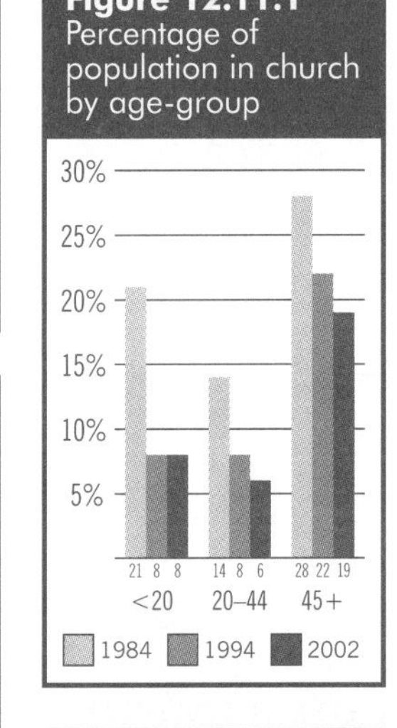

Figure 12.11.1 Percentage of population in church by age-group

Table 12.11.2 Sunday attendance by denomination

	Church of Scotland	Other Presbyterian	Episcopal	Baptist	Independent	Smaller Denoms.	Total Protestant	Roman Catholic	**Total Christian**
1984	5,250	460	220	510	650	210	7,300	12,080	19,380
%▼	*–26*	*–22*	*–45*	*–31*	*+3*	*+57*	*–20*	*–22*	*–21*
1990	3,980	360	120	350	670	330	5,810	9,440	15,250
%▼	*–17*	*–8*	*–8*	*–37*	*–3*	*+12*	*–14*	*–23*	*–19*
1994	3,320	330	110	220	650	370	5,000	7,300	12,300
%▼	*–15*	*–15*	*+45*	*–32*	*+22*	*+24*	*–7*	*–21*	*–15*
2002	**2,830**	**280**	**160**	**150**	**790**	**460**	**4,670**	**5,800**	**10,470**
1984▶	*27*	*3*	*1*	*3*	*3*	*1*	*38*	*62*	*100%*
1994▶	*27*	*3*	*1*	*2*	*5*	*3*	*41*	*59*	*100%*
2002▶	***27***	***3***	***2***	***1***	***8***	***4***	***45***	***55***	***100%***
Number of churches									
1984	21	5	3	3	9	3	44	13	57
1994	18	5	3	3	12	7	48	14	62
2002	**18**	**5**	**3**	**3**	**12**	**7**	**48**	**14**	**62**

Table 12.11.3 Sunday attendance by churchmanship

	Reformed Evangelical	Mainstream Evangelical	Charismatic Evangelical	TOTAL Evangelical	Reformed	Low church	Liberal	Broad	Catholic*	**ALL Churches**
1994	790	710	200	1,700	1,850	150	560	1,030	7,010	12,300
%▼	*–25*	*+51*	*0*	*+9*	*–36*	*–60*	*–25*	*–3*	*–15*	*–15*
2002	**590**	**1,070**	**200**	**1,860**	**1,190**	**60**	**420**	**1,000**	**5,940**	**10,470**
1994▶	*6*	*6*	*2*	*14*	*15*	*1*	*5*	*8*	*57*	*100%*
2002▶	***6***	***10***	***2***	***18***	***11***	***1***	***4***	***9***	***57***	***100%***
Number of churches										
1994	9	10	5	24	9	1	4	8	16	62
2002	**9**	**10**	**5**	**24**	**9**	**1**	**4**	**8**	**16**	**62**

Table 12.11.4 Sunday attendance by environment

	City Centre	Urban Priority Area	Housing Scheme	Suburban	Town	New Town	Rural Area: Dormitory	Rural: Other Areas	**ALL Churches**
1994	0	340	2,480	1,900	6,040	0	1,250	290	12,300
%▼	–	*+3*	*–25*	*–2*	*–20*	–	*+5*	*–14*	*–15*
2002	**0**	**350**	**1,870**	**1,860**	**4,830**	**0**	**1,310**	**250**	**10,470**
1994▶	*0*	*3*	*20*	*16*	*49*	*0*	*10*	*2*	*100%*
2002▶	***0***	***3***	***18***	***18***	***46***	***0***	***13***	***2***	***100%***
Number of churches									
1994	0	3	14	6	26	0	9	4	62
2002	**0**	**3**	**14**	**6**	**26**	**0**	**9**	**4**	**62**

**Catholic: One kind of churchmanship, not to be identified solely with the Roman Catholic church.*

Figure 12.11.2 Financial giving in the past year

Increased	61%
Remained stable	21%
Decreased	18%

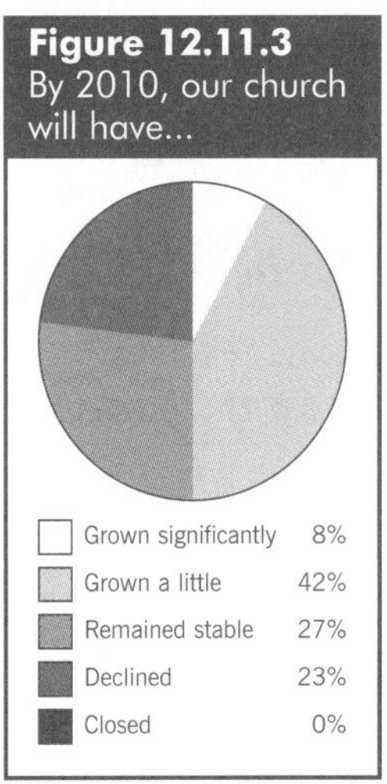

Figure 12.11.3 By 2010, our church will have...

Table 12.11.5 Age and gender of churchgoers 1984, 1994 and 2002

Age Group	Population 1984 Male %	Female %	Total %	Churchgoers in 1984 Male %	Female %	Total %	Population 1994 Male %	Female %	Total %	Churchgoers in 1994 Male %	Female %	Total %	Population 2002 Male %	Female %	Total %	Churchgoers in 2002 Male %	Female %	Total %
<12 } 12–14 }	*12*	*12*	*24*	*12*	*15*	*27*	*10*	*10*	*20*	*4*	*7*	*11*	*8* *2*	*8* *2*	*16* *4*	*5* *2*	*6* *3*	*11* *5*
15–19	*5*	*4*	*9*	*3*	*4*	*7*	*3*	*3*	*6*	*2*	*3*	*5*	*4*	*3*	*7*	*1*	*2*	*3*
20–29	*7*	*8*	*15*	*3*	*5*	*8*	*8*	*8*	*16*	*3*	*4*	*7*	*7*	*6*	*13*	*3*	*4*	*7*
30–44	*10*	*10*	*20*	*5*	*10*	*15*	*11*	*11*	*22*	*7*	*10*	*17*	*10*	*13*	*23*	*4*	*7*	*11*
45–64	*10*	*11*	*21*	*7*	*15*	*22*	*10*	*11*	*21*	*13*	*21*	*34*	*11*	*11*	*22*	*13*	*21*	*34*
65/65+	*4*	*7*	*11*	*6*	*15*	*21*	*6*	*9*	*15*	*8*	*18*	*26*	*6*	*9*	*15*	*10*	*19*	*29*
All ages	*48*	*52*	*100*	*36*	*64*	*100*	*48*	*52*	*100*	*37*	*63*	*100*	*48*	*52*	*100*	*38*	*62*	***100***

12.12 Dundee City[1]

[1] *Excluding 12 churches now included in Angus*

Table 12.12.1

OVERALL FIGURES	1984	1994	**2002**
Total population	143,780	146,290	144,070
Usual Sunday church attendance	20,620	17,750	14,030
% attending on Sunday	*14·3*	*12·1*	*9·7*
Number of churches	97	98	99
Population per church	1,480	1,490	1,460

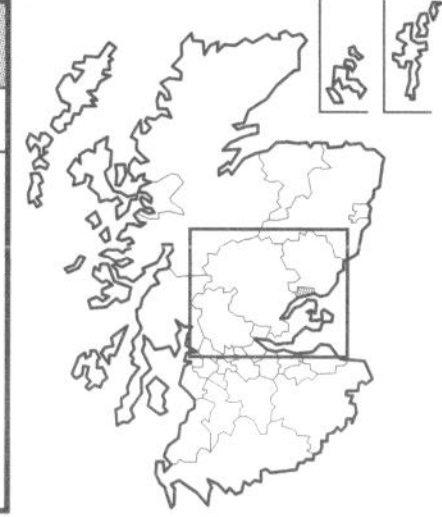

Table 12.12.2 Sunday attendance by denomination

	Church of Scotland	Other Presbyterian	Episcopal	Baptist	Independent	Smaller Denoms.	Total Protestant	Roman Catholic	**Total Christian**
1984	7,770	150	950	800	760	610	11,040	9,580	20,620
%▼	*–7*	*+7*	*+13*	*–20*	*+62*	*+20*	*0*	*–21*	*–10*
1990	7,240	160	1,070	640	1,230	730	11,070	7,580	18,650
%▼	*–6*	*0*	*+4*	*–3*	*+5*	*–4*	*–4*	*–7*	*–5*
1994	6,800	160	1,110	620	1,290	700	10,680	7,070	17,750
%▼	*–25*	*+19*	*–19*	*+35*	*+8*	*–27*	*–17*	*–28*	*–21*
2002	**5,080**	**190**	**900**	**840**	**1,390**	**510**	**8,910**	**5,120**	**14,030**
1984▶	*38*	*1*	*4*	*4*	*4*	*3*	*54*	*46*	*100%*
1994▶	*38*	*1*	*6*	*4*	*7*	*4*	*60*	*40*	*100%*
2002▶	***36***	***1***	***6***	***6***	***10***	***4***	***63***	***37***	***100%***
Number of churches									
1984	40	3	11	6	9	11	80	17	97
1994	36	4	12	6	9	12	79	19	98
2002	**36**	**5**	**12**	**6**	**9**	**12**	**80**	**19**	**99**

Table 12.12.3 Sunday attendance by churchmanship

	Reformed Evangelical	Mainstream Evangelical	Charismatic Evangelical	TOTAL Evangelical	Reformed	Low church	Liberal	Broad	Catholic*	**ALL Churches**
1994	1,610	1,170	1,450	4,230	1,210	2,070	1,820	1,610	6,810	17,750
%▼	*–65*	*+43*	*–8*	*–16*	*–42*	*–52*	*–7*	*–1*	*–20*	*–21*
2002	**560**	**1,670**	**1,340**	**3,570**	**700**	**1,000**	**1,700**	**1,600**	**5,460**	**14,030**
1994▶	*9*	*7*	*8*	*24*	*7*	*12*	*10*	*9*	*38*	*100%*
2002▶	***4***	***12***	***10***	***26***	***5***	***7***	***12***	***11***	***39***	***100%***
Number of churches										
1994	13	11	9	33	9	9	11	11	25	98
2002	**12**	**13**	**9**	**34**	**9**	**9**	**11**	**11**	**25**	**99**

Table 12.12.4 Sunday attendance by environment

	City Centre	Urban Priority Area	Housing Scheme	Suburban	Town	New Town	Rural Area: Dormitory	Rural: Other Areas	**ALL Churches**
1994	2,130	1,240	4,620	4,990	4,080	0	510	180	17,750
%▼	*–25*	*–46*	*–10*	*–13*	*–32*	–	*–15*	*–22*	*–21*
2002	**1,600**	**670**	**4,160**	**4,340**	**2,770**	**0**	**350**	**140**	**14,030**
1994▶	*12*	*7*	*26*	*28*	*23*	*0*	*3*	*1*	*100%*
2002▶	***11***	***5***	***30***	***31***	***20***	***0***	***2***	***1***	***100%***
Number of churches									
1994	14	9	18	34	14	0	5	4	98
2002	**14**	**9**	**18**	**35**	**14**	**0**	**5**	**4**	**99**

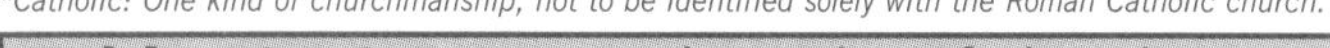

**Catholic: One kind of churchmanship, not to be identified solely with the Roman Catholic church.*

Figure 12.12.1 Percentage of population in church by age-group

	1984	1994	2002
<20	14	12	9
20–44	10	9	6
45+	18	16	13

Figure 12.12.2 Financial giving in the past year

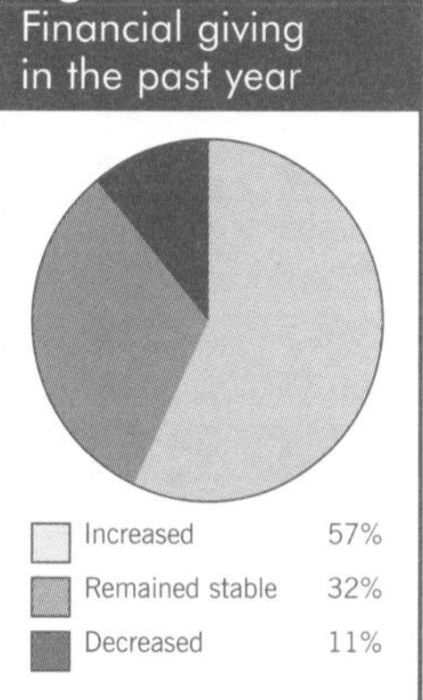

Figure 12.12.3 By 2010, our church will have...

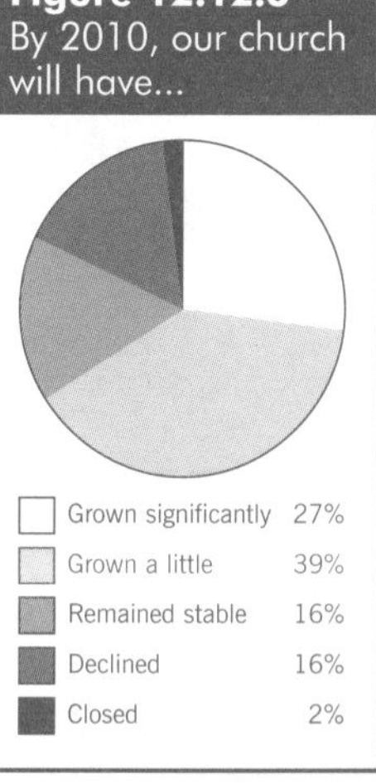

Table 12.12.5 Age and gender of churchgoers 1984, 1994 and 2002

Age Group	Population 1984 Male %	Female %	Total %	Churchgoers in 1984 Male %	Female %	Total %	Population 1994 Male %	Female %	Total %	Churchgoers in 1994 Male %	Female %	Total %	Population 2002 Male %	Female %	Total %	Churchgoers in 2002 Male %	Female %	Total %
<12	*10*	*10*	***20***	*9*	*13*	***22***	*9*	*9*	***18***	*7*	*9*	***16***	*7*	*7*	***14***	*5*	*6*	***11***
12–14													*2*	*2*	***4***	*1*	*2*	***3***
15–19	*5*	*4*	***9***	*3*	*3*	***6***	*3*	*3*	***6***	*3*	*4*	***7***	*3*	*3*	***6***	*2*	*5*	***7***
20–29	*7*	*8*	***15***	*3*	*6*	***9***	*9*	*8*	***17***	*4*	*6*	***10***	*7*	*6*	***13***	*4*	*6*	***10***
30–44	*9*	*9*	***18***	*5*	*10*	***15***	*10*	*10*	***20***	*6*	*10*	***16***	*11*	*11*	***22***	*5*	*8*	***13***
45–64	*11*	*12*	***23***	*9*	*15*	***24***	*11*	*12*	***23***	*9*	*16*	***25***	*11*	*12*	***23***	*9*	*16*	***25***
65/65+	*5*	*10*	***15***	*7*	*17*	***24***	*6*	*10*	***16***	*10*	*16*	***26***	*7*	*11*	***18***	*11*	*20*	***31***
All ages	*47*	*53*	***100***	*36*	*64*	***100***	*48*	*52*	***100***	*39*	*61*	***100***	*48*	*52*	***100***	*37*	*63*	***100***

[1] For other parts of Lothian, see Pages 12.21 and 12.22

Table 12.13.1

OVERALL FIGURES	1984	1994	**2002**
Total population	434,580	441,620	450,050
Usual Sunday church attendance	53,210	50,430	40,670
% attending on Sunday	*12·2*	*11·4*	*9·0*
Number of churches	229	237	241
Population per church	1,900	1,860	1,870

Table 12.13.2 Sunday attendance by denomination

	Church of Scotland	Other Presbyterian	Episcopal	Baptist	Independent	Smaller Denoms.	Total Protestant	Roman Catholic	**Total Christian**
1984	25,830	1,200[1]	3,020	4,410	1,700	2,450	38,610	14,600	53,210
%▼	*–2*	*+9*	*+25*	*–6*	*+35*	*+28*	*+3*	*–23*	*–4*
1990	25,260	1,310[1]	3,770	4,130	2,300	3,130	39,900	11,260	51,160
%▼	*–2*	*–11*	*+8*	*–14*	*+22*	*+20*	*0*	*–8*	*–1*
1994	24,710	1,170[1]	4,080	3,540	2,810	3,750	40,060	10,370	50,430
%▼	*–26*	*–19*	*+9*	*+5*	*+5*	*–30*	*–18*	*–26*	*–19*
2002	**18,310**	**950**	**4,460**	**3,700**	**2,960**	**2,640**	**33,020**	**7,650**	**40,670**
1984▶	*49*	*2*	*6*	*8*	*3*	*5*	*73*	*27*	*100%*
1994▶	*40*	*2*	*8*	*7*	*6*	*7*	*79*	*21*	*100%*
2002▶	***45***	***2***	***11***	***9***	***7***	***7***	***81***	***19***	***100%***
Number of churches									
1984	98	8[1]	28	19	17	28	198	31	229
1994	89	9[1]	30	17	26	35	206	31	237
2002	**89**	**9[1]**	**30**	**17**	**27**	**38**	**210**	**31**	**241**

Table 12.13.3 Sunday attendance by churchmanship

	Reformed Evangelical	Mainstream Evangelical	Charismatic Evangelical	TOTAL Evangelical	Reformed	Low church	Liberal	Broad	Catholic*	**ALL Churches**
1994	4,990	6,360	3,090	14,440	7,620	1,280	6,230	9,510	11,350	50,430
%▼	*–43*	*+20*	*+1*	*–6*	*–36*	*–23*	*+1*	*–48*	*–13*	*–19*
2002	**2,820**	**7,660**	**3,110**	**13,590**	**4,900**	**980**	**6,290**	**4,980**	**9,930**	**40,670**
1994▶	*10*	*13*	*6*	*29*	*15*	*3*	*12*	*19*	*22*	*100%*
2002▶	***7***	***19***	***8***	***34***	***12***	***2***	***16***	***12***	***24***	***100%***
Number of churches										
1994	24	38	22	84	26	12	36	41	38	237
2002	**24**	**40**	**23**	**87**	**26**	**12**	**37**	**41**	**38**	**241**

Table 12.13.4 Sunday attendance by environment

	City Centre	Urban Priority Area	Housing Scheme	Suburban	Town	New Town	Rural Area: Dormitory	Rural: Other Areas	**ALL Churches**
1994	12,100	4,530	4,030	21,870	6,560	0	1,010	330	50,430
%▼	*–14*	*–28*	*–25*	*–19*	*–21*	–	*–21*	*–18*	*–19*
2002	**10,400**	**3,240**	**3,020**	**17,750**	**5,190**	**0**	**800**	**270**	**40,670**
1994▶	*24*	*9*	*8*	*43*	*13*	*0*	*2*	*1*	*100%*
2002▶	***25***	***8***	***7***	***44***	***13***	***0***	***2***	***1***	***100%***
Number of churches									
1994	57	31	29	89	24	0	5	2	237
2002	**58**	**31**	**29**	**91**	**25**	**0**	**5**	**2**	**241**

*Catholic: One kind of churchmanship, not to be identified solely with the Roman Catholic church. [1] Revised figure

Figure 12.13.1 Percentage of population in church by age-group

30% 25% 20% 15% 10% 5%

11 11 7 <20; 10 8 6 20–44; 15 15 14 45+

1984 1994 2002

Figure 12.13.2 Financial giving in the past year

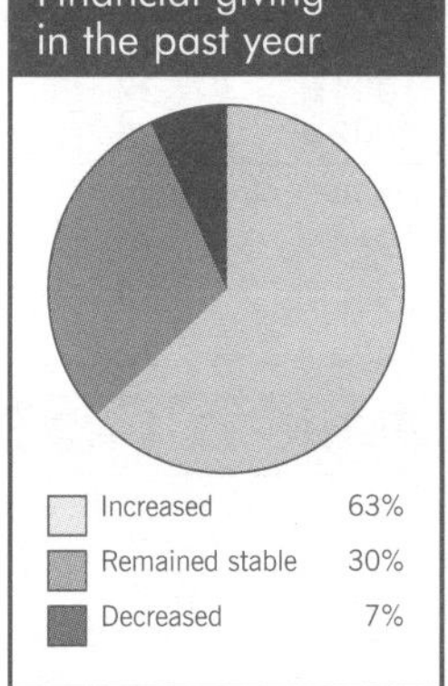

Increased 63%
Remained stable 30%
Decreased 7%

Figure 12.13.3 By 2010, our church will have...

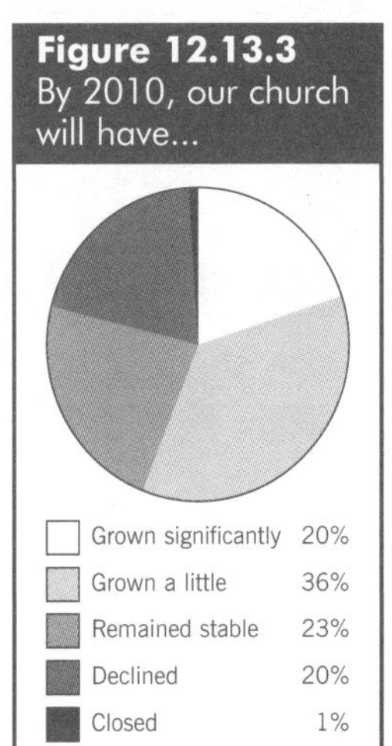

Grown significantly 20%
Grown a little 36%
Remained stable 23%
Declined 20%
Closed 1%

Table 12.13.5 Age and gender of churchgoers 1984, 1994 and 2002

Age Group	Population 1984			Churchgoers in 1984			Population 1994			Churchgoers in 1994			Population 2002			Churchgoers in 2002		
	Male %	Female %	Total %	Male %	Female %	Total %	Male %	Female %	Total %	Male %	Female %	Total %	Male %	Female %	Total %	Male %	Female %	Total %
<12 12–14	*9*	*9*	***18***	*7*	*11*	***18***	*8*	*8*	***16***	*8*	*9*	***17***	*7* *2*	*6* *2*	***13*** ***4***	*5* *3*	*6* *2*	***11*** ***5***
15–19	*4*	*4*	***8***	*2*	*3*	***5***	*3*	*3*	***6***	*2*	*3*	***5***	*3*	*3*	***6***	*1*	*2*	***3***
20–29	*8*	*8*	***16***	*5*	*7*	***12***	*10*	*9*	***19***	*5*	*6*	***11***	*8*	*8*	***16***	*4*	*5*	***9***
30–44	*9*	*9*	***18***	*6*	*10*	***16***	*11*	*11*	***22***	*7*	*10*	***17***	*13*	*12*	***25***	*7*	*9*	***16***
45–64	*11*	*12*	***23***	*8*	*15*	***23***	*10*	*11*	***21***	*9*	*14*	***23***	*10*	*11*	***21***	*10*	*15*	***25***
65/65+	*6*	*11*	***17***	*8*	*18*	***26***	*6*	*10*	***16***	*8*	*19*	***27***	*6*	*9*	***15***	*10*	*21*	***31***
All ages	*47*	*53*	***100***	*36*	*64*	***100***	*48*	*52*	***100***	*39*	*61*	***100***	*49*	*51*	***100***	*40*	*60*	***100***

12

12.14 Falkirk[1]

[1] Formerly part of Central Region

Table 12.14.1

OVERALL FIGURES	1984	1994	**2002**
Total population	142,240	142,000	145,730
Usual Sunday church attendance	21,740	17,790	14,100
% attending on Sunday	*15·3*	*12·5*	*9·7*
Number of churches	81	90	93
Population per church	1,760	1,580	1,570

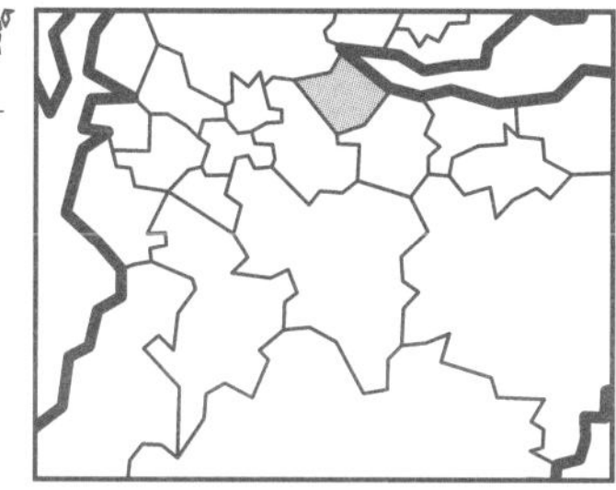

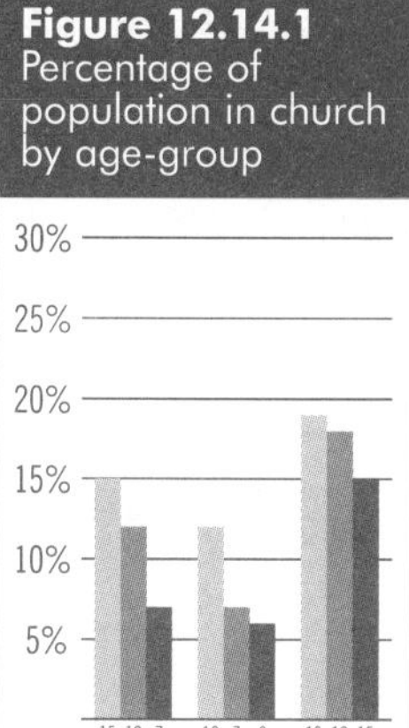
Figure 12.14.1 Percentage of population in church by age-group

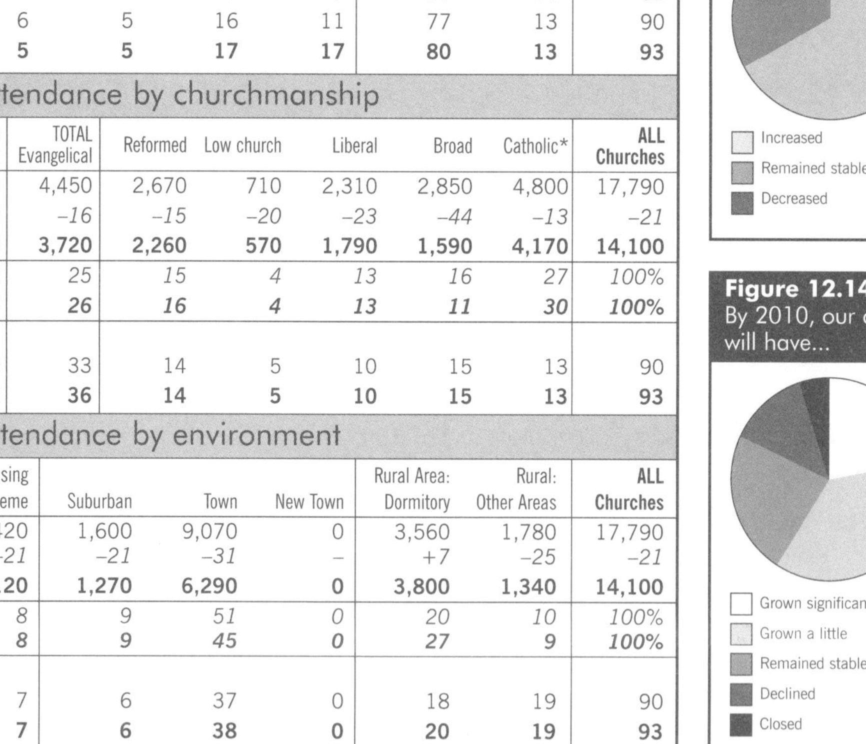

Table 12.14.2 Sunday attendance by denomination

	Church of Scotland	Other Presbyterian	Episcopal	Baptist	Independent	Smaller Denoms.	Total Protestant	Roman Catholic	**Total Christian**
1984	8,800	250	500	650	930	600	11,730	10,010	21,740
%▼	*–16*	*–12*	*–20*	*–15*	*+9*	*+28*	*–12*	*–11*	*–11*
1990	7,420	220	400	550	1,010	770	10,370	8,950	19,320
%▼	*–13*	*–9*	*0*	*–23*	*–11*	*+12*	*–11*	*–4*	*–8*
1994	6,440	200	400	400	900	860	9,200	8,590	17,790
%▼	*–24*	*+5*	*–25*	*–25*	*–10*	*+28*	*–17*	*–25*	*–21*
2002	**4,910**	**210**	**300**	**300**	**810**	**1,100**	**7,630**	**6,470**	**14,100**
1984►	*41*	*1*	*2*	*3*	*4*	*3*	*54*	*46*	*100%*
1994►	*37*	*1*	*2*	*2*	*5*	*5*	*52*	*48*	*100%*
2002►	***35***	***1***	***2***	***2***	***6***	***8***	***54***	***46***	***100%***
Number of churches									
1984	39	3	6	5	7	7	67	14	81
1994	36	3	6	5	16	11	77	13	90
2002	**32**	**4**	**5**	**5**	**17**	**17**	**80**	**13**	**93**

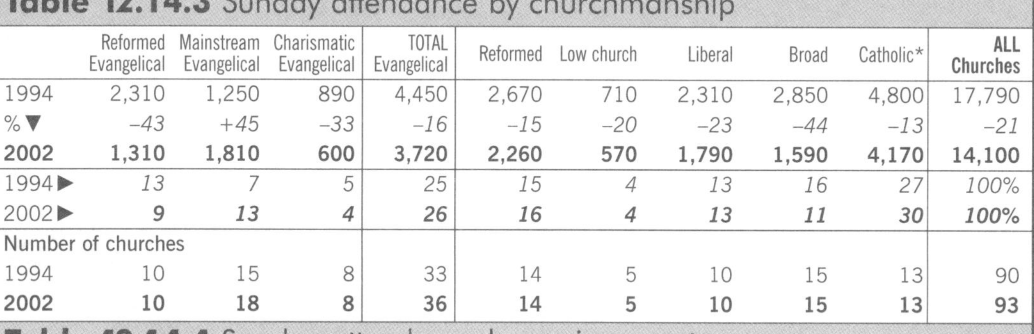

Table 12.14.3 Sunday attendance by churchmanship

	Reformed Evangelical	Mainstream Evangelical	Charismatic Evangelical	TOTAL Evangelical	Reformed	Low church	Liberal	Broad	Catholic*	**ALL Churches**
1994	2,310	1,250	890	4,450	2,670	710	2,310	2,850	4,800	17,790
%▼	*–43*	*+45*	*–33*	*–16*	*–15*	*–20*	*–23*	*–44*	*–13*	*–21*
2002	**1,310**	**1,810**	**600**	**3,720**	**2,260**	**570**	**1,790**	**1,590**	**4,170**	**14,100**
1994►	*13*	*7*	*5*	*25*	*15*	*4*	*13*	*16*	*27*	*100%*
2002►	***9***	***13***	***4***	***26***	***16***	***4***	***13***	***11***	***30***	***100%***
Number of churches										
1994	10	15	8	33	14	5	10	15	13	90
2002	**10**	**18**	**8**	**36**	**14**	**5**	**10**	**15**	**13**	**93**

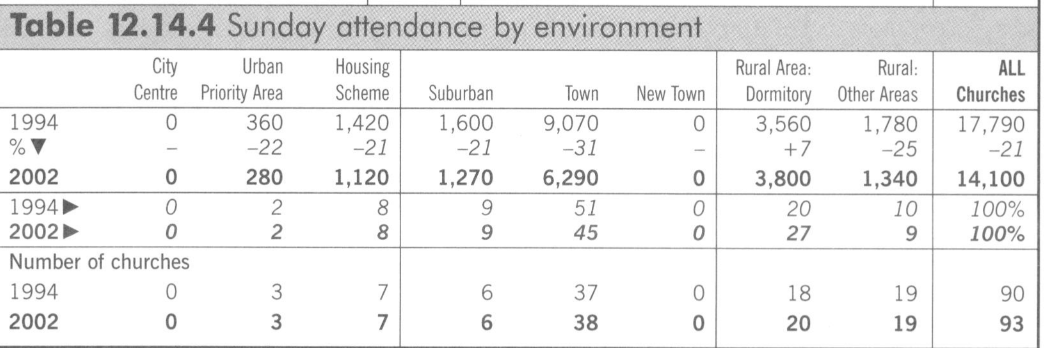

Table 12.14.4 Sunday attendance by environment

	City Centre	Urban Priority Area	Housing Scheme	Suburban	Town	New Town	Rural Area: Dormitory	Rural: Other Areas	**ALL Churches**
1994	0	360	1,420	1,600	9,070	0	3,560	1,780	17,790
%▼	–	*–22*	*–21*	*–21*	*–31*	–	*+7*	*–25*	*–21*
2002	**0**	**280**	**1,120**	**1,270**	**6,290**	**0**	**3,800**	**1,340**	**14,100**
1994►	*0*	*2*	*8*	*9*	*51*	*0*	*20*	*10*	*100%*
2002►	***0***	***2***	***8***	***9***	***45***	***0***	***27***	***9***	***100%***
Number of churches									
1994	0	3	7	6	37	0	18	19	90
2002	**0**	**3**	**7**	**6**	**38**	**0**	**20**	**19**	**93**

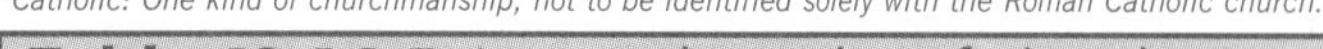
*Catholic: One kind of churchmanship, not to be identified solely with the Roman Catholic church.

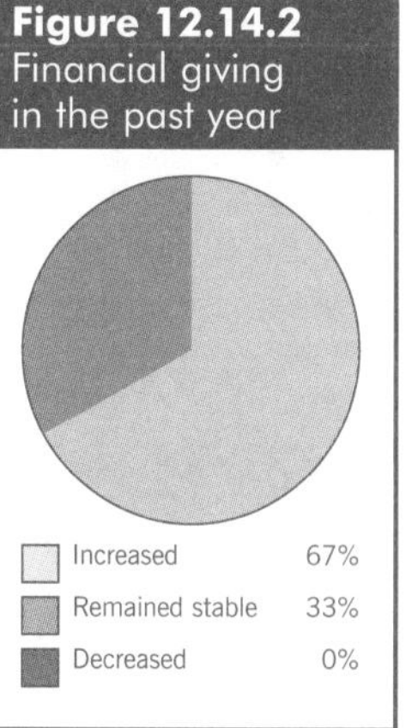
Figure 12.14.2 Financial giving in the past year

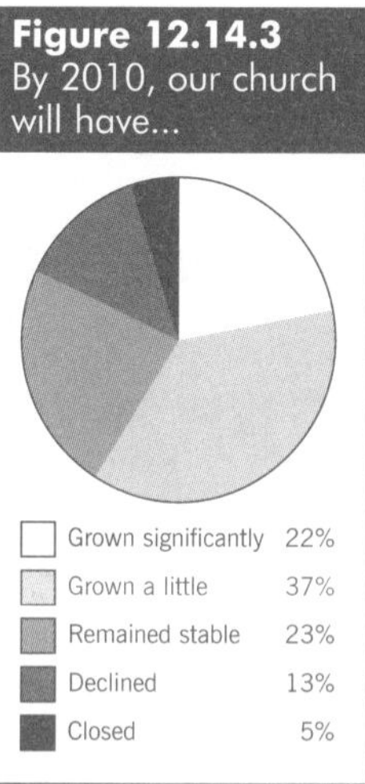
Figure 12.14.3 By 2010, our church will have...

Table 12.14.5 Age and gender of churchgoers 1984, 1994 and 2002

Age Group	Population 1984 Male %	Female %	Total %	Churchgoers in 1984 Male %	Female %	Total %	Population 1994 Male %	Female %	Total %	Churchgoers in 1994 Male %	Female %	Total %	Population 2002 Male %	Female %	Total %	Churchgoers in 2002 Male %	Female %	Total %
<12	*11*	*11*	***22***	*11*	*13*	***24***	*10*	*9*	***19***	*8*	*11*	***19***	*8*	*7*	***15***	*5*	*7*	***12***
12–14													*2*	*2*	***4***	*1*	*2*	***3***
15–19	*5*	*4*	***9***	*3*	*3*	***6***	*3*	*3*	***6***	*2*	*2*	***4***	*3*	*3*	***6***	*1*	*2*	***3***
20–29	*7*	*7*	***14***	*3*	*6*	***9***	*8*	*8*	***16***	*2*	*4*	***6***	*6*	*6*	***12***	*3*	*4*	***7***
30–44	*10*	*10*	***20***	*6*	*11*	***17***	*10*	*11*	***21***	*6*	*10*	***16***	*12*	*12*	***24***	*6*	*9*	***15***
45–64	*11*	*11*	***22***	*8*	*16*	***24***	*11*	*12*	***23***	*9*	*18*	***27***	*12*	*12*	***24***	*11*	*18*	***29***
65/65+	*5*	*8*	***13***	*7*	*13*	***20***	*6*	*9*	***15***	*10*	*18*	***28***	*6*	*9*	***15***	*11*	*20*	***31***
All ages	*49*	*51*	***100***	*38*	*62*	***100***	*48*	*52*	***100***	*37*	*63*	***100***	*49*	*51*	***100***	*38*	*62*	***100***

12

Table 12.15.1

OVERALL FIGURES	1984	1994	**2002**
Total population	352,200	351,200	351,100
Usual Sunday church attendance	40,600	33,660	28,040
% attending on Sunday	*11·5*	*9·6*	*8·0*
Number of churches	251	259	258
Population per church	1,400	1,360	1,360

Table 12.15.2 Sunday attendance by denomination

	Church of Scotland	Other Presbyterian	Episcopal	Baptist	Independent	Smaller Denoms.	Total Protestant	Roman Catholic	**Total Christian**
1984	21,260	660	1,620	2,370	2,190	1,790	29,890	10,710	40,600
%▼	*−16*	*−12*	*−27*	*−18*	*+30*	*−6*	*−13*	*−15*	*−13*
1990	17,890	580	1,180	1,940	2,840	1,680	26,110	9,050	35,160
%▼	*−7*	*−5*	*−18*	*−7*	*+29*	*+8*	*−3*	*−9*	*−4*
1994	16,630	550	970	1,800	3,670	1,820	25,440	8,220	33,660
%▼	*−21*	*−36*	*+8*	*+8*	*−11*	*+8*	*−15*	*−23*	*−17*
2002	**13,150**	**350**	**1,050**	**1,950**	**3,260**	**1,960**	**21,720**	**6,320**	**28,040**
1984▶	*52*	*2*	*4*	*6*	*5*	*5*	*74*	*26*	*100%*
1994▶	*49*	*2*	*3*	*5*	*11*	*6*	*76*	*24*	*100%*
2002▶	***47***	***1***	***4***	***7***	***11***	***7***	***77***	***23***	***100%***
Number of churches									
1984	111	9	19	18	33	29	219	32	251
1994	112	8	18	19	38[1]	31	226	33	259
2002	**110**	**8**	**18**	**20**	**38**	**31**	**225**	**33**	**258**

Table 12.15.3 Sunday attendance by churchmanship

	Reformed Evangelical	Mainstream Evangelical	Charismatic Evangelical	TOTAL Evangelical	Reformed	Low church	Liberal	Broad	Catholic*	**ALL Churches**
1994	3,270	3,340	2,600	9,210	4,790	1,210	4,940	5,860	7,650	33,660
%▼	*−20*	*+38*	*−23*	*0*	*−9*	*−10*	*−27*	*−25*	*−30*	*−17*
2002	**2,600**	**4,620**	**2,000**	**9,220**	**4,370**	**1,090**	**3,610**	**4,400**	**5,350**	**28,040**
1994▶	*10*	*10*	*7*	*27*	*14*	*4*	*15*	*17*	*23*	*100%*
2002▶	***9***	***16***	***7***	***33***	***15***	***4***	***13***	***16***	***19***	***100%***
Number of churches										
1994	21	39	23	83	36	15	42	44	39	259
2002	**19**	**40**	**23**	**82**	**36**	**15**	**42**	**44**	**39**	**258**

Table 12.15.4 Sunday attendance by environment

	City Centre	Urban Priority Area	Housing Scheme	Suburban	Town	New Town	Rural Area: Dormitory	Rural: Other Areas	**ALL Churches**
1994	90	310	3,700	1,350	17,480	3,360	3,670	3,700	33,660
%▼	*−11*	*−3*	*−10*	*+25*	*−28*	*−17*	*+6*	*−11*	*−17*
2002	**80**	**300**	**3,340**	**1,690**	**12,670**	**2,800**	**3,880**	**3,280**	**28,040**
1994▶	*0*	*1*	*11*	*4*	*54*	*10*	*11*	*11*	*100%*
2002▶	***0***	***1***	***12***	***6***	***45***	***10***	***14***	***12***	***100%***
Number of churches									
1994	3	5	29	10	109	18	36	49	259
2002	**3**	**5**	**28**	**10**	**111**	**18**	**35**	**48**	**258**

*Catholic: One kind of churchmanship, not to be identified solely with the Roman Catholic church. [1] Revised figure

Table 12.15.5 Age and gender of churchgoers 1984, 1994 and 2002

Age Group	Population 1984 Male %	Female %	Total %	Churchgoers in 1984 Male %	Female %	Total %	Population 1994 Male %	Female %	Total %	Churchgoers in 1994 Male %	Female %	Total %	Population 2002 Male %	Female %	Total %	Churchgoers in 2002 Male %	Female %	Total %
<12 } 12–14	*11*	*11*	***22***	*10*	*15*	***25***	*10*	*9*	***19***	*7*	*10*	***17***	*8*	*7*	***15***	*6*	*8*	***14***
12–14													*2*	*2*	***4***	*1*	*2*	***3***
15–19	*5*	*4*	***9***	*2*	*4*	***6***	*3*	*3*	***6***	*2*	*3*	***5***	*3*	*3*	***6***	*1*	*2*	***3***
20–29	*7*	*7*	***14***	*3*	*5*	***8***	*8*	*8*	***16***	*3*	*4*	***7***	*6*	*6*	***12***	*2*	*3*	***5***
30–44	*9*	*10*	***19***	*5*	*10*	***15***	*11*	*11*	***22***	*5*	*10*	***15***	*11*	*12*	***23***	*5*	*8*	***13***
45–64	*11*	*11*	***22***	*8*	*15*	***23***	*11*	*11*	***22***	*10*	*17*	***27***	*12*	*12*	***24***	*10*	*17*	***27***
65/65+	*6*	*8*	***14***	*7*	*16*	***23***	*6*	*9*	***15***	*10*	*19*	***29***	*7*	*9*	***16***	*12*	*23*	***35***
All ages	*49*	*51*	***100***	*35*	*65*	***100***	*49*	*51*	***100***	*37*	*63*	***100***	*49*	*51*	***100***	*37*	*63*	***100***

Figure 12.15.1 Percentage of population in church by age-group

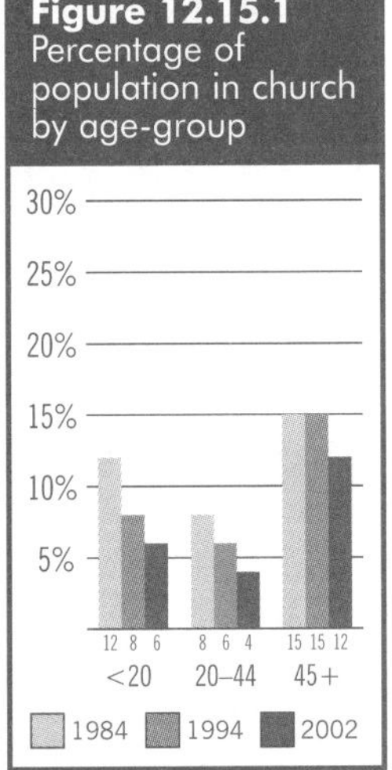

Figure 12.15.2 Financial giving in the past year

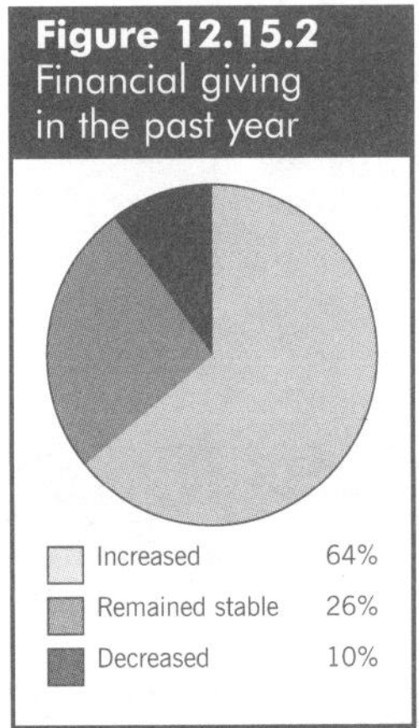

Figure 12.15.3 By 2010, our church will have...

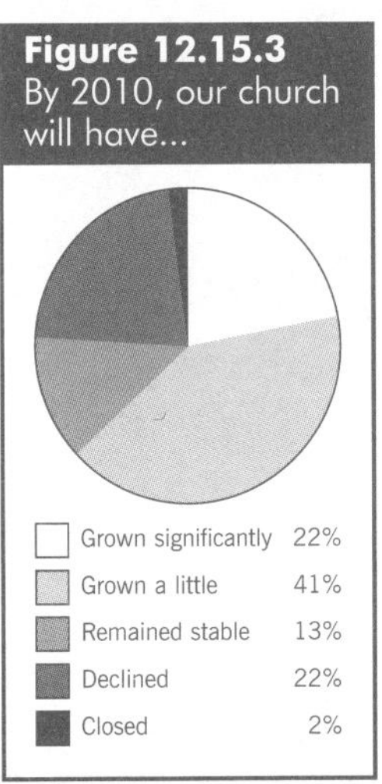

12.16 Glasgow City[1]

[1] *Including 4 churches which were in West Dunbartonshire and 15 churches which were in East Dunbartonshire*

Table 12.16.1

OVERALL FIGURES	1984	1994	**2002**
Total population	667,740	615,920	584,090
Usual Sunday church attendance	145,230	98,960	82,750
% attending on Sunday	*21·7*	*16·1*	*14·2*
Number of churches	401	400	400
Population per church	1,670	1,540	1,460

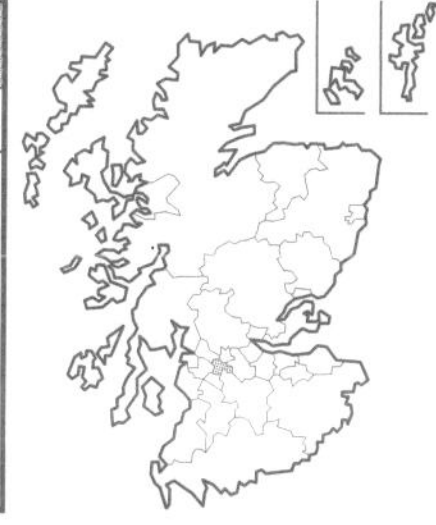

Figure 12.16.1 Percentage of population in church by age-group

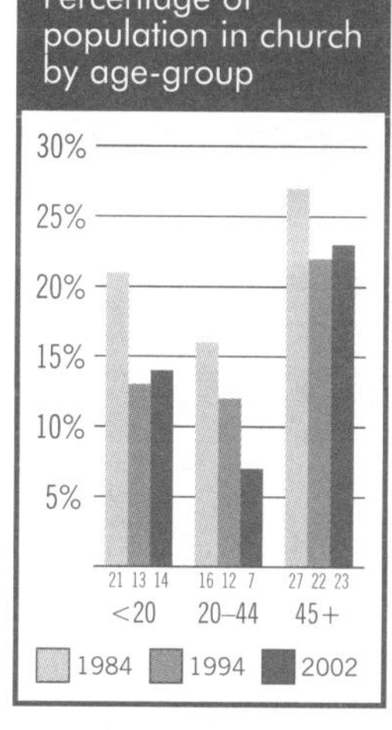

Table 12.16.2 Sunday attendance by denomination

	Church of Scotland	Other Presbyterian	Episcopal	Baptist	Independent	Smaller Denoms.	Total Protestant	Roman Catholic	**Total Christian**
1984	41,790[2]	2,660	1,590	3,330	3,940	4,670	57,980	87,250	145,230
%▼	*–17*	*–15*	*–19*	*–8*	*+13*	*–16*	*–14*	*–22*	*–19*
1990	34,730[2]	2,260	1,290	3,080[2]	4,460	3,920	49,740	67,930	117,670
%▼	*–15*	*–35*	*–4*	*+3*	*+4*	*–14*	*–13*	*–18*	*–16*
1994	29,540[2]	1,480	1,240[2]	3,180[2]	4,620	3,370	43,430	55,530	98,960
%▼	*–24*	*–15*	*+6*	*–3*	*–13*	*–17*	*–26*	*–14*	*–19*
2002	**22,390**	**1,170**	**1,320**	**3,100**	**4,010**	**2,800**	**34,790**	**47,960**	**82,750**
1984▶	*29*	*2*	*1*	*2*	*3*	*3*	*40*	*60*	*100%*
1994▶	*30*	*2*	*1*	*3*	*5*	*3*	*44*	*56*	*100%*
2002▶	***27***	***1***	***2***	***4***	***5***	***3***	***42***	***58***	***100%***
Number of churches									
1984	150[2]	26[2]	18	24[2]	39[2]	50	307	94[2]	401
1994	141[2]	25[2]	16	24[2]	54[2]	43	303	97[2]	400
2002	**140**	**25**	**16**	**23**	**53**	**46**	**303**	**97**	**400**

Table 12.16.3 Sunday attendance by churchmanship

	Reformed Evangelical	Mainstream Evangelical	Charismatic Evangelical	TOTAL Evangelical	Reformed	Low church	Liberal	Broad	Catholic*	**ALL Churches**
1994	5,640	7,140	3,520	16,300	13,230	2,630	3,870	8,220	54,710	98,960
%▼	*–43*	*+30*	*+9*	*0*	*–13*	*–24*	*–15*	*–40*	*–19*	*–19*
2002	**3,190**	**9,310**	**3,850**	**16,350**	**11,560**	**2,010**	**3,290**	**4,960**	**44,580**	**82,750**
1994▶	*6*	*7*	*4*	*17*	*13*	*3*	*4*	*8*	*55*	*100%*
2002▶	***4***	***11***	***5***	***20***	***14***	***2***	***4***	***6***	***54***	***100%***
Number of churches										
1994	44	80	28	152	56	20	32	48	92	400
2002	**43**	**79**	**29**	**151**	**58**	**20**	**33**	**46**	**92**	**400**

Table 12.16.4 Sunday attendance by environment

	City Centre	Urban Priority Area	Housing Scheme	Suburban	Town	New Town	Rural Area: Dormitory	Rural: Other Areas	**ALL Churches**
1994	21,420	13,420	22,530	35,370	4,930	0	1,290	0	98,960
%▼	*–22*	*–34*	*–37*	*+6*	*–14*	*–*	*+9*	*–*	*–19*
2002	**16,650**	**8,830**	**14,260**	**37,370**	**4,240**	**0**	**1,400**	**0**	**82,750**
1994▶	*22*	*13*	*23*	*36*	*5*	*0*	*1*	*0*	*100%*
2002▶	***20***	***11***	***17***	***45***	***5***	***0***	***2***	***0***	***100%***
Number of churches									
1994	60	88	84	128	32	0	8	0	400
2002	**60**	**88**	**84**	**128**	**32**	**0**	**8**	**0**	**400**

**Catholic: One kind of churchmanship, not to be identified solely with the Roman Catholic church. [2] Revised figure*

Figure 12.16.2 Financial giving in the past year

Increased	59%
Remained stable	26%
Decreased	15%

Figure 12.16.3 By 2010, our church will have...

Grown significantly	21%
Grown a little	34%
Remained stable	19%
Declined	24%
Closed	2%

Table 12.16.5 Age and gender of churchgoers 1984, 1994 and 2002

Age Group	Population 1984 Male %	Female %	Total %	Churchgoers in 1984 Male %	Female %	Total %	Population 1994 Male %	Female %	Total %	Churchgoers in 1994 Male %	Female %	Total %	Population 2002 Male %	Female %	Total %	Churchgoers in 2002 Male %	Female %	Total %
<12 / 12–14	*10*	*10*	**20**	*10*	*13*	***23***	*10*	*9*	**19**	*7*	*9*	***16***						
<12													*7*	*7*	**14**	*6*	*7*	***13***
12–14													*2*	*2*	**4**	*2*	*3*	***5***
15–19	*5*	*4*	**9**	*2*	*3*	***5***	*3*	*3*	**6**	*2*	*3*	***5***	*3*	*3*	**6**	*2*	*3*	***5***
20–29	*8*	*8*	**16**	*4*	*5*	***9***	*9*	*9*	**18**	*5*	*5*	***10***	*8*	*8*	**16**	*3*	*4*	***7***
30–44	*8*	*8*	**16**	*5*	*9*	***14***	*10*	*10*	**20**	*7*	*11*	***18***	*13*	*13*	**26**	*6*	*9*	***15***
45–64	*11*	*12*	**23**	*8*	*17*	***25***	*10*	*11*	**21**	*9*	*16*	***25***	*9*	*10*	**19**	*9*	*15*	***24***
65/65+	*6*	*10*	**16**	*7*	*17*	***24***	*6*	*10*	**16**	*9*	*17*	***26***	*6*	*9*	**15**	*10*	*21*	***31***
All ages	*48*	*52*	***100***	*36*	*64*	***100***	*48*	*52*	***100***	*39*	*61*	***100***	*48*	*52*	***100***	*38*	*62*	***100***

Highland, including Argyll and Bute[1] 12.17

[1] Including 19 churches formerly in the Dumbarton District of Strathclyde

Table 12.17.1

OVERALL FIGURES	1984	1994	**2002**
Total population	281,090	286,250	285,110
Usual Sunday church attendance	51,880	43,430	36,200
% attending on Sunday	*18·5*	*15·2*	*12·7*
Number of churches	531	531	520
Population per church	530	540	550

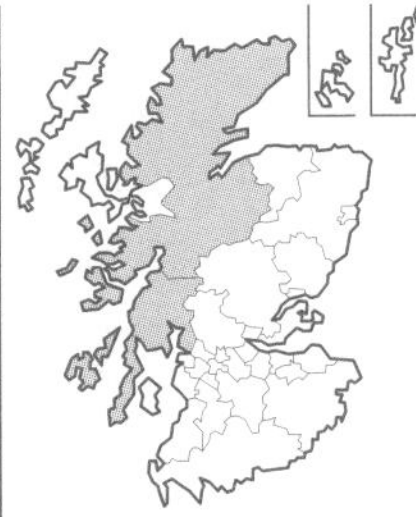

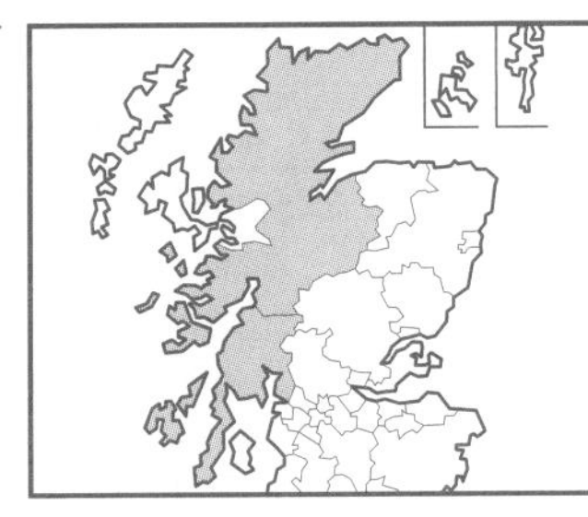

Table 12.17.2 Sunday attendance by denomination

	Church of Scotland	Other Presbyterian	Episcopal	Baptist	Independent	Smaller Denoms.	Total Protestant	Roman Catholic	**Total Christian**
1984	25,580	6,000	1,750	1,310	1,190	1,380	37,210	14,670	51,880
%▼	*–12*	*0*	*+3*	*+5*	*–2*	*+68*	*–6*	*–21*	*–10*
1990	22,530	5,980	1,790	1,370	1,170	2,320	35,160	11,540	46,700
%▼	*–11*	*–5*	*+2*	*+5*	*+32*	*+18*	*–5*	*–13*	*–7*
1994	20,160	5,700	1,830	1,440	1,550	2,730	33,410	10,020	43,430
%▼	*–22*	*–2*	*+6*	*0*	*0*	*–23*	*–15*	*–22*	*–17*
2002	**15,760**	**5,600**	**1,940**	**1,440**	**1,550**	**2,090**	**28,380**	**7,820**	**36,200**
1984▶	*49*	*12*	*3*	*3*	*2*	*3*	*72*	*28*	*100%*
1994▶	*47*	*13*	*4*	*3*	*4*	*6*	*77*	*23*	*100%*
2002▶	***44***	***15***	***5***	***4***	***4***	***6***	***78***	***22***	***100%***
Number of churches									
1984	198	153	42	17	20	19	449	82	531
1994	197	146	50	20	24	31	468	63[2]	531
2002	**196**	**136**	**50**	**21**	**23**	**33**	**459**	**61**	**520**

Table 12.17.3 Sunday attendance by churchmanship

	Reformed Evangelical	Mainstream Evangelical	Charismatic Evangelical	TOTAL Evangelical	Reformed	Low church	Liberal	Broad	Catholic*	**ALL Churches**
1994	9,830	5,190	1,700	16,720	8,580	3,320	2,620	4,840	7,350	43,430
%▼	*–28*	*+9*	*–1*	*–14*	*–13*	*–20*	*–14*	*–33*	*–16*	*–17*
2002	**7,080**	**5,650**	**1,690**	**14,420**	**7,480**	**2,650**	**2,260**	**3,240**	**6,150**	**36,200**
1994▶	*22*	*12*	*4*	*38*	*20*	*8*	*6*	*11*	*17*	*100%*
2002▶	***19***	***16***	***5***	***40***	***21***	***7***	***6***	***9***	***17***	***100%***
Number of churches										
1994	159	53	21	233	95	37	27	58	81	531
2002	**152**	**53**	**21**	**226**	**94**	**37**	**27**	**58**	**78**	**520**

Table 12.17.4 Sunday attendance by environment

	City Centre	Urban Priority Area	Housing Scheme	Suburban	Town	New Town	Rural Area: Dormitory	Rural: Other Areas	**ALL Churches**
1994	430	0	2,180	660	17,120	0	4,620	18,420	43,430
%▼	*+35*	–	*–17*	*–17*	*–36*	–	*–30*	*+4*	*–17*
2002	**580**	**0**	**1,820**	**550**	**10,910**	**0**	**3,250**	**19,090**	**36,200**
1994▶	*1*	*0*	*5*	*1*	*39*	*0*	*11*	*43*	*100%*
2002▶	***2***	***0***	***5***	***1***	***30***	***0***	***9***	***53***	***100%***
Number of churches									
1994	3	0	11	3	100	0	42	372	531
2002	**3**	**0**	**11**	**3**	**99**	**0**	**42**	**362**	**520**

*Catholic: One kind of churchmanship, not to be identified solely with the Roman Catholic church. [2] Revised figure

Figure 12.17.1 Percentage of population in church by age-group

Age group	1984	1994	2002
<20	17	16	10
20–44	13	9	7
45+	25	20	19

Figure 12.17.2 Financial giving in the past year

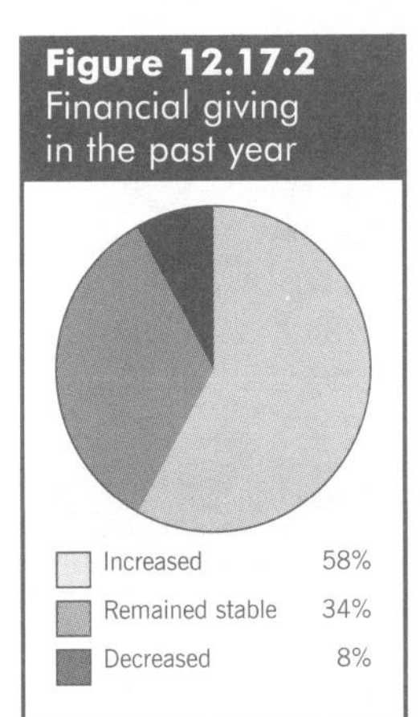

Figure 12.17.3 By 2010, our church will have...

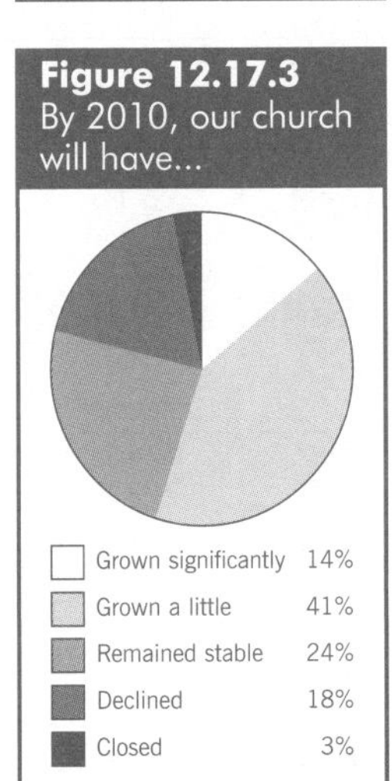

Table 12.17.5 Age and gender of churchgoers 1984, 1994 and 2002

Age Group	Population 1984			Churchgoers in 1984			Population 1994			Churchgoers in 1994			Population 2002			Churchgoers in 2002		
	Male %	Female %	Total %	Male %	Female %	Total %	Male %	Female %	Total %	Male %	Female %	Total %	Male %	Female %	Total %	Male %	Female %	Total %
<12 }	*11*	*11*	**22**	*10*	*13*	**23**	*10*	*9*	**19**	*10*	*11*	**21**	*7*	*7*	**14**	*7*	*6*	**13**
12–14 }													*2*	*2*	**4**	*1*	*2*	**3**
15–19	*5*	*4*	**9**	*2*	*3*	**5**	*3*	*2*	**5**	*2*	*3*	**5**	*3*	*3*	**6**	*1*	*2*	**3**
20–29	*7*	*7*	**14**	*3*	*4*	**7**	*7*	*7*	**14**	*2*	*4*	**6**	*6*	*5*	**11**	*2*	*2*	**4**
30–44	*10*	*9*	**19**	*6*	*10*	**16**	*11*	*11*	**22**	*6*	*9*	**15**	*11*	*11*	**22**	*5*	*8*	**13**
45–64	*10*	*11*	**21**	*9*	*15*	**24**	*12*	*12*	**24**	*11*	*16*	**27**	*13*	*13*	**26**	*12*	*17*	**29**
65/65+	*6*	*9*	**15**	*9*	*16*	**25**	*6*	*10*	**16**	*9*	*17*	**26**	*7*	*10*	**17**	*14*	*21*	**35**
All ages	*49*	*51*	**100**	*39*	*61*	**100**	*49*	*51*	**100**	*40*	*60*	**100**	*49*	*51*	**100**	*42*	*58*	**100**

12.18 Inverclyde[1]

[1] Formerly part of Renfrew and Inverclyde District of Strathclyde; 1984, 1990 and 1994 figures estimated pro rata to number of churches

Table 12.18.1

OVERALL FIGURES	1984	1994	**2002**
Total population	100,770	94,160	83,730
Usual Sunday church attendance	22,280	18,640	14,340
% attending on Sunday	*22·1*	*19·8*	*17·1*
Number of churches	56	57	59
Population per church	1,800	1,650	1,420

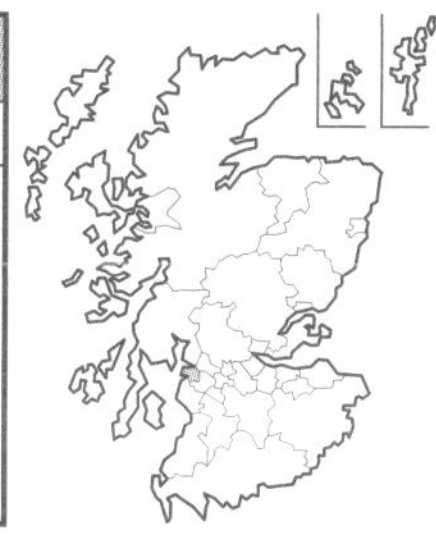

Figure 12.18.1 Percentage of population in church by age-group

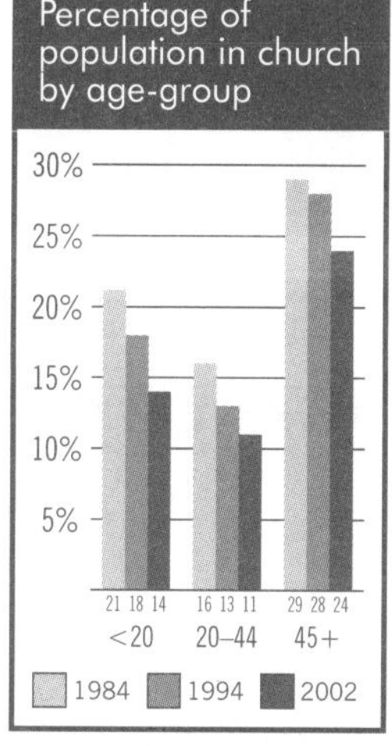

Table 12.18.2 Sunday attendance by denomination

	Church of Scotland	Other Presbyterian	Episcopal	Baptist	Independent	Smaller Denoms.	Total Protestant	Roman Catholic	**Total Christian**
1984	7,630	220	360	370	770	870	10,220	12,060	22,280
%▼	*–8*	*–14*	*–53*	*–8*	*–19*	*+10*	*–9*	*–12*	*–10*
1990	7,030	190	170	340	620	960	9,310	10,670	19,980
%▼	*–13*	*–16*	*–18*	*–12*	*–3*	*+11*	*–10*	*–4*	*–7*
1994	6,140	160	140	300	600	1,070	8,410	10,230	18,640
%▼	*–29*	*–12*	*+7*	*+87*	*–65*	*+10*	*–22*	*–24*	*–23*
2002	**4,330**	**140**	**150**	**560**	**210**	**1,180**	**6,570**	**7,770**	**14,340**
1984▶	*34*	*1*	*2*	*2*	*3*	*4*	*46*	*54*	*100%*
1994▶	*33*	*1*	*1*	*1*	*3*	*6*	*45*	*55*	*100%*
2002▶	***30***	***1***	***1***	***4***	***2***	***8***	***46***	***54***	***100%***
Number of churches									
1984	24	2	3	3	7	6	45	11	56
1994	21	2	3	3	7	9	45	12	57
2002	**21**	**2**	**3**	**4**	**3**	**14**	**47**	**12**	**59**

Figure 12.18.2 Financial giving in the past year

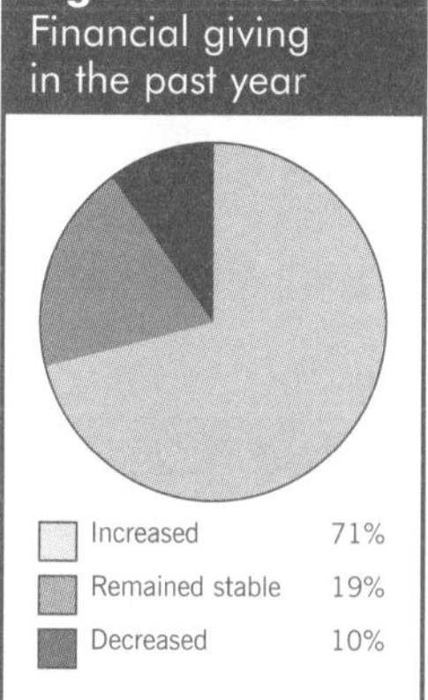

Table 12.18.3 Sunday attendance by churchmanship

	Reformed Evangelical	Mainstream Evangelical	Charismatic Evangelical	TOTAL Evangelical	Reformed	Low church	Liberal	Broad	Catholic*	**ALL Churches**
1994	840	880	800	2,520	3,130	1,130	1,230	1,110	9,520	18,640
%▼	*–39*	*+14*	*–11*	*–12*	*–38*	*–29*	*–20*	*–28*	*–20*	*–23*
2002	**510**	**1,000**	**710**	**2,220**	**1,930**	**800**	**980**	**800**	**7,610**	**14,340**
1994▶	*4*	*5*	*4*	*13*	*17*	*6*	*7*	*6*	*51*	*100%*
2002▶	***3***	***7***	***5***	***15***	***13***	***6***	***7***	***6***	***53***	***100%***
Number of churches										
1994	4	8	8	20	12	4	9	3	9	57
2002	**4**	**9**	**8**	**21**	**12**	**4**	**10**	**3**	**9**	**59**

Table 12.18.4 Sunday attendance by environment

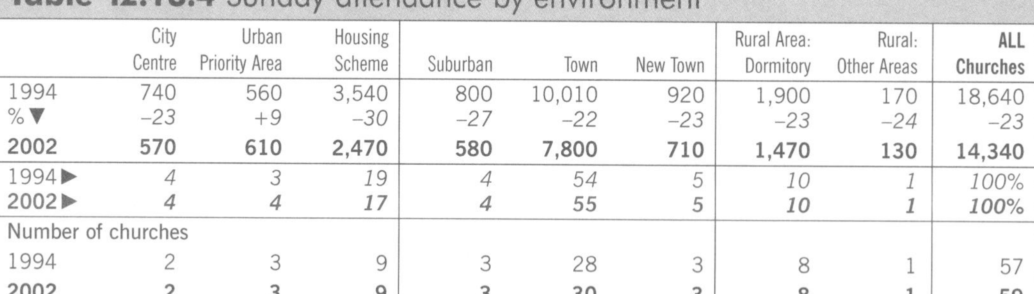

	City Centre	Urban Priority Area	Housing Scheme	Suburban	Town	New Town	Rural Area: Dormitory	Rural: Other Areas	**ALL Churches**
1994	740	560	3,540	800	10,010	920	1,900	170	18,640
%▼	*–23*	*+9*	*–30*	*–27*	*–22*	*–23*	*–23*	*–24*	*–23*
2002	**570**	**610**	**2,470**	**580**	**7,800**	**710**	**1,470**	**130**	**14,340**
1994▶	*4*	*3*	*19*	*4*	*54*	*5*	*10*	*1*	*100%*
2002▶	***4***	***4***	***17***	***4***	***55***	***5***	***10***	***1***	***100%***
Number of churches									
1994	2	3	9	3	28	3	8	1	57
2002	**2**	**3**	**9**	**3**	**30**	**3**	**8**	**1**	**59**

*Catholic: One kind of churchmanship, not to be identified solely with the Roman Catholic church.

Figure 12.18.3 By 2010, our church will have...

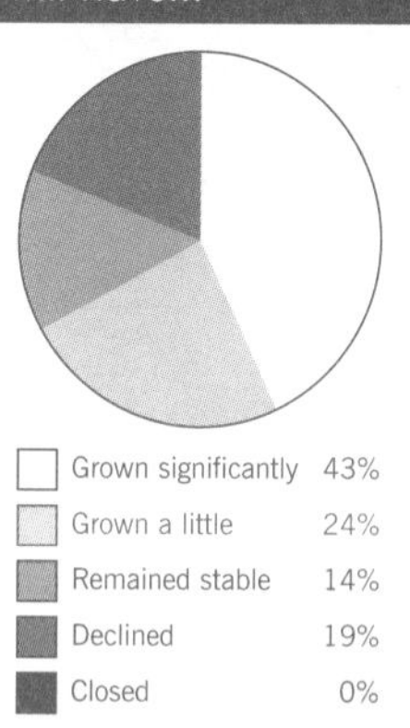

Table 12.18.5 Age and gender of churchgoers 1984, 1994 and 2002

Age Group	Population 1984			Churchgoers in 1984			Population 1994			Churchgoers in 1994			Population 2002			Churchgoers in 2002		
	Male %	Female %	Total %	Male %	Female %	Total %	Male %	Female %	Total %	Male %	Female %	Total %	Male %	Female %	Total %	Male %	Female %	Total %
<12 } 12–14 }	*11*	*11*	**22**	*11*	*13*	**24**	*10*	*9*	**19**	*9*	*9*	**18**	8	7	**15**	*7*	*7*	**14**
													2	2	**4**	*2*	*2*	**4**
15–19	5	5	**10**	*2*	*4*	**6**	3	3	**6**	*2*	*3*	**5**	3	3	**6**	*1*	*2*	**3**
20–29	8	7	**15**	*3*	*6*	**9**	8	8	**16**	*3*	*5*	**8**	6	6	**12**	*3*	*3*	**6**
30–44	9	10	**19**	*5*	*11*	**16**	11	11	**22**	*6*	*11*	**17**	11	12	**23**	*6*	*10*	**16**
45–64	11	11	**22**	*9*	*16*	**25**	11	12	**23**	*12*	*18*	**30**	12	12	**24**	*11*	*16*	**27**
65/65+	4	8	**12**	*7*	*13*	**20**	5	9	**14**	*7*	*15*	**22**	6	10	**16**	*11*	*19*	**30**
All ages	48	52	**100**	*37*	*63*	**100**	48	52	**100**	*39*	*61*	**100**	48	52	**100**	*41*	*59*	**100**

[1] *Formerly Motherwell & Monklands and Cumbernauld & Kilsyth Districts of Strathclyde*

Table 12.19.1

OVERALL FIGURES	1984	1994	**2002**
Total population	330,860	329,720	321,470
Usual Sunday church attendance	77,800	60,400	52,360
% attending on Sunday	*23·5*	*18·3*	*16·3*
Number of churches	210	214	212
Population per church	1,580	1,540	1,520

Figure 12.19.1
Percentage of population in church by age-group

	<20	20–44	45+
1984	22	18	31
1994	18	13	23
2002	16	9	24

Table 12.19.2 Sunday attendance by denomination

	Church of Scotland	Other Presbyterian	Episcopal	Baptist	Independent	Smaller Denoms.	Total Protestant	Roman Catholic	**Total Christian**
1984	18,070	580	380	2,110	4,990	2,670	28,800	49,000	77,800
%▼	*–5*	*–17*	*–21*	*–33*	*+2*	*–24*	*–8*	*–18*	*–14*
1990	17,170	480	300	1,410	5,080	2,030	26,470	40,260	66,730
%▼	*–2*	*+2*	*+3*	*–4*	*+7*	*–9*	*–1*	*–15*	*–9*
1994	16,790	490	310	1,350	5,420	1,850	26,210	34,190	60,400
%▼	*–17*	*–18*	*–16*	*–21*	*–1*	*+13*	*–12*	*–14*	*–13*
2002	**13,890**	**400**	**260**	**1,070**	**5,380**	**2,090**	**23,090**	**29,270**	**52,360**
1984▶	*23*	*1*	*1*	3	6	3	37	63	*100%*
1994▶	*28*	*1*	*0*	2	9	3	43	57	*100%*
2002▶	***27***	***1***	***0***	**2**	***10***	***4***	**44**	**56**	***100%***
Number of churches									
1984	67	7	6	8	46	28	162	48	210
1994	64	7	5	9	49	28	162	52	214
2002	**64**	**7**	**5**	**9**	**48**	**27**	**160**	**52**	**212**

Figure 12.19.2
Financial giving in the past year

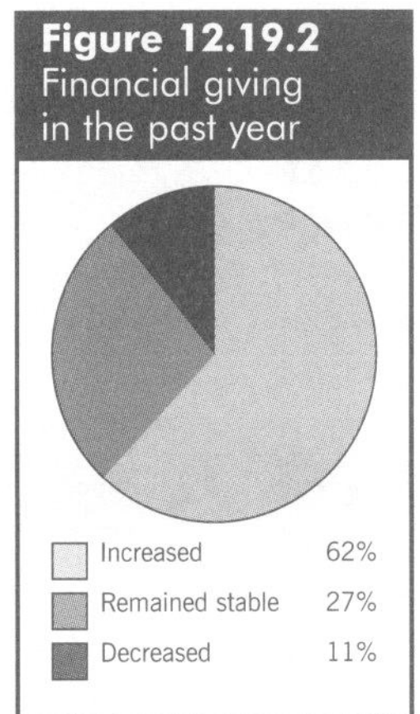

Increased	62%
Remained stable	27%
Decreased	11%

Table 12.19.3 Sunday attendance by churchmanship

	Reformed Evangelical	Mainstream Evangelical	Charismatic Evangelical	TOTAL Evangelical	Reformed	Low church	Liberal	Broad	Catholic*	**ALL Churches**
1994	6,520	4,840	3,160	14,520	5,660	670	2,940	4,470	32,140	60,400
%▼	*–33*	*+10*	*–5*	*–13*	*–22*	*–66*	*–34*	*–11*	*–9*	*–13*
2002	**4,390**	**5,300**	**3,010**	**12,700**	**4,390**	**230**	**1,950**	**3,970**	**29,120**	**52,360**
1994▶	*11*	*8*	*5*	*24*	9	*1*	5	*8*	53	*100%*
2002▶	***8***	***10***	**6**	***24***	**8**	***0***	***4***	***8***	***56***	***100%***
Number of churches										
1994	42	48	14	104	36	7	11	24	32	214
2002	**42**	**48**	**14**	**104**	**36**	**5**	**11**	**24**	**32**	**212**

Figure 12.19.3
By 2010, our church will have...

Grown significantly	19%
Grown a little	37%
Remained stable	18%
Declined	24%
Closed	2%

Table 12.19.4 Sunday attendance by environment

	City Centre	Urban Priority Area	Housing Scheme	Suburban	Town	New Town	Rural Area: Dormitory	Rural: Other Areas	**ALL Churches**
1994	0	7,250	12,680	4,230	22,950	5,440	4,830	3,020	60,400
%▼	–	*–24*	*–13*	*–7*	*–11*	*–16*	*–12*	*–13*	*–13*
2002	**0**	**5,490**	**11,030**	**3,930**	**20,470**	**4,580**	**4,240**	**2,620**	**52,360**
1994▶	*0*	*12*	*21*	*7*	*38*	*9*	*8*	*5*	*100%*
2002▶	***0***	***10***	***21***	***8***	***39***	***9***	***8***	***5***	***100%***
Number of churches									
1994	0	20	37	11	91	22	19	14	214
2002	**0**	**20**	**36**	**11**	**90**	**22**	**19**	**14**	**212**

**Catholic: One kind of churchmanship, not to be identified solely with the Roman Catholic church.*

Table 12.19.5 Age and gender of churchgoers 1984, 1994 and 2002

Age Group	Population 1984			Churchgoers in 1984			Population 1994			Churchgoers in 1994			Population 2002			Churchgoers in 2002		
	Male %	Female %	Total %	Male %	Female %	Total %	Male %	Female %	Total %	Male %	Female %	Total %	Male %	Female %	Total %	Male %	Female %	Total %
<12 } 12–14	*12*	*12*	***24***	*11*	*15*	***26***	*10*	*10*	***20***	*9*	*11*	***20***	*8*	*7*	***15***	*7*	*8*	***15***
													2	*2*	***4***	*2*	*3*	***5***
15–19	*5*	*5*	***10***	*2*	*4*	***6***	*3*	*3*	***6***	*3*	*3*	***6***	*3*	*3*	***6***	*2*	*2*	***4***
20–29	*8*	*7*	***15***	*3*	*6*	***9***	*8*	*8*	***16***	*5*	*6*	***11***	*7*	*7*	***14***	*3*	*4*	***7***
30–44	*9*	*9*	***18***	*6*	*10*	***16***	*11*	*11*	***22***	*7*	*10*	***17***	*12*	*12*	***24***	*6*	*9*	***15***
45–64	*10*	*12*	***22***	*8*	*14*	***22***	*11*	*12*	***23***	*10*	*16*	***26***	*11*	*12*	***23***	*11*	*16*	***27***
65/65+	*4*	*7*	***11***	*7*	*14*	***21***	*5*	*8*	***13***	*7*	*13*	***20***	*6*	*8*	***14***	*10*	*17*	***27***
All ages	*48*	*52*	***100***	*37*	*63*	***100***	*48*	*52*	***100***	*41*	*59*	***100***	*49*	*51*	***100***	*41*	*59*	***100***

12

12.20 Lanarkshire: South[1]

[1] Previously East Kilbride and Hamilton & Clydesdale in Strathclyde

Table 12.20.1

OVERALL FIGURES	1984	1994	**2002**
Total population	336,840	309,490	302,610
Usual Sunday church attendance	43,940	37,480	28,870
% attending on Sunday	*13·0*	*12·1*	*9·5*
Number of churches	159	163	163
Population per church	2,120	1,900	1,860

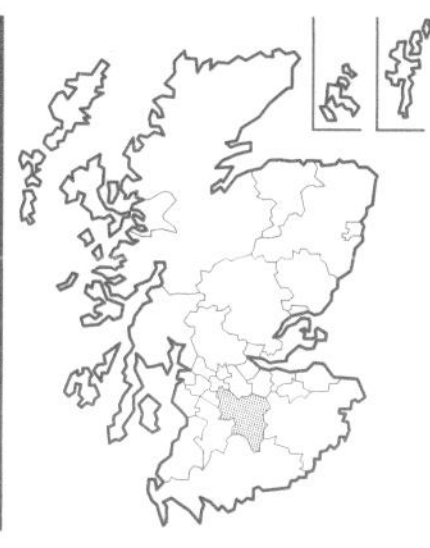

Figure 12.20.1 Percentage of population in church by age-group

Table 12.20.2 Sunday attendance by denomination

	Church of Scotland	Other Presbyterian	Episcopal	Baptist	Independent	Smaller Denoms.	Total Protestant	Roman Catholic	**Total Christian**
1984	16,630	330	440	2,120	3,450	900	23,870	20,070	43,940
%▼	*–8*	*–61*	*–25*	*–19*	*–3*	*–46*	*–11*	*–10*	*–11*
1990	15,230	130	330	1,710	3,330	490	21,220	18,020	39,240
%▼	*–10*	*+23*	*+15*	*–10*	*+8*	*–2*	*–6*	*–2*	*–4*
1994	13,730	160	380	1,540	3,580	480	19,870	17,610	37,480
%▼	*–22*	*+25*	*–21*	*–16*	*–21*	*+8*	*–20*	*–26*	*–23*
2002	**10,730**	**200**	**300**	**1,300**	**2,830**	**520**	**15,880**	**12,990**	**28,870**
1984▶	*38*	*0*	*1*	*5*	*8*	*2*	*54*	*46*	*100%*
1994▶	*37*	*0*	*1*	*4*	*10*	*1*	*53*	*47*	*100%*
2002▶	***37***	***1***	***1***	***4***	***10***	***2***	***55***	***45***	***100%***
Number of churches									
1984	68	3	5	9	37	14	136	23[2]	159
1994	64[2]	2	3	7	48	16[2]	140	23	163
2002	**64**	**4**	**3**	**6**	**46**	**17**	**140**	**23**	**163**

Figure 12.20.2 Financial giving in the past year

Table 12.20.3 Sunday attendance by churchmanship

	Reformed Evangelical	Mainstream Evangelical	Charismatic Evangelical	TOTAL Evangelical	Reformed	Low church	Liberal	Broad	Catholic*	**ALL Churches**
1994	4,790	5,180	810	10,780	11,910	600	3,170	3,910	7,110	37,480
%▼	*–35*	*+8*	*–23*	*–13*	*–42*	*–57*	*–2*	*–23*	*–10*	*–23*
2002	**3,120**	**5,610**	**620**	**9,350**	**6,910**	**260**	**3,100**	**2,840**	**6,410**	**28,870**
1994▶	*13*	*14*	*2*	*29*	*32*	*2*	*8*	*10*	*19*	*100%*
2002▶	***11***	***19***	***2***	***32***	***24***	***1***	***11***	***10***	***22***	***100%***
Number of churches										
1994	26	37	10	73	41	8	16	14	11	163
2002	**26**	**37**	**9**	**72**	**41**	**8**	**17**	**14**	**11**	**163**

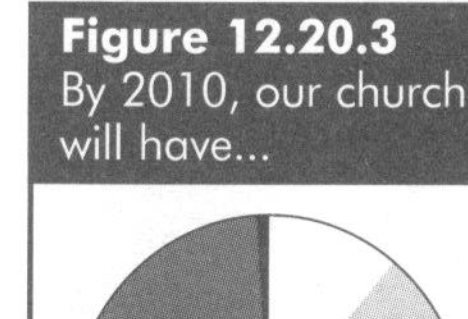

Figure 12.20.3 By 2010, our church will have...

Table 12.20.4 Sunday attendance by environment

	City Centre	Urban Priority Area	Housing Scheme	Suburban	Town	New Town	Rural Area: Dormitory	Rural: Other Areas	**ALL Churches**
1994	0	4,180	3,000	1,120	9,370	10,820	4,870	4,120	37,480
%▼	–	*–23*	*–30*	*–23*	*–11*	*–33*	*–22*	*–22*	*–23*
2002	**0**	**3,220**	**2,090**	**860**	**8,430**	**7,290**	**3,780**	**3,200**	**28,870**
1994▶	*0*	*11*	*8*	*3*	*25*	*29*	*13*	*11*	*100%*
2002▶	***0***	***11***	***7***	***3***	***29***	***25***	***14***	***11***	***100%***
Number of churches									
1994	0	6	15	9	41	28	25	39	163
2002	**0**	**6**	**15**	**9**	**40**	**28**	**26**	**39**	**163**

*Catholic: One kind of churchmanship, not to be identified solely with the Roman Catholic church. [2] Revised figure

Table 12.20.5 Age and gender of churchgoers 1984, 1994 and 2002

Age Group	Population 1984 Male %	Female %	Total %	Churchgoers in 1984 Male %	Female %	Total %	Population 1994 Male %	Female %	Total %	Churchgoers in 1994 Male %	Female %	Total %	Population 2002 Male %	Female %	Total %	Churchgoers in 2002 Male %	Female %	Total %
<12 } 12–14	*12*	*11*	***23***	*12*	*17*	***29***	*10*	*10*	***20***	*9*	*11*	***20***	*8*	*7*	***15***	*6*	*8*	***14***
													2	*2*	***4***	*2*	*4*	***6***
15–19	*5*	*4*	***9***	*2*	*4*	***6***	*4*	*3*	***7***	*3*	*3*	***6***	*2*	*2*	***4***	*2*	*2*	***4***
20–29	*7*	*8*	***15***	*3*	*6*	***9***	*8*	*7*	***15***	*4*	*6*	***10***	*6*	*6*	***12***	*1*	*2*	***3***
30–44	*10*	*10*	***20***	*6*	*10*	***16***	*11*	*11*	***22***	*8*	*11*	***19***	*12*	*12*	***24***	*2*	*2*	***4***
45–64	*11*	*11*	***22***	*8*	*15*	***23***	*11*	*12*	***23***	*9*	*16*	***25***	*12*	*12*	***24***	*5*	*8*	***13***
65/65+	*4*	*7*	***11***	*6*	*11*	***17***	*5*	*8*	***13***	*7*	*13*	***20***	*6*	*9*	***15***	*11*	*19*	***30***
All ages	*49*	*51*	***100***	*37*	*63*	***100***	*49*	*51*	***100***	*40*	*60*	***100***	*49*	*51*	***100***	*10*	*20*	***30***

[1] Formerly Other Lothian. for City of Edinburgh see Page 12.13

Table 12.21.1

OVERALL FIGURES	1984	1994	**2002**
Total population	159,930	165,550	171,310
Usual Sunday church attendance	20,470	16,420	13,670
% attending on Sunday	*12·8*	*9·9*	*8·0*
Number of churches	112	119	120
Population per church	1,430	1,390	1,430

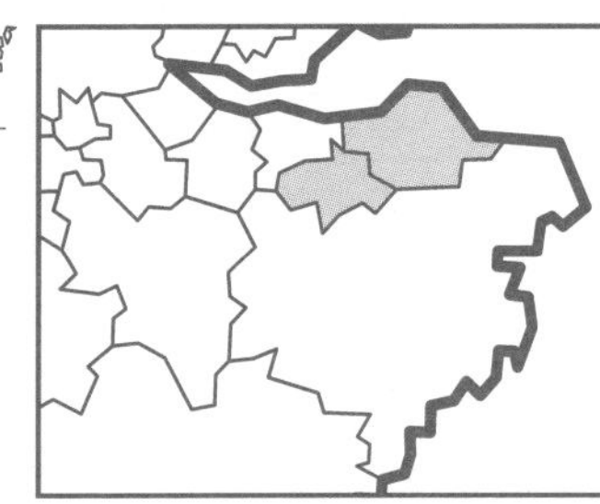

Table 12.21.2 Sunday attendance by denomination

	Church of Scotland	Other Presbyterian	Episcopal	Baptist	Independent	Smaller Denoms.	Total Protestant	Roman Catholic	**Total Christian**
1984	9,070	100	720	670	700	1,230	12,490	7,980	20,470
%▼	*–7*	*–30*	*–6*	*–12*	*+34*	*+14*	*–3*	*–18*	*–9*
1990	8,400	70	680	590	940	1,400	12,080	6,530	18,610
%▼	*–7*	*–14*	*+4*	*0*	*+5*	*–8*	*–5*	*–23*	*–12*
1994	7,780	60	710	590	990	1,290	11,420	5,000	16,420
%▼	*–20*	*0*	*–6*	*+12*	*–4*	*–26*	*–16*	*–17*	*–17*
2002	**6,250**	**60**	**670**	**660**	**950**	**950**	**9,540**	**4,130**	**13,670**
1984▶	*44*	*1*	*4*	*3*	*3*	*6*	*61*	*39*	*100%*
1994▶	*48*	*0*	*4*	*4*	*6*	*8*	*70*	*30*	*100%*
2002▶	***46***	***0***	***5***	***5***	***7***	***7***	***70***	***30***	***100%***
Number of churches									
1984	58	2	11	4	8	12	95	17	112
1994	57	2	10	6	14	14	103	16	119
2002	**57**	**2**	**10**	**6**	**14**	**15**	**104**	**16**	**120**

Table 12.21.3 Sunday attendance by churchmanship

	Reformed Evangelical	Mainstream Evangelical	Charismatic Evangelical	TOTAL Evangelical	Reformed	Low church	Liberal	Broad	Catholic*	**ALL Churches**
1994	2,580	1,310	1,040	4,930	2,420	660	2,670	2,130	3,610	16,420
%▼	*–27*	*+40*	*–14*	*–6*	*–28*	*–33*	*–29*	*–12*	*–14*	*–17*
2002	**1,890**	**1,840**	**890**	**4,620**	**1,750**	**440**	**1,890**	**1,880**	**3,090**	**13,670**
1994▶	*16*	*8*	*6*	*30*	*15*	*4*	*16*	*13*	*22*	*100%*
2002▶	***14***	***13***	***7***	***34***	***13***	***3***	***14***	***14***	***22***	***100%***
Number of churches										
1994	15	17	10	42	17	7	17	19	17	119
2002	**15**	**17**	**11**	**43**	**17**	**7**	**17**	**19**	**17**	**120**

Table 12.21.4 Sunday attendance by environment

	City Centre	Urban Priority Area	Housing Scheme	Suburban	Town	New Town	Rural Area: Dormitory	Rural: Other Areas	**ALL Churches**
1994	0	330	990	160	7,550	0	5,910	1,480	16,420
%▼	*–*	*–18*	*–24*	*–6*	*–25*	*–*	*–3*	*–26*	*–17*
2002	**0**	**270**	**750**	**150**	**5,680**	**0**	**5,720**	**1,100**	**13,670**
1994▶	*0*	*2*	*6*	*1*	*46*	*0*	*36*	*9*	*100%*
2002▶	***0***	***2***	***5***	***1***	***42***	***0***	***42***	***8***	***100%***
Number of churches									
1994	0	2	11	1	45	0	36	24	119
2002	**0**	**2**	**11**	**1**	**46**	**0**	**36**	**24**	**120**

*Catholic: One kind of churchmanship, not to be identified solely with the Roman Catholic church.

Table 12.21.5 Age and gender of churchgoers 1984, 1994 and 2002

Age Group	Population 1984			Churchgoers in 1984			Population 1994			Churchgoers in 1994			Population 2002			Churchgoers in 2002		
	Male %	Female %	Total %	Male %	Female %	Total %	Male %	Female %	Total %	Male %	Female %	Total %	Male %	Female %	Total %	Male %	Female %	Total %
<12	*12*	*11*	**23**	*12*	*17*	**29**	*10*	*9*	**19**	*8*	*12*	**20**	*8*	*7*	**15**	*6*	*7*	**13**
12–14													*2*	*2*	**4**	*2*	*1*	**3**
15–19	*5*	*4*	**9**	*2*	*3*	**5**	*3*	*3*	**6**	*4*	*3*	**7**	*3*	*3*	**6**	*1*	*1*	**2**
20–29	*7*	*8*	**15**	*2*	*6*	**8**	*7*	*7*	**14**	*3*	*4*	**7**	*7*	*6*	**13**	*2*	*3*	**5**
30–44	*10*	*11*	**21**	*5*	*9*	**14**	*11*	*11*	**22**	*6*	*9*	**15**	*11*	*11*	**22**	*6*	*9*	**15**
45–64	*10*	*11*	**21**	*8*	*15*	**23**	*12*	*12*	**24**	*10*	*16*	**26**	*12*	*13*	**25**	*10*	*16*	**26**
65/65+	*5*	*6*	**11**	*7*	*14*	**21**	*6*	*9*	**15**	*8*	*17*	**25**	*6*	*9*	**15**	*12*	*24*	**36**
All ages	*49*	*51*	**100**	*36*	*64*	**100**	*49*	*51*	**100**	*39*	*61*	**100**	*49*	*51*	**100**	*39*	*61*	**100**

Figure 12.21.1 Percentage of population in church by age-group

	1984	1994	2002
<20	14	11	6
20–44	8	6	5
45+	18	13	12

Figure 12.21.2 Financial giving in the past year

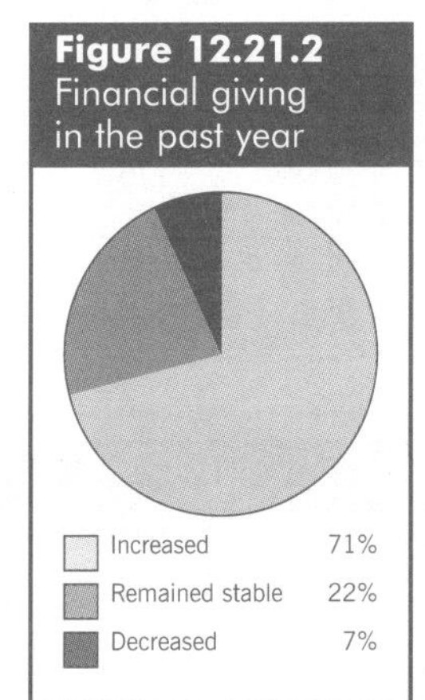

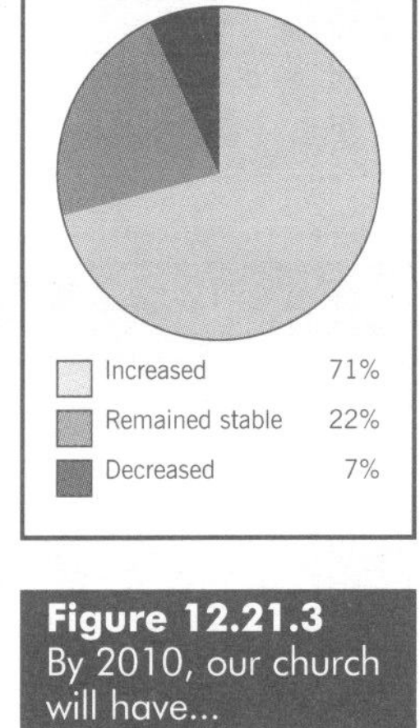

Increased	71%
Remained stable	22%
Decreased	7%

Figure 12.21.3 By 2010, our church will have...

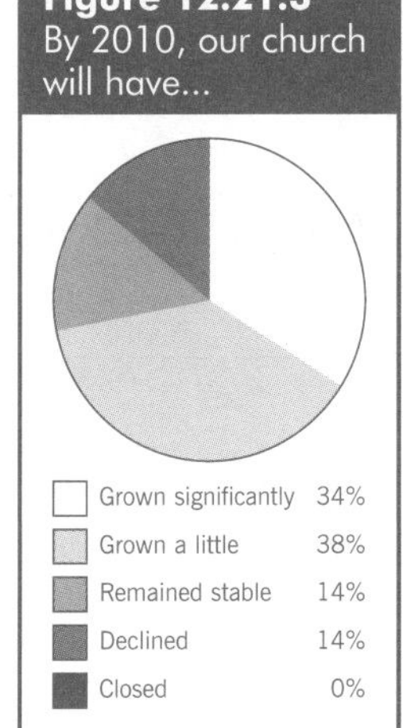

Grown significantly	34%
Grown a little	38%
Remained stable	14%
Declined	14%
Closed	0%

12

12.22 Lothian: West[1]

[1] Sometimes called Livingston

Table 12.22.1			
OVERALL FIGURES	1984	1994	**2002**
Total population	144,450	146,730	160,630
Usual Sunday church attendance	17,650	13,630	10,970
% attending on Sunday	*12·2*	*9·3*	*6·8*
Number of churches	75	83	85
Population per church	1,930	1,770	1,890

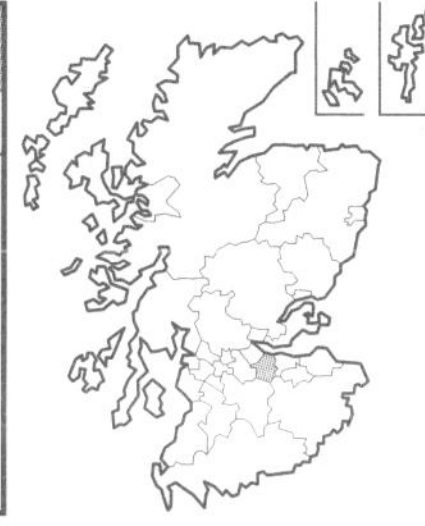

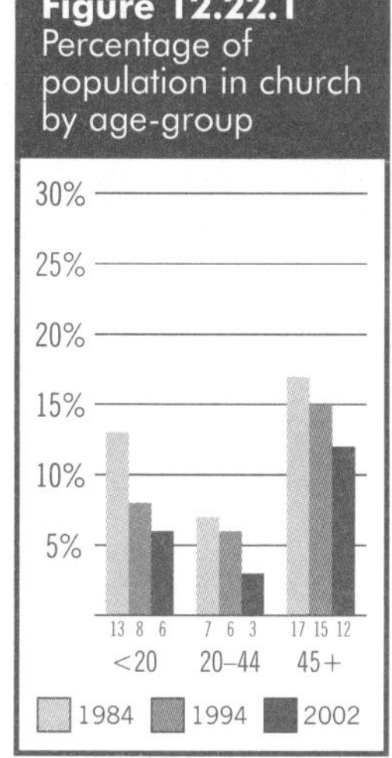

Figure 12.22.1
Percentage of population in church by age-group

Table 12.22.2 Sunday attendance by denomination

	Church of Scotland	Other Presbyterian	Episcopal	Baptist	Independent	Smaller Denoms.	Total Protestant	Roman Catholic	**Total Christian**
1984	7,290	350	190	500	470	1,110	9,910	7,740	17,650
%▼	*–4*	*–17*	*–21*	*–2*	*+6*	*+3*	*–3*	*–25*	*–13*
1990	7,010	290	150	490	500	1,140	9,580	5,830	15,410
%▼	*–11*	*–17*	*+7*	*–12*	*+16*	*–3*	*–8*	*–17*	*–12*
1994	6,250	240	160	430	580	1,110	8,770	4,860	13,630
%▼	*–22*	*–25*	*0*	*+23*	*+29*	*–36*	*–18*	*–22*	*–20*
2002	**4,850**	**180**	**160**	**530**	**750**	**710**	**7,180**	**3,790**	**10,970**
1984▶	*41*	*2*	*1*	*3*	*3*	*6*	*56*	*44*	*100%*
1994▶	*46*	*2*	*1*	*3*	*4*	*8*	*64*	*36*	*100%*
2002▶	***44***	***2***	***1***	***5***	***7***	***6***	***65***	***35***	***100%***
Number of churches									
1984	29	3	3	3	8	12	58	17	75
1994	28	3	3	4	14	15	67	16	83
2002	**28**	**3**	**3**	**4**	**14**	**17**	**69**	**16**	**85**

Table 12.22.3 Sunday attendance by churchmanship

	Reformed Evangelical	Mainstream Evangelical	Charismatic Evangelical	TOTAL Evangelical	Reformed	Low church	Liberal	Broad	Catholic*	**ALL Churches**
1994	560	3,670	470	4,700	1,180	1,080	1,070	1,000	4,600	13,630
%▼	*–64*	*+5*	*–6*	*–4*	*–36*	*–23*	*–76*	*–22*	*–17*	*–20*
2002	**200**	**3,870**	**440**	**4,510**	**760**	**830**	**260**	**780**	**3,830**	**10,970**
1994▶	*4*	*27*	*3*	*34*	*9*	*8*	*8*	*7*	*34*	*100%*
2002▶	***2***	***35***	***4***	***41***	***7***	***8***	***2***	***7***	***35***	***100%***
Number of churches										
1994	5	20	7	32	8	6	8	11	18	83
2002	**5**	**22**	**7**	**34**	**8**	**6**	**8**	**11**	**18**	**85**

Table 12.22.4 Sunday attendance by environment

	City Centre	Urban Priority Area	Housing Scheme	Suburban	Town	New Town	Rural Area: Dormitory	Rural: Other Areas	**ALL Churches**
1994	0	90	950	0	4,960	2,180	3,680	1,770	13,630
%▼	–	*–22*	*–19*	–	*–25*	*–17*	*–15*	*–15*	*–20*
2002	**0**	**70**	**770**	**0**	**3,700**	**1,820**	**3,110**	**1,500**	**10,970**
1994▶	*0*	*1*	*7*	*0*	*36*	*16*	*27*	*13*	*100%*
2002▶	***0***	***1***	***7***	***0***	***34***	***16***	***28***	***14***	***100%***
Number of churches									
1994	0	2	7	0	21	17	25	11	83
2002	**0**	**2**	**7**	**0**	**22**	**17**	**26**	**11**	**85**

*Catholic: One kind of churchmanship, not to be identified solely with the Roman Catholic church.

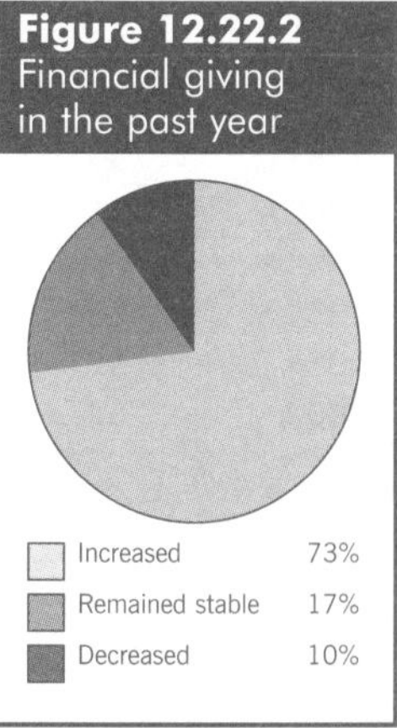

Figure 12.22.2
Financial giving in the past year

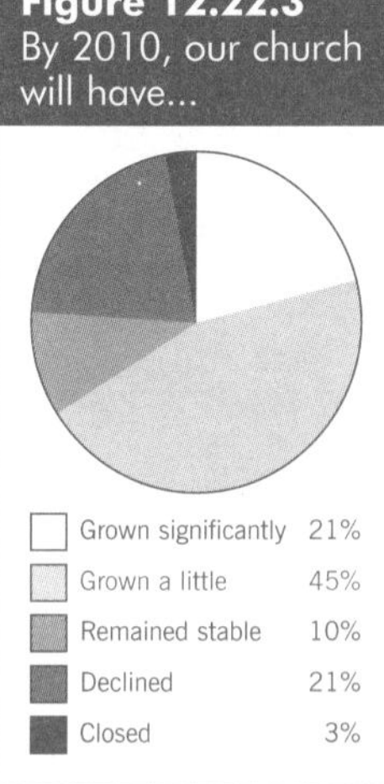

Figure 12.22.3
By 2010, our church will have...

Table 12.22.5 Age and gender of churchgoers 1984, 1994 and 2002

Age Group	Population 1984 Male %	Female %	Total %	Churchgoers in 1984 Male %	Female %	Total %	Population 1994 Male %	Female %	Total %	Churchgoers in 1994 Male %	Female %	Total %	Population 2002 Male %	Female %	Total %	Churchgoers in 2002 Male %	Female %	Total %
<12 } 12–14 }	*12*	*11*	***23***	*12*	*17*	***29***	*11*	*10*	***21***	*9*	*11*	***20***	*8*	*8*	***16***	*7*	*8*	***15***
12–14													*2*	*2*	***4***	*2*	*2*	***4***
15–19	*5*	*4*	***9***	*2*	*3*	***5***	*3*	*3*	***6***	*1*	*2*	***3***	*3*	*3*	***6***	*1*	*2*	***3***
20–29	*7*	*8*	***15***	*2*	*6*	***8***	*8*	*8*	***16***	*3*	*4*	***7***	*7*	*7*	***14***	*2*	*3*	***5***
30–44	*10*	*11*	***21***	*5*	*9*	***14***	*12*	*12*	***24***	*7*	*10*	***17***	*13*	*13*	***26***	*6*	*9*	***15***
45–64	*10*	*11*	***21***	*8*	*15*	***23***	*11*	*11*	***22***	*11*	*18*	***29***	*11*	*12*	***23***	*11*	*18*	***29***
65/65+	*5*	*6*	***11***	*7*	*14*	***21***	*4*	*7*	***11***	*7*	*17*	***24***	*5*	*6*	***11***	*11*	*18*	***29***
All ages	*49*	*51*	***100***	*36*	*64*	***100***	*49*	*51*	***100***	*38*	*62*	***100***	*49*	*51*	***100***	*40*	*60*	***100***

[1] *Formerly part of Grampian: Other Region. 1984, 1990 and 1994 figures pro rata to number of churches*

Table 12.23.1

OVERALL FIGURES	1984	1994	**2002**
Total population	73,160	84,330	87,100
Usual Sunday church attendance	12,790	11,170	9,170
% attending on Sunday	*17·5*	*13·2*	*10·5*
Number of churches	97	100	97
Population per church	750	840	900

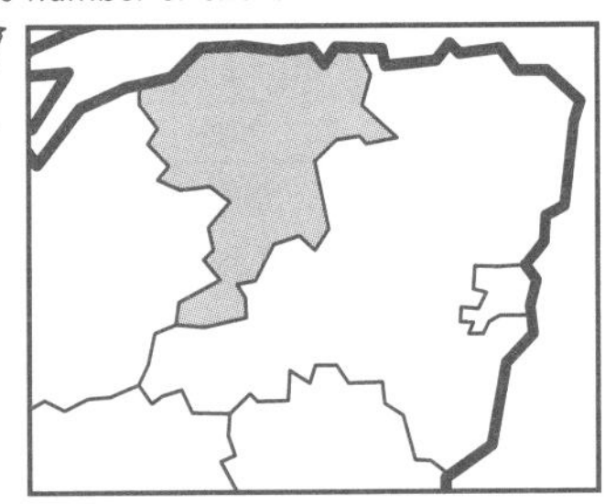

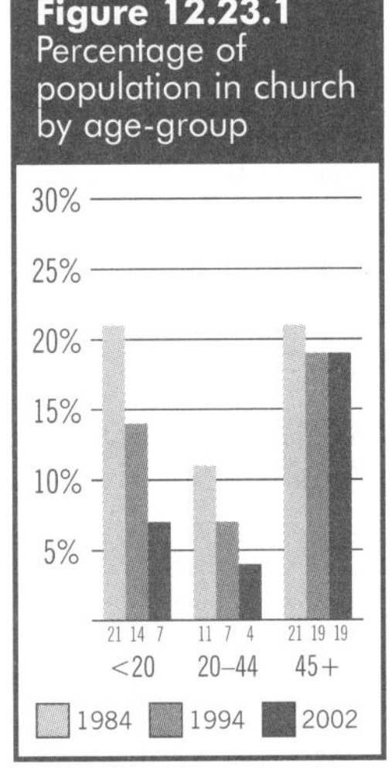

Figure 12.23.1 Percentage of population in church by age-group

Table 12.23.2 Sunday attendance by denomination

	Church of Scotland	Other Presbyterian	Episcopal	Baptist	Independent	Smaller Denoms.	Total Protestant	Roman Catholic	**Total Christian**
1984	6,010	180	580	1,310	770	1,220	10,070	2,720	12,790
%▼	*–8*	*+11*	*0*	*–23*	*–9*	*–10*	*–9*	*–11*	*–10*
1990	5,530	200	580	1,010	700	1,100	9,120	2,420	11,540
%▼	*–5*	*–5*	*–2*	*–6*	*+9*	*0*	*–3*	*–2*	*–3*
1994	5,240	190	570	950	760	1,100	8,810	2,360	11,170
%▼	*–22*	*+5*	*–11*	*–20*	*–9*	*–20*	*–19*	*–14*	*–18*
2002	**4,110**	**200**	**510**	**760**	**690**	**880**	**7,150**	**2,020**	**9,170**
1984▶	*47*	*1*	*5*	*10*	*6*	*10*	*79*	*21*	*100%*
1994▶	*47*	*2*	*5*	*8*	*7*	*10*	*79*	*21*	*100%*
2002▶	***45***	***2***	***6***	***8***	***7***	***10***	***78***	***22***	***100%***
Number of churches									
1984	37	3	14	4	10	12	80	17	97
1994	34	3	14	6	11	12	80	20	100
2002	**32**	**3**	**13**	**6**	**11**	**12**	**77**	**20**	**97**

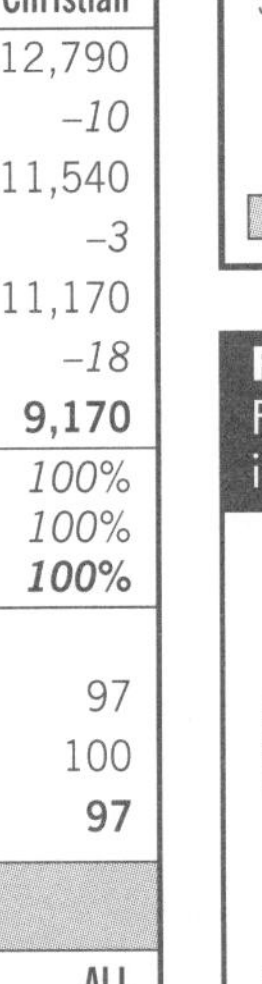

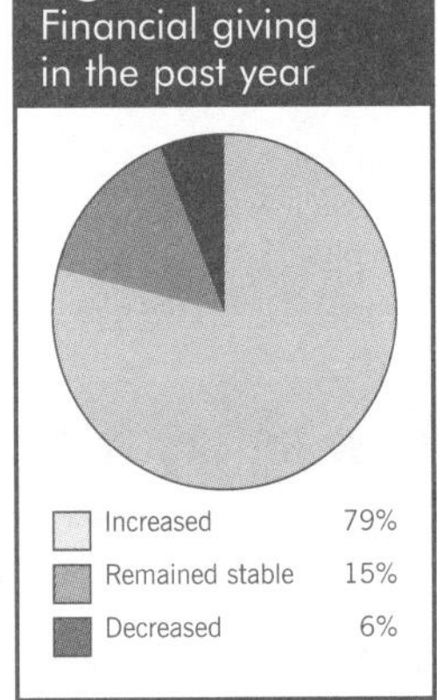

Figure 12.23.2 Financial giving in the past year

Table 12.23.3 Sunday attendance by churchmanship

	Reformed Evangelical	Mainstream Evangelical	Charismatic Evangelical	TOTAL Evangelical	Reformed	Low church	Liberal	Broad	Catholic*	**ALL Churches**
1994	820	2,100	700	3,620	1,990	940	1,350	2,220	1,050	11,170
%▼	*–49*	*–7*	*–31*	*–21*	*–12*	*–16*	*–19*	*–18*	*–19*	*–18*
2002	**420**	**1,960**	**480**	**2,860**	**1,750**	**790**	**1,090**	**1,830**	**850**	**9,170**
1994▶	*7*	*19*	*6*	*32*	*18*	*8*	*12*	*20*	*10*	*100%*
2002▶	***5***	***21***	***5***	***31***	***19***	***9***	***12***	***20***	***9***	***100%***
Number of churches										
1994	7	18	6	31	17	8	12	19	13	100
2002	**5**	**18**	**6**	**29**	**17**	**8**	**11**	**19**	**13**	**97**

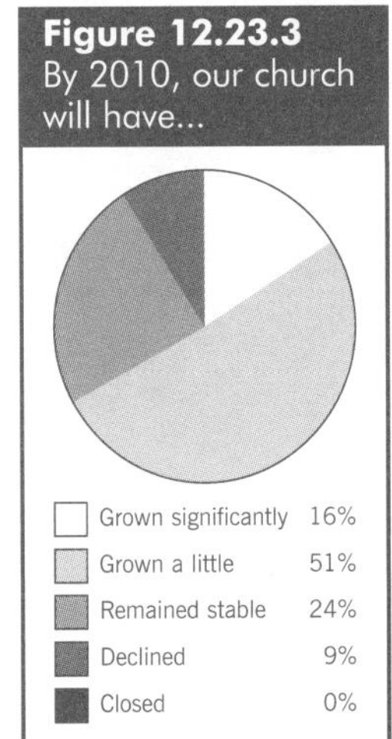

Figure 12.23.3 By 2010, our church will have...

Table 12.23.4 Sunday attendance by environment

	City Centre	Urban Priority Area	Housing Scheme	Suburban	Town	New Town	Rural Area: Dormitory	Rural: Other Areas	**ALL Churches**
1994	0	150	170	0	5,220	0	2,120	3,510	11,170
%▼	–	*–13*	*–12*	–	*–21*	–	*–26*	*–9*	*–18*
2002	**0**	**130**	**150**	**0**	**4,130**	**0**	**1,560**	**3,200**	**9,170**
1994▶	*0*	*1*	*2*	*0*	*47*	*0*	*19*	*31*	*100%*
2002▶	***0***	***1***	***2***	***0***	***45***	***0***	***17***	***35***	***100%***
Number of churches									
1994	0	1	2	0	30	0	19	48	100
2002	**0**	**1**	**2**	**0**	**29**	**0**	**19**	**46**	**97**

**Catholic: One kind of churchmanship, not to be identified solely with the Roman Catholic church.*

Table 12.23.5 Age and gender of churchgoers 1984, 1994 and 2002

Age Group	Population 1984			Churchgoers in 1984			Population 1994			Churchgoers in 1994			Population 2002			Churchgoers in 2002		
	Male %	Female %	Total %	Male %	Female %	Total %	Male %	Female %	Total %	Male %	Female %	Total %	Male %	Female %	Total %	Male %	Female %	Total %
<12 } 12–14 }	*12*	*11*	***23***	*13*	*18*	***31***	*11*	*10*	***21***	*12*	*13*	***25***	8	8	**16**	5	8	**13**
													2	2	**4**	*1*	*1*	***2***
15–19	*4*	*4*	***8***	2	4	**6**	3	3	**6**	*1*	*2*	***3***	3	3	**6**	*1*	*1*	***2***
20–29	*7*	*7*	***14***	3	5	**8**	7	7	**14**	2	*4*	**6**	8	5	**13**	*0*	*1*	***1***
30–44	*11*	*10*	***21***	6	9	**15**	*12*	*11*	**23**	5	*9*	**14**	*10*	*11*	**21**	*4*	*7*	***11***
45–64	*10*	*10*	***20***	8	*13*	**21**	*11*	*11*	**22**	*10*	*18*	**28**	*12*	*12*	**24**	*11*	*21*	***32***
65/65+	6	8	***14***	7	*12*	***19***	6	8	***14***	9	*15*	***24***	7	9	**16**	*15*	*24*	***39***
All ages	*50*	*50*	***100***	*39*	*61*	***100***	*50*	*50*	***100***	*39*	*61*	***100***	*50*	*50*	***100***	*37*	*63*	***100***

12

12.24 Orkney Islands

Table 12.24.1

OVERALL FIGURES	1984	1994	**2002**
Total population	18,790	19,760	19,160
Usual Sunday church attendance	2,840	2,920	2,480
% attending on Sunday	*15·1*	*14·8*	*12·9*
Number of churches	45	44	44
Population per church	420	450	440

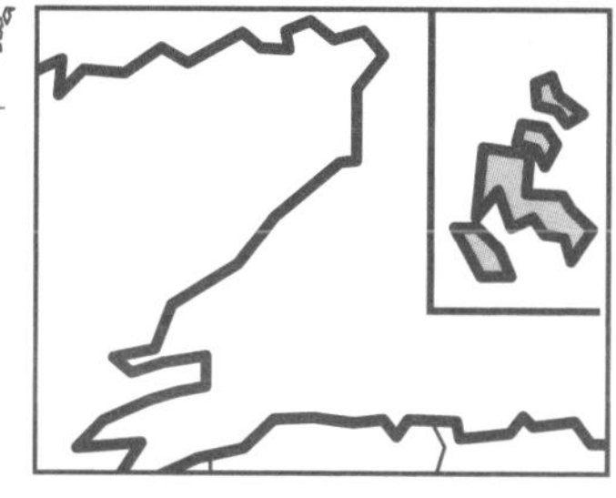

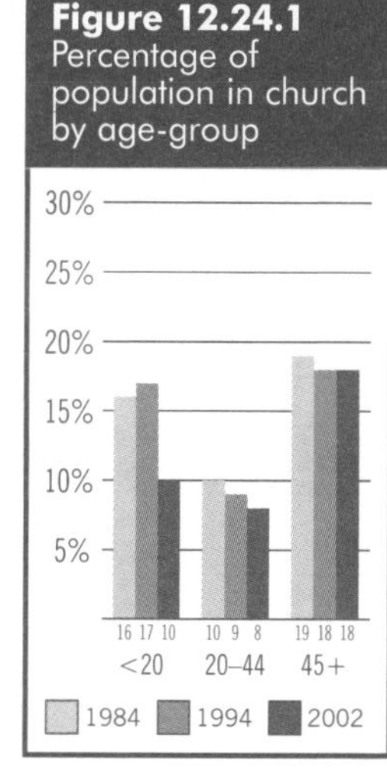

Figure 12.24.1 Percentage of population in church by age-group

Table 12.24.2 Sunday attendance by denomination

	Church of Scotland	Other Presbyterian	Episcopal	Baptist	Independent	Smaller Denoms.	Total Protestant	Roman Catholic	**Total Christian**
1984	1,880	120	110	220	380	60	2,770	70	2,840
%▼	*+4*	*–8*	*–18*	*–18*	*+5*	*0*	*+1*	*+29*	*+1*
1990	1,950	110	90	180	400	60	2,790	90	2,880
%▼	*+3*	*–18*	*–33*	*+6*	*–12*	*+17*	*–1*	*+67*	*+1*
1994	2,010	90	60	190	350	70	2,770	150	2,920
%▼	*–19*	*–33*	*–33*	*+16*	*–9*	*0*	*–16*	*–7*	*–15*
2002	**1,630**	**60**	**40**	**220**	**320**	**70**	**2,340**	**140**	**2,480**
1984▶	66	*4*	*4*	*8*	*14*	*2*	98	*2*	*100%*
1994▶	69	*3*	*2*	*7*	*12*	*2*	95	*5*	*100%*
2002▶	**66**	***3***	***2***	***9***	***13***	***1***	**94**	***6***	***100%***
Number of churches									
1984	28	2	2	2	9	1	44	1	45
1994	25	2	2	2	9	2	42	2	44
2002	**25**	**2**	**2**	**2**	**9**	**2**	**42**	**2**	**44**

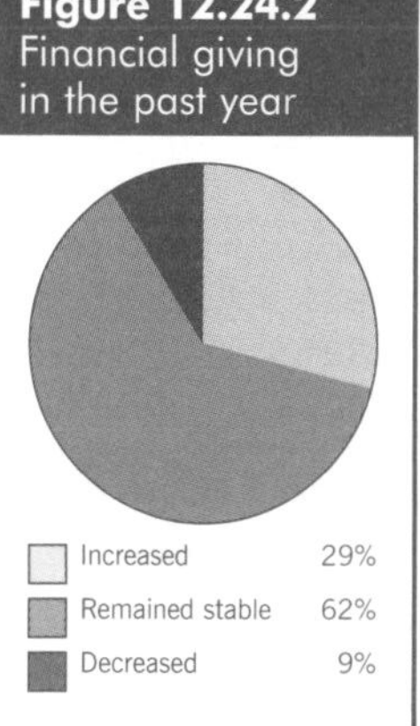

Figure 12.24.2 Financial giving in the past year

Table 12.24.3 Sunday attendance by churchmanship

	Reformed Evangelical	Mainstream Evangelical	Charismatic Evangelical	TOTAL Evangelical	Reformed	Low church	Liberal	Broad	Catholic*	**ALL Churches**
1994	100	510	290	900	570	20	330	1,000	100	2,920
%▼	*+40*	*+6*	*–31*	*–2*	*–35*	*+200*	*+3*	*–27*	*0*	*–15*
2002	**140**	**540**	**200**	**880**	**370**	**60**	**340**	**730**	**100**	**2,480**
1994▶	*3*	*18*	*10*	*31*	*20*	*1*	*11*	*34*	*3*	*100%*
2002▶	***6***	***22***	***8***	***36***	***15***	***2***	***14***	***29***	***4***	***100%***
Number of churches										
1994	2	12	4	18	8	1	6	10	1	44
2002	**2**	**12**	**4**	**18**	**8**	**1**	**6**	**10**	**1**	**44**

Table 12.24.4 Sunday attendance by environment

	City Centre	Urban Priority Area	Housing Scheme	Suburban	Town	New Town	Rural Area: Dormitory	Rural: Other Areas	**ALL Churches**
1994	0	0	0	0	940	0	20	1,960	2,920
%▼	–	–	–	–	*–21*	–	*0*	*–12*	*–15*
2002	**0**	**0**	**0**	**0**	**740**	**0**	**20**	**1,720**	**2,480**
1994▶	*0*	*0*	*0*	*0*	*32*	*0*	*1*	*67*	*100%*
2002▶	***0***	***0***	***0***	***0***	***30***	***0***	***1***	***69***	***100%***
Number of churches									
1994	0	0	0	0	7	0	1	36	44
2002	**0**	**0**	**0**	**0**	**7**	**0**	**1**	**36**	**44**

**Catholic: One kind of churchmanship, not to be identified solely with the Roman Catholic church.*

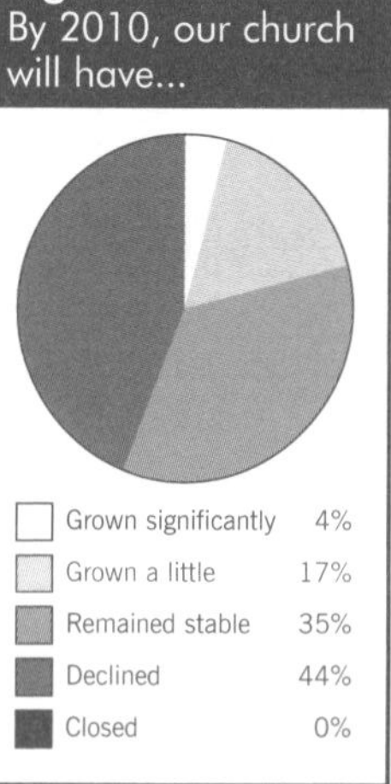

Figure 12.24.3 By 2010, our church will have...

Table 12.24.5 Age and gender of churchgoers 1984, 1994 and 2002

Age Group	Population 1984			Churchgoers in 1984			Population 1994			Churchgoers in 1994			Population 2002			Churchgoers in 2002		
	Male %	Female %	Total %	Male %	Female %	Total %	Male %	Female %	Total %	Male %	Female %	Total %	Male %	Female %	Total %	Male %	Female %	Total %
<12 } 12–14	*11*	*11*	***22***	*9*	*17*	***26***	*10*	*10*	***20***	*12*	*14*	***26***	*8*	*7*	***15***	*5*	*9*	***14***
12–14													*2*	*2*	***4***	*2*	*2*	***4***
15–19	*4*	*4*	***8***	*3*	*2*	***5***	*3*	*3*	***6***	*2*	*2*	***4***	*3*	*3*	***6***	*1*	*1*	***2***
20–29	*6*	*6*	***12***	*3*	*4*	***7***	*7*	*6*	***13***	*2*	*4*	***6***	*5*	*5*	***10***	*1*	*2*	***3***
30–44	*10*	*10*	***20***	*6*	*9*	***15***	*11*	*10*	***21***	*5*	*9*	***14***	*11*	*11*	***22***	*6*	*10*	***16***
45–64	*10*	*11*	***21***	*9*	*15*	***24***	*12*	*12*	***24***	*9*	*15*	***24***	*14*	*13*	***27***	*12*	*16*	***28***
65/65+	*8*	*9*	***17***	*9*	*14*	***23***	*7*	*9*	***16***	*10*	*16*	***26***	*7*	*9*	***16***	*11*	*22*	***33***
All ages	*49*	*51*	***100***	*39*	*61*	***100***	*50*	*50*	***100***	*40*	*60*	***100***	*50*	*50*	***100***	*38*	*62*	***100***

12

[1] Formerly part of Tayside: Other Region; 1984, 1990 and 1994 figures estimated pro rata on 2002 figures

Table 12.25.1

OVERALL FIGURES	1984	1994	**2002**
Total population	137,560	136,980	134,770
Usual Sunday church attendance	17,200	15,970	13,520
% attending on Sunday	*12·5*	*11·7*	*10·0*
Number of churches	144	150	146
Population per church	960	910	920

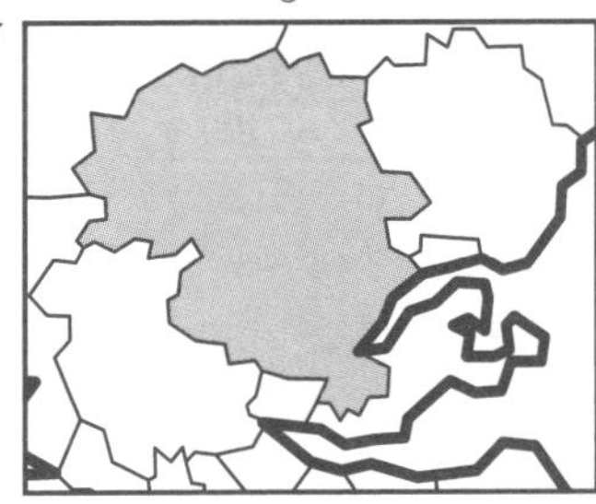

Table 12.25.2 Sunday attendance by denomination

	Church of Scotland	Other Presbyterian	Episcopal	Baptist	Independent	Smaller Denoms.	Total Protestant	Roman Catholic	**Total Christian**
1984	11,920	250	900	280	540	770	14,660	2,540	17,200
%▼	*–10*	*0*	*+10*	*–21*	*+46*	*+18*	*–6*	*+1*	*–5*
1990	10,690	250	990	220	790	910	13,850	2,560	16,410
%▼	*–6*	*+8*	*+5*	*–5*	*+14*	*+12*	*–2*	*–5*	*–3*
1994	10,090	270	1,040	210	900	1,020	13,530	2,440	15,970
%▼	*–23*	*0*	*–23*	*+114*	*+10*	*–14*	*–17*	*–4*	*–15*
2002	**7,780**	**270**	**800**	**450**	**990**	**880**	**11,170**	**2,350**	**13,520**
1984▶	69	*1*	*5*	*2*	*3*	*5*	*85*	*15*	*100%*
1994▶	63	*2*	*7*	*1*	*6*	*6*	*85*	*15*	*100%*
2002▶	**58**	***2***	***6***	***3***	***7***	***7***	***83***	***17***	***100%***
Number of churches									
1984	83	6	15	3	13	12	132	12	144
1994	81	6	16	3	17	13	136	14	150
2002	**76**	**5**	**16**	**3**	**15**	**16**	**131**	**15**	**146**

Table 12.25.3 Sunday attendance by churchmanship

	Reformed Evangelical	Mainstream Evangelical	Charismatic Evangelical	TOTAL Evangelical	Reformed	Low church	Liberal	Broad	Catholic*	**ALL Churches**
1994	1,450	1,210	400	3,060	2,690	610	3,410	3,580	2,620	15,970
%▼	*–45*	*+40*	*+10*	*–4*	*–20*	*+11*	*–27*	*–17*	*–11*	*–15*
2002	**800**	**1,700**	**440**	**2,940**	**2,140**	**680**	**2,480**	**2,960**	**2,320**	**13,520**
1994▶	*9*	*8*	*2*	*19*	*17*	*4*	*21*	*22*	*17*	*100%*
2002▶	***6***	***13***	***3***	***22***	***16***	***5***	***18***	***22***	***17***	***100%***
Number of churches										
1994	10	15	6	31	30	9	30	33	17	150
2002	**8**	**16**	**6**	**30**	**27**	**9**	**30**	**33**	**17**	**146**

Table 12.25.4 Sunday attendance by environment

	City Centre	Urban Priority Area	Housing Scheme	Suburban	Town	New Town	Rural Area: Dormitory	Rural: Other Areas	**ALL Churches**
1994	320	60	840	450	7,260	0	3,110	3,930	15,970
%▼	*–16*	*–33*	*–14*	*–18*	*–10*	–	*–23*	*–18*	*–15*
2002	**270**	**40**	**720**	**370**	**6,520**	**0**	**2,390**	**3,210**	**13,520**
1994▶	*2*	*0*	*5*	*3*	*46*	*0*	*19*	*25*	*100%*
2002▶	***2***	***0***	***5***	***3***	***48***	***0***	***18***	***24***	***100%***
Number of churches									
1994	3	1	6	3	45	0	24	68	150
2002	**3**	**1**	**6**	**3**	**43**	**0**	**24**	**66**	**146**

*Catholic: One kind of churchmanship, not to be identified solely with the Roman Catholic church.

Figure 12.25.1 Percentage of population in church by age-group

Figure 12.25.2 Financial giving in the past year

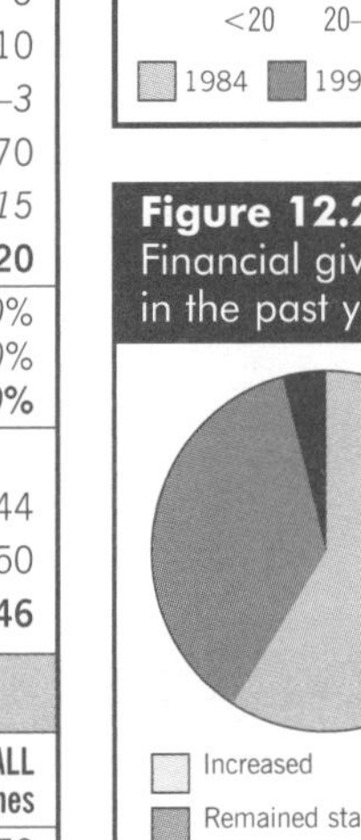

Increased	59%
Remained stable	37%
Decreased	4%

Figure 12.25.3 By 2010, our church will have...

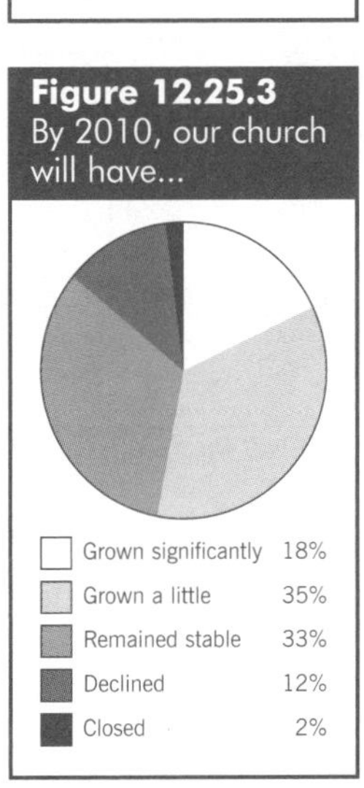

Grown significantly	18%
Grown a little	35%
Remained stable	33%
Declined	12%
Closed	2%

Table 12.25.5 Age and gender of churchgoers 1984, 1994 and 2002

Age Group	Population 1984			Churchgoers in 1984			Population 1994			Churchgoers in 1994			Population 2002			Churchgoers in 2002		
	Male %	Female %	Total %	Male %	Female %	Total %	Male %	Female %	Total %	Male %	Female %	Total %	Male %	Female %	Total %	Male %	Female %	Total %
<12	*10*	*10*	**20**	*10*	*12*	**22**	*10*	*9*	**19**	*9*	*11*	**20**	*7*	*7*	**14**	*6*	*12*	**18**
12–14													*2*	*2*	**4**	*1*	*1*	**2**
15–19	*4*	*4*	**8**	*2*	*3*	**5**	*3*	*3*	**6**	*2*	*3*	**5**	*3*	*3*	**6**	*1*	*1*	**2**
20–29	*7*	*6*	**13**	*3*	*6*	**9**	*7*	*7*	**14**	*2*	*4*	**6**	*5*	*6*	**11**	*1*	*2*	**3**
30–44	*9*	*10*	**19**	*6*	*10*	**16**	*10*	*10*	**20**	*5*	*10*	**15**	*10*	*11*	**21**	*5*	*9*	**14**
45–64	*11*	*12*	**23**	*9*	*15*	**24**	*11*	*12*	**23**	*10*	*17*	**27**	*13*	*13*	**26**	*11*	*17*	**28**
65/65+	*7*	*10*	**17**	*8*	*16*	**24**	*7*	*11*	**18**	*10*	*17*	**27**	*8*	*10*	**18**	*13*	*20*	**33**
All ages	*48*	*52*	**100**	*38*	*62*	**100**	*48*	*52*	**100**	*38*	*62*	**100**	*48*	*52*	**100**	*38*	*62*	**100**

12

12.26 Renfrewshire and East Renfrewshire[1]

[1] *Formerly Strathkelvin District of Strathclyde*

Table 12.26.1

OVERALL FIGURES	1984	1994	**2002**
Total population	282,870	271,780	261,880
Usual Sunday church attendance	58,800	50,640	40,860
% attending on Sunday	*20·8*	*18·6*	*15·6*
Number of churches	135	152	152
Population per church	2,100	1,790	1,720

Figure 12.26.1 Percentage of population in church by age-group

Table 12.26.2 Sunday attendance by denomination

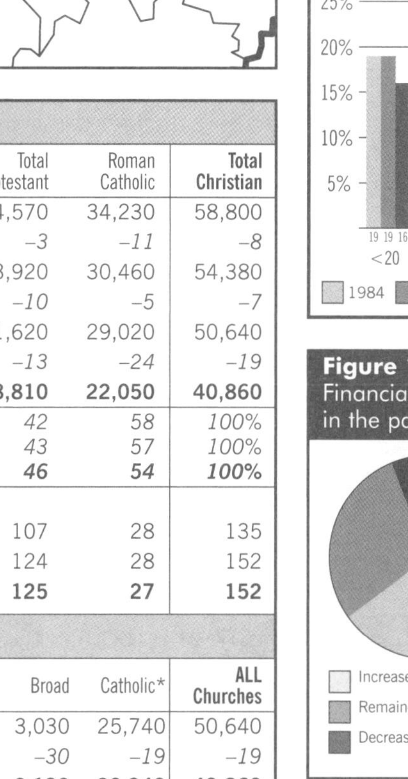

	Church of Scotland	Other Presbyterian	Episcopal	Baptist	Independent	Smaller Denoms.	Total Protestant	Roman Catholic	**Total Christian**
1984	18,810	370	500	1,270	1,890	1,730	24,570	34,230	58,800
%▼	*−12*	*+3*	*−6*	*+12*	*+57*	*+20*	*−3*	*−11*	*−8*
1990	16,620	380	470	1,420	2,960	2,070	23,920	30,460	54,380
%▼	*−13*	*−34*	*−13*	*−10*	*−2*	*+11*	*−10*	*−5*	*−7*
1994	14,490	250	410	1,280	2,890	2,300	21,620	29,020	50,640
%▼	*−19*	*−12*	*+7*	*+6*	*−15*	*+15*	*−13*	*−24*	*−19*
2002	**11,700**	**220**	**440**	**1,360**	**2,450**	**2,640**	**18,810**	**22,050**	**40,860**
1984►	*32*	*1*	*1*	*2*	*3*	*3*	*42*	*58*	*100%*
1994►	*29*	*0*	*1*	*3*	*6*	*5*	*43*	*57*	*100%*
2002►	***29***	***1***	***1***	***3***	***6***	***6***	***46***	***54***	***100%***
Number of churches									
1984	56	4	8	10	17	12	107	28	135
1994	48	3	8	12	32[2]	21	124	28	152
2002	**47**	**3**	**9**	**12**	**27**	**27**	**125**	**27**	**152**

Table 12.26.3 Sunday attendance by churchmanship

	Reformed Evangelical	Mainstream Evangelical	Charismatic Evangelical	TOTAL Evangelical	Reformed	Low church	Liberal	Broad	Catholic*	**ALL Churches**
1994	2,300	2,380	2,180	6,860	8,550	3,090	3,370	3,030	25,740	50,640
%▼	*−3*	*+18*	*−28*	*−3*	*−31*	*−19*	*−17*	*−30*	*−19*	*−19*
2002	**2,230**	**2,820**	**1,580**	**6,630**	**5,870**	**2,490**	**2,800**	**2,130**	**20,940**	**40,860**
1994►	*4*	*5*	*4*	*13*	*17*	*6*	*7*	*6*	*51*	*100%*
2002►	***6***	***7***	***4***	***17***	***14***	***6***	***7***	***5***	***51***	***100%***
Number of churches										
1994	11	24	20	55	30	11	23	9	24	152
2002	**11**	**25**	**20**	**56**	**30**	**11**	**23**	**9**	**23**	**152**

Table 12.26.4 Sunday attendance by environment

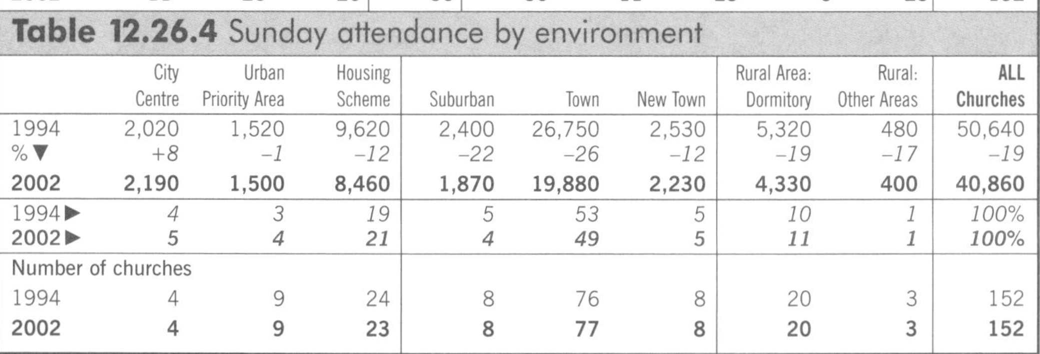

	City Centre	Urban Priority Area	Housing Scheme	Suburban	Town	New Town	Rural Area: Dormitory	Rural: Other Areas	**ALL Churches**
1994	2,020	1,520	9,620	2,400	26,750	2,530	5,320	480	50,640
%▼	*+8*	*−1*	*−12*	*−22*	*−26*	*−12*	*−19*	*−17*	*−19*
2002	**2,190**	**1,500**	**8,460**	**1,870**	**19,880**	**2,230**	**4,330**	**400**	**40,860**
1994►	*4*	*3*	*19*	*5*	*53*	*5*	*10*	*1*	*100%*
2002►	***5***	***4***	***21***	***4***	***49***	***5***	***11***	***1***	***100%***
Number of churches									
1994	4	9	24	8	76	8	20	3	152
2002	**4**	**9**	**23**	**8**	**77**	**8**	**20**	**3**	**152**

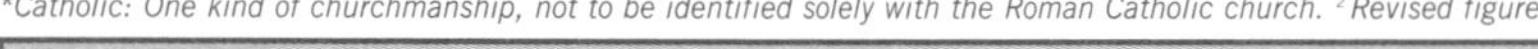

**Catholic: One kind of churchmanship, not to be identified solely with the Roman Catholic church.* [2] *Revised figure*

Figure 12.26.2 Financial giving in the past year

Increased	65%
Remained stable	29%
Decreased	6%

Figure 12.26.3 By 2010, our church will have...

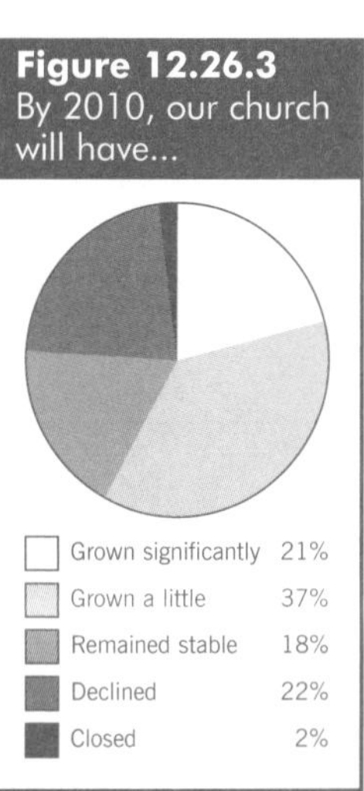

Grown significantly	21%
Grown a little	37%
Remained stable	18%
Declined	22%
Closed	2%

Table 12.26.5 Age and gender of churchgoers 1984, 1994 and 2002

Age Group	Population 1984			Churchgoers in 1984			Population 1994			Churchgoers in 1994			Population 2002			Churchgoers in 2002		
	Male %	Female %	Total %	Male %	Female %	Total %	Male %	Female %	Total %	Male %	Female %	Total %	Male %	Female %	Total %	Male %	Female %	Total %
<12 } 12–14	*11*	*11*	***22***	*11*	*13*	***24***	*10*	*9*	***19***	*9*	*11*	***20***	*8*	*7*	***15***	*7*	*8*	***15***
													2	*2*	***4***	*2*	*3*	***5***
15–19	*5*	*5*	***10***	*2*	*4*	***6***	*3*	*3*	***6***	*2*	*3*	***5***	*3*	*3*	***6***	*2*	*3*	***5***
20–29	*8*	*7*	***15***	*3*	*6*	***9***	*8*	*8*	***16***	*3*	*5*	***8***	*6*	*6*	***12***	*3*	*3*	***6***
30–44	*9*	*10*	***19***	*5*	*11*	***16***	*11*	*11*	***22***	*6*	*10*	***16***	*12*	*12*	***24***	*7*	*9*	***16***
45–64	*11*	*11*	***22***	*9*	*16*	***25***	*11*	*12*	***23***	*12*	*17*	***29***	*12*	*12*	***24***	*11*	*16*	***27***
65/65+	*4*	*8*	***12***	*7*	*13*	***20***	*5*	*9*	***14***	*7*	*15*	***22***	*6*	*9*	***15***	*10*	*16*	***26***
All ages	*48*	*52*	***100***	*37*	*63*	***100***	*48*	*52*	***100***	*39*	*61*	***100***	*49*	*51*	***100***	*42*	*58*	***100***

Table 12.27.1

OVERALL FIGURES	1984	1994	**2002**
Total population	23,270	22,830	21,800
Usual Sunday church attendance	3,700	3,130	2,890
% attending on Sunday	*15·9*	*13·7*	*13·3*
Number of churches	62	64	65
Population per church	380	360	340

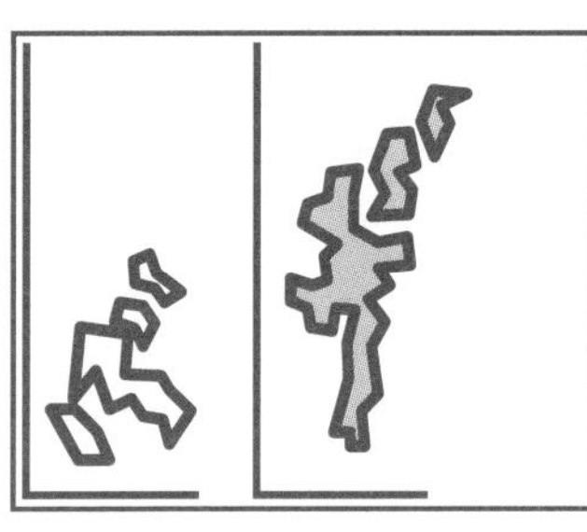

Table 12.27.2 Sunday attendance by denomination

	Church of Scotland	Other Presbyterian	Episcopal	Baptist	Independent	Smaller Denoms.	Total Protestant	Roman Catholic	**Total Christian**
1984	1,230	110	110	430	740	990	3,610	90	3,700
%▼	*–3*	*+9*	*–27*	*–33*	*–8*	*–14*	*–11*	*+22*	*–10*
1990	1,190	120	80	290	680[1]	850[1]	3,210	110	3,320
%▼	*–3*	*–17*	*–25*	*0*	*–7*	*–8*	*–6*	*0*	*–6*
1994	1,160	100	60	290	630[1]	780[1]	3,020	110	3,130
%▼	*–18*	*–20*	*0*	*+10*	*–10*	*+4*	*–8*	*–9*	*–8*
2002	**950**	**80**	**60**	**320**	**570**	**810**	**2,790**	**100**	**2,890**
1984▶	*33*	*3*	*3*	*12*	*20*	*27*	*98*	*2*	*100%*
1994▶	*37*	*3*	*2*	*9*	*20*	*25*	*96*	*4*	*100%*
2002▶	***33***	***3***	***2***	***11***	***20***	***28***	***97***	***3***	***100%***
Number of churches									
1984	14	4	2	5	10	26	61	1	62
1994	17	3	2	4	14	23	63	1	64
2002	**18**	**3**	**2**	**4**	**14**	**23**	**64**	**1**	**65**

Table 12.27.3 Sunday attendance by churchmanship

	Reformed Evangelical	Mainstream Evangelical	Charismatic Evangelical	TOTAL Evangelical	Reformed	Low church	Liberal	Broad	Catholic*	**ALL Churches**
1994	50	1,320	310	1,680	250	0	640	370	190	3,130
%▼	*0*	*–20*	*+29*	*–10*	*+40*	*0*	*–12*	*–22*	*–5*	*–8*
2002	**50**	**1,060**	**400**	**1,510**	**350**	**0**	**560**	**290**	**180**	**2,890**
1994▶	*2*	*42*	*10*	*54*	*8*	*0*	*20*	*12*	*6*	*100%*
2002▶	***2***	***37***	***14***	***53***	***12***	***0***	***19***	***10***	***6***	***100%***
Number of churches										
1994	2	33	4	39	5	0	8	11	1	64
2002	**2**	**33**	**4**	**39**	**6**	**0**	**8**	**11**	**1**	**65**

Table 12.27.4 Sunday attendance by environment

	City Centre	Urban Priority Area	Housing Scheme	Suburban	Town	New Town	Rural Area: Dormitory	Rural: Other Areas	**ALL Churches**
1994	0	0	20	60	1,470	0	100	1,480	3,130
%▼	–	–	*0*	*0*	*+6*	–	*–20*	*–21*	*–8*
2002	**0**	**0**	**20**	**60**	**1,560**	**0**	**80**	**1,170**	**2,890**
1994▶	*0*	*0*	*1*	*2*	*47*	*0*	*3*	*47*	*100%*
2002▶	***0***	***0***	***1***	***2***	***54***	***0***	***3***	***40***	***100%***
Number of churches									
1994	0	0	1	1	14	0	3	45	64
2002	**0**	**0**	**1**	**1**	**15**	**0**	**3**	**45**	**65**

**Catholic: One kind of churchmanship, not to be identified solely with the Roman Catholic church. [1] Revised figure*

Figure 12.27.1 Percentage of population in church by age-group

30%
25%
20%
15%
10%
5%
18 14 8 | 10 8 7 | 21 20 23
<20 | 20–44 | 45+
1984 | 1994 | 2002

Figure 12.27.2 Financial giving in the past year

Increased	49%
Remained stable	49%
Decreased	2%

Figure 12.27.3 By 2010, our church will have...

Grown significantly	16%
Grown a little	33%
Remained stable	23%
Declined	28%
Closed	0%

Table 12.27.5 Age and gender of churchgoers 1984, 1994 and 2002

Age Group	Population 1984 Male %	Female %	Total %	Churchgoers in 1984 Male %	Female %	Total %	Population 1994 Male %	Female %	Total %	Churchgoers in 1994 Male %	Female %	Total %	Population 2002 Male %	Female %	Total %	Churchgoers in 2002 Male %	Female %	Total %
<12 } 12–14	*12*	*12*	***24***	*12*	*18*	***30***	*11*	*11*	***22***	*11*	*14*	***25***	*9*	*8*	***17***	*5*	*6*	***11***
													3	*2*	***5***	*1*	*1*	***2***
15–19	*4*	*4*	***8***	*3*	*3*	***6***	*4*	*3*	***7***	*2*	*2*	***4***	*3*	*3*	***6***	*2*	*2*	***4***
20–29	*8*	*7*	***15***	*3*	*5*	***8***	*8*	*7*	***15***	*2*	*3*	***5***	*6*	*5*	***11***	*3*	*3*	***6***
30–44	*11*	*10*	***21***	*5*	*9*	***14***	*12*	*10*	***22***	*7*	*10*	***17***	*12*	*11*	***23***	*4*	*7*	***11***
45–64	*9*	*9*	***18***	*6*	*11*	***17***	*11*	*10*	***21***	*10*	*17*	***27***	*13*	*12*	***25***	*13*	*22*	***35***
65/65+	*6*	*8*	***14***	*8*	*17*	***25***	*5*	*8*	***13***	*7*	*15*	***22***	*5*	*8*	***13***	*11*	*20*	***31***
All ages	*50*	*50*	***100***	*37*	*63*	***100***	*51*	*49*	***100***	*39*	*61*	***100***	*51*	*49*	***100***	*39*	*61*	***100***

12

12.28 Stirling and Clackmannanshire[1]

[1] *Formerly part of Central Region*

Table 1228.1

OVERALL FIGURES	1984	1994	**2002**
Total population	131,760	131,530	134,050
Usual Sunday church attendance	22,150	17,020	14,180
% attending on Sunday	*16·8*	*12·9*	*10·6*
Number of churches	110	117	117
Population per church	1,200	1,120	1,150

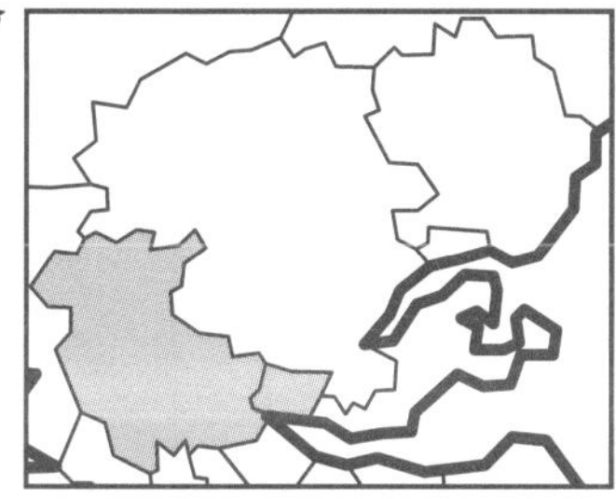

Table 12.28.2 Sunday attendance by denomination

	Church of Scotland	Other Presbyterian	Episcopal	Baptist	Independent	Smaller Denoms.	Total Protestant	Roman Catholic	**Total Christian**
1984	11,950	490	670	790	1,320	850	16,070	6,080	22,150
%▼	*–16*	*–8*	*–4*	*–16*	*–6*	*–4*	*–14*	*–15*	*–14*
1990	10,090	450	640	660	1,240[2]	820[2]	13,900	5,160	19,060
%▼	*–13*	*–11*	*+2*	*–27*	*–2*	*0*	*–11*	*–9*	*–11*
1994	8,770	400	650	480	1,210[2]	820[2]	12,330	4,690	17,020
%▼	*–21*	*+3*	*–15*	*+67*	*–13*	*–24*	*–16*	*–18*	*–17*
2002	**6,920**	**410**	**550**	**800**	**1,050**	**620**	**10,350**	**3,830**	**14,180**
1984▶	*54*	*2*	*3*	*4*	*6*	*4*	*73*	*27*	*100%*
1994▶	*51*	*2*	*4*	*3*	*7*	*5*	*72*	*28*	*100%*
2002▶	***49***	***3***	***4***	***5***	***8***	***4***	***73***	***27***	***100%***
Number of churches									
1984	53	6	8	6	10	10	93	17	110
1994	49	6	8	6	18	13	100	17	117
2002	**49**	**5**	**8**	**6**	**18**	**14**	**100**	**17**	**117**

Table 12.28.3 Sunday attendance by churchmanship

	Reformed Evangelical	Mainstream Evangelical	Charismatic Evangelical	TOTAL Evangelical	Reformed	Low church	Liberal	Broad	Catholic*	**ALL Churches**
1994	2,370	1,190	880	4,440	2,720	740	2,300	2,970	3,850	17,020
%▼	*–28*	*+32*	*–37*	*–14*	*–15*	*+27*	*–33*	*–14*	*–22*	*–17*
2002	**1,700**	**1,570**	**550**	**3,820**	**2,320**	**940**	**1,530**	**2,560**	**3,010**	**14,180**
1994▶	*14*	*7*	*5*	*26*	*16*	*4*	*14*	*17*	*23*	*100%*
2002▶	***12***	***11***	***4***	***27***	***16***	***7***	***11***	***18***	***21***	***100%***
Number of churches										
1994	13	19	10	42	19	7	13	20	16	117
2002	**12**	**19**	**10**	**41**	**19**	**8**	**13**	**20**	**16**	**117**

Table 12.28.4 Sunday attendance by environment

	City Centre	Urban Priority Area	Housing Scheme	Suburban	Town	New Town	Rural Area: Dormitory	Rural: Other Areas	**ALL Churches**
1994	0	510	1,360	1,400	8,310	0	3,400	2,040	17,020
%▼	–	*–18*	*–52*	*–1*	*–8*	–	*–24*	*–26*	*–17*
2002	**0**	**420**	**650**	**1,380**	**7,640**	**0**	**2,580**	**1,510**	**14,180**
1994▶	*0*	*3*	*8*	*8*	*49*	*0*	*20*	*12*	*100%*
2002▶	***0***	***3***	***4***	***10***	***54***	***0***	***18***	***11***	***100%***
Number of churches									
1994	0	4	9	8	48	0	23	25	117
2002	**0**	**4**	**9**	**8**	**47**	**0**	**24**	**25**	**117**

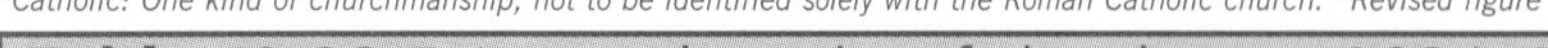

**Catholic: One kind of churchmanship, not to be identified solely with the Roman Catholic church.* [2] *Revised figure*

Table 12.28.5 Age and gender of churchgoers 1984, 1994 and 2002

Age Group	Population 1984 Male %	Female %	Total %	Churchgoers in 1984 Male %	Female %	Total %	Population 1994 Male %	Female %	Total %	Churchgoers in 1994 Male %	Female %	Total %	Population 2002 Male %	Female %	Total %	Churchgoers in 2002 Male %	Female %	Total %
<12 }	*11*	*11*	**22**	*11*	*13*	**24**	*10*	*9*	**19**	*9*	*11*	**20**	*8*	*7*	**15**	*7*	*9*	**16**
12–14 }													*2*	*2*	**4**	*1*	*2*	**3**
15–19	*5*	*4*	**9**	*3*	*3*	**6**	*3*	*3*	**6**	*2*	*2*	**4**	*3*	*3*	**6**	*1*	*2*	**3**
20–29	*7*	*7*	**14**	*3*	*6*	**9**	*8*	*8*	**16**	*2*	*4*	**6**	*7*	*6*	**13**	*2*	*3*	**5**
30–44	*10*	*10*	**20**	*6*	*11*	**17**	*10*	*11*	**21**	*6*	*10*	**16**	*11*	*11*	**22**	*5*	*9*	**14**
45–64	*11*	*11*	**22**	*8*	*16*	**24**	*11*	*12*	**23**	*8*	*18*	**26**	*12*	*13*	**25**	*10*	*18*	**28**
65/65+	*5*	*8*	**13**	*7*	*13*	**20**	*6*	*9*	**15**	*10*	*18*	**28**	*6*	*9*	**15**	*11*	*20*	**31**
All ages	*49*	*51*	**100**	*38*	*62*	**100**	*48*	*52*	**100**	*37*	*63*	**100**	*49*	*51*	**100**	*37*	*63*	**100**

Figure 12.28.1 Percentage of population in church by age-group

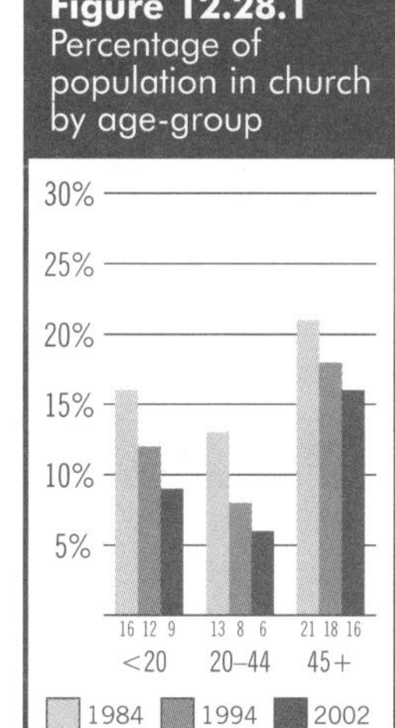

Figure 12.28.2 Financial giving in the past year

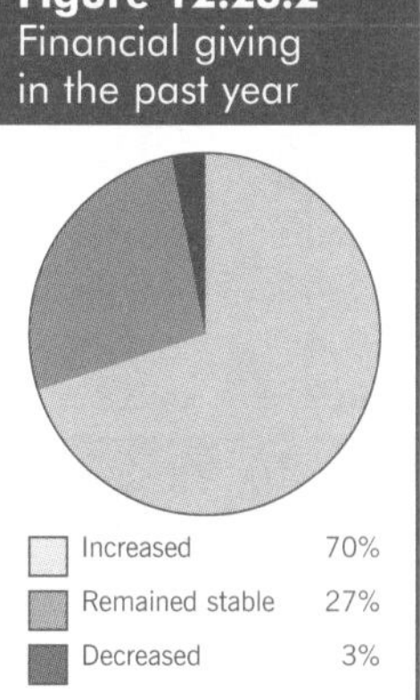

Figure 12.28.3 By 2010, our church will have...

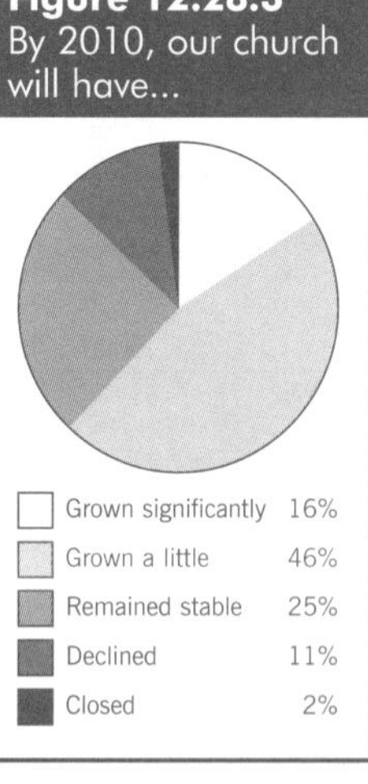

12

Table 12.29.1

OVERALL FIGURES	1984	1994	**2002**
Total population	41,550	41,280	41,110
Usual Sunday church attendance	21,090	16,510	16,120
% attending on Sunday	*50·8*	*40·0*	*39·2*
Number of churches	155	140	142
Population per church	270	290	290

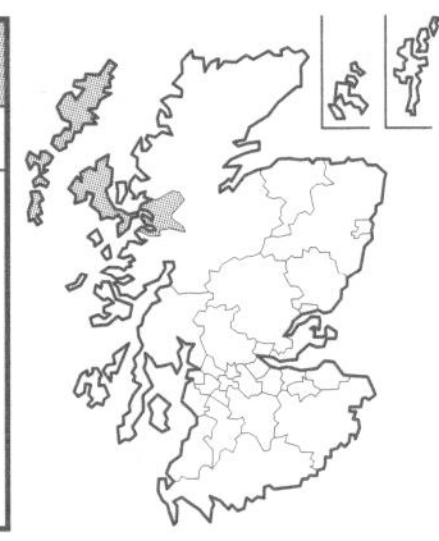

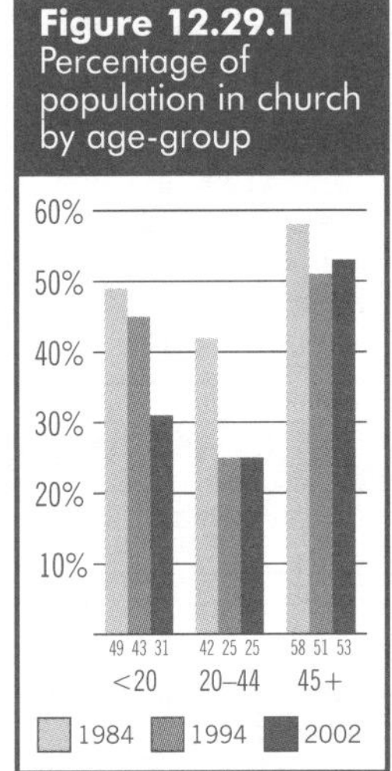

Figure 12.29.1 Percentage of population in church by age-group

Table 12.29.2 Sunday attendance by denomination

	Church of Scotland	Other Presbyterian	Episcopal	Baptist	Independent	Smaller Denoms.	Total Protestant	Roman Catholic	**Total Christian**
1984	6,830	11,980	210	0	120	60	19,200	1,890	21,090
%▼	*–20*	*–13*	*–24*	–	*–75*	*0*	*–16*	*–11*	*–16*
1990	5,460	10,380	160	0	30	60	16,090	1,690	17,780
%▼	*–14*	*–10*	*0*	–	*+67*	*+83*	*–11*	*+26*	*–7*
1994	4,720	9,340	160	0	50	110	14,380	2,130	16,510
%▼	*–15*	*+3*	*–25*	*n/a*	*+60*	*+27*	*–3*	*+2*	*–2*
2002	**3,990**	**9,600**	**120**	**20**	**80**	**140**	**13,950**	**2,170**	**16,120**
1984▶	*32*	*57*	*1*	*0*	*1*	*0*	*91*	*9*	*100%*
1994▶	*29*	*56*	*1*	*0*	*0*	*1*	*87*	*13*	*100%*
2002▶	***25***	***60***	***1***	***0***	***0***	***1***	***87***	***13***	***100%***
Number of churches									
1984	34	89	6	0	2	1	132	23	155
1994	34	80	6	0	1	3	124	16	140
2002	**35**	**79**	**6**	**1**	**2**	**3**	**126**	**16**	**142**

Table 12.29.3 Sunday attendance by churchmanship

	Reformed Evangelical	Mainstream Evangelical	Charismatic Evangelical	TOTAL Evangelical	Reformed	Low church	Liberal	Broad	Catholic*	**ALL Churches**
1994	10,320	960	30	11,310	2,330	0	500	100	2,270	16,510
%▼	*–3*	*+7*	*+33*	*–2*	*+6*	–	*–6*	*+150*	*–19*	*–2*
2002	**10,020**	**1,030**	**40**	**11,090**	**2,470**	**0**	**470**	**250**	**1,840**	**16,120**
1994▶	*62*	*6*	*0*	*68*	*14*	*0*	*3*	*1*	*14*	*100%*
2002▶	***62***	***7***	***0***	***69***	***15***	***0***	***3***	***2***	***11***	***100%***
Number of churches										
1994	77	14	1	92	23	0	3	4	18	140
2002	**76**	**15**	**1**	**92**	**24**	**0**	**3**	**5**	**18**	**142**

Table 12.29.4 Sunday attendance by environment

	City Centre	Urban Priority Area	Housing Scheme	Suburban	Town	New Town	Rural Area: Dormitory	Rural: Other Areas	**ALL Churches**
1994	0	0	0	0	4,130	0	170	12,210	16,510
%▼	–	–	–	–	*+37*	–	*+12*	*–16*	*–2*
2002	**0**	**0**	**0**	**0**	**5,650**	**0**	**190**	**10,280**	**16,120**
1994▶	*0*	*0*	*0*	*0*	*25*	*0*	*1*	*74*	*100%*
2002▶	***0***	***0***	***0***	***0***	***35***	***0***	***1***	***64***	***100%***
Number of churches									
1994	0	0	0	0	13	0	3	124	140
2002	**0**	**0**	**0**	**0**	**13**	**0**	**3**	**126**	**142**

**Catholic: One kind of churchmanship, not to be identified solely with the Roman Catholic church.*

Figure 12.29.2 Financial giving in the past year

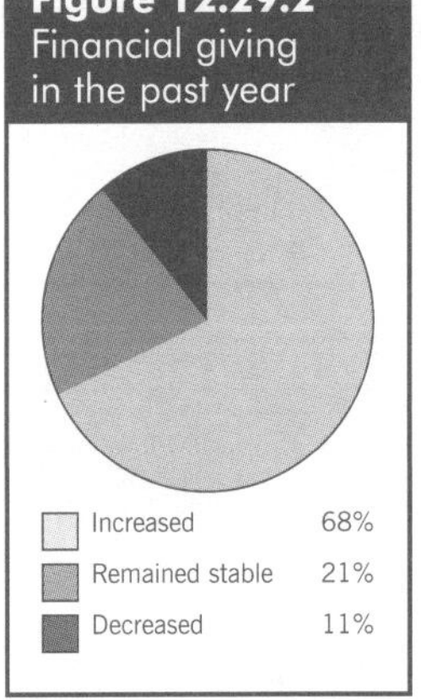

Figure 12.29.3 By 2010, our church will have...

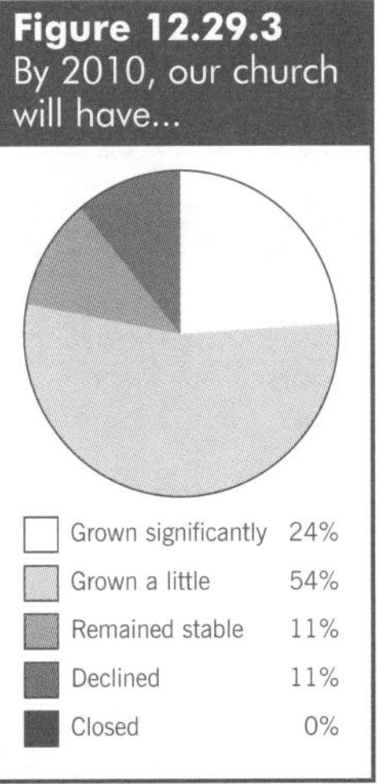

Table 12.29.5 Age and gender of churchgoers 1984, 1994 and 2002

Age Group	Population 1984			Churchgoers in 1984			Population 1994			Churchgoers in 1994			Population 2002			Churchgoers in 2002		
	Male %	Female %	Total %	Male %	Female %	Total %	Male %	Female %	Total %	Male %	Female %	Total %	Male %	Female %	Total %	Male %	Female %	Total %
<12 } 12–14	*12*	*11*	***23***	*10*	*13*	***23***	*10*	*9*	***19***	*10*	*11*	***21***	*7*	*7*	***14***	*5*	*6*	***11***
													2	*2*	***4***	*2*	*2*	***4***
15–19	*4*	*4*	***8***	*3*	*4*	***7***	*3*	*3*	***6***	*3*	*3*	***6***	*3*	*3*	***6***	*2*	*2*	***4***
20–29	*7*	*5*	***12***	*5*	*4*	***9***	*7*	*6*	***13***	*3*	*4*	***7***	*5*	*4*	***9***	*2*	*3*	***5***
30–44	*9*	*8*	***17***	*7*	*8*	***15***	*11*	*10*	***21***	*6*	*8*	***14***	*11*	*11*	***22***	*6*	*9*	***15***
45–64	*10*	*11*	***21***	*11*	*13*	***24***	*12*	*11*	***23***	*11*	*14*	***25***	*13*	*13*	***26***	*14*	*17*	***31***
65/65+	*8*	*11*	***19***	*8*	*14*	***22***	*7*	*11*	***18***	*10*	*17*	***27***	*8*	*11*	***19***	*12*	*18*	***30***
All ages	*50*	*50*	***100***	*44*	*56*	***100***	*50*	*50*	***100***	*43*	*57*	***100***	*49*	*51*	***100***	*43*	*57*	***100***

12

12.30 Church of Scotland

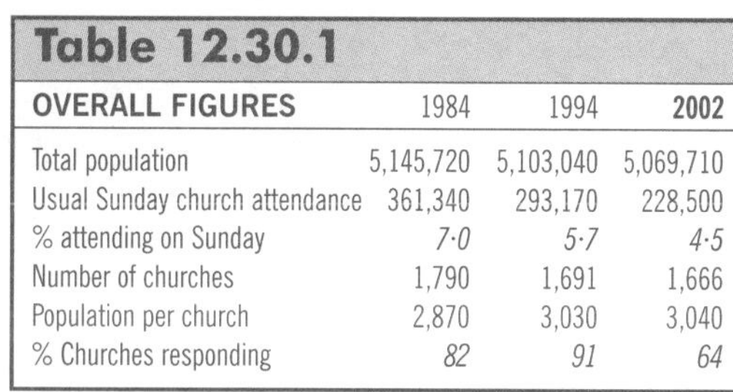

Table 12.30.1

OVERALL FIGURES	1984	1994	**2002**
Total population	5,145,720	5,103,040	5,069,710
Usual Sunday church attendance	361,340	293,170	228,500
% attending on Sunday	*7·0*	*5·7*	*4·5*
Number of churches	1,790	1,691	1,666
Population per church	2,870	3,030	3,040
% Churches responding	*82*	*91*	*64*

Figure 12.30.1
Frequency of attendance, 2002

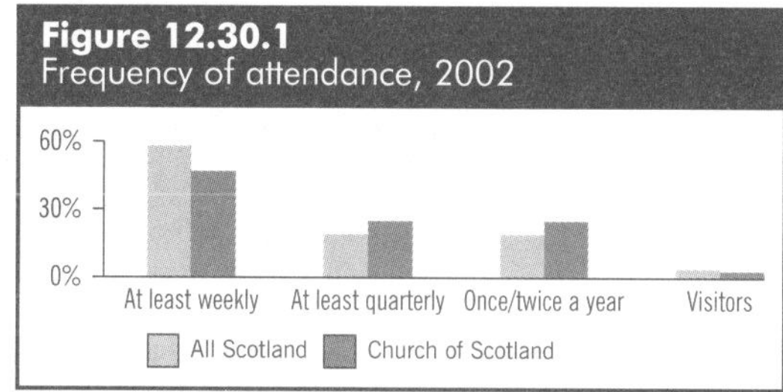

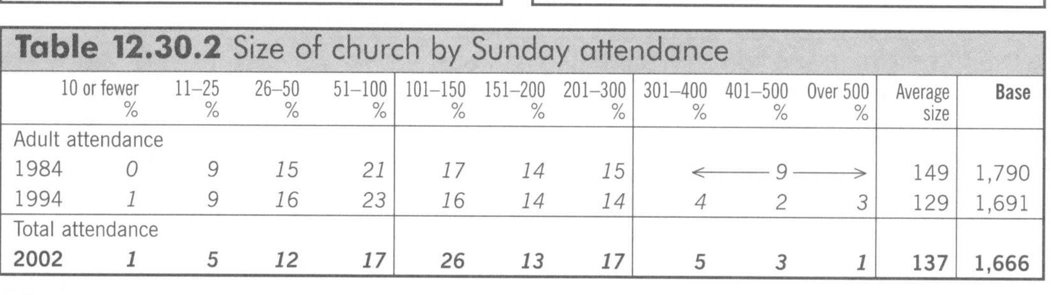

Table 12.30.2 Size of church by Sunday attendance

	10 or fewer %	11–25 %	26–50 %	51–100 %	101–150 %	151–200 %	201–300 %	301–400 %	401–500 %	Over 500 %	Average size	**Base**
Adult attendance												
1984	*0*	*9*	*15*	*21*	*17*	*14*	*15*	←	*9*	→	149	1,790
1994	*1*	*9*	*16*	*23*	*16*	*14*	*14*	*4*	*2*	*3*	129	1,691
Total attendance												
2002	***1***	***5***	***12***	***17***	***26***	***13***	***17***	***5***	***3***	***1***	**137**	**1,666**

Table 12.30.3 Frequency of attendance in 2002

	Twice weekly %	Weekly %	Fortnightly %	Monthly %	Quarterly %	Once or twice a year %	Visitors %
All Scotland	*12*	*46*	*7*	*6*	*6*	*19*	*4*
Church of Scotland	*4*	*43*	*9*	*7*	*9*	*25*	*3*

Table 12.30.4 Sunday attendance by churchmanship

	Reformed Evangelical	Mainstream Evangelical	Charismatic Evangelical	TOTAL Evangelical	Reformed	Low church	Liberal	Broad	Catholic*	**ALL Churches**
1994	50,790	11,320	5,070	67,180	98,900	23,270	32,610	69,520	1,690	293,170
%▼	*–41*	*+19*	*–16*	*–18*	*–22*	*–22*	*–20*	*–27*	*–35*	*–22*
2002	**29,830**	**21,030**	**4,240**	**55,100**	**77,140**	**18,040**	**26,030**	**51,090**	**1,100**	**228,500**
1994▶	*17*	*4*	*2*	*23*	*34*	*8*	*11*	*24*	*0*	*100%*
2002▶	***13***	***9***	***2***	***24***	***34***	***8***	***11***	***22***	***1***	***100%***
Number of churches										
1994	209	63	17	289	550	162	284	389	17	1,691
2002	**195**	**67**	**17**	**279**	**549**	**159**	**282**	**382**	**15**	**1,666**

Table 12.30.5 Sunday attendance by environment

	City Centre	Urban Priority Area	Housing Scheme	Suburban	Town	New Town	Rural Area: Dormitory	Rural: Other Areas	**ALL Churches**
1994	11,060	14,440	21,700	52,480	93,180	6,860	42,380	51,070	293,170
%▼	*–26*	*–39*	*–37*	*–13*	*–24*	*–30*	*–20*	*–17*	*–22*
2002	**8,230**	**8,840**	**13,740**	**45,640**	**71,140**	**4,790**	**33,760**	**42,360**	**228,500**
1994▶	*4*	*5*	*7*	*18*	*32*	*2*	*15*	*17*	*100%*
2002▶	***4***	***4***	***6***	***20***	***31***	***2***	***15***	***18***	***100%***
Number of churches									
1994	36	105	118	139	347	17	254	675	1,691
2002	**36**	**105**	**114**	**138**	**343**	**17**	**256**	**657**	**1,666**

**Catholic: One kind of churchmanship, not to be identified solely with the Roman Catholic church.*

Table 12.30.6 Age and gender of churchgoers 1984, 1994 and 2002

Age Group	Population 1984 Male %	Female %	Total %	Churchgoers in 1984 Male %	Female %	Total %	Population 1994 Male %	Female %	Total %	Churchgoers in 1994 Male %	Female %	Total %	Population 2002 Male %	Female %	Total %	Churchgoers in 2002 Male %	Female %	Total %
<12 } 12–14	*11*	*10*	***21***	*11*	*13*	***24***	*10*	*9*	***19***	*11*	*14*	***25***						
<12													*7*	*7*	***14***	*5*	*8*	***13***
12–14													*2*	*2*	***4***	*1*	*2*	***3***
15–19	*5*	*4*	***9***	*2*	*3*	***5***	*3*	*3*	***6***	*1*	*1*	***2***	*3*	*3*	***6***	*1*	*2*	***3***
20–29	*7*	*8*	***15***	*3*	*6*	***9***	*8*	*8*	***16***	*2*	*4*	***6***	*7*	*6*	***13***	*2*	*2*	***4***
30–44	*9*	*10*	***19***	*5*	*10*	***15***	*10*	*11*	***21***	*5*	*9*	***14***	*12*	*12*	***24***	*3*	*8*	***11***
45–64	*11*	*11*	***22***	*9*	*16*	***25***	*11*	*12*	***23***	*9*	*17*	***26***	*12*	*12*	***24***	*10*	*18*	***28***
65/65+	*5*	*9*	***14***	*7*	*15*	***22***	*6*	*9*	***15***	*8*	*19*	***27***	*6*	*9*	***15***	*13*	*25*	***38***
All ages	*48*	*52*	***100***	*37*	*63*	***100***	*48*	*52*	***100***	*36*	*64*	***100***	*48*	*52*	***100***	*35*	*65*	***100***

Figure 12.30.2
Percentage of population in church by age-group

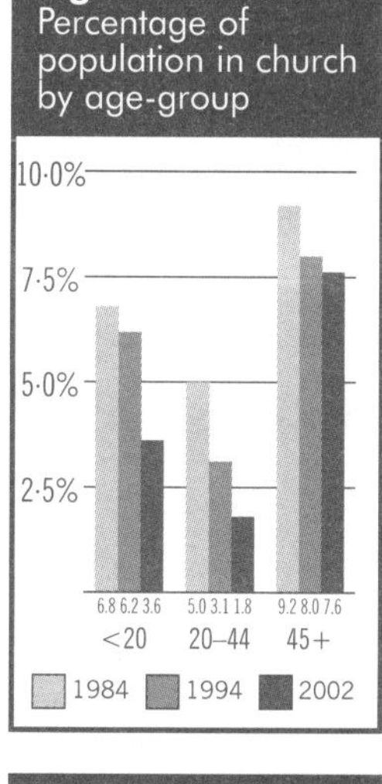

Figure 12.30.3
Financial giving in the past year

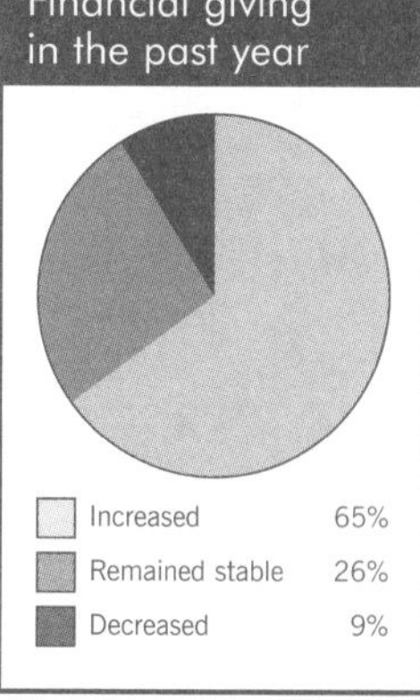

Figure 12.30.4
By 2010, our church will have...

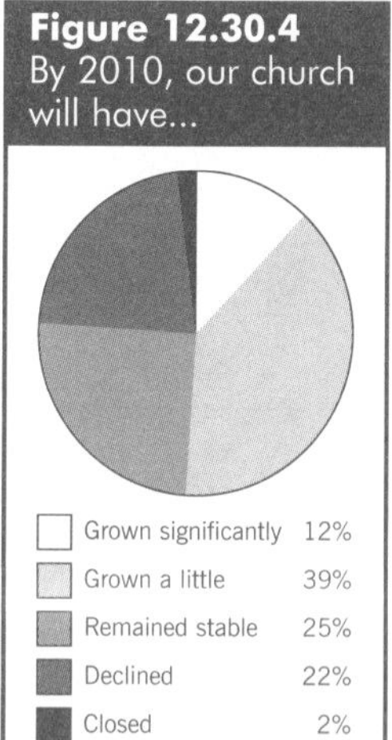

Table 12.31.1

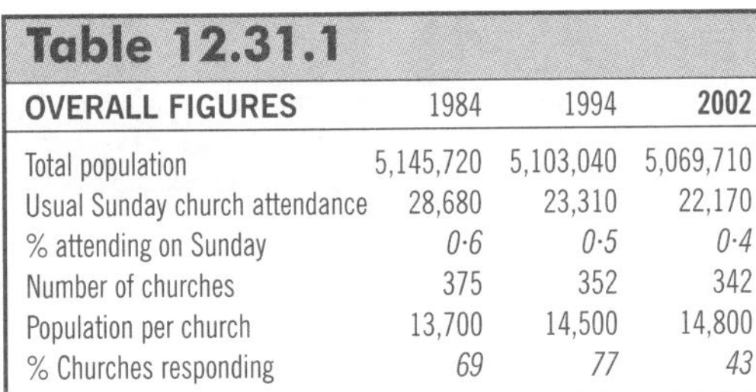

OVERALL FIGURES	1984	1994	**2002**
Total population	5,145,720	5,103,040	5,069,710
Usual Sunday church attendance	28,680	23,310	22,170
% attending on Sunday	*0·6*	*0·5*	*0·4*
Number of churches	375	352	342
Population per church	13,700	14,500	14,800
% Churches responding	*69*	*77*	*43*

Figure 12.31.1
Frequency of attendance, 2002

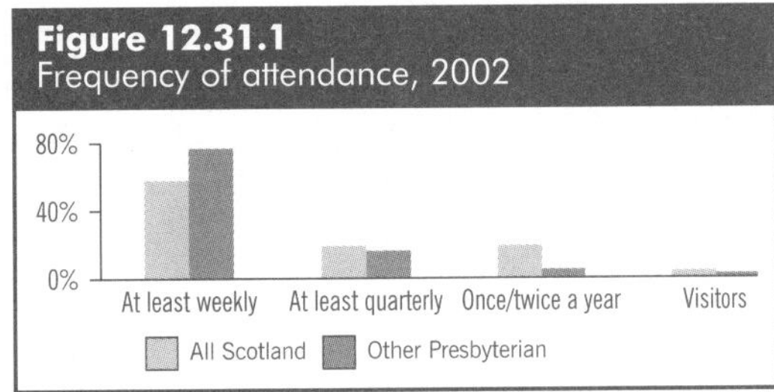

Figure 12.31.2
Percentage of population in church by age-group

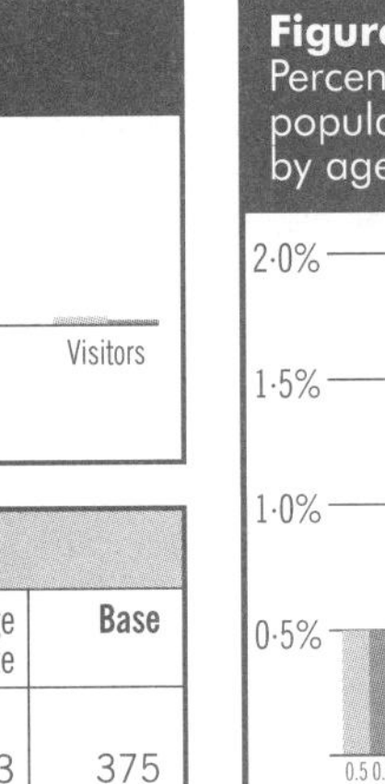

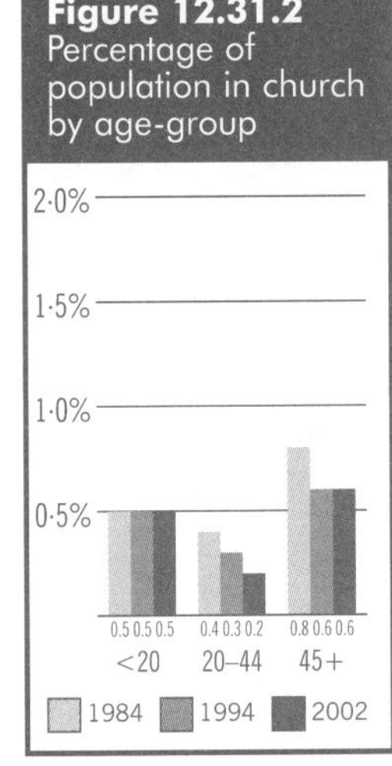

Table 12.31.2 Size of church by Sunday attendance

	10 or fewer %	11–25 %	26–50 %	51–100 %	101–150 %	151–200 %	201–300 %	301–400 %	401–500 %	Over 500 %	Average size	**Base**
Adult attendance												
1984	*14*	*30*	*26*	*17*	*4*	*4*	*3*	←	*2*	→	63	375
1994	*15*	*25*	*31*	*20*	*4*	*2*	*2*	*1*	*0*	*0*	52	352
Total attendance												
2002	***12***	***19***	***25***	***23***	***8***	***7***	***2***	***2***	***1***	***1***	**65**	**342**

Table 12.31.3 Frequency of attendance in 2002

	Twice weekly %	Weekly %	Fortnightly %	Monthly %	Quarterly %	Once or twice a year %	Visitors %
All Scotland	*12*	*46*	*7*	*6*	*6*	*19*	*4*
Other Presbyterian	*35*	*42*	*7*	*6*	*3*	*5*	*2*

Table 12.31.4 Sunday attendance by churchmanship

	Reformed Evangelical	Mainstream Evangelical	Charismatic Evangelical	TOTAL Evangelical	Reformed	Low church	Liberal	Broad	Catholic*	**ALL Churches**
1994	15,930	2,810	0	18,740	4,190	170	80	130	0	23,310
%▼	*–15*	*+32*	*0*	*–8*	*+7*	*–24*	*–12*	*+31*	*0*	*–5*
2002	**13,600**	**3,700**	**0**	**17,300**	**4,500**	**130**	**70**	**170**	**0**	**22,170**
1994►	*68*	*12*	*0*	*80*	*18*	*1*	*0*	*1*	*0*	*100%*
2002►	***61***	***17***	***0***	***78***	***20***	***1***	***0***	***1***	***0***	***100%***
Number of churches										
1994	232	46	0	278	66	4	2	2	0	352
2002	**221**	**46**	**0**	**268**	**67**	**4**	**2**	**2**	**0**	**342**

Table 12.31.5 Sunday attendance by environment

	City Centre	Urban Priority Area	Housing Scheme	Suburban	Town	New Town	Rural Area: Dormitory	Rural: Other Areas	**ALL Churches**
1994	1,410	260	1,770	2,080	5,730	430	1,590	10,040	23,310
%▼	*+5*	*–27*	*–34*	*+12*	*–1*	*–5*	*+2*	*–7*	*–5*
2002	**1,480**	**190**	**1,170**	**2,320**	**5,680**	**410**	**1,620**	**9,300**	**22,170**
1994►	*6*	*1*	*8*	*9*	*24*	*2*	*7*	*43*	*100%*
2002►	***7***	***1***	***5***	***10***	***26***	***2***	***7***	***42***	***100%***
Number of churches									
1994	14	7	18	28	63	7	21	194	352
2002	**14**	**7**	**18**	**28**	**62**	**7**	**21**	**185**	**342**

**Catholic: One kind of churchmanship, not to be identified solely with the Roman Catholic church. [1] Revised figure*

Figure 12.31.3
Financial giving in the past year

Increased	54%
Remained stable	35%
Decreased	11%

Figure 12.31.4
By 2010, our church will have...

Grown significantly	16%
Grown a little	37%
Remained stable	20%
Declined	21%
Closed	6%

Table 12.31.6 Age and gender of churchgoers 1984, 1994 and 2002

Age Group	Population 1984			Churchgoers in 1984			Population 1994			Churchgoers in 1994			Population 2002			Churchgoers in 2002		
	Male %	Female %	Total %	Male %	Female %	Total %	Male %	Female %	Total %	Male %	Female %	Total %	Male %	Female %	Total %	Male %	Female %	Total %
<12 } 12–14 }	*11*	*10*	*21*	*9*	*10*	***19***	*10*	*9*	*19*	*9*	*12*[1]	***21***	*7*	*7*	*14*	*11*	*7*	***18***
													2	*2*	*4*	*2*	*2*	***4***
15–19	*5*	*4*	*9*	*3*	*4*	***7***	*3*	*3*	*6*	*2*	*3*	***5***	*3*	*3*	*6*	*2*	*2*	***4***
20–29	*7*	*8*	*15*	*4*	*5*	***9***	*8*	*8*	*16*	*4*	*4*	***8***	*7*	*6*	*13*	*3*	*3*	***6***
30–44	*9*	*10*	*19*	*7*	*8*	***15***	*10*	*11*	*21*	*6*	*7*	***13***	*12*	*12*	*24*	*5*	*8*	***13***
45–64	*11*	*11*	*22*	*10*	*14*	***24***	*11*	*12*	*23*	*10*	*14*	***24***	*12*	*12*	*24*	*10*	*13*	***23***
65/65+	*5*	*9*	*14*	*10*	*16*	***26***	*6*	*9*	*15*	*11*	*18*[1]	***29***	*6*	*9*	*15*	*13*	*19*	***32***
All ages	*48*	*52*	*100*	*43*	*57*	***100***	*48*	*52*	*100*	*42*	*58*	***100***	*48*	*52*	*100*	*46*	*54*	***100***

12

12.32 Episcopal

Table 12.32.1

OVERALL FIGURES	1984	1994	**2002**
Total population	5,145,720	5,103,040	5,069,710
Usual Sunday church attendance	20,000	20,350	18,870
% attending on Sunday	*0·4*	*0·4*	*0·4*
Number of churches	306	311	309
Population per church	16,800	16,500	16,400
% Churches responding	*59*	*92*	*63*

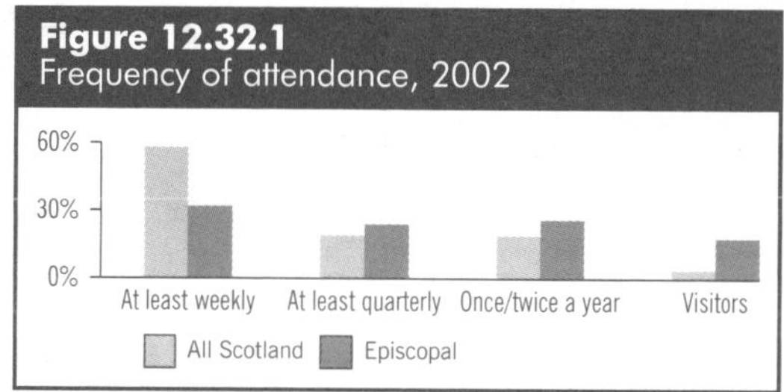

Figure 12.32.1
Frequency of attendance, 2002

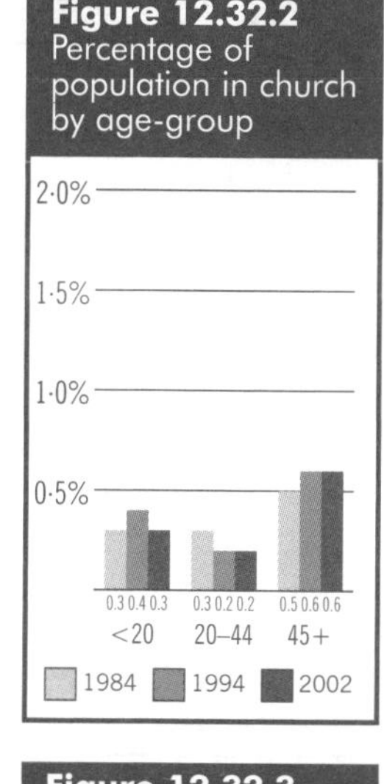

Figure 12.32.2
Percentage of population in church by age-group

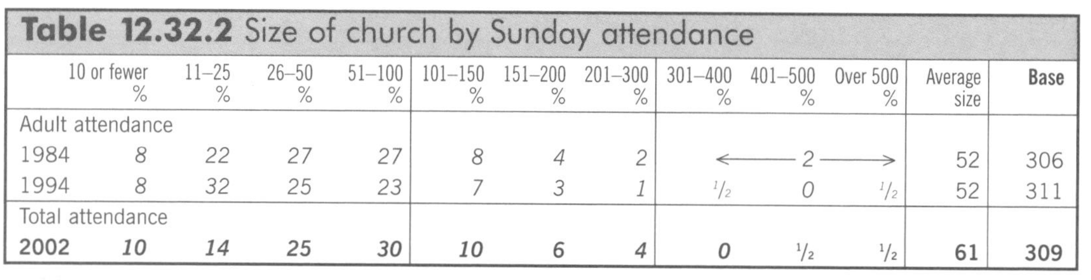

Table 12.32.2 Size of church by Sunday attendance

	10 or fewer %	11–25 %	26–50 %	51–100 %	101–150 %	151–200 %	201–300 %	301–400 %	401–500 %	Over 500 %	Average size	Base
Adult attendance												
1984	*8*	*22*	*27*	*27*	*8*	*4*	*2*	←	*2*	→	52	306
1994	*8*	*32*	*25*	*23*	*7*	*3*	*1*	*½*	*0*	*½*	52	311
Total attendance												
2002	***10***	***14***	***25***	***30***	***10***	***6***	***4***	***0***	***½***	***½***	**61**	**309**

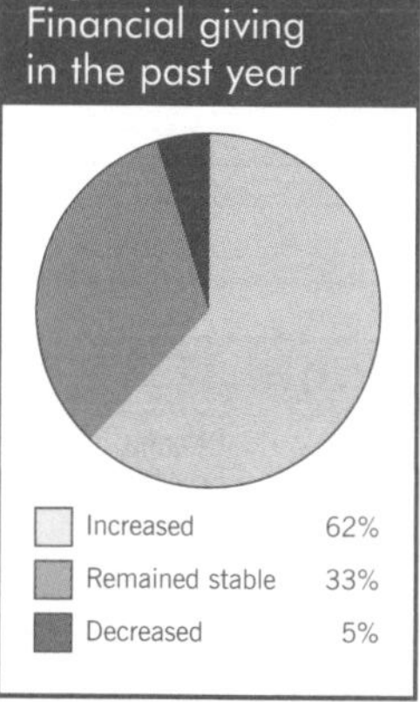

Figure 12.32.3
Financial giving in the past year

Table 12.32.3 Frequency of attendance in 2002

	Twice weekly %	Weekly %	Fortnightly %	Monthly %	Quarterly %	Once or twice a year %	Visitors %
All Scotland	*12*	*46*	*7*	*6*	*6*	*19*	*4*
Episcopal	*2*	*30*	*12*	*7*	*5*	*26*	*18*

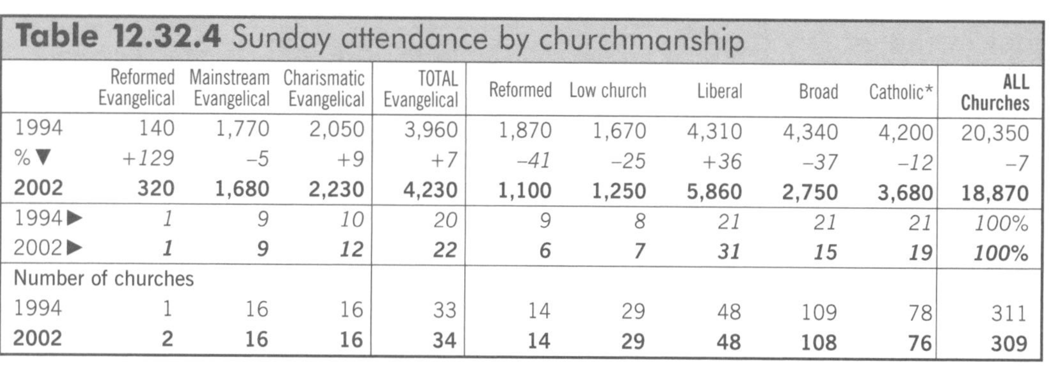

Table 12.32.4 Sunday attendance by churchmanship

	Reformed Evangelical	Mainstream Evangelical	Charismatic Evangelical	TOTAL Evangelical	Reformed	Low church	Liberal	Broad	Catholic*	**ALL Churches**
1994	140	1,770	2,050	3,960	1,870	1,670	4,310	4,340	4,200	20,350
%▼	*+129*	*−5*	*+9*	*+7*	*−41*	*−25*	*+36*	*−37*	*−12*	*−7*
2002	**320**	**1,680**	**2,230**	**4,230**	**1,100**	**1,250**	**5,860**	**2,750**	**3,680**	**18,870**
1994▶	*1*	*9*	*10*	*20*	*9*	*8*	*21*	*21*	*21*	*100%*
2002▶	***1***	***9***	***12***	***22***	***6***	***7***	***31***	***15***	***19***	***100%***
Number of churches										
1994	1	16	16	33	14	29	48	109	78	311
2002	**2**	**16**	**16**	**34**	**14**	**29**	**48**	**108**	**76**	**309**

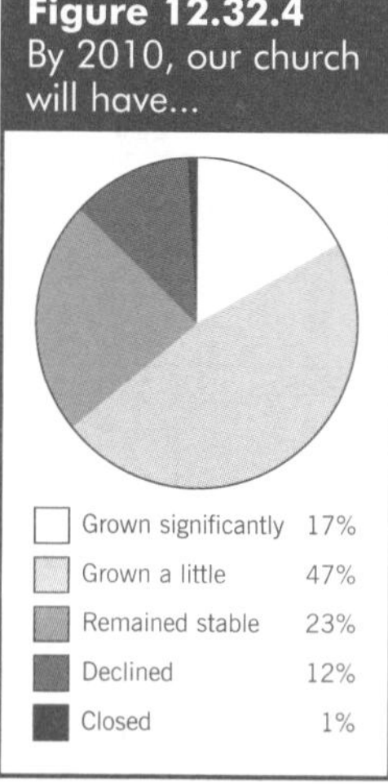

Figure 12.32.4
By 2010, our church will have...

Table 12.32.5 Sunday attendance by environment

	City Centre	Urban Priority Area	Housing Scheme	Suburban	Town	New Town	Rural Area: Dormitory	Rural: Other Areas	**ALL Churches**
1994	3,020	550	810	3,930	5,680	630	1,900	3,830	20,350
%▼	*+9*	*−53*	*−46*	*−7*	*−4*	*−8*	*−15*	*−6*	*−7*
2002	**3,290**	**260**	**440**	**3,650**	**5,440**	**580**	**1,620**	**3,590**	**18,870**
1994▶	*15*	*3*	*4*	*19*	*28*	*3*	*9*	*19*	*100%*
2002▶	***18***	***1***	***2***	***19***	***29***	***3***	***9***	***19***	***100%***
Number of churches									
1994	19	12	12	34	75	9	34	116	311
2002	**19**	**12**	**12**	**34**	**76**	**9**	**34**	**113**	**309**

Catholic: One kind of churchmanship, not to be identified solely with the Roman Catholic church.

Table 12.32.6 Age and gender of churchgoers 1984, 1994 and 2002

Age Group	Population 1984			Churchgoers in 1984			Population 1994			Churchgoers in 1994			Population 2002			Churchgoers in 2002		
	Male %	Female %	Total %	Male %	Female %	Total %	Male %	Female %	Total %	Male %	Female %	Total %	Male %	Female %	Total %	Male %	Female %	Total %
<12 } 12–14	*11*	*10*	***21***	*9*	*10*	***19***	*10*	*9*	***19***	*9*	*11*	***20***	*7*	*7*	***14***	*5*	*6*	***11***
													2	*2*	***4***	*1*	*2*	***3***
15–19	*5*	*4*	***9***	*2*	*4*	***6***	*3*	*3*	***6***	*2*	*3*	***5***	*3*	*3*	***6***	*1*	*2*	***3***
20–29	*7*	*8*	***15***	*4*	*4*	***8***	*8*	*8*	***16***	*3*	*4*	***7***	*7*	*6*	***13***	*3*	*4*	***7***
30–44	*9*	*10*	***19***	*7*	*12*	***19***	*10*	*11*	***21***	*6*	*9*	***15***	*12*	*12*	***24***	*6*	*8*	***14***
45–64	*11*	*11*	***22***	*9*	*16*	***25***	*11*	*12*	***23***	*10*	*16*	***26***	*12*	*12*	***24***	*12*	*16*	***28***
65/65+	*5*	*9*	***14***	*7*	*16*	***23***	*6*	*9*	***15***	*9*	*18*	***27***	*6*	*9*	***15***	*12*	*22*	***34***
All ages	*48*	*52*	***100***	*38*	*62*	***100***	*48*	*52*	***100***	*39*	*61*	***100***	*48*	*52*	*100*	*40*	*60*	***100***

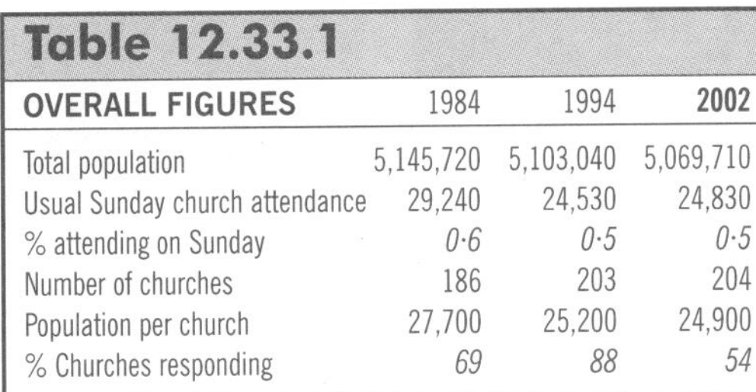

Table 12.33.1

OVERALL FIGURES	1984	1994	**2002**
Total population	5,145,720	5,103,040	5,069,710
Usual Sunday church attendance	29,240	24,530	24,830
% attending on Sunday	*0·6*	*0·5*	*0·5*
Number of churches	186	203	204
Population per church	27,700	25,200	24,900
% Churches responding	*69*	*88*	*54*

Figure 12.33.1
Frequency of attendance, 2002

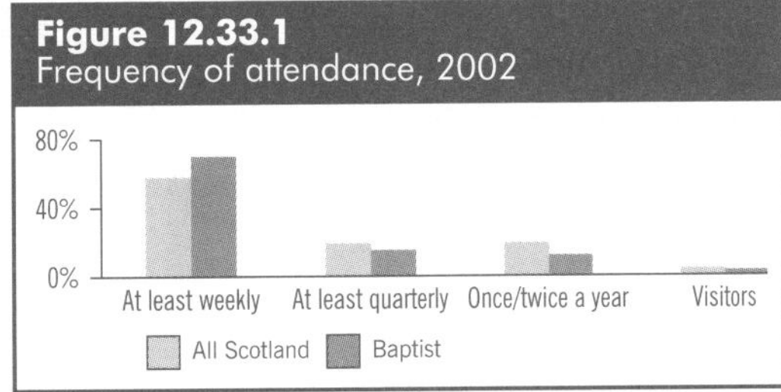

Figure 12.33.2
Percentage of population in church by age-group

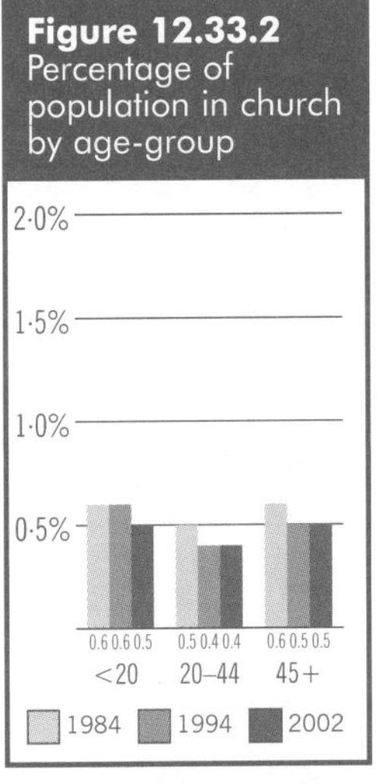

Table 12.33.2 Size of church by Sunday attendance

	10 or fewer %	11–25 %	26–50 %	51–100 %	101–150 %	151–200 %	201–300 %	301–400 %	401–500 %	Over 500 %	Average size	**Base**
Adult attendance												
1984	*0*	*11*	*15*	*38*	*14*	*9*	*6*	←——	*7*	——→	117	186
1994	*4*	*11*	*24*	*30*	*14*	*6*	*7*	*2*	*1*	*1*	90	203
Total attendance												
2002	***1***	***7***	***13***	***28***	***21***	***12***	***9***	***4***	***2***	***3***	**122**	**204**

Table 12.33.3 Frequency of attendance in 2002

	Twice weekly %	Weekly %	Fortnightly %	Monthly %	Quarterly %	Once or twice a year %	Visitors %
All Scotland	*12*	*46*	*7*	*6*	*6*	*19*	*4*
Baptist	*25*	*45*	*5*	*6*	*4*	*12*	*3*

Figure 12.33.3
Financial giving in the past year

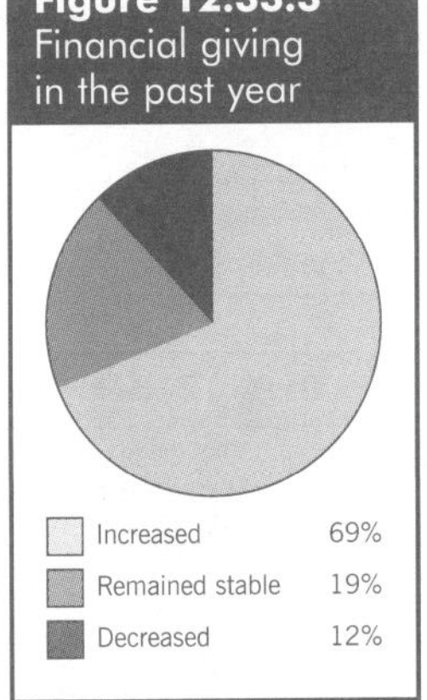

Table 12.33.4 Sunday attendance by churchmanship

	Reformed Evangelical	Mainstream Evangelical	Charismatic Evangelical	TOTAL Evangelical	Reformed	Low church	Liberal	Broad	Catholic*	**ALL Churches**
1994	4,500	16,300	3,350	24,150	0	0	380	0	0	24,530
%▼	*–11*	*+1*	*+20*	*+2*	–	–	*–18*	–	–	*+1*
2002	**4,020**	**16,490**	**4,010**	**24,520**	**0**	**0**	**310**	**0**	**0**	**24,830**
1994▶	*18*	*66*	*14*	*98*	*0*	*0*	*2*	*0*	*0*	*100%*
2002▶	***16***	***67***	***16***	***99***	***0***	***0***	***1***	***0***	***0***	***100%***
Number of churches										
1994	47	134	18	199	0	0	4	0	0	203
2002	**47**	**134**	**19**	**200**	**0**	**0**	**4**	**0**	**0**	**204**

Figure 12.33.4
By 2010, our church will have...

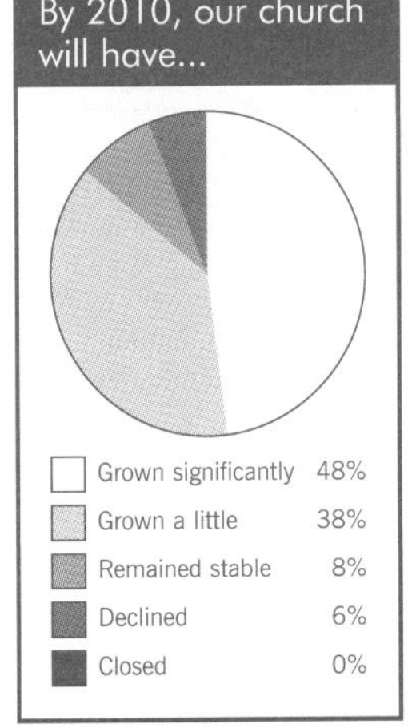

Table 12.33.5 Sunday attendance by environment

	City Centre	Urban Priority Area	Housing Scheme	Suburban	Town	New Town	Rural Area: Dormitory	Rural: Other Areas	**ALL Churches**
1994	2,550	1,330	1,000	4,280	11,740	1,670	790	1,170	24,530
%▼	*+16*	*–8*	*–15*	*+21*	*–5*	*–2*	*–11*	*+1*	*+1*
2002	**2,950**	**1,230**	**850**	**5,170**	**11,110**	**1,640**	**700**	**1,180**	**24,830**
1994▶	*10*	*5*	*4*	*18*	*48*	*7*	*3*	*5*	*100%*
2002▶	***12***	***5***	***3***	***21***	***45***	***6***	***3***	***5***	***100%***
Number of churches									
1994	16	10	14	37	96	16	6	8	203
2002	**16**	**10**	**14**	**36**	**94**	**16**	**6**	**12**	**204**

Catholic: One kind of churchmanship, not to be identified solely with the Roman Catholic church.

Table 12.33.6 Age and gender of churchgoers 1984, 1994 and 2002

Age Group	Population 1984			Churchgoers in 1984			Population 1994			Churchgoers in 1994			Population 2002			Churchgoers in 2002		
	Male %	Female %	Total %	Male %	Female %	Total %	Male %	Female %	Total %	Male %	Female %	Total %	Male %	Female %	Total %	Male %	Female %	Total %
<12 }	*11*	*10*	***21***	*10*	*14*	***24***	*10*	*9*	***19***	*12*	*13*	***25***	7	7	**14**	*7*	*8*	***15***
12–14 }													2	2	**4**	*2*	*3*	***5***
15–19	5	4	*9*	4	5	*9*	3	3	*6*	3	4	*7*	3	3	*6*	2	3	*5*
20–29	7	8	*15*	7	8	*15*	8	8	*16*	5	6	*11*	7	6	*13*	5	7	*12*
30–44	9	10	*19*	7	10	*17*	10	11	*21*	7	10	*17*	12	12	*24*	9	11	*20*
45–64	11	11	*22*	7	11	*18*	11	12	*23*	10	14	*24*	12	12	*24*	10	15	*25*
65/65+	5	9	*14*	5	12	*17*	6	9	*15*	5	11	*16*	6	9	*15*	7	11	*18*
All ages	48	52	**100**	40	60	**100**	48	52	**100**	42	58	**100**	48	52	**100**	42	58	**100**

12.34 Independent

Table 12.34.1

OVERALL FIGURES	1984	1994	**2002**
Total population	5,145,720	5,103,040	5,069,710
Usual Sunday church attendance	39,370	48,020	45,010
% attending on Sunday	*0·8*	*0·9*	*0·9*
Number of churches	438	577	559
Population per church	11,700	8,900	9,100
% Churches responding	*56*	*50*	*28*

Figure 12.34.1
Frequency of attendance, 2002

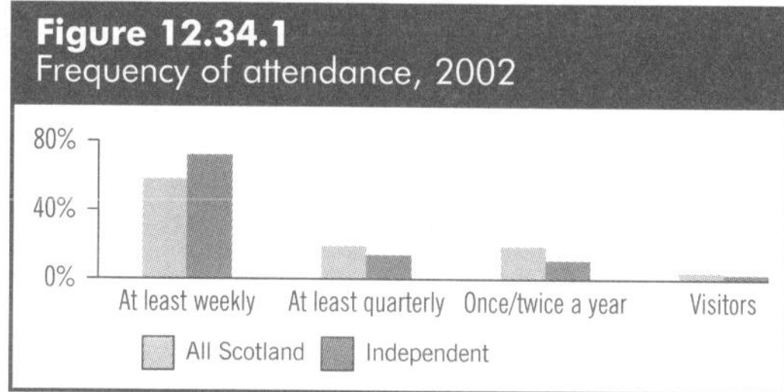

Figure 12.34.2
Percentage of population in church by age-group

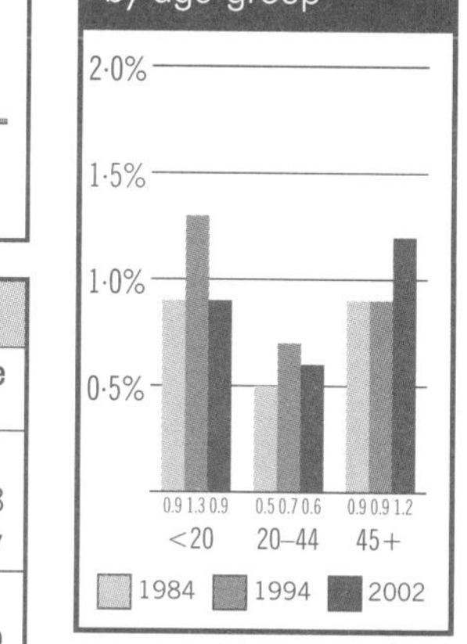

Table 12.34.2 Size of church by Sunday attendance

	10 or fewer %	11–25 %	26–50 %	51–100 %	101–150 %	151–200 %	201–300 %	301–400 %	401–500 %	Over 500 %	Average size	**Base**
Adult attendance												
1984	*5*	*13*	*29*	*31*	*10*	*9*	*3*	*0*	*0*	*0*	61	438
1994	*5*	*23*	*36*	*20*	*8*	*4*	*3*	*1*	*0*	*0*	60	577
Total attendance												
2002	***2***	***15***	***21***	***34***	***11***	***7***	***5***	***3***	***1***	***1***	**81**	**559**

Figure 12.34.3
Financial giving in the past year

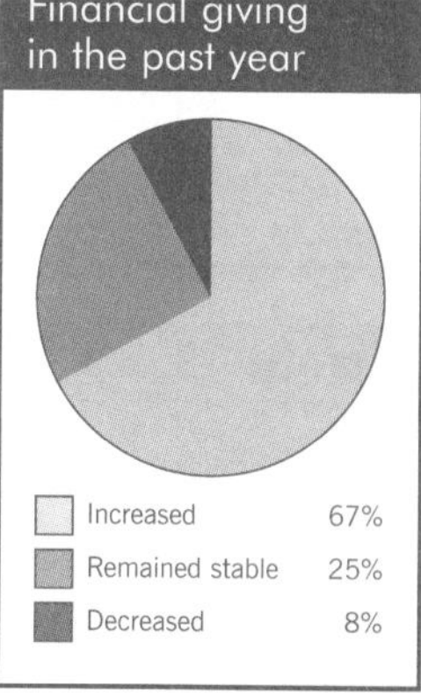

Table 12.34.3 Frequency of attendance in 2002

	Twice weekly %	Weekly %	Fortnightly %	Monthly %	Quarterly %	Once or twice a year %	Visitors %
All Scotland	*12*	*46*	*7*	*6*	*6*	*19*	*4*
Independent	*26*	*46*	*5*	*3*	*6*	*11*	*3*

Table 12.34.4 Sunday attendance by churchmanship

	Reformed Evangelical	Mainstream Evangelical	Charismatic Evangelical	TOTAL Evangelical	Reformed	Low church	Liberal	Broad	Catholic*	**ALL Churches**
1994	5,890	22,920	13,360	42,170	1,800	630	2,840	580	0	48,020
%▼	*–24*	*+8*	*–19*	*–5*	*–19*	*–5*	*–23*	*+17*	*–*	*–6*
2002	**4,460**	**24,770**	**10,840**	**40,070**	**1,460**	**600**	**2,200**	**680**	**0**	**45,010**
1994▶	*12*	*48*	*28*	*88*	*4*	*1*	*6*	*1*	*0*	*100%*
2002▶	***10***	***55***	***24***	***89***	***3***	***1***	***5***	***2***	***0***	***100%***
Number of churches										
1994	66	291	142	499	24	7	34	13	0	577
2002	**66**	**280**	**142**	**488**	**21**	**7**	**30**	**13**	**0**	**559**

Figure 12.34.4
By 2010, our church will have...

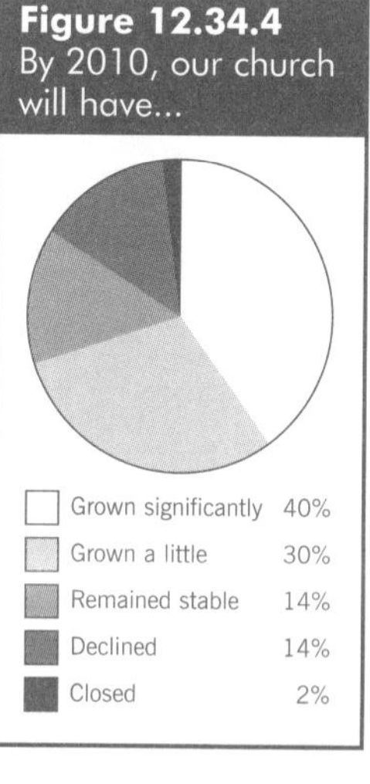

Table 12.34.5 Sunday attendance by environment

	City Centre	Urban Priority Area	Housing Scheme	Suburban	Town	New Town	Rural Area: Dormitory	Rural: Other Areas	**ALL Churches**
1994	3,090	1,130	4,930	7,430	21,170	2,130	3,600	4,540	48,020
%▼	*+2*	*+18*	*–21*	*–2*	*–8*	*–6*	*–6*	*+1*	*–6*
2002	**3,160**	**1,330**	**3,880**	**7,290**	**19,380**	**2,000**	**3,380**	**4,590**	**45,010**
1994▶	*6*	*2*	*10*	*16*	*44*	*4*	*8*	*10*	*100%*
2002▶	***7***	***3***	***9***	***16***	***43***	***4***	***8***	***10***	***100%***
Number of churches									
1994	18	18	67	69	228	20	55	102	577
2002	**18**	**18**	**66**	**67**	**217**	**20**	**56**	**97**	**559**

**Catholic: One kind of churchmanship, not to be identified solely with the Roman Catholic church.*

Table 12.34.6 Age and gender of churchgoers 1984, 1994 and 2002

Age Group	Population 1984			Churchgoers in 1984			Population 1994			Churchgoers in 1994			Population 2002			Churchgoers in 2002		
	Male %	Female %	Total %	Male %	Female %	Total %	Male %	Female %	Total %	Male %	Female %	Total %	Male %	Female %	Total %	Male %	Female %	Total %
<12 }	*11*	*10*	***21***	*12*	*16*	***28***	*10*	*9*	***19***	*13*	*15*	***28***	*7*	*7*	***14***	*7*	*8*	***15***
12–14 }													*2*	*2*	***4***	*2*	*2*	***4***
15–19	*5*	*4*	***9***	*4*	*4*	***8***	*3*	*3*	***6***	*3*	*4*	***7***	*3*	*3*	***6***	*3*	*3*	***6***
20–29	*7*	*8*	***15***	*4*	*6*	***10***	*8*	*8*	***16***	*5*	*6*	***11***	*7*	*6*	***13***	*4*	*5*	***9***
30–44	*9*	*10*	***19***	*6*	*8*	***14***	*10*	*11*	***21***	*8*	*10*	***18***	*12*	*12*	***24***	*7*	*8*	***15***
45–64	*11*	*11*	***22***	*7*	*12*	***19***	*11*	*12*	***23***	*8*	*12*	***20***	*12*	*12*	***24***	*11*	*14*	***25***
65/65+	*5*	*9*	***14***	*7*	*14*	***21***	*6*	*9*	***15***	*6*	*10*	***16***	*6*	*9*	***15***	*9*	*17*	***26***
All ages	*48*	*52*	***100***	*40*	*60*	***100***	*48*	*52*	***100***	*43*	*57*	***100***	*48*	*52*	***100***	*43*	*57*	***100***

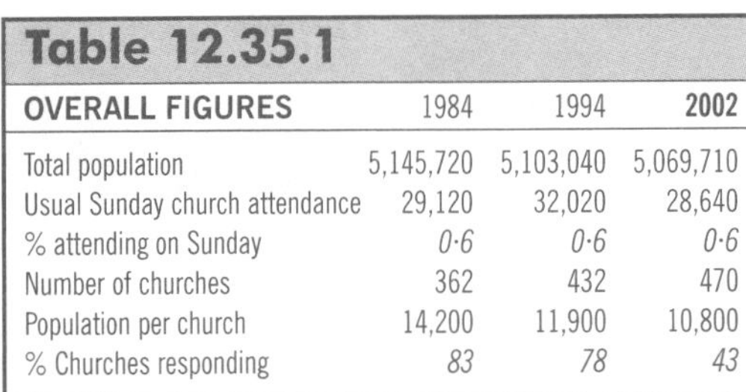

Table 12.35.1

OVERALL FIGURES	1984	1994	**2002**
Total population	5,145,720	5,103,040	5,069,710
Usual Sunday church attendance	29,120	32,020	28,640
% attending on Sunday	*0·6*	*0·6*	*0·6*
Number of churches	362	432	470
Population per church	14,200	11,900	10,800
% Churches responding	*83*	*78*	*43*

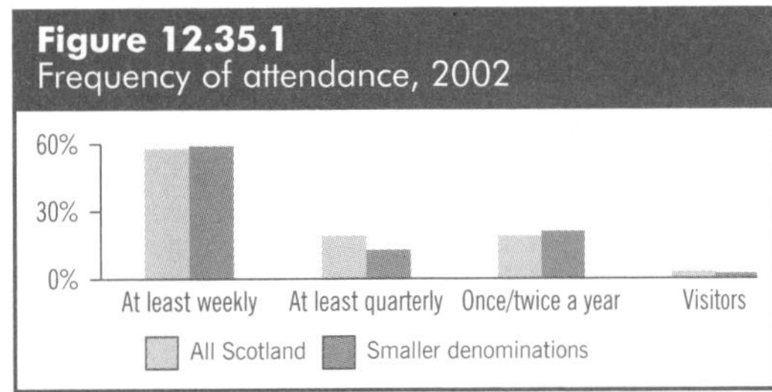

Figure 12.35.1 Frequency of attendance, 2002

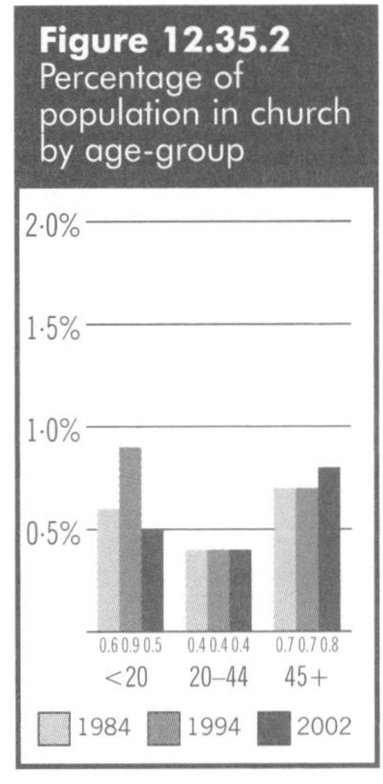

Figure 12.35.2 Percentage of population in church by age-group

Table 12.35.2 Size of church by Sunday attendance

	10 or fewer %	11–25 %	26–50 %	51–100 %	101–150 %	151–200 %	201–300 %	301–400 %	401–500 %	Over 500 %	Average size	**Base**
Adult attendance												
1984	*12*	*22*	*28*	*24*	*11*	*2*	*2*	*0*	*0*	*0*	52	362
1994	*14*	*27*	*27*	*22*	*4*	*2*	*3*	*1*	*0*	*0*	52	432
Total attendance												
2002	***11***	***16***	***23***	***28***	***10***	**5**	**6**	***1***	***0***	***0***	**61**	**470**

Table 12.35.3 Frequency of attendance in 2002

	Twice weekly %	Weekly %	Fortnightly %	Monthly %	Quarterly %	Once or twice a year %	Visitors %
All Scotland	*12*	*46*	*7*	*6*	*6*	*19*	*4*
Smaller denominations	*18*	*41*	*6*	*6*	*5*	*21*	*3*

Figure 12.35.3 Financial giving in the past year

Increased	59%
Remained stable	35%
Decreased	6%

Table 12.35.4 Sunday attendance by churchmanship

	Reformed Evangelical	Mainstream Evangelical	Charismatic Evangelical	TOTAL Evangelical	Reformed	Low church	Liberal	Broad	Catholic*	**ALL Churches**
1994	2,680	9,930	7,360	19,970	810	1,850	4,900	3,830	660	32,020
%▼	*–32*	*–1*	*–2*	*–5*	*+5*	*+1*	*–16*	*–30*	*–62*	*–11*
2002	**1,830**	**9,810**	**7,240**	**18,880**	**850**	**1,860**	**4,130**	**2,670**	**250**	**28,640**
1994▶	*8*	*31*	*23*	*62*	*3*	*6*	*15*	*12*	*2*	*100%*
2002▶	***7***	***34***	***25***	***66***	***3***	***7***	***14***	***9***	***1***	***100%***
Number of churches										
1994	63	118	88	269	14	35	56	45	13	432
2002	**63**	**138**	**92**	**293**	**16**	**38**	**60**	**50**	**13**	**470**

Figure 12.35.4 By 2010, our church will have...

Grown significantly	32%
Grown a little	34%
Remained stable	17%
Declined	15%
Closed	2%

Table 12.35.5 Sunday attendance by environment

	City Centre	Urban Priority Area	Housing Scheme	Suburban	Town	New Town	Rural Area: Dormitory	Rural: Other Areas	**ALL Churches**
1994	3,390	2,100	2,970	3,110	13,700	2,220	1,570	2,960	32,020
%▼	*+4*	*+7*	*–19*	*–4*	*–19*	*–10*	*+7*	*–10*	*–11*
2002	**3,510**	**2,240**	**2,410**	**2,980**	**11,160**	**2,000**	**1,680**	**2,660**	**28,640**
1994▶	*11*	*6*	*9*	*10*	*43*	*7*	*5*	*9*	*100%*
2002▶	***12***	***8***	***9***	***10***	***39***	***7***	***6***	***9***	***100%***
Number of churches									
1994	43	30	52	39	151	26	22	69	432
2002	**45**	**30**	**55**	**48**	**170**	**26**	**23**	**73**	**470**

**Catholic: One kind of churchmanship, not to be identified solely with the Roman Catholic church.*

Table 12.35.6 Age and gender of churchgoers 1984, 1994 and 2002

Age Group	Population 1984			Churchgoers in 1984			Population 1994			Churchgoers in 1994			Population 2002			Churchgoers in 2002		
	Male %	Female %	Total %	Male %	Female %	Total %	Male %	Female %	Total %	Male %	Female %	Total %	Male %	Female %	Total %	Male %	Female %	Total %
<12 } 12–14 }	*11*	*10*	***21***	*11*	*15*	***26***	*10*	*9*	***19***	*13*	*17*	***30***						
<12													*7*	*7*	***14***	*5*	*7*	***12***
12–14													*2*	*2*	***4***	*2*	*2*	***4***
15–19	*5*	*4*	***9***	*3*	*4*	***7***	*3*	*3*	***6***	*2*	*3*	***5***	*3*	*3*	***6***	*2*	*2*	***4***
20–29	*7*	*8*	***15***	*4*	*6*	***10***	*8*	*8*	***16***	*5*	*6*	***11***	*7*	*6*	***13***	*4*	*5*	***9***
30–44	*9*	*10*	***19***	*6*	*9*	***15***	*10*	*11*	***21***	*6*	*8*	***14***	*12*	*12*	***24***	*7*	*9*	***16***
45–64	*11*	*11*	***22***	*7*	*13*	***20***	*11*	*12*	***23***	*7*	*12*	***19***	*12*	*12*	***24***	*10*	*16*	***26***
65/65+	*5*	*9*	***14***	*7*	*15*	***22***	*6*	*9*	***15***	*7*	*14*	***21***	*6*	*9*	***15***	*9*	*20*	***29***
All ages	*48*	*52*	***100***	*38*	*62*	***100***	*48*	*52*	***100***	*40*	*60*	***100***	*48*	*52*	***100***	*39*	*61*	***100***

12

12.36 Roman Catholic

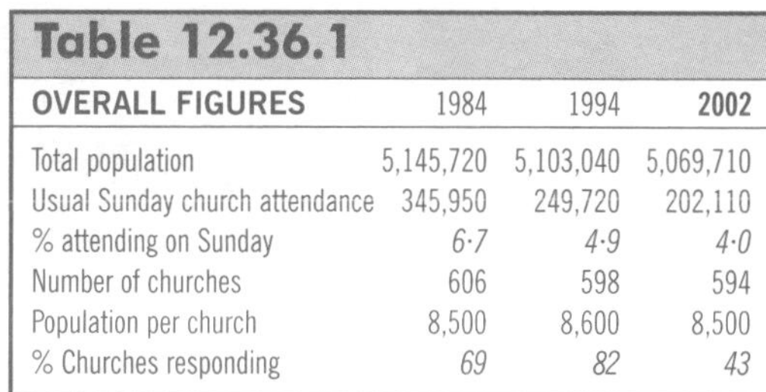

Table 12.36.1

OVERALL FIGURES	1984	1994	**2002**
Total population	5,145,720	5,103,040	5,069,710
Usual Sunday church attendance	345,950	249,720	202,110
% attending on Sunday	*6·7*	*4·9*	*4·0*
Number of churches	606	598	594
Population per church	8,500	8,600	8,500
% Churches responding	*69*	*82*	*43*

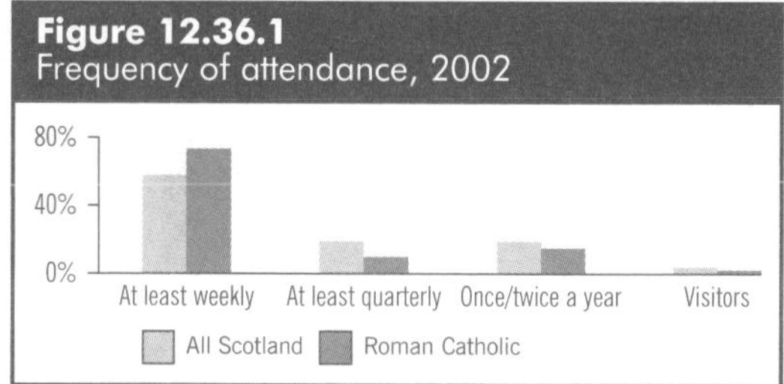

Figure 12.36.1
Frequency of attendance, 2002

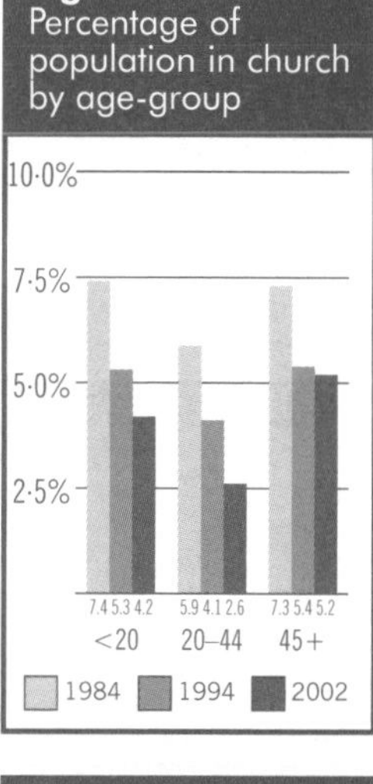

Figure 12.36.2
Percentage of population in church by age-group

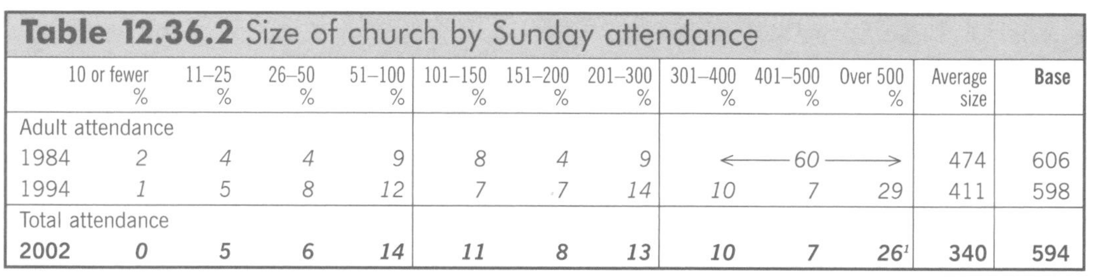

Table 12.36.2 Size of church by Sunday attendance

	10 or fewer %	11–25 %	26–50 %	51–100 %	101–150 %	151–200 %	201–300 %	301–400 %	401–500 %	Over 500 %	Average size	**Base**
Adult attendance												
1984	*2*	*4*	*4*	*9*	*8*	*4*	*9*	←	*60*	→	474	606
1994	*1*	*5*	*8*	*12*	*7*	*7*	*14*	*10*	*7*	*29*	411	598
Total attendance												
2002	***0***	***5***	***6***	***14***	***11***	***8***	***13***	***10***	***7***	***26*[1]**	**340**	**594**

Table 12.36.3 Frequency of attendance in 2002

	Twice weekly %	Weekly %	Fortnightly %	Monthly %	Quarterly %	Once or twice a year %	Visitors %
All Scotland	*12*	*46*	*7*	*6*	*6*	*19*	*4*
Roman Catholic	*5*	*68*	*5*	*4*	*1*	*15*	*2*

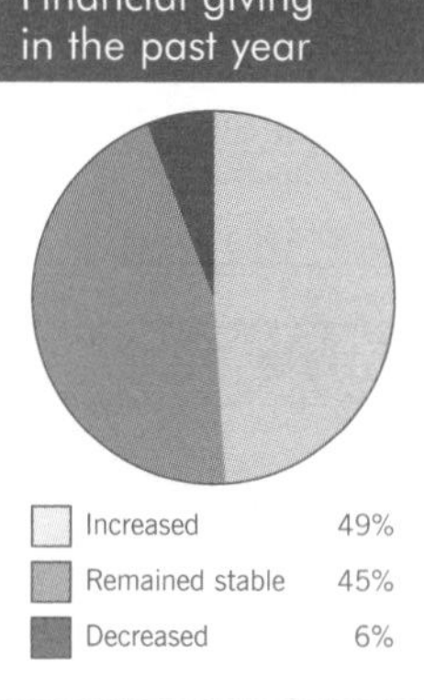

Figure 12.36.3
Financial giving in the past year

Table 12.36.4 Sunday attendance by churchmanship

	Reformed Evangelical	Mainstream Evangelical	Charismatic Evangelical	TOTAL Evangelical	Reformed	Low church	Liberal	Broad	Catholic*	**ALL Churches**
1994	0	2,790	0	2,790	0	2,110	24,180	5,700	214,940	249,720
%▼	–	*+11*	–	*+11*	–	*–5*	*–41*	*–30*	*–17*	*–19*
2002	**0**	**3,100**	**0**	**3,100**	**0**	**2,000**	**14,160**	**3,980**	**178,870**	**202,110**
1994▶	*0*	*1*	*0*	*1*	*0*	*1*	*10*	*2*	*86*	*100%*
2002▶	***0***	***2***	***0***	***2***	***0***	***1***	***7***	***2***	***88***	***100%***
Number of churches										
1994	0	2	0	2	0	2	58	18	518	598
2002	**0**	**3**	**0**	**3**	**0**	**2**	**58**	**18**	**513**	**594**

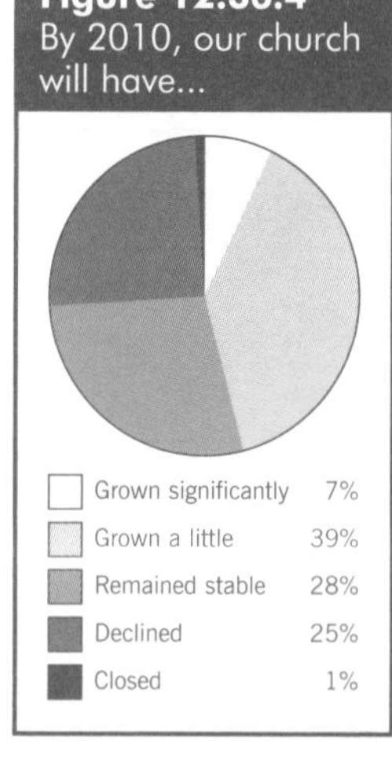

Figure 12.36.4
By 2010, our church will have...

Table 12.36.5 Sunday attendance by environment

	City Centre	Urban Priority Area	Housing Scheme	Suburban	Town	New Town	Rural Area: Dormitory	Rural: Other Areas	**ALL Churches**
1994	21,810	18,530	50,970	25,220	77,740	15,280	17,030	23,140	249,720
%▼	*–22*	*–24*	*–19*	*–7*	*–22*	*–26*	*–10*	*–18*	*–19*
2002	**16,990**	**14,110**	**41,260**	**23,450**	**60,600**	**11,380**	**15,320**	**19,000**	**202,110**
1994▶	*9*	*8*	*20*	*10*	*31*	*6*	*7*	*9*	*100%*
2002▶	***8***	***7***	***20***	***12***	***30***	***6***	***8***	***9***	***100%***
Number of churches									
1994	36	30	102	48	161	18	66	137	598
2002	**36**	**30**	**101**	**48**	**159**	**18**	**66**	**136**	**594**

**Catholic: One kind of churchmanship, not to be identified solely with the Roman Catholic church.* [1] *Actual average size 933*

Table 12.36.6 Age and gender of churchgoers 1984, 1994 and 2002

Age Group	Population 1984 Male %	Female %	Total %	Churchgoers in 1984 Male %	Female %	Total %	Population 1994 Male %	Female %	Total %	Churchgoers in 1994 Male %	Female %	Total %	Population 2002 Male %	Female %	Total %	Churchgoers in 2002 Male %	Female %	Total %
<12 } 12–14	*11*	*10*	***21***	*11*	*13*	***24***	*10*	*9*	***19***	*9*	*10*	***19***	7	7	**14**	*6*	*7*	***13***
12–14													2	2	**4**	*3*	*3*	***6***
15–19	5	4	**9**	*3*	*4*	***7***	3	3	**6**	*4*	*4*	***8***	3	3	**6**	*3*	*2*	***5***
20–29	7	8	**15**	*5*	*8*	***13***	8	8	**16**	*5*	*7*	***12***	7	6	**13**	*3*	*4*	***7***
30–44	9	10	**19**	*7*	*10*	***17***	10	11	**21**	*8*	*11*	***19***	12	12	**24**	*7*	*10*	***17***
45–64	11	11	**22**	*9*	*13*	***22***	11	12	**23**	*11*	*15*	***26***	12	12	**24**	*12*	*16*	***28***
65/65+	5	9	**14**	*8*	*9*	***17***	6	9	**15**	*6*	*10*	***16***	6	9	**15**	*9*	*15*	***24***
All ages	*48*	*52*	***100***	*43*	*57*	***100***	*48*	*52*	***100***	*43*	*57*	***100***	*48*	*52*	***100***	*43*	*57*	***100***

12

13

Alphabetical Index

This cumulative index uses the style Edition/Section/Page. Thus "3/6.15" means *Religious Trends* 3, Section 6, Page 15. See also Subject Index on Page 7.13.

13

13.2 Alphabetical Index

13

13.4 Alphabetical Index

13

13

13

13

13

13.12 Alphabetical Index

13

13.14 Alphabetical Index

13

13